Table of Contents

W9-DIR-951

Unit III   How Was Our Nation's Government Set Up?

Unit IV   How Did the Nation Grow in Size and Strength?

Unit VIII How Can the United States Meet the Future?

Appendix

List of Maps

List of Charts and Graphs

INTRODUCTION: A LOOK AT THE LAND AND PEOPLE OF THE UNITED STATES

What are the various regions of the United States?

The United States of America is big. It extends from the Atlantic Ocean to the Pacific Ocean, and from Canada in the north to the Gulf of Mexico in the south. It includes the Hawaiian Islands in the Pacific Ocean, and Alaska to the northwest of Canada. It covers more than 3,600,000 square miles (5.8 million square kilometers) of land. It is the fourth largest country in the world, after the Soviet Union, China, and Canada.

The United States is rich in natural resources. Its broad central plains are both level and fertile. It has rich deposits of coal, iron, oil, copper, and other minerals in different parts of the nation. Our land has many beautiful rivers, lakes, and streams. Great waterfalls provide power for our factories, towns, and cities. Our hills and mountains are covered with forests.

The United States is a land of great beauty. It has two great mountain ranges, the Appalachian Mountains in the East and the Rocky Mountains in the West. In the western highlands are great salt lakes, plateaus, and even long stretches of desert. Between our two great mountain ranges lies a grassy plain drained by the mighty Mississippi River. Our five Great Lakes are among the largest fresh-water lakes in the world. Our coastlines extend for thousands of miles and border the earth's two largest oceans. Along the coasts are rolling hills and valleys, lowlands of rich soil, and deep natural harbors.

The United States is divided by its geography into **regions,** or sections. The people in each of these regions have different ways of living because of the differences in the land and climate. There are regions of manufacturing, mining, cattle raising, cotton growing, and wheat and corn farming.

The land along the eastern coast is called the Atlantic Coastal Plain, which is narrow in the north but wider in the south. It is bordered on the west by the Appalachian Mountains. The coastal plain is roughly divided into two sections, north and south.

In New England, the northern part of the plain, the soil is rocky and sandy. Because the soil made farming difficult, the early settlers turned to fishing, shipbuilding, and trading.

In the Southeast, the southern part of the plain, the days are warmer and the growing season is longer. This section has fertile

PACIFIC OCEAN · COASTAL RANGES · BASIN · ROCKY MOUNTAINS · GRE PLAI

farmland with fields of cotton, tobacco, soybeans, and rice.

Beyond the Appalachian Mountains are the Central Plains, which extend all the way from the northern to the southern border of the nation. The land is fertile and grassy. Most of America's corn and wheat is grown on the Central Plains. Farther south, the long, hot growing season, the rainy climate, and the rich soil have encouraged cotton growing.

Farther west are the Great Plains, a dry, sunny region extending from Canada into Texas. The Great Plains include parts of North and South Dakota, Nebraska, Kansas, Oklahoma, Montana, Wyoming, New Mexico, Texas, and Colorado. There is little rain here because of the western mountains. The winds come from the Pacific Ocean in the west. As they pass over the mountains, the air loses most of its moisture. At one time, American Indians lived freely on the plains and depended on the buffalo for food, clothing, and shelter. Now cattle ranchers, sheepherders, and wheat farmers share the plains. Farther south, in Texas and Oklahoma, are rich oil fields.

The snowy peaks of the Rocky Mountains mark the end of the Great Plains and the beginning of the western highlands. West of the Rockies is the Great Basin, a region of plateaus and desert. Along the Pacific Coast are the coastal mountain ranges. The people in the western highlands make a liv-

North Carolina countryside

ing chiefly from mining (gold, silver, lead, zinc, and copper) and from raising cattle and sheep. The western highlands cover about one-third of the United States.

The Pacific Coast is one of the many beautiful regions of our nation. In southern California, the winds are warm and rain falls largely in the winter months. In the irrigated valleys, there are fruit orchards and cattle ranches. Farther north, where the rainfall is heavier, the land is rich with forests.

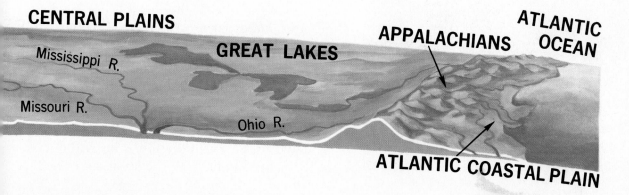

CENTRAL PLAINS

Mississippi R.

Missouri R.

GREAT LAKES

Ohio R.

APPALACHIANS

ATLANTIC OCEAN

ATLANTIC COASTAL PLAIN

The Great Plains

The United States is the leading manufacturing nation of the world. This is no accident. Our nation is blessed with the raw materials that feed hungry machines: cotton, tobacco, the meat and hides from animals, and products of our mines and oil wells. Our resources of coal, oil, gas, water, and now the atom, give us the power to run these machines. To turn out products we

Oregon coast

have skilled workers in our mines and factories, stores, and offices. Our transportation system makes possible the exchange of goods from farm to factory to small town and big city. Our system of making goods is run with as much freedom as possible.

The United States is also people — 238 million of many different races and religions. They have come from almost every nation in the world. All Americans, except American Indians, are immigrants or descend from immigrants. Regardless of where they come from, they all share the same dreams, namely to live in freedom and to make a better life for themselves.

The United States is a land of town and city dwellers. For a long time, most Americans lived on farms. Today, most of our people live in cities and towns. People have settled in cities because they can make their living in the many businesses found there.

The first great factory cities began in the Northeast — near the coal fields, the great harbors and waterways, and many of the important transportation routes. The next great cities grew up in the Midwest to handle the goods from the farms and the plains. Today, large cities are sprouting in the South, the Southwest and West. People are moving there in great numbers to live in the sun and to work in the new oil, space, and computer industries.

The people and sections of the United States are **interdependent.** In the early years of our nation, members of farm families made everything they needed. Today, the farmers depend on other people for food, clothing, and farm machines. Likewise, people in the city depend on farmers for food and on other workers for the goods they use. All our people depend on our great transportation and communication systems which make possible the exchange of goods from place to place. No American can live as he or she would like without help from others in the nation and the world.

4

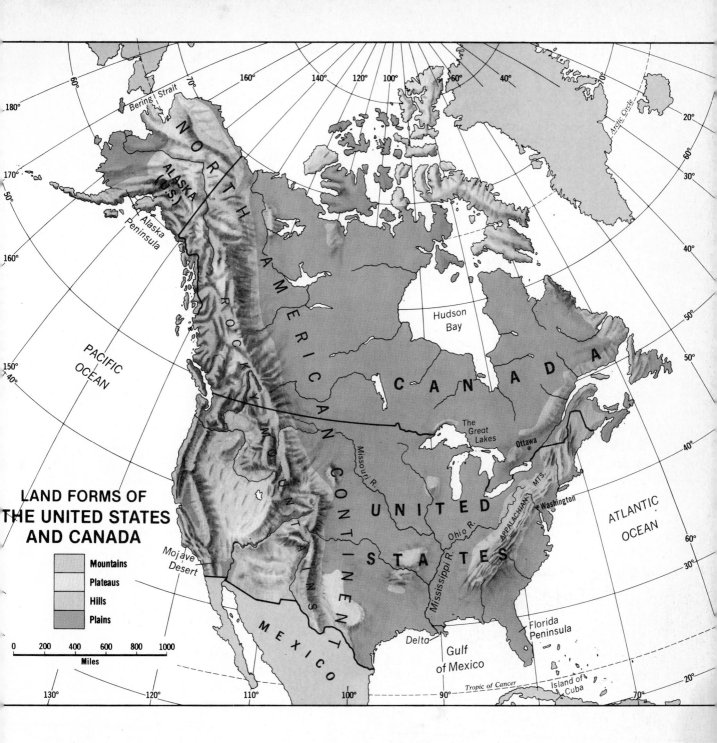

LAND FORMS OF
THE UNITED STATES
AND CANADA

Mountains
Plateaus
Hills
Plains

0   200   400   600   800   1000
Miles

PACIFIC
OCEAN

NORTH AMERICAN CONTINENT

ALASKA
(U.S.)

Alaska
Peninsula

Bering Strait

Hudson
Bay

C A N A D A

The
Great
Lakes

Ottawa

U N I T E D

S T A T E S

M E X I C O

Missouri R.

Mississippi R.

Ohio R.

APPALACHIAN MTS.

Washington

Mojave
Desert

Delta

Gulf
of Mexico

Florida
Peninsula

Island of
Cuba

ATLANTIC
OCEAN

Tropic of Cancer

Arctic Circle

ROCKY MOUNTAINS

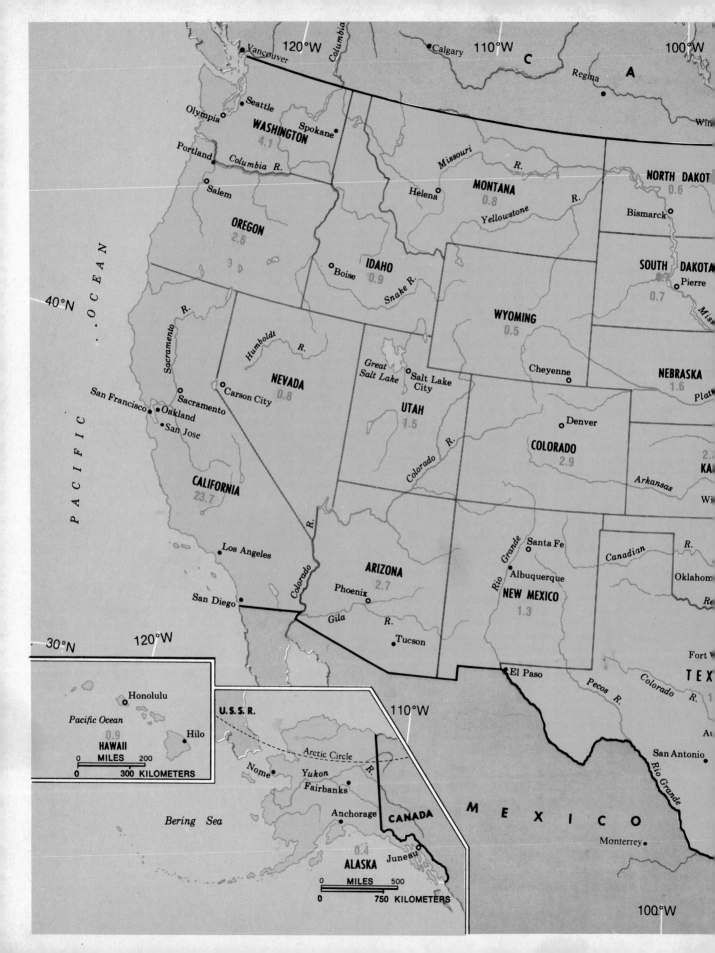

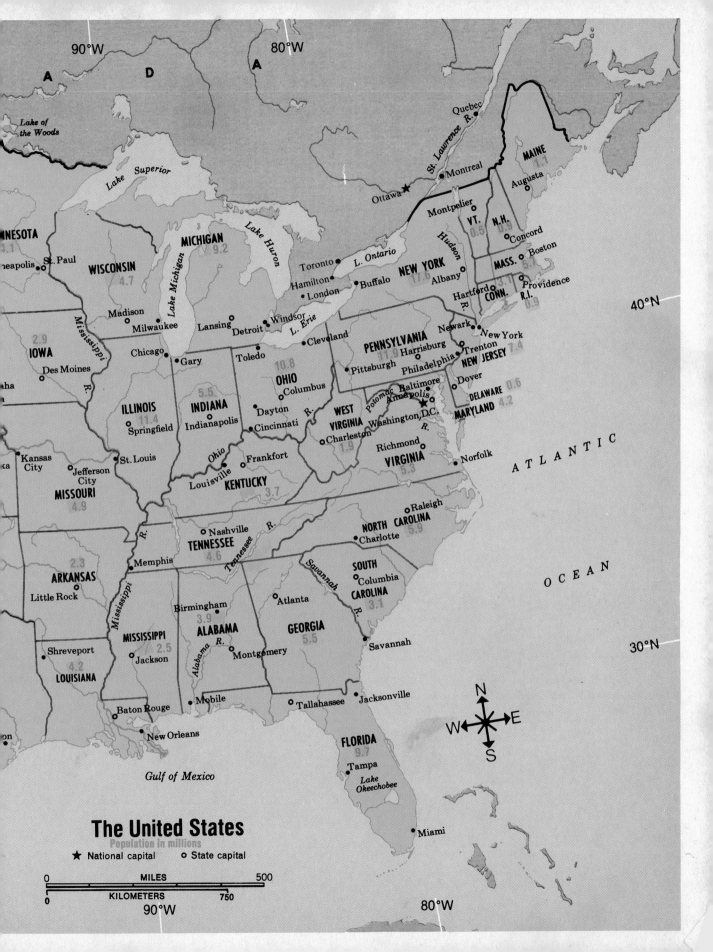

The United States
Population in millions
★ National capital   ○ State capital

MILES
0 | 500

KILOMETERS
0 | 750

The World Today

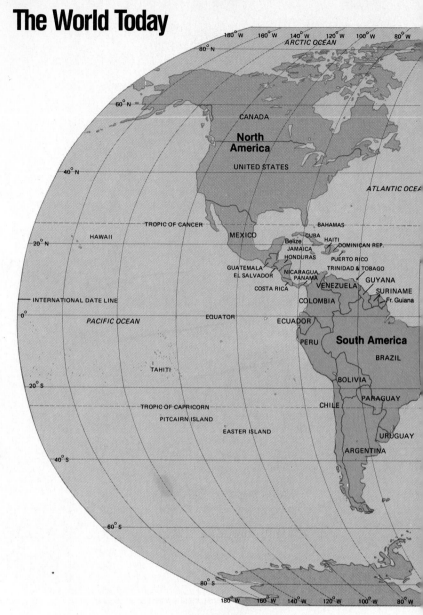

Abbreviations

ALB. Albania
AUST. Austria
BANG. Bangladesh
BEL. Belgium
BUL. Bulgaria
CEN. AFR. REP. Central African Republic
CZECH. Czechoslovakia
DEN. Denmark
E. GER. East Germany

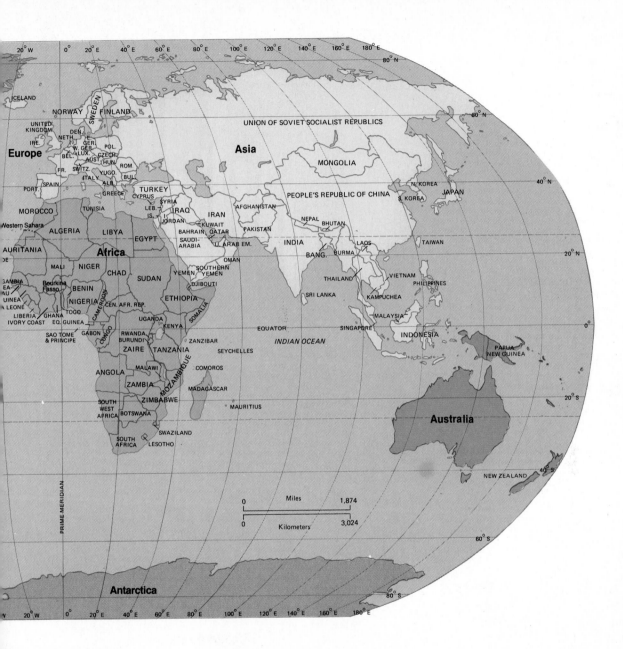

EQ. GUINEA Equatorial Guinea
FR. France
HUN. Hungary
IRE. Ireland
IS. Israel
LEB. Lebanon
LUX. Luxembourg
NETH. Netherlands
N. KOREA North Korea

POL. Poland
PORT. Portugal
ROM. Romania
S. KOREA South Korea
SWITZ. Switzerland
U. ARAB. EM. United Arab Emirates
W. GER. West Germany
YUGO. Yugoslavia

United States Population, 1790-1980

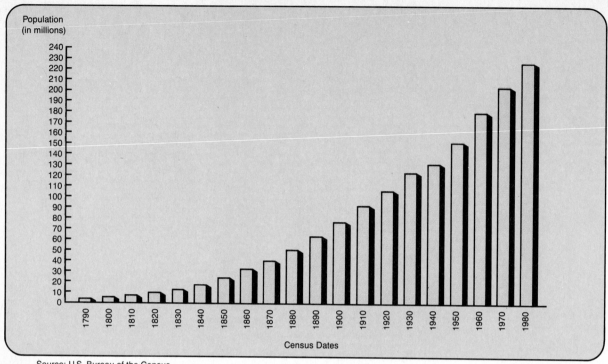

Population (in millions)

Census Dates

Source: U.S. Bureau of the Census

Westward Shift of the United States Population Center

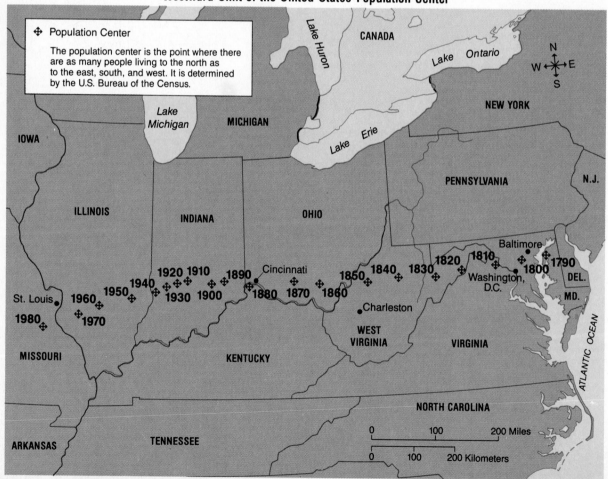

⊕ Population Center

The population center is the point where there are as many people living to the north as to the east, south, and west. It is determined by the U.S. Bureau of the Census.

Population Density by States, 1980

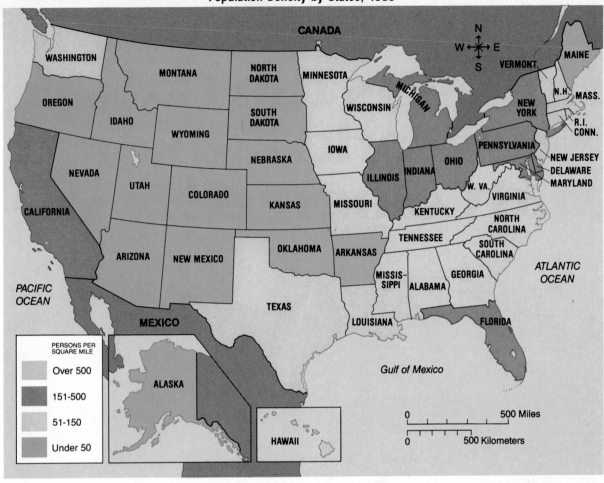

PERSONS PER SQUARE MILE

- Over 500
- 151-500
- 51-150
- Under 50

World's 15 Most Populous Countries

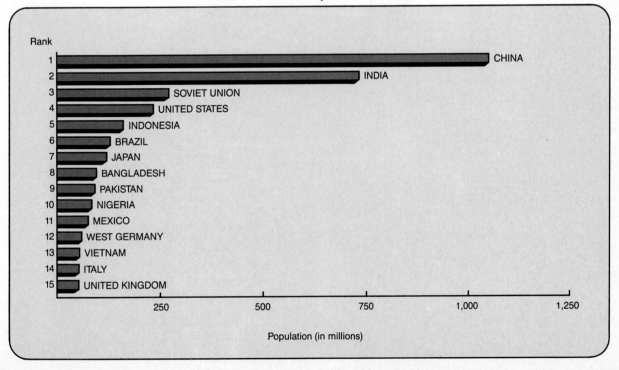

Rank

1. CHINA
2. INDIA
3. SOVIET UNION
4. UNITED STATES
5. INDONESIA
6. BRAZIL
7. JAPAN
8. BANGLADESH
9. PAKISTAN
10. NIGERIA
11. MEXICO
12. WEST GERMANY
13. VIETNAM
14. ITALY
15. UNITED KINGDOM

250   500   750   1,000   1,250

Population (in millions)

Unit I

How Was the New World Explored and Colonized?

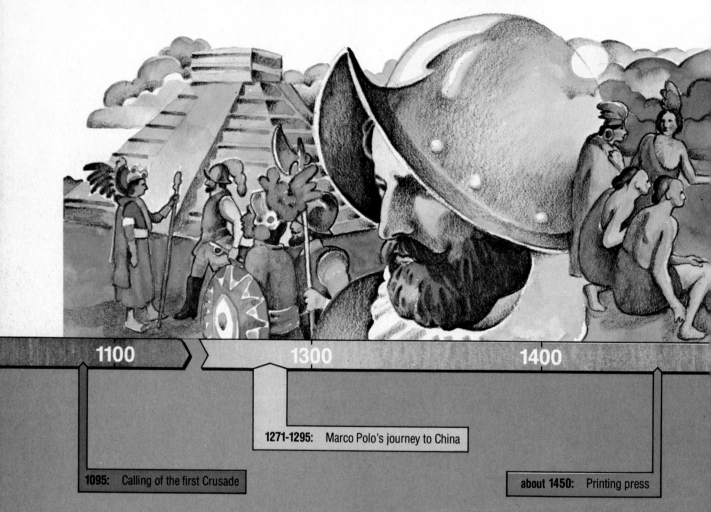

1100 · 1300 · 1400

1271-1295: Marco Polo's journey to China

1095: Calling of the first Crusade

about 1450: Printing press

CHAPTER

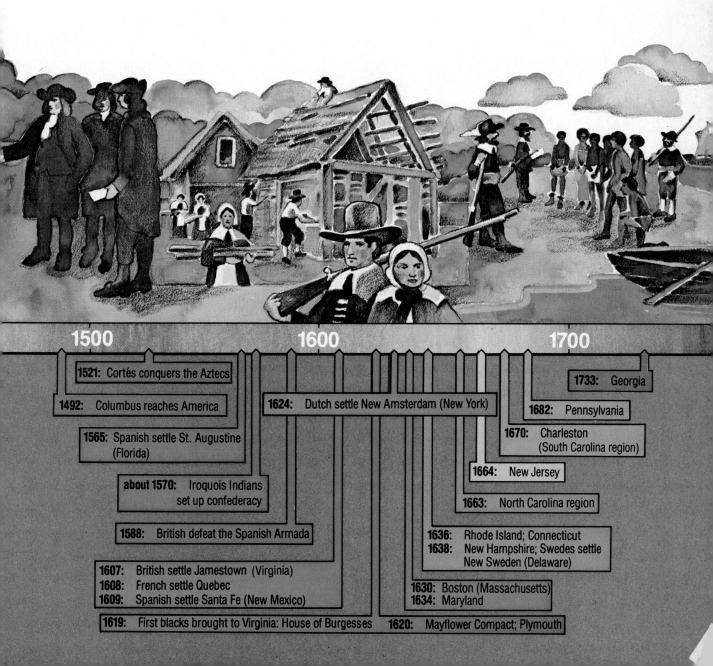

1500   1600   1700

1521: Cortés conquers the Aztecs

1492: Columbus reaches America

1624: Dutch settle New Amsterdam (New York)

1733: Georgia

1682: Pennsylvania

1565: Spanish settle St. Augustine (Florida)

1670: Charleston (South Carolina region)

about 1570: Iroquois Indians set up confederacy

1664: New Jersey

1663: North Carolina region

1588: British defeat the Spanish Armada

1636: Rhode Island; Connecticut
1638: New Hampshire; Swedes settle New Sweden (Delaware)

1607: British settle Jamestown (Virginia)
1608: French settle Quebec
1609: Spanish settle Santa Fe (New Mexico)

1630: Boston (Massachusetts)
1634: Maryland

1619: First blacks brought to Virginia; House of Burgesses   **1620:** Mayflower Compact; Plymouth

1 EUROPE DISCOVERS THE RICHES OF THE EAST

How did the people of Europe become interested in the Far East?

1. At the eastern end of the Mediterranean Sea is a small land once known as Palestine. To the people of Europe in the Middle Ages (A.D. 500–1350), Palestine was one of the most important places in the world. It was the Holy Land, the home of the Christian religion. In the Holy Land, Christ had lived, taught, and died. In the 7th century Muslims gained control of Palestine. Muslims are followers of the prophet Muhammad. Their religion is called Islam. In the 11th century the Turks captured Palestine. They were also Muslims. They were not friendly to the Christians who made long trips to see the holy places. In time, the Turks closed Palestine to visits by the Christians. This made the Christians of Europe angry. They felt that they should be allowed to travel freely in the land where their religion had begun.

2. The head of the Christian church was the pope. In 1095 he called a meeting of kings and nobles. He told them how the Turks were treating the Christians in Palestine. He called on all Christians to unite against the Turks and drive them from the Holy Land. Before long, kings and nobles in large numbers set out to fight the Turks.

The ruins of a Crusader fortress at Acre in Palestine built during the Middle Ages. How did the Crusades change the lives of people in Europe?

People from all over western Europe also left their homes to follow the kings and nobles. This was the first of many attempts to win back the Holy Land. These wars were called the **Crusades.** The name comes from the Latin word *crux*, or "cross," which the Crusaders wore on their clothing. The Crusades lasted almost 200 years. Many thousands died in battle. But the Christians could not hold on to the land they gained in the East.

3. The Crusades, however, changed the lives of the people of western Europe. The people of Europe had thought the world was small and flat. The Mediterranean Sea seemed to be the center of the world. During the Crusades many people left their homes and traveled to distant places for the first time. The Crusaders learned that the world was much larger than they had believed. They returned with stories of Asian people whose ways of living were different from their own. From these eastern lands they brought silks, perfumes, jewels, and spices such as pepper and cinnamon. These spices kept food from spoiling and made it taste better. The people of western Europe wanted more of these things. Before long a lively trade developed between the people of Europe and the people of Asia.

4. At the same time there were several men who began to travel to the lands of the Far East described by the Crusaders. The best-known travelers were the merchants Marco Polo, his father, and his uncle. They came from the Italian city of Venice. In the 13th century these traders visited Cathay, which we call China. They lived at the court of its ruler, the Great Khan. When Marco Polo returned to Venice, he wrote an account of his travels. He told of the riches of the Far East and of seeing a large ocean east of China and India. Marco Polo's stories increased the Europeans' desire to trade with the East.

5. The spices and other goods came from India, China, and the islands near south-

Marco Polo in China. Polo's book told about China's great wealth, as well as its paper money, coal, and other things new to Europe.

eastern Asia. These faraway places were known as the Indies, or the lands of the Far East. The goods were brought to the cities at the eastern end of the Mediterranean Sea, either by land or by sea. The route over land crossed the deserts and mountains of Asia. The goods were carried on the backs of camels. On the water, the goods were carried by ships from China and India to the Red Sea. Both of these routes were very long and dangerous. As a result, the prices of the goods were high.

6. Italian merchants carried on most of the new trade with the lands at the eastern end of the Mediterranean Sea. They brought spices, rugs, and jewels to Italy first. The Italian cities of Venice and Genoa became very important. From these ports, goods were sold to other merchants all over Europe. In time, people from other parts of Europe became jealous of the rich Italian traders and wanted a share of their trade.

7. People began to study maps looking for routes that would bring goods from the East to cities other than Venice and Genoa. Even the merchants of the Italian cities soon wanted to find new routes for their trade. The Turks had conquered more land

and had cut off the land routes to the Italian ports. Was there another way to the East? Some people began to say that the earth was not flat, and that it was possible to go all the way to the East by water.

8. In about 1450 Johann Gutenberg invented a printing press with movable type. With this invention Europeans could print books more quickly than by copying by hand. As a result, books about geography and travel became cheaper and more plentiful.

African ivory sculpture showing Portuguese explorers. From this sculpture, what do you think Africans thought of the explorers?

tiful. Marco Polo's account of his travels was widely read. His book was eagerly read by people who were looking for new ways to get the riches of the Far East.

9. Two inventions, the compass and the astrolabe, were of great help to sailors. The compass tells sailors the direction in which they are traveling. The astrolabe helps the captain place the position of his ship exactly. With these inventions, captains could sail their ships farther from land and bring them home safely again.

10. Meanwhile, a young nobleman in Portugal was determined to find another route to the rich lands of Asia. Prince Henry, a young son of the king of Portugal, wanted Portugal to have a share of the rich Eastern trade. He thought it was possible to reach India and China by sailing around the continent of Africa. He started a school to train ship captains. Each year he urged his captains to sail farther and farther southward.

11. Prince Henry died in 1460, but his dream came true. In 1488 a Portuguese captain, Bartholomeu Dias, sailed around the southern tip of Africa. Ten years later, Vasco da Gama rounded Africa and sailed on to India. A new route had been found! The ships of da Gama brought back enough pepper, gems, and cloth to pay for the cost of the voyage more than 60 times.

12. The Portuguese were now the masters of the new all-water route to the Far East. The route was longer, but it meant great wealth for the Portuguese. They set up trading posts in India to trade with the people of the Far East. Goods were brought to Europe by Portuguese sailors and were sold for prices lower than those of the Italian merchants. Water transportation was not so costly as the hard trip by camel caravan. Since Portugal was now getting rich, other countries rushed to find a shorter route to the East.

UNDERSTANDING
CHAPTER 1

I. What is the main purpose of paragraphs 1 through 3?

   a. To describe how the people of Europe lived during the Middle Ages
   b. To tell how the Crusades changed the lives of people in western Europe
   c. To tell how the people of Europe stopped their food from spoiling
   d. To describe what the people of Europe wanted most from the East

II. Choose the correct answer or answers.

1. There was a growing demand for goods from the Far East because
   a. these goods were cheaper than those made in Europe
   b. the Crusaders had brought back goods that the people wanted
   c. it was so easy to travel to the East
2. About the year 1500, ships could sail farther from land because
   a. there were new inventions that helped sailors
   b. ships were no longer made of wood
   c. there were accurate maps of the oceans
3. There was a search for an all-water route to India because (2 answers)
   a. the overland routes were too long and dangerous
   b. other countries besides Italy wanted to share in the eastern trade
   c. Vasco da Gama had found riches in India
4. The travels of Marco Polo are important because they
   a. showed a new way to the Far East
   b. told of the riches of the Holy Land
   c. showed the people of Europe the riches of the Far East
5. The Crusaders left their homes because
   a. they wanted to recapture the Holy Land from the Turks
   b. they wished to reach India by water
   c. trade with the East was important to them

III. Decide whether each statement is true or false. The underlined words are clues to help you decide. If the statement is false, change the underlined word or words to make it true.

1. The Turks closed <u>Palestine</u> to visits from Christians.
2. <u>Prince Henry</u> sailed around the southern tip of Africa.
3. <u>The Mediterranean Sea</u> was part of the trade route between Europe and Asia.
4. The Crusaders came from the countries of <u>Asia</u>.
5. <u>Monarchs and merchants</u> wanted to find easier and faster ways to reach the Far East.
6. Marco Polo once visited <u>England</u>.
7. The Crusaders brought back stories of <u>India and China</u>.
8. Vasco da Gama made voyages to the land that is now called <u>North America</u>.
9. The first nation to find an all-water route to India was <u>Portugal</u>.
10. The port cities of <u>Spain</u> became the centers of trade with the Far East.
11. The years from about A.D. 500 to 1350 are sometimes called the <u>Classical Ages</u>.

MAP SKILLS *Early Trade Routes*
Study the map. Then answer the following questions.

Early Trade Routes

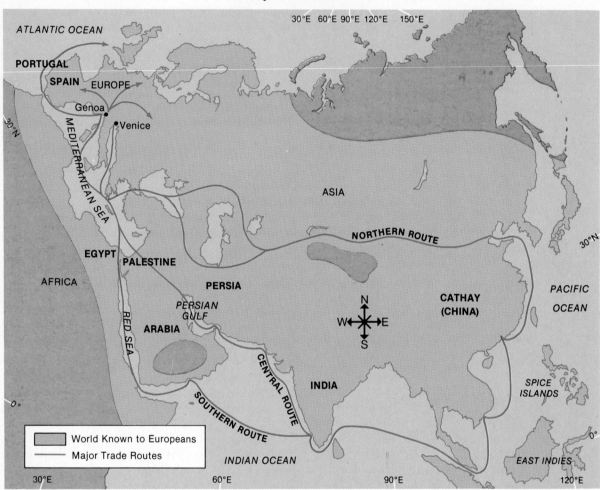

1. How many trade routes were there between Europe and the Far East?
   a. What were the names of these routes?
   b. How were they different?
   c. Which route do you think Marco Polo may have taken?
2. What body of water did the Crusaders cross to reach Palestine?
3. What cities probably supplied them with ships?
4. Where did the Italian merchants pick up the goods from Asia?
   a. How did these goods get to the rest of Europe?
   b. Why were these goods so expensive?
5. Why were China and the Spice Islands known as the Far East?
6. A continent is a large body of land.
   a. How many continents were known to the people of Europe during the Crusades?
   b. Which was the largest continent known to Europeans?

c. On which continent was Marco Polo's home?

d. Four continents were unknown to Europeans during the Crusades. Use an atlas or an encyclopedia to help you name them.

KNOWING THE KINDS OF MAPS AND THEIR FEATURES

Maps have many purposes. A **physical** map is one that shows the physical features of the earth. These are rivers, mountains, hills, and plains, for example. A **political** map shows countries, states, cities, and towns. **Historical** maps help us understand the historical background behind events. Most maps in this book are historical maps. The map of early trade routes on page 18 is an example. It shows the world known to Europeans at a certain time in history. It also shows how people moved their goods from one part of the world to other parts of the world at that time.

Real things, such as oceans, islands, or cities, are shown on maps in different ways. Some things are shown by using **labels.** For example, on the map on page 18 the label "Indian Ocean," stands for the real ocean. The city of Venice is also shown on the map with a label. Another way to show things on maps is by using **symbols.** For example, on the map on page 18, the city of Venice is also shown by a dot. This dot is a symbol for Venice. Look at the red lines on the same map. These red lines are symbols that stand for trade routes. The mapmaker has used the color red to make these trade routes stand out. The mapmaker has also used different colors to show the land and water areas. On the map on page 18, green is used to show land areas known to Europeans. Blue is used to show water and gray is used to show other land areas. In order to explain the meaning of different symbols, mapmakers include a **map key.** The map key on page 18 is found in the lower left-hand corner of the map. Map keys usually do not show the colors for land and water unless the map shows something special about the land or water.

Most maps also have a small compass to show direction. Find the map compass on page 18. Note that it has four major directions. These are N (north), S (south), E (east), and W (west). North points in the direction of the North Pole. South points in the direction of the South Pole. When you face north, east is to your right, west is to your left, and south is behind you. On most maps the direction north (N) points toward the top of the map. The map compass on page 18 also has four short lines. These stand for the intermediate directions. They are NE (northeast), SE (southeast), NW (northwest), and SW (southwest). The map compass is important in locating things on a map.

SUMMING UP

Arrange the events below in the order in which they took place.

1. Prince Henry's school for sailors is established.
2. Printing with movable type is invented.
3. The Crusades take place.
4. Many people read about the travels of Marco Polo.
5. The voyage of Vasco da Gama is completed.

2 COLUMBUS FINDS THE NEW WORLD

How did Columbus reach America?

Columbus arriving in the New World. What are the names of the first islands that he reached off the coast of America?

1. Christopher Columbus was born in Genoa, Italy, in 1451. Columbus first went to sea when he was in his early teens. He worked as a seaman on ships sailing the Mediterranean Sea. He probably sailed to England and Iceland also. During those trips he may have heard stories about land far to the west that may have been reached by Leif Ericson, the Viking. The Vikings were people who lived in northern Europe. They loved the sea and often sailed far from home. Some Vikings may have reached the New World about the year A.D. 1000. (See page 23.)

2. Columbus settled in Portugal where he worked as a mapmaker for a while. Then he became a sugar buyer in the Portuguese islands off Africa. He met sailors who believed there were islands farther west. Columbus read the works of ancient writers who thought the earth was round. He carefully studied maps and Marco Polo's book about China. Columbus became convinced that he could reach the Indies by sailing westward across the Atlantic Ocean.

3. For many years Columbus tried to get help from the rulers of France, Portugal, and Spain. Finally, the rulers of Spain agreed to give him money and ships. They hoped he would find a short route to the Indies and make Spain the richest country on earth. They gave him the power to govern any lands that he would discover.

4. Queen Isabella gave Columbus three small ships: the *Niña*, the *Pinta*, and the *Santa Maria*. At first, it was not easy to get a crew because many sailors were superstitious. They were frightened by stories of sea monsters and boiling waters. But finally Columbus got his crew and ships and prepared for the voyage. A few boys went on the voyage to help on deck and learn to be good sailors. On August 3, 1492, Columbus's fleet sailed from Palos, Spain. The ships stopped first at the Canary Islands for repairs and food. Columbus did not load too many supplies. Columbus felt that he would reach the Indies after a short voyage. He had a mistaken idea of the earth's size and of the real distance he had to sail before reaching land. On September 6, 1492, the fleet left the Canary Islands and sailed westward. (See the map on page 23.)

5. The voyage was long and the sailors became frightened. Columbus kept a daily record of his voyage. This kind of record is called a ship's log. Finally, on October 12, 1492, Columbus reached a small island off the coast of America, southeast of what is now Florida. He named it San Salvador. He called the people on the island Indians because he thought he was near the coast of India. Columbus continued to sail south-

west and reached the islands of Cuba and Hispaniola. These islands are south of Florida. He found a little gold but no rich and splendid cities. The people of these lands were poor.

6. Columbus returned to Spain. He brought back several Indians and some pieces of gold to show to the king and queen. They welcomed him as a hero. They were quite sure that on another voyage he would discover gold mines, jewels, and spices. They gave Columbus a new title — Admiral of the Ocean Sea. Spain would rule over the lands he had discovered.

7. The news of Columbus's discovery reached the king of Portugal. He refused to admit Spain's claim to the lands Columbus had discovered. The two Catholic countries asked the pope to settle the matter and agreed to obey his decision. He suggested that an imaginary line be drawn north and south through the New World, that is, the world new to Europeans. The lands west of this line would belong to Spain; the lands east of the line would belong to Portugal. The line was called the Line of Demarcation, or Line of Separation. Because of the pope's decision, the only land claimed by Portugal in the New World was Brazil. In 1500 Brazil was reached by Pedro Cabral, a Portuguese explorer.

8. During the following years, Columbus made three other voyages to the New World. On his second voyage he reached the islands of Puerto Rico and Jamaica. He also started the first settlement for Spain in the New World. This colony was located on the island of Hispaniola. On the third and fourth voyages Columbus traveled south and touched the northern coast of South America. Then, going north, he sailed along the coast of Central America.

9. Columbus was disappointed because he had not discovered the riches of the Indies. The king and queen of Spain were also disappointed. While Columbus was making his voyages, Vasco da Gama had found an all-water route around Africa to the riches of India for Portugal. In 1506 Columbus died a disappointed man. He thought he had only reached islands off the coast of Asia. He did not know that he had reached the New World.

10. Before long, many explorers came to the New World and sent back reports and maps to Europe. One of the earliest of these explorers was the Italian sailor Amerigo Vespucci. He made a number of voyages, some of them for Spain and some of them for Portugal. Vespucci wrote letters to his friends describing his voyages. He proved that South America was not part of the Indies. It was a continent new to Europeans. In 1507 a German mapmaker drew some maps of the New World. He named the new lands America in honor of Amerigo Vespucci.

Columbus holding an astrolabe. In the 15th century, sailors used it to figure out how far north or south their ships were.

21

Find the missing words.

1. The invention of the ▬▬▬ made books more plentiful.
2. The ▬▬▬ helped sailors to know their position at sea.
3. ▬▬▬ was an Italian trader who visited China.
4. The cheapest means of transportation was by ▬▬▬.
5. ▬▬▬ was an important port city of Italy.
6. The Crusaders tried to take away ▬▬▬ from the Turks.
7. From the East, the people of Europe got ▬▬▬, which they used to keep their food from spoiling.
8. ▬▬▬ reached India in 1498, after sailing around Africa.
9. The ▬▬▬ led to a demand for goods from the Far East.
10. ▬▬▬ sent ships to explore the coast of Africa.

I. What is the main purpose of Chapter 2?

a. To tell how the rulers of Spain helped Columbus
b. To describe how Columbus became a successful sailor
c. To describe the troubles of Columbus on his first voyage
d. To tell how Columbus came to reach the New World

II. Choose the correct answer.

1. Columbus sailed west because
   a. he thought he would find a new continent
   b. this route was not far from land
   c. he thought he would reach India
2. Columbus thought he had failed because
   a. he had not discovered a new continent
   b. he had not discovered the riches of the East
   c. Portugal had made more important discoveries before his voyage
3. Spain established a colony in the New World to
   a. search for gold
   b. farm the fertile lands discovered
   c. plan for future colonies all over the New World
4. The rulers of Spain were willing to help Columbus because they wanted
   a. land in the New World
   b. the riches of the East
   c. to increase the knowledge of the geography of the world
5. Columbus made several voyages to the New World because he
   a. wanted to find other lands for Portugal
   b. had not found the riches he expected
   c. wanted to start his own colony there
6. The Vikings may have reached the New World about the year
   a. 1000
   b. 1400
   c. 1492

MAP SKILLS *Columbus Sails to the New World*
Study the map. Then find the missing words.

Columbus Sails to the New World

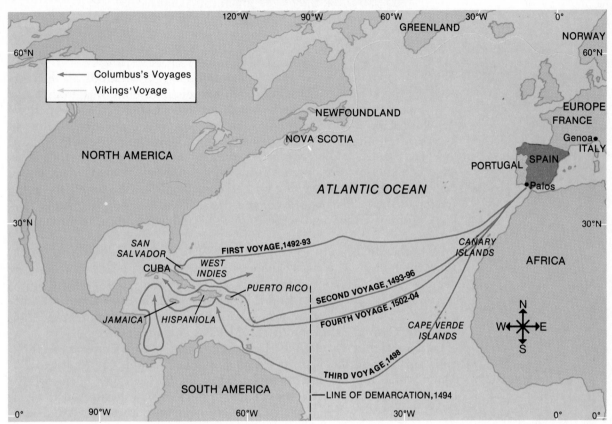

1. Columbus made ▬▬▬ voyages to the New World.
2. Columbus sailed ▬▬▬ (in which direction?) from Spain.
3. The first Spanish settlements in the New World were started in the ▬▬▬.
4. The Atlantic Ocean borders ▬▬▬ continents.
5. Columbus stopped at the ▬▬▬ before crossing the ocean.
6. The Line of Demarcation was drawn in a ▬▬▬ direction.
7. As a result of the Line, most of the land in the New World went to ▬▬▬.
8. The Portuguese claims lay ▬▬▬ (which side?) of the Line.

Answer these questions.

1. Did Columbus ever touch any land that is now part of the United States?
2. Did Columbus succeed in reaching Asia?

23

3. Why was the Line of Demarcation drawn?
4. Where in the New World may the Vikings have landed?
5. What islands were discovered by Columbus?
6. The islands discovered by Columbus were named the West Indies. Why do you think they were given this name?

USING LATITUDE AND LONGITUDE

There are special ways to locate places on maps. Two kinds of lines are used. These are called **longitude** and **latitude.** These are imaginary lines and do not actually appear on the earth's surface. **Longitude** lines run from the North Pole to the South Pole. They are also called meridians. Lines of longitude are numbered in degrees (°). The lines of longitude help to show how far a place is located east or west of a zero degree line (0°). The longitude line of zero degrees is called the **prime meridian.** Look at the map on page 23. Find the degree marks on the top and bottom of the map. Imaginary lines that would connect these lines from top to bottom are longitude lines. Through what countries would the prime meridian (0°) pass?

The other lines used to help locate places are called lines of **latitude.** Lines of latitude are also called parallels. They are also numbered in degrees (0°). Lines of latitude help to show how far a place is located north or south of a zero degree line. The latitude line of zero degrees is the **equator.** Look at the map on page 23. Find the degree marks on the sides of the map. Through what continents does the equator pass?

Latitude and longitude lines are used to locate places. For example, find the line showing the first voyage of Columbus on the map on page 23. Along which line of latitude was most of his first voyage? Along which latitude line was most of the Vikings' voyage? Now locate the Line of Demarcation shown on the map. Between which two lines of longitude did this line run? Along which line of longitude is Spain located?

People usually locate places by using latitude and longitude lines at the same time. It is possible then to locate places very specifically. For example, by looking at the map on page 23 you can see that Spain is located at about 0° longitude and 45° North latitude.

Christopher Columbus Use these three headings to make an outline about Christopher Columbus. From what you have read, enter two statements under each heading.

A. Columbus as a Boy

B. The Voyages of Columbus

C. The Results of the Voyages

Thinking It Through

Do you think Columbus's voyages were successful? Why or why not?

3 THE SEARCH FOR RICHES GOES ON

How did Spanish explorers reach new lands while searching for gold?

1. Spanish colonies or settlements in America began to grow. The land on the islands of Cuba and Puerto Rico was good for farming. The weather was warm the year round, and there was plenty of rain. The Spanish farmers divided their lands into large farms called **plantations**. The American Indians did the hard work on the farms. The American Indians were treated as slaves. Weakened by hard work and disease, thousands of Indians died. To make up for their loss of Indian workers, the Spanish began to use blacks brought from Africa. These blacks became slaves. Many were taken along as the Spanish began to explore other parts of the New World.

2. Most Spanish came to the New World not to farm but to find gold. One of these was Vasco de Balboa, the leader of a small settlement on the Isthmus of Panama. (See map on page 39.) An **isthmus** is a narrow strip of land that joins two larger bodies of land. The Indians told Balboa that there was a large body of water west of the isthmus, and a country rich with gold to the south.

3. In 1513 Balboa led a band of about 200 Spanish, 30 blacks, and a few Indians through the jungle and mountains of the isthmus. Balboa found a great sea on the other side. He called it the South Sea. Today we call it the Pacific Ocean. Balboa's discovery helped people understand that Asia had not been reached, for no large body of water lay west of Asia. The unknown lands that the Spanish were exploring came to be called the New World.

4. The new governor of the island of Puerto Rico was Juan Ponce de León. He had come to the New World on the second voyage of Columbus. He had become rich in the New World, but he was not happy because he was growing old. The Indians told him of a rich land to the north. They said that there was a spring of water in this land that would make him young again. In 1513 Ponce de León set out in search of the magic spring, the Fountain of Youth as the Indians called it. On Easter Sunday the Spanish fleet sighted land. They named the land Tierra Florida, which means "Land of Flowers." Ponce de León was the first Spanish explorer to visit the mainland of what became the United States.

5. Ponce de León marched through Florida looking for gold and the magic fountain. It is said that he bathed in every spring he found, but he did not become

In 1513 Balboa claimed for Spain the Pacific Ocean and the land it touched. A few years later a bitter enemy falsely accused him of rebellion. Balboa was beheaded.

Magellan and his fleet. After finally crossing into the Pacific Ocean, Magellan's crew wanted to return to Spain. Having come so far, why do you think they wanted to turn back instead of continuing onward to the Far East?

young again. Having no success, he returned to Puerto Rico. In 1521 he returned to Florida, but he was wounded in a fight with the Indians. He died in Cuba, believing that Florida was an island.

6. The explorer who proved without any doubt that the world was round was a Portuguese nobleman named Ferdinand Magellan. In an earlier voyage, he had sailed to the Spice Islands. (See map on page 18.) He believed that the world was round and that he could reach India by sailing west. Like Columbus, he received help from a Spanish monarch. The king gave him five old ships. Magellan set sail from Spain in 1519. Neither he nor his 265 sailors knew how long and dangerous their voyage would be.

7. Magellan and his little fleet crossed the Atlantic Ocean. He sailed south along the coast of South America looking for a passage through the continent. The weather became colder as the ships neared the southern tip of South America. One of his ships left him and another was lost in a storm. Finally, Magellan discovered a narrow waterway, or **strait,** at the southern end of the continent. Today, we call this waterway the Strait of Magellan. The waters were rough. After a month, the ships passed safely through the dangerous waters into another ocean. This was the ocean that Balboa had called the South Sea. Magellan found the waters so calm that he renamed it the Pacific, which means "peaceful."

8. The sailors begged Magellan to return to Spain, but he refused. For weeks they sailed over the vast sea. The ocean was larger than Magellan had expected. When there was no wind, the ships were helpless. The supply of food, water, and medicines soon gave out. The men suffered from hunger, thirst, and sickness. They chewed the leather of their shoes and the riggings

(ropes) of the ships. At one time they caught rats and ate them. After 98 days they touched an island where they found food and water. Finally, in March 1521, they reached the group of islands that we call the Philippines.

9. Things went badly in the Philippines. One of Magellan's ships was so wormy and rotten that it was left behind. Magellan himself took part in a fight with the natives and was killed. One of his captains took command and set out for Spain. The last ship, the *Victoria*, reached Spain in 1522, after three years of hardships. Only 18 men remained alive. This voyage around the world proved that the earth was round and that the New World was really a vast new land.

REVIEWING CHAPTER 2 **Decide whether each statement is true or false. The underlined words are clues to help you decide. If a statement is false, change the underlined word or words to make it true.**

1. Columbus hoped to find a route to the Indies.
2. Columbus made four voyages to the New World.
3. Columbus believed that he could reach India by sailing east.
4. Columbus believed the world was flat.
5. For a while, Columbus made his living by making maps.
6. Columbus called the people of the New World Indians.
7. The rulers of France and Portugal supplied Columbus with ships for his voyages.
8. The New World was named for Columbus.

UNDERSTANDING CHAPTER 3 **I. What is the main idea of paragraphs 6 through 9?**

a. Magellan and his crew faced hardships on their voyage.
b. Magellan's voyage proved the world was round.
c. Balboa discovered the South Sea.
d. The Pacific Ocean was named by Magellan.

II. Choose the correct answer.

1. The voyage of Magellan was important because it proved that
   a. the Pacific Ocean is smaller than the Atlantic Ocean
   b. the earth is round
   c. Asia is a separate continent
2. Spanish settlements began to grow in the New World because
   a. Spanish people came to find gold
   b. the land was fertile
   c. people came from other countries to live in Spanish colonies
3. Magellan's voyage did not help the ruler of Spain because
   a. the route he found was too long to carry on trade
   b. Magellan had been killed
   c. Portugal claimed India

4. Balboa's explorations were important because he was the first European to reach
   a. a shorter route to India
   b. the Pacific Ocean
   c. rich stores of gold and silver
5. The first Europeans to reach the Philippines had sailed from
   a. Portugal
   b. Spain
   c. Italy
6. The Strait of Magellan is at the southern end of
   a. Spain
   b. Africa
   c. South America

III. Decide whether each statement is true or false. The underlined words are clues to help you decide. If a statement is false, change the underlined word or words to make it true.

1. The Portuguese sailor who proved that the earth was round was <u>Balboa</u>.
2. The first European to see the Pacific Ocean was <u>Balboa</u>.
3. Because of <u>Magellan</u>, the people of Europe had a better idea of the size of the earth.
4. The Philippine Islands were claimed by <u>Spain</u>.
5. A <u>strait</u> is a narrow strip of water that connects two larger bodies of water.
6. The <u>French</u> were the first Europeans to explore North America.
7. The climate in the Spanish settlements in the New World was usually <u>warm</u>.
8. A narrow strip of land that joins two larger bodies of land is an <u>isthmus</u>.
9. Many Spanish people came to the New World to <u>find gold</u>.
10. <u>Ponce de León</u> was the first European explorer in Florida.

DEVELOPING IDEAS AND SKILLS

PICTURE SYMBOLS   These pictures should help you recall parts of the chapters you have read. What is the main idea of each picture?

MAKING A SUMMARY IN CHART FORM

A summary is a short restatement or digest of the main facts or points of a longer reading. There are many different ways to summarize information. One way to do a summary is in the form of a chart like the one below. The first thing to do in making the most of a chart is to look at the title. What is the title of the chart below? What kind of information are you being asked to summarize in this chart? Now, read the names that are listed on the left-hand side of the chart. Who are these people? If you do not remember them, go back and reread the chapter. After you know who they are and what they did, fill in the right-hand side of the chart. The information you write should be as short as possible. Use only one or two sentences to restate the important points.

When you have filled in one chart, you have done one type of summary. You can also recall information from the chapter more easily. Is there other information in the chapter that can be summarized in chart form? Try making up your own chart to summarize some of that information.

HOW THEY ADDED TO KNOWLEDGE ABOUT THE WORLD

1. Crusaders	
2. Marco Polo	
3. Prince Henry	
4. Columbus	
5. Magellan	

SUMMING UP

Thinking It Through

Magellan and his crew risked their lives in exploring the unknown. In much the same way, modern-day astronauts risk their lives when they take part in space flights. Why did Magellan undertake his voyage? What are the goals of today's space explorations? What do you think drives people to take part in explorations, even at the risk of death?

4 THE THIRST FOR GOLD

How did the Spanish conquer Mexico and Peru?

Aztec pyramids in Tenochtitlán. In what ways do these buildings show the advanced skills and knowledge of the Aztecs?

1. The central and eastern parts of Mexico were ruled by an American Indian people called the Aztecs. Their capital, Tenochtitlan (te NOCH tee TLAN), was built on an island in a valley surrounded by mountains. The ruler of the Aztecs, Montezuma, lived there. The Aztecs wore cotton clothes with beautiful feathers and turquoise stones. They had built fine buildings and temples of stone. They worshipped many gods in the form of stone idols. The Aztecs were feared as fighters. They had conquered other Indians living around them and had made them slaves.

2. Many young men came from Spain to the New World to seek their fortunes. One of these was Hernando Cortés. While living in Cuba, he heard of the riches of the Aztecs. In 1519 he gathered together an expedition and set out to conquer the Indians. When the Aztec chief, Montezuma, heard that the Spaniards had landed in Mexico, he sent them presents of gold and silver. The Aztecs thought these white men were gods. When Cortés saw the rich presents, he became more determined than ever to get hold of Montezuma's gold. After many months of fighting, Cortés captured the capital of the Aztec empire in 1521. Montezuma was killed in the fighting.

3. Cortés conquered the powerful Aztecs with only 600 men. There were several reasons why this happened. First, the Aztecs thought that the Spaniards were gods. According to an Aztec legend, or story, a god with light skin and a heavy beard had lived among them many years before. Before the god had left, he had promised to return. We have no way of knowing for sure, but this "god" may have been a Viking or a sailor from a ship that had blown off its course.

4. Second, the Aztecs had made enemies of the Indians living around them. They had forced these tribes to pay them large amounts of gold and give up their daughters to be put to death at the temples of the Aztec gods. As Cortés marched toward the valley where the Aztecs lived, he met the Indians who had been conquered by the Aztecs. These Indians were willing to help Cortés fight against their rulers.

5. Third, the Spaniards had better fighting equipment than the Aztecs. They wore steel armor, which protected them from arrows and spears. The Spaniards also had guns and horses, which the Aztecs had never seen. The horses and the loud noises of the cannons frightened the Indians. The Aztecs had no animals that they could ride. When the Aztecs saw the Spaniards riding into battle, they thought that each man and his horse were one strange and terrible animal.

6. Finally, Cortés himself was a reason for the Spanish success. Cortés was a true Spanish *conquistador* (Spanish word for "conqueror"). He was brave, reckless, and determined. He was strengthened by his religious beliefs. He had no doubts about fighting and conquering the Aztecs. At one point, he burned his ships so that his men could not run back. He was determined to lead them to success and riches.

7. Cortés called the land he conquered New Spain. Indians were forced to work in the gold and silver mines of Montezuma. Thousands of them died from the hard work. Thousands more died from the diseases, such as smallpox, which the Spanish brought to the New World. Mexico became a treasure house for Spain. The wealth of the conquered land was shipped to Spain. Spain kept control of Mexico for 300 years.

8. Francisco Pizarro was another conquistador of Spain who wanted to find gold. In 1531 he set out from Panama with a small army of 500 men. He sailed southward along the Pacific coast to Peru, the land of the Incas.

The ruins of the Inca city of Machu Picchu. An American discovered the ruins of this fortress city in 1911, almost 400 years after Pizarro conquered the Incas. In what mountains did the Incas build cities?

Cortés attacking the Aztecs. Why was Cortés able to defeat the Aztecs, even though he had only a small army?

9. The Indians of Peru lived in a range of mountains called the Andes. Their chief was called the Inca, and the people he ruled were called Incas. The Inca made all the laws for his people. The leaders lived in stone forts or palaces high in the mountains. The walls were built so well that some are standing today. Most of the people lived in the valleys below or along the mountainsides. They herded flocks of camel-like llama. The Incas were sun worshippers and made many objects of gold in the form of discs or circles. The Incas did not write but used a *quipu*, or knotted rope, to make a record of events. They also were good road builders.

10. Pizarro captured the Inca. The Indians brought Pizarro great amounts of gold and silver in the hope that he would free their chief. Pizarro took the treasure, but he did not free the Inca. Instead, he put the Inca chief to death. After this act of treachery, Pizarro easily conquered the Incas since they were without a leader. The Spanish became masters of Peru and forced the Indians to work in the mines. Spain now had two treasure houses, Mexico and Peru. The conquerors took so much gold and silver from these lands that Spain soon became the richest country in Europe.

Match each name in Column A with the correct description in Column B.

COLUMN A

1. Crusaders
2. Columbus
3. Prince Henry
4. Magellan
5. Vasco da Gama
6. Balboa
7. A. Vespucci

COLUMN B

a. Discovered the Pacific Ocean
b. First to sail around the world
c. First to find a new water route to India
d. Fought to recover the Holy Land from the Turks
e. Man for whom two continents are named
f. Set up a school for the study of navigation and geography
g. An Italian who made great discoveries for Spain

I. What is the main purpose of paragraphs 1 through 7?

a. To describe how the Aztecs lived
b. To describe the weapons of the Spanish soldiers
c. To tell how the Spanish treated the American Indians
d. To tell how Cortés conquered the Aztecs with only a small force

II. Choose the correct answer.

1. Cortés was able to conquer the Aztecs because
   a. the Aztecs refused to fight against him
   b. the Aztecs had a much smaller army
   c. Cortés had better fighting equipment than the Aztecs
2. Cortés and Pizarro helped Spain because they
   a. found gold and silver treasures
   b. found a short route to India
   c. conquered the colonies of Portugal
3. At first, Cortés was greeted by the Aztecs as a friend because they thought he
   a. was a god
   b. came to make a treaty of peace
   c. came to trade
4. As a result of the work of Cortés and Pizarro, Spain
   a. took control of all of North America
   b. became the richest country in Europe
   c. declared war on England

III. Decide whether each statement agrees or disagrees with what you have read. If the statement disagrees, explain why.

1. The Spanish defeated the American Indians because they made use of inventions that were not known to the Indians.
2. The American Indians in Mexico and Peru did not know how to govern themselves.

3. The American Indians of Mexico and Peru wandered from place to place in order to make a living.
4. The American Indians soon learned to hate the newcomers.
5. The American Indians forced the Spanish to work in the gold and silver mines.
6. Both the Incas and the Aztecs had conquered other tribes living near them.
7. The Aztecs and Incas were pleased that the Spaniards had brought new animals and equipment with them.
8. People were living in the New World long before the Europeans came.
9. The Spanish came to the New World to find gold.
10. The conquest of Mexico and Peru made Spain the richest country in Europe.

DEVELOPING IDEAS AND SKILLS

PICTURE STUDY There are five main figures in this picture of Cortés and Montezuma. What do you think each person may be thinking?

SUMMING UP

EXPLORING WITH CORTÉS You have read of the exploration of Cortés. Now your imagination will help you to form some ideas of what it must have been like to be with this famous explorer. Choose one of these activities. Using the following events, write a letter to a friend telling him or her about your part in this expedition. Imagine you are an Aztec of the 16th century. Describe some of these events from the Aztec point of view.

Preparing for the expedition
Sailing for Mexico
Meeting the first American
   Indian tribe
Sending presents to Montezuma

Entering the Aztec capital
Trading with the tribes
Capturing the Aztec leader
Fighting with the Aztecs
Conquering the Aztecs and Incas

5 THE SPANISH REACH THE SOUTH AND SOUTHWEST

Which lands did Coronado and De Soto explore?

1. The Spanish in Mexico heard stories from the Indians of another wonderful land to the north. It was called Cibola and had seven rich and splendid cities. The Spanish governor of Mexico was eager to conquer this land because he thought it might be as rich as Mexico. He sent Father Marcos de Niza and a band of soldiers northward to find the cities of gold.

2. Going with them was Estevanico, a black scout and explorer. (In 1528 Estevanico and two others had been shipwrecked on the Texas coast. They were captured shortly by American Indians. They had escaped and spent eight years

American Indians and Spanish missionaries and explorers, including Estevanico. What are these people showing each other?

wandering in what is now Texas, Arizona, and New Mexico. They finally reached a Spanish settlement.) De Niza sent Estevanico ahead to look over the area. For a while, Estevanico sent back reports. Suddenly the reports stopped. De Niza learned that Estevanico had been killed by Indians. De Niza heard more stories about wealthy cities. De Niza's reports about the seven cities of gold were greeted with enthusiasm in Mexico.

3. In 1540 the governor chose Francisco de Coronado to follow up de Niza's expedition. Coronado gathered a large group of soldiers and horses to carry the needed supplies. He took herds of sheep and cattle to provide food for his men on the trip. These were the first horses and cattle to graze on the plains of the United States. The explorers marched through northern Mexico into what is now Arizona, and eastward into what is now New Mexico and Texas. After a long journey, the Spanish came to the first city of Cibola. It was a village of Indians.

4. These Indians lived in houses of sun-dried brick, or **adobe.** The houses were three and four stories high. The higher stories were reached by ladders that were pulled up at night or when an unfriendly tribe appeared. The Spanish called the villages *pueblos*. Thus, they called the people who lived there Pueblo Indians. The Pueblo Indians were farmers. They raised crops of corn, beans, and squash in this dry land. They irrigated their farmland by using the waters of nearby rivers. They hunted the desert animals with bows and arrows and different kinds of traps. They used the meat for food and the skins for clothing. The Pueblos also spun and wove cotton cloth for their clothing. They made dishes and large jars of pottery in which they stored food and water. They wove baskets and mats from strips of the yucca plant. They also made beautiful objects of silver and turquoise, a greenish-blue stone.

Indians of the Southwest lived in apartment dwellings often several stories high. Why did the Indians build their houses of dried earth rather than of wood or stone?

5. Coronado was disappointed when he did not find the city of gold. Coronado divided his men into groups and sent them to explore different parts of the new territory. One party discovered a deep canyon. It was about eight miles across. Later it became known as the Grand Canyon of the Colorado River.

6. Still trying to find gold, Coronado met an Indian who told him of Quivira, a rich land to the northeast. Coronado started for Quivira in the spring. His expedition was now headed east. He left the desert and marched into what is now Texas and Oklahoma. Here he found vast stretches of level land covered with grass. The buffalo, an animal the Spaniards had not seen before, roamed these grassy plains.

7. Coronado met with other American Indians here. However, these Indians were different from the Pueblo Indians who lived farther west. These Indians were hunters. They were expert with the bow and arrow. They depended on the buffalo for their food, clothing, and materials. They had no fixed homes because they followed the buffalo herds as the herds roamed over the plains. They carried their belongings on two poles pulled by a dog. When they stopped to hunt, they put up a **tepee,** a tent made of buffalo skins.

8. From these Indians, Coronado learned that Quivira was farther north. He decided to continue with only a few men. On the march northward they came to what is now Kansas. Surely, Coronado thought, this must be Quivira. But again he found only an Indian village of straw-covered huts.

9. Certain he was not being told the truth by the Indians, he returned to Mexico. He thought he had failed because he had not found any riches. However, he had explored a large territory and had added to the knowledge of this new land called America. His journey gave Spain a claim to a large section of the present United States.

10. About the same time that Coronado was making his discoveries, another Spaniard was exploring the southeastern part of what is now the United States in search of gold. Hernando de Soto had been with Pizarro when Pizarro conquered the Incas. However, De Soto wanted more gold. In 1539 he landed on the Florida coast. With about 600 men and many horses, De Soto marched across the country looking for gold. This part of North America is warm and rainy because of the winds from the Gulf of Mexico. The land was then covered with thick forests and deep swamps. The Spanish had to cut their way through these forests. The Muskogee Indians lived in the woodlands. De Soto took their food for his soldiers. He forced some Indians to guide the expedition and carry supplies. The Muskogees attacked the Spanish and made their journey difficult.

St. Augustine in 1673. The artist exaggerated the size of this Spanish settlement.
Why were so many early settlements built near water?

11. De Soto and his men marched northward and then westward. In 1541, after a long, hard journey, they came to the Mississippi River. De Soto was disappointed that he did not find gold. For three years he had attacked and been attacked by Indians he had met along the way. Because of the hardships of the march, De Soto became sick and died soon afterward. He did not know that he had been the first European to see one of the world's greatest rivers. He was buried at night in the great river so that the Indians would not know that he had died.

12. The Spanish also wanted to find a strait through the continent of North America. Ships were sent northward along the Pacific coast to look for this strait. In 1542 a daring sailor, Juan Cabrillo, set out from Mexico to find the passage to the Atlantic Ocean. This was about the same time as the explorations of Coronado and De Soto. Cabrillo sailed along the coast, looking for an opening in the land. He died from an injury received during the voyage,

and his chief pilot, Ferrelo, took command. Ferrelo continued northward. Unable to find the passage he was searching for, Ferrelo returned to Mexico. But Spain claimed all of the land explored by Cabrillo and Ferrelo and called it Upper California. In 1602 another Spanish captain sailed along the same route, naming San Diego Bay and Monterey, which Cabrillo had reached earlier.

13. Spanish settlements began to grow in the lands north of Mexico. In 1565 the settlement of St. Augustine was built in Florida. Therefore, St. Augustine is the oldest European-built city in the United States. A second settlement was begun in 1609 on the dry western lands explored by Coronado. These lands were now called New Mexico by the Spanish. The settlement was named Sante Fe. It is considered the second oldest city in the United States.

14. Spain had gained a great empire in the New World. That Spanish empire lasted almost 300 years. How was this possible? The **conquistadors,** or Spanish con-

querers, were the most successful of all the European explorers. They were brave and well trained. The American plains were very much like the Spanish homeland—hot, dry, and treeless. The Spanish knew how to live in this new land by using adobe, brick, and stone. Finally, the Spanish explorers were very good horsemen. They rode freely and confidently over the countryside on the horses they brought from Spain. They helped Spain gain the largest empire in the New World.

REVIEWING CHAPTER 4

Choose the correct answer.

1. Spanish explorers were chiefly interested in
   a. trade with the Indians
   b. gold and silver
   c. finding fertile farmland
2. Cortés is remembered for his conquest of
   a. Mexico
   b. Peru
   c. Cuba
3. Cortés conquered the civilization of the
   a. Aztecs
   b. Incas
   c. Seminoles
4. Pizarro is remembered for the conquest of
   a. Mexico
   b. Peru
   c. Panama
5. Cortés was able to defeat the Indians because he
   a. had more men
   b. had better equipment for fighting
   c. was more familiar with the land
6. The leader of the expedition that first sailed around the world was
   a. Balboa
   b. Pizarro
   c. Magellan
7. The first European to see the Pacific Ocean was
   a. Magellan
   b. Balboa
   c. Pizarro
8. Montezuma was the leader of the
   a. Aztecs
   b. Incas
   c. Andes

UNDERSTANDING CHAPTER 5

I. What is the main purpose of paragraphs 1 through 8?

a. To explain how American Indians lived on the Great Plains
b. To describe the preparations made by Coronado before he started his expedition
c. To describe the land and people of the territory explored by Coronado
d. To name the different Indian nations that Coronado met

II. Choose the correct answer.

1. The members of De Soto's expedition were the first Europeans to reach the
   a. Florida coast
   b. Mississippi River
   c. Pacific Ocean

2. Coronado's search for the seven cities of Cibola led to
   a. the exploration of the southwest part of the United States
   b. new riches in gold for Spain
   c. a trail that led to a short route to the Pacific Ocean
3. Because some American Indians lived on the plains, they
   a. made homes of wood and brick
   b. raised corn, beans, and squash
   c. depended on buffalo for food and clothing
4. Because some American Indians lived on the desert, they
   a. used horses for farm work
   b. had to irrigate their land
   c. used skins of animals for tents
5. The Spanish explored the California coast because they
   a. were looking for gold
   b. wanted to settle the land
   c. were looking for a shorter route to the Atlantic

III. Fact or Opinion

A fact is a true statement. It can be proved. An opinion is what a person or group of people thinks about a subject. An opinion can tell the following:

   a. What a person thinks will happen
   b. What someone thinks should happen
   c. The feeling that a person has about a subject
   d. What a person believes about a subject

Read each statement carefully. If the statement is a fact, write F in your notebook. If it is an opinion, write O. Support your choice.

1. Coronado was looking for gold.
2. Because of De Soto's travels, the Spanish claimed the Mississippi Valley.
3. The Plains Indians were hunters.
4. The United States should be named after Columbus.
5. The Grand Canyon is on the Colorado River.
6. Nations should own colonies so they can become rich.

DEVELOPING IDEAS AND SKILLS

MAP SKILLS *Spanish Explorations in America*

Study the map on page 39. Then decide whether the statements that follow are true or false. If a statement is false, rewrite it so that it is true.

1. Florida is an island.
2. Coronado traveled southwest from Mexico.
3. The Spanish did not explore South America.
4. Much of the southern part of the United States was explored by the Spanish.
5. The Aztecs ruled the northern part of Mexico, or New Spain.
6. Coronado discovered the Mississippi River.
7. Cortés sailed northward from Cuba to reach the Aztec lands.
8. Spanish settlements bordered the Caribbean Sea.

Spanish Exploration in America

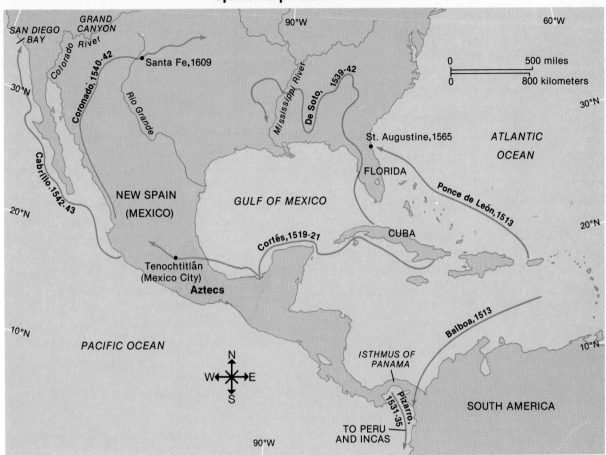

9. De Soto explored land in what is now the United States.
10. Pizarro sailed along the east coast of South America.

GAINING SKILL: ## USING THE SCALE ON MAPS

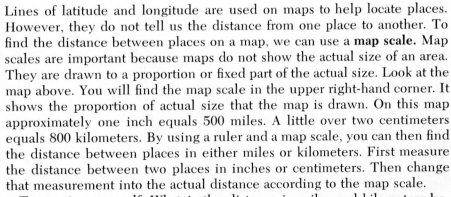

Lines of latitude and longitude are used on maps to help locate places. However, they do not tell us the distance from one place to another. To find the distance between places on a map, we can use a **map scale.** Map scales are important because maps do not show the actual size of an area. They are drawn to a proportion or fixed part of the actual size. Look at the map above. You will find the map scale in the upper right-hand corner. It shows the proportion of actual size that the map is drawn. On this map approximately one inch equals 500 miles. A little over two centimeters equals 800 kilometers. By using a ruler and a map scale, you can then find the distance between places in either miles or kilometers. First measure the distance between two places in inches or centimeters. Then change that measurement into the actual distance according to the map scale.

Try testing yourself. What is the distance in miles and kilometers between St. Augustine and Santa Fe? Between the southern tip of Florida and the island of Cuba? Between Mexico City and Santa Fe?

39

6 THE FRENCH JOIN THE SEARCH FOR A SHORTER ROUTE

How did France win land in the New World?

1. The French also wanted a share of the new riches. In 1523 the French king sent an Italian sea captain named Verrazano to the New World. Verrazano sailed up the east coast of North America looking for a northern route to the East. He failed. In 1534 the king sent Jacques Cartier.

2. Cartier also was looking for a shorter route to Asia. The route discovered by Magellan was too long and dangerous. While sailing northward along the east coast of North America, Cartier found a great gulf that led to the St. Lawrence River. He sailed up the river, hoping to reach the Pacific Ocean. Of course, he did not, but Cartier did find an American Indian village near a high hill. He called this place Montreal, which means "royal mountain." Before he left for home, Cartier named the country New France. Cartier's voyage gave France a claim to that part of the New World that we know as Canada.

3. Less than 70 years after Cartier reached the St. Lawrence River, another explorer and fur trader, Samuel de Champlain, came to New France. In 1603 Champlain brought a group of settlers up the St. Lawrence River. At the foot of a rocky cliff, Champlain laid out a fort and built several houses. These were located at a

The city of Quebec about 100 years after it was founded by Champlain. Near what important river was the city built?

point that the Indians called *kebec*, which means "a narrowing of the waters." The French called the settlement Quebec.

4. Champlain did many things to keep the French colony in the New World. He sent brave young men to live and trade with the Indians. He set up trading posts. He brought missionaries to teach the Catholic religion to the American Indians. While looking for a route to China, he explored the Great Lakes and found a lake that he named Lake Champlain. He lived among the Indians, chiefly the Algonquins and the Hurons. These tribes were his friends because he helped them fight their enemies, the powerful Iroquois. Champlain is often called the Father of New France.

5. The people of Europe wanted fish and furs. French fishermen fished for cod off the Newfoundland coast. Traders and trappers came to Canada in great numbers. They lived with the Indians, hunting and trapping. They learned the Indian languages. Forts and trading posts were built on the rivers. The Indians brought their furs to the trading posts to exchange them for the beads, guns, knives, hatchets, and wool blankets of the French. The main trading center was Montreal. The town had been permanently settled by the French in 1642. The skins were then taken from Montreal and sent to France.

6. Missionaries often went with the traders to preach to the Indians. They built churches in the wilderness. They learned the Indian languages and customs and brought European learning to the Indian villages. One of the most famous missionaries was Father Marquette. Father Marquette lived among the Indians near the Strait of Mackinac, between Lake Michigan and Lake Huron.

7. The French did not stop their search for a way through North America to Asia. The Indians had told them stories of a mighty river. The governor of New France sent Father Marquette and a young fur

Marquette and Joliet had the skills to explore the Mississippi River. Marquette knew Indian languages. Joliet could map rivers.

trader, Louis Joliet, to see if this river was the passage they were seeking. The river was the Mississippi, which De Soto had reached in 1541. Marquette and Joliet set out in 1673 on their journey with five men and two small canoes. Their Indian guides showed them the way. Marquette and Joliet went as far south as the Arkansas River. As the climate grew warmer, they became sure that the Mississippi River flowed into the Gulf of Mexico instead of the Pacific Ocean.

8. The explorations begun by Marquette and Joliet were continued by Robert de La Salle, a wealthy young Frenchman. In 1682 he sailed completely down the Mississippi to its mouth at the Gulf of Mexico. France then claimed all of the Mississippi River Valley. La Salle called it Louisiana, in honor of King Louis XIV. La Salle wanted to build a line of forts and settlements from the mouth of the Mississippi to the mouth of the St. Lawrence. France then would have control of the fur trade and a vast land

running through the center of the present United States and into Canada.

9. La Salle returned to France to get permission from King Louis to carry out his plan. The king approved because he dreamed of a strong French empire in the New World. La Salle outfitted an expedition of several hundred Frenchmen to begin a colony at the mouth of the Mississippi River. By mistake, he and his settlers landed in Texas. Soon after, La Salle was killed by one of his own party.

10. French explorers and fur traders now had explored the valleys of the St. Lawrence and Mississippi rivers. France had claimed all the land along these mighty rivers. The French settlements brought riches to France—not gold, but the valuable skins of the beaver and the otter.

La Salle claiming land for France. Why were the French interested in the New World?

REVIEWING SPANISH EXPLORATIONS

Choose the correct answer.

1. The Spanish explorer who conquered the Incas was
   a. Balboa
   b. Cortés
   c. Pizarro
2. Estevanico explored parts of
   a. Peru
   b. Brazil
   c. Texas
3. The Incas controlled an empire in
   a. Peru
   b. Mexico
   c. Quivira
4. The oldest European-built city in what is now the United States is
   a. Santa Fe
   b. St. Augustine
   c. Cibola
5. The first European explorer to reach the Mississippi River was
   a. De Soto
   b. Cabrillo
   c. Coronado
6. One of the explorers sent to find the seven cities of gold was
   a. Columbus
   b. Vasco da Gama
   c. Father Marcos de Niza
7. The Spanish explorer whose expedition was first to sail around the world was
   a. Prince Henry
   b. Magellan
   c. Vasco da Gama
8. The Aztecs were conquered by Spanish forces led by
   a. Cortés
   b. Montezuma
   c. Coronado

I. What is the main purpose of Chapter 6?

a. To describe how the French established colonies in America
b. To describe how the trappers traded with the Indians
c. To explain how Christianity came to New France
d. To outline La Salle's plans for uniting French colonies

II. Choose the correct answer or answers.

1. At first, French explorers came to the New World to
    a. search for a shorter route to Asia
    b. establish a home for religious freedom
    c. take part in the fishing and fur trade
2. Champlain is called the Father of New France because he
    a. made friends with the Huron Indians
    b. found a northern passage to Asia
    c. explored a great territory for France
3. La Salle wanted to build a line of forts to
    a. control the entire Mississippi River Valley
    b. control the gold supplies
    c. protect the missionaries from Indian raids
4. Champlain helped the Huron and Algonquin Indians because he
    a. needed their friendship for the safety of the colonists and their trade
    b. needed their help in finding gold
    c. was most interested in teaching them European ideas
5. The explorations of Cartier and Champlain were important because
    a. Quebec was established
    b. fur traders and missionaries opened a vast region for France
    c. they reached the mouth of the Mississippi River
6. French fishermen fished for cod off the coast of
    a. California
    b. Newfoundland
    c. Florida

III. Decide whether each statement is true or false. The underlined words are clues to help you decide. If a statement is false, change the underlined word or words to make it true.

1. French missionaries and fur traders made their way deep into the heart of South America.
2. French explorers entered the New World by way of the St. Lawrence River.
3. The French built forts and trading posts along the waterways.
4. Champlain founded the settlement of Quebec.
5. The French were the first Europeans to reach the Mississippi River.
6. The Great Lakes were explored by Champlain.
7. Father Marquette reached the mouth of the Mississippi River.
8. The French grew rich in the New World through the discovery of gold.

PICTURE SYMBOLS   These pictures should help you recall parts of the chapter you have read. What is the main idea of each picture?

SUMMING UP   **FRENCH EXPLORATIONS**   Complete this chart in your notebook.

FRENCH EXPLORER	WHAT HE WAS LOOKING FOR	WHAT HE DID
1. Cartier		
2. Champlain		
3. Marquette and Joliet		
4. La Salle		

Thinking It Through

Were the French successful in finding what they wanted in America? Explain.

7 THE ENGLISH COME TO STAY

What problems did early English settlers in America face? How was the colony at Jamestown able to succeed?

Sir Francis Drake as seen by an artist of his own time. Why do you think the artist included a globe in the painting?

1. The first person to explore the New World for England was John Cabot. He was an Italian sailor who was living in England when the news of Columbus's voyage reached there. The king of England gave him permission to go on a voyage of exploration. We know little about John Cabot because he did not keep careful records of his explorations. Cabot made two voyages to the New World, one in 1497 and the other in 1498. His first voyage was only five years after Columbus first landed in the West Indies. It is believed that Cabot reached the Atlantic Coast of North America at some point between what is now Massachusetts and Labrador, Canada. His voyages are important because they gave England a claim to the eastern coast of the North American continent.

2. At first, most English people were not interested in America. They seemed to forget about the voyages of Cabot. However, a few English sea captains had begun to trade with Spanish colonists. They got black slaves in Africa and sold them to plantation owners. But the Spanish government wanted its colonists to trade only with Spain. Therefore the Spanish navy attacked any English ships found near Spanish colonies in the New World.

3. Daring English sea captains such as Sir Francis Drake struck back. They attacked Spanish treasure ships and raided Spanish towns on the mainland. Elizabeth I, the queen of England, did not stop them.

To the Spanish, however, they were pirates. King Philip of Spain sent the Armada, a large fleet of warships, to punish England. But the great fleet of ships was destroyed, partly by the English navy and partly by a storm off the English coast. The defeat of the Armada ended Spain's almost complete control of the Atlantic Ocean. The English were now free to settle in the New World.

4. The first attempts by the English to set up colonies in the New World were made by Sir Humphrey Gilbert and Sir Walter Raleigh. Gilbert started a colony in Newfoundland, but it failed because of cold weather, hunger, and sickness. Raleigh made two attempts to start settlements on Roanoke Island near the coast of what is now North Carolina. The first attempt in 1585 did not succeed, and the group returned to England. The second attempt started the colony again in 1587, but the

group disappeared completely. To this day no one knows what happened to this "lost colony."

5. People began to understand that one person alone would not start a lasting colony. In 1606 two new stock companies were formed, the London Company and the Plymouth Company. Each company was given a **charter** by the king. This charter gave them the right to settle large areas of land in the New World. These companies raised money by selling shares of stock. A person who bought a share in the company would receive a share of any profit that the company made. The companies hoped to make money by finding gold, trading with the American Indians, and raising crops to sell in England.

6. The London Company sent the first group of colonists in December 1606. They brought with them tools, cloth, and household goods. Their charter allowed them to settle in what is now Virginia and North Carolina. In April 1607, they entered Chesapeake Bay. A few days later they found a river that they named the James, after their king. They set foot on a small peninsula and formed the first permanent English settlement in America. The new settlement was named Jamestown. It is now in the state of Virginia.

7. The colonists suffered terribly during the first summer. They lived in tents and slept on the ground. The land was wet and swampy. There were many insects. The water made them sick. The food spoiled in the hot weather. Many died from hunger and disease. Many settlers only wanted to look for gold and did no work.

8. Captain John Smith saved the colony. In 1608 he became the leader of the people. He made the settlers build a fort and enough cabins so that everyone would have a place to live. He traded with the Indians so that the settlement would have food. He ordered a well dug to have a supply of fresh water. He had no patience with the "gen-

Captain John Smith organizing work among the Jamestown settlers.

tlemen" who did little work. He passed a rule that men who would not work would not eat.

9. Captain Smith explored the rivers in the land nearby. He looked for gold and a passage to the Pacific Ocean. According to legend, on one trip into the forests, he was captured by the Indians. He was saved by Pocahontas, the daughter of the chief.

Pocahontas married John Rolfe and visited England where this portrait was painted.

10. The colony began to do better after a few years of hardship. The settlers were growing most of the food they needed. But it was not food that became the most important product of the colony. One of the settlers, John Rolfe, had learned how to grow a crop called tobacco. It was sold easily in England where smoking was becoming popular. Tobacco became so valuable that it was even used as money in Virginia. Large farms called plantations took the place of small farms. The owners, or **planters**, gained great wealth from their tobacco.

11. A great deal of labor and time was needed to grow tobacco. The planter could not ask neighbors for help because the neighbors were too busy working their own land. In the beginning, the planter used indentured servants as workers in the tobacco fields. **Indentured servants** were persons who agreed to work for the colony if the colonists paid for their trip to America. They were "bound" to work for a period of seven to fourteen years. At the end of this time they were given their freedom and a chance to become members of the colony. Most of the indentured servants left after their term of service because it was easy to get land.

12. The planters looked for a new source of labor that would last. In 1619 a Dutch ship brought 20 black Africans to Jamestown. (As you have already learned, these were not the first black people in the New World. Others had come much earlier with the Spanish explorers.) The blacks who arrived in 1619 were used as indentured servants to work in the tobacco fields. Over the years, many of the blacks were not freed at the end of their period as indentured servants. In the 1660s Virginia passed laws making most blacks and their children slaves. Black slaves soon became the chief source of labor in the southern colonies. By 1750 there were black slaves in all 13 English colonies.

13. In 1619 the London Company gave the Virginia settlers the right to make their own laws. Although the company would still appoint the governor, many of the laws would now be made by the free men of the Virginia colony. The men elected colonists to represent them in their own legislature, the House of Burgesses. This was the beginning of representative government in English America.

14. Still another event in 1619 changed life in Virginia. The London Company sent 90 young women to Virginia. They married and began to raise families.

REVIEWING CHAPTER 6

Who is described in each statement below?

Marquette and Joliet   Verrazano   La Salle   Cartier   Champlain

1. The first of the French to explore the Mississippi River
2. Called the Father of New France
3. Established fur-trading posts
4. Made a trip to the mouth of the Mississippi River
5. First European to reach the St. Lawrence River
6. Started the settlement of Quebec
7. Claimed the entire Mississippi Valley for France
8. Made the first explorations for the French in America although he was an Italian sea captain
9. Interested in teaching Christianity to the American Indians
10. Gave the name Louisiana to the land in the Mississippi Valley

I. What is the main purpose of paragraphs 4 through 14?

    a. To explain how trading companies were formed

    b. To describe the beginning of the first permanent English colony

    c. To tell what happened to the colonies founded by Sir Walter Raleigh

    d. To describe the work of John Smith

II. Choose the correct answer.

1. Why did the Jamestown colony have a difficult time at the very beginning?

    a. The climate was too cold for most European food crops.

    b. Too many settlers were searching for gold instead of planting crops.

    c. The Spanish attacked the colony.

2. Why is the year 1619 important in the history of Virginia?

    a. It marks the beginning of the Jamestown settlement.

    b. The first blacks were brought to English America in 1619.

    c. It was the year that cattle were brought to the New World.

3. Why did a trading company want to start a colony in Virginia?

    a. The company was given a charter.

    b. The king asked the company to start a colony.

    c. The company hoped to make money by finding gold and trading with the American Indians.

4. Why did the Jamestown colony finally succeed?

    a. All the American Indians moved farther inland.

    b. The raising of tobacco brought wealth to the settlement.

    c. All the settlers were good farmers.

5. Why is the House of Burgesses important in United States history?

    a. It was the beginning of representative government in the English colonies.

    b. It was the first written constitution in the New World.

    c. It guaranteed freedom of the press.

III. Decide whether each statement is true or false. The underlined words are clues to help you decide. If a statement is false, change the underlined word or words to make it true.

1. Sir Walter Raleigh was the first person to start an English colony in what is now the United States.

2. The first lasting English settlement was founded in what is now the state of Virginia.

3. The settlement of Jamestown was made before France claimed the Mississippi River Valley.

4. Jamestown's chief crop for trade with England was corn.

5. A person who agreed to work in order to pay for his or her way to America was called an indentured servant.

6. The year 1619 is an important one in the history of English settlements.

7. The first blacks were brought to Jamestown in Spanish trading ships.

8. The London Company allowed the colonists to make their own laws.

9. John Cabot claimed the coast of North America for England.

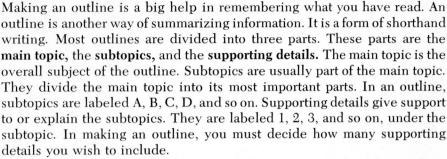

MAKING AN OUTLINE

Making an outline is a big help in remembering what you have read. An outline is another way of summarizing information. It is a form of shorthand writing. Most outlines are divided into three parts. These parts are the **main topic,** the **subtopics,** and the **supporting details.** The main topic is the overall subject of the outline. Subtopics are usually part of the main topic. They divide the main topic into its most important parts. In an outline, subtopics are labeled A, B, C, D, and so on. Supporting details give support to or explain the subtopics. They are labeled 1, 2, 3, and so on, under the subtopic. In making an outline, you must decide how many supporting details you wish to include.

Look at the example below. It shows the three main parts of an outline. The main topic of this outline is, "The Settlement of Jamestown." Copy this main topic into your notebook. Then copy the subtopics A, B, and C. Leave enough room after each subtopic to put the supporting details. Now look at the supporting details. These are numbered from 1 to 10. Under each subtopic, write the supporting details which explain or give support to the subtopic. Renumber the supporting details so that they begin with number 1 under each subtopic.

The Settlement at Jamestown

A. The Beginning of the Colony

B. The Troubles of the Colonists

C. The Colony Grows

     1. Blacks were brought to the colony.
     2. Trading companies were formed.
     3. There was a shortage of food and water.
     4. Tobacco became the chief crop.
     5. The climate was hot and damp.
     6. John Smith worked to save the colony.
     7. A settlement was made near the James River.
     8. The House of Burgesses marked the beginning of representative government in English America.
     9. Shares of stock were sold.
    10. Many settlers wanted to look for gold and did not work in the colony.

8 MORE SETTLERS START A NEW ENGLAND

Why did the Pilgrims and the Puritans come to America?

The Pilgrims leaving England for America. Why were they called Separatists? What was the name of their ship? When their ship did not land in Virginia as they had planned, what did they do?

1. During the 16th century, there was a great religious change in Europe. Some monarchs and rulers who had been members of the Catholic Church joined other religions. New churches were started. Because they were started in protest against some of the teachings and practices of the Catholic Church, they were called Protestant religions. Henry VIII of England was among those rulers who started their own church. He called it the Church of England, or the Anglican Church. He expected all English people to join it and pay for its support.

2. Many English people did not want to belong to this new church. Among them were the Pilgrims and Puritans. The Pilgrims wanted to separate from the Church of England and start a church of their own. That is why they were often called Separatists. The king would not allow this. He put many of them in jail because they would not support his church or obey its teachings. The Pilgrims decided to leave England and go to Holland where they would be free to practice their religious beliefs.

3. The Pilgrims were not happy in Holland. They were afraid their children would forget the English language and customs. A small group of them decided to go to the New World. The Virginia Company gave them a ship and supplies. In return for this help, the Pilgrims agreed to work for the company for seven years. The Pilgrims would send crops and animal skins and furs to the company. They would keep only what they needed for their own use.

4. In September 1620, the crew and 101 passengers set sail for America in a little ship called the *Mayflower*. There were about 35 Separatists from Holland on board. The Separatists were not interested in gold. They wanted to live in a land where they could worship God as they pleased. The non-Separatists on board included servants, crafts workers, and people who had invested in the colony. (Since then, most people have called everyone in the group Pilgrims. This is so even though not all of them were Separatists.) It took them ten weeks to cross the Atlantic Ocean in their little boat. Heavy storms drove the *Mayflower* off its course. The winds carried them far north of the Virginia settlement. In November 1620, the Pilgrims landed at Plymouth Rock in what is now Massachusetts.

5. The land they had reached was north of the land owned by the Virginia Company. They felt that they could not use their charter in the new location. Before going ashore, they held a meeting and drew up a new charter. Forty-one men signed the paper. In this paper they agreed that they would take part in making the laws of the community. They promised to obey these laws. This agreement, or **compact,** is called the Mayflower Compact. This paper gave the Pilgrims the right to govern themselves. The Pilgrims called their new settlement the Plymouth Colony.

6. The first winter was very difficult for the Pilgrims. The weather was very cold. More than half the settlers died from lack of food and shelter. The Pilgrims had built a small fort to defend their homes against the Wampanoag Indians. Captain Miles Standish was in charge of their defense. No attack came, for the Wampanoag Indians were friendly. Their chief, Massasoit, made an agreement with the Pilgrims to keep peace. The Indians showed the newcomers how to get food by planting beans, corn, and pumpkins. They also taught the settlers

What does this painting, *Pilgrims Going to Church,* show about life in the new colony?

how to hunt game in the woods and how to fish in the streams. With the help of the Wampanoags, the colony was saved.

7. When another fall came, the Pilgrims had fine crops and plenty of food. They decided to give thanks to God for their good fortune. Indians and a new shipload of settlers joined in the celebration of the first Thanksgiving Day. Before long the colonists were able to send a shipload of beaver skins to the Virginia Company. At the end

Massasoit, chief of the Wampanoag Indians. In 1621 he signed a treaty of peace with the settlers in the Plymouth Colony.

of three years, the Pilgrims paid in full their debt to the company. They now were able to govern themselves.

8. The Puritans were another group in England who decided to come to America for religious freedom. The Puritans were members of the Church of England, but they wanted to worship in a simple fashion. They felt that their church should be "purified" of altars, statues, and candles. English monarchs punished the Puritans for their ideas.

9. Many of the Puritans decided to come to America. They formed a stock company called the Massachusetts Bay Company. The company would supply ships and any goods needed to build settlements. The Puritans would fish, trade with the American Indians, and send to England anything of value they obtained in America. In 1628 the first group of these Puritans came to the New World to establish their own colony.

In Massachusetts, they began a settlement, which they called Salem.

10. In 1630 a larger group of Puritans came to America and settled around Massachusetts Bay. John Winthrop became the governor of the colony. He helped to establish the settlement at Boston in 1630. The first years in America were hard ones for these Puritan colonists. As time passed, they built better homes to protect themselves from the cold New England winters. As more Puritans came from England, the Massachusetts Bay Colony grew in size. Between 1630 and 1642, 16,000 people came to Massachusetts. Soon there were a number of towns in the colony. Roads were built to connect these spreading settlements. In 1691 the smaller Plymouth Colony was joined to the Massachusetts Bay Colony. Together they became known as Massachusetts. The colonists were beginning a New England here in America.

REVIEWING CHAPTER 7 — **Match each term in Column A with its correct description in Column B. There is one EXTRA item in Column B.**

COLUMN A

1. Indentured servants
2. House of Burgesses
3. Blacks
4. Charter
5. London Company
6. Tobacco
7. Jamestown

COLUMN B

a. Royal permission to start a colony
b. First permanent English settlement
c. Money crop of Virginia
d. Provided for the ships and supplies for the settlement at Jamestown
e. First representative assembly in America
f. Brought missionaries to the colonies
g. People who worked out their passage to the colonies
h. Brought to Virginia in 1619 by Dutch traders

I. What is the main purpose of paragraphs 2 through 7?

    a. To tell how the Pilgrim colony began

    b. To explain the first efforts at self-government in the new communities of New England

    c. To describe the friendship between the Puritans and the Indians

    d. To describe the voyage of the *Mayflower*

II. Choose the correct answer.

1. Why did the Pilgrims come to America?
   a. To search for a new route to Asia
   b. To find a place where they could worship as they pleased
   c. To trade with the American Indians
2. Why did the Pilgrims leave Holland?
   a. They could not practice their religion in Holland.
   b. The Dutch forced them to leave.
   c. They were afraid their children would forget the English language and customs.
3. Why did the Pilgrims celebrate Thanksgiving?
   a. They had paid their debt to the company that had given them ships and supplies.
   b. They had signed a treaty with the American Indians.
   c. They had food and had been able to live through the first difficult year in America.
4. Why did the Pilgrims sign the Mayflower Compact?
   a. They wanted to show the English king that they were free at last.
   b. They felt the old charter was not lawful.
   c. They were not satisfied with the government they had agreed on when they left England.
5. Why did the Puritans leave England?
   a. They had lost their farmland.
   b. They were not happy with the practices of the Church of England.
   c. They had heard of the riches of the fur trade.

III. Decide whether each statement is true or false. The underlined words are clues to help you decide. If a statement is false, change the underlined word or words to make it true.

1. The Pilgrims had planned to settle in <u>Virginia</u>.
2. The Pilgrims named their colony the <u>Massachusetts Bay Colony</u>.
3. The Pilgrims found the New England climate to be <u>warm and pleasant</u>.
4. Boston was founded by the <u>Puritans</u>.
5. The Pilgrims settled in <u>Holland</u> because of that country's religious freedom.
6. The first successful English colony in America was started at <u>Jamestown</u>.
7. John Winthrop was a leader of the <u>Puritan</u> colony.
8. <u>Wampanoag Indians</u> taught the Pilgrims how to hunt, fish, and plant corn.
9. The idea of self-government was first practiced in America in the settlement at <u>Plymouth</u>.
10. Miles Standish was a leader of the <u>Pilgrim</u> settlement.

MAP SKILLS *New World Explorers After Columbus*
Study the map. Then answer the questions that follow.

New World Explorers After Columbus

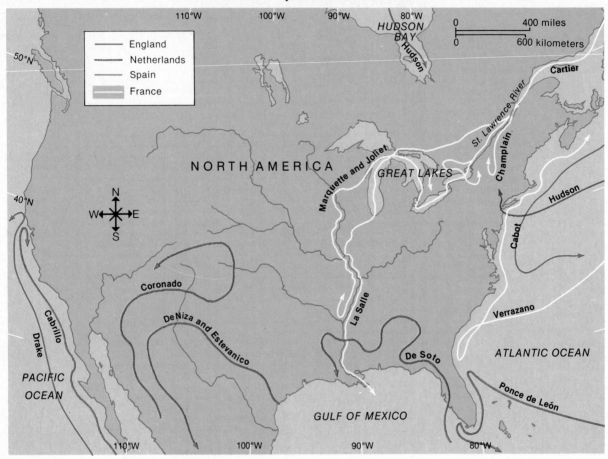

1. Which area of the United States was explored by both the French and the Spanish?
2. Who explored the eastern coast of North America for England?
3. Which country sent men to explore the Great Lakes area?
4. Which explorers sailed down the Mississippi River?
5. Which countries explored land that is now part of Canada?
6. Which section of the United States was explored by the Spanish?

SUMMING UP   **Thinking It Through**

What differences were there between the Jamestown settlers and the Massachusetts settlers? In what ways were these two groups similar?

9 HEROES OF RELIGIOUS FREEDOM

How did the search for religious freedom lead to the founding of new colonies in New England?

1. The Puritans had come to America to worship as they thought right. However, once in America, they were not willing to let others worship in a different way. There was no real religious freedom among the Puritans. They did not allow those who were not members of the Puritan faith to have a part in making laws. The leaders of the Puritan Church were the lawmakers of Massachusetts. They made laws for the community. Because of the Puritan rule, many people began to leave Massachusetts to start new settlements.

2. One of the people who disagreed with the Puritan leaders was a young minister named Roger Williams. Williams believed that the church should not be involved in government. Also, he felt that the land in America belonged to the Indians. Rulers could not give away this land by granting charters. He said that if white people wanted the Indians' land, they should pay the Indians for it. He also believed everyone had the right to worship God as he or she saw fit.

3. The Puritan leaders were angry with Roger Williams and made plans to send him back to England. He learned of their plans and escaped into the forest. Through the winter of 1636, Roger Williams lived with his Narragansett Indian friends. In the spring he was joined by other colonists who believed as he did. Together they founded a small settlement at the head of Narragansett Bay. The land was bought from the Narragansett Indians. He called the settle-ment Providence, because of God's help in keeping him safe from danger.

4. The men of Roger Williams's colony made the rules under which the people would live. Each person had a right to worship God in his or her own way. No one was forced to attend a certain church or support it. Members of different faiths were welcomed and treated kindly. The practice of religious freedom in America began in the colony of Roger Williams. In time, the colony was called Rhode Island.

5. In 1638 Roger Williams welcomed Anne Hutchinson and her large family to Rhode Island. In Massachusetts, Hutchinson had spoken out strongly against some of the Puritan ideas. She believed that people could pray to God directly, without the

Anne Hutchinson speaking up for her religious beliefs. What did the leaders of the Massachusetts Colony do about her?

Thomas Hooker and members of his congregation moving from Massachusetts in 1636. They founded Hartford in Connecticut. What other colonies were formed by people who had left Massachusetts?

help of the church ministers. In addition, she held meetings to discuss her ideas. The Puritan leaders of the Massachusetts colony brought Hutchinson to trial for her beliefs. She was ordered to leave the colony. Hutchinson took her family to Rhode Island, where there was religious freedom. She and her followers soon founded a new town in Rhode Island called Portsmouth. A few years later she moved to Long Island and then to another colony. At that time colonists and Indians were attacking each other's settlements near the Hudson River. Unfortunately, she and most of her family were killed in an Indian attack.

6. The Reverend Thomas Hooker also disapproved of the same Puritan practices that had led Roger Williams to Providence. Hooker hoped to begin a settlement where every man could take part in his government. He also hoped to find better farmlands for members of his **congregation,** or church. The rocky soil of Massachusetts made farming very difficult.

7. In 1636 Hooker left Massachusetts with a large part of his congregation. The little band headed west and started a new settlement at Hartford in what is now Connecticut. In 1639 the members of Hooker's congregation drew up a set of rules for governing themselves. They called it the Fundamental Orders. This was the first written **constitution,** or plan of government, in the English colonies.

8. Many other people left the older Puritan settlements because they were not satisfied with the Puritan Church or because they wanted more land. Generally, they settled at places that had well-protected harbors or along the fertile valleys of rivers. It was easier to travel along the river valleys, too. It was in this way that the colony of New Hampshire was settled in 1623. In 1638 the New Hampshire settlement of Exeter was started by the Reverend John Wheelwright. After he had defended his

sister-in-law Anne Hutchinson, the Puritans had ordered him out of Massachusetts.

9. At first the Puritan settlers in the New England colonies tried to deal fairly with the Indian tribes in the region. They paid for the land they used. They punished those settlers who tried to take advantage of the Indians. As the English colonies grew larger, settlers began to buy more land. The Indians were losing the hunting grounds they depended on. More and more often, settlers and Indians attacked each other's settlements.

10. When the Pequot Indians in southeastern Connecticut killed a white trader, the settlers and their Indian allies attacked the Pequots. Over 400 Pequot Indians were killed and most of the rest were sold into slavery. In 1643 the settlements of Massachusetts, Plymouth, Hartford, and New Haven joined together to protect themselves against Indian raids. They called this union the New England Confederation. For the first time in America, the colonies joined together to face a common problem. They remembered this feeling of working together for many years. The most serious fighting between settlers and Indians took place in 1675. It was known as King Philip's War. King Philip was the colonists' name for Metacomet, the chief of the Wampanoag Indians. He wanted to protect Indian land. He was the leader of several Indian tribes that attacked many New England towns and settlements. But the union of the settlers proved too strong for the tribes and King Philip was defeated. This was the last major attempt of the New England Indians to stop the spread of English settlers into their territory.

Choose the correct answer.

1. The Pilgrims established the Plymouth Colony in
   a. 1607
   b. 1620
   c. 1675
2. The Puritans and Pilgrims came from
   a. Spain
   b. England
   c. Russia
3. The Pilgrims started a government in an agreement called the
   a. Mayflower Compact
   b. House of Burgesses
   c. Fundamental Orders
4. The first Thanksgiving Day was celebrated by the
   a. Pilgrims
   b. Dutch
   c. Jamestown Colony

5. The Puritans and Pilgrims were helped by the
   a. monarch
   b. trading company
   c. French
6. The chief reason why the Pilgrims came to America was for
   a. trade with the American Indians
   b. religious freedom
   c. gold mines
7. A leader of the Plymouth settlement was
   a. John Smith
   b. Miles Standish
   c. John Rolfe
8. The Plymouth Colony became part of
   a. Connecticut
   b. Massachusetts
   c. New Hampshire

I. What is the main idea of paragraphs 1 through 4?

    a. Rhode Island wins the friendship of the Indians.
    b. A new colony is founded where people can worship as they please.
    c. Roger Williams escapes from Massachusetts.
    d. The Puritans have trouble with many settlers.

II. Choose the correct answer or answers.

1. Roger Williams is important in the history of America because he
    a. began a colony where freedom of worship was allowed
    b. believed that everyone should have a voice in the government
    c. thought the church should be a part of government
2. The New England Confederation was formed to
    a. make the colonies richer
    b. protect the colonies from Indian attack
    c. make trade easier among all the colonies
3. The Indians fought the settlers in New England because the
    a. settlers took their land and destroyed the forests
    b. settlers wished to take over the gold mines of the Indians
    c. Indians sided with the Spanish colonists
4. Anne Hutchinson left Massachusetts because
    a. the Puritans did not want to allow her religious practices
    b. she wanted to help the Indians
    c. she was not satisfied with the farmland
5. One of the reasons for settlements near rivers was that
    a. the settlers were far from Indian territory
    b. it brought the settlers closer to Europe
    c. it made travel easier
6. The settlement of Connecticut was led by
    a. Anne Hutchinson
    b. Thomas Hooker
    c. John Wheelwright

III. Decide whether each statement agrees or disagrees with what you have read. If the statement disagrees, explain why.

1. Some colonies in New England were started because people were not happy under the Puritan government.
2. Roger Williams practiced religious freedom in his colony.
3. The Indians in New England remained at peace with the settlers.
4. Settlements were begun in river valleys because the most fertile farmland was found there.
5. Some colonies joined together to fight Indian attacks.
6. Fertile farmland was found almost everywhere in Massachusetts.
7. Many settlements in New England were founded by people who did not come directly from England.
8. The Puritans are remembered because they guaranteed freedom of worship to all settlers.
9. The people of Connecticut had no laws to guide their settlement.

PICTURE STUDY *Roger Williams and the Narragansett Indians*

An artist painted this scene of Williams's 1636 escape from Massachusetts. What are the Narragansett Indians doing? Why? What feelings might Williams have had about the fighting between the colonists and the Wampanoag Indians in 1675? Explain your answer.

HEROES OF RELIGIOUS LIBERTY Fill in the columns for each of these leaders.

	WHY HE OR SHE LEFT	WHERE HE OR SHE SETTLED	WHAT HE OR SHE BELIEVED
1. Roger Williams			
2. Thomas Hooker			
3. Anne Hutchinson			

Thinking It Through

Why did the Puritans, who wanted religious freedom for themselves, refuse to give it to others?

59

10 EUROPEANS ARRIVE IN THE MIDDLE COLONIES

How were settlements in New York, New Jersey, Pennsylvania, and Delaware started?

1. In 1609, two years after Jamestown was settled, a Dutch ship sailed along the Atlantic coast. The ship was called the *Half Moon*. Its captain was Henry Hudson. Hudson was an English sailor who had been hired by Dutch merchants to find a passage through America to the Far East. More than a hundred years had passed since Columbus's voyage. Europeans still were looking for a shorter route to the Indies. Hudson did not find a shorter route. But he did sail up the mighty river that now bears his name.

2. Although Hudson did not find what he was sent for, he did explore the land along the Hudson River. He found that the woods were rich in fur-bearing animals. He reported that the American Indians were willing to trap these animals and sell them cheaply. When the Dutch merchants learned this, they formed the Dutch West India Company. This company wanted to trade with the American Indians for furs and to settle the land explored by Hudson. It sent colonists to establish settlements along the Hudson River.

3. The first permanent Dutch settlements in America were set up in 1624. Some of the Dutch went up the Hudson River. They settled in Fort Orange, where the city of Albany now stands. Some moved near the Connecticut River. Still others settled near the Delaware River. The governor of the Dutch colony, Peter Minuit, bought the island of Manhattan from the local Indians. Minuit paid $24 worth of colored beads and trinkets for the island. The Dutch built a fort and a village on the island, which then became known as New Amsterdam. These four settlements made up the colony of New Netherlands.

4. One of the most famous governors of New Netherlands was Peter Stuyvesant. He was an old soldier who had lost a leg during battles in the West Indies. He was not well liked because his rule was strict.

5. Sweden is a small country in northern Europe. In 1638 Swedish settlers built a fort at what is now Wilmington, Delaware. The fort was named Christina, in honor of the Swedish queen. Peter Minuit, who had helped set up the Dutch colony at New Amsterdam, also headed the Swedish colony at its start. More settlers arrived and the colony was called New Sweden. There were already Dutch settlers nearby. The earlier

Peter Stuyvesant and Dutch settlers reacting to the English attack on New Amsterdam. Stuyvesant surrendered New Netherlands in 1664. He retired to his Manhattan farm.

Dutch settlers called for help. They did not want the Swedish settlers taking away their fur trade. Moreover, New Netherlands had already claimed the land along the Delaware River. In 1655, Peter Stuyvesant marched south with his soldiers. He captured the Swedish colony and brought it under Dutch rule.

6. Trouble also developed between the Dutch and the English. England claimed all the land along the eastern coast because of the voyages of John Cabot in the late 1490s. The Dutch colony allowed traders from English colonies to send their tobacco and goods to New Netherlands. Then these products could be shipped to Europe without paying British taxes. England didn't want its colonists to escape paying the taxes. The quarrel between the Dutch and the English grew steadily worse. In 1664 war broke out between the two countries. An English fleet sailed into the harbor of New Amsterdam and demanded the surrender of the Dutch. Stuyvesant wanted to fight, but the Dutch settlers would not support him. New Netherlands became an English colony.

7. The king of England turned the colony over to his brother, the duke of York. The name was changed to New York in honor of the new ruler. At the same time, England had gained land across the Hudson River. The Dutch and Swedes had settled there, but it was now English territory. The duke of York gave this land to two English nobles, who named their colony New Jersey.

8. While the Dutch were losing New Amsterdam to the English, a remarkable young man named William Penn was living in England. He had become a member of a religious group called the Society of Friends, or Quakers. The Quakers' beliefs were different from those of the Church of England. The religious practices of the Quakers were simple. When they met to worship God, there was no preacher. Ev-

African slaves being sold in New Amsterdam. Most male slaves worked in nearby fields. Most female slaves were house servants.

eryone was free to speak. They believed that all people were equal before God. They refused to take off their hats for anyone. They would not swear loyalty to the king. They hated wars and refused to fight in them. They thought it was wrong to keep slaves. Because of their beliefs, the king forbade the Quakers to preach in England. If the Quakers disobeyed the king, they were put in prison or fined heavily. At one time William Penn went to jail for his religious beliefs.

9. Penn had a rich and famous father, Admiral Penn. The king owed a large sum of money to the admiral. Penn tried to collect the money after his father's death, but he did not succeed. William suggested that the king give him a grant of land in America in return for the debt. Penn

William Penn making a peace treaty with the Lenni-Lenape Indians. What else did Penn do to attract settlers from Europe?

wanted the land for the Quakers so they could be free to worship as they wished. The king agreed. The land given to Penn became known as Pennsylvania ("Penn's Woods").

10. William Penn came to Pennsylvania in 1682. Although he had a charter giving him the land, he paid the Indians for it. He wanted to live in peace and friendship with the Indians. His peace treaty with the Indians was never broken during his lifetime. For the capital of his colony, he chose the place where the city of Philadelphia now stands. Philadelphia means "brotherly love" in ancient Greek.

11. Penn opened his colony to others besides Quakers. He sent out notices to England, Ireland, Scotland, and Germany, promising freedom of worship and cheap land to all who would come to Pennsylvania. Thousands came. They were allowed to buy land for as little as a penny an acre. They took part in the government of the colony. They worshiped in their own manner. They built towns, raised crops, and were happy and prosperous. Pennsylvania became one of the most successful of all the English colonies. It became known as a place where there was a great deal of religious freedom.

12. The little colony that the Swedes had started in 1638 became known as Delaware. The English gained this colony after their war with the Dutch. The duke of York gave it to William Penn to govern. In 1704 it became a separate colony.

Which statements apply to Roger Williams of Rhode Island? Which apply to the Puritans of the Massachusetts Bay Colony?

1. Allowed only members of the church to vote and take part in the government.
2. Did not welcome people of different religious beliefs.
3. Believed that the Indians were the owners of the land in the New World.
4. Believed that the government and the church should have separate powers.
5. Allowed people of all faiths to come to the colony.
6. Sent John Wheelwright from the colony because of Wheelwright's religious beliefs.
7. Allowed the members of the colony to make rules to govern themselves.
8. Welcomed Anne Hutchinson to settle in the colony and practice her religion.

I. What is the main purpose of paragraphs 1 through 8?

   a. To describe the Swedish settlements in America
   b. To tell about Dutch settlements in the New World
   c. To tell about the purchase of Manhattan Island
   d. To describe the land along the Hudson River

II. Choose the correct answer or answers.

1. William Penn had peace with the American Indians because
   a. they were afraid of him
   b. they were treated fairly
   c. Penn bought their friendship with trinkets
2. Two reasons why many people were attracted to the Pennsylvania colony are that
   a. they were able to obtain land cheaply
   b. the colony had a fine government
   c. everyone could do as he or she pleased
3. William Penn wanted land in the New World because he
   a. wanted a home for people in debt
   b. wanted to make money from the sale of land
   c. wished to establish religious freedom for the Quakers
4. The chief reason why the Dutch came to America was to
   a. trade with the American Indians for furs
   b. use the nearby waters for fishing
   c. teach the American Indians the Christian religion
5. Two reasons why Quakers were punished in England are
   a. they wanted to restore the Catholic Church
   b. their beliefs were different from those of the Church of England
   c. they did not swear loyalty to the king
6. The Dutch sent Henry Hudson to America to
   a. look for good farmland
   b. start a new colony
   c. find a new way to the Indies

III. Decide whether each statement is true or false. The underlined words are clues to help you decide. If a statement is false, change the underlined word or words to make it true.

1. The Dutch established settlements in the St. Lawrence River Valley.
2. William Penn welcomed people of different religious beliefs to his colony.
3. Pennsylvania was started as a home for the Quakers.
4. New Netherlands was a colony founded by the Dutch.
5. Peter Stuyvesant was a governor of a Dutch colony in America.
6. The first settlers in Delaware were the English.
7. New Amsterdam was taken from the Dutch by the English.
8. The Dutch claimed New Netherlands because of the explorations of John Cabot.
9. Fort Orange was a trading post in the Swedish colony.
10. Many people came to Pennsylvania because they could buy land cheaply.

DEVELOPING IDEAS AND SKILLS

In each of the following groups are three events important in the history of the colonies. Arrange the events in each group in the order in which they took place.

1. Founding of Jamestown
   Defeat of the Spanish Armada
   First representative assembly
2. Puritans came to Massachusetts
   Roger Williams founds Rhode Island
   Dutch settlements begin
3. Pennsylvania is founded
   Dutch colonies become English colonies
   New Amsterdam is founded

SUMMING UP

UNDERSTANDING WILLIAM PENN Making decisions is an important skill. Here are some statements about William Penn. You may agree or disagree with each statement or you may decide you don't have enough information to make a decision. Be ready to support your decision.

1. He was a violent man.
2. He was always wealthy.
3. He found better ways of living.
4. He ruled his colony wisely.
5. He was friendly with the Indians.
6. As a young man he was interested in religion.
7. He began a colony for Quakers.
8. He learned an American-Indian language.

Thinking It Through

William Penn opened Pennsylvania to all Europeans. In what ways was he different from other colonial leaders?

11 THE LAST ENGLISH COLONIES ARE ESTABLISHED

How were English colonies founded in the South?

1. As you have learned, the rulers of England sometimes gave large grants of land to nobles and other friends. These people became the owners, or **proprietors,** of land in America. Their colonies were known as **proprietary colonies.** The colonies of New York, New Jersey, Pennsylvania, New Hampshire, and Delaware at first were ruled by proprietors. Many of the southern colonies also were ruled in the same way. The earliest of these in the South was Maryland.

2. In Massachusetts, the Puritans and Pilgrims had come from England to America for religious freedom. The Catholics were another religious group in England who were punished for their beliefs. Catholics did not want to pay for the support of the Church of England. George Calvert, known as the first Lord of Baltimore, was a Catholic and a friend of King Charles I. He wanted to start a colony for English Catholics who then would be able to practice their religion in peace. King Charles I planned to grant Lord Baltimore a piece of land north of Virginia.

3. Before the king could grant him a charter, Lord Baltimore died. The king presented the charter to his son, the second Lord Baltimore. Baltimore now became the proprietor of the land. He sent two ships with 300 settlers to America. They started

Early settlers in Maryland. The land was divided into large sections for use by the settlers. Why did Lord Baltimore want to start a colony?

the first settlement in 1634. It was called St. Marys. Soon other settlements were made, and the colony became known as Maryland. It was named in honor of Henrietta Maria, the king's wife.

4. In Maryland, the Protestants soon had the same rights as Catholics. In 1649 a Toleration Act was passed giving freedom of worship to all Christians. The colonists had no trouble with the Indians, for Lord Baltimore treated them fairly and won their friendship. The settlers cleared the fertile land for farms and raised crops of corn and tobacco. Because of all this, the colony prospered and grew rapidly.

5. In 1663 King Charles II gave a section of land that lay south of Virginia to eight other friends. These nobles called their colony Carolina in honor of their ruler. Charles is "Carolus" in Latin. In 1670 they founded a settlement at Charleston in southern Carolina. The proprietors were

An early settlement in the proprietary colony of Carolina. What is meant by the term *proprietary colony?*

surprised to learn that settlers were already living in the northern part of the colony. Some people from Virginia had moved there 17 years before in search of better farmland. These backwoods people and small farmers did not get along with the noble landlords. There were many arguments. Finally, in 1689 South Carolina and North Carolina split into two separate colonies. The king also took away the rights of the proprietors and placed a royal governor over the Carolinas.

6. Georgia was the last of the 13 British colonies founded in what later became the United States. It was settled in 1733. King George II wanted to protect South Carolina from attacks by the Spanish and Indians in Florida and by the French in the Louisiana. At the same time, the jails in England were filled with people who could not pay back the money they owed. They were called **debtors.** The debtors found it hard to pay their debts while they were in jail. Unless they had friends to help them, debtors might stay in prison all of their life.

7. James Oglethorpe was a rich man in the British government. He wanted to help debtors by starting a colony for them in America. He hoped they would be able to start a new life there. He planned to locate the colony between South Carolina and Florida. This would protect the other colonies from the Spanish, French, and Indians. King George II gave him the land for a settlement, which Oglethorpe called Georgia in honor of the king.

8. Oglethorpe paid the debts of a few people in jail and arranged for their trip to America. But most of the early English settlers in Georgia were poor tradespeople and crafts workers, not debtors. Settlers also came from Scotland and New England. Jews from England, Spain, and Portugal and German Protestants came. In 1733 the first settlement was made at Savannah, near the river of the same name. Many colonists raised cotton, rice, or **indigo.** Indigo is a

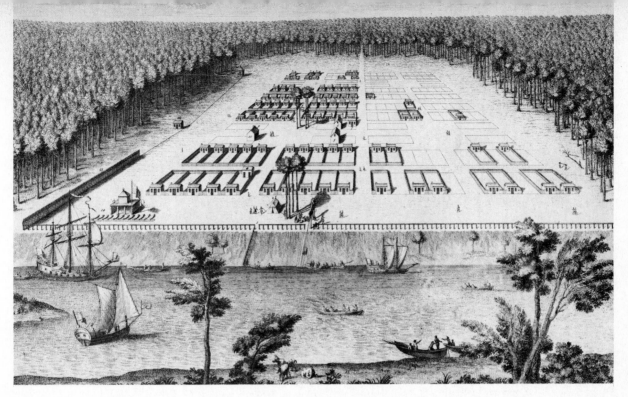

Earliest known view of Savannah, Georgia, 1734. The town was fortified against Spanish attacks. What were the reasons for starting this colony?

blue dye made from the indigo plant. Georgia did not grow as rapidly as the other English colonies.

9. By 1733 England had 13 colonies along the Atlantic Coast. They stretched from Georgia in the south to Maine (at that time part of Massachusetts) in the north. The population had grown to almost 1 million people. More and more people were coming to live in the colonies to find better lives for themselves than they had in Europe.

REVIEWING
CHAPTER 10

Match each name in Column A with its correct description in Column B.

COLUMN A

1. William Penn
2. John Cabot
3. Peter Stuyvesant
4. Leni-Lenape
5. Henry Hudson
6. Duke of York

COLUMN B

a. Explored the coast of North America for England
b. Took over New Amsterdam after the Dutch lost it to the English
c. Dutch governor of New Amsterdam
d. First explored the land around what is now New York City
e. Established a home for Quakers
f. Indian nation in Pennsylvania.

67

I. **What is the main purpose of paragraphs 1 through 4?**

    a. To describe the beginning of the Maryland colony

    b. To state the religious beliefs of Catholics

    c. To explain the powers of the proprietor

    d. To describe the land and products of Maryland

II. **Choose the correct answer.**

1. Some people had moved from Virginia to the Carolinas because
    a. the king had taken away their rights
    b. there had been serious trouble with the Indians
    c. they wanted better land

2. King George II was interested in having an English settlement south of the Carolinas for
    a. a defense against the Dutch
    b. protection against the French and the Spanish
    c. a home for Quakers

3. James Oglethorpe wanted a colony in America to
    a. establish a home for those in prison because they owed money
    b. buy and sell land for profit
    c. establish a government where everyone was considered equal

4. The Maryland colony was begun to
    a. provide a home for those who fled from Massachusetts
    b. establish a home where Catholics could practice their religion in peace
    c. find riches in gold

5. Many settlers moved to the Maryland colony because
    a. religious freedom for Christians was guaranteed there
    b. the land was perfect for growing cotton
    c. the government was the best in the colonies

III. **Decide whether each statement below is a fact or an opinion. Support your decision.**

1. James Oglethorpe founded the Georgia colony.
2. The proprietary colony was the best form of government for a colony.
3. Georgia was the last of the English colonies established in what later became the United States.
4. The Toleration Act of 1649 was passed in the Maryland colony.
5. The colonies should have paid the Indians for the land they took.
6. Georgia had fewer people than the other southern colonies.
7. North Carolina and South Carolina should have remained one colony.
8. Directly south of Georgia was Spanish territory.

MAP SKILLS *European Settlements, 1652,* and *the 13 Colonies, 1750*
Study the maps. Then choose the answer that best completes the sentence.

1. The American Indians that lived near Jamestown were the
    a. Iroquois   b. Powhatan   c. Pequot

2. New Sweden became a part of the colony of
    a. New York   b. North Carolina   c. Delaware

3. An important settlement in Maryland was
   a. Wilmington b. Exeter c. St. Marys
4. In 1652 the St. Lawrence River was located in
   a. the colony of New York b. Plymouth c. New France
5. The colony of Georgia protected the other colonies from the
   a. Dutch b. Spanish c. Portuguese
6. Maine belonged to the colony of
   a. Massachusetts b. Vermont c. New Hampshire
7. One of the colonies that was considered a southern colony was
   a. Delaware b. Maryland c. New Jersey
8. By 1750 the frontier was located near
   a. the Appalachian Mountains
   b. the Atlantic coast
   c. Rhode Island

European Settlements, 1652

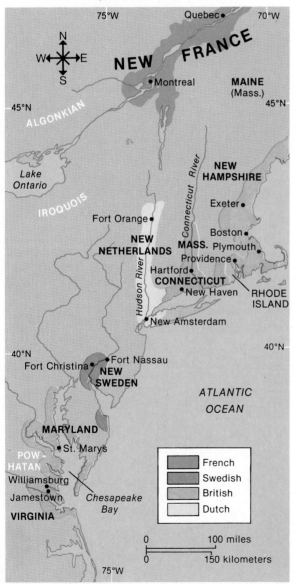

The 13 Colonies, 1750

9. The town of New Amsterdam was located near the
   a. James River   b. Ohio River   c. Hudson River
10. The powerful Indians that lived between New York and New France were the
   a. Iroquois   b. Narrangansett   c. Wampanoag

SUMMING UP **ENGLISH COLONIES**   Complete the following chart in your notebook.

COLONY	DATE FOUNDED	WHY FOUNDED	LEADER(S)
1. Virginia			

2. Massachusetts
  a. Plymouth
  b. Boston			

3. New York			
4. Maryland			
5. Connecticut			
6. Rhode Island			
7. Delaware			
8. New Hampshire			
9. North and South Carolina			
10. New Jersey			
11. Pennsylvania			
12. Georgia			

Thinking It Through

Georgia was started as a place where people could build lives for themselves. How and where can people get a "second chance" at life today?

12 NATIVE AMERICANS AND NEWCOMERS

What peoples made up the early colonies?

1. When the first European explorers and colonists reached North America, they found people whom they called Indians. Columbus gave the Indians that name because he thought he had landed in the East Indies, islands off the Asian mainland. These Native Americans were divided into hundreds of tribes, many of whom spoke different languages and followed different ways of life. They had crossed from Asia to Alaska thousands of years before, and they had very slowly spread throughout the Americas. Some American Indian tribes were mainly wandering hunters. Others settled in villages and became farmers. Many Indian nations had well-organized governments. For example, the Iroquois lived in what is now the northeastern part of the United States. Each of the five (then six) powerful Iroquois nations elected representatives to meet in tribal council. These tribal councils sent delegates to the Great Council Fire. That council made decisions and took action on very important matters.

2. The colonists found the first few years in the New World very hard. Many of them died from sickness or lack of food. The colonists had to learn to build homes with materials close at hand. They had to learn how to hunt in the forest, how to grow food in the New World, and how to make clothing for themselves. Above all, they had to learn how to deal with the Indians already living in the land.

3. At first, the Indians and Europeans got along together peacefully. In fact, the Indians generally were of great help to the colonists. White fur traders gave Indians useful

American Indians of the Northeast. In what ways did they use plants and animals to provide food, clothing, shelter, and transportation?

71

The Touro Synagogue in Newport, Rhode Island. It was the first Jewish house of worship in the colonies. Settlers from many countries came to the 13 colonies.

metal tools in return for furs. Indians showed settlers how to hunt in the forest and how to trap small animals such as beavers, foxes, and rabbits. They taught the settlers how to spear and hook fish in the streams. Most importantly, they taught the settlers how to grow Indian crops. Indian corn, or **maize,** was the most valuable of all Indian crops to the colonists. The colonists learned to boil or roast it, and they ate the first grains of corn as a vegetable. They ground hard, dried grains to make cornmeal. Many colonial families came to depend on cornmeal to make bread, cake, and cereal. Indians also showed the colonists how to drain the sap from maple trees and use it to make maple sugar and syrup. White settlers learned from the Indians how to make medicine from plants.

4. As the number of colonists increased in the New World, things changed. The colonists began to move inland and settled on Indian hunting grounds. They cut down the

forests and fenced the land to use it for farming. The Indians, on the other hand, did not believe that any person could own the land. They felt it belonged to the Great Spirit and could not be sold. As more and more whites came, the Indians became angry and fought to protect their way of life. Some attacked and tried to destroy the homes and farms of the colonists. There were also white settlers who attacked Indians. Some Indian tribes made agreements with whites to attack enemy tribes. Many people on all sides lost their lives.

5. Despite all the hardships, the number of people coming from Europe increased. Most of the people who settled in the English colonies came from England. But settlers came from other countries as well. Jews from many countries settled in New York, Rhode Island, and South Carolina. Many French people settled in the Carolinas. For a time, Swedes had their own colony in Delaware. Germans and Scotch-Irish settled in Pennsylvania. Many Dutch colonists lived in New York. By 1750 there were more than 1 million people living in the English colonies. As landowners, small-shopkeepers, or craft workers, they all had a chance to live better than they had lived in Europe. In time, they no longer looked upon themselves as English or Dutch or whatever they had been. Instead, they and their children became "Americans."

6. Most white settlers had come to the English colonies because they wanted to. This was not true, however, of another group, the blacks. Blacks were brought from Africa against their will. One of the first groups of blacks landed at Jamestown in 1619. By then, the slave trade was already more than 100 years old. Portugal had brought Africans to Europe in the early 16th century. Some blacks had gone with French and Spanish explorers on their travels in the New World. Thus, blacks had taken part in opening the New World long before the settling of Jamestown in 1607.

7. In general, black people had been taken by slave traders on the west coast of Africa. Many had been captured in war by stronger African tribes inland and then had been taken to the coast. There they were sold to white slave dealers. Next, the captured people were forced onto crowded slave ships. The trip across the Atlantic was horrible for most Africans. On the average, one-third of them died before they reached America. Here is a brief account of the trip by one slave who was brought from Africa.

8. "Once on board, we were taken below deck and chained together. At the end of two weeks, the ship's hold was so full of prisoners, that no one could lie down. We had to sit all the time because the room was not high enough to stand. When the prison could hold no more, the ship sailed. The weather was hot below and many of us died. Many of us jumped overboard. They preferred to drown or be eaten by sharks than be slaves in a foreign land. We had scarcely enough food to keep us alive. More than one-third of us died on the passage. When we arrived, we were not able to stand. I was sold to a trader with several others."

9. The first blacks brought to North America were sold as indentured servants. Their labor and skills became very valuable to the large tobacco and rice farms of the South. To prevent them from leaving, the planters began to draw up new laws. By 1700 the governments of most southern colonies had laws turning black people into slaves. Under these laws, black persons could be bought, sold, worked, and punished. Their children were also denied freedom. As slavery increased, many white colonists began to feel that they were "better" than or superior to black people. This false belief that one race is better than another is called **racial prejudice.**

10. Not all black people who lived in early colonial America were slaves. There were also free blacks. They were free for several reasons. Many earned a living as skilled crafts workers or as trusted servants. Although free blacks were better off than blacks in slavery, they had many limits on their lives. They usually could not own property. They usually had to live in their own neighborhoods, separate from whites. Free blacks could not bear witness against whites in a court of law. Despite their difficulties, however, they gave much to colonial life.

Slave ships were often so crowded that many did not survive the ocean voyage.

Decide whether each statement is true or false. The underlined words are clues to help you decide. If a statement is false, change the underlined word or words to make it true.

1. <u>Georgia</u> was the last of the 13 original colonies to be founded.
2. James Oglethorpe founded the colony of <u>South Carolina</u>.
3. The colony of Georgia was begun as a home for <u>debtors</u>.
4. <u>Virginia</u> settlers moved south in search of more land for their crops of corn and tobacco.
5. The first settlement in Georgia was called <u>Charleston</u>.
6. Maryland was established by <u>Lord Baltimore</u> as a home for Catholics.
7. The king of England was interested in <u>Maryland</u> because it lay near Spanish and French territory.
8. The soil and climate of Maryland were good for growing <u>indigo</u>.
9. The Toleration Act gave <u>everyone</u> the right to worship in his or her own way.
10. The land south of Virginia was called the <u>Carolinas</u>.
11. Many of the southern colonies started out as <u>proprietary</u> colonies.

I. What is the main idea of paragraphs 1 through 4?

a. To explain why the American Indians came to the New World
b. To describe how the American Indians helped the early settlers
c. To describe the American Indian way of life and how the Indians and European settlers acted toward each other

II. Choose the correct answer.

1. The earliest people in the New World were called Indians because
   a. they came from India
   b. Columbus gave them that name because he thought he had landed in the East Indies
   c. they had found a direct route to India
2. All these were problems of the early white settlers EXCEPT
   a. building homes in the wilderness
   b. obtaining cheap land
   c. providing enough food for themselves and their families
3. Two of the most valuable of the colonists' crops were
   a. tobacco
   b. corn
   c. tomatoes
4. The Africans were different from other colonists in that they
   a. came to the New World against their will
   b. belonged to a different race
   c. both of these statements
5. Many Europeans came to the New World to
   a. worship God in their own way
   b. obtain land cheaply
   c. both of these statements

6. In the 1700s slavery spread
   a. only in the southern colonies
   b. only in Virginia and the Carolinas
   c. to all 13 colonies

III. Do you agree or disagree with the following statements? Give reasons for your answers.

   a. The first Americans were people from Europe.
   b. The American Indians forced the first white settlers to work for them.
   c. Europeans came to America thousands of years after the American Indians arrived.
   d. In order to live in America, the colonists had to farm the land.
   e. The colonists got little help from the Indians.
   f. Despite the hardships of the New World, more and more people came.
   g. The Africans chose to come to America.
   h. Most black Africans could look forward to living lives similar to those of the white colonists.

DEVELOPING IDEAS
AND SKILLS

PICTURE STUDY *Slavery*

Slavery was common in colonial America and the young United States. Between the early 1600s and the early 1800s, millions of Africans were taken from their homelands to America.

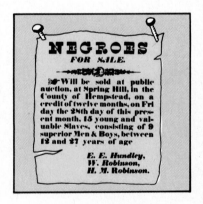

Look at the pictures above. Then answer the following questions.

1. Why are the Africans in chains?
2. What kind of crossing did they have?
3. What happened to them once they were in the New World?
4. How do you think they felt about their new land?
5. Why did so many Americans accept slavery for Africans?

Population of the 13 Colonies

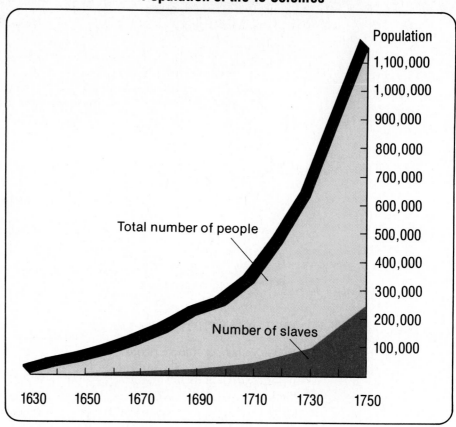

A. Use the graph above to find the correct answer.
1. What is indicated by the numbers listed along the righthand edge of the graph?
2. What was the population of the colonies in 1690?
3. What was the population of the colonies in 1750?
4. What was the population in 1730?
5. How many people were slaves in 1750?

B. Do you agree or disagree?
This graph shows us the following:

1. The countries from which the colonists came
2. Which colonists came against their will
3. Where the colonists chose to live
4. How many people were living in the 13 colonies from 1630 to 1750
5. Why people came to the colonies

Thinking It Through

What things or events in the New World caused the colonists to become a "new" people?

Study this time line. Then answer the questions that follow. Use the information in this unit to help you. You also may look at the time line on pages 12 and 13 if you need additional help.

In which period of time (A, B, C, D, E, or F) did the following take place?

1. The Mayflower Compact is signed.
2. Jamestown is founded.
3. Columbus reaches America.
4. Pizarro conquers the Incas.
5. Oglethorpe starts the Georgia colony.
6. The English seize New Amsterdam.
7. The first blacks are brought to Jamestown.
8. De Soto reaches the Mississippi River.
9. St. Augustine is built in Florida.
10. The Narragansett Indians help Roger Williams when he leaves the Massachusetts colony.

EXTENDING YOUR READING

Using the Parts of a Book

Your history book has certain parts that are very important. Knowing what these parts are will make the book more useful to you. First, there is the title page. On this page you can find the title of the book, the name of the author, and the name of the company that published it.

Next is the table of contents, which lists the unit titles and chapters. There also is a listing of maps and special sections. The table of contents gives you an idea of what the book is about.

At the end of the book are the glossary and the index. A glossary is a word list. It gives the meanings of many of the words used in the book. An index is a list of the important persons, places, and topics in the book and the pages on which they are discussed. An index is arranged in alphabetical order.

Now that you have read this introduction, answer these questions about the parts of this book.

1. On which page can you find the author's name?
2. What kind of book does the title suggest?
3. On which page can you find the unit titles and chapter titles?
4. How can the unit titles and chapter titles help you?
5. On which pages can you find the meaning of many words used in the book?

Now look at the table of contents. Answer the following questions.

1. How many units are there in the book?
2. In which unit can you read about inventions?
3. In which unit can you read about the settlement of the West?

Part of the index of the book is shown below. Answer the questions that follow it.

Africa, 16, 21, 72-73, 87, 276, 406, 429, 436, 444, 451, 454, 462, slavery, 276
Airplane, 363, 349, 444; first flight over Atlantic Ocean, 394; jets, 521; in World War II, 439-441
Air pollution, 512, 530, 531
Alabama, 195, 215, 221, 312, 336
Alamo, battle at, 240-241. *See also* Texas.
Alaska, 215, 235, 237, 245, statehood, 419; U.S. purchase of, 406
Albany Plan for Union of the English Colonies, 119, 120
Aldrin, Edwin, 522
Allegheny Mountains, 103
Allen, Ethan, 134

Answer the following questions.

1. How does an index differ from a table of contents?
2. Why is an index used?
3. How are the main topics and subtopics arranged?
4. What is a "cross reference"? Identify one above.
5. Where is the index located?
6. What does the dash—mean?
7. Why are the topics followed by page numbers?

BOOKS FOR UNIT I

AUTHOR	TITLE, PUBLISHER	DESCRIPTION
1. Alderman, Clifford	*Colonists for Sale,* Macmillan	The story of indentured servants in America.
2. Asimov, Isaac	*The Shaping of America,* Houghton Mifflin	Rivalries in Europe and painful Indian—colonial relations.
3. Cochran, Hamilton	*Pirates of the Spanish Main,* Golden	Exciting stories of sea fights and treasure ships.
4. Crawford, D.	*Four Women in a Violent Time,* Crown	Fighting against intolerance in the 1640s.
5. Crouse, A. and B.	*Peter Stuyvesant of Old New York*, Random House (Landmark Books)	The story of the last Dutch governor of New Amsterdam.

BOOKS FOR UNIT 1

	AUTHOR	TITLE, PUBLISHER	DESCRIPTION
6.	Daugherty, James	*Landing of the Pilgrims*, Random House (Landmark Books)	The adventures of a people who came to the New World in search of religious freedom.
7.	Garst, Shannon	*Three Conquistadors*, Julian Messner	Three Spanish explorers (Coronado, Cortés, Pizarro) in the New World.
8.	Guillet, E. and M.	*The Pathfinders of North America*, St. Martin's Press	True stories of the explorers of America from earliest times until now.
9.	Jones, Virgil C.	*Birth of Liberty*, Holt, Rinehart and Winston	James River in Virginia and the place in history of those who lived near it.
10.	Kjelgaard, Jim	*Explorations of Pere Marquette*, Random House (Landmark Books)	The adventures of a man who was both missionary and explorer.
11.	Longsworth, Polly	*I Charlotte Forten, Black and Free*, Crowell	Black girl reared by a wealthy family joins the abolitionist movement.
12.	Shepherd, Elizabeth	*The Discoveries of Esteban, the Black*, Dodd, Mead	The slave from Africa who commanded the respect of a band of Indians and guided a Spanish expedition.
13.	Tunis, Edwin	*Frontier Living*, World	Conditions of daily living along the western frontier.
14.	Tunis, Edwin	*Colonial Craftsmen*, World	The work of colonial artisans; the system, the work, the product.
15.	White, Anne T.	*The American Indian*, Random House	Adapted from the *Heritage Book of Indians*. Complete and beautifully illustrated.

Unit II

How Did the Colonies Win Their Freedom?

| 1640 | 1650 | 1660 | 1740 |

1735 Zenger Trial

1649 Toleration Act (Maryland)

1660 First Navigation Law of 1660

1639 Fundamental Orders of Connecticut

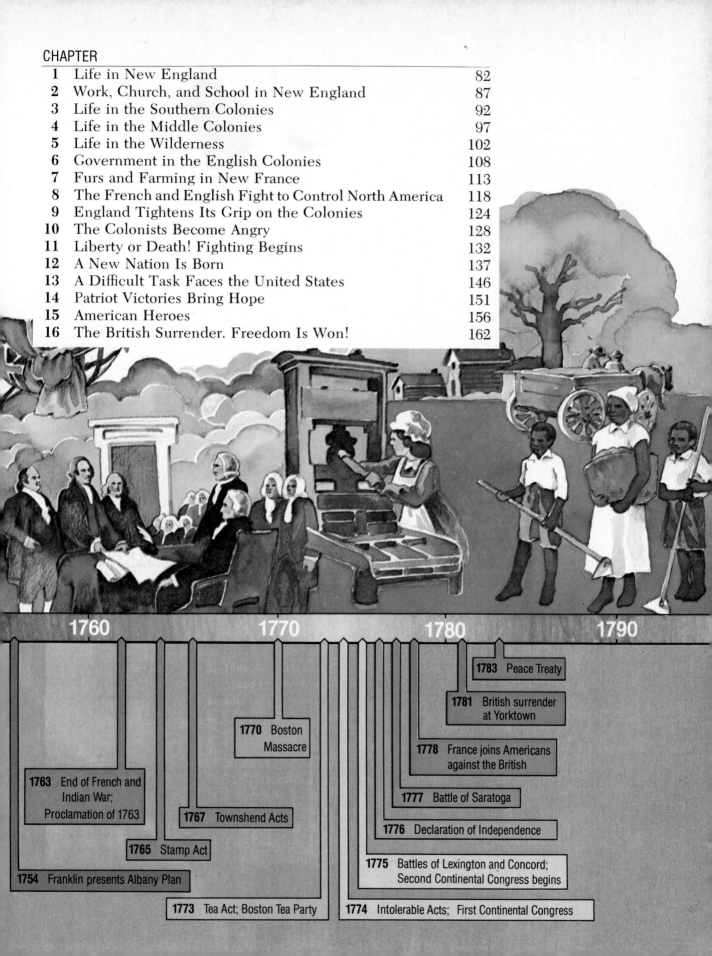

CHAPTER

1760   1770   1780   1790

1783 Peace Treaty

1781 British surrender at Yorktown

1778 France joins Americans against the British

1777 Battle of Saratoga

1776 Declaration of Independence

1775 Battles of Lexington and Concord; Second Continental Congress begins

1774 Intolerable Acts; First Continental Congress

1773 Tea Act; Boston Tea Party

1770 Boston Massacre

1767 Townshend Acts

1765 Stamp Act

1763 End of French and Indian War; Proclamation of 1763

1754 Franklin presents Albany Plan

1 LIFE IN NEW ENGLAND

How did the people of New England make a living?

1. By 1750 the population of the 13 colonies was growing fast. Most of the people lived on the land between the Atlantic Ocean and a line of mountains to the west called the Appalachians. This stretch of land is called the Atlantic Coastal Plain. It is narrow in the northern part and wider in the southern part. The 13 English colonies may be divided into four sections: New England, the Middle Colonies, the Southern Colonies, and the border strip, or frontier.

2. Geography played an important part in the way the people of each section made their living. New England was a section of small farms. Because much of the soil was rocky, many people turned to the ocean and the forests to make a living. The Middle Colonies were drained by the mighty Hudson and Delaware rivers. The land in these river valleys was divided into small farms

New England, 1750

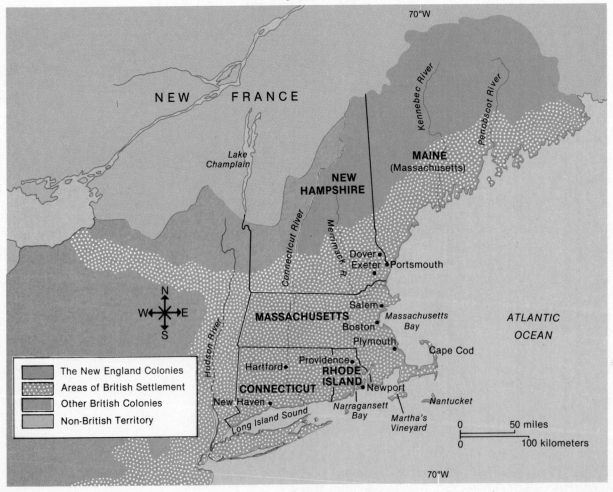

- The New England Colonies
- Areas of British Settlement
- Other British Colonies
- Non-British Territory

Women in colonial society. Women played an important role in colonial life. This painting shows women performing many kinds of work. Identify the kinds of work shown.

and large estates. The people of the Middle Colonies had a variety of occupations. The most fertile land in the Atlantic Coastal Plain was between the ocean and the mountains in the South. The Southern Colonies had large plantations worked by black slaves. They raised crops of rice, tobacco, and indigo. There were also many small farms. The frontier stretched from Maine to Georgia along the line of mountains. This border strip was settled by brave hunters and farmers who worked hard to clear the land.

3. Most of the early homes in New England were simple cottages made of brush (for the roof) and wood (for the sides). These homes had dirt floors. They had holes cut in the boards for windows and doors. The window spaces were covered with oiled paper. The settlers built furniture by splitting logs and smoothing the flat sides with an ax. Sometimes they built a fence of pointed logs around the settlement. The fence was called a **palisade** or **stockade.** It protected the settlers from Indians whose land and hunting grounds they had taken.

4. After a while, most towns had sawmills to supply lumber. The New England settlers began to build better and more comfortable houses of lumber and brick. Some rich people brought articles for their homes from England: window glass, rugs, and better-looking furniture. The settlements grew larger.

5. The kitchen was the chief room in the New England house. In the kitchen, there was a huge fireplace that was used to warm

Women working in the garden of a colonial home. Why was it necessary for every member of a colonial family to work on the farm?

6. Most of the people in New England were farmers. Their farms were usually small. The winters were long and cold, and so the growing season was short. The land was hilly and the fields were full of stones. While the farming was slow and difficult, the settlers depended on their land to supply them with most of their food.

7. Every New England family had to take care of its own needs. Most people built their own houses. This was usually done by the men in the family. Women had to spin thread, weave cloth, and sew all the clothing. The family had to get its food from the forests or its small farm or garden. The family cared for its members when they were sick or had reached old age.

8. Everyone in the family worked to supply what was needed. It took all day to complete the work to be done. Everyone was busy because the work had to be done by hand. The adults, usually the men, cleared the land, worked the fields, and hunted game in the forest. The boys chopped wood, kept the fires, and fed the animals. The women sewed clothes, cooked, and washed. They also prepared food for the winter by salting it down or pickling. The girls worked in the gardens and cleaned the cabin. In the evening, the father and the boys might whittle or carve some simple household article out of wood. In this way, they made the bowls and spoons for the family. Before going to sleep, one of the parents might place some hot coals into brass or copper warming pans in order to warm the beds.

and light the cabin and to cook the family meals. The settlers cooked food in large iron pots held by iron hooks over the fire. They baked bread in a small oven built at one end of the fireplace. Most colonial families did not have much furniture: a few chairs, tables, and a high-backed bench called a settee. They also had a spinning wheel for spinning wool or flax. Besides the fire, the cabin was lighted by candles made from tallow, the fat of animals. The candles were made by pouring the hot tallow into long tin molds.

UNDERSTANDING CHAPTER 1

I. **What is the main purpose of Chapter 1?**

    a. To tell how the early settlers built their homes
    b. To describe the home life of the farm family in early New England
    c. To describe the New England kitchen
    d. To explain the duties of each member of the colonial family

II. Choose the correct answer or answers.

1. Two reasons why members of farm families had to work all day are that
   a. there were few machines to help them
   b. they wanted to sell their crops in the market
   c. there were many jobs to get done
2. Life in early New England was hard because
   a. each family had to provide its own food, clothing, and shelter
   b. people had to work on land they rented
   c. the rough waters made it difficult to fish
3. Farming was not easy in New England because the
   a. cost of land was too high
   b. land was not well suited to farming
   c. farmers could not get their crops to market
4. The colonists built a palisade because
   a. they wanted to live apart from each other
   b. they feared the Indians whose land or hunting grounds they had taken
   c. they were often attacked by the French settlers
5. Two reasons why forests were important to the settlers are that the settlers
   a. used wood to manufacture paper
   b. obtained food there
   c. could use the wood for house furniture
6. Most early settlers in New England
   a. did not have much furniture
   b. raised indigo, tobacco, and rice
   c. lived west of the Appalachian Mountains

III. Decide whether each statement agrees or disagrees with what you have read. If the statement disagrees, explain why.

1. Some New England settlers did not farm for a living.
2. The most fertile farm land was found in the Southern Colonies.
3. New England families had to trade with other people to get the things they needed to live.
4. Every member of the colonial family in New England had to work.
5. The settlers in New England lived on large farms.
6. The kind of work that the settlers did depended on the geography of the land on which they settled.
7. The Atlantic Coastal Plain is narrower in the South than in the North.
8. Most of the work on a New England farm was done by hand.
9. Farm life in colonial days was easier than it is now.
10. The family depended on the farm to supply its members with their food.

An event in history can come to life even though it may have taken place long ago. Visual aids such as pictures, charts, and diagrams help bring events to life. They can often fill in the details of history more quickly and more clearly than words alone. They can show how people lived in the past. They can show how they dressed, what they did, and what their homes were like. But visual aids are helpful only if you study them closely, note the details, and challenge them with questions.

For example, look at the drawing above. (A drawing is another kind of visual aid.) Who are the people in the picture? How are they dressed? What are they doing? How different is this kitchen from the ones we have today? What else can you describe about them and their life? It is often possible to check the accuracy of the drawing by reading the text or looking at other aids. Compare the drawing above with the picture on page 83. What things do they each show that are similar? What things are different?

Pictures are an important part of studying history. They can be used to give new meaning to history and bring to life what we read. They can also help us remember what we have read. As you read the following chapters, think about the pictures and other visual aids you see. Use them to help better understand what you read.

SUMMING UP   **Thinking It Through**

"Geography helps decide how people live, work, and play."

How does this statement apply to life in New England?

2 WORK, CHURCH, AND SCHOOL IN NEW ENGLAND

How did Puritan beliefs affect life in New England?

1. Because it was not easy to make a living from the soil, people in New England soon turned to other occupations. Mountain streams and the nearby sea had plenty of fish. Forests were a rich source of wood. Thus, New Englanders were able to make a living from fishing and shipbuilding.

2. The New England settlers used fish as a source of food and an item of trade. They exchanged fish for furs and game from the forests. The settlers needed ships to catch the fish and to carry on their trade. The forests supplied wood for the shipbuilding industry. The New Englanders sent fish, furs, and lumber to towns along the Atlantic Coast. The towns of Salem and Boston were leading seaports in this trade.

3. In time, ships began to travel farther from the coast of North America. A three-sided trade developed between New England, the West Indies, and the coast of Africa. It was called the molasses-rum-slave trade. The New England captain would take a cargo of rum to Africa. On the African coast, the captain would exchange the rum for black slaves. He would bring the slaves to the West Indies. In exchange for the slaves, the captain would take molasses to New England. There it would be turned

New England Trade Routes

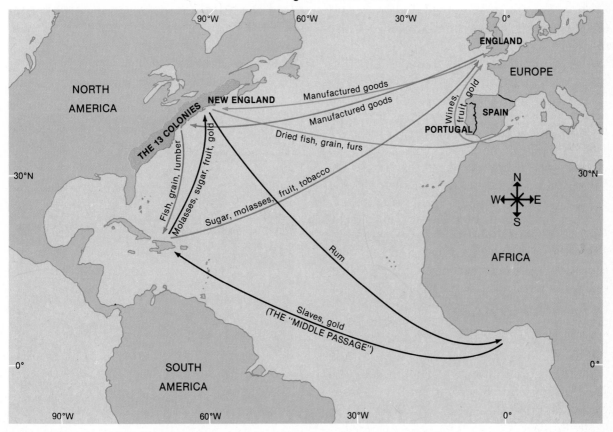

The stocks and pillory of a New England town. These punishments were meant to embarrass wrongdoers. Do you think this kind of punishment would work today?

5. Under their rule, laws in the Puritan colonies were strict and punishments were harsh. For example, there were laws against card playing, dancing, and wearing fancy clothes. People who broke the laws might be whipped or put in the **stocks** or **pillory.** In the stocks, the legs of the law-breaker were locked in a wooden frame. In the pillory, the head and hands of the law-breaker were locked in a wooden frame. A liar or drunkard might be placed in a wooden chair and ducked in a stream. More serious crimes were punished by cutting off the lawbreaker's nose or arms. Puritan leaders did not believe in "sparing the rod."

6. The Puritans thought that education was important. They wanted their children to read the Bible and grow up with an understanding of their religious duties. As early as 1647, Massachusetts passed an education law. The law required each village of 100 families to provide an elementary school. In these schools, pupils learned to read the Bible, write, and do arithmetic.

into rum, and the trade would begin all over again. Soon, New Englanders were also bringing slaves to the Southern Colonies. The New England shipbuilders, ship-owners, merchants, and traders benefited from this trade. There were several thousand black slaves in the New England Colonies. But most black slaves were sold to and lived in the Southern Colonies.

4. The people of New England, many of whom were Puritans, were very religious. They read the Bible daily. They did not permit work on Sunday. They expected everyone to attend church services. The churches were unheated and uncomfortable. People sat on hard, wooden benches. Women and men sat apart. Boys were placed in a balcony above the main section of the church and were punished if they made any noise. The ministers gave two long sermons on Sunday. They told their followers how they should behave and what they should believe. The ministers of the Puritan Church were often the leaders of the community.

A one-room schoolhouse, built in 1763. Why was education so important to New Englanders?

A colonial tinsmith's shop. Men and women are making kitchen pots and pans. Why did workers have to be apprentices before working on their own?

School was held six days a week. The teacher was strict, and pupils were whipped if they did not know their lessons. The teacher did not receive any pay, but he lived for free with the families of his pupils. The chief book was the *New England Primer*. It was used to teach religion and reading. Books were scarce and many classes used the same book. The books were taken apart and individual pages were fastened to a piece of wood with a handle. On the pages might be the Lord's Prayer or the alphabet. Each page was covered with a thin sheet of cow horn. This kind of book was called a hornbook.

7. In addition to the elementary school, there was another school called the dameschool. In this school, a woman was given a small fee for teaching children how to read, write, and count. The pupils met at the home of the teacher. In larger towns, an academy or high school developed. In 1636 Harvard, the first college in the colonies, was opened. Colleges usually prepared students for careers as ministers of the church.

8. A boy could get another kind of education by becoming an apprentice. Parents would "lend" their children to a skilled crafts worker. The skilled worker would teach a trade such as shoemaking, carpentry, or shipbuilding. In addition to teaching the trade, the master was expected to teach the boy counting and reading. The apprentice would live with and work for the master until he was 21. On the other hand, only a few girls became apprentices. But girls were sometimes sent to other people's houses to work and learn household skills.

9. The Puritans did have some fun. They enjoyed working together to build a new house or school. They held quilting parties and husking bees. They enjoyed taking part in the affairs of the community at a town meeting. At these gatherings, they discussed the need for building new roads, a school, or a church. Men who were both church members and property owners made the decisions. As the years passed, life improved in the New England Colonies.

THE NEW ENGLAND COLONIES Are the following statements true or false? Rewrite each false statement to make it true.

1. The New England family depended on its own farm to supply most of its food.
2. As the years passed, the colonists built better homes and improved their ways of living.
3. The spinning wheel was run by water power.
4. There were a few things in the New England home that were made of iron.
5. Settlers in New England had large farms.
6. Every member of the New England family had to work.
7. The people in each section of the British colonies made a living in a different way because of the geography of the land.
8. The farmers kept their meat from spoiling by salting.
9. New England had the most fertile soil of all the colonies.
10. Most of the work in New England was done by machine.

I. What is the main purpose of Chapter 2?

a. To describe the church meetings in New England
b. To tell about life in a Puritan community
c. To describe how the settlers made a living
d. To tell about the first schools in the colonies

II. Choose the correct answer.

1. Education was important to the Puritans because they wanted their children to
   a. be smarter than other colonists
   b. read the Bible and lead good lives
   c. keep busy all day
2. Some of the New England settlers turned to fishing and trading because
   a. they could not grow cotton successfully
   b. it was difficult to make a living from the soil
   c. there was not enough help on the large farms
3. New England became a center for shipbuilding because
   a. there was plenty of wood in the forests
   b. there was a need to carry fish to other ports
   c. both of these reasons
4. Harvard College was founded by the Puritans to
   a. prepare young men to learn a trade
   b. give the colony trained teachers
   c. train men to become ministers
5. Two kinds of trade that benefited shipowners were
   a. sending of gold to the Southern Colonies
   b. sending of fish to towns in the West Indies and along the Atlantic coast
   c. the molasses-rum-slave trade

III. **Decide whether each statement agrees or disagrees with what you have read. If the statement *disagrees*, explain why.**

1. The settlers tried to make use of the natural resources of their land.
2. The Puritan town meeting is an example of how early settlers governed themselves.
3. Trade was carried on with Africa because the settlers needed slaves in New England.
4. An apprenticeship was another form of education.
5. As fishing and trading increased, shipbuilding became important.
6. Life in the Puritan settlement centered around the church.

DEVELOPING IDEAS AND SKILLS **PICTURE SYMBOLS**   These pictures should help you recall parts of the chapter you have read. What is the main idea of each picture?

SUMMING UP **NEW ENGLAND**   Complete the following chart in your notebook.

NEW ENGLAND

1. Climate and soil
2. Size of farms
3. Kinds of work
4. Type of settlement
5. How work was done
6. Government

Thinking It Through

To the Puritans, what was the purpose of education? What do you think is the purpose of your education?

3 LIFE IN THE SOUTHERN COLONIES

What was life like on a southern plantation?

1. The Southern Colonies included Maryland, Virginia, the Carolinas, and Georgia. These colonies differed from New England and the Middle Colonies in climate and soil. The growing season in the South was longer and the soil was richer. Nearly everyone made a living by farming. The fertile coastal plain was at its widest point. Therefore, many of the farms were much larger than those in New England. These large farms were called **plantations.** The chief crops were tobacco, rice, and indigo. You may recall that indigo is the plant from which a blue dye is made.

2. The first settlers in Jamestown lived in any kind of shelter they could make. They made tents from the sails of their old ships and huts from the sod or soil. Their first wooden houses were little more than one-room shacks. Later, they built better cabins. However, the furnishings inside the cabins were very much like those of the early New England settlers.

3. As time passed, the plantations became very important in the South. They were located near rivers and streams so the tobacco could be shipped easily to market. There were smaller farms nearby. Plantations were far apart because of their size. As a result, there were fewer towns in the Southern Colonies than in some of the colonies to the north.

4. Plantation owners were called planters. The planter's family did not live in a log cabin, but in a house made of wood and brick. The planter usually built a large two-story building. The house had wide

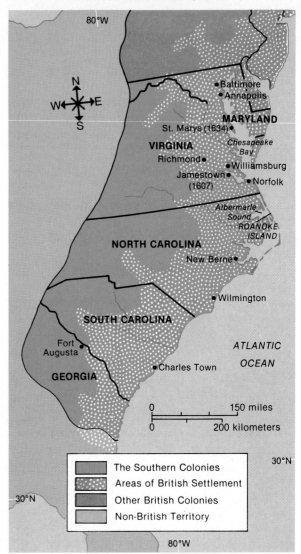

The Southern Colonies, 1750

porches and beautiful pillars in front. Near the planter's house were the smaller houses of the slaves who were house servants. There were also cabins for the slaves who worked in the fields. The plantation was like a small village.

5. Everyone on the plantation had a job to do. The owner of the plantation was in charge of all the work. The owner's wife took care of such household duties as cooking, candle making, sewing, and jelly making. Most slaves worked in the fields. Some

were house servants. Others worked in the shops as carpenters, blacksmiths, or shoe-makers. The plantation grew most of its own food. The land provided materials for almost everything that was needed. As a result, the plantation supported itself.

6. Tobacco growing, while profitable, was not easy work. Can you imagine all the jobs that had to be done? The soil had to be prepared. The plants had to be placed in the soil. The soil had to be kept soft and the weeds removed. The leaves had to be picked and cared for. The tobacco leaves had to be dried, packed in large barrels, and sent to market. At first, the planter made use of indentured servants. But as more land was taken up for tobacco, the planter used black slaves. Some planters soon had from 50 to 100 slaves working with tobacco.

As the use of slaves spread, few indentured servants could be found in the tobacco fields.

7. Most of the people in the South, however, were not plantation owners. They were small farmers who had few or no slaves at all. Members of the farm family did all the work of raising crops and looking after household needs. Many also grew tobacco, which they sold to the nearest large planter. Others sold tar, pitch, and tur-pentine to English shipbuilders. They took these products from the pine trees in the great forests of the South. Pitch was used to keep the wooden ships watertight. Tar was used to keep the wood and ropes from rot-ting. These products were called **naval stores,** for they were used by the English navy.

An unknown artist's painting of a southern plantation. In what ways does this painting match what you have learned about southern plantations?

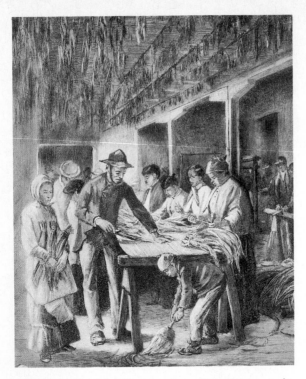

Growing tobacco. Tobacco was an important crop in Virginia, Maryland, and North Carolina. Slaves were used to plant, harvest, dry, and ready the tobacco for sale.

The End of the Hunt. This painting shows southern gentlemen out for a day's hunt. Why did southern planters have time for recreation?

8. The planters had a very active social life. Since slaves did the hard work, planters had more time for leisure and pleasure than did New England farmers. Because the plantations were far apart, guests were always welcome. It was common for visitors to stay for several days. During that time, fox hunts, parties, and dances were held. Men and women wore elegant clothes to the plantation parties. The greatest sports in the South were hunting and horse racing. The southern planters often thought of themselves as English lords and ladies far from home. But there were differences. In England, the farmers who worked on the lord's land paid him rents and services, but they were free. A planter's workers, however, were slaves who had no rights. In the colonies, the planters had far greater power than most people in England.

9. There were fewer schools in the South than in New England, because there were fewer towns of any size. Children could not be expected to travel many miles to school and return home each day. The planter's children were taught in their own home. The teacher, who lived at the plantation, was called a **tutor.** When the boys were older they might be sent to school in England or to William and Mary College in Virginia. This was the first college founded in the Southern Colonies. It opened in 1693. The girls did not go to college. They were taught at home how to manage the large household. The children of the small farmer had little or no opportunity to get an education. Almost no effort was made to teach the indentured servants or the slaves. In fact, some colonies had laws against teaching slaves to read or write.

Decide whether each statement is true or false. The underlined words are clues to help you decide. If a statement is false, change the underlined word or words to make it true.

1. The <u>Puritans</u> wanted their children to receive an education.
2. The *Bible* and the *New England Primer* were the chief books used in Puritan schools.
3. <u>Yale</u> was the first college founded in this country.
4. Many slaves in Africa were paid for with <u>molasses</u>.
5. <u>Apprenticeship</u> was a form of education.
6. Most of the teachers in the early schools were <u>well paid</u>.
7. New England <u>shipowners</u> benefited from the molasses-rum-slave trade.
8. <u>Public schools</u> were started in New England in 1647.
9. Students were <u>punished</u> when they did not know their lessons.
10. Harvard College trained young men for the <u>church</u>.

I. What is the main purpose of Chapter 3?

a. To tell about the social life of the planters
b. To describe what a plantation was like
c. To describe the climate of the South
d. To describe life in the Southern Colonies

II. Choose the correct answer.

1. Why did the southern colonists turn to farming for a living?
   a. The fertile soil and warm climate made farming easy.
   b. There were no other natural resources in the South.
   c. The planters did not like to trade.
2. Why were there fewer schools in the South?
   a. The people wanted to keep their children at work on the farm.
   b. The people had little interest in education.
   c. There were fewer towns than in the colonies in the North.
3. Why did the southern planters have more leisure time than New England farmers?
   a. The planters had slaves to do the hard work.
   b. The planters did not care for their plantations.
   c. The planters depended upon their neighbors for help.
4. Why did plantation farming become important in the South rather than in New England?
   a. The land in the South was level and more fertile.
   b. The New England settler disliked slavery.
   c. The New England settler was interested in fishing.
5. Why were the forests in the South important?
   a. The Southern Colonies had a great shipbuilding industry.
   b. The southern colonists obtained tar, pitch, and turpentine from the pine trees.
   c. Maple sugar had become an important product in Virginia.

III. Decide whether each statement agrees or disagrees with what you have read. If the statement disagrees, explain why.

1. Nearly everyone in the South made a living by farming.
2. Fishing became important in the South.
3. The plantation usually was located in a clearing in the woods, far from transportation.
4. Since homes were far apart, the South had fewer towns than the other colonies.
5. Black slavery was the chief means of labor.
6. Southern forests provided naval stores.
7. Most of the people of the South were small farmers.
8. The soil and the climate made farming difficult in the South.
9. Small farmers had little use for slaves.

PICTURE SYMBOLS These pictures should help you recall parts of the chapter you have read. What is the main idea of each picture?

NEW ENGLAND AND THE SOUTHERN COLONIES Complete the following chart in your notebook.

	SOUTHERN COLONIES	NEW ENGLAND
1. Climate and soil		
2. Labor		
3. Size of farms		
4. Type of settlement		
5. Chief crops		
6. Occupations		
7. Schools		

4 LIFE IN THE MIDDLE COLONIES

How did an American spirit develop in the Middle Colonies?

1. The Middle Colonies included New York, New Jersey, Pennsylvania, and Delaware. They were located between New England and the Southern Colonies. Most of the people who settled in New England and the South were from England. The people who settled in the Middle Colonies came from several different countries. They came from Holland, Sweden, Germany, Scotland, and Ireland, as well as from England. There were black slaves from Africa in all the Middle Colonies. All these groups spoke different languages and had different customs. There were also different religious groups, such as Quakers and Catholics, among these settlers.

2. The soil and climate were better for farming in the Middle Colonies than in New England, although not as good as in

The Middle Colonies, 1750

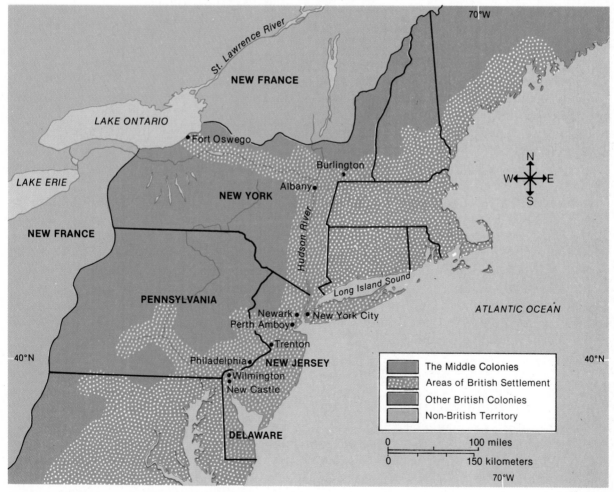

LAKE ONTARIO

NEW FRANCE

St. Lawrence River

70°W

•Fort Oswego

LAKE ERIE

Burlington

Albany•

NEW YORK

NEW FRANCE

Hudson River

Long Island Sound

PENNSYLVANIA

ATLANTIC OCEAN

Newark• •New York City

Perth Amboy•

•Trenton

40°N

Philadelphia• **NEW JERSEY**

•Wilmington

New Castle

40°N

DELAWARE

	The Middle Colonies
	Areas of British Settlement
	Other British Colonies
	Non-British Territory

0   100 miles

0   150 kilometers

70°W

the South. There was no one outstanding crop on farms in the middle section as there was in the South. Grains were plentiful. Wheat, rye, oats, and barley were the chief products. These colonies sold so much grain, flour, and bread that people in the other sections called the Middle Colonies the "Bread Colonies." Manufactured articles included glass, barrels, leather, and shoes. Ironworks were started to make axes, saws, and guns. Philadelphia and New York became shipbuilding and trading centers.

3. The people in the different colonies hardly knew each other. Most people stayed at home because the roads were poor. The few trips that they made to the villages were on horseback. When stagecoach travel started between the large towns, roads were widened. A **stagecoach** was a large wagon or carriage drawn by horses. The stagecoach stopped at stations or stages along the way. Passengers could get off to refresh themselves at these stages. A fresh team of horses was supplied for the next part of the journey. Many times, the passengers had to help the driver push the wheels of the stagecoach out of the mud. The trips often would take many days.

4. In addition, mail service was slow. A person never knew how long it might take for his or her letter to reach its destination. Letters were carried by travelers rather than by regular mail riders. Mail was often lost or left in stores and inns for weeks. A traveler left the mail at the last stop on his or her journey. It would stay there until another traveler appeared. If that traveler was going farther, he or she would take the letters along.

5. As travel and communication improved, the colonists themselves began to change. They forgot that they were once Dutch, Swedish, German, or English. People began to dress alike, to eat the same kinds of foods, and to think about the same problems. They began to consider them-

Philadelphia, Pennsylvania. By 1770 it was the largest city in the 13 colonies.

selves Americans. Benjamin Franklin has been called the "first American." We ought to know something about him to understand why.

6. Benjamin Franklin was born in Boston in 1706, the son of a candlemaker. He liked books and decided to become a printer to be near the books he loved. At the age of 12, he became apprenticed to his older brother, James, to learn the printing trade. When he was 17, he ran away from home and went to Philadelphia. He got a job with a printer and spent his spare time studying and reading. Franklin worked hard and saved his money. He was able to buy his own printing shop at the age of 22. He became very well known for printing *Poor Richard's Almanac*.

7. Franklin was known for his common sense. Many of his wise sayings appeared in the *Almanac* and are remembered to this day. Examples are "A penny saved is a penny earned," "Honesty is the best policy," and "Early to bed and early to rise makes a man healthy, wealthy, and wise."

8. Franklin was one of the earliest inventors in the colonies. By flying a kite, he discovered that lightning is a giant electrical spark. He made the rocking chair and a new kind of street lamp. His stove proved to be better for warming homes than the fireplace.

9. Franklin helped make life better for people in other ways. He and his friends started the first public library in Philadelphia. Through his efforts, police and fire departments were begun in Philadelphia. He got the people to pave the muddy streets and brighten the dark city with his new street lamp.

10. In 1753 he became the first postmaster general of the colonies. Before long, mail service was improved. The mail was delivered faster and to more distant parts of the colonies. He allowed newspapers to be sent as cheaply as letters. As a result of his efforts, people of the colonies got to know each other better.

11. Women played an important part in colonial life. Most colonial women worked in the home. This work was very hard. A woman had to be skilled in many things to take care of her home and family. One important skill was making clothes for the family members. Women also quilted bedspreads, hooked rugs, and sewed curtains.

12. If her husband was a crafts worker, a colonial woman often helped him in the

Benjamin Franklin.

shop. Women could sometimes get jobs outside their home as well. Some women were tavern keepers, school teachers, or traders. Other women worked in saw mills or grist mills. Some women also made and sold wine. Many women were printers and published their own newspapers.

REVIEWING CHAPTER 3 **THE SOUTHERN COLONIES** Are the following statements true or false? Rewrite each false statement to make it true.

1. The South was a section of large farms.
2. Corn and wheat were the most important crops.
3. Nearly everyone in the South made a living by farming.
4. The South had a great ship-building industry.
5. The South had a longer growing season than the Middle Colonies.
6. As the use of indentured servants spread, fewer slaves worked in the fields.
7. Great quantities of tobacco were grown.
8. There was a great interest in public education.

I. **What is the main purpose of paragraphs 1 through 5?**
  a. To tell about the means of travel in colonial days
  b. To identify the products of the Middle Colonies
  c. To describe the people who came to live in the Middle Colonies
  d. To describe the life of the people in the Middle Colonies

II. **Choose the correct answer.**

1. How were the Middle Colonies different from New England and the South?
   a. The towns governed themselves.
   b. Settlers came from many countries of Europe.
   c. Farming was important in the Middle Colonies.
2. Why were these colonies called the "Bread Colonies"?
   a. Philadelphia became famous for its bakeries.
   b. These colonies sent large amounts of food to other colonies.
   c. The Middle Colonies bought wheat from New England.
3. Why did people travel so little in colonial times?
   a. Roads were poor.
   b. The stagecoach had not yet become popular.
   c. Robbers made it risky to go from one town to another.
4. Why is Benjamin Franklin considered to be the "first American"?
   a. He was known for his common sense.
   b. He printed his own newspaper.
   c. He helped the people of the colonies to get to know one another better.
5. How did newcomers from Europe change after settling in the Middle Colonies?
   a. They did not want religious freedom in America.
   b. They crowded together in the large cities.
   c. They began to think of themselves as Americans.

III. **Decide whether each statement agrees or disagrees with what you have read. If the statement disagrees, explain why.**

1. The Middle Colonies attracted people from many countries.
2. Manufacturing was important in the Middle Colonies.
3. Nearly all the people in the Middle Colonies were Quakers.
4. Benjamin Franklin was famous for many useful inventions.
5. The Middle Colonies were better suited to farming than the New England Colonies.
6. Mail service was slow because mail deliverers were poorly paid by the government of the colony.
7. Pennsylvania was one of the Middle Colonies.

PICTURE SYMBOLS *Benjamin Franklin*
These pictures should help you recall parts of the chapter you have read.
What is the main idea of each picture?

SUMMING UP **UNDERSTANDING PEOPLE** Judging people is an important skill. Here are some statements about Benjamin Franklin. You may agree or disagree with each statement or decide that you don't have enough information to make a judgment.

	AGREE	DISAGREE	DON'T KNOW
1. He had little common sense.			
2. He invented many things.			
3. He was a soldier.			
4. He had little use for books.			
5. He liked to make life better for others.			
6. He ran away from home because of trouble in school.			
7. He was interested only in the Pennsylvania colony.			
8. He was a writer.			

Thinking It Through

Benjamin Franklin was a man of many talents. In your opinion, what was his most important contribution to the people of his time? Explain.

5 LIFE IN THE WILDERNESS

How did early settlers survive on the frontier?

1. Some people did not want to live in the older and more settled colonies along the Atlantic Coast. They moved inland to live on the frontier. The frontier was a border strip separating the older settlements from the wilderness. Only a few people lived there. The people who went into this unknown country to make their homes were **pioneers.** We are going to learn how those pioneers lived on our first frontier, the foothills of the Appalachian Mountains.

2. What kinds of people moved to the wilderness? Some were young men looking for adventure. Others were people who did not like the rules of the older communities and wanted to be free to live in their own way. Some came to the frontier to be trappers or fur traders. However, most wanted land of their own, and there was plenty of free land on the frontier. Many newcomers to America were able to start a new life in the wilderness.

3. As the pioneers traveled westward, they took the easiest means of travel. They followed the rivers and valleys and the **gaps,** or low places, through the mountains. Some went up the Hudson River to the Mohawk Valley. Others followed the James and Potomac rivers into the valleys of Virginia and Maryland. Usually, several families traveled together in order to help

A colonial scutching bee, or party. Flax stems were tied together and beaten until they became soft. The soft fibers were used to make cloth.

each other. They carried their household goods in packs on the backs of horses. When they found a good place, each family built a log cabin in the wilderness.

4. The settlers on the frontier could never really feel safe. They faced dangers from wild animals. In addition, American Indians did not want strangers moving onto their land. Most of the first settlements were made into forts. A fence of pointed logs, called a **stockade,** was built around the cabins. At each corner of the stockade a higher cabin was built. This was the **blockhouse.** The blockhouse had openings where a guard could watch for Indians. It was not safe to leave the stockade alone. Indians might fight to protect their land. Also, they might fight to stop white people from killing the animals needed for food and clothing.

5. Living conditions on the frontier were difficult, but the settlers were not unhappy. Pioneers had to be all-around people. The men had to hunt, fish, farm, and cut timber. They had to be handy at all kinds of crafts. There was little time for play. Frontier women had to be strong. They not only took care of the home, but often worked in the fields. They had to raise the children and care for them. They had to make the family's clothing, cook the food, milk the cows, plant the garden, and do the laundry. Women had help from their children. Each child had jobs to do. Some of these might be feeding the chickens or gathering firewood. Older children helped take care of younger children. Everyone in the pioneer family worked long hours. There was no time to be idle.

6. Frontier houses were log cabins with dirt floors. The openings between the logs were filled with mud. Windows were no more than openings cut in the logs. The pioneers made furniture from logs that they had split. They made clothes from animal skins. Some of the Indians helped the new settlers. They taught the pioneers to do

Building a log cabin in the wilderness.

many useful things. They showed the settlers how to grow corn and hunt game in the forest. They taught them to tan and shape the skins into clothes and moccasins. They showed the pioneers how to use plants for food and medicine.

7. After 1750 a few daring hunters and trappers began to cross the Allegheny Mountains, as one part of the Appalachians is called. They hunted wild animals—deer, bear, and fox—for their meat, skins, and fur. Often, these hunters stayed in the forest for a year or two. These men were called **long hunters** because of the long rifles they carried.

8. The greatest of the long hunters and Indian fighters was Daniel Boone. Boone spent many of his early years hunting and exploring the Indian territory of Kentucky. In 1775 a land company asked him to open a trail to Kentucky and build a fort there. Boone chose 30 expert woodsmen to help him. They worked their way through a pass in the mountains called the Cumberland Gap. Then they "blazed" a trail, the Wilderness Road, to the banks of the Kentucky River. There they built a settlement. It was

George Caleb Bingham's painting showing Daniel Boone leading pioneers through the Cumberland Gap. His courage became well known through story and legend.

named Boonesboro, after Daniel Boone. Within a few months, Boone brought his family and other settlers to Boonesboro.

9. While Boonesboro was getting its start, other settlements began in what is now Kentucky and Tennessee. A group of settlers led by James Robertson followed Boone's trail through the mountains and established a settlement at what is now Nashville, Tennessee, on the Cumberland River.

The western settler was becoming a new kind of American. In the wilderness, people were judged by their courage in facing the dangers of the forest. They learned to depend on their own skills. Wealth, fine clothes, or schooling did not matter. Pioneers were rough, but they believed that each person was the equal of another. They also saw that success came to the person who was ambitious and willing to work.

REVIEWING CHAPTERS 1-4

As you read in Chapters 1-4, early settlements were formed in three sections: New England, the Middle Colonies, and the Southern Colonies. Which section is described in each statement below?

1. Many fishermen and sailors
2. Large plantations, fine mansions, slavery
3. Few towns
4. Little attention to public education

5. Members of the Quaker religion
6. A region of rocky, small, but well-kept farms
7. Slaveholders and small farmers
8. A bread-producing region

9. Crops of tobacco, indigo, and rice
10. Centers for manufacturing and trade
11. Large interest in religion and public education
12. Time for leisure

I. **What is the main purpose of Chapter 5?**

a. To describe the early settlements in Kentucky
b. To tell how people lived on the frontier
c. To tell about the hardships of the pioneer farmer
d. To describe the work of some of the brave people who moved west

II. **Choose the correct answer.**

1. People moved to the frontier for all of these reasons EXCEPT:
   a. The best land near the coast was settled.
   b. The government had bought land from the Indians.
   c. Many people were looking for adventure.
2. The pioneers built stockades in the wilderness because they
   a. were English people who were claiming new land for their country
   b. wanted to protect their supply of furs
   c. wanted to protect themselves from Indians whose land they had taken
3. The long hunters helped America grow because they
   a. brought back information about plants in the new lands
   b. blazed new trails in the wilderness
   c. provided food for the new settlements
4. The people of the frontier developed a spirit of democracy because they
   a. learned to accept other people as their equals
   b. had others do all the work
   c. possessed great courage and skill

III. **Decide whether each statement agrees or disagrees with what you have read. If the statement disagrees, explain why.**

1. Trade was the main reason that frontier settlers built their homes close to the stockade.
2. The frontier was quickly changed into a land of towns and farms.
3. Many settlers came to the frontier in spite of dangers there.
4. Without help from American Indians, white people would have had an even harder life in the wilderness.
5. The frontier was a region of wide, grassy plains.
6. A wealthy person who moved to the frontier usually was placed in charge of a settlement.
7. Daniel Boone is famous for exploring the frontier.

8. The pioneers were separated from the more settled sections of the colonies.
9. Hunting and trapping were as important as farming to the pioneer.

MAP SKILLS *The First Frontier*
Study the map. Then decide whether the statements which follow are true or false. If a statement is false, rewrite it so that it is true.

The First Frontier

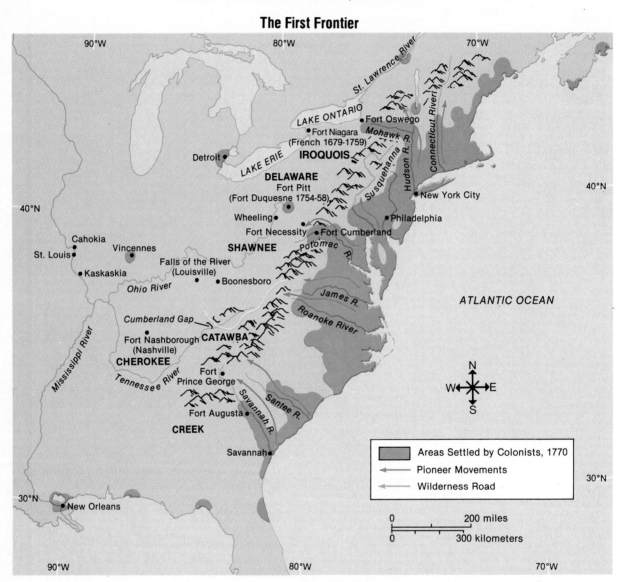

1. Many early settlements were located near rivers and bays.
2. All the rivers flow in a westward direction.
3. Philadelphia is located inland.
4. Settlers often traveled along the rivers to reach new land.

5. The frontier was always west of the pioneers.
6. Settlers moved inland from older settlements toward the mountains.
7. There were few waterways on the Atlantic Coastal Plain.
8. The Ohio River is west of the Appalachian Mountains.
9. The Mohawk River flows into the Hudson River.
10. The Cumberland Gap is shown on this map.

GAINING SKILL: ## USING THE GLOSSARY

Even the best readers often come across a word or words whose meaning is unknown to them. A good reader tries to understand the difficult word by looking at the meaning of nearby words and groups of words. This is known as using the context of words to discover their meaning.

Often, however, you will not be able to figure out the meaning of an unfamiliar word from its context. When that happens, you should look up the word in a dictionary. Make sure you look up the word exactly as it is spelled. (It is often helpful to write down the word as you look it up in the dictionary.) You should also know exactly which letter follows another in the alphabet.

A special kind of dictionary is found in the back of this book. It is called a **glossary.** A glossary lists some of the difficult words used in a book, and gives their meanings. Many of the words found in the glossary of this book are historical terms. For example, the word **pioneers** appears in paragraph 1 on page 102. The meaning of that word can be found in the glossary of this book. Now find the glossary definitions for some of the other words in this chapter.

You might try making a glossary of your own. Whenever you find a word you don't know, write it down. If you cannot find the meaning in the book's glossary, then look in a dictionary. After you find the word, write its meaning in your notebook.

SUMMING UP **MOVING WEST** Using the following headings, make an outline about frontier settlement. Write at least two subtopics under each heading.

A. Reasons why people moved to the frontier

B. Conditions on the frontier

C. Early settlements

Thinking It Through

What hardships did the pioneers face in the wilderness? What new ideas did they learn from these hardships? What new qualities did they develop from these hardships?

6 GOVERNMENT IN THE ENGLISH COLONIES

What kind of government developed in the colonies?

Meeting of Virginia's House of Burgesses at Jamestown in 1619. This was the first meeting of representatives in English America. Each of 11 towns chose two people to act as representatives at the assembly. Why are there no women in this picture?

1. In 1215 some English nobles forced the king to sign the Magna Carta, or "Great Charter." This charter gave them a share in the government. From that time on, the English people struggled to limit the power of their rulers. The people gradually won more rights for themselves. The settlers in Jamestown and Massachusetts had charters that granted them most of the same rights as people living in England. Once in America, the colonists demanded even more power to govern themselves.

2. In 1619 the London Company granted the Virginia settlers permission to establish an assembly of two lawmaking bodies. These two lawmaking bodies were called houses. The upper house was made up of the governor and a council, both appointed by the London Company. The lower house was made up of members elected by the settlers. This lower house was called the House of Burgesses. In it were 22 representatives. This was the settlers' first representative government in America. The settlers now had a share in making laws for the colony. The example of Virginia was later followed by other colonies.

3. You may remember that in 1620 the Pilgrims made an agreement called the Mayflower Compact. This agreement gave the Pilgrims the right to govern themselves. In 1633 Puritan leaders of the Massachusetts Bay Colony made plans for holding regular meetings in each town. In the town meetings, all the men who were landowners and church members of the commu-

nity could vote or hold office. In this way, Massachusetts began to have a kind of democratic government.

4. In 1639 the Connecticut colonists drew up a plan of government called the Fundamental Orders. This was the first written constitution in America. The Orders called for a governor, a council, and a lower house elected by the people. Connecticut became a **self-governing colony.** The people were allowed to elect their own governor and make their own laws. Later, Rhode Island also became self-governing.

5. By 1750 there were three kinds of colonies: royal, proprietary, and self-governing. In the royal colony, the governor was appointed by the king. In the proprietary colony, he was appointed by the trading company or proprietor who founded the colony. In the self-governing colony, the governor was elected by the voters or citizens of the colony. The governor's power

was greater in the royal and proprietary colonies. In these colonies, he could **veto,** or disapprove, bills passed by the lower house of the legislature. A council usually was chosen by the king or governor. It helped the governor. If a bill was approved by the lower house, it meant nothing until the council approved it also. The council acted much like the Senate in our national Congress.

6. Most colonies had a lower house, or representative assembly, chosen by the men of the colony. Only men who owned property or belonged to a particular church were allowed to represent the people. However, most people (except slaves) could own property if they were willing to clear the land. The assemblies were composed of people who had been sent by their neighbors to look after their interests. By 1750 the assemblies had won the right to pass tax laws and to decide how these taxes were to be used. Sometimes the assembly was able to control the governor's salary.

7. Many troubles arose between the governor and the assemblies. In the royal and proprietary colonies, the governor represented the king or the proprietor. He had to enforce their laws. Many times, he vetoed bills passed by the assembly because he thought the bills would not please the king or proprietor. Naturally, members of the assembly became angry at this. On some occasions, the representatives refused to pay the governor's salary or raise money for the soldiers the governor needed.

8. Religious freedom in the colonies grew with the rise of self-government. However, some colonies did not permit members of all religions to have a share in

A town meeting in a northern colony. On the local level, town governments were usually run by wealthy local leaders. All the colonies had laws that limited voting rights, usually to white men who owned property.

government. In Massachusetts, every man had to be a member of the Puritan Church in order to vote or hold office. Everyone had to attend Puritan services and pay taxes for the support of this church.

9. When Roger Williams left Massachusetts to begin the Rhode Island settlement, he allowed complete religious freedom for his people. He thought it unwise to force people to attend or support a church in which they did not believe.

10. In 1649 Maryland passed a law granting freedom of worship to all who believed in Christ. This was known as the Toleration Act. In the Quaker colonies of Pennsylvania and Delaware, William Penn allowed people to worship as they saw fit. There were about 2,000 Jews in the colonies, most of them living in New York, Rhode Island, Pennsylvania, and South Carolina. They were not permitted to vote or hold office in most of the colonies.

11. A famous trial in 1735 helped to establish freedom of the press in America. John Peter Zenger was arrested for writing articles that criticized the New York governor. Zenger's lawyer argued that the people have the right to fight injustice by speaking the truth. The jury found Zenger not guilty. From that time on, our newspapers have been free to write on government affairs. Our newspapers often speak out against actions of our government leaders.

12. The colonies were not fully democratic. Women could not vote. Many men could not vote because they did not own property or belong to a particular church. Indentured servants could not vote. There was black slavery. All the colonies had laws to limit the activities of blacks—both free and slave. Except for the Quakers, most white colonists accepted black slavery. From time to time there were slave revolts. But these revolts were easily stopped. It should be remembered, however, that England gave more liberty to its colonists than did any other nation with settlements in America. The French and Spanish colonies were ruled by governors appointed by their king. Settlers had no part in making laws.

REVIEWING CHAPTERS 1-5

Complete the following statements by using the words or phrases listed below.

plant tobacco
plantation owners
themselves
log or frame houses

shelter
difficult
gardens
roads

pioneer farmers
indentured servants
naval stores
cleared their land

1. Life for colonists in America was ▬▬▬.

2. The most important needs of the early colonists were food, clothing, and ▬▬▬.

3. The early settlers got their food by hunting animals or by raising vegetables in their ▬▬▬.

4. Pioneer farmers ▬▬▬ to raise crops.

5. ▬▬▬ were most likely to have all the things they needed to make a living.

6. The earliest homes were usually ▬▬▬.

7. The New England colonists depended on ▬▬▬ to do most of their work.

8. The colonists traded fish, tobacco, and ▬▬▬ for the things they needed.

9. Most colonists did not travel far from their homes because of the poor ▬▬▬ .

10. The life of the ▬▬▬ would have been more difficult without the help of the Indian.

I. **What is the main purpose of Chapter 6?**

   a. To describe the kinds of government that developed in the colonies
   b. To explain the plan of government of Thomas Hooker
   c. To tell how the British colonies grew
   d. To show how freedom of the press grew in America

II. **Choose the correct answer.**

1. In royal and proprietary colonies, governors and the assemblies had many differences because
   a. the governor represented the king or the proprietor
   b. the assembly represented the colonists
   c. both these reasons
2. English people in America enjoyed greater freedom than did people in England because they
   a. had a bill of rights
   b. were far from the king and Parliament
   c. were granted many freedoms by the king
3. English colonies were different from Spanish and French colonies in which way?
   a. There were no Catholics in English colonies.
   b. Only English colonies had black slaves.
   c. English colonists had more freedom than French or Spanish colonists.
4. Freedom of worship grew slowly in Massachusetts because
   a. only one religion was allowed there for some time
   b. the Toleration Act was passed
   c. the royal governor refused to allow freedom of religion
5. The English colonies were not entirely democratic because
   a. they did not allow any religious freedom
   b. they did not allow all people to vote
   c. only the English governor could make laws

III. **Decide whether each statement below is a fact or an opinion.**

1. The first colonial representative assembly met in 1619.
2. We remember John Zenger for his fight for freedom of the press.
3. Freedom of the press is our most important right.
4. England gave more liberties to its colonists than did any other nation at this time.
5. All colonists should have the right to vote.
6. The governor's first duty in a colony was to represent the king.
7. The town meetings in New England began about 1633.
8. People should not take part in town meetings unless they are educated.

Decide whether these statements about the cartoon are true or false.

"Flowers of Freedom"

1. The British did not allow any freedom in the colonies.
2. Everyone in the colonies had the right to vote.
3. This garden is growing in England.
4. Most colonies made their own laws.
5. People of different religions could live in the British colonies.

SUMMING UP **Thinking It Through**

Many people could not vote or hold office in colonial times. Which groups were they? Do you feel this was fair? Why or why not?

7 FURS AND FARMING IN NEW FRANCE

How was life in the French settlements different from life in the English colonies?

1. The first French explorers came to the New World looking for a water passage to Asia. They found instead that they could make a profit by fishing and trading for furs. They did not join the search for gold. French fishermen spent part of the year fishing in North American coastal waters. They spent the rest of the year at home in France. The French also pushed far up the St. Lawrence River to trade for furs with the American Indians. These daring men made the wilderness their home. French trappers soon adopted many of the Indian customs. They married Indian women and dressed in Indian clothing. One of the earliest leaders of the fur trade was Samuel de Champlain. In 1608 Champlain founded Quebec, the first permanent French settlement in America.

2. Wherever the French trappers went, missionaries went with them. The French wanted to make the Indians Christians. Many of these brave missionaries lived among the Indians. They learned the Indian language, established schools, and taught the Indians to read and write. The missionaries faced great dangers in the wilderness. Some of the priests were tortured and killed by unfriendly tribes. Their service to France was great, however. They won for France the friendship of many Indian tribes. One of the most famous missionaries was Father Marquette.

3. In the 1650s, the king of France took direct control of his colonies in America. He appointed a governor and a council to rule the colony of New France. The governor was all-powerful and the settlers had no voice in their government. The king also sent soldiers to protect the settlers in New France.

4. The king wanted more people to come to the colony of New France. He decided to turn the fertile St. Lawrence Valley into a vast farm land. He gave grants of land in the valley to wealthy friends and nobles. These men were expected to bring settlers to work the land. The **seigneurs,** as the landowners were called, divided the land into smaller farms. The seigneurs saw that the land was cleared and the farmers protected against Indian attacks. In return for these services, the farmers were expected to work for the landowner a few days each year and give him a share of the crops.

5. The farmers in New France were called **habitants.** Their farms were long and narrow with one end at the bank of the river. They built their homes along the roads facing the river. Each family raised what it needed—wheat, vegetables, and fruit. Cattle grazed on the pastures that had been cleared on the hillside.

6. Homes were built of stone and wood, like those of the New England settlers. The cabin was furnished poorly. There was a great stone fireplace for cooking and warmth. The kitchen was also the living room. Tables and chairs were homemade and very rough. The children slept above in the loft, or attic. Each farm also had a barn for animals and farming tools.

7. The French farmer was very religious and gave part of the year's crop to the Church. The Catholic Church was very active in each village. The few schools in New France were started by the missionary priests. While people of many faiths lived in the English colonies, France allowed only members of the Catholic faith to come to the French settlements.

8. French farmers never did come in great numbers to New France. The French

were more interested in the fur trade than in farming. Once a year, a great fur fair was held in Montreal. In the spring, the Indians brought their furs to the trading posts. They loaded their canoes for the long trip to Montreal. When the canoes reached Montreal, the Indians traded their furs for guns, knives, and other goods. The fair lasted for most of the summer. When the fair was over, the Indians returned to the woods. The trading ships, richly laden with furs and often fish, started the return voyage to France.

9. Because of the explorations of La Salle, the French had settled the Mississippi River Valley. La Salle had called this land Louisiana, in honor of King Louis XIV. (See map on page 117.) The most important settlement in this territory was New Orleans, founded in 1718 at the mouth of the mighty river. The king's governor lived there.

10. The French claimed a vast territory in North America. For the most part, it was a great wilderness marked by a thin line of forts and trading posts. By 1750 there were only 80,000 French people living in New France. Most of these colonists were fur traders who did not make lasting settlements. The few farmers in New France were located in the St. Lawrence River Valley. New France was large in size, but it was actually weaker than the neighboring English colonies.

The Habitant Farm. French farm families like the one in this painting settled along the banks of the St. Lawrence River. What crops did they raise?

George Catlin's painting of La Salle meeting the Taensa Indians near what is now Natchez, Mississippi. La Salle continued his expedition south down the Mississippi River. In 1682 he claimed the whole river valley for France.

REVIEWING CHAPTER 6

Decide whether each statement describes a democratic or an undemocratic feature of colonial life. Explain your answers.

1. Only members of the Puritan Church could vote in Massachusetts.
2. There were black slaves in the colonies.
3. In several colonies, the people had the power to make their own laws.
4. John Peter Zenger was found not guilty in his trial.
5. Women were not permitted to vote in the colonies.
6. The people of New England held town meetings to discuss their problems.
7. The House of Burgesses gave Virginia settlers a chance to make laws for themselves.
8. Rhode Island granted freedom of worship to all colonists.
9. The king chose the governors of royal colonies.

I. What is the main purpose of Chapter 7?

   a. To describe the work of the missionaries
   b. To describe the homes of the French settlers
   c. To tell how colonists came to New France
   d. To tell how the people lived in New France

II. Choose the correct answer.

1. Why were there few people in New France?
   a. Many people wanted to make money and return to France.
   b. Trading is a less settled way of life than farming.
   c. Both of these reasons.
2. How did the king of France encourage farming in the New World?
   a. He paid settlers to come to New France to farm.
   b. He sold land to the French people at low prices.
   c. He gave large pieces of land in the New World to his friends.
3. Why was New France not as strong as it seemed?
   a. The settlements were widely scattered.
   b. The colonies covered a small area near the Atlantic Coast.
   c. The settlers had great power in running their own affairs.
4. In the main, French people came to the New World to
   a. make homes and farm the land
   b. search for gold
   c. take part in the fur trade
5. One way in which missionaries were important in New France was by
   a. dividing large lands into small farms
   b. teaching the Indians to read and write
   c. discovering great stores of gold and silver
6. In New France the seigneurs were
   a. called habitants
   b. long, narrow farms
   c. landowners

III. Decide whether each statement agrees or disagrees with what you have read. If the statement disagrees, explain why.

1. There was a great amount of religious freedom in New France.
2. Farming was the most important occupation in New France.
3. Early French settlements were located chiefly on waterways.
4. The spread of the Christian religion was important to the French settlers.
5. Homes of the early French and English settlers were alike in many ways.
6. France and England held about the same amount of territory in North America.
7. Both English and French colonists were able to make their own laws.
8. Most early French settlements grew into large-sized towns.

MAP SKILLS *North America in 1750*
Study the map. Then decide whether the statements that follow are true or false. If a statement is false, rewrite it so that it is true.

North America in 1750

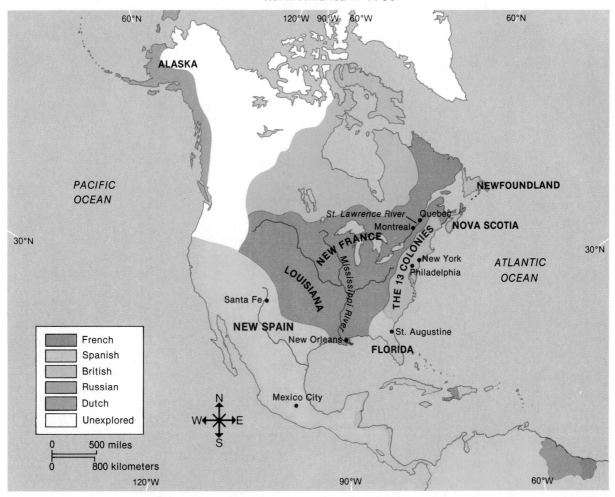

1. England had claimed most of North America by 1750.
2. All of North America had been explored by 1750.
3. Most of the Spanish claims were in the eastern part of North America.
4. The great river valleys were claimed by France.
5. Florida was one of the 13 English colonies.
6. Four nations had claimed land in North America by 1750.
7. Spanish claims bordered the Atlantic and Pacific oceans.

SUMMING UP Imagine that you are a fur trader or a farmer in New France. Write a letter to your friend about your adventures.

117

8 THE FRENCH AND ENGLISH FIGHT TO CONTROL NORTH AMERICA

How did France lose its vast territory in the New World?

The barracks and a cannon at Fort William Henry on Lake George, New York. Why do you think this fort has been restored and preserved as an historic site? Are there any historic sites near your community?

1. Starting in the last years of the 17th century, England and France fought four wars for the control of Europe, India, and North America. During the early wars, some of the fighting spread to the colonies in America. However, it was the fourth war that most deeply involved the colonies. It was called the Seven Years' War in Europe, and the French and Indian War in America. It brought victory to England and gave the English control over most French territory in the New World.

2. The war began in America. Both nations claimed the rich lands of the Ohio River Valley. The French said that the land belonged to them because of the explorations of La Salle. The English claimed the Ohio Valley as part of the Virginia Colony. The French built a line of forts and trading posts in the valley to defend their growing fur trade. However, they could not stop the English pioneers from coming there in search of farmland. With the English king's help, an Ohio land company had been formed in Virginia to send colonists to the valley.

3. The French took steps to drive the British out of the Ohio territory. They built forts, including Fort Duquesne, where the city of Pittsburgh now stands. The French urged their American Indian friends to attack English settlers on the frontier. The English governor of Virginia sent a young officer named George Washington to ask the French to leave the territory. They refused. Then the English sent Washington with a small army of Virginians to capture Fort Duquesne. The small band fought bravely, but they were defeated. This battle in 1754 marks the beginning of the French and Indian War.

4. The danger of attacks by the French and their Indian allies in the Ohio Valley grew. Benjamin Franklin suggested that the 13 English colonies work together to protect themselves. He thought that they

could defend themselves more easily if they were under one government. In 1754 delegates from the friendly Iroquois Indians and some of the English colonies met in Albany, New York. Franklin presented his plan. It followed the example of the way the six Iroquois nations had joined together. It was called the Albany Plan for Union of the English Colonies. Both the colonies and the king refused to approve the plan.

5. There were several important differences between the French and English colonies. The French had control of a vast territory stretching from the mouth of the Mississippi to the mouth of the St. Lawrence. The English held the land between the Atlantic Coast and the Appalachian Mountains. The English territory was smaller in size, but easier to defend. There were more people living in the English colonies. The 13 colonies had more than 1,000,000 settlers compared with 80,000 French people in the French territory. Many of the French were scattered in forts and trading posts. The English lived in settled communities and were ready to defend their homes. Except for the Iroquois and the Cherokee, most of the American Indians were friendly with the French. They were willing to fight against the English. Few English people had really tried to understand the life of the Indians. Most English settlers had found it easier to drive the Indians away.

6. General Braddock led the British soldiers in America. Braddock, with George Washington and some other Virginians, set out in a second attempt to capture Fort Duquesne. The British army marched

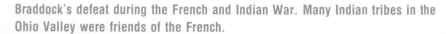

Braddock's defeat during the French and Indian War. Many Indian tribes in the Ohio Valley were friends of the French.

through the wilderness in bright red uniforms. Washington warned Braddock that the French would not fight in the open. Braddock would not listen to this warning. As the British approached Fort Duquesne, they were attacked by the French and Indian fighters. The French forces fired from behind trees and bushes, but Braddock refused to let his troops take cover. Many British were killed, including Braddock. Washington took command and ordered a retreat. After Braddock's defeat, the Indians were able to attack the cabins of the unprotected settlers on the frontier. The control of the Ohio Valley had fallen to the French.

7. Most of the early battles were won by the French. In 1757 William Pitt became the leader of the English government. He called upon the British to fight harder. He appointed younger men, such as Amherst and Wolfe, to command the British armies in America. Fort Duquesne was captured and renamed Fort Pitt. The British armies captured French forts on the Great Lakes and forced the French to retreat to Montreal and Quebec.

8. The deciding battle of the war took place at Quebec in 1759. The French had fortified the city. It was impossible to attack the city directly because it was protected by high cliffs. A British army commanded by General Wolfe surrounded Quebec. General Montcalm, the French commander at Quebec, had more soldiers than the English had, but he was growing short of food.

He could expect no help from France until the winter ended.

9. Wolfe realized that he had to take the city by surprise. One night, he discovered a path that led to the top of the cliffs. By morning, Wolfe and his army had climbed to the top and were on the plains facing the city. The French were caught by surprise. In the battle that followed, both generals were killed. The British won a great victory. This battle marked the real end of the war, although fighting went on for three more years.

10. In 1763 the war ended. France lost all of its territory in the New World except a few islands near Newfoundland and some islands in the West Indies. The British got Canada and all the French territory east of the Mississippi, except New Orleans. In return England gave Spain the French territory west of the Mississippi and the city of New Orleans.

11. The war was important to the English colonists. They discovered they could fight as well as England's regular soldiers. They gained confidence in themselves. During the war, George Washington gained valuable experience as a military leader. Although the colonies had not accepted Franklin's Albany Plan of Union, they learned that they had to work together to protect themselves. Finally, the colonies began to feel more independent of England, now that the French had been removed from the West.

REVIEWING CHAPTER 7 **Decide whether each statement describes the English Colonies or New France. Explain your answers.**

1. The territory was made up of farms, villages, and cities near the Atlantic Coast.

2. The territory covered a vast area; settlements were scattered and difficult to reach.

3. The chief occupations were trapping, hunting, and trading.
4. Only Catholics were allowed to come to the colonies.
5. The chief occupations were farming, fishing, and ship-building.
6. People were gradually getting a large share of self-government.
7. Many settlers made enemies of the American Indians by cutting down the forests and driving away the animals.
8. New settlers could settle in the lands of the Mississippi River Valley.
9. The governor was all-powerful and the settlers had no voice in their government.

UNDERSTANDING CHAPTER 8

I. What is the main purpose of Chapter 8?

a. To describe how the French and English fought a war
b. To show how Benjamin Franklin planned to unite the English colonies
c. To explain how England gained control of North America
d. To describe the early work of George Washington

II. Choose the correct answer.

1. Why was the French and Indian War fought?
   a. Both England and France claimed the same territory.
   b. The English captured the French city of Quebec.
   c. England insisted on stopping French ships.
2. Why did the French claim the Ohio Valley?
   a. The land had been explored by La Salle.
   b. The land had been explored by Champlain.
   c. The land was first claimed by De Soto.
3. Why did England want the Ohio Valley?
   a. The Indians there wanted help against the French.
   b. They wanted the land for farming.
   c. There were stories of gold to be found there.
4. Why was the Battle of Quebec important?
   a. The French were able to keep the war in progress for several years.
   b. It meant the end of British rule in Canada.
   c. It brought victory to the English in North America.
5. Why was the war important to the English colonies?
   a. It taught the colonies to cooperate with one another.
   b. The colonies had made profits from trading with the French.
   c. The colonies gained their freedom from the king.
6. What was one advantage the English had over the French in fighting the war?
   a. The English claimed more land.
   b. The English had a larger number of people living in America.
   c. The English controlled Louisiana.

III. Decide whether each statement is true or false. The underlined words are clues to help you decide. If a statement is false, change the underlined word or words to make it true.

1. Most of the American Indians sided with the <u>English</u> in the war.
2. The battle at <u>Fort Duquesne</u> in 1754 marked the beginning of the French and Indian War.
3. When peace was made, England gained control of Canada and <u>the land east of the Mississippi River</u>.
4. The Battle of Quebec was the <u>last major battle of the war</u>.
5. The war was fought over claims to the <u>Mississippi Valley</u>.
6. <u>William Pitt</u> sent young leaders and fresh troops to join the fight against the French.
7. As a result of the war, <u>England</u> lost its colonies in America.
8. <u>George Washington</u> was in command of the English army at Quebec.

DEVELOPING IDEAS
AND SKILLS

MAP SKILLS *North America in 1763*
Study the map and compare it with the one on page 117. Then find the missing words.

North America in 1763

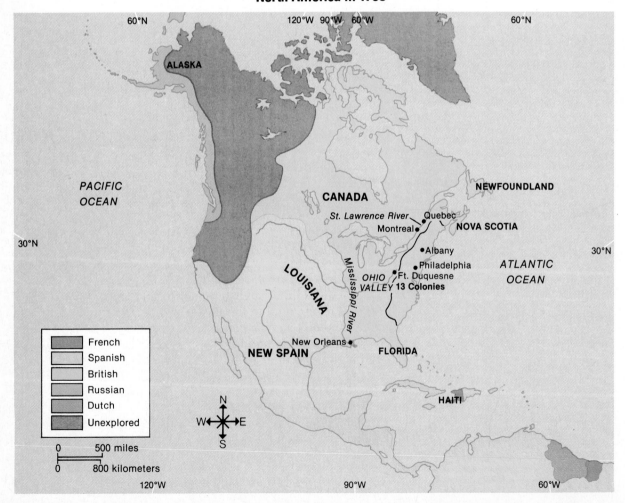

1. Between 1750 and 1763, ▬▬▬ doubled its territory in North America.
2. Part of the English territory was once claimed by ▬▬▬ .
3. ▬▬▬ added to its territory in the western part of North America.
4. The ▬▬▬ River separated English and Spanish territory in 1763.
5. In 1763 the Ohio Valley was under ▬▬▬ control.
6. Spain and ▬▬▬ claimed land along the Pacific Coast.
7. After the French and Indian War, Canadian territory was controlled by ▬▬▬ .
8. ▬▬▬ held territory in mainland North America in 1750, but not in 1763.

SUMMING UP **FRENCH AND INDIAN WAR** Using the headings below, make an outline of the French and Indian War. Write at least two subtopics under each heading.

A. Causes of the French and Indian War

B. Battles of the War

C. Results of the War

9 ENGLAND TIGHTENS ITS GRIP ON THE COLONIES

How did Britain try to gain strict control over its colonies?

1. After the French and Indian War, England decided to change the way it treated the colonies. First, the British felt the colonies needed more protection from the American Indians. Second, the war had left England with a large debt. England believed the colonies should pay part of this debt. Finally, England believed the colonies did not have enough respect for English laws.

2. In 1763 a remarkable Indian leader, Chief Pontiac, tried to drive the British from the land around the Ohio River. He captured many British forts. Pontiac was defeated only when England sent more soldiers to America. The British felt they should keep 10,000 soldiers in America to protect the colonies. This would cost a large sum of money. The British government wanted the colonies to help pay this cost.

3. To avoid more trouble with the Indians, the British issued the Proclamation of 1763, closing the lands west of the Appalachian Mountains to the settlers. (See map on page 106.) The British did not expect to keep this law for long. They wanted to give the Indians some time to calm down. In time, England would reopen the land to pioneers. The proclamation also required fur

British troops landing at Boston Harbor. British soldiers were sent to America to protect the colonists from Indian attacks. How do you think the colonists felt about having the soldiers stationed in America?

traders to have a license to trade with the Indians. A large British force was sent to the frontier to enforce the new laws.

4. The pioneers were angry with the new laws. They wanted the rich farmland west of the mountains. Land companies wanted to sell this land to the settlers. The fur traders wanted to be free to deal with the Indians. They hated the law that limited their trading.

5. England had a large debt when the French and Indian War ended. The money to carry on this war had come from taxes paid by the people in England. A tax is money that people pay to their government for certain services. These taxes were raised by Parliament, the lawmaking body of England. The people of England accepted the taxes because they had representatives in Parliament. The debt would grow larger now that soldiers were being kept in America. Since the British army would protect the colonists, Parliament thought the colonists should help share the debt. In order to raise money, Parliament decided to tax the colonies in America.

6. The tax laws seemed just to the people in England. They thought Parliament had a right to tax the colonists as well as themselves. But the colonists objected. They were not directly represented in Parliament. They had their own assemblies to tax them. Therefore, they would not agree to this "taxation without representation."

7. Finally, Parliament believed that control over the colonies should be tightened. In England, people felt that the colonies did not obey English laws. As early as 1660, Parliament had passed the Navigation Acts controlling trade between the colonies and England. Under these laws, all goods shipped from the colonies to England had to be carried in British ships. In time, Parliament passed other trade laws. The colonists had to send certain products to England before they could sell them to other countries. These products included

Harbor, Charleston, South Carolina. Why was it easy for colonists to smuggle goods into the colonies? Why did the British want to stop the smuggling?

tobacco and cotton. Colonists could make certain goods — hats, clothes, and iron goods — only for their own use. They were not allowed to sell them abroad. The laws also forced the colonists to buy many of their goods only from England.

8. These laws were passed because it was believed that the wealth of the colonies should go to the parent country. This idea was called **mercantilism.** Although many colonists didn't think these laws were fair to the colonies, there was no trouble for many years. England did not enforce the Navigation Laws strictly. Many of the colonists disobeyed the laws by smuggling goods in secret, without paying the tax on them. This was illegal.

9. In 1760 England's new king, George III, decided to enforce the Navigation Laws. He felt too much money was being lost because the laws were not obeyed. Since the colonies had not followed these laws for so long, there was bound to be trouble when the laws were strictly enforced.

In each group below, match the name in Column A with its correct description in Column B.

COLUMN A

1. Wolfe
2. Montcalm
3. Braddock
4. Pitt
5. Washington

COLUMN B

a. French commander at Quebec
b. English commander at Quebec
c. sent to ask the French to leave the Ohio Valley
d. defeated at Fort Duquesne
e. leader of the English government

COLUMN A

1. Quebec
2. Fort Duquesne
3. Albany
4. Ohio Valley
5. Louisiana

COLUMN B

a. where Franklin offered a Plan of Union
b. territory claimed by both France and England
c. French territory given to Spain in 1763
d. where the city of Pittsburgh now stands
e. where the English defeated the French forces in 1759

I. **What is the main purpose of Chapter 9?**

a. To describe the trade laws passed by Parliament
b. To tell how the British tried to control the colonies
c. To describe British policy in the colonies before the French and Indian War
d. To describe the closing of the frontier

II. **Choose the correct answer.**

1. Why did the colonists dislike the Proclamation of 1763?
a. It limited settlements to the land east of the Appalachian Mountains.
b. It placed a tax on tea.
c. It favored the French settlers in Canada.
2. Why did England make the Proclamation of 1763?
a. To keep settlers west of the mountains
b. To raise money to pay for the French and Indian War
c. To keep peace with the American Indians
3. Why did England pass the Navigation Laws?
a. To punish the colonies for trading with the French
b. To encourage farming in the colonies
c. To control colonial trade in the interest of England
4. Why did England tax the colonies after the French and Indian War?
a. To pay the salaries of members of Parliament
b. To pay the cost of the war
c. To get money for new roads and schools

5. Why was there little argument between England and the colonies before 1763?
   a. English laws controlling trade were not strictly enforced.
   b. Few colonists criticized the king.
   c. The colonies had been able to protect themselves.

III. **Decide whether each statement is true or false. The underlined words are clues to help you decide. If a statement is false, change the underlined word or words to make it true.**

1. The Proclamation of 1763 <u>opened</u> land west of the Appalachian Mountains for settlement.
2. Britain felt the colonies needed stronger protection against the <u>Indians</u>.
3. The British passed laws to prevent <u>smuggling</u> by the colonies.
4. Britain felt that the colonies should share the cost of the <u>French and Indian War</u>.
5. Colonists felt that the Parliament <u>had the right to tax them</u>.
6. Colonists <u>agreed</u> that the reason for their settlement was to make England richer.
7. The Navigation Acts were passed to make the <u>colonies</u> richer.

DEVELOPING IDEAS AND SKILLS

In this cartoon are five main figures. From your reading, describe what each of these people may be thinking.

SUMMING UP

Thinking it Through

Did England have the right to ask the colonists to pay for the soldiers sent to the colonies? Why or why not? Did the colonies have the right to be represented in Parliament? Why or why not?

127

10 THE COLONISTS BECOME ANGRY

What action did the colonists take to fight British tax laws?

1. In 1765 Parliament passed a tax law called the Stamp Act. The Stamp Act was supposed to raise money to pay for the troops protecting the colonies. Under this law the colonists had to buy stamps and put them on important papers such as wills, deeds, and newspapers. The stamps did not cost much, but the colonists did not like paying for them. They did not want their tax laws made for them by the British government, which was 3,000 miles away. The members of Parliament were elected by the voters in England. The colonists did not elect representatives to Parliament.

2. Patrick Henry, a young Virginia lawmaker, spoke out strongly against the Stamp Act. He said that the colonists were English and had the same rights as people living in England. Therefore, colonists could not be taxed unless they were represented in making the tax laws. Only the colonists could tax themselves. "Should the colonists obey a law for which they had no vote?" asked Patrick Henry.

3. Nine colonies sent representatives to a meeting in New York City to protest the Stamp Act. This meeting was known as the Stamp Act Congress. After much discussion, the members of this congress declared that Parliament had no right to tax the colonies. They asked Parliament to **repeal,** or do away with, the Stamp Act, but the British government refused.

4. Some of the colonists founded secret clubs such as the Sons of Liberty and the Daughters of Liberty. The Sons of Liberty broke into the homes of the stamp-tax collectors to burn or destroy the stamps. The merchants of New York, Philadelphia, and Boston agreed not to buy English goods until the hated tax was repealed. This refusal to buy goods is called a **boycott.** The Daughters of Liberty organized boycotts. They also held spinning and weaving **bees** to replace British cloth with homemade cloth. British merchants lost so much business that they urged Parliament to repeal the law. Parliament finally gave in and repealed the Stamp Act. However, they continued to claim the right to tax the colonies whenever they wished.

5. In 1767 Parliament passed new tax laws proposed by Charles Townshend, one of the king's ministers. The Townshend Acts placed taxes on some articles brought into the colonies—paper, paint, and tea. The tax money was to be used to pay the salaries of the colonial governors. The taxes

The colonists tarring and feathering a tax collector. Why did the colonists resent the British taxes? What kinds of taxes did the colonists oppose?

The Boston Massacre, 1770. Why were British troops in Boston at that time?

were not high, but again the colonies objected to being taxed by Parliament. In addition, paying the salaries of the governors had given colonial assemblies some power over the governors. If Parliament were to pay the salaries, the colonial assemblies would lose some of that power. The Townshend Acts also gave British officials the right to search homes of Americans who might be smuggling goods into the country. These warrants to search homes were called **writs of assistance.**

6. The British government sent soldiers to Boston to help collect the new taxes. The colonists did not like having the British soldiers in their city. They made the soldiers feel uncomfortable whenever they appeared in the streets. Crowds teased the British whenever there was an opportunity. In March 1770, some soldiers, angered by a few boys who had thrown snowballs at them, fired into a crowd of colonists. Five people, including Crispus Attucks, a runaway slave, were killed. The colonists called this incident the Boston Massacre.

7. After the Boston Massacre, Samuel Adams became a leader in Boston and the colonies. Adams is sometimes called the "Father of the American Revolution" for his part in urging the colonists to fight for their rights. Through his efforts, town meetings were held in Boston. The colonists asked the king to remove the troops from the city and repeal the Townshend Acts. Soon, the English government did take away all the Townshend taxes except the tax on tea. This one tax would remain to show the Americans that Parliament had the right to tax the colonists.

8. The tax on tea caused further trouble. In 1773 Parliament allowed the British East India Company to send tea to America and sell it at a very low price. In this way, even with the tax included, the tea could be sold at a lower cost than the colonial merchants could sell it. But the colonists refused to buy the tea, even at the lower price. They felt buying the tea would be admitting that Parliament had a right to tax them.

9. The people of Boston even refused to unload ships carrying the tea. The boats remained in the harbor. One night in December 1773, the Sons of Liberty, disguised as American Indians, boarded the ships. They threw chests of tea into the bay. This became famous as the Boston Tea Party.

The Boston Tea Party, 1773. Why did the colonists refuse to buy the low-priced tea?

Complete the following sentences.

1. England wanted the colonists to share the cost of the _____.

2. The British wanted to send troops to the frontier to protect the colonists from the _____.

3. The American Indian chief who led a revolt against the British was _____.

4. _____ was the lawmaking body of England.

5. _____ were passed to control colonial shipping and trade.

6. Under the new laws, goods shipped from the colonies to England had to be carried on _____ ships.

7. By 1763 England had helped free the colonists from threat of attacks by the _____ and _____.

8. Colonial merchants brought in goods without paying the tax on them. This is called _____.

I. What is the main purpose of Chapter 10?

    a. To describe Patrick Henry's speech against the Stamp Act
    b. To show how the colonists protested the right of Parliament to tax the colonies
    c. To describe the protest against the Stamp Act
    d. To tell about early fighting in Boston

II. Choose the correct answer.

1. The patriots held the Boston Tea Party because they
    a. wanted to surprise the British soldiers
    b. did not like the tax on tea
    c. wanted to welcome the new British governor

2. Parliament passed the Townshend Acts to
    a. pay the salaries of colonial governors
    b. help the colonies improve their trade
    c. pay for better roads in Massachusetts

3. The colonists protested the Stamp Act because they
    a. could not afford to pay for the stamps
    b. did not believe they should be taxed unless they had representatives in Parliament
    c. did not want the port of Boston closed

4. Parliament repealed the Stamp Act because
    a. they agreed they had no right to tax the colonies
    b. the colonies threatened to boycott English goods
    c. they had collected enough money

III. Decide whether each statement agrees or disagrees with what you have read. If the statement disagrees, explain why.

1. The Boston Tea Party showed how much the colonists disliked the tax on tea.

2. Parliament repealed the Stamp Act because it felt it had no right to tax the colonies.

3. Patrick Henry led the fight against the Stamp Act.

4. The people of Boston welcomed the protection of British soldiers.
5. British troops searched homes looking for smuggled goods.
6. Samuel Adams became known as the "Father of the American Revolution."
7. The king of England wanted to allow the colonies to have a greater voice in making their own laws.
8. The Boston Massacre made the colonists stop their protests against the Townshend Acts.

DEVELOPING IDEAS AND SKILLS **Answer the following questions about the cartoon.**

1. Who is the person holding the key?
2. Who is the person in the stocks?
3. Why was he placed in the stocks?
4. When did this take place?
5. How did the man get free from the stocks?

SUMMING UP **BRITISH LAWS TO CONTROL THE COLONIES**   Each of England's rules to control the colonies brought some action on the part of the colonists. Make a chart of these laws, using the headings below.

LAWS	WHAT THE LAW SAID	HOW THE COLONISTS REACTED
a. Proclamation of 1763		
b. Navigation Laws		
c. Stamp Act		
d. Townshend Acts		

11 LIBERTY OR DEATH! FIGHTING BEGINS

What events led to the American Revolution?

Patrick Henry. When he spoke out against the Stamp Act and against King George III before the Virginia House of Burgesses, some representatives cried, "Treason!" Henry replied, "If this be treason, make the most of it." What did he mean?

1. Parliament passed three new laws to punish the people of Boston for the Boston Tea Party. The laws were so harsh that the colonists called them the Intolerable Acts. The first law said that the people could no longer hold town meetings. The second ordered the colonists to shelter British soldiers. These troops not only could move into taverns and unoccupied buildings, but also into people's homes. The third law closed the port of Boston until the colonists paid for the tea. No ships were allowed to come to Boston Harbor. This meant that the people of Boston soon would be without food.

2. Samuel Adams wanted the other colonies to know about British actions against the colonists in Massachusetts. After the Boston Massacre in 1770, he started the Committees of Correspondence. One committee sent letters to the other colonies telling them what was taking place in Massachusetts. The other colonies set up their own committees. When each committee received the letters, it would write to others in the thirteen colonies. In 1774 the colonists worked together in this way to resist the Intolerable Acts. Food and money were sent to help the people of Boston.

3. In 1774 the Massachusetts Colony called a meeting of the leaders of all the colonies. All the colonies except Georgia sent representatives. This meeting of the First Continental Congress was held in Philadelphia. Samuel Adams, George Washington, and Patrick Henry were some of the important men present. The members of the Congress again stated the rights they had won over the years. They asked Parliament to repeal the unjust trade laws and to be willing to settle disputes peacefully. They drew up a list of actions by the king that denied their rights. They also agreed not to buy British goods until these differences with England were settled.

4. Patrick Henry made another speech before the Virginia Convention in 1775 defending the First Continental Congress. It was a very powerful speech. Here it is, in part: "There is no longer any room for hope. If we wish to be free . . . we must fight! I repeat it, sir, we must fight! . . . Gentlemen may cry peace, peace—but there is no peace. The war has already begun! . . . Why stand we here idle? What is it that gentlemen wish? What would they

have? Is life so dear, or peace so sweet, as to be purchased at the price of chains and slavery? Forbid it, Almighty God! I know not what course others may take; but as for me, give me liberty or give me death!"

5. Meanwhile, the colonists in Massachusetts began to gather guns and ammunition. They formed small groups called Minutemen. The Minutemen were ready to fight on a minute's notice. In April 1775, the British commander in Boston sent soldiers to seize guns and powder that were being kept at the nearby village of Concord. While marching to Concord, the troops were to arrest Samuel Adams and John Hancock, thought to be hiding in Lexington. The Minutemen were ready. Two patriots, Paul Revere and William Dawes, had ridden through the countryside and warned the farmers that the British were coming. When the British reached Lexington, they found 70 Minutemen waiting for them. The British ordered the farmers to return to their homes, but they refused. Suddenly, shots were fired! The Minutemen had to retreat because they were few in number. The British marched to Concord where they burned some of the war supplies. As they started back to Boston, they met another group of Minutemen at Concord

The Battle of Breed's Hill, 1775. Both black and white Americans fought the British. More than 5,000 blacks served in the American army.

Bridge. More shots were fired and men on both sides were killed. As the British troops returned to Boston, the Minutemen fired on them. The American Revolutionary War began here at Lexington and Concord.

6. Other colonists left their homes and families to join the Minutemen. They camped outside Boston to watch the British soldiers who occupied the city. They had few guns and little training, but their courage made up for the lack of supplies. The Minutemen hoped to force the British to leave Boston. In June 1775, the colonial troops prepared Breed's Hill against attack. The hill overlooks Boston Harbor. The British saw the Americans on the hill with their guns pointing at Boston. The British commander, General Howe, decided to capture the hill and remove the danger to his soldiers.

7. The British troops charged the hill twice but were driven back by the gunfire of the colonists. At the third British attack, the Americans had to retreat because their supply of ammunition ran short. It was a costly victory for the British, however. Nearly a thousand British soldiers were killed or wounded. The Americans lost only 140 men. The battle showed that the colonists could hold their own against the well-trained regular British troops. This famous battle was called the Battle of Bunker Hill. But it was really fought on Breed's Hill. In the darkness, the Americans had placed their cannons on Breed's Hill instead of the position on Bunker Hill they had planned to use.

8. The British remained in Boston for almost a year. The colonial troops kept the British shut up in the city until they felt strong enough to drive them out. Ethan Allen and the Green Mountain Boys captured Fort Ticonderoga in the spring of 1775. The cannons they captured were dragged 300 miles (480 kilometers) over the mountains to help in the second battle for Boston in 1776. This time, the British commander decided not to try to take the hills occupied by the Americans. He and his troops quietly left the city.

REVIEWING CHAPTERS 9 AND 10 **The colonists and England argued over many issues before the American Revolution. Decide whether each statement below is the opinion of the *British* or the *colonists*. Support your decisions.**

1. The Navigation Laws should be strictly enforced.
2. The colonists should not be allowed to settle west of the Appalachian Mountains.
3. The colonists should provide food and shelter for British soldiers.
4. The British Parliament should make laws for all the colonies.
5. The Stamp Act and the Townshend Acts are unfair.
6. The colonies should trade almost entirely with England.
7. The colonists should be taxed only by their own elected assemblies.
8. Officers should not be allowed to search homes for smuggled goods.
9. The colonists should pay part of the cost of the French and Indian War.
10. The colonists should have more self-government.
11. The British Parliament should pay the salaries of colonial governors.

I. What is the main purpose of Chapter 11?

    a. To describe how the American Revolution began
    b. To tell how Parliament tried to punish the people of Boston
    c. To describe what happened at Lexington and Concord
    d. To tell of the meeting of the First Continental Congress

II. Choose the correct answer.

1. Why were the Intolerable Acts passed?
    a. To punish the people of Boston
    b. To raise money for the English king
    c. To punish Patrick Henry and Samuel Adams
2. Why did the First Continental Congress meet?
    a. To ask for the repeal of unjust laws
    b. To raise an army to fight for independence
    c. To prepare an expedition to the West
3. Why did the British march to Lexington and Concord?
    a. To break up the meeting of the Continental Congress
    b. To search farmhouses for smuggled goods
    c. To capture some ammunition
4. Why is Samuel Adams called the Father of the American Revolution?
    a. He wrote the Declaration of Independence.
    b. He urged the colonists to fight for their rights.
    c. He was the leader of the fighting at Lexington.
5. Why is the Battle of Bunker Hill important?
    a. It was really not fought on Bunker Hill.
    b. It ended the chances of the colonies for the control of Boston.
    c. It showed that colonial troops could hold their own against the British army.

III. Decide whether each statement agrees or disagrees with what you have read. If the statement disagrees, explain why.

1. The Committees of Correspondence helped to bring the colonies closer together.
2. The First Continental Congress forced the king to repeal the unjust laws.
3. The Battle of Lexington was the beginning of the war for independence from England.
4. The colonies declared their freedom immediately after the fighting at Lexington.
5. The First Continental Congress taxed all the colonies to pay for an army to fight for independence.
6. The port of Boston was closed until the people paid for the damages of the Boston Tea Party.
7. Patrick Henry made the famous "liberty or death" speech.
8. Crispus Attucks was killed in the Boston Massacre.

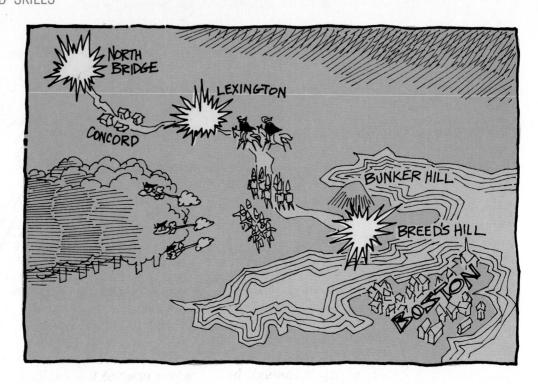

Complete the following paragraph. You may use both the map above and the facts you have learned from reading this chapter:

On the night of April 18, 1775, some of the king's troops secretly marched from Boston into the town of (1) ———. They had planned to arrest Samuel Adams and John Hancock. However, Adams and Hancock had been warned in advance by (2) ——— and (3) ———. Shooting broke out. The troops then marched to (4) ——— where more shooting began at the nearby North Bridge. The king's troops then began a retreat to (5) ———. They were under fire all the way. Hoping to force the British to leave Boston, the colonists strengthened their position on what they thought was (6) ——— Hill. The British troops attacked. After the battle was over, the colonists realized they had really fought on (7) ——— Hill instead.

SUMMING UP   **Thinking It Through**

Patrick Henry challenged the colonists with the words, "Is life so dear, or peace so sweet, as to be purchased at the price of chains and slavery?" In your own words, explain the meaning of this question. What meaning does this challenge have for us today?

12 A NEW NATION IS BORN

Why did the 13 colonies declare their freedom from England?

Signing the Declaration of Independence, 1776. How do you think the people of England felt about this declaration?

1. When the First Continental Congress met at Philadelphia in 1774, most colonists did not believe they should be free from England. But by the summer of 1776, after the fighting around Boston, the colonists had decided they were fighting a war for independence. What had changed their minds? First, the British had hired German soldiers, or Hessians, to help put down revolt in the colonies. Second, a powerful pamphlet, *Common Sense*, had been written by Thomas Paine. Paine was English. He had just come to the colonies. In his **pamphlet** (a booklet in paper covers), he argued that the colonies would gain their rights only by separating from England. His fighting words were read by many. Third, a large number of people in the colonies had come from countries other than England. They felt that they did not owe loyalty to the British.

2. In the summer of 1776, leaders of the colonies met again. This meeting of the Second Continental Congress also was held in Philadelphia. This congress tried once more to make peace with King George III. Again the British government refused to repeal the laws that controlled the trade of the colonies. When their efforts failed, the members of this congress voted for independence. They appointed a committee of five men to draw up a **declaration,** or statement, of independence. The members of the committee were Thomas Jefferson of Virginia, Benjamin Franklin of Pennsylvania, John Adams of Massachusetts, Roger Sherman of Connecticut, and Robert Liv-

ingston of New York. Thomas Jefferson wrote most of the declaration. It was later approved by the committee with a few changes. This Declaration of Independence was adopted by the Second Continental Congress on July 4, 1776. It marked the beginning of a new nation called the United States of America. United States citizens celebrate the nation's independence each year on July 4.

3. The Declaration of Independence is one of the most important documents in history. It declared the colonies free of England. It started a new nation. The Declaration told the world that this new nation believed that "all men are created equal" and have a "right to life, liberty, and the pursuit of happiness." Jefferson wrote that the people form governments to make these rights possible. Should a government take these rights away, the people have a duty and a right to change the government.

4. In 1776 the colonists went to war against England. Let us look back at those events that led to the American Revolution.

Patriots carrying a Loyalist on a pole. Support of the British was strongest in Georgia, New York, Pennsylvania, and the Carolinas.

a. Since 1660 the British government had passed trade laws for the colonies. For a long time many of these laws were not enforced. Under a new king, George III, the British government began to enforce the laws. Colonial merchants were hurt by these attempts to control their growing trade. They wanted to be free of these trade laws.

b. Many pioneer farmers disliked the English rule that kept them from settling west of the Appalachian Mountains.

c. The colonists believed they should be taxed only by their own representatives. To pay the taxes ordered by Parliament would be surrendering to "taxation without representation."

d. Many of the people in the colonies no longer thought of themselves as English people but as Americans. The struggle to live in a strange land had forced them to think for themselves. Above all, they wanted the right of self-government. They wanted the right to choose their own leaders and make their own laws.

5. When the fighting began, most colonists did not support the war for independence. Only about one-third of the nearly 3 million people in the 13 colonies in 1775 supported a fight for freedom. They were called **patriots.** Another third did not take sides. The last one-third remained loyal to the English king. People in this group were known as **Loyalists,** or **Tories.** The patriots naturally looked upon the Tories as traitors. Likewise, the Tories called the patriots traitors for defying the king.

6. But there was no turning back now. The Continental Congress had declared the colonies to be free. In the Declaration of Independence, Jefferson had written a long list of reasons why it was impossible to continue under British rule. He had described to the world the kind of government that

people in America wanted. He had told of the attempts by the Americans to settle their disagreements with the king. The last sentence of the Declaration said that "for the support of this declaration, with a firm reliance on the protection of Divine Providence, we mutually pledge to each other our lives, our fortunes, and our sacred honor." The leaders of the American colonies were willing to give up everything to protect their freedom and gain their independence.

Match each term in Column A with its correct description in Column B.

COLUMN A

1. Navigation Laws
2. Stamp Act
3. Writs of assistance
4. Sons and Daughters of Liberty
5. Committees of Correspondence
6. Minutemen
7. First Continental Congress

COLUMN B

a. patriot soldiers
b. meeting to protest acts of the king
c. secret patriot clubs
d. control of colonial shipping
e. kept colonies informed on what the British were doing
f. tax on legal papers
g. right to search homes

I. What is the main purpose of Chapter 12?

a. To describe the beginning of the new nation
b. To describe the meeting of the Second Continental Congress
c. To discuss the ideas of the Declaration of Independence
d. To discuss why the colonies separated from England

II. Choose the correct answer.

1. Which was NOT a reason why the colonists decided to declare themselves independent?
   a. The British government tried to enforce the Navigation Laws.
   b. Thomas Paine wrote *Common Sense*.
   c. England withdrew its troops from Boston.
2. Why is July 4 celebrated as a holiday in the United States?
   a. It marks the beginning of religious freedom in the Americas.
   b. It marks the beginning of the United States of America.
   c. It celebrates the repeal of the Stamp Act.
3. Why is the Declaration of Independence important?
   a. It ended the fighting with the British.
   b. It gave courage to the people of the colonies.
   c. It marked the beginning of a new kind of government in the world.
4. What was the main reason why the Revolutionary War was fought?
   a. To gain independence for the United States
   b. To add more territory to the United States
   c. To get rid of the hated Navigation Laws

5. The colonists began to believe they ought to be free from England after the
    a. fighting around Boston
    b. Declaration of Independence
    c. passing of the Stamp Act
6. All of these are part of the Declaration of Independence EXCEPT
    a. a statement that all men and women should have the right to vote
    b. a list of reasons why Americans could not continue to belong to England
    c. a statement that "all men are created equal"

III. **Decide whether each statement agrees or disagrees with what you have read. If the statement disagrees, explain why.**

1. All the colonists thought of England as their own country.
2. The Declaration of Independence called for a new kind of government.
3. The Revolution ended with the writing of the Declaration of Independence.
4. The pamphlet *Common Sense* urged the colonists to revolt against England.
5. Loyalists were people who supported England during the Revolution.
6. Most of the colonists believed they should be free from England.
7. One of the chief reasons for the war was the issue of "taxation without representation."

DEVELOPING IDEAS AND SKILLS   In July 1776, some New Yorkers pulled down a statue of King George III. Thirteen years before, the colonists and the British had fought side by side in the French and Indian War. Why had the colonists' feelings toward the British changed? For your answers, look at the chart on page 142.

READING TO FIND INFORMATION

Many exercises in this textbook require you to find information to complete the exercise or answer a question. When you read to find this information, you should look for every item that helps answer the question or complete the exercise. Ignore all facts or statements that do not relate to the question or exercises, even though that information may also be important. How is this done? **Skim** the reading first. To skim material, read quickly through the chapter and look for key words or phrases that help tell you what the reading is about. Try to find the information you need.

When you think you have found the information, read the first sentence or two of the paragraph it is in. Then read the entire paragraph more closely until you find the correct information. If you need to prove your answer, write the paragraph number next to the question.

For example, look at question 2 in Part II of Understanding Chapter 12 on page 139. Skim pages 137–138 until you find the information you need. Then read that paragraph more closely. You should have found the answer at the end of paragraph 2 on page 137.

SUMMING UP

DECLARATION OF INDEPENDENCE   In your notebook, complete the *outline* of some of the important facts and ideas of the Declaration of Independence.

A. Why the Declaration Was Made
    1.
    2.
B. When and Where It Was Written
    1.
    2.
C. Important Ideas in the Declaration
    1.
    2.
    3.
D. Results of the Declaration
    1.
    2.

Thinking It Through

Why do you think the Congress wrote out the reasons for declaring the colonies free of England?

What other methods could the colonists have used to try to gain their rights without a war?

CAUSES of the AMERICAN REVOLUTION

Stricter British enforcement of Navigation Laws

Colonists resist British tax laws

YE CUSTOM HOUSE

TEA TAX

Proclamation of 1763 closes the western lands

The colonists did not want to shelter British soldiers

The colonists were becoming Americans 3,000 miles away

LONDON TIMES

NEW YORK GAZETTE

Desire to make their own laws

Rise of many skilled colonial leaders

AMERICAN REVOLUTION

THE DECLARATION OF INDEPENDENCE

I. Introduction

The world has a right to know why the colonists want to separate from Great Britain.

When, in the course of human events, it becomes necessary for one people to dissolve the political bands which have connected them with another, and to assume, among the powers of the earth, the separate and equal station to which the laws of nature and of nature's God entitle them, a decent respect to the opinions of mankind requires that they should declare the causes which impel them to the separation.

II. Ideas About Government

People are born with certain rights. Governments are formed to protect these rights. When the government takes away these rights, it is the duty of the people to change their government.

We hold these truths to be self-evident; that all men are created equal; that they are endowed by their Creator with certain unalienable rights; that among these are life, liberty, and the pursuit of happiness. That, to secure these rights, governments are instituted among men, deriving their just powers from the consent of the governed; that, whenever any form of government becomes destructive of these ends, it is the right of the people to alter or to abolish it, and to institute a new government, laying its foundation on such principles, and organizing its powers in such form as to them shall seem most likely to effect their safety and happiness. Prudence, indeed, will dictate that governments long established should not be changed for light and transient causes; and accordingly all experience hath shown that mankind are more disposed to suffer while evils are sufferable, than to right themselves by abolishing the forms to which they are accustomed. But when a long train of abuses and usurpations, pursuing invariably the same object, evinces a design to reduce them under absolute despotism, it is then right, it is their duty, to throw off such government, and to provide new guards for their future security. Such has been the patient sufferance of these colonies; and such is now the necessity which constrains them to alter their former systems of government. The history of the present King of Great Britain is a history of repeated injuries and usurpations, all having in direct object the establishment of an absolute tyranny over these states. To prove this, let facts be submitted to a candid world.

III. Grievances Against the King

The king has not ruled wisely. He has forced upon the colonies many things to which they cannot agree. He has closed our legislatures. He has sent soldiers to the colonies in time of peace. He has enforced laws that cut off our trade. He has taxed us without our consent. He has taken away colonial charters. He has encouraged the American Indians to attack the settlers on the frontier. He has brought German soldiers to fight against the colonists.

He has refused his assent to laws the most wholesome and necessary for the public good.

He has forbidden his governors to pass laws of immediate and pressing importance, unless suspended in their operation till his assent should be obtained; and when so suspended, he has utterly neglected to attend to them.

He has refused to pass other laws for the accommodation of large districts of people, unless those people would relinquish the right of representation in the legislature, a right inestimable to them, and formidable to tyrants only.

He has called together legislative bodies at places unusual, uncomfortable, and distant from the depository of their public records, for the sole purpose of fatiguing them into compliance with his measures.

He has dissolved representative houses repeatedly for opposing, with manly firmness, his invasions on the rights of the people.

He has refused, for a long time after such dissolutions, to cause others to be elected, whereby the legislative powers, incapable of annihilation, have returned to the people at large for their exercise; the state remaining, in the mean time, exposed to all the dangers of invasions from without and convulsions within.

He has endeavored to prevent the population of these states; for that purpose obstructing the laws for the naturalization of foreigners, refusing to pass others to encourage their migration hither, and raising the conditions of new appropriations of lands.

He has obstructed the administration of justice, by refusing his assent to laws for establishing judiciary powers.

He has made judges dependent on his will alone for the tenure of their offices, and the amount and payment of their salaries.

He has erected a multitude of new offices, and sent hither swarms of officers to harass our people and eat out their substance.

He has kept among us, in times of peace, standing armies, without the consent of our legislatures.

He has affected to render the military independent of, and superior to, the civil power.

He has combined with others to subject us to a jurisdiction foreign to our constitutions and unacknowledged by our laws, giving his assent to their acts of pretended legislation:

For quartering large bodies of armed troops among us;

For protecting them, by a mock trial, from punishment for any murders which they should commit on the inhabitants of these states;

For cutting off our trade with all parts of the world;

For imposing taxes on us without our consent;

For depriving us, in many cases, of the benefits of trial by jury;

For transporting us beyond seas, to be tried for pretended offences;

For abolishing the free system of English laws in a neighboring province, establishing therein an arbitrary government, and enlarging its boundaries, so as to render it at once an example and fit instrument for introducing the same absolute rule into these colonies;

For taking away our charters, abolishing our most valuable laws, and altering, fundamentally, the forms of our governments;

For suspending our own legislatures, and declaring themselves invested with power to legislate for us in all cases whatsoever.

He has abdicated government here, by declaring us out of his protection and waging war against us.

He has plundered our seas, ravaged our coasts, burned our towns, and destroyed the lives of our people.

He is at this time transporting large armies of foreign mercenaries to complete the works of death, desolation, and tyranny already begun with circumstances of cruelty and perfidy scarcely paralleled in the most barbarous ages, and totally unworthy the head of a civilized nation.

He has constrained our fellow-citizens, taken captive on the high seas, to bear arms against their country, to become the executioners of their friends and brethren, or to fall themselves by their hands.

He has excited domestic insurrection among us, and has endeavored to bring on the inhabitants of our frontiers the merciless Indian savages, whose known rule of warfare is an undistinguished destruction of all ages, sexes and conditions.

IV. The Colonies Have Asked to Be Heard

The colonists asked the king and Parliament to correct these wrongs, but they did not listen.

In every stage of these oppressions we have petitioned for redress in the most humble terms; our repeated petitions have been answered only by repeated injury. A prince whose character is thus marked by every act which may define a tyrant is unfit to be the ruler of a free people.

Nor have we been wanting in our attentions to our British brethren. We have warned them, from time to time, of attempts by their legislature to extend an unwarrantable jurisdiction over us. We have reminded them of the circumstances of our emigration and settlement here. We have appealed to their native justice and magnanimity; and we have conjured them, by the ties of our common kindred, to disavow these usurpations, which would inevitably interrupt our connections and correspondence. They, too, have been deaf to the voice of justice and consanguinity. We must, therefore, acquiesce in the necessity which denounces our separation, and hold them as we hold the rest of mankind, enemies in war, in peace friends.

V. Forming a New Nation

Therefore, we declare the colonies to be independent of the king. A new nation is formed, the United States of America. The signers give their lives and their fortunes to keep America free.

We, therefore, the representatives of the United States of America, in General Congress assembled, appealing to the Supreme Judge of the world for the rectitude of our intentions, do, in the name and by the authority of the good people of these colonies, solemnly publish and declare, That these united colonies are, and of right ought to be, free and independent states; that they are absolved from all allegiance to the British crown, and that all political connection between them and the state of Great Britain is, and ought to be, totally dissolved; and that, as free and independent states, they have full power to levy war, conclude peace, contract alliances, establish commerce, and do all other acts and things which independent states may of right do. And, for the support of this declaration, with a firm reliance on the protection of Divine Providence, we mutually pledge to each other our lives, our fortunes, and our sacred honor.

13 A DIFFICULT TASK FACES THE UNITED STATES

What were the strengths and weaknesses of the British and American forces at the beginning of the Revolutionary War?

1. The British had some important advantages in fighting a war with the American colonies:

a. The British had more people. There were about 10 million people in Great Britain compared with almost 3 million who lived in America.

b. The British had a strong navy that they could use to **blockade,** or close, American ports. The British navy could guard British ships carrying troops and supplies. The Americans had no real navy.

c. The British army was well trained and well equipped. The British had many factories. The British army could depend on these factories for guns, cannons, and ammunition. The American army was poorly trained and poorly equipped.

d. The British government could raise money to carry on the war. But the Second Continental Congress, the governing body for the colonies, had trouble raising money. This congress did not have the power to tax the states, as the colonies were now called. Even when asked for money, the states usually refused.

e. The British could count on the help of one-third of the people in America, the Loyalists, or Tories. Another third of Americans did not take sides.

2. The British had some disadvantages, too. Many British people did not agree with the idea of a war with their colonies. They

British soldiers wore their red coats into battle against the Americans. How was this a disadvantage when fighting in the forests?

American soldiers preparing to meet the British at Concord. What do you think these men were thinking at this moment?

did not think of the people in America as enemies. In addition, the British had to move troops and materials of war 3,000 miles (4,800 kilometers) to reach the fighting in America. Also, other countries were ready to help the colonists in their fight against the British.

3. The United States of America had some advantages. The people of the new nation were fighting on their own land and defending their own homes. They were better fighters in the wilderness than the British. The guns used by American soldiers had a longer range and were more accurate than any used by the British. The Americans had the advantage of a great military leader in George Washington.

4. The Second Continental Congress made preparations to carry on the war. It appointed George Washington as commander in chief of the newly organized army. Washington was born in Virginia on February 22, 1732. He was the son of a wealthy planter. Washington did not attend school for long. At the age of 14, he learned to survey, or measure, land. As a young man he took part in the Indian wars and became an officer. When he was 21, he delivered the message from the governor of Virginia to the French commander in the Ohio Valley warning the French to leave. He was with Braddock in the defeat near Fort Duquesne. After the French and Indian War, he expected to live peacefully on his plantation at Mount Vernon. However, he had a great desire to serve his country. When the call came for a meeting of the colonies in 1774, Washington became a representative to the First Continental Congress. In 1775 the Second Continental Congress appointed him commander of the American army. He received no pay. He proved to be a leader with great skill and courage. He refused to give up even when he received few supplies or little money to fight the war. He took command of the army in Massachusetts after the Battle of Bunker Hill.

George Washington. When the Revolutionary War began, he was chosen to be commander of the American army. After the war, he was elected the nation's first president. How has this country honored his memory?

5. The Second Continental Congress had to raise large sums of money to pay, equip, and clothe the American army. But it did not have the power to raise money by taxing the states. It could only ask the states to give money to the new government. Thus this congress raised money in other ways. First, it issued paper money (called continentals). People used this money because they had faith that the patriot army would win. But early British victories caused the money to drop in value until it became worthless. Another way the government raised money was by borrowing from foreign countries. Finally, it received large amounts of money in gifts from wealthy patriotic Americans. Men like Robert Morris collected money from patriots and sent it to Washington's armies. Haym Salomon helped Morris get loans from France for the new country. Salomon also gave his own fortune to the new government.

6. The government also sent representatives to Spain, Russia, and France to seek help. The man it sent to Paris, France, was

147

Benjamin Franklin. Americans thought the French would help them because of earlier French defeats at the hands of the English. Perhaps France might want to recover its lost territory in America. The French government was friendly to Franklin and agreed to send some supplies in secret to the patriots.

REVIEWING THE
BEGINNING OF THE
WAR

Choose the correct answer.

1. The first fighting in the American Revolution took place at
   a. Lexington
   b. Bunker Hill
   c. Philadelphia
2. The Declaration of Independence was approved by the
   a. First Continental Congress
   b. Second Continental Congress
   c. Committees of Correspondence
3. All of the following were events leading to the Revolution EXCEPT
   a. the Stamp Act
   b. the Battle of Quebec
   c. the Navigation Laws
4. Those in the colonies who supported the king were called
   a. patriots
   b. Sons and Daughters of Liberty
   c. Tories
5. The Declaration of Independence was written by
   a. Samuel Adams
   b. Thomas Jefferson
   c. George Washington

UNDERSTANDING
CHAPTER 13

I. What is the main purpose of Chapter 13?

   a. To present the advantages of the British
   b. To describe how the Second Continental Congress planned to carry on the war
   c. To describe how the United States tried to get outside help
   d. To discuss the problems faced by the United States in trying to win independence

II. Choose the correct answer or answers.

1. Congress sent Benjamin Franklin to France to
   a. keep him from being captured by the British
   b. bring back the newest weapons of war
   c. ask for help
2. Two ways in which the Second Continental Congress tried to raise money to carry on the war were
   a. issuing paper money
   b. taxing the colonists
   c. asking for gifts from wealthy citizens
3. Washington was chosen to lead the American army because he
   a. was the richest man in the nation
   b. had military experience
   c. was recommended by King George

4. The French were pleased to see the Revolution begin because
   a. they disliked the Americans
   b. they thought they might regain some territory lost to England
   c. they hoped to sell supplies to both sides in the war

III. Decide whether each statement below is a fact or an opinion. Explain your answers.

1. Some patriots were not soldiers.
2. Loyal colonists should not criticize their government.
3. The Americans received help from France in the Revolution.
4. Parliament should have had the right to tax all the people under British rule.
5. George Washington was in command of the patriot armies.
6. Britain had enemies who wanted to see it defeated by the Americans.
7. People are created equal in every way.
8. The British could not easily send troops to the fighting in the colonies.

DEVELOPING IDEAS AND SKILLS

Answer the following questions about the cartoon.

1. Who is the larger figure? Why is he laughing?
2. Who is the smaller figure?
3. What advantages does the size of the larger figure represent?
4. When was the Declaration of Independence written?
5. What did it say?
6. What is the meaning of this cartoon?
7. If you were to draw a cartoon showing the outcome, what would it show?

UNDERSTANDING CARTOONS

Many newspapers include a special kind of drawing that helps explain, at a glance, ideas about historical events. This kind of drawing is called a **cartoon.** A single cartoon can illustrate an idea that would take many words to explain.

Cartoons, like other kinds of visual aids, must be studied carefully in order to understand what they are saying. Some cartoons have titles. Others may have captions. You should read the title or caption first to get a general idea of the cartoon's meaning. Then look closely at the cartoon. What are the people in the cartoon doing? Can you recognize any of them? (A cartoonist often uses special signs or symbols to help identify the main figures. For example, a tall man with a beard and a high hat stands for the United States.) What situation or event is the artist trying to illustrate? Does the artist succeed in making certain ideas or events stand out more clearly? These are some of the questions you should ask yourself while studying the cartoon.

You will find several cartoons in this textbook. Like the other visual aids in the book, the cartoons are used to help you recall or understand what you have read. A cartoon often seems simple in order to get its ideas across. (Remember, however, that it is not designed to explain all the sides of an issue.) Look at the cartoon on page 149. See if you are able to answer the questions that follow it.

ENGLAND AND THE COLONIES Complete the following chart in your notebook.

	ENGLAND	AMERICAN COLONIES
1. Population		
2. Military Strength		
3. Wealth		
4. Government		

Thinking It Through

Which side seemed to be in the better position to win a war? Why? What were some advantages of the other side?

14 PATRIOT VICTORIES BRING HOPE

What early battles did the American army win?

This painting is called *Washington Crossing the Delaware*. Do you think it shows realistically what happened when Washington and his troops crossed the Delaware River in 1776? Explain your answer.

1. After the Battle of Bunker Hill, the fighting shifted from Boston to New York. The British wanted to capture the harbor at New York, where they could receive war supplies from England. Washington moved his army to Long Island to stop the British. A number of battles were fought on Long Island and in New York City. Washington did not have nearly as many men as the British commander, General Howe. The Americans had to leave New York and retreat into New Jersey.

2. Washington's long retreat continued through New Jersey into Pennsylvania. Many people thought he would surrender, but he did not. With his small army, he could not risk a real battle with the British troops. On Christmas night in 1776, Washington went back across the icy Delaware River into New Jersey and attacked a group of Hessians camped at Trenton. You will remember that the Hessians were German soldiers paid to fight for the English cause. The German soldiers were celebrating Christmas and were surprised by the Americans. They surrendered with all their supplies. A week later, Washington again surprised and defeated another British army at Princeton, New Jersey. These quick moves by Washington caused a British general to call him "the Old Fox."

3. The next year, 1777, brought a great victory for the American army. The British planned to divide the 13 states and end the fighting. With an army of 8,000, General Burgoyne was to march south from Montreal by way of Lake Champlain and Albany. General Howe was to bring his troops north from New York to join him. A third army, under Colonel St. Leger, was to march eastward across New York State to meet both armies. (See the map on page 154.)

4. At first, the British plan seemed to be working. General Burgoyne captured Fort Ticonderoga in northern New York State. But then the British troops were slowed by thick forests. They also were attacked by bands of patriots along the way. A group of patriot farmers from Vermont defeated a part of Burgoyne's army. In the meantime, Colonel St. Leger was cut off at Oriskany, New York. In the bloody battle that followed, the British were forced to retreat. The third member of the plan, General Howe, decided not to go north at all. He tried to capture Philadelphia instead.

5. As General Burgoyne moved south, his army grew weaker. His supplies were giving out. The American army grew larger and stronger. General Gates, in command of the Americans, surrounded the British at

Washington reviewing the troops at Valley Forge, Pennsylvania, during the difficult winter of 1777–1778.

Saratoga, New York. The battle that followed ended in defeat for the British. Saratoga proved to be the turning point of the war. When news of the American victory reached the French king, he promised to enter the war on the side of the United States. Without his help, the Americans might not have had the supplies to continue their fight for freedom.

6. The British army under General Howe spent a comfortable winter in Philadelphia. Washington and his tired army were forced to camp at Valley Forge, Pennsylvania, about 30 miles away. American soldiers deserted the army in large numbers. The brave men who remained became sick because they had little food or clothing. There was little protection against the cold. Washington tried to hold the army together and to keep the soldiers' spirits high. He wrote to the Second Continental Congress many times, begging for money to feed and pay his soldiers. In May 1778, Washington received the news that France had signed a treaty with the United States and was going to war against England.

7. Washington had the help of many brave soldiers who came from Europe to help the patriots. One of these was Marquis de Lafayette, a young French nobleman who came to America in 1777. Lafayette served the American cause until the end of the war. Baron von Steuben came from Germany and drilled the soldiers at Valley Forge. Thaddeus Kosciusko was a Polish engineer. He helped the army of the young nation build forts for protection against the British troops.

8. A dark event in the history of the war was the desertion of General Benedict Arnold. Arnold had been one of the finest American leaders. He had tricked the English into thinking the Americans had a large force at Oriskany. His bravery had saved the victory at Saratoga. He had asked Washington to make him commander at West Point, and Washington had granted his request. But he needed money and felt he had not received proper rewards for his part in the war. In 1780 it was discovered that he had planned to sell secrets of the defense of West Point to the British. He escaped to the British lines and spent his remaining days in England. The patriot army could not afford to lose such able leaders as General Arnold.

When the Revolutionary War began, the newly formed American army was untrained. This painting shows Baron von Steuben, the famous German soldier, teaching American troops how to use their muskets. What other Europeans came to help the new nation?

Which statements describe the Americans at the beginning of the war? Which describe the British? Explain your answers.

1. They had a smaller population.
2. They had a strong navy to carry men and supplies.
3. They were able to hire foreign soldiers to fight for them.
4. They had a new government with few powers.
5. They were fighting on land they knew well.
6. They had many factories to supply their armies with guns.
7. They had no regular army; their soldiers would serve only a few months.
8. They had no gold or money to pay their soldiers and buy supplies.

I. What is the main purpose of Chapter 14?

a. To discuss how people from foreign nations helped Americans
b. To describe the early years of the Revolution
c. To describe the winter at Valley Forge
d. To tell about the Battle of Saratoga

II. Choose the correct answer.

1. The British wanted New York City because it
   a. had an excellent harbor, which would help them to get their supplies from England
   b. was the place where the Loyalists gathered
   c. was the capital of the new nation
2. Washington's leadership helped the Americans through
   a. the victories at Trenton and Princeton
   b. his march into South Carolina and Georgia
   c. the building of a navy to strike at British ships
3. The Battle of Saratoga was important in winning the war because it
   a. persuaded the French to come to the aid of the Americans
   b. caused a change in the government of England
   c. led to the beginning of a new government in the United States
4. The British plan to cut the United States in two failed because
   a. Washington received equipment in time
   b. France came to the aid of the United States
   c. none of the British generals successfully carried out his part in the plan
5. The best reason we can give for the treason of Benedict Arnold is that he
   a. felt that he had not received what he deserved
   b. did not believe that the colonies should be fighting for independence
   c. had not been given a chance to take part in the war

III. Decide whether each statement is true or false. The underlined words are clues to help you decide. If a statement is false, change the underlined word or words to make it true.

1. Washington wrote to <u>France</u> asking for money.
2. Burgoyne's surrender at <u>West Point</u> was the turning point of the war.
3. <u>Lafayette</u> was a French nobleman who came to America to help the American cause.
4. Soldiers at <u>Valley Forge</u> suffered from a lack of clothing and shelter.
5. American soldiers were trained and drilled by <u>Kosciusko</u>.
6. Washington was driven from Long Island by <u>Burgoyne</u>.
7. "The Old Fox" was a named given to <u>General Washington</u>.
8. General Burgoyne was slowed in his march through <u>New York</u> by a group of patriots from Vermont.

DEVELOPING IDEAS
AND SKILLS **MAP SKILLS**   *Northern Battles of the American Revolution*

Study the map. Then decide whether the statements that follow are true or false. Support your decisions.

Battles of the American Revolution in the North

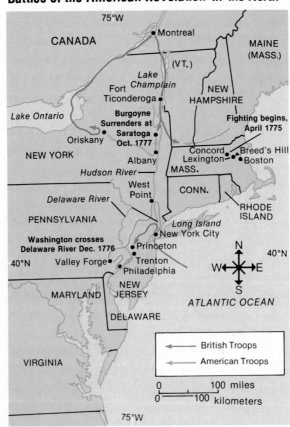

154

1. Most of the Revolutionary War battles were sea battles.
2. Valley Forge is across the river from Trenton.
3. The Revolutionary War began in Massachusetts.
4. Saratoga is located north of New York City.
5. British troops could land at Boston and New York City.
6. West Point guards the Hudson north of New York City.
7. An army could attack both Trenton and Princeton within a few days.
8. Some British troops came south from Canada.
9. The distance between New York City and Saratoga is 100 miles (160 kilometers).
10. The British were able to control New York by holding three river forts.

SUMMING UP **SOLDIERING WITH WASHINGTON**   Imagine you are a soldier serving in Washington's army. Keep a diary of your experiences. Here are some of the events you might want to describe in your diary.

Meeting Washington
Spying for Washington
The winter at Valley Forge
Crossing the Delaware River to Trenton
Meeting Lafayette
Hearing the news of Arnold's treason
Bringing a message to Saratoga

Thinking It Through

All people act according to the set of values or beliefs they feel are important. From what you have read, what values did George Washington hold? What values did Benedict Arnold hold?

15 AMERICAN HEROES

What successes did the Americans have at sea and on the frontier?

The British surrendering to George Rogers Clark at Vincennes, 1779. What hardships had Clark's troops faced? Why were Clark's victories important?

1. Fighting went on west of the Appalachian Mountains while the patriots were stopping the British in the East. The land north of the Ohio River was known as the Northwest Territory. British soldiers there occupied the fur-trading posts they had taken from the French. The British urged the Indians to attack American settlers who lived near the borders of Kentucky and western Pennsylvania.

2. A Virginia frontiersman named George Rogers Clark set out to stop the attack of the British and their American Indian and Loyalist allies. He also planned to drive the English from the Northwest Territory. He wanted the territory to be part of the new nation. Clark explained his plan to the governor of Virginia and was given permission to lead an expedition to the West.

3. He raised a small army of about 200 frontiersmen. These men had spent most of their lives in the forest, hunting game and fighting Indians. They were "good shots" with a rifle. Clark loaded them on boats and floated them down the Ohio River. They marched across the hills in what is now the state of Illinois. On July 7, 1778, Clark and his little army attacked and captured the British fort at Kaskaskia.

4. During the winter, Clark set out for the British fort at Vincennes. Vincennes is in present-day Indiana. This was the beginning of one of the most terrible marches in our history. The frontier patriots had to endure many hardships before they reached Vincennes, about 200 miles away. There had been a flood during the winter months, and Clark and his men had to march through icy water. They had to cut trees

Battles of the American Revolution in the Northwest

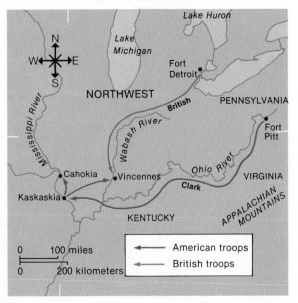

and build rafts to cross the overflowing streams. They carried no food with them, so they depended on the wild animals of the forest for their meals. Once their food ran out, and they nearly starved. Clark's band of heroes finally surprised the British at Vincennes and easily captured the fort. The British had not expected the Americans to attack in such terrible weather.

5. The victories of George Rogers Clark reduced the number of British and Indian attacks on the frontier settlers. As a result, the United States claimed the land bounded by the Great Lakes, the Ohio River, and the Mississippi River. When the treaty of peace was signed after the Revolutionary War, the United States was able to make this territory part of the new nation. The Northwest Territory later became the states of Ohio, Indiana, Illinois, Michigan, and Wisconsin.

6. When the war began, the Americans had no navy. Colonial merchants owned a few ships. The government put guns on these ships. It gave the owners or captains permission to look for and capture British ships. These ships were called **privateers.** Any British ship that was captured could be sold. The profits could then be shared by the captain and crew and the owners of the privateer.

7. The United States did build a few of its own ships during the war. By the time the fighting was over, most of these ships had been either sunk or captured by the British navy. After France entered the war, the Americans mainly depended on the French fleet to fight the British. The most famous American sea captain of the Revolution was John Paul Jones.

8. John Paul Jones was born in Scotland. He spent so much time on the Scottish coasts that he soon became an expert sailor. At the age of 12, he went to sea as an apprentice. He came to America when still a young man and lived on a southern plantation. In 1775 he joined the United States

John Paul Jones leading a naval battle against the British. Why were victories at sea important to the Americans?

Navy. Before long, he was commanding his own ships. He attacked the British wherever he found them.

9. On June 14, 1777, John Paul Jones took command of a new ship called the *Ranger.* On that same day, Congress chose a flag to represent the new nation. It had 13 red and white stripes and 13 stars on a blue field. It was called "the Stars and Stripes." It was flown, for the first time, on John Paul Jones's ship. Therefore, June 14 is celebrated in our nation as Flag Day.

10. Captain Jones's most famous battle was with the British ship *Serapis.* This was one of the mighty warships of the British navy. Jones commanded an old ship called *Bonhomme Richard,* which he had received from the French. He gave the order to attack the *Serapis.* His ship caught fire

during the battle and the captain of the *Serapis* asked Jones if he wished to surrender. Jones replied, "I have not yet begun to fight." He brought his ship alongside the *Serapis* and tied the two warships together. The American sailors boarded the British vessel and fought hand-to-hand with the British sailors. The *Bonhomme Richard* sank in the battle, but Jones and the American sailors took command of the *Serapis*. This was but one example of the courage displayed by the young American navy.

11. Men were not the only heroes of the Revolution. Many women played an important part as well. For example, the first official copies of the Declaration of Independence were printed by Mary Katherine Goddard. Women took care of farms, shops, and small businesses while their husbands were fighting. They helped supply food and clothing to the patriot armies. Some collected money for the government and the army. They also collected metal objects that could be melted down to make cannon balls and musket shot. Others fought bravely in the field, alongside the men. Mary Ludwig married John Hays and followed him to his army camp. At first she worked as a cook and nurse. During the Battle of Monmouth in 1778 she spent hours carrying water back and forth to the troops. She got the name Molly Pitcher (Mary with her pitcher). When her husband was wounded during the battle she put down her water pitchers and took up a gun to fight. Because of her bravery and action, George Washington made her a sergeant. Another daring army woman was Deborah Sampson. She enlisted as a soldier disguised as a man. She remained disguised for a year and fought in several battles. A surprised doctor found out she was a woman after she was wounded. She got better, but had to leave the army. Molly Pitcher and Deborah Sampson, and many other women, played an important role in the American victory in the Revolutionary War.

Molly Pitcher (Mary Ludwig Hays) at the Battle of Monmouth, New Jersey.

Which person in the following list is identified in each description?

Samuel Adams   Robert Morris   Marquis de Lafayette
Patrick Henry   Paul Revere   Loyalist
George Washington   Thomas Paine   General Howe
              Thomas Jefferson

1. I lived in America, but I did not want to become free from England.
2. I was commander in chief of the American armies.
3. I wrote the pamphlet *Common Sense*.
4. I organized the Committees of Correspondence and urged the colonists to fight.
5. I was a leading British general.
6. I wrote the Declaration of Independence.
7. I made some famous speeches against the laws of Parliament.
8. I raised money for the patriot cause.
9. I came from France to help the Americans win their freedom.
10. I warned the farmers that the British were coming to Concord.

I. What is the main purpose of Chapter 15?

    a. To tell about the deeds of George Rogers Clark
    b. To review American victories on the sea and on the frontier
    c. To tell about the battles of John Paul Jones
    d. To describe American Indian attacks on the frontier

II. Choose the correct answer.

1. How did Congress build a small navy?
    a. By arming merchant ships
    b. By borrowing money from the states to build warships
    c. By borrowing ships from France
2. One reason why George Rogers Clark wanted to capture land in the Northwest was
    a. to control trade on the Ohio River
    b. to stop American Indian attacks on American settlers
    c. to drive the French from the Great Lakes
3. What were the results of the campaigns of George Rogers Clark?
    a. United States warships were free to sail the Great Lakes.
    b. England moved its troops back to Canada.
    c. The Northwest Territory became part of the United States after the war.
4. The United States could not hope to drive the British navy from the seas because
    a. the United States had no navy at the beginning of the war
    b. the United States had but ten large warships
    c. American merchants remained loyal to Great Britain

III. The following list contains headlines or slogans that might have appeared in newspapers during the period of the Revolution. Name the event described by each headline.

1. "I Have Just Begun to Fight!"
2. A Christmas Present
3. "The Redcoats Are Coming!"
4. "Give Me Liberty or Give Me Death!"
5. Tea Party Held
6. The Liberty Bell Rings

Choose the correct answer.

1. The first printer to publish the Declaration of Independence with the names of the signers was
   a. Abigail Adams
   b. Mary Ludwig Hays
   c. Mary Katherine Goddard
2. Which statement best describes this selection?
   a. Colonial women took an active part in the Revolutionary War.
   b. Women supplied materials to both armies.
   c. Women often fought alongside men in battles.
3. Mary Ludwig was honored by General Washington for
   a. bringing water to the men during battle
   b. taking her husband's place in battle
   c. both of these statements
4. Most women helped the patriot cause by
   a. writing pamphlets against the British
   b. acting as spies for the army
   c. taking care of the farms and shops
5. Deborah Sampson is remembered as a Revolutionary hero because she
   a. took part in the battles
   b. was a friend of General Washington
   c. gave money to the patriot leaders
6. Some women helped the revolutionary cause by
   a. leading armies into battle
   b. raising money for the Revolutionary government
   c. voting for independence

Understanding Our Country's Flag What do you know about our country's flag? You may agree or disagree with each statement below or indicate you don't have enough information to make a judgment. You may use an almanac if you need help.

	AGREE	DISAGREE	DON'T KNOW
1. The first flag of the United States had 13 stars and 13 stripes.			
2. The colors of the first flag were red, white, and blue.			
3. Today's flag looks the same as our first flag.			
4. Our flag is sometimes called the Stars and Stripes.			
5. Flag Day is celebrated on July 4.			
6. Each state has a star in the flag.			
7. The flag flies over all public schools.			
8. Objects may be placed above the flag.			

16 THE BRITISH SURRENDER. FREEDOM IS WON!

How did the Americans defeat the British?

1. The British generals decided to take the war to the southern states. They were able to capture parts of Georgia and South Carolina because there were no large American armies in the South. The British were troubled, however, by small groups of patriot farmers and backwoodsmen. These small bands hid in the forests and swamps. They struck suddenly and captured British food and guns. Just as suddenly, they disappeared. One of these bands of raiders was led by Francis Marion, a planter from South Carolina. He was called the "Swamp Fox."

2. In 1780 the British General Cornwallis started northward into North Carolina. Washington sent General Greene to command the armies in the South and stop the British. Cornwallis chased Greene far into North Carolina. But the British general could not get enough supplies to continue his march, and so he returned to the coast. Finally, he marched northward into Virginia to try to capture the American forces under Lafayette. Lafayette was able to escape the British, and Cornwallis again headed toward the coast. He camped at Yorktown on Chesapeake Bay, where he would be near supplies coming to him on British ships. However, instead of the British fleet, the French fleet from the West Indies appeared and blocked Cornwallis's chances of getting help.

3. Meanwhile, George Washington, with an army of American and French soldiers, hurried south from New York. Washington planned to join forces with Lafayette. Washington was successful, and he and Lafayette closed in on Cornwallis. The British were trapped by the French and American soldiers on land, and by the French fleet at sea. On October 19, 1781, Cornwallis surrendered at Yorktown. The fighting of the American Revolutionary War was over. It had lasted six and a half years.

4. The treaty of peace that ended the war was signed at Paris almost two years later, on September 3, 1783. England recognized the independence of the United States. England gave the territory south of Canada and east of the Mississippi River to the new American nation.

5. The new nation had won its freedom. It had fought bravely for its independence.

Battles of the American Revolution in the South

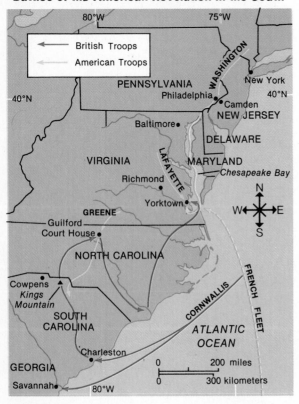

The British surrendering to the Americans at Yorktown, Virginia, in 1781. What nation had helped trap Cornwallis's troops?

How had the young nation succeeded in defeating the mighty British army? Let us recall some of the reasons for the American victory.

a. The Americans were fighting on their own soil and in defense of their own homes. They had a strong desire to win.

b. The Americans were better fighters in the wilderness.

c. During the war, the United States was led by such able men as George Washington, George Rogers Clark, and John Paul Jones. It had the help of other able people who were not soldiers—Robert Morris and Benjamin Franklin. They helped get money, materials, and foreign aid for the patriot armies. Also, the United States had soldiers who never gave up the fight for freedom despite their many hardships.

d. Of the 300,000 soldiers who served in the war, about 5,000 were blacks. Most of these blacks were from the North.

They served throughout the war, playing a large part in the Battle of Bunker Hill near Boston and Stony Point in New York. Jews, although a small group, generally supported the patriot side. When fighting broke out, Jews were in the Continental Army, both as officers and common soldiers. Jewish merchants armed their ships with cannons and sent them out to attack the British. Jews like Haym Salomon raised large sums of money for the patriot cause.

e. Many women contributed to victory. They kept the farms and businesses running while their husbands, fathers, sons, and brothers were fighting. The United States also was helped by men who came from Europe to fight in the battle for liberty: Lafayette, Kosciusko, von Steuben, and others.

f. The French government sent money, ships, and soldiers to aid the American cause. It was the French fleet that blocked Cornwallis at Yorktown.

6. What happened to the Tories—those people who were loyal to the British king? During the war they raised many troops to fight for the king. Many of them lost their lives, their fortunes, and their families for the cause. All the states had passed laws allowing the states to seize the property of Loyalists. The states then obtained millions of dollars from the sale of Loyalist property. The peace treaty provided that Congress should urge the states to pay back the Loyalists for their property. In most cases this was not done. So at the end of the war, the British government really did nothing to help the Loyalists. As a result, about 100,000 to 200,000 of them fled to Canada.

7. The American Revolution was one of the most important events in the history of the world. It was the beginning of many changes in the Americas. Before the Revolutionary War, there was not a free country in the New World. Now, for the first time, a

The peace talks in 1783. Benjamin West never completed this painting. The British officials would not allow their portraits to be included. Why do you think they refused?

colony had successfully revolted against the ruling country. By the early 1800s, the Spanish and Portuguese colonies in Central and South America had taken up the fight for freedom. It also influenced England to govern its colony in Canada more wisely.

8. The war for independence was also the beginning of what may be called the Democratic Revolution. Before the Revolutionary War, many people were denied important rights. A monarch could arrest his or her subjects or take away their lands without reason. A monarch could put a tax on the people without their consent. Peo-

ple could not openly criticize their rulers. After the Revolutionary War, people in many nations wanted equal treatment before the law. They claimed the right to choose people to represent them in making laws and raising taxes. They asked to read newspapers that discussed the government. They gained the protection of fair courts. The Democratic Revolution is still going on today. Many people around the world are demanding freedom. Their desire is for the rights Americans won in their Revolution, namely, "life, liberty, and the pursuit of happiness."

Find the missing words.

1. The first battle of the Revolution was fought at _____.
2. The battle that is called the "turning point" of the war was fought at _____.
3. Washington's soldiers suffered during the winter at _____.
4. The _____ were German soldiers hired to fight for the British.
5. _____ was an American naval hero in the Revolution.
6. One of the English forts captured by George Rogers Clark was at _____.
7. Armed merchant ships were called _____.
8. The _____ River is an important waterway in the Northwest Territory.

I. What is the main purpose of paragraphs 1 through 4?

   a. To review the reasons for American victory
   b. To describe the final battles of the war
   c. To tell about the adventures of the Swamp Fox
   d. To explain what was written in the treaty of peace

II. Choose the correct answer.

1. Why did Cornwallis surrender?
   a. He was satisfied with the amount of territory he had won for the British.
   b. He was given orders to stop fighting.
   c. He was trapped and could receive no help.
2. Which was a result of the war?
   a. The United States remained under the rule of England.
   b. France regained territory in the New World.
   c. The independence of the United States was recognized.
3. One reason why Americans won freedom is
   a. they received help from France
   b. they won most of the battles that were fought
   c. the British decided the war was lasting too long
4. Francis Marion helped the American cause by
   a. raising and training an army to help Washington
   b. surprising British troops and capturing their supplies
   c. doing both a and b
5. In which way did France help in the defeat of Cornwallis?
   a. The French fleet kept the British from getting help.
   b. A French army turned defeat into victory at Saratoga.
   c. The French navy blockaded ports in Georgia and South Carolina.

III. Decide whether each statement agrees or disagrees with what you have read. If the statement disagrees, explain why.

1. In 1783 the territory of the United States extended as far west as the Pacific Ocean.
2. Francis Marion knew a great deal about fighting in swamps and forests.

3. The Treaty of Paris recognized the independence of the United States of America.
4. The Americans won the Battle of Yorktown with the help of the French.
5. The capture of Cornwallis at Yorktown ended fighting in the Revolution.
6. The Americans had some outstanding leaders during the war.
7. The treaty of peace was signed by Washington and Cornwallis immediately after the surrender.

DEVELOPING IDEAS AND SKILLS

MAP SKILLS *North America in 1783*

Study the map. Then decide whether these statements are true or false.

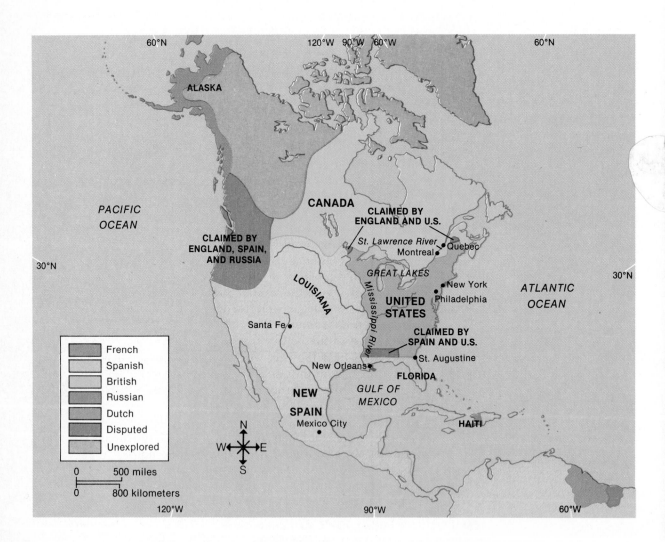

1. Most of North America was owned by Spain and England.
2. Spanish territory lay north of the Great Lakes.
3. The United States extended as far south as the Gulf of Mexico.

4. The new boundary of the United States in the west was the Mississippi River.
5. In 1783 the only independent country in the New World was the United States.
6. New Orleans was part of the United States.
7. Part of North America was disputed by three countries.

SUMMING UP

The American Revolution   Complete this chart of the battles of the Revolution in your notebook.

BATTLES OF THE REVOLUTION

NORTHEAST	NORTHWEST	ON THE SEA	IN THE SOUTH

Thinking It Through

How might American and British history have been different if the colonies had lost the Revolution?

Using a Time Line

Study this time line. Then answer the questions that follow. Use the information you have studied in this unit to help you. You may also look at the time line on pages 80 and 81 if you need additional help.

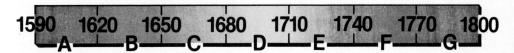

In which period of time (**A, B, C, D, E, F, or G**) did the following take place?

1. Massachusetts passed an education law requiring each village to provide an elementary school.
2. The French and Indian War ended.
3. The British Parliament passed the Navigation Laws.
4. The British and colonists clashed during the Boston Massacre.
5. The Toleration Act was passed in Maryland.
6. The Declaration of Independence was signed.
7. Franklin presented the Albany Plan.
8. The Revolutionary War ended and a peace treaty was signed.

Building a Home Library

You will get hours of enjoyment from reading about the heroes and events that you have studied in this unit. Many of these hours can be spent in your leisure time at home. You will want to have some books nearby so that you will be able to read about those events that have interested you most.

In your own library you should have several kinds of books. You should have biographies or stories of the lives of great men and women. Other books will describe the lives of young people who lived during the period in our history that you have just read about. You will want books to which you can refer again and again to refresh your memory of the facts of this period in history.

Your school textbook gives you a brief account of the story of your country and its great people. It is not possible in one book to tell the exciting life stories of many of our leaders. But these stories can form part of your home library. Many books can be obtained without great cost. Many books come in inexpensive paperback editions. You can ask your teacher to recommend some books that will give you a start on your home library. The library teacher in your school can also help. You can look over lists of books and decide on the book you want for your birthday or holiday gift.

Some of the books that you may want in your home library are listed for you below and on the next page. These are only suggestions of the kind of good and exciting reading you can enjoy at home, when you choose.

BOOKS FOR UNIT II

AUTHOR	TITLE, PUBLISHER	DESCRIPTION
1. Alter, Robert E.	*Listen, the Drum,* Putnam	A novel about George Washington's first command in the Ohio River Valley
2. Bishop, Jim	*The Birth of the United States,* William Morrow	A "You are there" account of the first four days of July, 1776
3. Cousins, Margaret	*Ben Franklin of Old Philadelphia* Random House	The life and contributions of a famous American
4. DePauw, L. G.	*Founding Mothers,* Houghton Mifflin	Women in the years of the Revolution
5. Dobler, Lavina, and Toppin, Edgar	*Pioneers and Patriots,* Doubleday	About the lives of six black men and women who aided in the fight for independence and the growth of the nation
6. Earle, Alice M., Editor	*Diary of Anna Green Winslow,* Corner House	Life of a Boston school girl of 1771 told in her own words
7. Ellsberg, Edward	*I Have Just Begun To Fight,* Dodd, Mead	The story of John Paul Jones, sea rover and naval hero

AUTHOR	TITLE, PUBLISHER	DESCRIPTION
8. Forbes, Esther	*Johnny Tremain,* Houghton Mifflin	A silversmith's apprentice and his adventures in the American Revolution
9. Green, Robert J.	*Patriot Silver,* St. Martin's Press	The tale of a young man who becomes a follower of Francis Marion, the Swamp Fox
10. Hawke, Donald F.	*Honorable Treason,* Viking	The Declaration of Independence and the men who signed it—their struggles and personal problems
11. Holbrook, Stewart	*America's Ethan Allen,* Houghton Mifflin	The patriot leader from Vermont who captured Fort Ticonderoga
12. Judson, Clara I.	*George Washington,* Wilcox and Follett	An interesting biography of our first president
13. Lester, Julius	*To Be a Slave,* Dial Press	How it felt to be a slave—beginning with Africa and ending with the Civil War
14. Pearson, Michael	*Those Yankee Rebels,* Putnam	The Revolution from the British point of view—sometimes funny, sometimes sad account of how a war was lost
15. Sentman, G. A.	*Drummer of Vincennes,* Winston	George Rogers Clark's expedition against the British at Vincennes
16. Smith, Robert	*The Infamous Boston Massacre,* Crowell Collier	Describes the events in the angry town of Boston which led to the American Revolution
17. Tunis, Edwin	*Colonial Living,* World	About homes, customs, food, and dress in colonial America

Unit III
How Was Our Nation's Government Set Up?

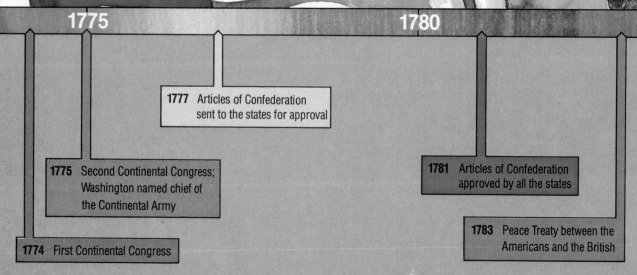

1775

1780

1777 Articles of Confederation
sent to the states for approval

1775 Second Continental Congress;
Washington named chief of
the Continental Army

1774 First Continental Congress

1781 Articles of Confederation
approved by all the states

1783 Peace Treaty between the
Americans and the British

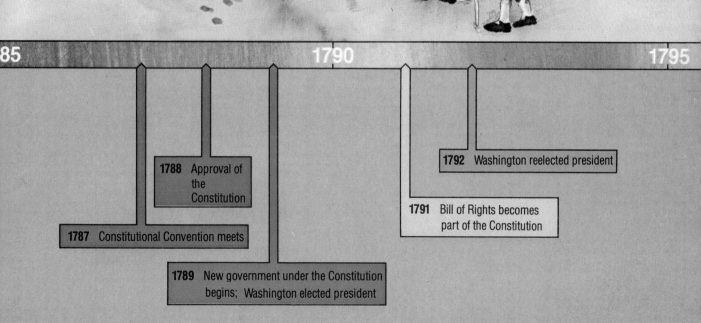

85   1790   1795

1788 Approval of
          the
          Constitution

1787 Constitutional Convention meets

1792 Washington reelected president

1791 Bill of Rights becomes
          part of the Constitution

1789 New government under the Constitution
          begins; Washington elected president

1 THE NEW NATION HAS TROUBLES

How did the new nation prepare to govern itself after the Revolution?

1. The young nation was very weak after the Revolutionary War. The people of the United States were not yet really united. The Second Continental Congress had been the government during most of the war. A committee of that congress had prepared a plan of government for the United States called the Articles of Confederation. In 1781 this plan was approved by the states, as the colonies were now called. The Articles of Confederation became the framework of the new government. They set up a loose union of states. The Articles called this union a "league of friendship" between the states.

2. The Articles gave very few real powers to the new government. Congress could declare war but had no power to raise an army. Congress had no power to raise taxes. It could only ask the states for money and hope that the states would pay it. Because the states often held back the money, the government could not pay its debts. It owed money to foreign nations and to soldiers who had fought in the war for independence. There was no president to enforce the laws. There was no system of courts to protect the rights of the people. The people wanted to establish a weak government. They were afraid they would lose their liberty under a strong government. They remembered too well the harsh rule of the English monarch.

3. Each state was jealous of its own rights and made its own laws. For example, the state of New York made the people of New Jersey and Connecticut pay taxes on products they brought into New York. New Jersey taxed a lighthouse built by New York on the New Jersey coast. Maryland and

Fort Niagara. The British captured the fort from the French in 1759. They held it until 1796, even though the fort was on United States soil.

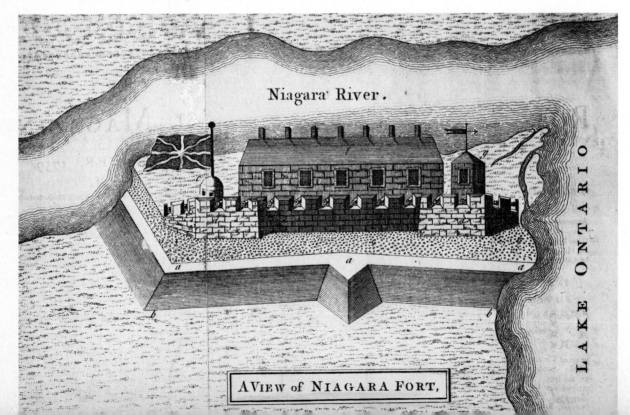

Niagara River.

LAKE ONTARIO

A VIEW of NIAGARA FORT,

Shays's Rebellion. Massachusetts farmers could not afford to pay their debts and taxes. Their armed protests were put down. People saw a need for stronger government.

Virginia argued over the right to use the Potomac River. New York and New Hampshire each claimed parts of Vermont. Congress did not have the power to settle these disputes.

4. Because of its weakness, the new nation was treated badly by other countries. The Spanish, who held Florida and the city of New Orleans, interfered with the trade of American farmers on the Mississippi River. Great Britain refused to leave its fur-trading posts in the Northwest Territory. Pirates stopped and searched American ships on the Mediterranean Sea. Congress was helpless. Americans began to realize that they needed a strong government.

5. Leaders in several states saw that changes must be made in the Articles of Confederation if the freedom of the new nation was to be saved. They called an impor-tant meeting. George Washington and 54 other representatives from every state except Rhode Island met at Philadelphia in May 1787. They gathered to change the Articles of Confederation. Soon they agreed that many changes were needed. They decided to write a completely new plan of government. Such a written plan of government is called a **constitution.** This meeting is known as the Constitutional Convention.

6. Many wise men attended the Constitutional Convention. George Washington was elected president of the convention. Benjamin Franklin, over 80 years of age, was the oldest delegate present. His common sense was very helpful when members of the meeting could not seem to agree. Most of the leaders who took part in the Revolution were present.

7. One of the most important men at the convention was James Madison of Virginia. As a young man, he spent most of his time reading and studying law. He did not take

James Madison. He helped write *The Federalist Papers.* He wrote these essays to convince people to support the new Constitution. Twenty years later he was elected the fourth president of the United States.

an active part in the Revolution. Because of his learning, he was named a delegate to this important meeting of the states. Madison soon led discussions on the powers that the new government should have. The meetings were held in secret. However, James Madison kept a private record of all that happened at the convention. His notes were published many years later. From these notes we know what took place while our Constitution was being written. Because of his work at the convention, Madison is often called the "Father of the Constitution."

UNDERSTANDING CHAPTER 1

I. What is the main purpose of Chapter 1?

    a. To tell how a new plan of government was worked out
    b. To describe the quarrels among the states
    c. To tell about the people who took part in the Constitutional Convention
    d. To describe the problems of setting up a workable government after the Revolutionary War

II. Choose the correct answer or answers.

1. Why did the states refuse to give much power to the national government?
    a. They were not able to trade on the Mississippi.
    b. They now wanted to return to British rule.
    c. They feared a government with too much power.
2. What was a serious weakness in the Articles of Confederation?
    a. Congress had no power to tax.
    b. Only a few states were represented in Congress.
    c. The government was too much like the English government.
3. Why did the leaders of the nation call for a convention?
    a. They wanted to change the Articles of Confederation.
    b. They wanted to raise taxes to pay debts.
    c. They wanted to provide for a strong navy to fight the pirates in Africa.
4. Why did some people see a need for a stronger national government? (2 reasons)
    a. The country was having trouble with other nations.
    b. There were serious quarrels among the states.
    c. The Indians were attacking the people on the frontier again.
5. James Madison helped the country at the convention by
    a. settling arguments when they arose
    b. leading discussions on the powers that the new government should have
    c. keeping no records of the meetings

III. Decide whether each statement agrees or disagrees with what you have read. If the statement disagrees, explain why.

1. The 13 states worked well together after achieving independence from Great Britain.
2. Each state wanted to have more power than the national government.
3. The Articles of Confederation had given Congress the power to tax the people.
4. In 1787 leaders of the United States met to make changes in the Articles of Confederation.
5. Other nations treated the young United States with great respect.
6. The Articles of Confederation failed because Congress had too much power.
7. George Washington became known as the "Father of the Constitution."

DEVELOPING IDEAS AND SKILLS **Study the chart. Then decide whether you agree or disagree with the statements below. Give reasons for your answers.**

WEAKNESSES OF THE ARTICLES OF CONFEDERATION

1. A weak Congress could declare war, but couldn't raise an army. No way to raise money.
2. States printed their own money; taxed goods sent in from other states.
3. Treated badly by other nations.

---

1. After the Revolution, the United States was governed by the Articles of Confederation.
2. The new government was weak.
3. Under this government, the states went their separate ways.
4. The new government helped to unite Americans.
5. This government could make laws but had little power to carry them out.
6. Other countries made problems for the new nation.

SUMMING UP What problems developed in the United States because of the weaknesses of the central government? Benjamin Franklin said, "It is time for thirteen clocks to strike as one." What do you think he meant?

Thinking It Through

Under the Articles of Confederation, the states could choose to give or not give money to the central government. Should citizens have that right today?

2 THE CONSTITUTION BECOMES THE LAW OF THE LAND

What kind of government was set up under the Constitution?

1. The members of the Constitutional Convention decided that a strong central government was needed. The government must have the power to make laws and enforce them. One person would be the head of the government. He would be called the president. The people in each state would elect men to represent them in the government. These men would form the Congress of the United States and make the laws. Among Congress's powers would be the power to collect taxes and raise an army.

2. However, the delegates could not agree on the number of representatives each state should have in Congress. Under the Articles of Confederation, each state had one representative, regardless of the size of the state. Each state had one vote, no matter how many people lived in that state. The states with the most people did not want to continue this system of representation. They demanded that the number of representatives from a state in the new Congress be based on the number of people living in that state. The smaller states protested. They were afraid that if this were done, the larger states would pass whatever laws they wished. The larger states argued that a state with but a few people should not have the same voice in making laws as a state with a large population. Finally, each side gave in a little on its demands and an agreement was reached. This kind of an agreement is called a **compromise.**

3. The compromise provided that the Congress be made up of two groups, called **houses.** In one house, the number of representatives from each state would depend on the population of the state. This house was called the House of Representatives. This

The House of Representatives (left) and the Senate (right) in the early 19th century. Why did both houses of Congress have fewer members at that time than they do today? Do you think it was an advantage to have a smaller Congress? Why or why not?

pleased the large states. In the other house of Congress, each state would have an equal number of members who were called senators. Each state would send two senators to this house, called the Senate. Since all states, regardless of their population, would have equal representation in the Senate, the smaller states were satisfied. This became known as the Great Compromise.

4. The South consisted of six states at the time of the convention. Farming was the main occupation in this region. The North consisted of seven states. Many northerners carried on business and trade as a means of making a living. The difference in interests between the two sections was caused by the geography of each section, as you have learned.

5. The northern states wanted Congress to have the power to control trade among the states and with foreign countries. The South did not agree with the wishes of the North. The South feared that Congress would pass laws favoring northern businesses and shipping interests. The South knew that the North favored a **tariff,** or tax, on goods coming into the country. Northern business people favored a tax on imports so they could sell their products for lower prices than the foreign-made goods. However, if Congress taxed imports, the foreign goods that southerners bought would cost more.

6. The southern states had special interests, too. Black slaves were becoming the chief source of labor in the South. The southern states wanted to count them as part of the population. This would increase the number of representatives each southern state should have in the House of Representatives. However, they did not want to count slaves as part of the population when deciding the taxes each state should pay. On the other hand, northerners wanted to count slaves when deciding taxes. But northerners did not want the South to have

The Constitutional Convention. Meetings were held behind closed doors. Why do you suppose secrecy was so important to the Convention?

more representatives in Congress than they did. The North argued that slaves were not citizens and had no political rights.

7. Again a compromise was reached. The national government was granted the power to control all trade as the North had wished. It was also agreed that five slaves would be counted as three people when deciding the number of representatives from each state. This also would be true in deciding the taxes a state would pay. This became known as the Three-Fifths Compromise. It was further agreed that the national government could not stop the shipment of slaves into the country for a period of 20 years. This pleased **proslavery** people (those in favor of slavery) in the South.

8. The members of the Constitutional Convention worked throughout the hot summer of 1787. After four months of discussion, they completed the Constitution. It had to be approved by 9 of the 13 states before it could become the law of the land. All winter and into the spring, the people argued over the merits of the Constitution.

9. There were people who feared that the Constitution gave too much power to the national government. Thomas Jefferson of Virginia suggested that a bill of rights be added to the document. Jefferson wanted the rights of the people to be stated clearly. Men like James Madison, Alexander Hamilton, and John Jay made speeches and wrote articles defending the Constitution. By the end of June 1788, the nine states needed had approved the Constitution. Many people approved the Constitution provided that a bill of rights be added later. The Constitution became the supreme law of the new nation. In the spring of 1789 the new government began to work.

REVIEWING WHEN THINGS HAPPENED

Decide whether each item below dates *before*, *during*, or *after* the American Revolution.

1. Albany Plan of Union
2. Mayflower Compact
3. Declaration of Independence
4. Government under the Articles of Confederation
5. New England Confederation
6. Convention to write a Constitution
7. Fundamental Orders of Connecticut

UNDERSTANDING CHAPTER 2

I. What is the main purpose of Chapter 2?

a. To describe the different interests of the North and the South
b. To tell why the Bill of Rights was added to the Constitution
c. To describe how a new plan of government was worked out
d. To describe how the new government was accepted by the large states

II. Choose the correct answer.

1. The argument over the number of representatives from each state led to the
   a. creation of a system of courts
   b. election of Washington as president
   c. forming of two houses of Congress
2. The fact that one state had taxed the goods coming from another state led to the
   a. Bill of Rights
   b. first tariff law
   c. control of trade by Congress
3. Some people were worried about the Constitution because
   a. it had no bill of rights
   b. there was no provision for a president
   c. the states had unequal representation in the Senate
4. The members of the convention took a long time in working out a new plan of government because
   a. some differences among the states had to be settled
   b. not all states were represented at the convention
   c. large states wanted equal representation with small states

5. The Articles of Confederation were done away with because
   a. the states would no longer obey them
   b. they were no longer in effect after 1783
   c. people agreed that a stronger national government was needed

III. Decide whether each statement agrees or disagrees with what you have read. If the statement disagrees, explain why.

1. The Constitution divided Congress into two houses, the Senate and the House of Representatives.
2. The Constitution became the law of the land when it was approved by all 13 states.
3. The Constitution says that all states have the same number of representatives in the House of Representatives.
4. The Constitution was adopted by the states in 1789.
5. All 13 states promptly agreed to accept the Constitution.
6. Slavery was abolished, or done away with, when the Constitution was adopted.
7. There are many compromises in the Constitution.
8. The members of the convention in Philadelphia wrote a bill of rights.

DEVELOPING IDEAS AND SKILLS

Answer the following questions about the cartoon.

1. Who is the "jury"?
2. Who are the men that are arguing?
3. Why are they arguing?
4. What is the paper in their hands?
5. How was this argument settled?
6. When did this take place?

179

FINDING THE MAIN IDEA

Every paragraph has a main idea. The main idea is the one thing that all of the sentences in the paragraph say something about. It may be found at the beginning, in the middle, or at the end of a paragraph. Finding the main idea of a paragraph will help you understand and remember what you read. It will also help you find other information quickly. Once you have found the main idea of a paragraph, you can easily take notes on what you have read.

Reread paragraphs 1–9 in this chapter. Pick out the main idea in each paragraph. For example, can you find the main idea of paragraph 1 on page 176? It is found in the first sentence: "The members of the Constitutional Convention decided that a strong central government was needed." Now see if you can find the main idea of the other paragraphs. When you have them, write them down in your notebook. This will help you in studying. Continue this procedure as you read the other chapters in the book. Not only will you become more skillful in finding the main idea, you will have a better understanding of what is going on in your social studies class.

SUMMING UP

IMPROVING THE UNITED STATES GOVERNMENT The Constitution corrected some of the weaknesses of the government under the Articles of Confederation. In your notebook, list the weaknesses below. In the column next to each, describe the improvement made by the Constitution.

ARTICLES OF CONFEDERATION	CONSTITUTION
1. No person had the power to enforce the laws.	
2. Congress was unable to raise needed money.	
3. States taxed goods from other states.	
4. Large and small states had the same number of representatives in Congress.	
5. Congress was unable to raise an army.	

Thinking It Through

Why was the Constitutional Convention one of the great events in history?

3 OUR FEDERAL GOVERNMENT

How does the Constitution divide power among the different areas of government? How does it provide for changes in government?

Independence Hall, Philadelphia. Site of the Declaration of Independence (1776) and the Constitutional Convention (1787).

1. The men who wrote the Constitution had lived through a war with England. They could not easily forget how a strong king had taken away the rights of the people. They remembered the tax laws and the soldiers who searched homes without a warrant. On the other hand, they had found out that if a government is too weak, there is no law and order. For these reasons, they gave careful thought to the new government. Their ideas continue to guide us today, almost 200 years later. We should know some of these ideas.

2. First, the Constitutional Convention decided to establish a **federal** government. In this form of government, power is divided between the national government and the states. There are certain things that only the national government may do. There are others that only the states may do. In order to establish this federal government, the 13 states had to give up some of their powers. The federal plan was a compromise between a government that has all the power and a government that has almost no power.

3. Second, the members of the convention divided the powers of the national government into three separate branches: the **legislative,** the **executive,** and the **judicial.** They gave each branch certain powers. The authors of the Constitution were afraid to give any one branch too much power. So, they gave each branch powers to serve as a check on the other branches. For example, the president (executive branch) may **veto,** or disapprove, a bill passed by Congress (legislative branch) and keep it from becoming a law. In turn, Congress may refuse to pass laws that the president may want. The Supreme Court (judicial branch) may **check** both the president and Congress by declaring a law **unconstitutional.** In doing this, the Court is saying that Congress and the president have no right to pass such a law. The law is no longer in effect. In these ways the branches of government check one another. This is called **checks and balances.**

4. The president is the head of the executive branch of government. The president

181

is the chief executive. The president is elected for a term of four years and may be elected no more than twice. The president has a number of important powers. He or she must support the Constitution and enforce the laws passed by Congress. He or she is commander in chief of the army and navy and makes treaties with foreign nations. He or she may sign or veto laws passed by Congress. The president appoints the members of the Supreme Court and many other government officers with the "advice and consent" of the Senate.

5. Congress is the legislative, or lawmaking, branch of the government. Congress is the legislature. There are two houses in Congress, the Senate and the House of Representatives. There are two senators from each state. They hold office for six years. One-third of the Senate is elected every two years. There are 435 members in the House of Representatives. These representatives (or congressmen and congresswomen, as they are called) are elected for two-year terms. Congress's chief purpose is to make laws. It also has the power to tax, to control trade, and to declare war.

6. The third branch of the national government is the judicial branch. This branch, often called the judiciary, consists of the Supreme Court and a number of lower federal courts. The Supreme Court has nine judges, called **justices.** The justices of the Supreme Court are the most important judges in the country. They are appointed to the Court by the president, with the approval of the Senate. The Supreme Court makes certain that the president and Congress follow the Constitution. The Court settles disputes over the meaning of laws passed by Congress.

7. The delegates who met at Philadelphia in 1787 knew that the United States would grow and that its people's needs would change. They made it possible to change parts of the Constitution by peaceful means. The people of our country may change their government's powers to fit their needs. New parts may be added to the Constitution. These changes, or additions, are called **amendments.**

8. Amendments usually begin in the Congress. First, a suggested amendment must be passed by a two-thirds vote of both the Senate and House of Representatives. It then goes to the states for their approval. Each state may have its legislature vote on the change, or each may call a convention to vote on the amendment. The proposed amendment must be approved by three-fourths of the states before it is added to the Constitution. Amendments do not have to be approved by the president. Since 1789 over 3,000 amendments have been suggested, but only 26 have met with the approval of the Congress and three-fourths of the states.

9. When the Constitution was approved, it was understood that the first Congress would add a bill of rights. The Congress added ten amendments to the Constitution shortly after the representatives met for the first time. These first ten amendments are called the Bill of Rights. Every American should know and understand those rights that are guaranteed in the Constitution. People are guaranteed the right to worship as they please and to speak or write their opinions freely. They are protected against unjust arrest or punishment. They have the right to a speedy and public trial by jury. They are protected from unreasonable search of their homes and have the right to hold peaceful meetings.

10. George Washington was elected the first president under the Constitution. On April 30, 1789, he took the oath of office in New York City. One of Washington's first jobs was to choose men to help him carry out the duties of the presidency. He appointed Alexander Hamilton as secretary of treasury to advise him on money matters. He appointed Thomas Jefferson as secretary of state to help in matters concerning

University rally against the Vietnam War.

Courtroom proceedings.

Synagogue.

Newspaper stand.

Which of our constitutional rights are represented in these pictures?

Washington going to his first inauguration as president of the United States. The president is the head of the executive branch of government. What are some of the important powers of the president?

George Washington's first cabinet. Identify Washington and Jefferson in this painting.

foreign countries. He made an old soldier-friend, General Henry Knox, secretary of war. He named Edmund Randolph as the first attorney general, the president's adviser in matters of law. These men became known as the president's cabinet.

11. The most important men in the cabinet were Alexander Hamilton and Thomas Jefferson. They had different ideas about the powers of the national government. Hamilton believed in a strong national government. He did not think the average person had the ability to take part in the affairs of government. He wanted to limit government jobs to those who were well educated or rich. The followers of Hamilton became known as Federalists.

12. On the other hand, Jefferson believed that the power of the national government should be limited. He believed

that the government should not spend too much money. He wanted the farmer and the worker to have a greater voice in government. He wanted everyone to get an education so people would know and understand what their government was doing. He wanted to make sure the government was not being led by too many rich people. His followers were called anti-Federalists or Democratic-Republicans. The supporters of Hamilton and Jefferson formed our first political parties.

13. Washington was elected for a second term as president in 1792. He refused to accept a third term and John Adams of Massachusetts became the second president of the United States. Washington returned to his home at Mount Vernon, Virginia. In December 1799, he died after a severe cold. He was buried on his estate at Mount Vernon. At Washington's funeral, Henry Lee, a member of Congress, said in praise of him, "First in war, first in peace, and first in the hearts of his countrymen."

REVIEWING
CHAPTER 2

Choose the correct answer.

1. The Constitution provides for a Congress made up of the Senate and the
   a. Supreme Court
   b. House of Representatives
   c. General Assembly
2. Each state has how many senators?
   a. one
   b. two
   c. three
3. The first plan of government for the United States after the Revolutionary War was called the
   a. Articles of Confederation
   b. Constitution
   c. Continental Congress
4. Some states would not approve the Constitution until
   a. the states received greater power
   b. it was agreed that a bill of rights would be added later
   c. they received payment for their debts
5. One of the major compromises of the Constitution was over the question of
   a. Indian affairs
   b. the settlement of boundary lines
   c. the control of trade by the national government
6. In a compromise
   a. one side gives up everything it asks for
   b. the two sides refuse to agree
   c. each side gives in a little
7. The "Father of the Constitution" was
   a. George Washington
   b. James Madison
   c. Benjamin Franklin
8. The Constitutional Convention was held in
   a. 1776
   b. 1783
   c. 1787

I. **What is the main purpose of paragraphs 3 through 6?**

    a. To describe the difference between a democracy and a dictatorship
    b. To explain the meaning of checks and balances
    c. To explain the ideas of government described in the Constitution
    d. To give us an understanding of the Bill of Rights

II. **Choose the correct answer.**

1. The men who wrote the Constitution divided the national government into three branches because
    a. they were afraid to give one branch too much power
    b. they thought the government would pass laws quickly
    c. they wanted to make sure the national government was not as strong as the state governments
2. The Bill of Rights is important because it
    a. makes rules for the sale of public land
    b. controls trade among the states
    c. guarantees the rights of the American people
3. The Constitution can be changed by
    a. voting for new government officials
    b. asking the Supreme Court
    c. adding new parts, or amendments
4. The Constitution established which kind of government?
    a. A federal government
    b. Rule by a monarch
    c. Rule by a few educated people
5. Hamilton and Jefferson disagreed over the following:
    a. The powers of the national government
    b. The election of Washington
    c. The forming of a cabinet

III. **Decide whether each statement is true or false. The underlined words are clues to help you decide. If a statement is false, change the underlined word or words to make it true.**

1. The United States government is made up of <u>three</u> branches.
2. Congress may not interfere with <u>the religion of any citizen</u>.
3. <u>Freedom of assembly</u> means that a person may speak her or his opinions freely.
4. A <u>federal</u> government is one in which powers are divided between the national and state governments.
5. The Constitution guarantees every citizen the right to <u>trial by jury</u>.
6. The president's veto of a bill passed by Congress is an example of the government's <u>checks and balances</u>.
7. The <u>cabinet</u> is a group of advisers to the president.
8. <u>Washington</u> was inaugurated as the nation's first president.
9. The first ten amendments to the Constitution are called the <u>Bill of Rights</u>.
10. <u>Hamilton</u> thought everyone should be educated so that the nation could be governed wisely.

PICTOGRAPH STUDY *How a Bill Becomes a Law*
Study the following pictograph. Then tell whether each statement is true or false. The underlined words are clues to help you decide. If a statement is false, change the underlined word or words to make it true.

How a Bill Becomes Law

1. Introduced in either Senate or House of Representatives. Bills to raise money for government must start in House of Representatives.

2. Sent to committee for discussion, changes, and a vote.

3. If bill is approved by committee, it is presented to all members of the house. Discussed, changed, and voted upon. If passed by a majority (more than half the members voting), bill is sent to other house.

4. Same method is used in other house —committee and vote. If majority of house vote in favor of bill, it goes to the president.

5. If the two houses passed bills that are not exactly the same, bills must be sent to special committee to work out differences. Then final bill goes back to both houses for vote. If bill wins, it is sent to president.

6. President has 10 days to study bill. (a) If president signs bill, it becomes law of the land. (b) If president does nothing about bill, it becomes law after 10 days if Congress is still in session. (c) President can veto, or refuse to sign, bill. If that is done, president must send written message to Congress telling why bill was vetoed.

7. Congress may accept veto. In that case, bill does not become law. But Congress may wish to pass bill "over" the veto. Another vote may be taken. If ⅔ of members of each house vote for bill, it becomes law regardless of president's wishes.

1. If the bills approved by each house are different, the bills may be sent to <u>the Supreme Court</u> to work out differences.
2. Bills dealing with money must start in <u>the House of Representatives</u>.
3. If both houses pass the same bill, it goes to the <u>Attorney General</u>.
4. The president may either sign or <u>veto</u> the bill.
5. Even if the bill is vetoed it can still become a law. But then the Senate and the House of Representatives have to pass it by a <u>nine-tenths</u> majority.

PICTOGRAPH STUDY *Our Federal Government*
Study the pictograph. Then tell whether each statement at the top of the
next page is true or false. If the statement is false, rewrite it to make it true.

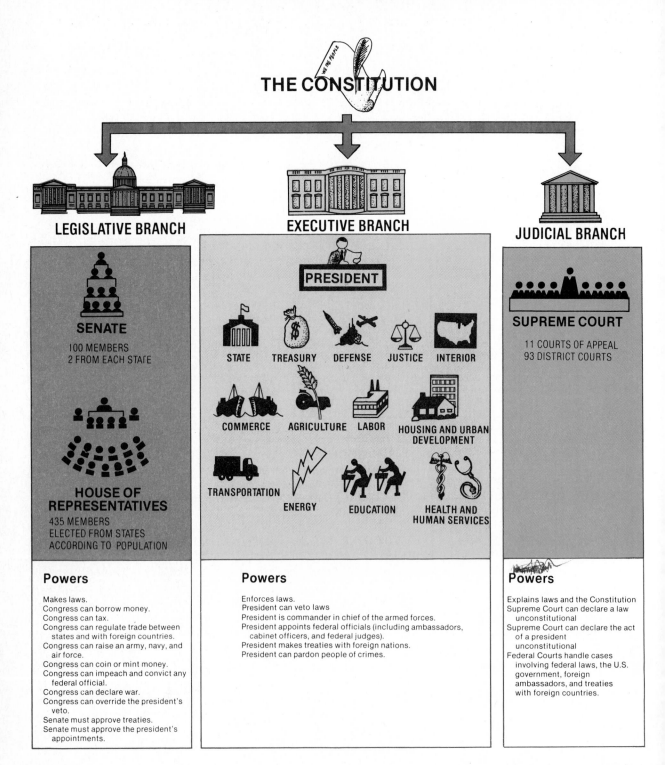

THE CONSTITUTION

LEGISLATIVE BRANCH

SENATE

100 MEMBERS
2 FROM EACH STATE

HOUSE OF REPRESENTATIVES

435 MEMBERS
ELECTED FROM STATES
ACCORDING TO POPULATION

EXECUTIVE BRANCH

PRESIDENT

STATE   TREASURY   DEFENSE   JUSTICE   INTERIOR

COMMERCE   AGRICULTURE   LABOR   HOUSING AND URBAN DEVELOPMENT

TRANSPORTATION   ENERGY   EDUCATION   HEALTH AND HUMAN SERVICES

JUDICIAL BRANCH

SUPREME COURT

11 COURTS OF APPEAL
93 DISTRICT COURTS

Powers

Makes laws.
Congress can borrow money.
Congress can tax.
Congress can regulate trade between
   states and with foreign countries.
Congress can raise an army, navy, and
   air force.
Congress can coin or mint money.
Congress can impeach and convict any
   federal official.
Congress can declare war.
Congress can override the president's
   veto.
Senate must approve treaties.
Senate must approve the president's
   appointments.

Powers

Enforces laws.
President can veto laws
President is commander in chief of the armed forces.
President appoints federal officials (including ambassadors,
   cabinet officers, and federal judges).
President makes treaties with foreign nations.
President can pardon people of crimes.

Powers

Explains laws and the Constitution
Supreme Court can declare a law
   unconstitutional
Supreme Court can declare the act
   of a president
   unconstitutional
Federal Courts handle cases
   involving federal laws, the U.S.
   government, foreign
   ambassadors, and treaties
   with foreign countries.

1. Our national government is divided into three parts.
2. The Department of Education is part of the executive branch of government.
3. There are 11 departments to help the president.
4. The Senate has more members than the House of Representatives.
5. The Supreme Court is the highest court in the United States.
6. The Senate and the House of Representatives make the laws.
7. The Senate has direct control over departments in the executive branch.
8. Matters concerning preparations for war are handled by the Congress.

Using a Time Line

Study this time line. Then answer the questions that follow. Use the information you have studied in this unit to help you. You may also look at the time line on pages 170 and 171 if you need additional help.

In which period of time (**A, B, C, D,** or **E**) did the following take place?

1. The Articles of Confederation were approved.
2. The United States declared its independence.
3. The Bill of Rights was added to the Constitution.
4. The Constitutional Convention met.
5. The new government under the Constitution began to work.

EXTENDING YOUR
READING — III

Using Special Reference Books

There are a number of special books that can help you understand the story of America better. These special books are called reference books. The most important reference books for you to know and use are the dictionary, the encyclopedia, the almanac, and the atlas.

The dictionary gives you the meaning of words. To help you find the words you want, there is a guide word at the top of each page. There are special dictionaries for those who are interested in history: the biographical dictionary and the geographical dictionary.

The encyclopedia has more information about the topics in this book. Most encyclopedias have many volumes or books. The encyclopedia is arranged in alphabetical order. Like the dictionary, there are guide words to help you locate the topic quickly. The encyclopedia also has an index. In most encyclopedias, the index is in the last volume. There are many encyclopedias that are written especially for young people.

Another useful reference book is the almanac. The almanac is a book of facts and figures published each year; therefore, its information is up to date. It has information about all kinds of events that have taken place during the year. The almanac has an index to help you find what you want to read.

Finally, there is the atlas. An atlas is largely a collection of maps. A great deal of information about history and geography can be learned by looking at these maps. Most atlases have a table of contents and an index to help you locate the map you want.

Which of the following would you use to find:

1. The actual movement of Washington's armies during the American Revolution?
   a. encyclopedia   **b.** atlas   **c.** newspaper
2. If a unit on the Constitution was included in a book of American history?
   a. almanac   **b.** table of contents   **c.** dictionary
3. The meaning and pronunciation of the word *amendment*?
   a. atlas   **b.** dictionary   **c.** almanac
4. More information about George Washington?
   a. atlas   **b.** newspaper   **c.** encyclopedia
5. A first-hand account of the Constitutional Convention?
   a. a diary by one of the delegates   **b.** newspaper   **c.** encyclopedia
6. What is happening in Congress today?
   a. encyclopedia   **b.** textbook   **c.** newspaper
7. A list of the American presidents?
   a. newspaper   **b.** almanac   **c.** atlas
8. How a bill is passed?
   a. textbook   **b.** atlas   **c.** dictionary
9. The location of the city of Washington, D.C.?
   a. atlas   **b.** dictionary   **c.** newspaper
10. The most recent facts about immigration into the United States?
    a. encyclopedia   **b.** textbook   **c.** almanac

BOOKS FOR UNIT III

AUTHOR	TITLE, PUBLISHER	DESCRIPTION
1. Bradley, Duane	*Electing a President*, Van Nostrand Reinhold	Clear, simply written explanations of the importance of the presidency and how campaigns are carried on
2. Brown, H., and Guadagnolo, J.	*America Is My Country*, Houghton Mifflin	Gives the background of our basic documents, songs, landmarks, and holidays

BOOKS FOR UNIT III

AUTHOR	TITLE, PUBLISHER	DESCRIPTION
3. Coy, Harold	*First Book of Congress* *First Book of Presidents* *First Book of the Supreme Court* Watts	Three books on the branches of our government
4. Elting, Mary	*We Are the Government,* Doubleday	A simple account of how our government works
5. Fisher, Dorothy C.	*Our Independence and the Constitution,* Random House	A story about the writing of our basic documents
6. Gordon, Dorothy	*You and Democracy,* Dutton	A simply written book about living in a democracy
7. Holland, Janice	*They Built a City,* Scribner	The story of our capital, Washington, D.C.
8. Johnson, Gerald W.	*The Congress,* William Morrow	How Congress began, how it works, how it checks and balances
9. Judson, Clara I.	*Thomas Jefferson— Champion of the People,* Wilcox and Follett	The story of the man who wrote the Declaration of Independence and was our third president
10. Knapp, G. L.	*Uncle Sam's Government at Washington,* Dodd, Mead	The story of our national government and the men who wrote the Constitution
11. Morris, Richard B.	*First Book of the Constitution* Watts	The story of the people and events leading to the writing of the Constitution
12. Ross, George E.	*Know Your Government,* Rand	A detailed account of the three branches of our government

Unit IV
How Did the Nation Grow in Size and Strength?

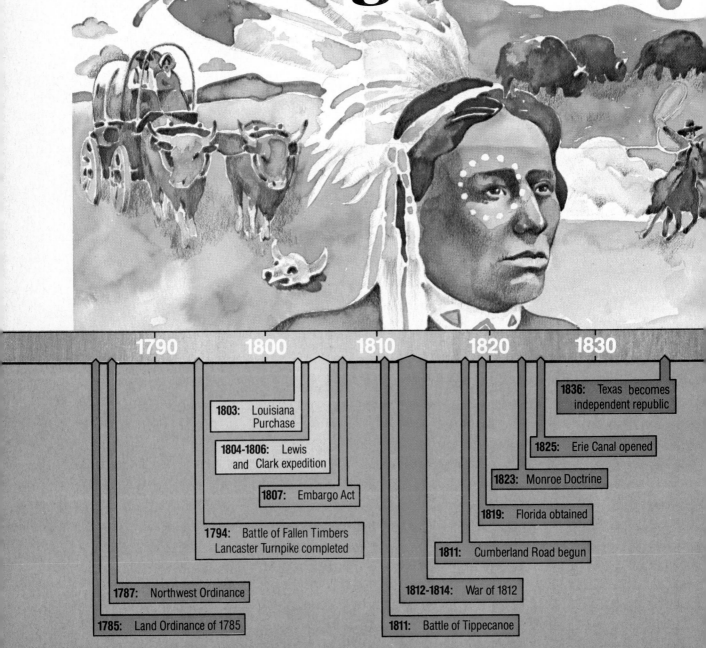

1790   1800   1810   1820   1830

1836: Texas becomes independent republic

1803: Louisiana Purchase

1804-1806: Lewis and Clark expedition

1825: Erie Canal opened

1807: Embargo Act

1823: Monroe Doctrine

1819: Florida obtained

1794: Battle of Fallen Timbers Lancaster Turnpike completed

1811: Cumberland Road begun

1787: Northwest Ordinance

1812-1814: War of 1812

1785: Land Ordinance of 1785

1811: Battle of Tippecanoe

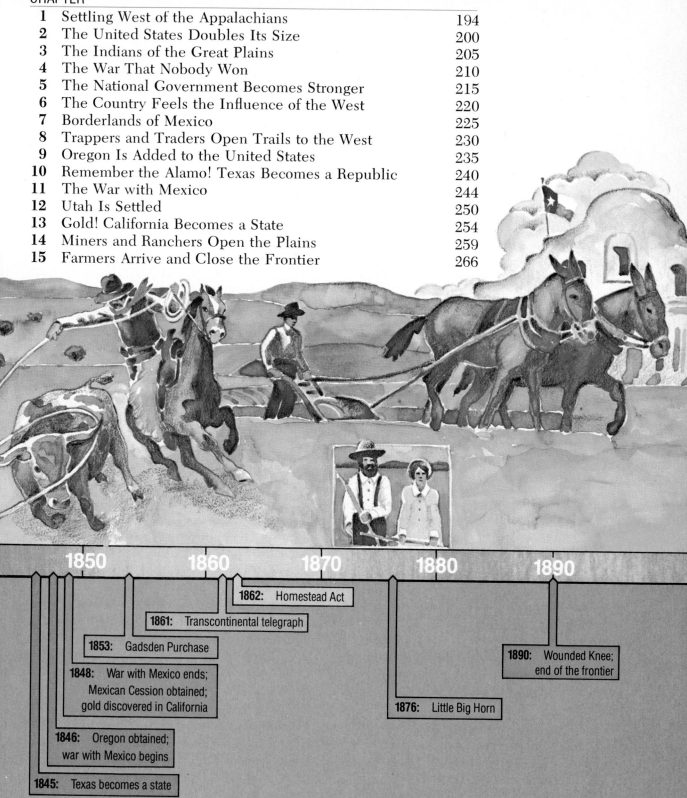

1850   1860   1870   1880   1890

1862: Homestead Act

1861: Transcontinental telegraph

1853: Gadsden Purchase

1848: War with Mexico ends;
Mexican Cession obtained;
gold discovered in California

1890: Wounded Knee;
end of the frontier

1876: Little Big Horn

1846: Oregon obtained;
war with Mexico begins

1845: Texas becomes a state

1 SETTLING WEST OF THE APPALACHIANS

How did the pioneers begin to settle the lands between the Appalachian Mountains and the Mississippi River?

1. The large section of land north of what is now Kentucky was called the Northwest Territory. It reached from the Ohio River to the Great Lakes. It extended as far west as the Mississippi River. This is the territory in which George Rogers Clark captured some of the British forts during the Revolutionary War. In 1781 it was agreed that this territory would be the property of the national government.

2. Under the Articles of Confederation, the government began to prepare the Northwest Territory for settlement. Congress passed the Land Ordinance of 1785. This law broke up the territory into squares of land called townships. Each township was then divided into 36 sections, each one mile square (1.6 kilometers square). Congress set aside one section in each township for the support of public education. The money from the sale of that section paid for the township's school.

3. Settlers could now get land in the territory by buying it at the government land office. They could choose the piece of land they wanted and the government would make a record of their purchase. The land could be bought for as little as one dollar per acre. But many settlers could not pay $640 for a square mile of land, so land companies were formed. These companies bought large areas of land and divided it into smaller parts. The smaller parts were sold to people who wished to settle in the Northwest.

4. In 1787 the Congress of the Confederation passed the Northwest Ordinance. This law described how the territory was to be governed. At first, Congress would choose the officers to govern the territory. As more settlers came to the region, free men could elect their own assembly. They also could send delegates to Congress. These delegates could not vote in Congress. But they could tell the lawmakers about the needs of the people in the Northwest Territory. When as many as 60,000 people had settled in a part of the territory, the people could ask to be admitted to the Union as a state. The law said that from three to five states could be made out of the Northwest Territory.

5. The Northwest Ordinance also had a bill of rights for the people of the territory. It granted freedom of speech, freedom of worship, and the right to trial by jury. It set aside lands for public education. It said that Indian lands were not to be taken unless the Indians agreed. Above all, it did not allow slavery in the territory.

6. The first town in the Northwest was started by General Rufus Putnam in 1788. Putnam had fought in the Revolution. He was one of the owners of an important land company. Starting at the present site of the city of Pittsburgh, Putnam and about 50 families traveled down the Ohio River. Near the spot where the Muskingum River joins the Ohio River, they founded the settlement of Marietta. Thousands of people followed their little group. They came in rafts, barges, houseboats, and flatboats. The settlers loaded their household goods on the flatboats and floated down the Ohio looking for a place to build their homes.

7. In the South, settlers also were looking for the easiest and shortest route to the West. The mountains farther south narrow down into a coastal plain. The pioneers took a route that went around the mountains to settle the rich land in what are now

Marietta, Ohio. This was the first town built by the settlers in the Northwest Territory. Why do you think the first houses were surrounded by a stockade? What nearby river helped this town grow as a shipping center?

the states of Alabama and Mississippi. They soon found that the land was good for growing cotton. In Louisiana, farmers grew sugar cane.

8. Many of the pioneers lived in much the same way as they had back East. They had small farms on which they raised all their food. They made most of their own clothes and other things they needed. They had to clear the land and build log huts to shelter themselves. In the North, the small farmers grew corn and wheat. In the South, the pioneer farmers grew cotton, rice, and sugar.

9. At first, the roads that took settlers to the West were poor. But in time better roads were built. The first of these roads was completed in 1794. It was called the Lancaster Turnpike. It ran from Philadelphia to Lancaster, Pennsylvania. The road was built of crushed rock and gravel. At some places on the road a *pole,* or pike, was stretched across the road. Travelers had to

pay a small amount before they could pass this pike. This payment was called a toll. When the toll was paid, the pike was turned to let the travelers pass. The Lancaster Turnpike was a success. After a while many other roads like it were built. The national government began building one of the most important new roads in 1811. This was the Cumberland Road. It ran from Cumberland, Maryland, to Wheeling on the Ohio River. Later it was extended into Illinois and became known as the National Road.

10. These roads joined the cities of the East with the frontier settlements. Conestoga wagons loaded with household goods and tools traveled over the early roads. These wagons, with their high wooden sides, were first built in the Conestoga Valley of Pennsylvania. They had large wheels to keep the wagons from sinking in the mud. The wagons were covered with white canvas (a kind of heavy cloth) over a

Lancaster Turnpike, Pennsylvania. Most turnpikes were built by private companies. There were tollgates or pikes every 6 to 10 miles (10 to 16 kilometers). A cart or wagon might be charged from 10¢ to 25¢.

wooden frame. They were pulled by either horses or oxen.

11. In the early 1800s, canals were built in many parts of the country. Canals are waterways built by people. Canals connect larger bodies of water. In that way long trips could be made entirely by water. Travel by canal was slow, but it was cheaper than land travel. Probably the most important canal was the Erie Canal in New York State. It made possible an all-water route from New York City to the Great Lakes. Boats could travel up the Hudson River to Albany and then westward for over 350 miles (560 kilometers) on the canal to Buffalo.

12. As more white settlers moved west, trouble grew between whites and Indians. Many Indian tribes living on land between the Appalachian Mountains and the Mississippi River had signed treaties. The treaties were supposed to protect their land. But white settlers moved onto Indian land anyway. The Indians were not happy with the settlers who cleared their forests and destroyed their hunting grounds. They began to attack the new settlements. President Washington sent General Anthony Wayne with an army to end the Indian raids. The Indians were defeated at the Battle of Fallen Timbers in 1794. They had to give up much of their land in what is now Ohio and Indiana. In 1825 Congress set aside land west of the Mississippi River for American Indians. By 1840 many tribes east of the river had been forced to give up their land. In exchange they were given land west of the Mississippi River.

UNDERSTANDING
CHAPTER 1

I. What is the purpose of Chapter 1?

a. To tell how the Northwest Territory was organized

b. To describe how the lands between the Appalachians and the Mississippi River were settled

c. To tell how the Indians were defeated at the Battle of Fallen Timbers

196

II. Choose the correct answer.

1. People traveled to the Northwest because they
   a. wanted to find cheap and fertile land
   b. wished to convert the American Indians to Christianity
   c. hoped to drive the Spanish from Mississippi
2. The Northwest Ordinance is important because it
   a. brought lasting peace with the Indians
   b. provided a plan for governing territories
   c. brought an end to slavery in the United States
3. The first town built in the Northwest Territory was
   a. Marietta, Ohio
   b. Pittsburgh, Pennsylvania
   c. Lancaster, Pennsylvania
4. Indian raids in the Northwest led to
   a. another war in England
   b. the passage of the Northwest Ordinance
   c. Washington's sending an army to stop the attacks
5. The turnpikes were built to
   a. provide better routes to the West
   b. send armies into Indian country
   c. help railroad travel
6. Pioneers who settled what is now Alabama and Mississippi found the land was good for growing
   a. sugar cane
   b. cotton
   c. corn
7. The Erie Canal made it easier for settlers to travel from
   a. New York State to the Great Lakes region
   b. Cumberland, Maryland, to Wheeling on the Ohio River
   c. Virginia to Alabama and Mississippi

III. Do you agree or disagree? Give reasons for your answers.

1. The Ohio River was an important means of travel from East to West.
2. Farming families worked hard to make a living on the frontier.
3. Farmers wanted to earn money by selling their surplus crops.
4. Early pioneer families took over Indian lands, even though this often was against signed treaties.
5. The new frontier was east of the Appalachian Mountains.
6. The Northwest Ordinance contained a plan for admitting new states to the Union.
7. Sugar was an important crop in Louisiana.
8. Some cotton planters traveled West because the soil was worn out in their old plantations.
9. New routes to the West were needed because the old trails were too rough for travel.
10. Some pioneers used Conestoga wagons to carry their families and goods overland.

MAP SKILLS *A. Settling the New Frontier, 1783–1800*
Study the map. Then complete the statements below.

Settling the New Frontier, 1783-1800

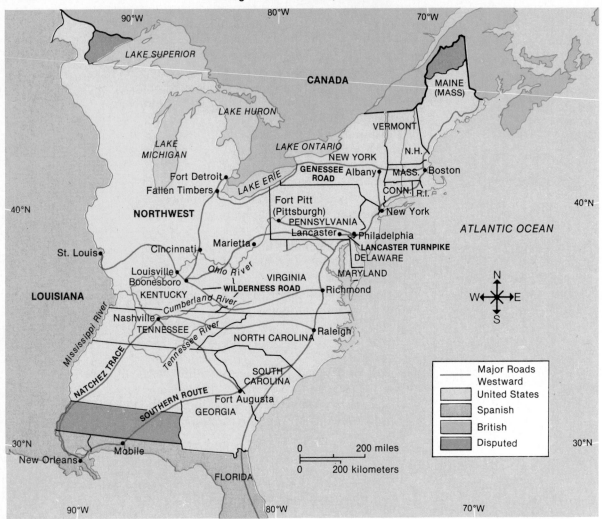

1. The southern border of the Northwest Territory was the ▬▬▬ River.
2. Fallen Timbers is located ▬▬▬ of Lake Erie.
3. Settlers could reach Boonesboro by traveling on the ▬▬▬.
4. Pioneers traveling on the Southern Route from North Carolina to Fort Augusta in Georgia passed through the state of ▬▬▬.
5. The direction in which the Mississippi River flows is ▬▬▬.

MAP SKILLS B. Roads and Waterways about 1840

Study the map. Then complete the statements below.

Roads and Waterways about 1840

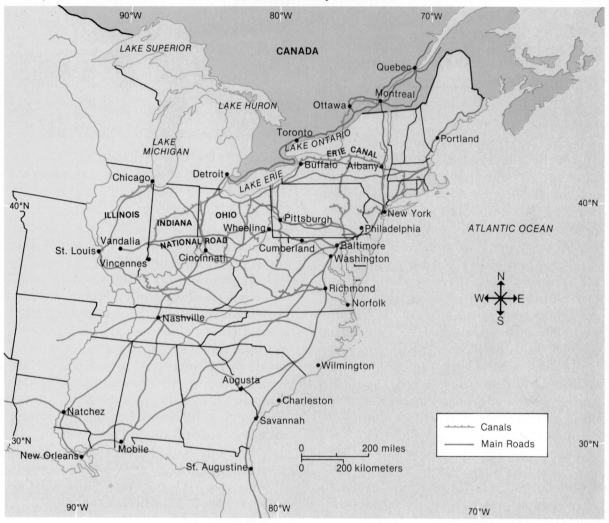

1. A family could reach Ohio on an all-water route from Albany by traveling on the _____ and Lake _____.
2. The National Road ran from Cumberland in Maryland to _____ in Illinois.
3. Surplus crops could be sent from Indiana to New Orleans on the Ohio River and the _____ River.
4. By comparing the two maps, A and B, you can see that travelers who used the Genesee Road in 1800 probably used the _____ 40 years later.
5. In 1840 most of the canals were in the _____ part of the country.

SUMMING UP   What problems did pioneer families face in moving West? What problems do people have in moving today? Are they the same as or different from those of the pioneer family?

2 THE UNITED STATES DOUBLES ITS SIZE

How did the United States obtain land west of the Mississippi River?

A flatboat on the Mississippi River. What do you think the artist was trying to show about life on the river?

1. Settlers continued to move across the Appalachian Mountains into the Ohio and Mississippi valleys. By 1803 the "middle border" states of Kentucky, Ohio, and Tennessee had been admitted to the Union. In time, farmers in this region were able to raise more crops than they needed. These extra crops are called **surplus crops.** Farmers wanted to get their surplus crops to market and sell them. Then they would be able to make enough money to buy the tools and articles they could not make themselves. The best markets for these crops were in New York, Philadelphia, and Pittsburgh. These cities were far away. To send crops there meant going over land and through the Appalachian Mountains. Instead, the farmers loaded their goods on flatboats and floated them down the Mississippi River to New Orleans. New Orleans was a big port city. From there the goods were sent on ships to seaports on the Atlantic Coast or to Europe.

2. During the second half of the 1700s, New Orleans belonged to Spain. The Spanish were not always friendly. Spanish officials in New Orleans troubled western farmers by stopping their goods at New Orleans. Shortly before 1800, a general named Napoleon came to power in France. He took New Orleans and much of the great Spanish territory west of the Mississippi from Spain. Our government feared that Napoleon would try to build a French empire in America. Western farmers were worried that he would interfere with their trade at New Orleans. They asked President Jefferson to help them.

3. Jefferson sent James Madison to France to see if the United States could buy New Orleans. Jefferson knew that Napoleon needed money to carry on his wars in Europe. Madison and the American officials in Paris were surprised when Napoleon offered to sell not only New Orleans, but the vast lands west of the Mississippi as well. At first, Jefferson did not know what to do. The Constitution had not given him the power to buy land. However, he could not let this bargain pass by. With the approval of Congress, Jefferson bought the Louisiana Purchase for $15 million in 1803.

4. Jefferson's decision to buy the Louisiana territory was very important to the growth of the young nation. It doubled the size of the United States. It opened a rich territory to Americans who wanted land for farming and fur trapping. The United States now controlled the entire Mississippi River, including the port of New Orleans. This meant that western farmers could send their goods freely and safely to market. In time, all or part of 14 states would be made from the Lousiana Purchase.

5. The people of the United States knew very little about the Louisiana Purchase.

President Jefferson wanted to open this great land for settlement. First, he had to find out what the territory was like. He selected two young officers, Meriwether Lewis and William Clark, to explore the land. Lewis and Clark kept a record of their expedition. From their notes, we have a clear idea of their travels.

6. The expedition left St. Louis in 1804. The explorers traveled about 1,600 miles (about 2,500 kilometers) up the Missouri River to what is now the state of South Dakota. They reached the village of the Mandans, a friendly Indian tribe. A French trapper and his Indian wife were living there. Her name was Sacajawea, which means "bird woman." Sacajawea was about 16 years of age. She belonged to a tribe of Indians that lived farther west, near the Rocky Mountains. She had been captured in an Indian war and carried away from her tribe. The trapper had married her and brought her to the Mandan village to live. Lewis and Clark hired Sacajawea and her husband as guides. They would be very useful in guiding them farther west.

Sacajawea, Shoshone guide for the Lewis and Clark expedition. What were some of the skills that a guide probably needed?

7. With Sacajawea's help, the expedition followed the Missouri River. They reached the spot in the Rocky Mountains where the mighty Missouri River begins as a tiny stream. Lewis and Clark continued across

New Orleans, Louisiana, in 1803. Why was this city such an important port for farmers and merchants?

UNDER MY WINGS EVERY THING PROSPERS

the mountains until they reached the Columbia River. There they made canoes and paddled downstream. In November 1805, the explorers and their guides came to the Pacific Ocean. This last part of their journey had taken them through what is now the states of Idaho, Washington, and Oregon.

8. In March 1806, Lewis and Clark decided to return to St. Louis. The party separated so that more territory could be explored. Lewis went north and Clark followed a southern route. They met again where the Yellowstone River flows into the Missouri River. In September 1806, they finished their journey. They had been gone more than two years and had traveled 8,000 miles (12,800 kilometers).

9. The expedition of Lewis and Clark was of great value to the young nation. They made maps of the Louisiana Purchase. The explorers were able to describe the land and the people in the new territory. They also collected information about plants and animals. Lewis and Clark reported that the land was rich in fur-bearing animals. Their explorations also gave the United States a claim to territory as far west as the Pacific Ocean.

10. Zebulon Pike was another important explorer of the Louisiana Purchase. He was an army officer. In 1805 he was ordered to find the beginnings of the Mississippi River. Pike traveled northward from St. Louis, but his exploring party failed to reach its goal. However, Pike did gather much useful information about the land along the way.

11. In 1806 Pike set out to explore another part of the newly purchased land. He traveled west from St. Louis into what is now Colorado. A famous mountain there is named Pikes Peak in his honor. Pike traveled south from Colorado into Spanish territory. The Spanish thought he was a spy and arrested him in Santa Fe. After he was set free, Pike returned home and wrote a book about his explorations. Like Lewis and Clark, Pike added much to the knowledge about the Lousiana Purchase, its land and resources.

Choose the correct answer.

1. The Northwest Ordinance was passed in
   a. 1781
   b. 1785
   c. 1787

2. Many pioneers traveled to the Northwest Territory by
   a. train
   b. steamboat
   c. flatboat

3. The Indians in Ohio and Indiana were forced to give up much of their land after
   a. the Battle of Marietta
   b. the Battle of Fallen Timbers
   c. General Wayne bought the land

4. People moved to Ohio because they wanted
   a. cheap land
   b. religious freedom
   c. gold

5. The first town that the settlers started in the Northwest was
   a. Cincinnati
   b. Boonesboro
   c. Marietta

6. An important road that ran from Maryland into Illinois was the
   a. Lancaster Turnpike
   b. National Road
   c. Conestoga Road

I. What is the main purpose of paragraphs 1 through 4?

    a. To tell how the United States acquired the Louisiana Purchase
    b. To describe the size of the Louisiana Purchase
    c. To tell why Jefferson wanted Louisiana
    d. To tell how the farmers used the port of New Orleans

II. Choose the correct answer or answers.

1. Jefferson purchased Louisiana because
    a. he wanted to extend the power of the United States
    b. American troops drove Napoleon from Louisiana
    c. farmers needed the free use of the Mississippi River
2. Sacajawea is remembered because she
    a. guided Lewis and Clark to the Pacific
    b. saved Lewis and Clark from death at the hands of the Indians
    c. helped in the discovery of the Mississippi River
3. The Louisiana Purchase has proven to be valuable to the United States because it
    a. drove the British from North America
    b. was rich in minerals, forests, and furs
    c. opened more territory for the use of slaves
4. Lewis and Clark followed which two water routes through the Louisiana Purchase?
    a. Missouri River
    b. Mississippi River
    c. Columbia River
5. The expedition of Lewis and Clark was important because the explorers
    a. opened the Southwest for settlement
    b. discovered gold
    c. made maps of the Louisiana Purchase
6. On part of his second expedition, Zebulon Pike crossed land owned by
    a. France
    b. England
    c. Spain

III. Decide whether each statement is true or false. The underlined words are clues to help you decide. If a statement is false, change the underlined word or words to make it true.

1. The explorations of Lewis and Clark helped to interest the nation in the <u>New Mexico</u> territory.
2. The United States purchased Louisiana from <u>Spain</u>.
3. The <u>Mississippi River</u> was the eastern border of the Louisiana Purchase.
4. <u>Napoleon</u> was the ruler of France.
5. Napoleon offered to sell <u>all</u> of the Louisiana territory.
6. Western farmers depended on the river port of <u>Cincinnati</u> to trade their goods.
7. Pike tried to find the beginnings of the <u>Columbia River</u>.
8. Lewis and Clark explored as far west as the <u>Rocky Mountains</u>.

MAP SKILLS *Explorations of the Louisiana Purchase*
Study the map. Then decide whether the statements are true or false. If a statement is false, rewrite it so it is true.

Explorations of the Louisiana Purchase

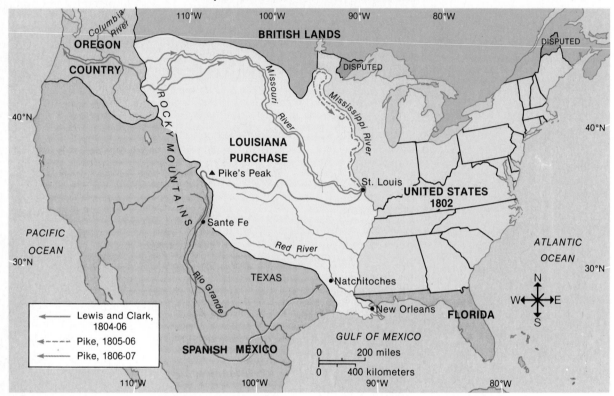

1. The Louisiana Purchase doubled the size of the United States.
2. The Louisiana Purchase extended the United States boundary to the Pacific Ocean.
3. Lewis and Clark traveled into the Oregon country.
4. Lewis and Clark did not reach the Pacific Ocean.
5. Lewis and Clark traveled in a northwest direction.
6. The United States now controlled the entire Mississippi River.
7. Pike's explorations took him north from St. Louis.
8. Santa Fe was a Spanish settlement.
9. Pike traveled through land that is now part of Mexico and Texas.

THE LOUISIANA PURCHASE Complete the following outline in your notebook.

A. Why It Was Needed
B. How It Was Bought
C. Results of the Purchase

3 THE INDIANS OF THE GREAT PLAINS

How did the Plains Indians live?

1. The section of our country between the Mississippi River and the Rocky Mountains is called the Great Plains. Lewis and Clark found Indian tribes on the Great Plains whose way of life, or **culture,** was different from those of Indians in the East. These tribes were divided into small bands, or groups, of 300 to 500 people. Each band had a chief. Some of the Plains Indians lived in villages and grew corn and beans. But most Plains Indians were nomads or wanderers. In the spring and summer, they followed great herds of buffalo and lived off them. When the Spanish first saw them, the Plains Indians had no horses. The Spanish brought horses with them. The Plains Indians quickly learned to ride them. As a result, hunting and fighting became their main occupations.

2. Five strong nations of Indians lived on the Great Plains of the West. These were the Cheyenne, Sioux, Arapaho, Comanche, and Apache. Their tribes stretched from the upper Mississippi in the east to the Rocky Mountains in the west, and from Canada in the north to the Platte River in the south. Both men and women wore their hair in long braids. The men pulled out by the roots all the hair on their faces. At times they painted their faces and eyebrows, as well as their bodies, with colors. Many wore large brass rings in their ears and around their arms.

3. The men wore moccasins, leggings, a loincloth, a buffalo robe, and if they could get it, a woolen blanket. The women usually wore a long shirt, fastened around the

A buffalo hunt. Plains Indians used almost every part of the buffalo. Compare their way of life with that of the Indians pictured on page 71.

A Comanche village in Texas. List all the activities described in the text that are shown in this painting.

waist with a strap. The women made moccasins of deer hides with soles of untanned buffalo hides. They dressed the upper part of the moccasin with beads. They often decorated their clothing with beads and porcupine quills. They obtained these beads and other products, such as gun powder, lead, and guns, from white traders in exchange for buffalo skins.

4. The guns that they got from the traders were not the best. However, Plains Indian males from the age of six years on up knew how to use bows and arrows. They were able to shoot their arrows with unbelievable accuracy. They used their bows and arrows for hunting and fighting. Plains Indians were often at war.

5. Plains Indians lived in cone-shaped tents called tepees. These tepees were made of buffalo hides, skillfully sewn together by the women. Some 20 poles meeting at the top formed the framework, with a hole left at the top through which the smoke escaped. There was also an opening for a door, covered by a hide. Those inside generally turned short pieces of dry wood to keep the fire low and the smoke down.

6. Plains Indians lived chiefly on buffalo meat and wild game. Besides those foods, they also grew a few vegetables, such as the Indian potato and the wild beet. They also gathered grapes, plums, and cherries, which grew wild around them. When the Plains Indians had plenty to eat, they might eat all day and night. Then there would be dancing and games. War games were very important. They were considered good training for real battles and for hunting. During the winter, the Plains Indians ate the dried buffalo meat they had saved. Many people were very hungry by the end of the winter. When the buffalo herds appeared, the men would go buffalo hunting.

7. When the buffalo herds moved, the Indians also moved their camps. They loaded their horses and dogs with their goods. The dogs were able to drag very heavy loads on A-shaped frames, called **travois.** The women carried the small children on their back. They attached the children to their backs with buffalo skin.

Traveling, painted by Keahbone, a modern Kiowa Indian artist. What other animal besides the horse was used to pull travois?

8. Plains Indian boys and girls did not go to school. They did not learn to read books. Instead, they were trained in the old beliefs and customs of the tribe. Boys learned to hunt and become warriors. They learned to make weapons and tools, to follow and kill animals for food, to track their enemies, and to make fires. They went on raids to take horses from other Indian bands. Girls learned to cook, sew, soften animal skins for clothing, and make moccasins and clothing. They wove blankets and mats and made bowls and jars out of clay. They had to learn how to build shelters. Women often were in charge of setting up the tepees after the group had moved. A family's well-being depended upon all its members.

9. Plains Indians believed in spirits found in nature. They believed that the spirits controlled things happening on earth. The chief spirit was the sun. However, they also worshiped the earth, the moon, rocks, winds, and waters. Each tribe had a medicine man, who tried to win favors from the spirits. A medicine man also was called on when a person was sick or a tribe was thinking of war.

10. From the 1750s to the 1850s, the Plains Indians controlled much of the Great Plains. Their way of life depended more and more on the buffalo and the horse. They began to get more blankets, metal tools, and guns from white people or from other tribes that traded with white people.

REVIEWING CHAPTER 2

Decide whether each statement is true or false. The underlined words are clues to help you decide. If a statement is false, change the underlined word or words to make it true.

1. The Louisiana Purchase was made by <u>President Adams</u>.
2. The Louisiana Purchase was explored by <u>Lewis and Clark</u>.
3. The purchase of Louisiana gave the United States control of the <u>Ohio River</u>.
4. All or part of <u>fourteen</u> states was made from the Louisiana Purchase.
5. Lewis and Clark traveled through the <u>Louisiana Pur-</u>

<u>chase and the Oregon country</u>.
6. The Louisiana Purchase <u>doubled</u> the size of the United States in 1803.
7. Western farmers wanted the government to buy <u>New Orleans</u>.
8. Zebulon Pike explored parts of the Louisiana Purchase and <u>Spanish</u> territory.

UNDERSTANDING CHAPTER 3

I. What is the main purpose of Chapter 3?

a. To describe how the Plains Indians defended their lands
b. To describe the way of life of the Plains Indians
c. To describe the houses build by the Plains Indians

II. Choose the correct answer.

1. Why was the buffalo important to the Plains Indians?
   a. Buffaloes were used to carry their goods.
   b. Buffaloes were the main source of food and clothing.
   c. Buffaloes were worshiped by the Plains Indians.
2. What became the most important way that the Plains Indians made a living?
   a. Farming
   b. Fishing
   c. Hunting
3. Why were most Plains Indians always on the move?
   a. They did not want to live near the white settlers.
   b. They were looking for new sources of water.
   c. They had to follow the buffalo herds.
4. Where did the Plains Indians live?
   a. On the Atlantic Coast
   b. On the Pacific Coast
   c. Between the Mississippi River and the Rocky Mountains
5. In what kind of shelter did the Plains Indians live?
   a. Cone-shaped tents
   b. Long rectangular houses
   c. Sun-dried homes of clay
6. What animals did the Plains Indians keep?
   a. Cows and pigs
   b. Horses and dogs
   c. Oxen and sheep

III. Do you agree or disagree? Give reasons for your answers.

1. Many of the Plains Indians were often at war.
2. Each tribe of Indians had many smaller bands.
3. The cow was important to the Plains Indians.
4. The Plains Indians got most food, clothing, and shelter through trade with the pioneers.
5. The children of the Plains Indians went to school while their parents were out hunting.
6. Most Plains Indians used covered wagons to carry their goods from place to place.

DEVELOPING IDEAS
AND SKILLS

PICTURE STUDY *Plains Indians*
Study the picture on the next page. Then answer the questions.

1. What kind of houses do the Plains Indians live in?
2. What kinds of work are the women doing?
3. What animals are found in this camp? How are they used?
4. Is the village fixed or on the move?
5. How were buffalo important to the Plains Indians?

Complete the following outline in your notebook.

THE PLAINS INDIANS

I. Tribes
    a.
    b.
II. Occupations
    a.
    b.
III. Use of the Buffalo
    a.
    b.
IV. Animals
    a.
    b.
V. Religion
    a.
    b.

Thinking It Through

The Plains Indians and the pioneer farmers had different ideas on how to live on and use the land. How might the two ways of life have existed peacefully together?

4 THE WAR THAT NOBODY WON

Why did the United States and England become involved in a second war?

1. The westward march of the United States was slowed by war in Europe. England and France were at war. Neither country wanted the United States to supply the other with goods. Therefore, the two warring nations stopped American ships on the ocean to search for war supplies. Both England and France often seized the food and cotton carried by American ships. Not only did Great Britain remove cargoes, but it seized American sailors and forced them to serve on British ships. The English government claimed that these sailors were deserters from the British navy. This act of seizure was known as the **impressment** of seamen. Since American citizens were being captured, the United States government and people became angry. The United States had not taken sides in the European war. As a **neutral** nation, the United States had felt its ships were free to sail the seas.

2. Thomas Jefferson did not want war. He believed that one way to stay out of war was to keep our ships off the ocean. In 1807 he helped pass a law that declared an **embargo.** This meant that American ships could not leave port or trade at all. This law was called the Embargo Act. The law did not stop the war, for England and France found they could get the goods they needed from other countries. The Embargo Act hurt the business of merchants in the Northeast. The Embargo Act was ended in 1809.

3. James Madison, the next president, also tried to keep peace. His ideas were criticized by a new group of young men in Congress. They were called the War Hawks, because they talked continually of war. The leading War Hawks were Henry Clay of Kentucky and John Calhoun of South Carolina. They protested the seizing of American seamen and the stopping of American trade. They also accused the British in Canada of giving guns to the Indians and urging them to attack settlers in the West. Finally, the War Hawks suggested that the United States add, or **annex,** Canada to our nation. Led by these warlike young congressmen, the United States declared war on England in 1812.

4. The people of the United States were divided on the question of war with England. Many people in the South and West wanted war, but others in New England did not support it. New England merchants had continued to send their ships to sea, running the risk of capture. They knew they would make a huge profit if even only a few ships reached port. Now a war with England would make matters worse. It would ruin their trade completely. During the war, some of the New England states threatened to withdraw from the Union if the government did not end the fighting.

5. In the beginning, the American armies met failure. The soldiers were not trained and equipped to fight another war. An army that was sent to invade Canada was easily defeated. But other American forces attacked York (now called Toronto), the capital city of Upper Canada. They set fire to government buildings and the governor's house. One of the earliest successes of the United States was a victory in a naval battle fought on Lake Erie. A young commander, Oliver H. Perry, was sent to fight English ships on the lake. He built a fleet of nine ships from wood found along the shores of the lake. Perry won the battle and sent a famous message to the nation, "We have

met the enemy, and they are ours." Lake Erie was now under American control.

6. Perry's victory forced the British to retreat to Canada. An American force under General William Henry Harrison followed them. He overtook the British and defeated them in the Battle of the Thames River. In this battle, a remarkable Shawnee Indian, Tecumseh, was killed alongside the British. Tecumseh was not a chief. He had many followers, however. He was a leader because of his strength, his bravery, and his speaking ability. He thought that land was like air and water. It should be free for all to use. The white man, however, wanted to own the land and take it from the Indians. Tecumseh wanted to organize the Indian tribes. He wanted to unite them against the whites who were moving in and taking the land. He wanted the Indians to agree that there would be no sales of the land. He was successful in getting pledges from many northwestern tribes. Then Tecumseh joined with the British in the War of 1812. He thought this might help stop the Americans from moving west. The British, however, did not give Tecumseh much support. They left Tecumseh and his Indian followers to fight alone. When Tecumseh was killed, his warriors took his body and buried it in a secret grave. With his death, Indian resistance in the Old Northwest fell apart.

7. The most famous American warship was the *Constitution*. This sturdy ship was named "Old Ironsides" because cannon balls seemed to bounce off its wooden hull. The *Constitution* won its greatest victory over the *Guerrière*. The early success of a few courageous ship captains was not enough, however. The larger British ships drove our small navy from the seas and blockaded our ports.

8. In August 1814, the British landed at Chesapeake Bay, which separates eastern Maryland from western Maryland and Virginia. The British marched against Washington, D.C. There was no resistance and the president and Congress fled the city. The British set fire to the president's house, the Capitol, and other government buildings. The British fleet then sailed up the bay to Baltimore. This city was defended by Fort McHenry. The British bombarded the fort, but it refused to surrender. A young American lawyer, Francis Scott Key, was on board a British ship trying to arrange for an exchange of prisoners. During the night, he watched the bombing of the fort. In the morning, the American flag was still flying over the fort. Overjoyed, Francis Scott Key wrote the words of a poem that has become "The Star-Spangled Banner." At the same time, a young naval

Francis Scott Key watching Fort McHenry from aboard ship. The defense of the fort against the British inspired Key to write the words to "The Star-Spangled Banner."

The Battle of New Orleans, 1815. This was the greatest American land victory of the war. The British losses were 2,036 people killed and wounded. Only 8 American soldiers were killed and 13 wounded. The victory helped restore national pride. Who was the general who became a military hero because of this battle?

officer, Thomas McDonough, defeated a British fleet on Lake Champlain. This success saved New York from invasion by the British.

9. The war came to an end in December 1814. There was nothing in the peace treaty about the seizure of American seamen. It was a peace without victory. However, before the treaty of peace became known, another battle was fought at New Orleans. The treaty had been signed in Belgium, and word of the signing did not reach New Orleans in time to stop the battle. The British attacked New Orleans. The city was defended by **frontiersmen** under the command of General Andrew Jackson. They were aided by a volunteer force of seamen under the famous French pirate, Jean Lafitte. The British lost many soldiers during their unsuccessful attack. This was one of the few victories on land for the Americans during the war.

10. The War of 1812 is sometimes called the Second War for Independence. Americans had to defend the freedom they had won almost 30 years before. They took great pride in the victories of their navy, and Andrew Jackson became a hero of the nation. The people now saw the need for a strong government that could protect their country in time of war. They were more willing to support the national government. The war also helped manufacturing to develop in this country. During the war, the American people could not get manufactured goods from Europe. They started factories in New England to supply the nation with needed goods. Finally, the older nations of Europe began to look upon the United States with more respect.

Decide whether each statement is true or false. The underlined words are clues to help you decide. If a statement is false, change the underlined word or words to make it true.

1. The Plains Indians raised their children to follow tribal <u>beliefs and customs</u>.
2. The Plains Indians depended on <u>deer</u> for most of their food.
3. When Plains Indian families moved to a new place, the women set up the <u>bark huts</u>.
4. The Plains Indians obtained metal tools, blankets, and guns from white traders in exchange for <u>animal skins</u>.

I. What is the main purpose of paragraphs 5 through 8?

    a. To identify the events of the War of 1812
    b. To describe the Battle of New Orleans
    c. To present the arguments of the War Hawks
    d. To explain why the United States went to war against Great Britain

II. Choose the correct answer.

1. The demands of the War Hawks led to
    a. war with France
    b. war with England and the invasion of Canada
    c. the election of a new president
2. The Embargo Act led to
    a. complaints by factory owners in the South
    b. a tariff on foreign goods
    c. hard times for New England shippers
3. The War of 1812 led to which two results?
    a. The growth of the national spirit
    b. The growth of manufacturing in the United States
    c. The loss of French territory in America
4. One reason the United States declared war on England in 1812 was
    a. taxation without representation
    b. the impressment of American seamen
    c. the burning of Washington
5. The bombardment of Fort McHenry led to the
    a. end of the War of 1812
    b. writing of "The Star-Spangled Banner"
    c. burning of the city of Washington
6. The Battle of New Orleans caused
    a. Andrew Jackson to become a national hero
    b. the signing of the treaty of peace
    c. the adding of Florida to the territory of the United States

III. Decide whether each statement agrees or disagrees with what you have read. If the statement disagrees, explain why.

1. The War Hawks wanted peace with England.
2. The United States was prepared for another war with England.
3. Many merchants in the Northeast depended upon British trade.

4. The British navy often stopped American ships to see if they were carrying war supplies to France.
5. The United States wanted to remain neutral during the war between France and England.
6. Manufacturing developed in the United States during the War of 1812.
7. The War of 1812 was fought only on American soil.
8. The war ended without bringing victory to either side.
9. Tecumseh defeated William Henry Harrison during the War of 1812.
10. "The Star-Spangled Banner" was written during the American Revolution.

Picture Symbols

These pictures should help you recall parts of the chapter you have read. Describe the main idea of each picture.

WAR OF 1812   Complete this outline in your notebook.

A. Causes of the War
   1.
   2.
B. War on Land
   1.
   2.
C. War on the Sea
   1.
   2.
D. Results of the War
   1.
   2.

Thinking It Through

The title of this chapter is "The War Nobody Won." Paragraph 9 describes the end of the War of 1812 as a "peace without victory." What do these statements mean?

5 THE NATIONAL GOVERNMENT BECOMES STRONGER

What leaders, events, and decisions strengthened the national government in the years after the War of 1812?

1. The War of 1812 brought the people of the United States closer together. They were proud of the government that had defended their rights. They felt that nothing could stop the new nation. This feeling of self-confidence grew as the national government became stronger at home and abroad.

2. In 1817 James Monroe became the fifth president of the United States. Florida still belonged to Spain. Seminole Indians from Florida often crossed the border into United States territory. They attacked American settlements and fled back to Spanish territory in Florida. Spain was too weak to stop these raids. In addition, black slaves were escaping from Georgia to the Spanish side of the border. President Monroe sent General Andrew Jackson south to drive the Seminole Indians from American territory. Jackson pushed the Seminole Indians into Florida, followed them, and captured two Spanish forts.

3. Spain wanted the American government to punish Jackson for marching into Spanish territory. The government refused. President Monroe did not want trouble with Spain, but he said that the invasion of Florida was necessary to protect American settlers. Spain realized that it could not defend Florida. So in 1819 it signed the treaty giving Florida to the United States. The United States then paid the $5 million owed by the Spanish government to Ameri-can citizens. This was for damage caused to American ships during previous wars. The United States received not only the present state of Florida, but land in Alabama and Mississippi along the coast of the Gulf of Mexico. The whole South was now open to American settlement.

4. At about this time, the Spanish and Portuguese colonies in Latin America overthrew their rulers and declared themselves independent countries. The rulers of some countries in Europe did not want to see this happen. They were afraid that the idea of revolt might spread to their own nations. Spain asked for their help in regaining its colonies. But President Monroe and the American people were glad to see the Spanish colonies win freedom. The United States did not want the European powers to help Spain. Great Britain, too, wished to see the colonies of Latin America independent, for then these people would be free to trade with Britain.

5. Americans also were watching the Russians, who were moving south on the western coast of North America. Russian fur traders had crossed into Alaska from Asia. Alaska was Russian territory. During the War of 1812, a Russian fur-trading company had built a fortified village near San Francisco. Russia claimed land as far south as the Oregon country.

6. President Monroe and his secretary of state, John Quincy Adams, decided to act. On December 2, 1823, Monroe sent a message to Congress. The ideas in this message are known as the Monroe Doctrine. The Monroe Doctrine stated the following. (1) The United States would not allow European powers to set up any new colonies in the Americas. (2) European nations are not to interfere with the governments of independent American countries. (3) In turn, the United States would stay out of European affairs and would not take action against European colonies already in the Americas.

President James Monroe with his cabinet. What are the main points of the Monroe Doctrine?

7. The whole matter turned out well for the United States. The people supported President Monroe, for they were glad to see their government speak out against the older and more powerful governments of Europe. Great Britain sided with the United States, because it wished to trade with the new Latin American republics. The European nations did not try to end the revolts in the Spanish colonies. Russia withdrew all its claims to the western coast of North America except for Alaska. The nations of the world realized that the United States would soon be a power in world affairs.

8. At home, the national government was strengthened through the decisions of the Supreme Court. Shortly before leaving office in 1801, President John Adams had appointed John Marshall of Virginia as chief justice of the Supreme Court. Marshall believed the federal government should have more power than state governments. His decisions as chief justice from 1801 to 1835 were based on this belief.

9. In 1819 a dispute arose between the state of Maryland and the United States government. Maryland had taxed a branch of the United States Bank in the state of Maryland. Marshall ruled that Congress had the power to establish a bank and a state could not interfere with it. A state may not tax an agency or part of the federal government. He said that the power to tax could be used to destroy the bank. This decision strengthened the national government.

10. Marshall's decisions changed our government in another way. Early in his term of office, Marshall established the right of the Supreme Court to **review** laws passed by Congress. This meant that the Supreme Court could decide whether laws passed by Congress are in keeping with the Constitution. If they were not, the Supreme Court could declare such laws **unconstitutional.** Once declared unconstitutional, such laws are no longer in effect.

11. The power to decide that the laws passed by Congress were unconstitutional was not written in the Constitution. Under Marshall, the Supreme Court ruled that it needed this power to keep Congress from passing any law it wished. By adding this power, the Supreme Court became a powerful branch of the United States government.

Chief Justice John Marshall. He ruled that the Supreme Court could use its power to declare a law unconstitutional.

Match the name in Column A with its correct description in Column B. There is one extra description in Column B.

COLUMN A

Oliver Perry
Thomas Jefferson
Tecumseh
James Madison
Henry Clay
Francis Scott Key
Andrew Jackson

COLUMN B

1. I was president of the United States during the War of 1812.
2. I wrote our national anthem, "The Star-Spangled Banner."
3. I won the Battle of Tippecanoe.
4. I defeated the British on Lake Erie.
5. I became the third president of the United States.
6. I was the hero of the victory at New Orleans.
7. I wanted war with England in order to take Canada.
8. I joined the British side during the War of 1812.

I. What is the main purpose of Chapter 5?

  a. To tell how the United States added Florida
  b. To explain the reasons for the Monroe Doctrine
  c. To explain how the national government grew in strength
  d. To describe the work of John Marshall on the Supreme Court

II. Choose the correct answer.

1. What was the reason why President Monroe issued his famous message?
  a. To open the Louisiana Purchase for settlement
  b. To end slavery in the American nations
  c. To keep European nations from regaining their colonies in the Americas

2. Why did Great Britain support President Monroe?
  a. Britain wanted to build up trade with the new nations in the Americas.
  b. Britain was against its old enemy, Germany.
  c. The United States had a treaty with Great Britain.

3. Why did Andrew Jackson invade Florida?
  a. The United States had declared war on Spain.
  b. The United States wanted to punish the Seminole Indians for raiding American territory.
  c. The United States wanted to capture escaped prisoners from Georgia.

4. The decisions of Chief Justice Marshall led to the
  a. increased power of the national government
  b. rise of political parties
  c. growth in power of the states

5. Which of these was an important statement in the Monroe Doctrine?
   a. The United States will not trade with new nations in the Americas.
   b. The United States will not allow European nations to make new colonies in the Americas.
   c. The United States will encourage new European colonies in the Americas.

III. **Decide whether each statement agrees or disagrees with what you have read. If the statement disagrees, explain why.**

1. President Monroe ordered European nations to free their colonies in the Americas.
2. Andrew Jackson became famous for his defense of the Seminole Indians.
3. The Monroe Doctrine is part of the Constitution.
4. Some European rulers did not like to see colonies gain their freedom.
5. The Supreme Court may declare laws passed by Congress unconstitutional.
6. The Monroe Doctrine was intended in part to warn Russia about extending its territory on the west coast of North America.
7. Thomas Jefferson probably agreed with John Marshall's ideas on government.

DEVELOPING IDEAS AND SKILLS

Answer the following questions about the cartoon.

1. Who is the man building the fence?
2. Why is he building the fence?
3. What name would you give to the fence?
4. What do people looking over the fence want?
5. How did the fence help the Americas?

Growing Stronger Every Year

Match each event in Column A with its date in Column B. There is one extra date in Column B.

COLUMN A

1. Louisiana Purchase
2. Acquisition of Florida
3. Second War with England
4. Monroe Doctrine
5. Northwest Ordinance

COLUMN B

a. 1776
b. 1787
c. 1803
d. 1812
e. 1819
f. 1823

Thinking It Through

What might have happened if European nations had challenged the Monroe Doctrine?

6 THE COUNTRY FEELS THE INFLUENCE OF THE WEST

How did farmers and workers gain a role in government?

1. When George Washington was elected president, only men who owned property or were wealthy could vote. By 1824 more than half the states had done away with these limits on voting rights. What caused this change? The first reason was the settlement of the West. The second reason was the rise of factories in the cities of the East.

2. In the West, the life of the pioneers was hard and dangerous. Their homes were simple and rough. They did not feel better or more important than their neighbors. They had to be able to take care of their needs in the wilderness. When they held meetings, the men expected to take part in the discussions and vote. The belief that all people are equal was strong on the frontier. As the western states came into the Union, most of them gave the right to vote and hold office to all white men.

3. The example of the western states led the factory workers of the East to seek the same rights. The growth of factories brought the workers together to discuss their common problems. They wanted better working conditions and a larger voice in governing themselves. Gradually the eastern states did away with property or religious qualifications for voting and holding public office.

4. The first six presidents came from the eastern states of Virginia and Massachusetts. By 1824 one-third of the American people were living west of the Appalachian Mountains. The people of these states wanted to have a president from their section of the country. In 1828 the first president from the West was elected. He was Andrew Jackson—frontiersman, Indian fighter, and hero of New Orleans.

President-elect Andrew Jackson on his way to Washington, D.C. How does this picture show that his election was a victory for the "common people"?

5. Andrew Jackson was born in a frontier settlement. All his life, Jackson was ready to fight. He took part in the American Revolution when he was only 13 years old. As a young man, he was a lawyer in Tennessee. He was elected to Congress when Tennessee became a state. He was more famous as a soldier, however. After he defeated the British in the Battle of New Orleans, he became a national hero. Later, he led the drives against the Creek and Seminole Indians in the Southeast. Like many westerners at that time, he believed in equality for men only if they were white.

6. Jackson's election as president has been called the Revolution of 1828, because it seemed a victory for the "common man." Much of Jackson's support came from people who had just been given the right to vote—the farmers of the West and the workers of the East. Unlike Jefferson, Jackson believed in a strong central government to serve the will of the people. Again unlike Jefferson and his supporters, Jackson and his followers were self-made men who had little schooling.

7. Once in office, Jackson began to carry out his ideas. He believed all male citizens had the ability to hold office, and that many of them should be given the chance to do so. He dismissed many of the old government office-holders and replaced them with friends who helped elect him. This practice of giving jobs to faithful party workers is called the **spoils system.** The spoils system was continued by other presidents since Jackson. As a result, government jobs were given to some people who were not able to do them well.

8. When Jackson was president, his followers believed that the common people should have a major voice in choosing the officers of their government. For a long time, candidates for president and vice-president were chosen by small groups of congressmen. They held private meetings to decide who would run for president.

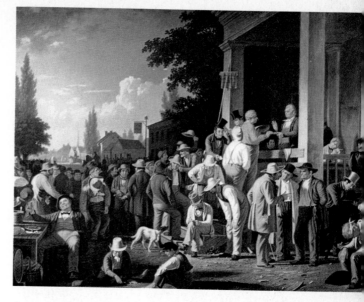

A local official being sworn into office. Why do you think no women are included in this 19th-century scene?

Only after these few men had chosen candidates were the people given the opportunity to vote through their **electors.** By this method, the people actually had little to say in choosing the president.

9. The people of the West thought this was not democratic. During Jackson's term of office, a new way of choosing presidential candidates was begun. Political parties held **conventions,** or large meetings, of delegates. The delegates represented the members of the party throughout the country. The delegates chose the candidates for their party. Since 1840 the **nominating convention** has been the method used to select candidates for the presidency.

10. Andrew Jackson shared the beliefs of most westerners. He wanted Indian land for white settlers. Many Indians still lived in the southern states of Alabama, Georgia, Mississippi, and Tennessee. Jackson wanted to move them to lands west of the Mississippi. This would open land in the South to planters and small farmers. While

this idea was popular with the pioneers, it was hard for the Indians. Many tribes had signed treaties with the United States to protect their land. Now they were forced to sign new treaties that took away their land and gave them new land in the West.

11. One of the Indian tribes hit the hardest was the Cherokee nation. The Cherokee and another tribe, the Creek, held a large amount of land in northwest Georgia. They were a farming people. The Cherokees also had a government, a constitution, and a written language. This language had been devised by a Cherokee named Sequoyah. It took Sequoyah twelve years to complete his new written alphabet and language. After the language was finished in 1821, books were printed and a Cherokee newspaper was begun. Tribal history, beliefs, and treaties were written down.

12. The Cherokees had a treaty with the United States saying that they owned the land. White settlers, however, wanted their land. The Cherokees took their case to the Supreme Court of the United States. They hired lawyers to resist removal from their land. The Court said that the Cherokees owned the land and had a right to keep it. President Jackson, however, refused to support the Court's decision. He sent an army and forced the Cherokees from their homes. They were allowed to take only what they could carry. They then began a long march to new lands hundreds of miles away in the West. Thousands died along the way from cold, hunger, and exhaustion. This march became known as the Trail of Tears.

13. The government's policies resulted in wars with the Indians. The first of these was the Black Hawk War. Black Hawk was a young leader of the Sac and Fox. When the old head of the tribe agreed to move his people from their homes in Illinois, Black Hawk objected but he went. The Sac and Fox had difficulties in their new home in Iowa. The Sioux Indians bothered them. White settlers burned their crops. So, in 1832, Black Hawk led a band of his tribe back to Illinois to their old land. The white settlers there fled in panic and called on the army to help. Black Hawk and his people fled from the army. But finally they were trapped and massacred.

14. Another place where the Indians resisted was in Florida. When the government tried to move the Seminole Indians from their land, the Seminoles refused. An army was sent in 1837 but was defeated by the Seminoles. New armies were then sent. The Seminoles hid in the swamps. For the next five years they fought the armies. Finally, in 1842 some of the Seminole Indians agreed to leave their lands. Others, however, went deeper into the Florida wilderness. These Indians were never defeated.

REVIEWING CHAPTER 5

Which statement describes James Monroe? Which one describes John Marshall? Explain your answers.

1. I said that the Supreme Court has the power to declare laws unconstitutional.

2. I warned European countries not to establish any more colonies in the Americas.

UNDERSTANDING CHAPTER 6

I. What is the main purpose of Chapter 6?

a. To describe Jackson's feelings toward the American Indians
b. To show how Jackson filled positions in the government
c. To discuss Jackson's policies toward farmers, workers, and American Indians
d. To describe changes in the nation's population between 1800 and 1828

II. Choose the correct answer.

1. The growth of settlements in the West led to
   a. demands for laws forbidding slavery
   b. a desire for public schools
   c. a belief that all white men should have the right to vote
2. The fact that new states were created in the West led to
   a. the election of Andrew Jackson
   b. the growth in power of American Indians
   c. a demand to make Texas part of the United States
3. Andrew Jackson began
   a. the spoils system
   b. war with England
   c. better relations between North and South
4. The spoils system led to
   a. better government
   b. higher tariffs
   c. some people's holding government jobs who were not suited for their jobs
5. The demand for more democracy in the selection of a president led to
   a. election of the president by Congress
   b. conventions to nominate candidates for president
   c. more frequent elections
6. The movement of American Indians to the west of the Mississippi resulted in
   a. peace between the Spanish and the American Indians
   b. the opening of new land for white settlers
   c. the death of Jackson

III. Decide whether each statement agrees or disagrees with what you have read. If the statement disagrees, explain why.

1. The election of Jackson was a victory for wealthy southern planters.
2. The new states in the West allowed all adult men and women to vote by 1828.
3. The nominating convention gave more people the chance to choose candidates for president.
4. Jackson believed in filling government positions with his friends and those who supported him.
5. Jackson believed in helping the American Indians to keep land owned by their tribes.
6. Jackson considered himself to be a servant of the common people.
7. Jackson was the first president to come from the West.
8. Jackson believed in giving more power to the states.
9. Jackson distrusted the workers in the eastern states.
10. Jackson and Jefferson had the same ideas of democracy.
11. Jackson's policies forced the Cherokee Indians to move westward on the Trail of Tears.

MAP SKILLS *The United States in 1830*

Study the map. Then decide whether the following statements are true or false. If a statement is false, rewrite it so that it is true.

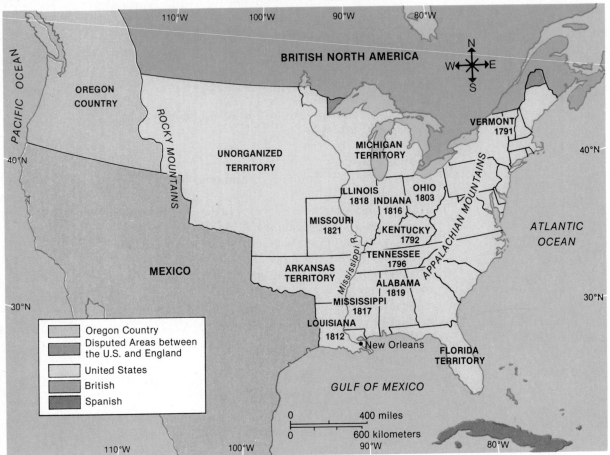

The United States, 1830

1. By 1830 most of the Louisiana Purchase had been organized into states.
2. In 1830 the United States territory reached to the Pacific Coast.
3. There were no states west of the Mississippi River.
4. Much of what later became part of the United States was still controlled by Spain.
5. The entire Northwest Territory had been made into states.
6. Most of the states admitted to the Union after 1789 were west of the Appalachian Mountains.

SUMMING UP   **Thinking It Through**

Did democracy exist for all people during Jackson's time? What groups of people did not have full rights as citizens? What general statement can you make about American democracy during the Jacksonian period?

7 BORDERLANDS OF MEXICO

How did people live in Spanish America?

1. In the 1500s the Spanish empire in the Americas was divided into two parts: the Kingdom of New Spain and the Kingdom of Peru. The Kingdom of New Spain included Mexico and the islands of the West Indies. Its capital was Mexico City. The Kingdom of Peru included Peru, Panama, and all the Spanish lands of South America. Its capital was the city of Lima. Each kingdom was governed by a viceroy, or governor, who was appointed by the king of Spain. The viceroy was the direct representative of the king in the New World.

2. The monarch divided the lands of New Spain into great estates and gave them to captains, or **conquistadors**. Many American Indians lived on these estates. They farmed the land on the estates, watched the cattle, and worked the gold and silver mines for their lords. The lords were expected to treat them kindly, to teach them Christianity, and to give them small plots of ground to farm for themselves. In most cases, the lords did not do so. In time, the Indians became slaves. They could not leave the land. They were forced to work very hard without pay. When too many Indians died, blacks were brought from Africa to work as slaves. (*Negro* is the Spanish word for "black.")

3. The Catholic Church also helped to keep the Spanish in power. In church schools, the people were taught to be faithful to the Church and loyal to the Spanish monarch. The Church began universities in Mexico City and Lima to prepare people for service in the government or in the Church. The Church also sent Catholic missionaries beyond the settlements into Indian territory. The Church believed it was its duty to bring the Catholic religion to the conquered Indians.

4. **Missions** were built in the new lands. The missions were run by Catholic priests. The missions usually included workshops,

A picture by an Indian artist showing the harsh life of the Indians under Spanish rule. What is happening in this picture?

chalchicueyeca

mills, and farmlands as well as a church and the living quarters. The missions also had schools where the Indians could be taught how to farm or do other skills. The Indians were usually taught how to weave cloth and sew articles of clothing. The mission could support itself with this work. Occasionally, a mission could even grow enough grain to export to Europe. Missions sometimes also produced pottery, wine, or olive oil. To protect the missions, the Spanish built **presidios,** or forts. In time these missions and presidios grew into towns and cities. These towns became the center of settled regions of ranches, farms, and villages.

5. The Spaniards did not drive the Indians out of the lands they settled. Instead, they used them to do the hard work. The Indians learned to wear Spanish clothing and to speak the Spanish language. Many went to Spanish churches and were taught by Spanish priests. Some married the Spanish. (The people who were part Spanish and part Indian were called **mestizos.**) They wove cotton and woolen cloth, fashioned pottery, carved stones, and shaped metals. In turn they showed the Spanish how to grow tobacco, beans, potatoes, squash, and maize (corn).

6. The government of New Spain decided to settle its lands north of what is now Mexico. In 1769 the viceroy sent two men, Gaspar de Portolá and Father Junípero Serra, to build forts and missions in the territory of California. After many hardships, they built the first fort and mission at San Diego. After setting up a mission and fort near Monterey Bay, Portolá returned to

Spanish mission. Often the priests' living quarters, the church, and the workshops were surrounded by walls. Indian homes and farmlands were outside the walls.

Mexico without Serra. Serra continued his work. Although lame, he was able to found nine more missions in California. A road, El Camino Real (The King's Highway), led from one mission to another. A total of 21 missions were built.

7. The missionaries taught the Indians of California the Christian religion. They taught them to read and write. They showed them how to farm and care for herds of cattle, sheep, and horses. They brought new crops that grew well in the warm climate of California: grapes, oranges, olives, and figs. They taught Indian women to spin, weave, and sew. Towns, or pueblos, slowly grew around the missions.

8. In 1821 Mexico gained its freedom from Spain. At that time Mexico was much larger than it is today. Its land included what are now the states of Texas, Arizona, New Mexico, and California. Mexico wanted more people to come to its borderlands, as these lands were called. It was willing to give land to anyone who wanted to settle in the territory. One of the early settlers was John Sutter of Switzerland. The governor gave him land for a huge ranch in central California. On the ranch, Sutter raised cattle and wheat. He built an adobe fort called Fort Sutter. The fort was a resting place for hunters who wandered into California.

9. There were other settlements in Arizona, New Mexico, and Texas. These settlements were not as well populated as those in California. The land was very dry and the Indians were not friendly. To encourage more settlements on the eastern borderlands, the Mexican government opened the land to American farmers and traders. Thus began the movement of farmers and planters into the area known as Texas. Before long this led to conflict.

REVIEWING CHAPTER 6

Decide whether each statement is true or false. The underlined words are clues to help you decide. If a statement is false, change the underlined word or words to make it true.

1. Andrew Jackson was the first president from a <u>western</u> state.
2. Andrew Jackson drove the American Indians from the <u>Northwest Territory</u>.
3. Most presidents before Jackson had come from <u>New York State</u>.
4. Jackson was born and brought up on the <u>frontier</u>.
5. Andrew Jackson was elected with the support of the <u>farmers and factory workers</u>.
6. Jackson's policy toward the American Indians was <u>popular</u> with the pioneers.
7. When George Washington was elected president, <u>all adult men</u> could vote.

UNDERSTANDING CHAPTER 7

I. What is the main purpose of Chapter 7?

a. To describe crops the Indians gave to the Spanish
b. To describe how cattle were raised in the New World
c. To tell how people lived in the Spanish colonies

II. Choose the correct answer.

1. Which two names are connected with Spanish settlement in California?
   - a. Cabral
   - b. Portolá
   - c. Serra
2. El Camino Real was the name of
   - a. a mission
   - b. a road
   - c. an estate
3. The Spanish brought which TWO crops to California?
   - a. cotton
   - b. oranges
   - c. grapes
4. Which one of these would NOT have been seen in Spanish California?
   - a. highways
   - b. missions
   - c. women voters
5. Under the Spanish, the Indians
   - a. learned the Spanish language and the Catholic religion
   - b. were supplied with weapons to fight the Russian fur traders
   - c. were allowed to buy up large estates and missions
6. Father Junípero Serra founded the first mission and fort in Spanish California at
   - a. Los Angeles
   - b. San Diego
   - c. Mexico City
7. Arizona, Texas, and New Mexico were once part of
   - a. California
   - b. Mexico
   - c. Peru

III. Do you agree or disagree? Decide whether each statement agrees or disagrees with what you have read. If the statement disagrees, explain why.

1. By the 1500s the Spanish empire included only the Kingdom of New Spain.
2. The Spanish king appointed a viceroy to govern New Spain, and divided the lands into estates that he gave to captains or conquistadors.
3. Catholic missions were used as schools to teach Indians to farm, but they were never used as forts.
4. The government of New Spain decided to settle the lands north of Mexico in what is now Arizona and Oklahoma.
5. The Missionaries taught the Indians the Christian religion and how to farm and care for cattle, sheep, and horses.
6. When Mexico gained its freedom from Spain in 1821, it wanted to settle more of its border lands.
7. John Sutter of Switzerland settled land in what is now New Mexico.

PICTURE SYMBOLS   These pictures should help you recall parts of the chapter you have read. What is the main idea of each picture?

SUMMING UP   How did the way of life in the Spanish colonies differ from that in the English colonies? Complete the following chart.

	SPAIN	ENGLAND
1. Size of population		
2. Ways of making a living		
3. Chief sources of labor		
4. Treatment of American Indians		
5. Language and religion		

Thinking It Through

In what ways were the American Indians helped by the Spanish? In what ways were they hurt by the Spanish?

8 TRAPPERS AND TRADERS OPEN TRAILS TO THE WEST

How did the mountain men prepare the way for settlement of the Far West?

1. Americans were beginning to think the United States should extend all the way to the Pacific Ocean. Between 1820 and 1840, many people began to move into the land beyond the Mississippi River. They found that the **mountain men** were the best guides they could have. Who were these mountain men?

2. During the 1820s the most valuable fur was beaver. It was used in making hats for men. A number of fur companies were formed. The companies hired men to travel far into western country to trap beaver. These men crossed the plains into the mountains, looking for fur. These mountain men became the best white trappers and explorers in the early years of the Far West.

3. The mountain men hunted alone or in small groups. They took with them horses, traps, and rafts. They brought their furs to a trading post and exchanged them for goods from the eastern states. After they finished trading, the trappers returned to their winter camps and to another year of trapping.

4. The mountain man lived most of his life in the wilderness. He was always in danger from wild animals. The American Indians did not want white people moving into their hunting grounds. They often attacked the mountain men. In order to stay alive, the mountain man learned the ways of the Indians. He lived chiefly on buffalo meat. He carried a knife, tomahawk, and rifle with him. He became a hard and cruel Indian fighter. Like the Indians, he scalped his enemies when the fight was over.

5. Jim Bridger, Jed Smith, and Jim Beckwourth were three famous mountain men. They were explorers as well as trappers. Bridger was the first white person to locate the Great Salt Lake in what is now Utah. He and Smith found the famous South Pass through the Rockies in southern Wyoming. The South Pass became the chief route of wagon trains to California and Oregon. Jed Smith explored as far west as California. Beckwourth was a runaway black slave. One tribe, the Crow Indians, made him their chief. In 1850 he discovered a pass through the Sierra Nevada, which are high mountains in California.

6. Although these mountain men did not know it, they were preparing the way for

A hunter's shack in the Rocky Mountains. What is happening in this picture?

settlers who soon followed their trails. Forts were built along the trails. The Oregon Trail followed a line of forts: Laramie, Bridger, and Hall. Wagon trains used these forts as stopping places where they could get supplies and guides through the mountains.

7. Farther south, a few traders were pioneering a trail to the Southwest. As you have already learned, in 1806 Zebulon Pike, an army explorer, had gone into the Spanish territory of New Mexico. He had visited the Spanish settlement at Santa Fe. When he returned, he wrote about his travels in the Southwest. He suggested that American goods were wanted in Santa Fe. American trade with this old city began in 1821, when Mexico gained its independence from Spain.

8. Santa Fe was in territory that became part of the new republic of Mexico. The first goods for Santa Fe were carried on pack horses and mules. Only a few traders made these early journeys, and they were often attacked by Indians. To protect themselves, the traders formed larger groups of covered wagons. The groups were called **wagon trains.** These were the first covered wagons to cross the western plains. The route the traders and their wagons followed became known as the Santa Fe Trail. It was about 800 miles (1,280 kilometers) long.

9. The trip to Santa Fe began at towns along the Missouri River. At first, the wagons traveled across the prairies. The prairie grasslands were often so muddy that the wagons could hardly move. Farther west, the country changed to the dry, flat land of the plains. The plains were the home of the buffalo and the "Horse Indians." In this region, Indian attacks were likely. When attacked, the wagons were drawn into a square and the animals were driven inside. Not every wagon train was successful in driving off these attacks. Death and destruction often took place on the Santa Fe Trail. A good guide was im-

Travelers on early trails across the Great Plains. They faced the danger of Indian attacks. What kind of threat did settlers pose to the Indians?

portant to the safety of the train and its people. Kit Carson, one of the most famous of the early westerners, started as a scout on this treacherous trail. After the plains, the wagon train crossed a strip of sand more than 50 miles (80 kilometers) wide. This strip was called the Cimarron Desert. Beyond the desert, the trail climbed steeply to a pass in the Rocky Mountains. From the top of the pass, the travelers could see Santa Fe, the end of the long and dangerous journey.

10. The traders brought clothing and other goods to the Mexican town. They returned with buffalo hides, mules, furs, and bars of gold and silver. Despite the dangers, the trade with Santa Fe went on. The profit from the trip more than made up for the dangers met along the way. The traders on the southern trail helped the westward march of the American people. They were the first to use the covered wagon on the plains. They learned how to protect themselves against Indian attacks. Many people came to believe that Mexico

231

could not hold on to this territory for long. The traders of the Sante Fe Trail sped the day when the Southwest would become part of the United States.

11. There was another group that traveled west. These were the peddlers. The peddlers brought goods from the towns to the farmer or fur trapper who lived at the edge of the frontier. The peddler was important to these people who could not afford to make the long journey to buy household goods.

REVIEWING
CHAPTER 7

Choose the correct answer.

1. Universities were begun in Mexico City and Lima by
   a. the Catholic Church
   b. American settlers
   c. Father Junípero Serra
2. El Camino Real was a road that led from
   a. Sante Fe to Mexico City
   b. one mission to another in California
   c. Lima to Mexico City
3. Mexico gained its freedom from Spain in
   a. 1776
   b. 1821
   c. 1848
4. John Sutter owned land in
   a. New Mexico
   b. Texas
   c. California
5. The Mexican government wanted American farmers and traders to settle in
   a. Texas
   b. Veracruz
   c. the Northwest Territory
6. The first Spanish fort and mission built in California was at
   a. San Francisco
   b. San Diego
   c. Santa Fe

UNDERSTANDING
CHAPTER 8

I. What is the main purpose of Chapter 8?

   a. To discuss the beginning of trade in the Southwest
   b. To describe the adventures of the mountain men
   c. To describe the changes on the Santa Fe Trail
   d. To tell about the people who opened the West after 1820

II. Choose the correct answer.

1. The explorations of the mountain men led to
   a. the opening of the West to pioneers who wanted land
   b. war with Spain
   c. the discovery of gold
2. The discovery of South Pass led to
   a. trade with Santa Fe
   b. wagon trains to California and Oregon
   c. the beginning of missions in California
3. The demand for beaver fur led to
   a. war with France over fur-trading posts
   b. increased trade along the Florida coast
   c. exploration of the West by mountain men

4. Zebulon Pike's explorations led to
   a. trouble with Peru
   b. the settlement of Americans in Oregon
   c. trade with Santa Fe
5. Many people traveled over the route to Santa Fe to
   a. settle in the land with a wonderful climate
   b. dig for gold and copper
   c. trade with the Mexicans and the American Indians

III. Decide whether each statement below is a fact or an opinion. Support your decision.

1. The mountain men explored the mountains and trails in search of furs.
2. What is now the southwestern part of the United States once belonged to Spain, and then to Mexico.
3. Americans should have built many forts along the Santa Fe Trail.
4. The traders and the American Indians should have cooperated.

DEVELOPING IDEAS
AND SKILLS

MAP SKILLS *Western Trails Before 1854*

Study the map. Then decide whether the statements on page 234 are true or false. If a statement is false, rewrite it so that it is true.

Western Trails Before 1854

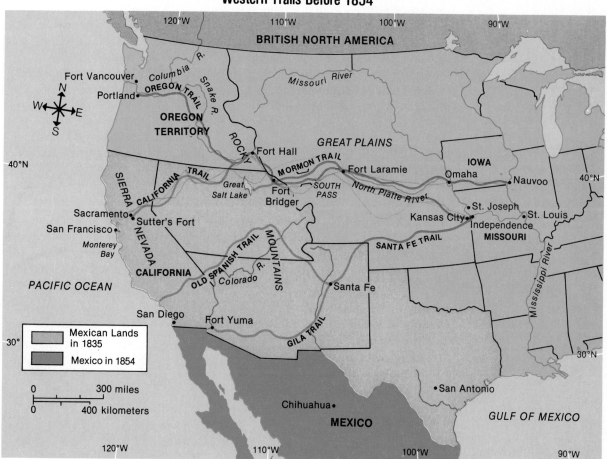

1. The Oregon Trail led to the Southwest.
2. Settlers leaving from Omaha had to cross the Rocky Mountains in order to reach the Pacific Coast.
3. The Oregon Trail followed the route of the Missouri River.
4. Most wagon trains started from towns east of the Mississippi River.
5. South Pass was an opening through the Rocky Mountains.
6. Most forts were located far from the trails.
7. Santa Fe was in Mexican territory in 1835.

Answer the following questions.

1. How did the forts help people moving west?
2. Travelers to the Far West did not stop and settle the central part of the United States. Why?
3. Why did Sante Fe welcome American trade?

USING PRIMARY AND SECONDARY SOURCES

Information about events comes from many sources. Most of these can be divided into two main groups. These are **primary sources** and **secondary sources.** A primary source is any firsthand information about an event. Letters, diaries, and documents written at the time of an event are examples of primary sources. Actual photos of an event or pictures drawn by someone who was there are also primary sources. Primary sources are very valuable as sources of information. They reveal the actual feelings and views of people who took part in events or who saw them.

Another way to obtain information about events is through secondary sources. A secondary source is an account of an event written or drawn by someone who was not present when the event took place. That person got his or her information about the event from another source, either a primary or secondary one. This textbook is an example of a secondary source. However, it can contain or include examples of primary sources. Can you find such examples in this textbook?

A DIARY   Suppose you were trapping with the mountain men or traveling on the Santa Fe Trail. Keep a diary of your adventures. Some of your entries might include the following:

Following the signs of beaver
Meeting American Indians
Living on a wagon train
Coming to Santa Fe
Trading for furs
Exploring with Bridger
Finding a pass through the mountains

Thinking It Through

What kind of life did the mountain men lead?

9 OREGON IS ADDED TO THE UNITED STATES

Why did the United States lay claim to the Oregon Territory?

Headstone dedicated to the first white women to cross the Great Plains. What hardships must these people have faced on their journey? What qualities must they have had in order to survive?

1. West of the Rocky Mountains in the far Northwest lay the large territory called Oregon. It extended from California north to Alaska. Russia, Spain, England, and the United States all claimed this region. The Russians had sent an expedition to explore the region in 1741. The Spanish claimed that an agreement with Portugal in 1494 gave them the right to own Oregon. The English based their claim on the voyages of Drake, Cook, and Vancouver. The Americans argued that the region had been explored by Lewis and Clark. They also claimed that Captain Robert Gray, an American sailor, had found the mouth of the Columbia River in 1792. Gray claimed the Columbia and all the land around it for the United States.

2. Both English and American fur traders had gone into Oregon and established fur-trading posts. In 1792 an English trader named Alexander Mackenzie explored the country for a British company. By 1808 his company had built a trading post. In 1811 an American trader, John Jacob Astor, started a trading post at the mouth of the Columbia River. He called the settlement Astoria. Astor bought furs from the Indians and shipped them across the Pacific to China. There, they were exchanged for tea. He sold the tea shipments in the United States for a large profit.

3. During the War of 1812, Astor had to give up his settlement at Astoria to the British. After the war, England and the United States agreed that the two countries should share the Oregon country until such time as they could make a fair division of the land. During the years that followed, the Oregon country belonged to neither nation. Spain and Russia had given up their claims to Oregon.

4. At first, few Americans went to Oregon. The British were pleased, for they were getting rich from the fur trade with the Indians. Over a thousand British people lived in Oregon. In 1832 a curious event brought an end to this situation. Four friendly Indian chiefs traveled overland from Oregon to St. Louis to ask for missionaries to teach them the Christian religion. Shortly thereafter, several missions were begun in Oregon—one by Jason Lee and another by Samuel Parker. Soon a third was set up by Marcus and Narcissa Whitman and Henry and Elizabeth Spalding. A few years later, Father Pierre DeSmet also came to the Oregon country. So it was that the first white Americans who followed trappers into Oregon were missionaries.

A wagon train moving west. Why did many settlers prefer to travel west in groups such as this one?

They had moved west to teach the Christian religion to the Indians and to heal their sick.

5. The missionaries wrote letters to friends in the East, describing the riches of the Oregon country. When easterners heard of the great forests and the good farmlands, they became interested in the Oregon country. Thousands of settlers started across the plains to reach the fertile and beautiful valleys of the far Northwest.

6. The Oregon pioneers followed the trail that had been traced by the mountain men and the fur trappers. By the 1840s it became known as the Oregon Trail. The wagon caravans began their journey from towns along the Missouri River. Independence and St. Joseph, two Missouri cities today, were the usual places for "jumping off" to Oregon. In 1843 about 2,000 people began the movement westward over the Oregon Trail.

7. The settlers traveled in large groups. The wagon train was a means of protection against the attacks of the Indians, whose hunting grounds were being disturbed. The big covered wagons were drawn by mules or oxen. The journey, about 2,000 miles (3,200 kilometers) long, took about six months. The most important member of the wagon train was the captain, or wagon master. He was elected by the people of the train. Each day he had to choose which route to take, the safest crossings for streams, and the best place to camp for the night. He also had to protect the wagons against the Indians. At night, the wagons parked in a circle. The people camped inside the circle to talk, wash their clothes, and cook their meals.

8. After long weeks traveling over the plains, the caravans neared the mountains. In order to pass through the Rockies, the trains used the South Pass, which had been discovered by the mountain men. To some people, the trip was just one danger and hardship after another. Wild animals, sickness, and bitter weather beset the pioneers. Others who made the trip overlooked the dangers and saw the excitement of the journey to their new home.

9. By 1844 so many Americans had moved to Oregon that they wanted the territory to belong to the United States. In the presidential election of that year, the candidate of the Democratic party was James

A campsite of westward pioneers. Why was group singing a welcome activity for pioneers?

K. Polk. He ran for election on the slogan, "54° 40' or Fight!" This meant that the Democratic party wanted the United States to annex the Oregon country as far north as the 54th parallel, almost to Alaska. Polk was elected.

10. There was talk of fighting with Great Britain over the Oregon country. However, Britain made an offer to divide the territory at the 49th parallel. The southern half of Oregon would belong to the United States; the northern part would belong to Britain. Congress accepted the offer. In 1846 the Oregon Territory was added to the United States. The boundary between the United States and the British territory of Canada was fixed at the 49th parallel. The United States now extended from the Atlantic to the Pacific Ocean. The western movement, which had begun at the border strip along the Appalachians, had carried the nation across the continent.

REVIEWING CHAPTER 8

Decide whether each statement is true or false. The underlined words are clues to help you decide. If a statement is false, change the underlined word or words to make it true.

1. The discovery of the South Pass helped in the movement of settlers to the Far West.
2. Mountain men explored in the Rocky Mountains.
3. The South Pass was used by pioneers going to the Southwest.
4. Mountain men found the trails that became part of the Oregon Trail.
5. Many Americans began to believe that the United States would soon reach the Pacific Ocean.
6. Zebulon Pike's explorations caused interest in the Southwest.
7. Mountain men traveled in large groups.
8. Buffalo hides were brought back from Sante Fe by traders lucky enough to reach there.

UNDERSTANDING CHAPTER 9

I. What is the main purpose of Chapter 9?

a. To describe life on the Oregon Trail
b. To discuss how Oregon was added to the United States
c. To tell how fur-trading posts were established
d. To describe the early sea voyages to Oregon

II. Choose the correct answer.

1. How did the United States and Great Britain settle their claims to Oregon?
a. The British gave up their claims.
b. The territory was divided between the two countries at the 49th parallel.
c. The two countries asked France to settle the question.

2. How did the United States get Oregon?
   a. As a result of war
   b. By treaty with Great Britain
   c. By purchase from Great Britain and Russia
3. How did John Jacob Astor give the United States a claim to Oregon?
   a. He drove British fur traders from the Oregon country.
   b. He brought settlers to the Oregon country to farm.
   c. He started a fur-trading post in the Oregon country.
4. What was one of the reasons the United States claimed Oregon?
   a. Francis Drake had explored the western coast of North America.
   b. The land was part of the Louisiana Purchase.
   c. Robert Gray and Lewis and Clark explored there.
5. Why did the Americans go to Oregon after 1840?
   a. To find better homes and cheaper land
   b. To search for gold
   c. To enjoy freedom of worship

III. **Decide whether each statement is true or false. The underlined words are clues to help you decide. If a statement is false, change the underlined word or words to make it true.**

1. Jason Lee and Marcus and Narcissa Whitman went to Oregon to <u>study plant and animal life</u>.
2. John Jacob Astor was interested in Oregon because of the <u>fur trade</u>.
3. The voyage of Sir Francis Drake had given <u>Great Britain</u> a claim to the Oregon country.
4. <u>Lewis and Clark</u> had explored the Oregon country for the United States.
5. President <u>Robert Gray</u> wanted to annex the Oregon country.
6. Many pioneers who moved to Oregon followed the <u>Sante Fe Trail</u>.
7. The addition of Oregon extended the territory of the United States to the <u>Pacific Ocean</u>.

DEVELOPING IDEAS
AND SKILLS

MAP SKILLS *The Oregon Trail*

Study the map on page 233. Then complete the following sentences.

1. Pioneers going west on the Oregon Trail started from towns in ▬▬▬▬.
2. First, they had to cross the ▬▬▬▬.
3. They followed the North Platte River to ▬▬▬▬ in the Rocky Mountains.
4. At ▬▬▬▬, they turned north and followed the Snake River.
5. The city that rose up at the end of the Oregon Trail was ▬▬▬▬.
6. Another settlement in the Oregon Territory was ▬▬▬▬.
7. Among the Oregon settlements were the missions of ▬▬▬▬ and ▬▬▬▬.

THE OREGON TERRITORY Complete this chart in your notebook.

RELATION TO OREGON

1. Sir Francis Drake

2. Robert Gray

3. Lewis and Clark

4. John Jacob Astor

5. Marcus and Narcissa Whitman

6. "54° 40′ or Fight!"

Thinking It Through

How did both the United States and Great Britain gain from the Oregon settlement?

10 REMEMBER THE ALAMO! TEXAS BECOMES A REPUBLIC

How did Texas win its independence from Mexico?

Santa Anna, leader of Mexico. A Texas army led by Sam Houston captured Santa Anna at the Battle of San Jacinto.

1. In early 1821 Moses Austin, a pioneer, miner, and trader, decided to bring American settlers into Texas. Texas was then Spanish territory. The Spanish agreed and promised to give land to the people Austin brought with him. Later that same year, Mexico revolted against Spain and won its independence. Mexico promptly claimed the Spanish territory of Texas and the land west of it. After Moses Austin died, his son Stephen decided to carry on his father's plans. He promised that the colonists would be loyal to the Mexican government. As a result, the Mexican government opened Texas to settlement and sold land very cheaply to the Americans.

2. By 1830 there were nearly 20,000 Americans in the Mexican province of Texas. This large number of Americans troubled the Mexican government. The Mexicans began to fear that the American colonists would soon have too much power. In 1830 the Mexican government closed Texas to further settlement by Americans. Slowly, disagreements developed between the Americans and their rulers. They disagreed in matters of language, religion, customs, and ideas of government. Americans began to dislike living under Mexican law. When Mexico passed a law forbidding slavery in Texas, plantation owners who had moved to the cheap land refused to obey the law.

3. In 1834 an ambitious general, Santa Anna, seized control of the Mexican government and made himself ruler of the country. Americans were not used to his kind of government and resisted him. The Texans decided they would take action. On March 2, 1836, they declared themselves independent of Mexico. As this was taking place, Santa Anna was trying to force the Americans to obey the Mexican government.

4. Santa Anna marched on San Antonio to trap a small band of Texans who had refused to be loyal to him. The Texas rebels retreated to an old Spanish mission called the Alamo. They turned the mission into a fort. When Santa Anna appeared with a force of several thousand men, the Texans refused to surrender. Finally, the Mexicans broke through the fort. In the fighting that followed, all the Texans and

over 1,500 Mexicans were killed. "Remember the Alamo" became the battle cry of the Texans. Three weeks later, Santa Anna put to death nearly 400 prisoners who had surrendered to him near the little village of Goliad.

5. Texans were more determined than ever to be free from Mexico. General Sam Houston had begun to train an army to defend Texas against the armies of Santa Anna. Sam Houston was born on a farm in Virginia, but his family settled on the frontier of Tennessee. As a young man, Houston spent three years living with the Cherokee Indians and learning their ways. He joined the army and fought under Andrew Jackson. Leaving the army, he studied law in Tennessee. He was elected to Congress from that state and later served as governor. He had left Tennessee to make a new home on the plains of Texas.

6. A few weeks after the battle of the Alamo, a Texas army under Sam Houston surprised the Mexicans at the San Jacinto River. The enemy was completely destroyed and Santa Anna was captured. The Mexican leader was not allowed to return to Mexico until he had signed a treaty agreeing to the independence of Texas. The Texans were now free. The new country was called the Lone Star Republic because its flag had a single gold star against a blue background. Houston was elected the first president of the Republic of Texas. The city of Austin became its capital.

7. The new nation had a constitution modeled after that of the United States. Texas was soon involved in foreign affairs. It signed treaties with France and England. It also got loans from European countries to help develop its trade.

8. Most of the people living in Texas were Americans, and they wanted to join the United States. The United States was not sure about admitting Texas as a state. Some people did not want to bring more

The Battle of the Alamo, 1836. Among the defenders of the Alamo were James Bowie, William B. Travis, the commanders; and Davy Crockett, the frontiersman. List two cities in Texas that were named after important Texas leaders of the 1820s and 1830s.

slave land into the nation. Others feared a war with Mexico if the United States annexed Texas. Many thought Texas should be in the Union because they wanted the United States to expand to the lands beyond Texas. Some argued that the Texans were Americans and had a right to live under the United States government if they wanted to. Because of this division of opinion among Americans in the United States, Texas remained an independent republic for nine years. In 1845 Texas became a state.

Match each person in Column A with the correct identification in Column B. There is one extra item in Column B.

<table>
<tr><td align="center">COLUMN A</td><td align="center">COLUMN B</td></tr>
</table>

COLUMN A

1. Francis Drake
2. Lewis and Clark
3. Marcus and Narcissa Whitman
4. James Polk
5. John Jacob Astor
6. Alexander Mackenzie
7. Robert Gray

COLUMN B

a. Explored the Louisiana Purchase
b. Discovered the Columbia River
c. President who favored adding Oregon to the United States
d. Explored the west coast of North America for Great Britain
e. Explored the Santa Fe Trail
f. An English trader who explored Oregon
g. Started a mission in Oregon
h. Started an American fur-trading post in Oregon

I. What is the main purpose of Chapter 10?
  a. To describe the life of Sam Houston
  b. To discuss how Texas became free from Mexico
  c. To describe the battle at the Alamo
  d. To tell how the first settlers came to Texas

II. Choose the correct answer.

1. Texas revolted against the rule of Mexico because
   a. the Mexican government passed harsh tax laws
   b. the Mexican government opened the land to slavery
   c. there were many differences in language and ideas of government
2. Many Americans had moved to Texas because
   a. land was cheap
   b. settlers had learned of the good soil and climate from the journey over the Oregon Trail
   c. the land had been described by Lewis and Clark
3. The Alamo has an honored place in American history because
   a. a small band of men showed great bravery there
   b. the battle there won freedom for Texas
   c. freedom of speech was defended there
4. Mexico did not want more Americans coming to Texas because
   a. there was no more land to sell
   b. it began to fear the power of the Americans
   c. Spain had ordered the government to close the borders
5. Some Americans did not favor annexing Texas because
   a. they feared a war with Mexico
   b. Texas was too far from other American territory
   c. few Americans lived there

242

III. Decide whether each statement agrees or disagrees with what you have read. If the statement disagrees, explain why.

1. When Texas broke away from Mexico, it immediately became part of the United States.
2. The Austin family did much to bring Americans to Texas.
3. The customs and religion of the Americans in Texas were different from those of the people of Mexico.
4. Some of the settlers who moved to Texas were plantation owners.
5. Santa Anna tried to force Americans in Texas to obey the Mexican government.
6. At the Alamo, the Texans were outnumbered by the Mexican army.
7. The final battle for Texan independence was won under the leadership of Sam Houston.
8. In 1830 Mexico closed Texas to further American settlement.

DEVELOPING IDEAS AND SKILLS

Complete the statements below. Write the answers in your notebook. Use the text from pages 225–245 and the map on page 233.

1. Mexico won its freedom from Spain in the year _____.
2. The capital of Mexico is _____.
3. The lands north of the Rio Grande were called the _____.
4. The early settlements in California were started as _____.
5. The northern boundary of Mexico was the _____.
6. Sutter's Fort was located near _____.
7. Great Salt Lake was in _____ territory.

SUMMING UP

Thinking It Through

Suppose Texas had not won its freedom from Mexico. How might American history have been different?

11 THE WAR WITH MEXICO

Why did the United States declare war against Mexico? What were the results of this war?

1. Although Santa Anna withdrew his armies from Texas, the Mexican Congress did not recognize the independence of the new republic. Mexico made it clear that it would go to war if the United States annexed Texas. There was also a dispute over the boundary of Texas. The Texans claimed the river called the Rio Grande as their southern boundary. The Mexican government said that the boundary was the Nueces River, some 50 to 100 miles (80 to 160 kilometers) to the north.

2. Meanwhile, the Republic of Texas carried on, hoping that soon it would be admitted to the United States. In 1844 James Polk was elected president of the United States. He wanted to bring Texas into the Union. Early in 1845, Congress admitted Texas as a slave state, recognizing the Rio Grande as the southern boundary of the new state. In January 1846, President Polk sent Zachary Taylor to defend the boundary. This meant that Taylor and the American soldiers entered territory that was also claimed by Mexico. The Mexicans attacked. On May 12, 1846, after receiving news of the attack, Congress declared war on Mexico.

3. The Mexican government was certain it could win the war. Mexico's army was five times larger than that of the United States. Mexico felt that its soldiers were better fighters in the deserts of Mexico. It was certain that the northern states would not support the war, because Texas was a slave state. Mexico was mistaken.

4. General Taylor crossed the Rio Grande and defeated the Mexican troops at Monterrey and Buena Vista. In the Southwest, a small army under General Stephen W. Kearny marched westward from Santa

General Winfield Scott marched American troops into Mexico City, the capital of Mexico. He became an American hero. Many considered him the greatest American general since George Washington.

Fe. When Kearny reached California, he found that a group of Americans under Captain John Frémont had broken away from Mexican rule. They had set up their own government, called the Bear Flag Republic. Frémont also had been helped by an American fleet in the Pacific. A third army under General Winfield Scott had landed at Veracruz and marched inland toward Mexico City, the capital of Mexico. After fighting for several months, Scott reached Mexico City. When the city was captured, Mexico was ready for peace.

5. The Mexican War was what some people call a "popular" war. Many newspapers and political leaders wanted this war. They believed it was the destiny of the United States to acquire new territories such as Texas. They wanted the American people to get excited about the war and to support it. Many did. Some people, however, did not. They feared that slavery would be extended. They believed that President Polk had forced the war on the American people.

6. A peace treaty was signed in February 1848. Mexico recognized Texas as part of the United States. The border between the United States and Mexico was set at the Rio Grande. Mexico also gave the United States a vast territory in the Southwest, extending as far as the Pacific Ocean. This was known as the Mexican Cession. From this land came the states of New Mexico, Arizona, California, Utah, Nevada, and parts of Colorado and Wyoming. The United States paid $15,000,000 for the land and another $3,250,000 to American citizens for debts owed by the Mexican government.

7. Five years later, in 1853, the United States arranged to buy a strip of land in the southern part of New Mexico and Arizona. Railroad men thought this land was needed for a railroad route to California. For this land, the United States paid Mexico the sum of $10,000,000. The territory is called the Gadsden Purchase, after our ambas-

Vaqueros. What did the American settlers new to the Southwest learn from these Mexican-American cowboys? What language do the words *ranch* and *rodeo* come from?

sador to Mexico, James Gadsden. He arranged to buy the land. This purchase completed the boundaries of all the states that would form the Union until the admission of Alaska and Hawaii in the 20th century.

8. After the Mexican War, thousands of Americans moved to the southwestern part of the United States. They were looking for gold, silver, and land. The Mexicans who lived there were under the rule of the United States. Some of them had owned much of the land, using it for cattle and sheep ranches. Others had been laborers who had worked on the large ranches and estates. They were proud of their Spanish and American Indian ways of living.

9. As more and more Americans rushed to the Southwest, many Mexican Americans there became "second-class citizens." Many of them lost their ranches, farmlands, and mines to the "Anglos" or "gringos," as the Mexican Americans called them. As the Anglos increased their control over the land, there were many fights. Nevertheless, Mexican-American **vaqueros,** or cowboys, taught the new settlers how to brand, rope, and round up cattle. They also taught the Anglos about irrigation and mining.

245

Choose the correct answer.

1. A state that was an independent republic before it joined the Union was
   a. Florida
   b. Louisiana
   c. Texas
2. "Remember the Alamo" refers to the
   a. celebration of Texan independence
   b. massacre of the defenders of a fort
   c. opening of Texas for settlement

3. Texan independence was finally won at
   a. the Alamo
   b. San Jacinto
   c. Goliad
4. The president of the Texas Republic was
   a. Sam Houston
   b. Davy Crockett
   c. Moses Austin
5. Santa Anna was captured at the battle near the
   a. Nueces River
   b. Rio Grande
   c. San Jacinto River

I. What is the main purpose of Chapter 11?

a. To review the battles of the Mexican War
b. To discuss how Texas and the Southwest became part of the United States
c. To describe the purchase of the last territory in the Southwest
d. To describe Spanish foreign policy

II. Choose the correct answer.

1. One of the reasons why Texas was admitted as a state in 1845 was
   a. it had great wealth in oil
   b. many Americans lived there
   c. Mexico already had agreed to Texan independence
2. All of these were results of the Mexican War EXCEPT:
   a. Mexico paid the United States for the damages of the war.
   b. California became part of the United States.
   c. The great Southwest was added to the United States.
3. One of the reasons for the Gadsden Purchase was to
   a. complete the territory of California
   b. provide a home for the Mexican Americans
   c. obtain land for a railroad through the Southwest
4. All of these were causes of the war with Mexico EXCEPT:
   a. Texas was admitted as a state.
   b. The Alamo was attacked by Mexican soldiers.
   c. There was a dispute over the boundary between Texas and Mexico.
5. After the war with Mexico, Mexicans in the Southwest
   a. became citizens of the United States
   b. worked the land for others
   c. did both of the above

III. Decide whether each statement is true or false. The underlined words are clues to help you decide. If a statement is false, change the underlined word or words to make it true.

1. The United States claimed the southern boundary of Texas was the <u>Rio Grande</u>.
2. President <u>Jackson</u> favored making Texas a state.
3. General <u>Scott</u> captured Mexico City.
4. The United States gained territory in <u>New Mexico and Nevada</u> as a result of the Mexican War.
5. <u>General Taylor</u> was a leader in freeing California from Mexican rule.
6. The United States <u>bought land</u> from Mexico in order to build a railroad.
7. The territory won by the United States after the war with Mexico was called the <u>Gadsden Purchase</u>.

DEVELOPING IDEAS AND SKILLS

MAP SKILLS *Texas and the Mexican War*

Study the following map. Then find the missing words.

Texas and the Mexican War

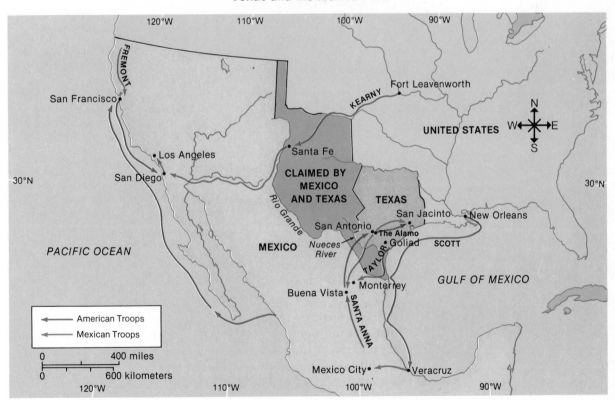

1. The Alamo is a mission near the present city of _____ .
2. Santa Anna had to march _____ to attack the Alamo.
3. Most of the Mexican War was fought on _____ soil.

247

4. General ▬▬▬ brought his armies across the Gulf of Mexico.
5. General Taylor crossed the ▬▬▬ to invade Mexico.
6. ▬▬▬ marched westward to conquer the northern provinces of Mexico.
7. General Scott stopped at the coastal city of ▬▬▬ before he marched inland.
8. General Kearny left from ▬▬▬ in his march to California.

SUMMING UP **MAP SKILLS** *Growth of the United States, 1783–1853*

Study the following map. Then decide whether the following statements are true or false. If a statement is false, rewrite it so that it is true.

Growth of the United States, 1783-1853

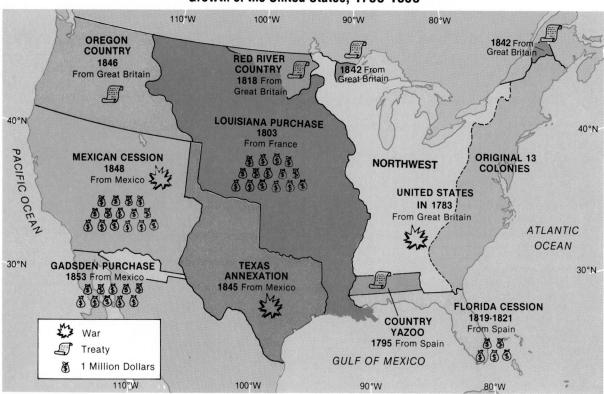

1. United States territory reached the Pacific Ocean by 1846.
2. The largest addition of territory was the Mexican Cession.
3. The last territory acquired by the United States was in Maine.
4. All the land east of the Mississippi River was obtained from Great Britain as a result of the Revolutionary War.
5. The greatest changes in the size of the United States took place before 1800.
6. The United States gained much of its territory through treaty and purchase.
7. Texas and Oregon were acquired about the same time.

8. In 1783 the western boundary of the United States was the Mississippi River.

9. The Louisiana Territory was purchased from France for 15 million dollars.

10. The United States grew in a north-south direction.

GROWTH OF THE UNITED STATES Complete this chart in your notebook.

TERRITORY	DATE ADDED TO THE U.S.	HOW
1. Northwest		
2. Louisiana		
3. Florida		
4. Oregon		
5. Texas		
6. California		
7. Gadsden Purchase		

Thinking It Through

Many Americans thought it was the destiny of the United States to acquire Texas and lands along the Pacific Coast. In other words, they felt that they were meant to obtain these lands. How did this way of thinking affect American attitudes toward war with Mexico?

Do you think the Mexican War could have been avoided? If so, how? What kind of settlement with Mexico would have been fair?

12 UTAH IS SETTLED

How did the Mormons create a homeland in the desert?

1. While the Mexican War was going on, another group of pioneers was moving into land that is now Utah. These people were Mormons. They were looking for a place to worship freely. The Mormon Church had been started in New York State in 1830 by Joseph Smith. The ideas of the Mormons were different in many ways from other religions. They felt that they were a chosen people. They believed in living, working, and sharing as a group, not as individuals. They felt that a Mormon man could have more than one wife. Many Americans strongly disliked the Mormon beliefs. They drove the Mormons from their homes in New York and then from their homes in Ohio and Missouri.

2. Next, the Mormons settled near Quincy, Illinois, starting a new town called Nauvoo. Things went well for a time. More followers came from Europe. They built a house of worship. Nauvoo became the largest city in the state. However, the Mormons were not left in peace. In 1844 Joseph Smith and his brother were arrested. While the two men were in jail, a mob broke in and killed them.

3. The Mormons now felt that they could never be safe within the United States.

Mormon pioneers. In the late 1840s several thousand Mormons traveled west across the plains. What does this picture show about the means of transportation they used?

They chose a new leader, Brigham Young. In 1846 he led them across the Mississippi River to Iowa. They spent the winter there, living in huts and caves. When spring came, Brigham Young and a small wagon train started westward in search of their new home. They took a route just north of the Oregon Trail. After crossing the Rockies, they turned south and made their way to the valley of the Great Salt Lake in what is now Utah. This place was in Mexican territory. The Mormons felt that they would be safe there.

4. Their first winter was very hard. Within a month, they "broke, watered, planted, and sowed upwards of 100 acres." Then they built adobe huts, set close together and fortified. Despite their efforts, most of their first year's crops failed. Nonetheless, more Mormons came to join them.

5. Brigham Young laid out a new city in the desert, called Salt Lake City. He showed the people how to irrigate the dry fields with water from the mountains. From Salt Lake City, Mormon pioneers left to start other settlements in Utah, Nevada, and southern California. According to Young, these settlements would be part of a new nation, called Deseret. The Mormons seemed to have found the religious freedom they wanted.

6. Things soon changed. When the Mexican War ended in 1848, Mormon lands

Brigham Young at the Great Salt Lake. The Mormons soon set to work farming the dry desert land of Utah.

became part of the United States. In 1850 the area became part of the Utah Territory. The Mormons, not wanting outsiders to control their way of life, said they would fight. When American troops entered Utah, the Mormons attacked them. They also attacked wagon trains passing through their territory. At a place named Mountain Meadows, Mormons attacked one wagon train, killing 120 people. Despite the attacks, the United States soon gained control. Utah became a state in 1896.

REVIEWING CHAPTERS
10 AND 11

I. Who is identified in each statement?

1. I led American settlers into Texas in 1820.
2. I led the army that captured Mexico City.
3. I was president of the United States during the Mexican War.
4. I was the Mexican leader who was defeated at San Jacinto.
5. I was the ambassador to Mexico who arranged to buy land.
6. I was the president of the Texas Republic.

Sam Houston   Zachary Taylor   Moses Austin
James Polk   Santa Anna   Winfield Scott
                   James Gadsden

II. Match each phrase with the place it describes.

1. Where over 100 defenders of a fort were killed
2. Was known as the Bear Flag Republic
3. Paid $15 million for it in 1848
4. Land settled by the Mormons
5. Southern boundary of the United States
6. City in Mexico

Rio Grande	Mexican Cession	California
Veracruz	Alamo	Utah

I. What is the main idea of Chapter 12?

   a. To tell us who the Mormons are
   b. To describe how Utah was settled
   c. To describe how American Indians made a living in the desert

II. Choose the correct answer.

1. The Mormons moved west in order to
   a. search for gold
   b. trade with the American Indians
   c. practice their religion freely
2. The Mormons were able to succeed in Salt Lake City because they
   a. found silver there
   b. were helped by the federal government
   c. learned how to bring water from the mountains to their fields
3. Brigham Young is remembered as the man who
   a. founded the Mormon religion
   b. led the Mormons to a new home near Salt Lake City
   c. built a mission for the American Indians
4. What name did the Mormons give their new home?
   a. The "Lost Colony"
   b. The Lone Star Republic
   c. Deseret
5. In order to live the way they thought was right, the Mormons
   a. moved to Mexican territory
   b. gave up their religious beliefs
   c. sailed for England
6. The place where the Mormons settled later became the state of
   a. California
   b. Oregon
   c. Utah

III. Decide whether each statement agrees or disagrees with what you have read. If the statement disagrees, explain why.

1. The Mormons had to move from place to place because people were against their religion.
2. The Mormons found the religious freedom they wanted in another part of the United States.

3. The Mormons learned how to irrigate desert land in order to survive.
4. The Mormons were treated well in New York and Illinois.
5. The Mormons moved westward to find a place of their own.
6. The Mormons wanted the United States army to help them after the Mexican War.
7. The Mormons showed that crops could grow in the dry lands of Utah.
8. The Mormons played a great part in opening up the lands of the East.

DEVELOPING NEW
IDEAS AND SKILLS

MAP SKILLS *The Mormon and Other Trails to the West*

Study the map on page 233. Then answer the questions that follow.

1. From what town did the Mormons begin their trip west on the Mormon Trail?
2. For much of its length the Mormon Trail covered a path just north of what other trail?
3. To what regions on the West Coast did most of the trails lead?
4. Pioneers traveling overland to San Francisco had to go through what important pass?
5. Through what mountains did the Mormons travel after they crossed the Great Plains?

SUMMING UP

Arrange these events in their proper order, beginning with the event that happened first.

The town of Nauvoo is started.
Utah becomes a state.
Joseph Smith leaves New York State.
Brigham Young begins to build Salt Lake City.
Joseph Smith is killed.

Thinking It Through

Why do some people want others to believe the same things they do? Should everyone have the same religious beliefs? What is the advantage or disadvantage of letting each person believe as he or she wishes?

13 GOLD! CALIFORNIA BECOMES A STATE

How did the discovery of gold change the course of California's history?

1. In January 1848, some men were building a sawmill near what is now Sacramento, California. The land belonged to John A. Sutter. A young man named James Marshall was in charge of the work. The men dammed a stream to furnish the mill with water power. Early one morning, Marshall found small yellow stones in the stream. They were gold! The discovery of gold took place just two weeks before the signing of the treaty ending the Mexican War. Not long after the discovery, California became part of the United States.

2. The people of California went wild when they heard news of the discovery of gold. They left their homes, families, and businesses and made their way to the gold fields. Workers on farms and ranches quit their jobs. Schools were closed as both teachers and pupils rushed to the diggings.

3. News of the discovery did not reach the East until 1849. Then, it did not take long for thousands of people to start a "gold rush" to California. These gold seekers of 1849 were called the **forty-niners.** The forty-niners went to California by three different ways. Some went by ship to the Isthmus of Panama and then by land across the isthmus. On the west coast of Panama, they waited for another boat to take them to San Francisco. Others sailed all the way around South America and northward to California. This was the safest route, but it was also the longest. Many did not take the time to be safe; they wanted to get to California first. These people went overland.

4. Most people took the overland route across the United States. They traveled in wagon trains drawn by mules and oxen. Sometimes, they had to fight with Indians,

California gold miners. Thousands of people rushed to California in search of gold. Would you have gone? Why or why not?

who did not want them crossing their hunting grounds. They met the same dangers from the weather and the desert as the thousands who had gone over these same routes in the years before. There was great danger in crossing the Great Plains. The travelers had to get through the mountains before the first snows of winter set in. If the trains left too early, the mud of the early spring weather bogged them down for weeks. But the dangers were not frightening enough to keep thousands from making the journey. Thinking of the gold that lay ahead drove the forty-niners on.

5. The newcomers to California were shocked by what they saw. People were living in any kind of shelter they could find or make. Boarding houses, saloons, and hotels had been thrown together to serve the needs of the gold seekers. Prices for food and mining tools were very high. Gold seekers bought their supplies and rushed to the gold fields.

6. Miners looked for gold in the bed of a river or a stream. When they found a place they wanted, they put up stakes to mark the land and claim it as their own. With their picks and shovels, the miners dug up the "pay dirt" and placed it in washing pans. They held the pans in the cold stream until the water washed away the lighter sand, leaving the gold behind. This was called digging and panning for gold. If the miners were lucky, they found gold. Most of the miners, however, were unlucky.

7. Most of the people who became rich from the gold rush were those who did not mine. The miners were willing to pay large sums of money to those who washed their clothes or cooked their meals. Storekeepers were paid in gold dust or nuggets for everything the miners needed. Many of the gold seekers gave up the search for gold and became farmers instead.

8. When gold was first discovered in 1848, there were only a few thousand people living in California. By 1849 California

The Pony Express. It began in 1860 but lasted only 18 months. What detail in this painting shows why this mail service ended so quickly?

had enough people to ask Congress to become a state. California was almost 2,000 miles (3,200 kilometers) from the settled part of the United States. It took months to make the trip from Missouri to California. The horse was still the fastest means of land transportation.

9. Stagecoach lines were begun to carry mail and passengers quickly to California. These wooden coaches were pulled by teams of four to six horses. They traveled by day and night, and the passengers had to sit up on the hard wooden benches. The coaches stopped every ten or fifteen miles to change horses and drivers. Each stop was called a **stage** of the trip. These stations were not very comfortable and the food was poor. The trip was not only rough, but dangerous. Sometimes, the stagecoaches were attacked by bandits. Many passengers were robbed or killed by bandits along the stagecoach route. American Indians also tried to prevent the movement of stagecoaches and wagon trains through their hunting grounds. In 1851 a 15-year agreement between the American Indians and the government resulted in fewer of these attacks.

255

10. The stagecoach was too slow for carrying mail. It took about 25 days to send a letter across the country. People in California did not like to wait so long for news about what was going on in the East. In 1860 the famous Pony Express began. It reduced the time for a letter to cover the 2,000 miles (3,200 kilometers) from Missouri to California to ten days.

11. The riders for the Pony Express were chosen carefully. These men needed great courage to ride over the lonely trails. There was no one to help them fight off American Indians and robbers. They carried the mail in leather bags hung on each side of the horse. There were stations along the route where horses and riders were changed. Buffalo Bill Cody was one of the most famous Pony Express riders. But the Pony Express lasted only 18 months. In 1861 a telegraph line was completed across the continent to San Francisco. The Pony Express could not carry messages as quickly as this invention.

"Buffalo Bill" (William F.) Cody. He was a rider for the Pony Express. He also worked as a buffalo hunter in railroad camps and as an army scout. Later he entered show business and toured in his Wild West Show.

REVIEWING CHAPTERS 11 AND 12

Match the items in Column B with those in Column A.

COLUMN A

1. Joseph Smith
2. Brigham Young
3. James Gadsden
4. James Polk
5. Sam Houston
6. Zachary Taylor
7. John C. Frémont
8. Marcus and Narcissa Whitman
9. John Astor
10. Winfield Scott

COLUMN B

a. The president who added Texas and Oregon to the United States
b. Bought strip of land from Mexico
c. Founded Mormon Church; killed in Illinois
d. Led successful invasion of Mexico during war
e. Commander of Texas armies
f. Led Mormons to Utah
g. Took possession of California during war
h. Started a mission in Oregon
i. Led army from New Orleans
j. Began a fur-trading post in Oregon

I. What is the main purpose of Chapter 13?

    a. To explain how the discovery of gold helped add a new state to the Union

    b. To identify the routes taken to find gold

    c. To describe the work of the Pony Express

    d. To explain the need for communication in the Far West

II. Choose the correct answer.

1. It took a long time for the news of the discovery of gold to reach the East because

    a. at first people thought there was really not much gold

    b. there was no fast means of communication across the country

    c. California still belonged to Mexico

2. The news of the discovery of gold led to

    a. higher prices for goods in eastern cities

    b. war with Mexico

    c. a rush of people to California

3. Most of the people who got rich during the gold rush were

    a. storekeepers

    b. miners

    c. farmers

4. The Pony Express was started because

    a. settlers needed digging tools in a hurry

    b. the railroads were overcrowded

    c. there was no fast mail service with the East

5. Who were the forty-niners?

    a. People who rushed to the gold fields

    b. People who settled on the Great Plains

    c. Riders of the Pony Express

III. Decide whether each statement below is a fact or an opinion. Support your answers.

1. The safest route to California was around South America.
2. Most people found no gold in California.
3. All disputes over claims should have been settled peacefully.
4. Buffalo Bill Cody was a famous Pony Express rider.
5. After 1850 passengers could travel to California by stagecoach.
6. The American Indians and white pioneers should have changed their ways of living in order to get along with each other.
7. Gold was discovered in California near the end of the Mexican War.
8. Miners should have taken the law into their own hands to protect their claims.

Answer these questions about the cartoon.

1. Who is the man in the cartoon?
2. Where is he going?
3. Why is he leaving his store?
4. What is he thinking about?
5. What route would you take? Why?

SUMMING UP **"CALIFORNIA, HERE I COME"** One of the people to go to California was a young writer named Mark Twain. At the time, he was a newspaper reporter. His job was to send to his paper reports about life in California. Imagine you had been a newspaper reporter at this time. Write a news story about one of the topics below.

1. Life on the route to California
2. Life in San Francisco
3. Life in the gold fields
4. The Pony Express
5. An interview with John Sutter

Thinking It Through

Moving West was not easy. Pioneers, who braved the dangers of the overland trails, or came across the Isthmus of Panama, or sailed around South America, put their lives on the line. Knowing the dangers the pioneers faced, would you have gone West? Explain your reasons.

14 MINERS AND RANCHERS OPEN THE PLAINS

What part did miners and ranchers play in settling the Great Plains?

Saloon scene in a western town. Many people in mining towns opened saloons, hotels, gambling houses, and food and supply stores. They often made more money than those who mined and found gold and silver. Why do you think this was so?

1. The open land between the Mississippi River and the Rocky Mountains was the last to be settled. When travelers head west from Missouri, they enter a region of higher and drier land. The land slopes upward to the Rocky Mountains. Pioneers who passed over this land thought it was too dry for raising good crops. They did not stop on the Great Plains. They believed this land could not compare with the riches to be found in gold and fur along the Pacific Coast. As a result, this great area was largely unsettled even when hundreds of thousands of people were living in California and Oregon. The Great Plains, however, was the homeland and hunting grounds of many American Indian tribes.

2. Miners were the first to stay in the mountains that bordered the plains. They had left California to look for gold in other streams. These men in search of rich deposits of ore were called **prospectors.** They discovered gold in many places in the Rocky Mountains. In Nevada, they found the Comstock Lode, one of the richest silver mines in the world. They discovered copper in Montana. Mining camps grew up wherever a rich "stake" was found. Some mining camps grew into villages and towns.

3. Life in such mining towns as Deadwood and Last Chance was hard and dangerous. The miners had to live in all kinds of rough shelters until they could build better homes. They had to do their own cooking, wash their own clothes, and doctor themselves when they were sick. At night, many of them would go to the saloons and gambling houses in the town. They drank whiskey and lost their gold to professional gamblers and card players.

4. Law and order were not well enforced by some peace officers. There were many street fights and gun duels. Many people in town were afraid to go out on the streets. Some of the honest men soon began to take the law into their own hands. They formed committees of **vigilantes** to protect themselves and their families. The vigilantes captured many lawbreakers and gunfighters and hanged them, often without a trial. In their rough way, the vigilantes brought peace to many mining towns.

Lawman comes to town. What was it about western mining towns that led to gun fights and violence in the streets? When police forces were set up, why did people want fair trials and an end to vigilante "justice"?

5. While prospectors and miners were moving into the mountains, cattle owners were coming to the Great Plains. Wild herds of cattle had been roaming over the southern part of the plains since the time of the Spanish explorers. Some Texans had fenced in parts of the herds and had begun to raise cattle. But the raising of cattle remained limited to the southern part of the plains, for there was no easy way of taking the cattle to the markets of the North and the East. The coming of the railroads changed this. In 1867 a railroad was built from the East to Kansas. Cattle raisers began to drive their herds north to the railroad. New towns (Abilene, Wichita, and Dodge City) were started where the cattle trails met the railroads. The cattle were loaded on trains for the meat-packing factories in Chicago and the East.

6. As the herds were driven north, the cattle grew fat on the grassy lands of the plains. The cattle raisers wanted their herds to graze on the open range, the unfenced land that belonged to the national government. However, buffalo roamed on the same plains and stood in the way of the cattle herds.

7. In the early 19th century there were over 60 million buffalo. Before long, there were few buffalo left. Passengers shot them from train windows. Bands of hunters went into the plains looking for buffalo. They killed the big animals and removed their hides. They loaded the valuable hides on wagons and sold them to tanneries in the East. There was also great demand for buffalo tongues as food.

8. When the Plains Indians saw what was happening to the buffalo, they became

The coming of the railroads. The railroads brought an end to the buffalo's freedom to roam the open range. What other changes did the railroads bring to the plains? How did these changes affect the way people lived?

alarmed. They decided to drive the white settlers away, before the settlers completely wiped out the buffalo. The Plains Indians fought the newcomers desperately. They attacked settlements and lonely ranch houses. They tortured and killed women and children, burned their homes, and stole their cattle. The settlers fought as cruelly as the Indians. They often killed Plains Indians without mercy.

9. One of the last battles between the Plains Indians and the United States soldiers took place in Montana in 1876. The Sioux Indians, led by two chiefs, Crazy Horse and Sitting Bull, surrounded General George Custer and his troops at the Little Big Horn River. Every one of Custer's men was killed. More troops were then sent into Indian country. By 1877 the Plains Indians were defeated and the western pioneers settled the plains.

10. As the Plains Indian tribes surrendered, they were forced into lands set aside for them by the government. These lands were known as **reservations.** The government gave the Plains Indians food and schooling. It attempted to teach the Plains Indians to farm, but the Indians wanted to keep their own ways of living.

11. Some Indians did not want to move onto reservations. The Nez Percé was one such tribe. They lived in what is now Idaho, Washington, and Oregon. The Nez Percé had borrowed many of the ways of living from the Plains Indians, including buffalo hunting. In the 1860s and 1870s more and more miners and settlers took over their land. When some young warriors attacked whites, the United States army came to protect the settlers. Chief Joseph had not wanted to fight. But the army attacked. Then Chief Joseph tried to lead his tribe into Canada, over 1,000 miles (1,600 kilometers) away. There were many battles along the way. Only 30 miles (48 kilometers) from the border, army troops defeated

American troops charging into battle against Plains Indians. This painting is by Frederic Remington, who went west in 1880 in search of adventure. He soon began to paint scenes of the West as he saw it. Why are his paintings important to us today?

the Nez Percé. When Chief Joseph surrendered, he said, "My heart is sick and sad. . . . From where the sun now stands, I will fight no more forever."

12. Chief Joseph's fight was the last Indian war, but not the end of the bloodshed. In 1890, army officers surrounded a Sioux Indian camp at Wounded Knee, a creek in South Dakota. Over 200 Sioux were killed, including many women and children. The Plains Indians and whites had different ways of life. The Plains Indians roamed the plains freely in search of buffalo, so important to their way of living. The buffalo meant food and clothing. The white settlers wanted the land for farming and cattle raising. Plains Indians were not willing to give up their tribal customs for this way of life. They fought to keep their homes and hunting grounds. The Plains Indians were able to hold the plains for a time, but in the end their way of life was destroyed.

Which person, date, or place is identified in each description below?

Sir Francis Drake	James Marshal	1848
Jed Smith	John Frémont	1836
John Sutter	forty-niners	Santa Fe Trail
Lone Star State	Bear Flag Republic	Pony Express

1. Owned a sawmill near Sacramento.
2. A fur trader who reached California overland through the South Pass.
3. Explorer, mapmaker, and general who helped to overthrow Mexican rule in California.
4. The year that gold was discovered in California.
5. A route across the plains from Missouri through New Mexico.
6. Name given to California when it revolted against Mexico.
7. Sailed into the bay of San Francisco in the 16th century.
8. Name given to people who rushed to California in search of gold.

I. What is the main purpose of Chapter 14?

   a. To tell how the Great Plains was settled
   b. To describe Indian life on the Great Plains
   c. To discuss the Indian Wars
   d. To describe how the cattle industry grew

II. Choose the correct answer.

1. Why did the Plains Indians fight the settlers who came to the plains?
   a. The Plains Indians wanted the territory for mining.
   b. The settlers killed off the buffalo and took the Plains Indians' land.
   c. The railroad ruined Indian farmland.
2. General Custer was defeated by the Sioux Indians at which place?
   a. Wounded Knee Creek
   b. Little Big Horn River
   c. Comstock
3. Why did people rush to the mountains?
   a. To find gold and other minerals
   b. To find cheaper land
   c. To make use of the vast forests
4. Why were vigilante committees formed?
   a. To keep law and order in mining towns
   b. To keep others from staking claims in the gold fields
   c. To speed communications with the East
5. Why did cattle raising become profitable?
   a. New kinds of cattle were brought to the plains.
   b. Sheepherders came to the grassy regions of the plains.
   c. The railroad brought the cattle to market.
6. "The Great Plains" refers to the region between the
   a. Rocky Mountains and the Pacific Ocean
   b. Mississippi River and the Rockies
   c. Appalachian Mountains and the Mississippi

7. Abilene, Wichita, and Dodge City were important as
   a. mining towns
   b. railroad centers for shipping cattle to the East
   c. fur trading centers

III. **Decide whether each statement agrees or disagrees with what you have read. If the statement disagrees, explain why.**

1. When the settlers found a use for the Great Plains, it meant war with the Plains Indians.
2. The Great Plains was the last territory in this country to be settled.
3. The Indians of the plains were mainly farmers.
4. Plains Indians wanted to live on reservations and learn new ways of living.
5. The Sioux victory against General Custer was one of the last victories for the Plains Indians.
6. Cattle raising became a great business on the plains.

DEVELOPING IDEAS AND SKILLS **MAP SKILLS** *American Indians*

Study the map. Then decide whether each statement on page 264 is true or false. If a statement is false rewrite it so that it is true.

American Indians

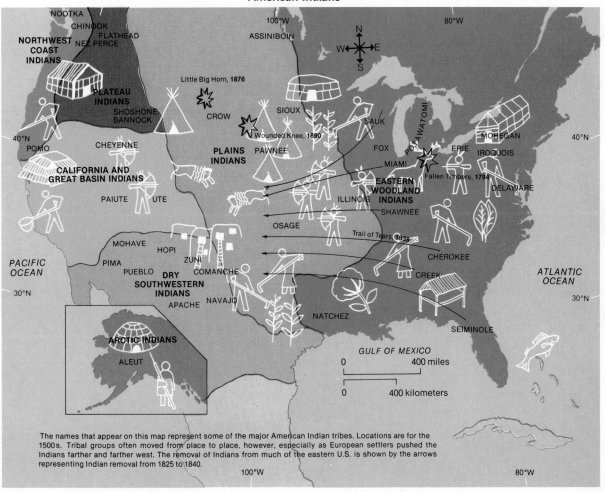

The names that appear on this map represent some of the major American Indian tribes. Locations are for the 1500s. Tribal groups often moved from place to place, however, especially as European settlers pushed the Indians farther and farther west. The removal of Indians from much of the eastern U.S. is shown by the arrows representing Indian removal from 1825 to 1840.

1. The Plains Indians depended on the buffalo for food.
2. Indians of the Southwest were farmers.
3. American Indians lived in the same kind of homes throughout the country.
4. Indians east of the Mississippi River farmed and hunted game in the woods.
5. The Cheyenne and Aleut Indians had similar life-styles.
6. The Seminole Indians once lived in the area now known as Florida.
7. Utah and Illinois are two states whose names come from the names of Indian tribes.
8. Wounded Knee Creek is in the region where Indians of California lived.
9. The Battle of Fallen Timbers took place after the Battle of Little Big Horn.
10. On the Trail of Tears the Cherokees moved from the East to the region where Plains Indians had lived.

SUMMING UP **THE PLAINS INDIANS** Here are some statements about the Plains Indian. You may agree or disagree with each statement or you may decide you haven't enough information to make a judgment. Be able to support your choice.

	AGREE	DISAGREE	DON'T KNOW
1. They wanted to find gold.			
2. They wanted chiefly to farm.			
3. They liked to roam the plains and woodlands.			
4. They are American citizens today.			
5. The Plains Indians had most of their land taken away from them in the 19th century.			
6. They depended upon the buffalo and the horse.			
7. There are more than 500,000 Plains Indians today.			
8. The Plains Indians wanted to be ranchers.			

Match the items in Column B with those in Column A.

COLUMN A
1. Comstock Lode
2. Chicago
3. Chief Joseph
4. prospectors
5. Last Chance
6. Crazy Horse
7. vigilantes
8. Abilene

COLUMN B
Leader of the Nez Percé
Town where cattle trails met the railroads
Mining town
Leader of the Sioux
One of the world's richest silver mines
Members of citizens' groups that try to punish lawbreakers, often without trials and by means that are against the law
Those who search for riches such as silver and gold
Town with meat-packing factories in the 19th century

Thinking It Through

The story of the American Indians is a very sad one. Again and again, Indians were pushed off their land and hunting grounds. Looking back, what might have been a better solution to the problems between settlers and Indians? Should any action be taken today? Explain your answer.

15 FARMERS ARRIVE AND CLOSE THE FRONTIER

How did the coming of farmers to the Great Plains bring an end to the American frontier?

1. Land that once belonged to the Plains Indians was now owned by the cattle ranchers. The cattle owners needed help to watch over their great herds of cattle. They hired hard-riding cowboys to look after the herds and lead them in the long drive to the railroads. A cowboy usually wore a heavy woolen shirt, a neckerchief of colored silk or cotton, leather trousers called chaps, pointed boots, and a big hat called a sombrero. He sometimes carried two guns called six-shooters. Everything he had— boots, spurs, saddle, and chaps—was for one purpose, riding his horse. Texas cowboys learned most of their skills from the vaqueros, the Mexican cowboys.

2. There were two roundups of cattle each year. In the spring, young calves were brought together in order to brand them with the owner's mark. In the fall, the cows were rounded together to pick out the animals to be sent to market.

3. The cattle were divided into droves, or herds, for the long drive to the railroad. The head of the cattle drive was the trail boss. The cowboys rode on each side of the herd. Behind the herd was the tail rider and a small group of spare horses. Each outfit had a chuck wagon and a hoodlum wagon pulled by horses or mules. The cook drove

Cowboys during roundup. They worked as herders on cattle ranches. Their job was most difficult in the days before the open range was fenced in. What were some of the dangers and difficulties facing the cattle drive?

the chuck wagon. This wagon was loaded with food, pots and pans, bedding, tents, medicines, and every article that was needed for the trail. The hoodlum wagon carried the water barrels, wood, and branding irons.

4. The cowboys had to guard the cattle night and day. The herds had to be defended against bands of American Indians, cattle thieves called rustlers, and wild animals. If the cattle did not have enough food and water, they became restless. A sudden shot or a thunderstorm could start a stampede.

5. More than 5,000 black cowboys rode the cow trails from Texas after the Civil War. Some of them were among the best riders on the range. They rode with other Texans, Mexicans, and American Indians. They shared the same jobs and dangers. After the trail drives stopped, many of the black cowboys went back to Texas and took up new jobs. One of the most famous black cowboys was Nat Love, who was called Deadwood Dick.

6. The days of the open range did not last long. The cattle ranchers had driven the buffalo from the range. They had taken the land from the Plains Indians. Now the cattle ranchers had to fight to hold the land for their cattle. Spanish-speaking sheepherders had used the plains for many years. Their flocks of sheep chewed the grass close to the ground and left nothing for the cattle to eat. More sheepherders came from the East. Bitter fights arose between the cattle ranchers and the sheepherders.

7. The railroads brought people to the plains in search of farmland. Once the plains were thought to be worthless. Now it was found that the dry lands west of the Mississippi were some of the best wheat lands in the world. Farmers were encouraged to move west by the national government's new land policy. Under the Land Ordinance of 1785, a farmer could buy 640 acres of land for as little as one

Settlers on the Great Plains. What two inventions helped the new farmers? With what materials did this family build its house?

dollar per acre. However, this was more than the average farmer could buy and work. In 1820 the farmer was able to buy 80 acres at $1.25 per acre. Even this was too expensive, and people of the West demanded free land to attract settlers. In 1862 the government passed the Homestead Act, which provided 160 acres of free land to any citizen who would farm it for five years.

8. As a result of the Homestead Act, farmers came to the Great Plains. These people were called **homesteaders.** Many settlers came from Norway, Sweden, Germany, and Russia. Settlers were helped by two important new inventions: barbed wire and the windmill. Barbed-wire fences were put up to keep the cattle from trampling or eating the settlers' crops. With the windmill, farmers could pump enough water, even in the drier parts of the plain, to make their crops grow.

9. The new farmers had hard times at first. Their first and most important concern was housing. Since there were few trees

on the prairies, these farmers had to build their houses of sod and prairie mud. These sod houses kept homesteaders cool in summer and warm in winter. Sometimes, however, the roofs of sod houses caused problems. When there was no rain, the roof would dry out and a fine layer of dust would cover the inside of the house. In wet weather, mud from the roof would drip on everything. The lives of homesteaders were hard in other ways. There were long distances between farmhouses, and the homesteader's life was a lonely one. Farmers had to defend their homes against the cattle ranchers who did not want to give up the open range. Angry ranchers sometimes tore down the fences and beat those farmers who did not leave. However, the farmers continued to come, and more and more land was fenced in. Gradually, most of the cattle ranchers and sheepherders had to move to other land.

10. The last of the Indian territory opened to settlers was Oklahoma. In 1889 the government opened this territory for settlement. Since this was the last large area that whites had not settled, thousands of people took part in the rush to get land. Crowds pushed and shoved at the border of the territory, waiting for the hour when they would be allowed to enter. The signal permitting them to cross the boundary led to a mad rush. The settlers knew that the first in the territory would have the choice of the best farmland. By 1890 all the good land was occupied by farmers. Very little open range remained. After this date, there was no large area in the United States that had not been settled in the steady march westward.

REVIEWING CHAPTER 14

Who is described in each item below—*miners, American Indians,* or *cattle ranchers?*

1. Depended on the buffalo for food, clothing, and shelter
2. Let their cows graze on the open range
3. Used horses for hunting and fighting
4. Depended on vigilantes to keep order
5. Discovered silver and copper in the West
6. Lived in crude shelters and temporary towns
7. Defeated Custer at the Little Big Horn
8. Were placed on reservations
9. Helped to kill off the buffalo
10. Drove cattle north to the railroads

UNDERSTANDING CHAPTER 15

I. What is the main purpose of Chapter 15?

a. To tell how the last frontier was settled
b. To discuss the arguments among settlers on the plains
c. To describe the life of the cowboy
d. To describe the coming of the homesteaders

II. Choose the correct answer.

1. Why was there a movement of settlers to the Great Plains?
   a. Plains Indians had agreed to sell the land.
   b. Railroads had opened the region and homesteaders started farms on the plains.
   c. Minerals had been discovered in many states.

2. How did farmers get their land after 1862?
   a. By buying it at a government land office
   b. From the land companies
   c. As a result of the Homestead Act
3. From whom did the cowboys learn many of their skills?
   a. Mexican vaqueros
   b. Swedish farmers
   c. Spanish-speaking sheepherders
4. Why did the open range come to an end?
   a. Plains Indians stole the herds.
   b. Homesteaders settled and closed in the land.
   c. The cattle could not live on the dry land.
5. Why were there bad feelings between sheepherders and cattle ranchers?
   a. The sheep ate the good grass so that it was too short for cattle.
   b. Sheepherders encouraged the Plains Indians to attack cattle.
   c. The cattle ranchers owned all the water holes.
6. What was the long drive?
   a. The route of the forty-niners to California
   b. The movement of cattle from Texas north to the railroads
   c. The placement of Indians on reservations.
7. The last of the Indian territory opened to settlers was
   a. Texas
   b. New Mexico
   c. Oklahoma
8. Many settlers to the Great Plains came from
   a. Norway, Sweden, Germany, and Russia
   b. Portugal, Italy, and Greece
   c. California, Oregon, and Idaho

III. Decide whether each statement agrees or disagrees with what you have read. If the statement disagrees, explain why.

1. The invention of barbed wire helped both the farmer and the rancher.
2. The cattle raisers were happy to see many people settle in the West.
3. By 1860 all the land in the West had been opened for settlement.
4. The railroads brought people to the plains in search of land for farms.
5. Houses in the plains were most often made of logs.
6. Cowboys led the herds of cattle on the long drive to the railroads.
7. Towns grew in places where the cattle were loaded on trains.
8. When Oklahoma was opened for settlement, few people wanted the land.

IV. Arrange these events in their proper order, beginning with the event that happened first.

The Homestead Act was passed.

The Land Ordinance law was passed, allowing land to be sold at a dollar an acre.

All the good land was settled.

Thousands rushed to get land in Oklahoma.

PICTURE STUDY What do you think the two groups of people are arguing about? What is the house made of and why? What inventions shown helped bring about the struggle?

SUMMING UP **CATTLE RANCHER VS. HOMESTEADER** What did cattle ranchers and homesteaders think about the issues below? Complete the chart in your notebook.

CATTLE RANCHERS	ISSUES	HOMESTEADERS
	Coming of the railroads	
	Use of barbed wire	
	Homestead Act	
	Indians on the plains	

Using a Time Line

Study this time line. Then answer the questions that follow. Use the information you have studied in this unit to help you. You may also look at the time line on pages 192 and 193 if you need additional help.

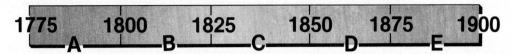

In which period of time (**A, B, C, D,** or **E**) did the following take place?

1. Jefferson bought Louisiana from France.
2. The Homestead Act was passed by Congress to help settlers.
3. The United States defeated Mexico in war.
4. The Northwest Ordinance was passed by Congress.
5. Gold was discovered in California.
6. The end of the frontier was reached.
7. Putman started the settlement named Marietta.

EXTENDING YOUR READING — IV

Building a Class Library

Your classroom should have a library of books that tell you more about the history of these United States. Not all the books you can and should read are available in your school. You and your classmates can help to build your own class library.

Find out what books the members of your class are most interested in. Then see if members of the class have any of these books at home. All of you have probably read books that you liked very much and are willing to share with your classmates. If each member of the class brings to school some of the books that he or she has read at home, you will find there will be many kinds of books available for the library.

Try to have a variety of books in the classroom. There should be biographies of famous people (including early pioneers), adventure stories, and stories about frontier, farm, and city life.

The class should have a system of lending these books to individual members of the class. The class librarian can record book titles and keep a record of students who borrow them. Students should keep their own record of the books they have read from the class library. You should try to read many kinds of books about many different periods of history. Some suggestions for your class library are listed on this page and the next.

BOOKS FOR UNIT IV

AUTHOR	TITLE, PUBLISHER	DESCRIPTION
1. Adams, Samuel H.	*The Erie Canal,* Random (Landmark Books)	The description of the people who helped build the Erie Canal.
2. Bauer, Helen	*California Rancho Days,* Doubleday	Describes life, customs, and activities in Spanish California.
3. Blassingame, W., and Glendenning, R.	*Men Who Opened the West,* Putnam	Biographies of some who blazed western trails.
4. Chambers, M. C.	*Boy Heroes of Chapultepec,* Winston	Story of a teenage Mexican boy during the Mexican War.
5. Chidsey, Donald B.	*And Tyler, Too,* Thomas Nelson	John Tyler, whose party did not want him to be president —a lively period in our history.
6. Dangerfield, George	*Defiance to the Old World,* Putnam	The story behind the Monroe Doctrine.
7. Daugherty, James	*Marcus and Narcissa Whitman: Pioneers of Oregon,* Viking	The hardships faced by two pioneers in setting up a mission in Oregon.
8. Daugherty, James	*Of Courage Undaunted,* Viking	A story drawn from the journals of Lewis and Clark.
9. Flexner, Eleanor	*Century of Struggle,* Belknap	The history of the women's suffrage movement.
10. Heiderstadt, Dorothy	*Indian Friends and Foes,* McKay	Biographies of American Indians from Pocahontas to Geronimo.
11. Judson, Clara I.	*Andrew Jackson, Frontier Statesman,* Wilcox and Follett	Story of the first president from the West.

AUTHOR	TITLE, PUBLISHER	DESCRIPTION
12. Katz, William L.	*Black West,* Doubleday	Narrative and illustrations of black explorers, fur traders, cowboys, and soldiers.
13. Langdon, William C.	*Everyday Things in American Life, 1776–1876,* Scribner's	Information about travel by flatboat, steamboat, roads, railroads, and the use of steam power.
14. Latham, F. B.	*The Law or the Gun,* American	A story of the Mormons.
15. Politi, Leo	*The Mission Bell,* Scribner's	The story of Father Serra and the founding of the California missions.
16. Reeder, C. R.	*The Story of the Mexican War,* Meridith Press	Personalities and campaigns of the war, including background of troubles between Texas and Mexico.

Unit V

How Did Differences in Our Ways of Life Lead to Civil War?

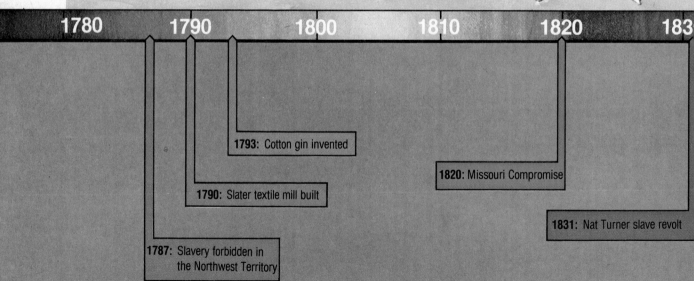

1780   1790   1800   1810   1820   183

1793: Cotton gin invented

1820: Missouri Compromise

1790: Slater textile mill built

1831: Nat Turner slave revolt

1787: Slavery forbidden in the Northwest Territory

CHAPTER

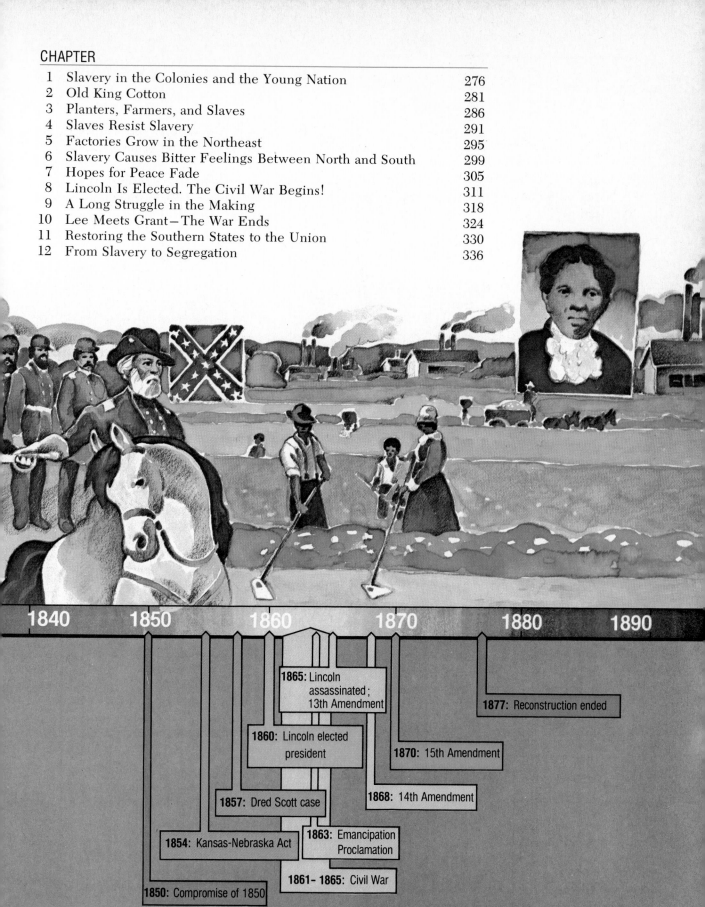

1840   1850   1860   1870   1880   1890

1865: Lincoln assassinated; 13th Amendment

1877: Reconstruction ended

1860: Lincoln elected president

1870: 15th Amendment

1857: Dred Scott case

1868: 14th Amendment

1854: Kansas-Nebraska Act

1863: Emancipation Proclamation

1861-1865: Civil War

1850: Compromise of 1850

1 SLAVERY IN THE COLONIES AND THE YOUNG NATION

What do we know about slavery in colonial times? How were slaves treated in the early days of our nation?

1. In the 1500s the Spanish and the Portuguese brought blacks from Africa to the New World. They sold the blacks as slaves in the West Indies and Brazil. The slaves worked on tobacco and sugar plantations there. In 1619 the first blacks to come to the British colonies were brought to Virginia from West Africa. Soon blacks were also brought to the other colonies. At first, these Africans were treated as indentured servants. After working a number of years, they were set free. Then they were sometimes given land, tools, clothing, and money, just as was done with white indentured servants. Some free blacks became successful farmers and crafts people. Still other free blacks continued to do farm work for white people. By the 1640s, however, many black workers were kept indentured for life.

2. In the early 1660s, new laws in Virginia and Maryland turned most blacks into slaves. However, white indentured

This painting shows slaves being taken south after they have been sold. Name two reasons why slavery was cruel.

276

servants continued to be set free after their term of service. Why did this happen? Let's go back and think about the first shiploads of servants to arrive in the colonies. The European servants were white. The Africans were black. Suppose a white indentured servant ran away. He or she could hide easily among the white people of neighboring communities. A runaway black servant could easily be pointed out and caught. Therefore, planters would risk less money using black indentured servants. Planters soon found that it cost them less to keep an indentured servant for life than to pay workers. The next step was to buy slaves. Thousands of slaves could be brought from Africa to supply the planters. If they had slaves, planters would not have to train new indentured servants every few years. They would not have to pay their slaves. They could keep the slaves' children as slaves.

3. Other reasons why blacks were forced into slavery were these. Blacks had different languages from whites. They had different ways of living. Their religion was different. Their skin color was different from that of whites. Because blacks seemed so different, many whites did not feel guilty about making blacks slaves. These whites began to feel they were better than blacks. Some began to act as if blacks were not human beings. They passed laws that treated slaves as property. The laws allowed white slave owners to treat their slaves cruelly. Whipping slaves was common. Slave families could be broken up. The children could be sold to different planters. Teaching reading and writing to slaves was against the law in many places. Even free blacks did not have all the rights that whites had.

4. Despite many hardships, some slaves and free blacks were able to obtain an excellent education. One example is Phillis Wheatley. She was born in 1753 in Africa. At the age of eight she was taken as a slave

Phillis Wheatley, a colonial poet. A slave ship had brought her to Boston. Wheatley began to write poetry at the age of 14.

to Boston. She became a maid in the Wheatley family. They saw how bright she was. The Wheatleys gave her a good education. By the age of 14, she was writing poetry. By 20, her poems were published in a book. She became a well-known poet. Benjamin Banneker is another example. He was born in 1731 in Maryland. He was a free black. At 22, he made the first clock ever built in the British colonies. Later, he helped plan the capital at Washington, D.C.

5. Some blacks planned revolts to escape from slavery. One of the early slave revolts took place in 1712 in New York City. On the night of April 6, some slaves set fire to one of their master's houses. Then they waited to kill those who came to put out the fire. They managed to kill nine whites before the governor sent troops to end the revolt. The slaves fled. Most were captured.

Almanacs by Benjamin Banneker were widely sold in the 1790s. He was astronomer, farmer, mathematician, and surveyor.

Some committed suicide rather than be taken. The captured slaves were tried. Most of them were put to death. Such revolts, however, often led to even stricter controls over slaves.

6. The number of slaves grew slowly during colonial times. In the North, some of the states began to free their slaves after the Revolutionary War. In 1787 Congress, under the Articles of Confederation, passed a law forbidding slavery in the Northwest Territory. By 1819 blacks were free in the northern states.

7. The new Constitution did not help the slaves. Delegates to the Constitutional Convention in 1787 knew the horrors of slavery. Nevertheless, they compromised. Each slave was counted as three-fifths of a person. This was for purposes of taxing and figuring out how many representatives each

Many slaves tried to escape. What do you think were their chances for success? Why? In what other way did blacks resist slavery?

state should have in Congress. The delegates did not even use the word *slave* in the Constitution. In short, the Constitution accepted the owning of slaves.

8. In 1793 slavery grew stronger. That year Congress passed a new law to help southern slave owners capture their **fugitive,** or runaway, slaves. The new law was called the Fugitive Slave Law. This law said that runaway slaves had to be returned to their owner. Anyone helping a runaway slave could be fined. The fine was as much as $500. In those days, a person had to work a year or more to earn that much.

UNDERSTANDING
CHAPTER 1

I. What is the main purpose of Chapter 1?

a. To describe the achievements of Benjamin Banneker
b. To describe how the first Africans were brought to Virginia
c. To describe how slavery developed during colonial times and during the early years of the nation

II. Choose the correct answer or answers.

1. As a result of the Constitution,
   a. slavery was ended in the United States
   b. each slave was counted as three-fifths of a person for purposes of representation and taxes
   c. the government had to help return slaves who had run away from their owners
2. In what two ways did Africans differ from most other people who first came to the colonies in the New World?
   a. They had a different skin color.
   b. They came against their will.
   c. They came to make a better life for themselves.
3. Phillis Wheatley is remembered as a person who
   a. fought in the American Revolution
   b. helped sew the first American flag
   c. became a well-known colonial poet
4. A fugitive is a person who
   a. owes money to another person
   b. spreads the Christian religion
   c. runs away
5. Some blacks showed their hatred of slavery by
   a. revolting against their owners
   b. refusing to vote
   c. going on protest marches

III. Decide whether each statement agrees or disagrees with what you have read. If the statement disagrees, explain why.

1. The first blacks to arrive in Virginia were slaves.
2. Colonial laws allowed slave owners to treat their slaves as property rather than human beings.

3. Despite their early hardships, most black slaves learned to read and write.
4. Slaves did not have the rights of free people.
5. The slaves found ways to protest against slavery.
6. The new Constitution put an end to slavery.
7. Some northern states freed their slaves after the Revolutionary War.
8. Slavery was prohibited in the Northwest Territory.

DEVELOPING IDEAS AND SKILLS **PICTURE SYMBOLS** These picture symbols should help you recall parts of the chapter you have read. Describe the main idea of each picture.

SUMMING UP List the advantages of slavery to slave owners. List the disadvantages of slavery to the slaves and the slave owners.

Thinking It Through

As recently as the past ten years, there were reports that slavery still existed in some parts of the world. Should a nation permit human beings to be bought and sold within its borders?' Should one nation try to stop slavery in another nation? Explain your answers.

2 OLD KING COTTON

How did the cotton gin help change the way of life in the South?

Processing the cotton for sale was as hard work as picking it. How did the cotton gin help? When was the cotton gin invented?

1. Despite the new slave law of 1793, it looked like slavery might be coming to an end. First, powerful Americans such as George Washington and Thomas Jefferson were beginning to say that it was wrong to keep other human beings as slaves. Second, most slaves worked on large tobacco plantations. The soil of these plantations was wearing out. Although planters could grow less tobacco, they still had to provide food, housing, and clothing for their slaves. This was becoming very costly.

2. Cotton was also grown. But it was not as important a crop as tobacco. Raising cotton was hard work. The cotton fibers contain little seeds. These seeds have to be removed before the cotton can be used to make cloth. Growing cotton was costly because it was difficult to remove the seeds by hand. It took a slave all day to separate the seeds from one pound of cotton.

3. In 1793 the problem of removing the seeds from the cotton fiber was solved by Eli Whitney. Whitney was a New Englander who went to teach young people in the South. While visiting a plantation, he learned of the problem of separating the seeds from the cotton. Whitney became interested in this problem. He quit teaching and devoted his time to making a machine that would clean the cotton. In 1793 he finished the machine. He called it the cotton engine, or cotton gin for short.

4. The first cotton gin had two rollers turned by hand. The first roller had sharp metal teeth. It drew in the cotton from the plant and left the seeds behind. The second roller turned in the opposite direction. It had brushes that cleaned the lint fibers from the saw teeth of the first roller. After this, the clean cotton was pushed out and made ready to be put into bales. The machine could clean 50 pounds a day if it was operated by hand. It could clean 500 pounds of cotton if it was run by water power. Demand for the cotton gin was great. All the planters wanted it. Later, Whitney's machine was copied by others. His ideas were stolen and his patent on the machine was worth little. Whitney became famous because of his machine, but he made little money from it.

5. The invention of the cotton gin changed the way of life in the South. First, it made cotton the most valuable crop. Within a few years, planters had turned their fields over to growing cotton. Of course, some farmers continued to raise rice and tobacco, but cotton became the "king crop" in the South. Second, the growing of so much cotton led to the search for new land. In order to make money, south-

This painting by Charles Parsons shows cotton being loaded for shipment to markets in Europe and the North.

ern farmers planted as much cotton as they could. Growing cotton year after year on the same land caused the soil to wear out. Planters thought it would be easier to get new land than to try to restore minerals to the soil they had used. They looked westward for new lands. Beginning in South Carolina and Georgia, the cotton country spread as far west as Texas.

6. Third, the invention of the cotton gin ended any chance of freedom for slaves in the South. Most owners of large plantations believed they could not raise large amounts of cotton without the work of black slaves. As more cotton was raised, the demand for slaves grew. The average price for a slave rose from $500 in 1798 to $1,500 in 1860. A very good worker might sell for as much as $2,000. When planters had as many as 50 slaves, they had a large amount of money invested in their slaves. They were not willing to give up this valuable "property."

7. In addition, the ship owners of the North profited from the increased slave trade. So did northern merchants who traded in molasses and rum, which were part of the slave trade. (See map on page 87.) According to the Constitution, Congress could not prevent the importing of slaves into the country until 1808. Northern ship owners also profited from shipping cotton to factories in Great Britain and the North.

8. Cotton growing was very important to the new factories of the North. During the War of 1812, a number of factories for making cloth were started in New England. They could use much of the cotton grown in the South. There were no large mills in the South, for planters wanted to invest their money in land and slaves. They made as much money by selling cotton as they could make by starting factories themselves.

Do you remember when it happened? Match each item in Column A with the correct date in Column B.

COLUMN A	COLUMN B
a. The first Africans were sold to colonists in Jamestown as indentured servants.	1. 1712
b. The Constitution counted each slave as 3/5 of a person.	2. 1793
c. A slave revolt took place in New York City.	3. 1619
d. Virginia and Maryland passed laws that made black people slaves.	4. 1787
e. Congress passed the first Fugitive Slave Law.	5. 1660s

I. What is the main purpose of paragraphs 5 and 6?

a. To describe how the cotton gin works
b. To show how the cotton gin changed the way of life in the South
c. To describe new crops grown in the South
d. To explain the new value of tobacco

II. Choose the correct answer.

1. Why didn't the South raise much cotton before 1793?
    a. Planters wanted to raise wheat and potatoes.
    b. The climate of the South was not good for growing cotton.
    c. Cotton growing was too costly.
2. Why did slavery greatly increase in the South after 1793?
    a. The cotton gin made cotton growing profitable, and therefore planters wanted more slaves to do the work.
    b. A new type of tobacco increased the demand for slaves.
    c. A new law said that planters had to own at least 50 slaves.
3. Why did planters look for new lands southwest of the Carolinas and Georgia?
    a. Cotton growing "wore out" the soil.
    b. Planters had a great desire for adventure.
    c. The government offered these lands to the planters at a very low price.
4. Why were there few factories in the South?
    a. There was no labor supply to do factory work.
    b. Planters would rather invest their money in land.
    c. There were no raw materials at hand.
5. What affect did the invention of the cotton gin have on the North?
    a. More northern farmers planted cotton.
    b. Factories for making cotton cloth were started in the North.
    c. Many northern white farmworkers moved to the South.

III. Decide whether each statement agrees or disagrees with what you have read. If the statement disagrees, explain why.

1. The invention of the cotton gin increased the demand for slaves.
2. Because people wanted to make money from growing cotton, they looked for more land.
3. Inventors always become rich.
4. Most planters believed cotton could be grown without using slaves.
5. Cotton lands extended as far west as what is now Alabama, Mississippi, Louisiana, and Texas in the years after 1800.
6. Northern ship owners, factory owners, and merchants did not benefit from slavery in the South.

DEVELOPING IDEAS AND SKILLS

A. MAP SKILLS *The Cotton Kingdom*
Study the map. Then decide whether these statements are true or false.

The Cotton Kingdom

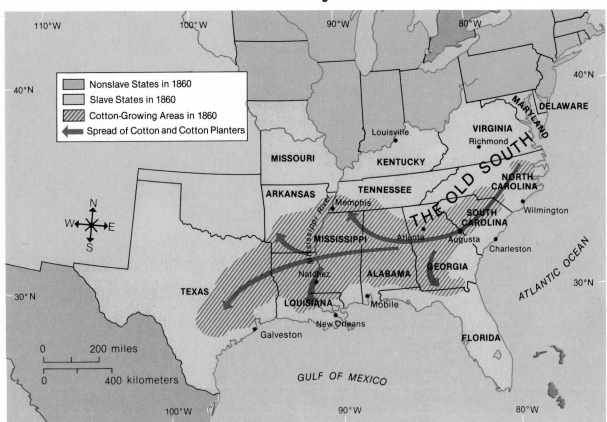

1. All the states in the Cotton Kingdom were west of the Mississippi River.
2. The cotton country moved steadily in a southwest direction.
3. Alabama and Mississippi were two of the new cotton states.
4. The new cotton states bordered the Gulf of Mexico.
5. Cotton planters in the new Cotton Kingdom came chiefly from Europe.

Answer the following questions.

1. Why did the planters leave the Old South?
2. Why was New Orleans important to the Cotton Kingdom?
3. Why was the new cotton area more fertile than land in the Old South?

B. PICTOGRAPH STUDY *Cotton and Slaves*

Study the graphs. Then decide whether these statements are true or false. Rewrite the false statements to make them true.

Cotton and Slaves

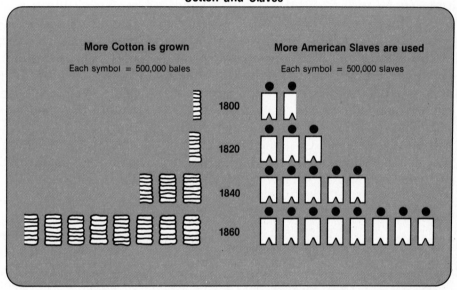

1. As more cotton was grown, planters used fewer slaves.
2. The amount of cotton grown more than doubled between 1840 and 1860.
3. The number of slaves more than doubled between 1840 and 1860.
4. About 50,000 bales of cotton were grown in 1800.
5. There were about 4 million slaves in 1860.

SUMMING UP   **THE COTTON GIN**   Complete this outline in your notebook.

A. How the cotton gin worked
    1.
    2.
    3.
    4.
B. How the cotton gin changed the South
    1.
    2.
    3.

3 PLANTERS, FARMERS, AND SLAVES

How did people live in the South before 1860?

1. In 1860 the population of the South was about 9 million. Of this number, about 3½ million were slaves. Most southern white families did not own any slaves. Most of those who did had only a few slaves. However, a group of 10,000 families owned as many as 50 slaves or more. Those who owned many slaves were called planters.

2. The planters lived on huge farms called plantations. The plantation home was usually a large brick or wooden house of 10 or 12 rooms. It had a wide porch with beautiful pillars in the front. Near the planter's house were the kitchen, school, barns, stables, cotton gin, shops, and rows of log cabins for the black slaves. The cotton fields stretched beyond the cabins and the shops.

3. The slave cabins were dark because they often had no windows. During the cool and rainy winter, the cabin was warmed by a fireplace. The family cooked its own meals. The food, mostly corn bread, molasses, and bacon, was provided by the planter. Some of the planters let slaves have a small garden and a few chickens and pigs. The furniture was homemade, and there was little of it. Slaves were not expected to have new clothes each year. What clothes they had were made on the plantation.

4. Since teaching slaves to read and write was against the law, few had these skills. Those who did were taught by other

A large southern plantation. How did life on a plantation differ from life on a small farm in the South?

slaves or by members of the planter's family. Religion played an important part in the life of slaves. Beautiful spirituals such as "Let My People Go" and "Nobody Knows the Trouble I've Seen" show the desire for freedom and the sadness of slave life. Because of poor food and housing, slaves were often sick. However, the slave owner would usually see that they had a doctor's care, since their work was valuable. The mistress of the plantation often served as a nurse.

5. Two kinds of slaves worked on the plantation, house slaves and field slaves. House slaves worked closely with the planter and the planter's family. They were separated from the other slaves. They lived in or near the master's house. They were raised to believe that it was a great honor to work as servants in the main house. On the other hand, most field hands had little to do with the slave owner. Many of them lived and died without once having set foot inside the slave owner's house.

6. On large plantations, planters usually hired overseers to manage the work. On smaller farms, the planters directed the work themselves. As a rule, slaves disliked the overseers because the overseers worked the slaves hard and sometimes beat them. An overseer's pay depended upon the amount of work he could get from the slaves.

7. Work on the plantation was carried on in three ways. One was the task system, in which each slave had a certain amount of work to do each day. The second was called the gang system. The workers were divided into groups and a good worker set the pace for the others. The third method depended on the use of the whip to drive the slaves to do more. Usually work began at daybreak and ended at sundown. Men, women, and children worked in the fields. On most plantations, black slaves had to endure great hardship and suffering. Their life span was much shorter than that of the whites around them.

8. The wife of a plantation owner had an important role on the plantation. She was kept very busy and seldom had as much free time as her husband. Besides raising her children, the planter's wife was in charge of the entire household. Even in the wealthiest families, she was expected to spin thread, weave cloth, and sew clothes. A plantation wife also supervised the preparation of food and assigned duties to household slaves. The women's role in running the day-to-day affairs of the plantation was an important one.

9. Growing cotton kept everyone busy. At the end of the short winter, the land was plowed and cotton was planted. Weeding the fields was the chief work in the summer. In the early fall the cotton was picked. After the picking, the cotton was taken to the gin for cleaning. Then it was packed into bales. The bales were shipped down the river to the cotton ports. These were New Orleans, Louisiana; Charleston, South Carolina; and Mobile, Alabama. Factories in England and the northern states were waiting for all the cotton the South could send. The factories then turned the cotton into manufactured goods. Eventually, the cotton goods were shipped to markets all over the world.

10. Most southern whites were people who ran small farms. These people owned or rented their land. Their farmland was the poorest land in the South. The good land was held by the large plantation owners. The home of an ordinary farm family was a log cabin or a frame house. The farm families did their own work and raised their own food. Since they had no slaves to work in the fields, they raised only a small amount of cotton. Small-farm owners did not object to slavery. If they had a successful year and a good crop, they might buy a slave. Then they were the envy of their neighbors. The aim of southern white farmers was to own a large plantation and to have many slaves working for them in the fields.

287

Find the missing words.

1. The leading crop in the South before 1790 was ▇▇▇▇.
2. The inventor of the cotton gin was ▇▇▇▇.
3. We know that ▇▇▇▇ did not approve of slavery, because of what he wrote in the Declaration of Independence.
4. The earliest American factories for weaving cloth began in the ▇▇▇▇ part of the United States.

5. The need for new lands for growing cotton opened settlements in ▇▇▇▇, ▇▇▇▇, and ▇▇▇▇.
6. The ▇▇▇▇ made cotton the most important crop in the South.
7. The invention of the cotton gin increased the ▇▇▇▇ for slaves.

I. What is the main purpose of Chapter 3?

    a. To describe the life of the black slaves
    b. To discuss how people lived in the South before 1860
    c. To explain the job of the overseer
    d. To describe the life of the small-farm owner in the South

II. Choose the correct answer.

1. The plantation was usually able to support itself because
    a. all food was grown and repair work done on the plantation
    b. the needs of the people on the plantation were few
    c. the plantations covered only a few acres
2. White owners and renters of small farms accepted slavery because
    a. the slaves often helped them on their farm
    b. they hoped someday to own slaves too
    c. they felt that there was nothing they could do to stop it
3. The largest group of people in the South in 1860 was
    a. plantation owners
    b. factory owners
    c. owners or renters of small farms
4. Which of these jobs was done last?
    a. Cotton was packed into bales.
    b. Cotton was picked.
    c. Cotton was cleaned.
5. On most plantations, black slaves had
    a. to endure great hardship and suffering
    b. life spans about equal to those of the whites around them
    c. to work about eight hours a day

III. Decide whether each statement agrees or disagrees with what you have read. If the statement disagrees, explain why.

1. All the farmers in the South owned slaves.
2. The owners of small farms had the best land in the South.

3. Many buildings were near the planter's house.
4. There were laws against teaching slaves to read and write.
5. Some planters gave the slaves money to buy the things they needed.
6. A slave could move to another plantation if he or she wished.
7. Many small-farm owners in the South lived in log cabins.
8. In 1860 more than one-third of the people in the South were slaves.
9. Planters cared little if their slaves became sick.
10. Most black spirituals show that slaves were not happy with the life forced upon them.

DEVELOPING IDEAS
AND SKILLS

PICTURE STUDY *A Cotton Plantation*

Study this picture. Then use the information you have gained from this picture and from Chapters 1, 2, and 3 of this unit to answer the following questions.

1. How was cotton transported from the plantations to the market?
2. Compare the housing of the slaves with those of the planters.
3. What kind of work did slaves do on cotton plantations?

4. Who is the man on horseback shown in the picture?
5. To what port cities was the cotton carried?
6. If you were a planter, how would the world appear to you? If you were a slave, how would the world seem to you?

SUMMING UP **THE SOUTH BEFORE 1860** Complete this outline in your notebook.

A. Groups living in the South before 1860.
1.
2.
3.
B. Steps in growing cotton
1.
2.
3.
C. What you would see on a plantation
1.
2.
3.
4.

Thinking It Through

Ralph Waldo Emerson once said, "If you put a chain around the neck of a slave, the other end fastens itself around your own." What does this statement mean?

4 SLAVES RESIST SLAVERY

How did many slaves show their hatred of slavery?

1. Slaves found many ways to fight their slavery. Many of them ran away to the North, to Canada, to Mexico, or to an Indian tribe. The main idea was to get out of slave territory. In some places, however, there were slave catchers. They moved through the free states looking for black people. Sometimes they caught a runaway slave. Just as often they grabbed someone else, a free black. Then they claimed the free black was the slave they had been hunting.

2. Slaves learned many ways to trouble their owner. They broke or lost tools they used. They allowed many farm animals to escape. A plantation building might burn mysteriously. Slaves pretended to be sick. They might do their work poorly or slowly. As one traveler in the South described it, "There are certain diseases which only the Negroes have. They break, waste, and destroy everything they handle; they burn or tear their clothing. They wander about at night, and sleep half the day. They slight their work, cutting up corn, tobacco and cloth. The overseers call it 'rascality.' They believe they do it on purpose." The purpose of all these activities was to make slave owners lose as much money as possible.

3. Many slaves showed their anger more openly. They planned and took part in slave revolts. There were slave revolts as early as the 1600s. During the years 1800–1860, there were more than 100 slave revolts. There may have been many more. But we do not know about all of them. That is because many blacks did not leave a written record of what they thought or did.

$150 REWARD

RANAWAY from the subscriber, on the night of the 2d instant, a negro man, who calls himself *Henry May*, about 22 years old, 5 feet 6 or 8 inches high, ordinary color, rather chunky built, bushy head, and has it divided mostly on one side, and keeps it very nicely combed; has been raised in the house, and is a first rate dining-room servant, and was in a tavern in Louisville for 18 months. I expect he is now in Louisville trying to make his escape to a free state, (in all probability to Cincinnati, Ohio.) Perhaps he may try to get employment on a steamboat. He is a good cook, and is handy in any capacity as a house servant. Had on when he left, a dark cassinett coatee, and dark striped cassinett pantaloons, new—he had other clothing. I will give $50 reward if taken in Louisvill; 100 dollars if taken one hundred miles from Louisville in this State, and 150 dollars if taken out of this State, and delivered to me, or secured in any jail so that I can get him again. WILLIAM BURKE.
Bardstown, Ky., September 3d, 1838.

Sign posted by a slave owner. Slave owners felt that their slaves were their property and should be returned. Others disagreed.

4. One of the largest slave revolts took place in 1822. It was led by Denmark Vesey of Charleston, South Carolina. Denmark Vesey was a free black and a skillful carpenter. He was respected by blacks and whites alike. In 1818 he held many secret meetings at his home. Under his plan, thousands of slaves were to march on the city of Charleston to capture it. However, a house slave revealed the plan to his master. About 135 of Vesey's men were arrested. More were tried. Thirty-seven of them were hanged. They died following Vesey's words, "Die like a man, silent, as you see me do."

5. The most violent slave revolt took place in 1831 in Virginia. It was led by Nat Turner, a very religious man. Turner believed that God had chosen him to lead his people to freedom. By the time the revolt was over more than 100 slaves and 55 whites were killed. Nat Turner and 19 others were captured, tried, and hanged. The Nat Turner uprising did much to end any idea whites might have had that blacks were happy being slaves.

Nat Turner was leader of the 1831 slave revolt. Turner was captured. What was one result of this revolt?

that their slaves were better off than factory workers in the North. They said that slaves did not have to worry about food, shelter, or clothing. They claimed that factory workers were never sure that they would be able to keep their jobs. Some white men and women thought otherwise. They found it difficult to get along with whites who believed in slavery. Some had to leave the South.

7. To control the slaves even further, each slave state passed stricter slave codes. Under the old slave laws, slaves had been treated as property not persons. This continued under the new slave codes. But the new laws made it very difficult for slave owners to free their slaves. Slaves were not allowed to be taught to read or write. They could not meet together unless a white person was present. They could not leave the plantation. They could not go to court and say anything against their owner. If slaves disobeyed any of these rules, they could be whipped or branded. These codes gave the planters complete power over the slaves. At the same time, however, the codes were an admission that slavery could be kept only through force.

6. After the Nat Turner revolt, most southerners no longer felt they had to apologize for slavery. They said openly that they would not free their slaves. They said the Bible approved of slavery. They argued

REVIEWING CHAPTER 3

Choose the correct answer.

1. Slavery developed in the South because
   a. slavery was more profitable in the South
   b. northerners were too poor to own slaves
   c. blacks wanted to live in the South
2. The plantation overseer was
   a. a manager
   b. an owner
   c. a worker

3. A spiritual is a
   a. meeting
   b. religious song
   c. reading
4. All of these were cotton ports in the South EXCEPT
   a. New Orleans
   b. Charleston
   c. Philadelphia

5. The cost of a good slave in 1860 was about
   a. $20
   b. $200
   c. $2,000

6. Cotton was shipped to factories in
   a. California
   b. the South
   c. England and the Northeast

I. **What is the main purpose of Chapter 4?**

a. To describe the tariff
b. To describe how the slaves protested against slavery
c. To describe the dangers facing runaway slaves

II. **Choose the correct answer or answers.**

1. Nat Turner was the
   a. leader of a slave revolt
   b. minister of a church in Charleston
   c. printer of antislavery books
2. What methods, other than revolts, did the slaves use to show their feelings about slavery?
   a. They pretended they were sick.
   b. They ran away when they had the chance.
   c. Both of these statements.
3. After the slave revolts, the white southerners
   a. decided to free their slaves
   b. became even more determined to keep their way of life
   c. closed all shops run by blacks
4. The new slave codes
   a. gave blacks the right to a free trial
   b. gave adult male blacks the right to vote
   c. made life even harder for slaves
5. What reasons did southern slave owners give for keeping slavery?
   a. They said that slaves could quickly learn to take care of themselves.
   b. They said that slaves in the South were better off than factory workers in the North.
   c. Both of these statements.

III. **Decide whether each statement agrees or disagrees with what you have read. If the statement disagrees, explain why.**

1. Blacks were happy as slaves and never thought of freeing themselves.
2. Other Americans never tried to help the slaves.
3. At first, southerners agreed that their way of life should be changed.
4. Slave codes made life easier for slaves on plantations.
5. Slaves learned different ways to trouble their owners.
6. As a result of the slave revolts, many people in the South wanted to give up slavery.
7. Slave catchers moved through the country looking for runaway slaves.
8. In the United States, a slave was treated as a piece of property.

PICTURE STUDY   Study the picture. Then answer the following questions.

1. What crop are the slaves harvesting?
2. What is the job of the man on the horse?
3. In what ways did slaves such as these fight back against slavery?

SUMMING UP   Abraham Lincoln did not like to see runaway slaves carried back into slavery. "I hate to see the poor creatures hunted down and caught," he said, "but I bite my tongue and keep quiet." Do you think it is right for people to stay silent when they think something bad is happening? Explain your answer.

5 FACTORIES GROW IN THE NORTHEAST

How did the Northeast become a manufacturing center?

Calico Printing machines in the early 1800s. What is meant by the term *Industrial Revolution*?

1. While the South was becoming more closely tied to slavery, great changes were taking place in the North. As you learned, most people had to make the things they needed by hand. For example, usually the women of the household spun yarn by using a spinning wheel. Then they wove the yarn into cloth with a hand loom. Making yarn on the wheel took much time. Women had to spend hour after hour at their wheels and looms to produce enough yarn and cloth to make clothes for their families. They needed a faster way to make yarn and weave it.

2. British inventors came to the rescue. In the mid-1760s James Hargreaves invented the spinning jenny. This machine could spin several threads at once. The old spinning wheel could not keep up with it. In 1769 James Watt, a Scottish inventor, built a new kind of steam engine. Now steam could be used to turn spinning wheels and other machines. In the 1780s Edmund Cartwright, an English inventor, invented a new kind of loom for weaving. It was run by steam power. With the help of these and other inventions, people could make cloth faster, more cheaply, and in greater amounts than ever before.

3. The new machines were becoming bigger and more expensive. Only rich people could buy them. The machines were placed in factories, and workers were hired to run them. The spinning and weaving of cloth had now been taken out of the home. This change in making goods—from hand to machine, from home to factory—is called the Industrial Revolution.

4. England did not want to share its new machines with other nations. It passed laws forbidding anyone to take plans or models of the new machines out of the country. In spite of these laws, the new inventions spread to America through the efforts of Samuel Slater. Slater had worked in the factories in England and had learned how to make a machine for spinning thread. Slater then had come to the United States. In 1790 he set up, from memory, a spinning machine and a power loom in Rhode Island.

5. The first factories in the United States were started in New England. There were several reasons for the beginning of factories in the northeastern states. For a long time, Americans bought their manufactured goods from England. During the War of 1812, people in the United States could not get these goods from England. At the same time, the war kept American ships at home. The seaports of Boston and Salem were not busy. Therefore, the traders and ship owners used some of their idle money to start the first factories.

6. The early factories had to be built near a source of water power. New England had many streams to provide the power. Later, when machines were run by steam, coal was needed. Nearby Pennsylvania had a vast supply of coal that was easy to reach.

7. The new machines could not be run without workers. The sandy New England soil had never been good farmland. Therefore, many people in New England were willing to leave their farmlands to work in the factories. Also, from 1820 to 1860, many people came to the United States from Europe. Most of these people settled in the cities of the Northeast where they could find work in the factories. Very few moved to the South looking for work. They would have a hard time finding jobs where there was a large supply of slave labor.

8. The population of the Northeast grew rapidly. By 1860 there were about 17,500,000 people in the Northeast, making it the most thickly settled part of the United States. Cities grew in size as people crowded together to be near their places of work. As the use of workers who were not slaves increased, the use of slave labor dropped. After the Revolutionary War, many northern slave owners freed their slaves. By the middle of the 19th century, there were about 250,000 free blacks living and working in the North.

9. In the Northeast a whole new class of people arose — the factory workers. The life of a factory worker was quite hard. The factory buildings were often dirty. Sometimes the work was dangerous and there were few safety precautions. The working day was also very long, often from 12 to 15 hours. Many of the workers in factories were women and children. The children were as young as seven or eight years of age. Their families sent them to work to help add to the family income. Child factory workers worked as long as everyone else. In spite of the long hours and hard work, pay was low for everyone. Men received about $5 per week; women about $2; and children about $1 per week. Although wages were low, prices were also low. A room and meals cost $1.25 or $2.00 per week. Women could get away from factory work by marrying someone with a good job. Men could escape by moving to cheap land in the West. Children had a more difficult time escaping. In time, laws and regulations improved the lives of factory workers and helped improve the factory system.

REVIEWING CHAPTER 4

Slave or Free Person

Which phrases describe the life of slaves and which describe the life and rights of free people? Put the letter S before those items that describe slaves and an F before those that describe free people.

1. Got paid for their work
2. Could not leave their place of work
3. Had the right to vote
4. Could not travel without permission
5. Could own property
6. Were the property of other people
7. Could go to school
8. Could get a job of their own choice

I. What is the main purpose of Chapter 5?

  a. To tell how the Northeast became a center of manufacturing
  b. To explain what is meant by the Industrial Revolution
  c. To tell about the effects of the invention of the steam engine
  d. To describe how the first factories were started

II. Choose the correct answer or answers.

1. New inventions spread to the United States because
    a. England wanted to share its inventions with other people
    b. Samuel Slater came to the United States and built the first of the new machines here
    c. James Watt came to America and explained his invention
2. New England became a center of manufacturing because
    a. it had the raw materials needed for making clothes
    b. southern planters put their money into northern factories
    c. many people in New England had the money to start factories
3. How did the machines change the way of living in the North?
    a. Jobs became harder and took more time.
    b. There was a rapid growth in cities and population.
    c. Many people decided to move to the South.
4. Why was labor available to the factories in the Northeast?
    a. There were many black slaves in the North.
    b. Farmland was poor, and so many people left their farms to work in the factories.
    c. Hard times had caused workers to leave the South.
5. Which two people helped to bring about the Industrial Revolution?
    a. Phillis Wheatley
    b. James Watt
    c. James Hargreaves

III. Decide whether each statement is true or false. The underlined words are clues to help you decide. If a statement is false, change the underlined word or words to make it true.

1. Because of the Industrial Revolution, work was now done by <u>labor-saving machines</u>.
2. The first source of power for machines was <u>water</u>.
3. The first American factories were located in New England because of the <u>fertile soil there</u>.
4. Before 1812 the United States depended largely on <u>England</u> for manufactured goods.
5. The early factory workers were paid <u>high</u> wages.
6. Factories were built near a <u>source of power</u>.
7. The Industrial Revolution began in <u>England</u>.

POPULATION OF PRINCIPAL CITIES   Read the chart below carefully. Then answer the following questions.

	POPULATION	
	1820	1850
1. Boston, Massachusetts	43,298	136,881
2. New York, New York	123,706	515,547
3. Philadelphia, Pennsylvania	112,772	340,045
4. Baltimore, Maryland	62,738	169,054
5. Charleston, South Carolina	24,780	42,985
6. New Orleans, Louisiana	27,176	116,375

1. Which was the most populated city in 1820?
2. Which was the most populated city in 1850?
3. Which city had the largest population growth between 1820 and 1850? What are some reasons for this growth?
4. Which city had the smallest population growth between 1820 and 1850?
5. What was the combined population growth of New York, Philadelphia, Boston, and Baltimore from 1820 to 1850?

What were the differences between the North and the South before 1860? Complete this chart in your notebook.

DIFFERENCES	NORTH	SOUTH
1. Population		
2. Ways of Making a Living		
3. Sources of Labor		
4. Other Differences		

Thinking It Through
What conditions are necessary for manufacturing to succeed?

6 SLAVERY CAUSES BITTER FEELINGS BETWEEN NORTH AND SOUTH

How did the slavery issue further divide North and South?

1. A serious argument over slavery took place in Congress when Missouri asked to be admitted to the Union in 1819. Missouri was a territory making up part of the Louisiana Purchase. Many settlers in Missouri came from southern states. Slavery was allowed in Missouri. When the Missouri request to be admitted reached the House of Representatives, a northern representative attached special conditions to it. No more slaves were to be brought into Missouri. In addition, all children born of slaves after Missouri became a state would become free when they reached the age of 25. These conditions would limit slavery in Missouri. The House of Representatives voted in favor of statehood for Missouri under these conditions. The northern states had more representatives in the House since they had a larger population than southern states. The Senate voted against this bill and so it did not become law.

2. In December 1819, Maine also asked to be admitted to the Union. The House of Representatives was ready to approve Maine's request. There was no slavery in Maine. However, at first the Senate would not allow Maine to enter the Union. There were 11 free states and 11 slave states in 1819. Therefore, both sections of the country had the same number of senators. Southern senators refused to admit Maine as a free state unless the northern senators would agree to admit Missouri as a slave state. In 1820 Henry Clay of Kentucky helped arrange a compromise that allowed both Maine and Missouri to enter the Union.

3. By means of the Missouri Compromise, as the new agreement was called, several laws were passed. Congress admitted Maine as a free state and Missouri as a slave state. Slavery had now spread to one more state. At the same time Congress set up a line westward across what was left of the Louisiana Purchase. This line, set at 36° 30′ North, divided free and slave territory. (See map on page 303.) In the future, any states formed north of the line would be free states. The states formed south of the line would be open to slavery. Northerners thought this line would help their fight against slavery.

4. An even bigger fight broke out over a **tariff** that Congress passed in 1828. A tariff is a tax on goods from abroad. Tariffs are sometimes used to help support American products. These taxes are added to the cost of foreign goods to make them more expensive. Therefore, American buyers tend to buy the less expensive goods made in the

Senator Daniel Webster defending the tariff in Congress. Why was the North in favor of the tariff and the South against it?

299

William Lloyd Garrison used his newspaper *The Liberator* to try to awaken white people to the evils of slavery. What did he mean when he said that people should not do evil so that good may come?

warships to Charleston, South Carolina. Fortunately, Congress worked out a compromise in 1833. Under this compromise, a new law made the tariff smaller—a little at a time—over the next ten years. South Carolina was satisfied and accepted the lower tariff.

6. In 1831 a man in Boston began to print a newspaper called the *Liberator*. He was William Lloyd Garrison. Garrison wanted to **abolish,** or do away with, slavery. He called on Congress to free all slaves and end slavery in the United States. Other men and women also wanted to get rid of slavery at once. They felt it was absolutely wrong for one person to own another. These people, both whites and free blacks, were called **abolitionists.** Wendell Phillips, Theodore Weld, Sarah and Angelina Grimké, David Walker, Sojourner Truth, Theodore Parker, and David Einhorn were some abolitionist leaders. They often asked

Frederick Douglass was the best-known black abolitionist. Douglass started the *North Star,* an antislavery newspaper. He also worked for the rights of northern blacks.

United States. The South, led by John C. Calhoun of South Carolina, was strongly against the tariff. Southerners felt the tariff favored the North, with its factories, over the South. They argued that the Constitution did not allow such laws. Vice-President Calhoun argued that when Congress passed such an unfair law, a state had the right to **nullify** it, or set it aside.

5. In 1832 Congress passed another tariff. South Carolina became angry. The people of that state sent delegates to a special convention. They declared the law unconstitutional. They would not collect the tariff in their state. They threatened to **secede,** or leave, the Union if the national government tried to force them to obey the tariff. Andrew Jackson, who was president at the time, proposed to enforce the law. He sent

people to disobey the laws of the government if these laws supported slavery. Einhorn said that when one group has no rights, other groups will soon lose theirs.

7. Many northerners did not like what the abolitionists were doing. Some northern factory owners were afraid they would lose business in the South. Many northern workers felt that blacks were not the equals of whites. For a while, some northerners used force to break up the abolitionists' meetings. An angry crowd once forced Garrision to take safety inside a jail. Elijah P. Lovejoy, another abolitionist, was murdered by a mob in Illinois. But this did not stop the abolitionist movement from growing. By 1840 it had over 150,000 members.

8. In 1852 Harriet Beecher Stowe wrote an antislavery book called *Uncle Tom's Cabin.* The book told the story of a cruel overseer called Simon Legree. Legree whipped Uncle Tom, a black slave, so badly that he died. The book was widely read in the North. It did much to convince northerners that slavery should be ended.

9. Some abolitionists worked secretly to help slaves escape. In doing so, they disobeyed the fugitive slave laws. The slaves were taken from one abolitionist house to another at night. They were dressed in disguises or hidden in farm wagons. Slaves were moved in secret farther and farther north until they reached safety in Canada. This chain of secret hiding places was called the Underground Railroad. Since the slaves were valuable, their owners demanded that the government force the abolitionists to obey the laws. But it was hard to enforce such laws when so many people in the North approved of the work of the Underground Railroad. Over 300 slaves were guided to freedom by Harriet Tubman, a courageous black woman.

10. Frederick Douglass was one of the most important black abolitionists. Although born a slave, he was taught to read and write. At his first opportunity, he escaped to the North. He eventually settled in Newport, Rhode Island, hoping to become a shipbuilder. White shipbuilders, however, did not want to work with a black person. Frederick Douglass found out that many northerners, even if they disapproved of slavery, did not care for blacks. Northern states did not let blacks vote or give evidence in court. Northern cities also kept blacks and whites apart, or **segregated,** in schools and other places. Frederick Douglass therefore began a lifelong struggle for equality. He toured the country giving lectures on the abolitionist struggle. He said, "The Negro must be free . . . not in Africa . . . but free in the United States!" He founded a freedom paper called *The North Star* in Rochester, New York.

Harriet Tubman was one of the heroic conductors of the Underground Railroad. She escaped slavery in 1849. Harriet Tubman helped more than 300 slaves escape to freedom and was a friend of the leading abolitionists. Why do you think many people called her "Moses"?

Decide whether the following statements apply to the North or to the South. Explain your answers.

1. Section of large farms or plantations
2. People worked in factories
3. Black slaves used for labor
4. Grew cotton and tobacco
5. Had largest cities in the nation
6. Had better land for farming
7. Developed busy canal and ocean-going trade
8. Built many miles of railroad

I. What is the main purpose of paragraphs 6 through 10?

  a. To describe the Missouri Compromise
  b. To tell about the work of the Underground Railroad
  c. To show how the North and South grew apart over slavery
  d. To describe the work of those who opposed slavery

II. Choose the correct answer.

1. South Carolina threatened to leave the Union if the
   a. national government enforced the tariff
   b. Supreme Court said the tariff was unconstitutional
   c. government did not permit them to raise more cotton
2. The desire to do away with slavery led to the
   a. work of abolitionist groups during the years 1820–1860
   b. passing of the Fugitive Slave Law
   c. election of President Jackson
3. The argument over whether states should be slave or free led to the
   a. Missouri Compromise of 1820
   b. Monroe Doctrine
   c. tariff laws from 1816 to 1833
4. The desire of some northerners to help runaway slaves led to the
   a. Missouri Compromise of 1820
   b. admission of Maine as a free state
   c. development of the Underground Railroad
5. The Missouri Compromise was passed in order to
   a. settle differences between North and South over the admission of free and slave states
   b. allow slavery in the states to be made from the Louisiana Purchase
   c. forbid slavery from spreading to more states

III. Decide whether each statement is true or false. The underlined words are clues to help you decide. If a statement is false, change the underlined word or words to make it true.

1. <u>Maine</u> was part of the Louisiana Purchase.
2. The Missouri Compromise admitted Missouri as a <u>slave</u> state.
3. The Underground Railroad was a <u>train</u> that brought the slaves to freedom.
4. Many northerners <u>refused to obey</u> the Fugitive Slave Laws.
5. Abolitionists were people who wanted to <u>keep slavery</u> in the South.

6. <u>John C. Calhoun</u> urged states to nullify laws they considered unconstitutional.
7. Runaway slaves were freed once they reached the <u>North</u>.
8. One of the leading abolitionists was <u>Frederick Douglass</u>.
9. <u>Sarah Grimké</u> guided over 300 slaves to freedom on the Underground Railroad.
10. Harriet Beecher Stowe wrote <u>*Uncle Tom's Cabin*</u>.

DEVELOPING IDEAS AND SKILLS **MAP SKILLS** *The Compromise of 1820*
Study the map. Then decide whether these statements are true or false. Explain your answers.

The Missouri Compromise of 1820

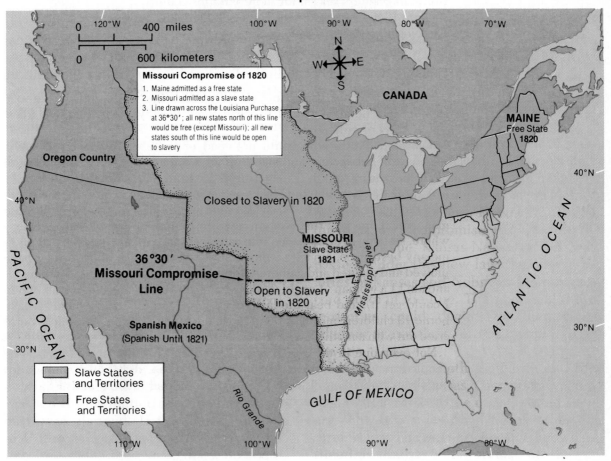

Missouri Compromise of 1820
1. Maine admitted as a free state
2. Missouri admitted as a slave state
3. Line drawn across the Louisiana Purchase at 36°30′; all new states north of this line would be free (except Missouri); all new states south of this line would be open to slavery

1. Most of the Louisiana Purchase was open to slavery.
2. Missouri was south of the line marked at 36° 30′.
3. Missouri was admitted to the United States as a slave state.
4. The Mississippi River divided the free and slave territories.
5. The southwest boundary of the United States in 1820 was the Rio Grande.

6. The fighting over slavery even extended to Congress. On May 19, 1856, Senator Charles Sumner of Massachusetts spoke out strongly against slavery. He called the proslavery leaders in Kansas "murderers and robbers." He also said some nasty things about a senator from South Carolina. Two days later, one of the South Carolina senator's friends, a member of the House, stopped at Sumner's desk. He beat Sumner with a cane until Sumner fell, bloodied, to the floor. It took over three years for Sumner to recover from the attack. The North was shocked. But many southerners believed that Sumner deserved the beating.

7. In 1857 an important case concerning slavery came before the United States Supreme Court. This was the case of Dred Scott, a black slave. Dred Scott had been taken by his master into free territory. When he was taken back to a slave state, Scott declared that he was a free man because he had lived in free territory. Helped by abolitionists, he took his case to the Supreme Court. The decision of the Court was an important one.

8. The Supreme Court ruled that Dred Scott was not free. It said that Congress cannot take a person's property, and a slave is just that—property. It said that slaves do not have the rights of citizens. Congress cannot keep slavery out of the territories because this would be the same as taking away a person's property. Therefore, ruled the Court, Congress had no right to pass the Missouri Compromise in the first place. Dred Scott was still a slave. This decision of the Court meant that Congress could not keep slavery out of new states when they were formed. You can imagine the feelings in the North and South over this decision. Many northerners joined the Republican party to work against the spread of slavery.

9. In 1858 an election for the office of United States senator was held in Illinois. The two candidates were Stephen A. Douglas and Abraham Lincoln. Douglas had written the Kansas-Nebraska Act. He was running for reelection to the office. Lincoln belonged to the new Republican party. The two men held a series of debates, or talks. In the debates, Lincoln argued that slavery was wrong and should not be allowed to spread. Douglas said it was up to the people in the territories to decide whether or not they should have slavery. Lincoln lost the election. How-

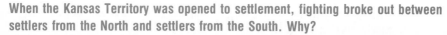

When the Kansas Territory was opened to settlement, fighting broke out between settlers from the North and settlers from the South. Why?

Election debate between Abraham Lincoln and Stephen Douglas. What was the stand of each on the slavery issue?

Virginia. He wished to give the slaves guns and ammunition to revolt against their masters. He called on the slaves to follow him, but few did. In a few days, he was captured by the United States Marines, led by Colonel Robert E. Lee. Brown was found guilty of treason for attacking government property and was hanged.

Federal troops enter the weapons storehouse at Harpers Ferry. Why had Brown and his followers taken over the storehouse?

ever, he became well known for his stand against slavery in the territories.

10. Another person working against slavery was John Brown of New England. He had taken part in the Kansas wars and in an Underground Railroad in Pennsylvania and Ohio. He thought these ways of fighting slavery were too slow. He wanted to use force to free the slaves. In 1859, with his five sons and a few followers, he captured a government storehouse at Harpers Ferry in

REVIEWING
CHAPTER 6

Choose the best answer.

1. Abolitionists were a group who favored
   a. extending slavery to the West
   b. the tariff laws
   c. freedom for black slaves
2. The *Liberator* was the name of a
   a. military hero
   b. pamphlet by Thomas Jefferson
   c. paper published by William L. Garrison
3. The Missouri Compromise dealt with
   a. inventions
   b. slavery
   c. tariffs

4. The Underground Railroad was the
   a. first railroad in the United States
   b. system of escape for black slaves
   c. secret means of sending messages to Washington
5. *Uncle Tom's Cabin* was written by
   a. Angelina Grimké
   b. Frederick Douglass
   c. Harriet Beecher Stowe

I. What is the main purpose of Chapter 7?

　　a. To describe the Lincoln-Douglas debates
　　b. To describe the raid of John Brown
　　c. To identify the events that led directly to the Civil War
　　d. To tell about the Compromise of 1850

II. Choose the correct answer.

1. Fighting broke out in Kansas as a result of
　　a. a dispute over gold claims
　　b. an argument over how the land should be used—for farming or raising cattle
　　c. bitter feelings between settlers who wanted Kansas to be a free state and others who wanted it to be a slave state
2. The Republican party was formed in order to
　　a. keep slavery from spreading to the territories
　　b. build a railroad through the Southwest to the Pacific Coast
　　c. obtain the right to vote for women
3. Abraham Lincoln became well known throughout the country as a result of his
　　a. heroism in the Mexican War
　　b. leadership of the abolitionists
　　c. debates with Stephen Douglas
4. The Dred Scott decision made northerners feel that the Supreme Court favored the South because it
　　a. declared the idea of states' rights to be unconstitutional
　　b. declared that a state could disobey a law of Congress
　　c. stated that Congress could not keep slavery out of the territories
5. John Brown raided Harpers Ferry in order to
　　a. hold some people for ransom
　　b. force Virginia to leave the Union
　　c. start a revolt among the slaves in the South

III. Decide whether each statement agrees or disagrees with what you have read. If the statement disagrees, explain why.

1. Dred Scott was declared to be a free man because he had lived for a time in a free state.
2. The Republican party was a group of men who wanted to keep slavery from spreading.
3. As a result of his debates with Douglas, Lincoln was elected as a senator from Illinois.
4. The Compromise of 1850 brought an end to arguments about slavery.
5. Lincoln did not want slavery in any new states that were made from the territories.
6. The Wilmot Proviso aimed at keeping slavery from any territory gained from Mexico.
7. The Compromise of 1850 was needed because the gold rush had brought many people to California.

MAP SKILLS *The Compromise of 1850*
**Study the map. Then decide whether these statements are true or false.
Explain your answers.**

The Compromise of 1850

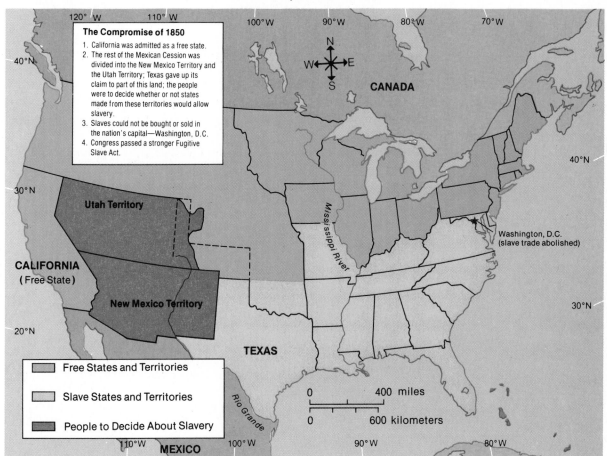

The Compromise of 1850

1. California was admitted as a free state.
2. The rest of the Mexican Cession was divided into the New Mexico Territory and the Utah Territory; Texas gave up its claim to part of this land; the people were to decide whether or not states made from these territories would allow slavery.
3. Slaves could not be bought or sold in the nation's capital—Washington, D.C.
4. Congress passed a stronger Fugitive Slave Act.

CANADA

Utah Territory

CALIFORNIA
(Free State)

New Mexico Territory

Mississippi River

Washington, D.C.
(slave trade abolished)

TEXAS

Rio Grande

Free States and Territories

Slave States and Territories

People to Decide About Slavery

0   400 miles

0   600 kilometers

MEXICO

1. According to the Compromise of 1850, the settlers in the New Mexico Territory would decide whether or not to allow slavery.
2. According to the Compromise of 1850, slavery was allowed in California.
3. After 1850 slaves could not be bought and sold in the nation's capital.
4. After 1850 all the land west of the Mississippi River was closed to slavery.
5. By 1850 the United States had obtained Mexican territory that stretched to the Pacific Ocean.
6. By 1850 the land taken from Mexico had been made into two territories and one state.

309

Arrange these events in their proper order, beginning with the event that took place first.

The Mexican War
The Missouri Compromise
The forming of the Republican party
Bleeding Kansas
John Brown's raid
The passing of a new Fugitive Slave Law
Lincoln-Douglas debates

Thinking It Through

Which section, North or South, seemed to get the better of the Compromise of 1850? Why?

If Lincoln believed slavery was wrong, why do you think he did not want to interfere with slavery in the South?

Letting states decide whether they would be free or slave was democratic, thought Stephen Douglas. Do you agree or disagree? Why?

8 LINCOLN IS ELECTED. THE CIVIL WAR BEGINS!

What were the strengths of the North and the South when war began?

1. The country was to elect a president in 1860. Lincoln was the candidate of the Republican party. The South made it known that it would leave the Union if Lincoln was elected.

2. On February 12, 1809, Abraham Lincoln was born in a log cabin in Kentucky. He grew up on the Indiana frontier. He had little formal education, but he was a bright boy and read many books. When Abe was 21, his family moved to Illinois. He got a job as a clerk in a store in New Salem. In 1831 he made a trip by flatboat down the Mississippi River. He visited New Orleans, where he saw a slave market for the first time. Young Abe Lincoln was shocked. His great dislike for slavery began on this journey to the famous cotton port of the South. Lincoln was well liked in his hometown. The villagers loved to gather in the store and listen to his funny stories. While working in the store, Lincoln studied law. He became a lawyer. In 1846 he was elected to the House of Representatives in Washington, D.C. After serving one term, he returned to Illinois to practice law.

3. Lincoln believed that slavery was wrong. He wanted to keep slavery out of territories that were still free. He did not believe that Congress should stop slavery in the southern states. He felt that southern planters depended on their slaves. After Congress passed the Kansas-Nebraska Act, Lincoln became a leader in the fight against the spread of slavery. In 1858 he ran for election as senator from Illinois against Stephen Douglas. Lincoln lost the election

Abraham Lincoln. What do you think Lincoln meant when he said, "A house divided against itself cannot stand"?

Confederate soldiers fire on Fort Sumter, South Carolina. After the fort had been fired upon for 34 hours, the Union soldiers surrendered.

for senator. But his debates with Douglas made him one of the best-known men in America.

4. In 1860 the Republican party chose him to run for the office of president of the United States. Lincoln won the election. The South did not trust him. South Carolina quickly moved to **secede,** or leave, the Union. Six more slave states followed: Mississippi, Florida, Alabama, Georgia, Louisiana, and Texas. These seven states formed a new government, the Confederate States of America. Richmond, Virginia, soon became the capital of the new government.

5. Jefferson Davis, a Mississippi planter, became president of the Confederate States. Jefferson Davis was born in Kentucky. His family moved to the slave-holding country of the deep South. Unlike Lin-

coln, Davis had received a fine education. He was a graduate of the United States Military Academy at West Point. Along with Grant, Lee, and many other military leaders, he served in the Mexican War. Davis also had more experience in government than Lincoln did. He had been U. S. secretary of war. Also, he had been a member of both the House of Representatives and the Senate. When his state of Mississippi seceded from the Union, Davis left the Senate to head the Confederate government.

6. On March 4, 1861, Lincoln was sworn in as president of the United States. In his **inaugural address** (his first public speech as president), he said he would not let the southern states leave the Union. "A husband and wife can be divorced," he said, "but the different parts of the country cannot do this." He promised the South that he

would not interfere with slavery there. He said the South had to strike the first blow. Near the end of the speech he said, "We are not enemies, but friends."

7. The South did strike the first blow. On April 12, 1861, Confederate guns fired on Fort Sumter in the harbor of Charleston, South Carolina. The small force of Union soldiers there had to surrender. Four more southern states joined the Confederacy—Virginia, Arkansas, Tennessee, and North Carolina. This was the beginning of the Civil War, sometimes called the War Between the States.

8. Let us compare the strengths of the North and the South as they prepared for war. There were 22 million people in the North. The South had less than half that

Robert E. Lee, brilliant leader of the southern armies. Although he did not believe in slavery, Lee could not bring himself to side against his home state of Virginia when North and South went to war. What were the South's military strengths?

number, 9 million. Of these, about 3.5 million were black slaves. Many of these slaves continued to work on the farms and plantations. The North had more factories to manufacture guns, ammunition, and other things needed for war. The North had more railroads to move soldiers and supplies from place to place. The North had more ships and planned to use them to blockade southern ports. The government of the United States was a working government. The Confederate government was just beginning. Because of these strengths, the North expected to end the war quickly.

9. It might seem that all the advantages were on the side of the Union government. The South would face larger armies with superior equipment. But the South had some advantages, too. We have learned from reading about the Revolutionary War the advantage of fighting on home ground. During the Civil War, the fighting was largely in the South. Southern armies were defending their homes and fields. They had skilled and intelligent leaders. Many Confederate generals had graduated from West Point. When war came, these generals left the United States Army to fight for their home states. Among these generals were Robert E. Lee, Thomas "Stonewall" Jackson, and Jeb Stuart.

10. Robert E. Lee was born in Virginia on January 19, 1807. He was two years older than Lincoln. He grew up in a comfortable home and later was a brilliant student at West Point. He got his early military experience in the Mexican War. At the beginning of the Civil War, Lee was asked to command the Union armies. He turned down the offer. He did not believe in slavery, but he did not want to lead an army against his state of Virginia. When Virginia seceded, Lee resigned from the United States Army and took command of Virginia's military forces. To Lee and other southerners, one's state was still more important than the national government.

313

Match each name in Column A with the correct identification in Column B.

Column A

1. Harriet Beecher Stowe
2. Harriet Tubman
3. John Brown
4. Dred Scott
5. William Lloyd Garrison
6. Henry Clay
7. Stephen Douglas
8. Frederick Douglass

Column B

a. published the *Liberator*
b. offered another compromise to end arguments between North and South
c. wrote *Uncle Tom's Cabin*
d. denied freedom by the Supreme Court
e. was a leader of the Underground Railroad
f. believed the people in the territories should decide whether they wanted to be free or slave
g. tried to free slaves by force
h. was a leading black abolitionist

I. **What is the main purpose of Chapter 8?**

   a. To describe how the Civil War began
   b. To describe the career of Robert E. Lee
   c. To describe how the Confederacy was formed
   d. To discuss the election of Abraham Lincoln

II. **Choose the correct answer.**

1. What was Lincoln's purpose in fighting the Civil War?
   a. To abolish slavery
   b. To keep the Union together
   c. To punish the South
2. The Civil War began directly after
   a. the firing on Fort Sumter
   b. John Brown's raid
   c. the Compromise of 1850 was not accepted in the South
3. The North expected the war to end quickly because
   a. the North had more resources and people to wage war
   b. the South would be fighting in strange territory
   c. slaves would be kept on the plantations of the South
4. Robert E. Lee turned down an offer to command the Union armies because he
   a. felt that war should not be fought
   b. believed that slavery would continue
   c. did not want to lead an army against his home state
5. The Confederacy was formed in 1861 in order to
   a. promote factories in the South
   b. defend the southern ideas of government and way of life
   c. oppose the election of Lincoln

III. **Decide whether each statement is true or false. The underlined words are clues to help you decide. If a statement is false, change the underlined word or words to make it true.**

1. The disagreement between the North and South over <u>tariffs</u> was the main cause of the Civil War.
2. There were <u>eleven</u> states in the Confederate States of America.
3. <u>Every</u> state that had slaves withdrew from the Union in 1861. (See map on page 316.)
4. Robert E. Lee became commander of the <u>Union armies</u> at the start of the Civil War.
5. The War Between the States began at <u>Fort Sumter</u>, South Carolina.
6. Abraham Lincoln was educated <u>in an eastern school</u>.
7. <u>Virginia</u> was one of the states that withdrew from the Union.
8. The <u>South</u> had few factories at the outbreak of the war.
9. Most slaves <u>left the South</u> when the war began.
10. Most of the fighting during the Civil War took place in the <u>South</u>.

DEVELOPING IDEAS AND SKILLS

PICTOGRAPH STUDY   *The Year 1860: A Comparison*

Study the graph. Then decide whether these statements are true or false.

The Year 1860: A Comparison

1. The population of the North was more than double the population of the South.
2. There was more farmland in the South than in the North.
3. The value of farmland was greater in the South than in the North.
4. There were no railroads and factories in the South.
5. The North had 3 1/2 times as many factories as the South.
6. This graph tells you why the South had so few factories.

The Union and the Confederacy, 1861

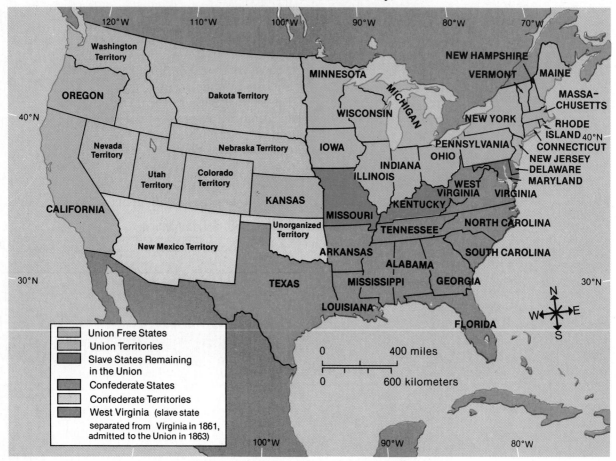

1. All states with slaves left the Union in 1861.
2. There were eight states in the Confederacy.
3. Two Union states were physically separated from the rest of the Union.
4. The Confederate states had a long coastline.
5. The entire nation was organized into states before the war.

SUMMING UP A. Issues between North and South. Complete the following chart in your
notebook.

NORTH'S OPINION	ISSUE	SOUTH'S OPINION
	Admission of Missouri	
	Dred Scott Decision	
	John Brown's Raid	

B. DEBATE: "The Civil War Could Have Been Avoided." Do you agree or disagree with this statement? In your notebook, list reasons for your opinion under one of these headings.

COULD HAVE BEEN AVOIDED	COULD NOT HAVE BEEN AVOIDED

Thinking It Through

When Lincoln took office as president of the United States in 1861, the outgoing president, James Buchanan, said to him, "If you are as happy on entering the White House as I am in leaving it, you are the happiest man in this country." Why did Buchanan feel this way?

If you had been president in 1861, what would you have done when southern forces fired on Fort Sumter?

9 A LONG STRUGGLE IN THE MAKING

What were the plans of the North and the South to win the war?

1. The first great battle of the war was fought in the East. Part of the South's plan for victory was to move quickly north to seize Washington, D.C. The South gathered forces near Manassas Junction in Virginia. In July 1861, the Union army moved south to try to capture Richmond, Virginia, the capital of the Confederate States. The Union army met the Confederate army near Manassas Junction at Bull Run, only 30 miles (48 kilometers) from Washington, D.C. The Confederate army stood firm "as a wall" under the command of General Thomas Jackson. He earned the nickname "Stonewall" Jackson. The Union force was defeated and forced to return to Washington. The people of the North realized then that victory would not be easy. The defeat caused President Lincoln and Congress to call for more soldiers. General George McClellan was appointed to train the army for a long, hard fight.

2. Failing to win at Bull Run, the North shifted its fighting to the West. Part of the Confederate plan was to use a large part of its troops to defend the South. But the North wanted to cut the South in two. A large part of the Confederacy lay west of the Mississippi River. If the North could control the Mississippi, the South would not be able to send goods across the river. The southern armies in the East depended on the southwestern states for supplies. After dividing the South at the Mississippi, the North hoped also to cut the eastern Confederacy in two.

3. The Confederacy had built strongly guarded forts at points along the Mississippi. The Union had to capture Fort Henry on the Tennessee River and Fort Donelson on the Cumberland River. General Ulysses S. Grant and Admiral David Farragut played leading parts in the capture of these forts.

4. Ulysses S. Grant became the greatest general on the side of the North during the war. He was born in Ohio in 1822. When he was 17 years old, he entered West Point. After graduation, Grant became a lieutenant and fought in the Mexican War. Later he left the army and went into business. He did not stay long at any job. He had little success as a storekeeper, farmer, or lumberman. When the war broke out, he was 39 years old and seemed to be a failure. Because the North needed military leaders, he was given command of a regiment in Illinois. Within a short time, he proved he was a great officer.

5. In February 1862, Grant forced the Confederates to give up Forts Henry and Donelson. His next important battle was at

This painting by Winslow Homer shows Confederate soldiers held prisoners by the Union army. What do you imagine prisoners such as these thought when they were captured?

Shiloh in southern Tennessee. On the first day of fighting, the southern army almost defeated the northern army. But, with fresh troops, Grant won back the lost ground and defeated the Confederates. In late April, Admiral Farragut led a Union fleet in the capture of New Orleans. All the other forts along the Mississippi fell into Union hands, except for those at Vicksburg. That stronghold would be hard to take.

6. General Grant began the campaign against Vicksburg toward the end of 1862. He was helped by another able general, William T. Sherman. Vicksburg was too well defended to be taken by a direct attack. Grant surrounded the city and kept the Confederate forces from receiving food or help. On July 4, 1863, the fort surrendered. It was a great victory for the Union cause. The fall of Vicksburg gave the Union control of the Mississippi. Texas, Arkansas, and most of Louisiana were cut off from other states in the Confederacy.

7. Another part of the Union war plan was to blockade ports in the South. The blockade would keep the southern states from selling their cotton in Europe. The South had to sell cotton in order to get money and goods for the needs of the army and the people. But the Union warships formed a "wall" around the South. Southern ships then tried to "run the blockade." Some got through and returned with medicines and war supplies. But, for the most part, the blockade ruined the South's trade. The blockade was one of the most important reasons for the defeat of the South.

8. In an effort to break the blockade, the Confederacy made an unusual warship. They covered one of their wooden ships with iron plates and sent it out to sea. As a wooden ship, it had been called the *Merrimac*. The ship was renamed the *Virginia* after it was iron-clad, but still many people called it the *Merrimac*. Early in 1862, the *Merrimac* sank one Union ship and ran three others aground. Wooden ships were

General William T. Sherman

helpless against it. However, a northern engineer, John Ericsson, had built a new ship called the *Monitor*. Its deck was low in the water, and it too was covered with iron. In the middle it had a revolving turret with two large cannons. The two ships met in battle on March 9, 1862. After four hours of fighting, the *Merrimac* returned to port, never to fight again. This was the first battle between iron-clad ships. Wooden ships were never again useful as warships. The battle also ended Confederate hopes of breaking the Union blockade.

9. During the fighting in the West, another Union army in the East under General McClellan tried to capture Richmond. This attempt failed, too. Lee then decided to lead his army into northern territory. The Confederate plan was to march troops through Maryland and into Pennsylvania. The South hoped to cut off the Northeast from the Northwest and so force the North

319

Antietam, Maryland, 1862. President Lincoln and General George B. McClellan in the general's tent. Why was the battle of Antietam a significant event of the war?

the **Emancipation Proclamation.** In this proclamation, Lincoln said that all slaves were free in the parts of the Confederate States still fighting. Until then, people in the North had felt they were fighting to keep the Union together. Now they also felt they were fighting to free the slaves. However, the North had to win the war if the proclamation were to mean anything. The proclamation did not free slaves in the border states. This was because Lincoln wanted to keep the border states on the northern side. Nor did it free slaves in parts of the South already under northern control.

Thousands of southern slaves, seeking freedom, fled north to the Union army after Lincoln announced the Emancipation Proclamation. In what ways did this weaken the South's war effort?

to give up. In Maryland, one of the bloodiest battles of the war was fought at Antietam. Lee was not defeated, but his march was stopped. He took his army back into Virginia. The first invasion of the North had failed.

10. Lincoln's hopes were strengthened by the Battle of Antietam. He thought this would be the right time to do something about slavery. He issued a message called

REVIEWING
CHAPTER 8 Abraham Lincoln, Jefferson Davis, and Robert E. Lee were three leaders during the Civil War. Which man does each item describe?

1. Military leader of the South during the war
2. President of the United States in 1861
3. President of the Confederate States of America
4. Debated against Stephen Douglas on the question of slavery
5. Refused an appointment as commander of the Union armies

6. Opposed the spread of slavery into the territories
7. Served in the House of Representatives and the Senate and fought in the Mexican War
8. Lived on the frontier, studied by himself
9. Became a lawyer and entered politics in Illinois
10. Was considered a brilliant army officer

I. **What is the main purpose of Chapter 9?**

a. To present the Confederate plan to invade the North
b. To describe the early fighting in the Civil War
c. To tell about the life of Ulysses S. Grant
d. To describe the fighting in the West

II. **Choose the correct answer.**

1. Vicksburg was an important victory for the North because it
   a. brought a quick end to the war
   b. led to the capture of General Lee and his army
   c. gave the North control of the Mississippi River
2. Lee's first invasion of the North was stopped in
   a. Virginia
   b. Maryland
   c. Ohio
3. The South tried to break the northern blockade by
   a. building iron-clad boats
   b. capturing northern ports
   c. persuading Mexico to enter the war
4. The battle of the *Monitor* and the *Merrimac* was important because it
   a. ended the northern blockade
   b. led to the defeat of the northern navy
   c. meant that the days of the wooden warships were over
5. The North blockaded southern ports to
   a. prevent the South from bringing in slaves
   b. prevent the South from selling its cotton to Europe
   c. destroy all southern ports because of the firing on Fort Sumter

III. **Decide whether each statement agrees or disagrees with what you have read. If the statement disagrees, explain why.**

1. The Emancipation Proclamation freed all slaves throughout the entire United States.
2. The first important battle of the Civil War was fought in the East.
3. The blockade of southern ports had a great deal to do with the defeat of the South.
4. General Lee was stopped in his first attempt to invade the North.
5. Lincoln issued the Emancipation Proclamation as soon as he heard of the first defeat of the Union army.
6. All the Confederate states were located east of the Mississippi River.
7. The North was fighting the war to keep the Union together.

MAP SKILLS *The Union and Confederate Plans*
Study the map. Then decide whether these statements are true or false.
Support your decision.

The Union and Confederate Plans

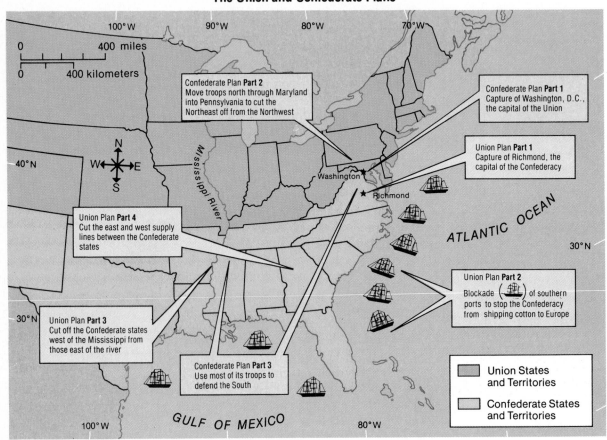

Confederate Plan **Part 2**
Move troops north through Maryland into Pennsylvania to cut the Northeast off from the Northwest

Confederate Plan **Part 1**
Capture of Washington, D.C., the capital of the Union

Union Plan **Part 1**
Capture of Richmond, the capital of the Confederacy

Union Plan **Part 4**
Cut the east and west supply lines between the Confederate states

Union Plan **Part 2**
Blockade (   ) of southern ports to stop the Confederacy from shipping cotton to Europe

Union Plan **Part 3**
Cut off the Confederate states west of the Mississippi from those east of the river

Confederate Plan **Part 3**
Use most of its troops to defend the South

Union States and Territories

Confederate States and Territories

1. The Union planned to do most of the fighting on its own soil.
2. The Confederacy depended on trade with Europe.
3. Part of the Union plan was to capture the Confederate capital.
4. Part of the Confederate plan was to capture the Union capital.
5. The Union blockade was limited to ports on the Atlantic Ocean.
6. If the Mississippi River were controlled by the North, the South would be divided in two.
7. The Confederacy planned to use a large part of its troops to defend its land.
8. The Union had a four-part plan to defeat the Confederacy.
9. This map shows how the Confederacy planned to defeat the Union.

Answer these questions about the cartoon.

1. Near what large city did this battle take place?
2. Who is watching this battle? Why?
3. What is the name of the battle?
4. Who won this battle?
5. What did the North learn from this battle?

"Easy Victory?"

SUMMING UP   Abraham Lincoln is often called "The Great Emancipator." Do you think this nickname is justified? Explain your answer.

10 LEE MEETS GRANT—THE WAR ENDS

How did the Civil War come to an end?

Sherman's march to the sea. About this march Sherman said, "If the people [of Georgia] raise a howl against my barbarity and cruelty, I will answer that war is war, and not popularity-seeking." Do you agree or disagree with Sherman? Explain.

1. In May 1863, Lee defeated the Union army at Chancellorsville, Virginia. After this victory, Lee once again led an army into the North. This time, he reached Pennsylvania. On July 1, he met the Union army at the little town of Gettysburg. A bloody battle was fought. In this battle, 140,000 men took part. The North held back Lee's armies for three days. At last, the southern forces weakened and began a return march to southern soil. The Battle of Gettysburg has been called the turning point of the war. Thousands of young men on both sides were killed in this terrible battle.

2. Southern hopes for victory received two crushing blows on July 4, 1863. Vicksburg surrendered to Grant, and Lee was stopped at Gettysburg. The Mississippi River was under northern control. The Confederacy was cut in two. The second invasion of the North had failed. How long could the Confederacy last?

3. In March of 1864, President Lincoln appointed General Grant to command all the Union armies. Grant had one aim: to force Lee to surrender. Grant's plan was simple. He would attack and attack until the Confederate army was unable to fight. Grant had more men, more supplies, and more equipment. During the summer of 1864, Grant slowly drove Lee farther and farther south toward Richmond.

4. In the meantime, two other Union generals were invading other parts of the South. General Philip Sheridan led a Union army through the Shenandoah Valley of Virginia. The rich farmlands of the valley were destroyed. General Sherman captured Atlanta in September 1864. From there his army marched across Georgia to the sea. His goal was Savannah, 200 miles (320 kilometers) to the southeast. Sherman's army destroyed not only railroads and bridges, but homes and farms as well. They took everything useful for the Union army. A few days before Christmas, Sherman entered Savannah. The "Deep South" was now separated from the rest of the Confederacy.

5. Through the summer of 1864, Grant forced Lee into battle. Lee's army became smaller and smaller. He could not replace his losses. Lee realized he could not defend Richmond any longer. He left the city on April 3, 1865, hoping to join with another Confederate army. Grant surrounded him, and Lee surrendered. On April 9, 1865, Grant accepted Lee's surrender at Appomattox Courthouse, Virginia. The end of the war had come.

6. The War Between the States had lasted four years. The South did not have as many men or supplies as the North. The North

had armed about 2,500,000 men; the South had armed 600,000. In the beginning, young men were eager to take part in the war. Both sides thought the fighting would be over quickly. As the war went on, fewer people volunteered. Both sides finally called men into service whether or not they volunteered. This is called a **draft.** In New York City, there were riots to protest the draft. A man in the North could avoid army service by paying $300 to the government, or by getting someone to take his place. Northern states even paid men to join the army. These payments were called **bounties.** Some men became bounty jumpers. They would join, collect the money, and then desert. Then they would enlist somewhere else to collect another bounty.

7. As the war continued, both sides punished each other terribly on the battlefield. Never before had so many American soldiers been killed or wounded. More than 110,000 Union soldiers and 90,000 Confederate soldiers died on the battlefield. Almost 400,000 other soldiers died of wounds and sickness. Most of the medical

A soldier killed at the Battle of Gettysburg. This picture was taken by a war photographer.

knowledge we have today had not yet been discovered. Doctors had only crude instruments for operations. They had very little medicine to cure diseases or to lessen the pain. Many Union and Confederate soldiers died in prison camps where conditions were terrible.

8. Women played an important role during the Civil War. They organized and provided relief for the wounded. Dorothea Dix organized a volunteer army nursing corps. She convinced the Union leaders that nurses were very important. She received a commission from the U. S. War Department to head the volunteer nurses. It became her job to set up military hospitals, to supply nurses, and to manage the flow of supplies. Clara Barton was a clerk in Washington, D.C. She set up a supply system for Union hospitals. As supplies were carried from one hospital to another, she often faced death from cannon fire. Clara Barton and other nurses also helped the wounded and dying in army camps and on the battlefield. She also reported the missing in action to Union families. Clara Barton later founded the American Red Cross to bring help to the suffering. Phoebe Levy Pember was one of the most outstanding hospital organizers in the South. She ran part of the military hospital in Richmond, Virginia. This hospital was one of the largest military hospitals in the world. In addition to these famous women, many others also played an important part in the Civil War. Women in both the North and the South made bandages and clothes for the soldiers. Because many men were off fighting, women worked in factories and on farms or plantations. They worked for long hours and little pay.

9. Many black soldiers took part in the Civil War. Before the summer of 1862 few blacks were fighting in the war. But then the North needed more soldiers. The Union army decided to draft black soldiers. The War Department began to draft black

troops. Several Northern states also began to organize their own black regiments. One famous black regiment was the 54th Massachusetts. This regiment led several raids into South Carolina. It also led an important attack on the fort guarding Charleston harbor. In that attack, more than one half of the 54th regiment was killed. A total of almost 200,000 blacks served in the Union army and navy. They fought in nearly every battle of the war. Even in the military, however, blacks did not get equal treatment with whites. They were sometimes assigned to do the worst chores around the camps. They were paid less than white soldiers until 1864 when Congress required equal pay for them. Black soldiers were often treated badly by both white soldiers and civilians. In spite of this, they fought bravely. Twenty black soldiers received the Congressional Medal of Honor, our government's highest award for bravery.

10. Conditions during the war were more severe in the South than in the North. The blockade stopped the South from getting the clothes, household goods, and medicines that the people needed. Women took charge of the farms and plantations. They had to sew the clothing, care for the wounded, and feed the armies that passed by. People had to do without many of the comforts they had had before the war. Most had enough food, for the South was a farm-ing region. However, railroads broke down and could not be repaired. It became harder and harder to carry food to the Confederate armies. Factories were built to make guns, but these factories could not take care of the needs of the entire Confederate army.

11. The North, too, felt the sorrow caused by the loss of life. However, very little fighting took place on northern soil. The factories developed new methods for supplying the vast number of soldiers. They turned out cannons, ammunition, uniforms, rails, and engines. As a result of the war, factories in the North would soon make it possible for the United States to be a leading industrial nation.

12. The Civil War turned the United States into a modern nation. In 1861 the national government at Washington, D.C., was not prepared to fight a war. The men in charge had no idea of how to carry on a long war. They changed orders from day to day. As the war continued, however, the government was reorganized. Washington grew from a small town to a large city. The War Department was soon able to supply the Union armies with everything from pots and pans to the largest cannon. New inventions were encouraged and used for the first time. These included machine guns, observation balloons, and ironclad warships. When the war ended, national government and industry had been strengthened.

A black infantry unit that served in the Union army.

In each group, one item or name does not belong with the others. Find the item that should not be in each group.

1. Northern generals: Sherman, Lee, Grant
2. Plans of the North: capture Washington, D.C.; blockade southern ports; control the Mississippi River
3. Advantages of the North: more factories to turn out guns, an experienced and working government, more farmland to supply food for the army
4. Purposes of the Emancipation Proclamation: to give northerners another reason for fighting, to free slaves in states that were fighting against the Union, to abolish slavery everywhere
5. Advantages of the South: outstanding army leaders, larger population, fighting on their own soil
6. Purposes of the blockade: to prevent the export of cotton to England, to prevent supplies from reaching the South, to attack southern warships
7. Union victories in the West: Antietam, Vicksburg, Fort Henry

I. What is the main purpose of Chapter 10?

   a. To tell about Sherman's march to the sea
   b. To explain how the Civil War came to an end
   c. To describe the conditions in the South during the war
   d. To describe the surrender of General Lee

II. Choose the correct answer.

1. How did Grant plan to defeat Lee?
   a. By defending the city of Washington
   b. By destroying the railroads in the South
   c. By following Lee's army and forcing the fight
2. Lincoln appointed Grant to command the Union forces because
   a. Grant had proved his value at Gettysburg
   b. Grant had won great victories in the West
   c. Grant was the oldest of the Union officers
3. Lee surrendered to Grant in April 1865 because
   a. valuable generals had been killed in battle
   b. his army was reduced in numbers and he could not replace his losses
   c. the leaders of the Confederate States had decided to return to the Union
4. Blacks were helpful to the northern cause because they
   a. raised food for soldiers on the plantations
   b. served in the armed forces
   c. inspected camps and cared for the sick and wounded

5. The turning point of the war took place at the Battle of
   a. Gettysburg
   b. Bull Run
   c. Atlanta
6. Some of the great loss of life in the war was caused by
   a. the use of poison gas, which was not expected
   b. the fact that there were no telegraph lines in the East
   c. the lack of medical supplies and modern operating instruments

III. Decide whether each statement is true or false. The underlined words are clues to help you decide. If a statement is false, change the underlined word or words to make it true.

1. The year <u>1863</u> marked the turning point of the war.
2. General Sherman captured <u>Atlanta</u> and marched to the sea.
3. After the fall of Vicksburg, <u>Grant</u> was placed in command of the Union armies.
4. The famous "march to the sea" ended at the port of <u>Savannah</u>.
5. The Civil War ended in the year <u>1865.</u>
6. <u>Clara Barton</u> was known for her work with wounded soldiers on the battlefields.
7. The War Between the States lasted <u>two</u> years.
8. Lee surrendered to Grant at <u>Appomattox Courthouse.</u>
9. <u>Both the North and South</u> found they had to draft soldiers into the army.
10. Very little fighting took place on <u>northern</u> soil during the war.

MAP SKILLS *The Civil War*
Study the maps. Then decide whether the statements on page 329 are true or false. Support your decision.

1861: The War Began

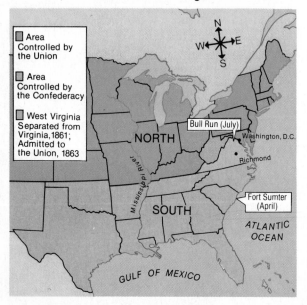

1862: The South Invaded the North

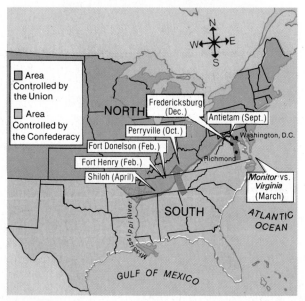

1863: Turning Point in the War

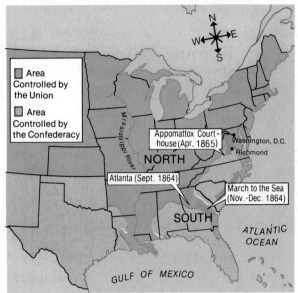

N W E S

Area Controlled by the Union

Area Controlled by the Confederacy

Gettysburg (July)

Chancellorsville (May)

Washington, D.C.

Richmond

NORTH

SOUTH

Mississippi River

Chattanooga (Nov.)

Vicksburg (May-July)

ATLANTIC OCEAN

GULF OF MEXICO

1864 and 1865: The North Wins the War

N W E S

Area Controlled by the Union

Area Controlled by the Confederacy

Appomattox Court-house (Apr. 1865)

Washington, D.C.

Richmond

NORTH

Atlanta (Sept. 1864)

March to the Sea (Nov.-Dec. 1864)

SOUTH

Mississippi River

ATLANTIC OCEAN

GULF OF MEXICO

1. The Battle of Gettysburg was one of the turning points of the Civil War.
2. The Civil War lasted five years.
3. Most of the fighting took place in the North.
4. The Confederacy was able to cut off the Northeast from the Northwest.
5. When the Union gained control of the Mississippi River at Vicksburg, it divided the South in two.
6. In 1862 the northward movement of Confederate troops was stopped at Perryville and Antietam.
7. In 1865 Union troops marched from Atlanta to the Atlantic Ocean.
8. Kentucky, Missouri, Delaware, and Maryland did not leave the Union.

SUMMING UP **IMPORTANT EVENTS OF THE CIVIL WAR** Complete the outline in your notebook.

A. The East
   1.
   2.
B. The West
   1.
   2.
C. On the Sea
   1.
   2.

11 RESTORING THE SOUTHERN STATES TO THE UNION

How were the Confederate states treated after the Civil War?

1. The Civil War came to an end on April 9, 1865. Four years of war had exhausted the nation. In the North, soldiers returned home to look for jobs. In the South, soldiers returned to find much of their land destroyed. They needed to do a great deal of work to rebuild their homes and to grow crops. Almost 4 million slaves had been freed. They also faced many problems at the war's end. They needed places to live and jobs to support themselves and their families. In March 1865, just before the war ended, Congress had passed a law setting up the Freedmen's Bureau. Its job was to provide work, food, medical supplies, and clothing for poor whites and freed blacks alike. It also supported the education of blacks.

2. Equally important was solving the problem, "How should the victorious North treat the defeated South?" Long before the end of the war, President Lincoln had made plans for the South for the time when peace would come. He did not want to punish the states that had seceded. He wanted them returned to the Union as soon as possible. Lincoln did not live to carry out his plans. On April 14, 1865, he was killed in a theater by John Wilkes Booth, an actor who favored the Confederacy. The Union lost its beloved leader only five days after the surrender of Lee.

3. The new president, Andrew Johnson, was a southern Democrat. He had once owned slaves himself. Following Lincoln's

The assassination of President Lincoln was a blow to both the North and the South. Why?

plan, he made it clear that he would welcome the southern states back into the Union. In state after state, former Confederate leaders put themselves into power again. They drew up new constitutions. They accepted the new 13th Amendment. (This amendment had been passed in 1865. It ended slavery.) These white southern leaders drew up a series of laws called the Black Codes. These state laws sharply limited the rights of the **freedmen.** Freedmen were the men, women, and children who had been slaves. The southern states elected representatives to Congress. Many of these representatives were former Confederate leaders.

4. When Congress met, many of its members were angry with President Johnson. The Republican party was in control. Some of its leaders, Charles Sumner and Thaddeus Stevens, disagreed sharply with Johnson. These members of Congress were called Radical Republicans. They felt that the president had no power to readmit states to the Union. Only Congress could do that. They wanted to punish the South for leaving the Union and bringing on such a costly war. They wanted to give full rights to the newly freed blacks. They felt that the Black Codes would set up a new form of slavery. Finally, they refused to seat former Confederate leaders in Congress.

5. Under the leadership of Sumner and Stevens, Congress went ahead with its own plan for the **Reconstruction,** or the rebuilding, of the South. It passed a bill that continued the Freedmen's Bureau. It also passed the Civil Rights Act of 1866, giving citizenship to all persons, except Indians, born in the United States. President Johnson vetoed, or rejected, both of these bills. He thought the laws were too hard on the South. However, Congress passed both bills over the president's veto. They became laws.

6. Many Republican members of Congress were afraid that the Civil Rights

Union soldiers were sent to the South to keep order after the Civil War. What feelings do you think southerners had toward these troops? Why?

Act of 1866 might be ruled unconstitutional. So they proposed the 14th Amendment to the Constitution. This amendment would make former slaves United States citizens. It also stated that no former Confederate leaders could vote or hold office. The Republicans supported this amendment. President Johnson did not. In the congressional elections of 1866, he "took his case" to the people. Johnson asked them to vote for men who would support his policies. The majority of the people did not. The Radical Republicans were now in full control of both houses of Congress.

7. With this new support, the Radical Republicans moved quickly to carry out the amendment and their plans for Reconstruction. The southern states were to draw up new constitutions. Former Confederate leaders and soldiers could not vote or hold office. Freed black men were given the

right to vote and hold office. The new state governments had to accept the 14th Amendment before they would be readmitted to the Union. Until they accepted it, the South was divided into five military districts. Each district was ruled by a United States general supported by federal troops.

8. By 1868 new state and local governments had been set up in the South. The new governments were made up mainly of two groups. The larger group was made up of white men, many of whom had opposed the Confederacy. Some of these whites were from the North. They were called **carpetbaggers** because they had carried their belongings to the South in small carpetbags. Southern whites who had not fought in the Civil War were also in the new governments. They favored Congress's Reconstruction program and were called **scalawags.** The smaller group in the new governments was made up of black men. Some were ministers, lawyers, and teachers. Others were ex-slaves.

9. Many in both the white and the black groups had very little training for their new jobs. As a result, some bad things were done as well as some good things. Some lawmakers, black and white, used their power to make money for themselves and their friends. On the other hand, they passed laws setting up free public schools for blacks and whites. They rebuilt streets, roads, and bridges. They made taxes fairer. Men no longer had to prove they owned property before being allowed to vote.

10. From 1868 to 1876, black men took part in government at all levels. The 15th Amendment protected the right of black American men to vote. Congress proposed this amendment in 1869 and it was approved in 1870. On the local level, blacks became mayors, sheriffs, and town clerks. They served in state legislatures. On the national level, 14 black men were elected to the House of Representatives. Some of them were former slaves. Two other blacks,

Voting in a state election during Reconstruction. Which amendment protected the right of black American men to vote?

Blanche K. Bruce and Hiram R. Revels, were sent to the United States Senate from Mississippi.

11. The differences between President Johnson and Congress grew worse. In 1868 Congress passed a law reducing his powers. The president decided to ignore this law. When he did, the House of Representatives **impeached** him. This means the House accused him of doing something wrong. They charged him with disobeying a law passed by Congress. Then he was tried by the Senate. If the Senate upheld the charges, he would lose the presidency. Johnson was not found guilty of the charge by only one vote! Johnson remained in office until the end of his term in 1869.

12. The new president, Ulysses Grant, agreed with Congress's policies. Federal troops remained in the South, giving support to the new governments. In the meantime, white southerners became more and

more opposed to Reconstruction. They blamed their problems on Congress, the federal troops, and the freedmen who now helped run the governments. They set out to win back their places in the state governments in the South. All over the South, white southerners formed secret groups or societies. The main purpose of these societies was to keep blacks from voting. The Ku Klux Klan was the most well known of the secret groups. Members of this group dressed in white robes. They rode at night to beat or kill those blacks who voted or held office in the new governments. They also attacked white supporters of blacks. By keeping blacks from voting, the whites soon gained control of the state governments.

13. Things had changed in the North, too. Sumner and Stevens had died. Few northerners continued to show their concern for the rights of black Americans. They often believed the reports about the dishonesty of black people in the state legislatures. They were becoming more interested in building railroads and making their mills and factories grow even larger. By 1877 the federal troops who occupied the South had left. The southern states were now under the control of white Democratic leaders. Reconstruction was over.

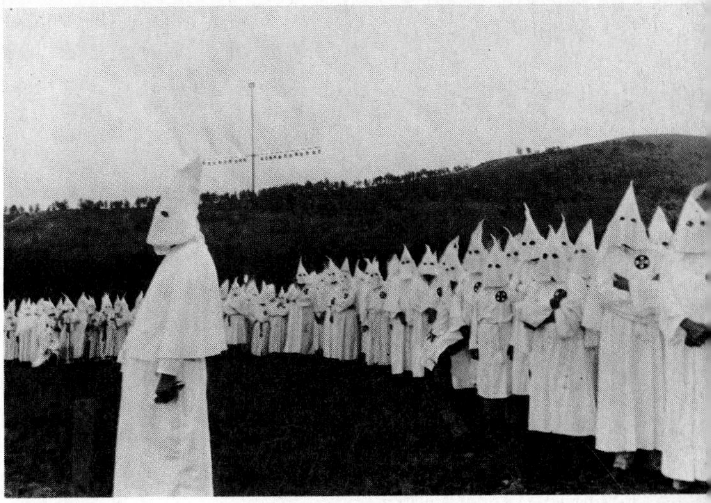

The Ku Klux Klan, a secret organization, used illegal threats and violence to frighten black people and also white people who supported Reconstruction. After the Reconstruction period, the KKK used terror to maintain white political control.

REVIEWING CHAPTER 10

Find the missing words.

1. The turning point of the Civil War was the Battle of ________.
2. Lincoln appointed ________ as the commander of the Union armies before the close of the war.
3. The Civil War ended in the year ________.
4. The Union general who captured Atlanta, Georgia, and marched to the sea was ________.
5. The last battles of the war took place around the city of ________.
6. The great Confederate general who surrendered to Grant was ________.
7. Both the North and South used a ________ to bring men into the army.
8. The North attempted to cut off the trade of the South by means of a ________.
9. During the war ________ set up a way of supplying Union hospitals.

I. What is the main purpose of Chapter 11?

    a. To discuss the impeachment of President Johnson
    b. To describe changes in the Constitution
    c. To explain the steps taken to restore the South to the Union
    d. To describe how blacks were kept from voting in the South

II. Choose the correct answer.

1. Lincoln could not carry out his plans for Reconstruction because he was
    a. disliked by the South
    b. killed shortly after the war
    c. defeated for reelection as president
2. President Johnson was impeached because he
    a. was accused of treason
    b. wanted to punish the South
    c. was charged with disobeying a law of Congress
3. Which of the following was NOT included in Congress's plan for Reconstruction?
    a. The South was to be divided into five military districts.
    b. Blacks were not to be active in the local governments.
    c. Southern states would have to accept the 14th Amendment before being readmitted to the Union.
4. The most important result of the Civil War was that
    a. the Union of states was saved
    b. factories were started in the South
    c. new territories were brought into the Union
5. Congress organized the Freedmen's Bureau to
    a. provide food, medical supplies, clothing, and schools to southern whites and blacks
    b. give citizenship to freed slaves
    c. give black people the right to vote

III. Decide whether each statement agrees or disagrees with what you have read. If the statement disagrees, explain why.

1. Lincoln wanted to let the states which had seceded take their place in the Union as soon as possible.
2. Johnson's plan to rebuild the South was opposed by Congress.
3. Blanche K. Bruce was a black senator from New York.
4. The 13th Amendment ended slavery in the United States.
5. The 15th Amendment said that no state has a right to leave the Union.
6. The Ku Klux Klan took the law into its own hands.
7. The 14th Amendment said that no person in the United States may be kept from voting because of his race or color.
8. Congress sent troops to the South to make sure its laws would be obeyed.

PICTURE SYMBOLS   These pictures should help you recall parts of the chapter you have read. Describe the main idea of each picture.

SUMMING UP   Put the following events in the order in which they happened.

Grant became president.
Federal troops left the South.
Amendment was passed to protect the voting right of blacks.
Lincoln was assassinated.
Johnson was impeached.

Thinking It Through

If you had been president in the years after the Civil War, how would you have treated the southern states that had left the Union? Explain.

Do you think the period of Reconstruction was successful in binding the nation's wounds, as Lincoln had hoped? Explain.

12 FROM SLAVERY TO SEGREGATION

What were some of the changes in the South after 1877? What were some of the problems black people faced?

Cotton mills in the South after Reconstruction. What were some of the problems these workers had to face?

1. The Industrial Revolution came to the South after 1865. In many small towns, business leaders raised enough money to start small factories. Before long, there were many cotton and flour mills and furniture and tobacco factories. Factory workers were chiefly poor whites from the hills. They worked 12 hours a day, six days a week for low wages. The workers depended on the factory owners for their jobs, their houses, and their food supplies.

2. Mining also expanded. Great coal fields were opened in the Appalachian highlands from Maryland to Alabama. Great deposits of iron were found all the way from Virginia through northern Alabama to Arkansas. Birmingham, Alabama, became a busy iron and steel center by 1890. Despite the destruction left by the war, the old railroads were quickly rebuilt while new ones were being built. By 1890 the South had a railroad system twice as large as that of 1860.

3. Despite the new mills and factories, farming remained the chief source of wealth in the South. The war, of course, had brought changes. The freeing of the slaves meant that the southern planters had to work out a new labor system. They had land to be farmed but no money to pay wages. The freed blacks and poor whites had no money to buy or rent the land. But they were willing to work. To get farming going again, the planters divided their land into small farms. Then they rented these pieces of land to farmers. The planters provided cabins, seed, and tools for the farmers, but no wages. When the cotton or tobacco crop was in, the farmers turned over part (usually one-third) of what they raised to the landowner as rent for the land. The farmers gave the landowner another part (often one-third) as rent for tools, seed, and fertilizer. In other words, the farmers *shared* part of their crops with the planters. For this reason, these farmers were called **sharecroppers.**

4. Poverty was not the only problem southern blacks had to live with. Many southern whites had not forgiven Congress for the Reconstruction laws. As soon as these whites regained control of the state governments, they drew up a new set of laws to keep whites and blacks apart, or segregated. These laws were called Jim Crow laws. The name Jim Crow may have come from a well-known song of the 1830s. One of the first Jim Crow laws said that

blacks and whites had to ride in separate railroad cars. Blacks took these laws to the Supreme Court. In 1896 the Court ruled that "separate but equal" railroad cars for black people were lawful. The decision opened the way for more Jim Crow laws. These laws separated blacks from whites in restaurants, hotels, schools, and hospitals. Under segregation laws, black people did not seem to benefit much from the ending of slavery.

5. Beginning in Mississippi in 1890, the states in the South adopted new constitutions. These new constitutions took the vote away from many blacks. Some states limited the right to vote to persons who could read and write an article of the United States Constitution. Other states taxed each person who wanted to vote. This **poll tax,** as it was called, was small. However, it kept many poor blacks from voting. Finally, some southern states passed laws that allowed a man to vote if his father or grandfather had voted in 1867. This law allowed many poor whites to vote even if they could not read or write or afford to pay the tax. Of course, many blacks did not qualify because their fathers and grandfathers had not been allowed to vote in 1867. Because of these laws, the number of black persons who were able to vote dropped sharply. This meant that black Americans had little or no voice in local government.

6. In addition, many blacks were not safe from personal harm. Blacks were sometimes **lynched.** This meant that they were judged guilty without a trial, and then killed by a mob. From 1880 to 1910, over 3,000 black people were lynched in the South, mostly by hanging. Often a single crime by a black person, or the rumor of a crime, sent white mobs streaming into black neighborhoods, ready to burn homes or kill innocent people. In many cases, this treatment continued without strong protest from people in the North.

7. In spite of their hardships, many blacks in the South wanted an education. Many of the first schools in black communities were started with money and teachers from the North. Among these schools was Hampton Institute in Virginia. One of its first students was Booker T. Washington. He was born a slave. To stay in school, he worked as a janitor. When Washington graduated, he became a teacher. Later he founded Tuskegee Institute in Alabama. Other blacks eager to learn went to his school. Washington believed that students should learn useful skills, such as carpentry, bricklaying, or mechanics, in addition to book learning. Such skills would help them earn a good living and permit them to buy their own homes and farms. In this

Freed slaves working on a peanut farm in the late 1800s. What problems did such workers have to face?

way, their white neighbors would come to respect them and grant them their rights. He also believed that blacks ought to live apart from white people.

8. Although Washington had many followers, not all black people believed as he did. One of these was William E. B. Du Bois. He had studied in Europe and at Harvard. Unlike Washington, he had not been born into slavery. Du Bois believed that blacks should receive the same education given to white people. He thought blacks should not be taught just skills needed for jobs in the trades. He thought blacks should study the arts and sciences. Then they could become doctors, lawyers, and teachers. Du Bois also felt that blacks should demand equal rights with whites. In 1909 he helped to organize the National Association for the Advancement of Colored People (NAACP). The NAACP tried to get lawmakers to end Jim Crow laws. It brought

A northern city between 1900 and 1915. Why did thousands of black people move to the North? How did the movement to the cities affect blacks?

W. E. B. Du Bois

civil rights cases to court. This organization still works today for equal rights for blacks.

9. After the Civil War many white and black people began moving from the farms to nearby cities. By 1900 thousands of southern blacks were also moving to cities in the North. They were looking for jobs in the many new factories being built. Among these cities were New York, Pittsburgh, Chicago, Philadelphia, and Detroit. Blacks new to the cities had to get used to a life much different from farm life. Most had little or no money. They had to live in the poorer areas. Jobs were hard to find. Blacks faced discrimination in housing and jobs. In fact, many practices were as discriminatory as those in the South. For all their disadvantages, however, the northern cities seemed to offer blacks a better life than they had in the rural South.

Choose the correct answer.

1. Lincoln felt that the southern states should
   a. be kept out of the Union
   b. not be punished harshly
   c. not be allowed representatives in Congress
2. After the death of Lincoln, the new president was
   a. Johnson
   b. Grant
   c. Taylor
3. The president following Lincoln in office decided to treat the South
   a. as most of Congress wished
   b. according to the plan of the Radical Republicans
   c. much as Lincoln would have treated this section

4. The 14th Amendment
   a. freed the slaves
   b. gave blacks the right to vote
   c. made black people citizens of the United States
5. All of these had some influence in the South after the Civil War EXCEPT
   a. freed men
   b. Ku Klux Klan
   c. Minutemen
6. The years 1865 to 1877 were called the
   a. Spoils System
   b. Reconstruction Period
   c. Era of Good Feeling

I. What is the main purpose of Chapter 12?

   a. To describe the breakup of the plantation system
   b. To describe changes in the South since 1865
   c. To discuss the beginning of education for blacks in the South
   d. To describe the new kinds of work in the South

II. Choose the correct answer.

1. Why did sharecropping start in the South?
   a. The planters needed money to start cotton mills.
   b. The planters wanted to increase the amount of cotton grown.
   c. The planters wanted to make use of their land but had no money to pay for workers.
2. In 1896 the Supreme Court ruled that
   a. separate railroad cars for blacks and whites were not against the law
   b. colleges for blacks must be built in the South
   c. blacks could not be denied the right to vote
3. All of the following are Jim Crow practices except
   a. having separate rest rooms for blacks and whites in a factory
   b. preventing blacks and whites from attending the same public school
   c. allowing blacks and whites to play together on a basketball team
4. Booker T. Washington felt that school should
   a. turn students into churchgoers
   b. train students in a foreign language
   c. provide students with a useful skill or trade
5. William E. B. Du Bois helped found the NAACP to
   a. fight for rights for black people
   b. help blacks start their own businesses
   c. build schools in the South

III. Decide whether each statement agrees or disagrees with what you have read. If the statement disagrees, explain why.

1. Sharecroppers pay rent in cash for the land they use.
2. Not all black leaders agreed with the views of Booker T. Washington.
3. Little industrial progress occurred in the South from the time of the Civil War until the 1970s.
4. Some states passed laws requiring a person to pay a tax before he could vote.
5. After the federal troops left, the southern states moved swiftly to give blacks more rights.
6. By the early 1900s, few blacks voted in the South and fewer still held public office.
7. Du Bois felt that education was the *only* way for blacks to get their rights.
8. The northern cities offered many blacks a better life than they had as southern sharecroppers.
9. The nation as a whole supported the blacks' fight for their rights.
10. Blacks faced no discrimination in the North.

DEVELOPING IDEAS AND SKILLS

Answer the following questions about the cartoon and what you have read in this chapter.

1. What new problems did the former slaves face?
2. What effect did these practices have on black people? White people?
3. In what other ways were blacks denied their rights after 1877?
4. Why didn't the federal government help?
5. How do you think blacks should gain their rights?

CONTRIBUTIONS OF BLACK AMERICANS The people listed below became famous before 1900. Why are they famous? You may use an encyclopedia to help you answer the question.

Booker T. Washington	Harriet Tubman	Peter Salem
Frederick Douglass	Phillis Wheatley	Sojourner Truth
Benjamin Banneker	Crispus Attucks	Jim Beckwourth
Robert Smalls	Blanche K. Bruce	Ida Wells
Hiram R. Revels	Nat Love	

Study this time line. Then answer the questions that follow. Use the information you have studied in this unit to help you. You may also look at the time line on pages 274 and 275 if you need additional help.

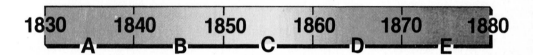

1830   1840   1850   1860   1870   1880
A   B   C   D   E

In which period of time (**A, B, C, D,** or **E**) did the following take place?

1. Nat Turner led a slave revolt.
2. President Lincoln was assassinated.
3. Harriet Beecher Stowe wrote *Uncle Tom's Cabin*.
4. Reconstruction ended.
5. The Emancipation Proclamation was signed.
6. The Supreme Court decided on the Dred Scott case.

Thinking It Through

Suppose you were a black person living in the South in the 1890s. How would you have reacted to the Jim Crow laws? Explain your answer.

Knowing the Public Library

Many history books are as exciting as any story book. Your teacher may interest you in reading one of these books. She or he may also ask you to visit the public library in order to write a report on a topic you are studying. Will you be able to find the books you want in the library?

The books in your library are arranged in two main parts: fiction and nonfiction. Books that tell stories about make-believe people and events are called fiction. They are arranged in alphabetical order according to the authors' last names. Other books, like biographies and histories, are called nonfiction books.

To help you find a nonfiction book easily, the libraries use a system of numbers. All books about history have a number in the 900s. The number can be found on the back of each history book. It is known as the call number. The call number tells you how to locate your book in the library.

There are three cards prepared for every book in the library. They are the title card, the author card, and the subject card. These are placed in the card index, or card catalog, of the library. Any one of these cards will tell you where the book is and several facts about the book.

THE AUTHOR CARD

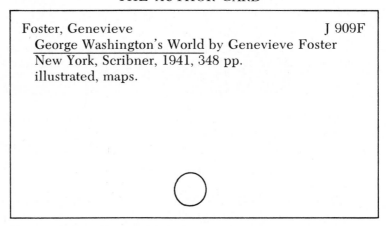

```
Foster, Genevieve                                    J 909F
    George Washington's World by Genevieve Foster
    New York, Scribner, 1941, 348 pp.
    illustrated, maps.
```

THE TITLE CARD

```
George Washington's World                            J 909F
    by Genevieve Foster
    New York, Scribner, 1941, 348 pp.
    illustrated, maps.
```

WASHINGTON, GEORGE   J 909F
  (or HISTORY, MODERN — 18TH CENTURY)
George Washington's World by Genevieve Foster
New York, Scribner, 1941, 348 pp.
illustrated, maps.

Answer these questions about the cards.

1. When you see the number 900 on a card, to which section of the shelves will you go to find the book?
2. Who is the author of the book?
3. From the title, what kind of book do you think this is?
4. Where was the book published? By what company?
5. In what year was the book published? Why is the date important?
6. What word tells you the book has pictures?

BOOKS FOR UNIT V

AUTHOR	TITLE, PUBLISHER	DESCRIPTION
1. Angell, Polly	*Pat and the Iron Horse*, American	An immigrant boy in the days of the canal boats and railroads.
2. Coy, Harold	*Chicano Roots Go Deep*, Dodd, Mead	Chicanos of the Southwest and present attempts to retain their culture.
3. Dagliesh, Alice	*Ride in the Wind*, Scribner's	Charles Lindbergh's early flight across the Atlantic.
4. Davis, A. F.	*American Heroine*, Oxford	The work of Jane Addams at Hull House.
5. Dowdell, Dorothy and Joseph	*The Japanese Helped Build America*, Messner	Courage of Japanese immigrants, fighting discrimination, and gifts to American culture.
6. Finkelstein, M., Sandifer, J., and Wright, E.	*Minorities, USA*, Globe	Stories of a variety of religious and ethnic minorities who have helped build America.
7. Hano, Arnold	*Roberto Clemente, Batting King*, Putnam	The Puerto Rican athlete who died helping victims of an earthquake.
8. Holland, Ruth	*Mill Child*, Crowell-Collier	The moving bitter story of child labor in America.
9. Hutmacher, J. Joseph	*Nation of Newcomers*, Delacorte	Clear, interesting study of ethnic minority groups in American history.
10. Johnson, R. P.	*Chief Joseph, The Story of an American Indian*, Dillon Press.	A fighter, guide, and peacemaker of a wandering and suffering people.
11. Leipold, L. Edmond	*Founders of Fortunes, Books I and II*, T. S. Denison	Biographies of "captains of industry" in the 19th and 20th centuries.
12. Leipold, L. Edmond	*Famous American Indians*, T. S. Denison	Biographies of Americans of Indian descent in war, art, athletics, and politics.

AUTHOR	TITLE, PUBLISHER	DESCRIPTION
13. Lens, S.	*The Labor Wars,* Doubleday	The struggle of American workers for justice in working conditions.
14. Marker, Dorothy	*The Little Giant of Schenectady,* American	The life of Charles Steinmetz and his remarkable work with electricity.
15. Meltzer, M.	*Taking Root,* Farrar, Straus	Jewish immigrants to the United States.
16. Miers, Earl S.	*Black Americans,* Grosset & Dunlap	Accounts of famous black Americans and their contributions.
17. Nathan, Adele G.	*Building of the First Transcontinental Railroad,* Random House (Landmark Books)	The story of the people responsible for the first railroad across the continent.
18. Shippen, Katherine	*Mister Bell Invents the Telephone,* Random House (Landmark Books)	One of the greatest inventions in the field of communication.
19. Sobol, Donald J.	*The Wright Brothers of Kitty Hawk,* Thomas Nelson and Sons	The experiment of two pioneers in aviation.
20. Time-Life Editors	*1870–1900,* Time-Life Books	Magnificent pictorial account of America: frontier, entertainment, cities, law and order.
21. Weems, John E.	*Death Song,* Doubleday	The last of the Indian wars, the closing decades of the 19th century.
22. Wilson, D.	*Bright Eyes: The Story of Susette la Flesche,* McGraw-Hill	Omaha Indian fighting racism and atrocities committed against her people.

Unit VI

How Did the United States Become a Leading Industrial Nation?

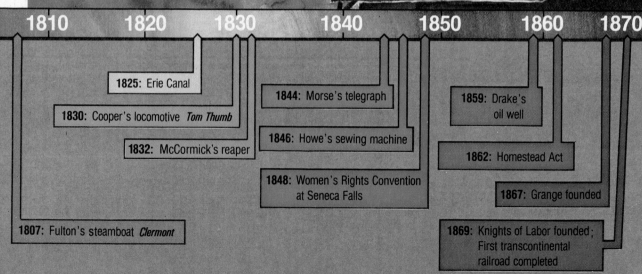

1810	1820	1830	1840	1850	1860	1870

1825: Erie Canal

1830: Cooper's locomotive *Tom Thumb*

1832: McCormick's reaper

1844: Morse's telegraph

1846: Howe's sewing machine

1848: Women's Rights Convention at Seneca Falls

1859: Drake's oil well

1862: Homestead Act

1867: Grange founded

1807: Fulton's steamboat *Clermont*

1869: Knights of Labor founded; First transcontinental railroad completed

CHAPTER

1880   1890   1900   1910   1920   1930   1940

1920: 19th Amendment

1886: American Federation of Labor founded

1924: Immigration law set up quotas

1883: Civil Service Act

1933: New Deal began

1879: Edison's light bulb

1935: Social Security Act

1876: Bell's telephone

1903: Wright brothers airplane flight at Kitty Hawk

1908: Ford's Model T car

1929–1941: Great Depression

1 AMERICANS CHANGE THEIR WAY OF LIFE

How did America's great natural and human resources change the American way of life after 1800?

1. About 180 years ago, the United States was a country of farms, villages, and towns. Most Americans were farmers, living in small cabins. Everyone in the farm family worked hard all day to provide the things that were needed. People had to clear their land, build their own homes, and care for the animals. They had to raise their own food, make their own clothing, and care for each other when they were sick. They did all this work by hand. Except for the spinning wheel and the hand loom, early farmers had no machines to help them. Only rich people who had servants or slaves to work for them had time for leisure.

2. The people who lived then did not have any of the comforts we have today. They had no electricity; they used the fireplace for lighting and warming the house and cooking the meals. They had poor roads, and most people did not travel far from their homes. Most families did not know what was happening outside their villages because there were few newspapers.

3. This kind of living has passed in America. Today, most Americans live in towns and cities. They can buy many kinds of food in nearby stores or supermarkets. Food often comes in packages, ready for use. Clothing is also ready-made. Americans work fewer hours per day and fewer hours per week. They have time to read, to relax, and to enjoy themselves. They send messages around the world in a matter of minutes. They travel in a few hours to places that once would have taken weeks or months to reach.

4. The farm has changed in many ways. Farm families of today do not make their own clothing, furniture, and household goods. They do not grow all the food they need. They depend on workers hundreds of miles away for these things. The farmer no longer does everything by hand, nor does everyone in the farm family have to work to provide the things it needs.

5. What has caused this change in the ways of living of Americans? There are many causes, but the most important is the invention and use of machines. This great change is called the Industrial Revolution. Machines are like steel giants. They have the strength of hundreds of people. They do not grow tired. They need only fuel. Oil, natural gas, coal, **hydroelectricity** (electricity produced by water power), and nuclear material are the main fuels. Today machines do much of the work once done by humans.

Corn picking near Omaha, Nebraska. How have machines made life easier for farmers?

Because of machines, fewer workers are needed in factories. In what ways, however, do machines create new jobs for people?

6. Because of machines, we need fewer workers on the farm and in the factory to grow the food and make the goods we need. This means that people are free to do other kinds of work. Some people are needed to service and run the machines. Others find it possible to go to school to become scientists, doctors, lawyers, and teachers. Machines have helped give us a better life.

7. A second reason for our improved way of living is the use we have made of our rich natural resources. Natural resources are found in or upon the earth. These are gifts of nature; they are not made by people.

First, there is the land. The United States has one of the most remarkably level plains in the world. It has mountains, plateaus, lakes, and great rivers. Second, there are the minerals found in the earth. The United States has rich deposits of coal, iron, oil, copper, and other minerals. These have been necessary in building our nation. Finally, the United States has a great water supply and great forests.

8. A third reason for our improved way of living is the people who have built this country. There are the people who have invented machines and shown us how to use our resources. There are the people who have built factories and businesses. There are the people who have brought us all closer to each other through the railroad, telegraph, and airplane. There are the men and women who have come to our country from other lands. There are the workers in factories, farms, and mines who have turned out the goods we have needed.

9. It has been said that Americans are never satisfied. The energy of Americans is shown in the movement west from the Atlantic Ocean to the Pacific. Pioneers took the great forest lands and made them into farms. Ranchers and herders made the dry lands of our plains useful. Our mineral resources have been used to make the greatest industries in the world. Perhaps these successes of the United States are a result of the fact that Americans believe they can accomplish whatever they set their minds to do.

UNDERSTANDING
CHAPTER 1

I. What is the main purpose of Chapter 1?

   a. To tell how people lived in early America

   b. To describe how machines have given us more leisure time

   c. To tell about the changes in our way of living since the early 19th century

   d. To describe our natural resources and their importance

II. Choose the correct answer.

1. There was little time for leisure or fun in the 1800s because
   a. machines needed constant watching
   b. there were no laws to limit the hours of work on the farm
   c. people had to make almost everything they needed themselves
2. The increased use of machinery in agriculture has resulted in
   a. a greater number of workers on farms
   b. increased crop production
   c. a smaller amount of money needed to begin farming
3. Which of these would be called a natural resource?
   a. Coal
   b. Glass
   c. Nylon
4. Before 1800 most farmers wore clothing that was
   a. brought from Europe
   b. made in American factories
   c. made mainly by women in their homes
5. The United States has all of these EXCEPT
   a. a region of level, grassy land
   b. great forests
   c. great rivers that flow from east to west

III. Decide whether each statement agrees or disagrees with what you have read. If the statement disagrees, explain why.

1. Machines have brought all parts of our nation closer together.
2. Fewer farmers are needed today to grow the food the country needs.
3. Because of the use of machines, we use larger amounts of coal, iron, and oil.
4. The use of the machine has given Americans more time for rest and fun.
5. One of the reasons why the United States has grown to be a great industrial nation is that Americans work hard.
6. Farmers now produce more of their own food than they did 180 years ago.
7. Because of the machine, Americans do not depend so much on each other as they once did.
8. Machines give us more of the things we need to feed and clothe ourselves.

DEVELOPING IDEAS
AND SKILLS

GRAPH STUDY *The United States and the World*

Study the graph. Then decide whether the following statements are true or false. If a statement is false, rewrite it so that it is true.

1. The land area of the United States is less than 10% of all the land in the world.
2. The United States has about 5% of the world's population.
3. The United States produces over one-half the world's automobiles.

4. The United States grows about one-half of all the corn grown in the world.
5. About three-quarters of the world production of coal is produced in the United States.
6. This graph compares the agricultural and industrial production of the United States with that of all other nations combined.

The United States and the World

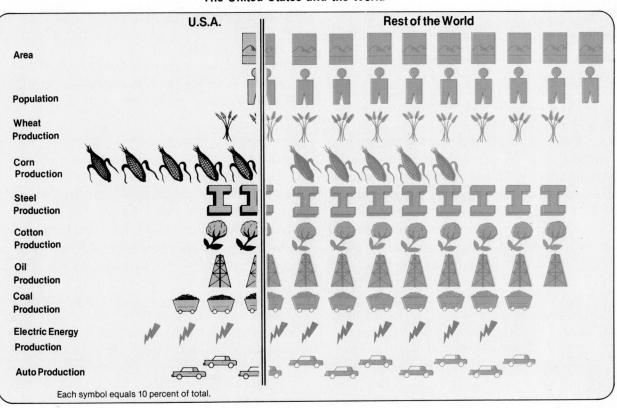

Each symbol equals 10 percent of total.

SUMMING UP **THE UNITED STATES THEN AND NOW** Complete this chart in your notebook. Show the differences in our way of life between the year 1800 and the present time.

	ABOUT 1800	NOW
Transportation		
Communication		
Manufacturing		
Tools and Machines		
How We Get Our Food		
Clothing		

2 INVENTIONS CHANGE OUR WAY OF LIVING BEFORE THE CIVIL WAR

Which inventions brought about changes in travel, communication, and farming during the first half of the 19th century?

A Hudson River steamboat. When Fulton first tried out his steamboat, many people thought it would not run. Why are people sometimes unwilling to believe that new inventions or ideas will be successful?

1. As the United States grew in size and population, the West grew too. By 1859 the West included all the land between the Appalachian Mountains and the Rocky Mountains. At first the roads that took settlers to the West were poor, but during the 19th century better roads were built. As time went by, however, more people wanted to travel West by water, because they found that this way of traveling was cheaper. Canals were built to make water travel easier. As you have already learned, the most famous canal was the Erie Canal. The Erie Canal ran over 350 miles across New York State and connected the Great Lakes with the Hudson River. Canal boats not only brought people to the West. They also carried crops from the West to the East and farm machinery from the East to the West.

2. Canal boats were pulled by long ropes attached to horses or mules walking nearby. The boats moved very slowly. Some Americans thought that the steam engine, improved by James Watt, could be used to move a boat. As early as 1787, John Fitch used a steam engine to do this. It was not very successful. Another young man, Robert Fulton, was interested in the same idea. Fulton bought a wood-burning engine in England. When he returned to America, he built a boat that had paddle wheels on each side. He connected the steam engine to the

paddle wheels. He called the boat the *Clermont*. In August 1807, Fulton was ready to try his boat on a trip up the Hudson River from New York to Albany. There were many who thought the boat would not run. They felt that a boat with a heavy iron engine on deck would sink. They nicknamed the boat "Fulton's Folly." But the *Clermont* made the trip successfully, averaging about five miles an hour (eight kilometers an hour)! The age of the steamboat had arrived. Soon, steamboats were used on rivers all over the country.

3. In England, horses were used in the mines to pull wagonloads of coal. It was easier to pull the heavy loads if the horses pulled the wagons on rails. Then George Stephenson, an English engineer, used a steam engine to pull such a train of wagons. Stephenson's engine was called a locomotive. Others called it the "iron horse." This was the first successful steam locomotive.

4. In America, the first successful locomotive was made by Peter Cooper in 1830. He called it the *Tom Thumb*. Cooper's locomotive raced against a horse to prove that it could pull trains better than the horse could. The first railroad company in this country to use the locomotive was the Baltimore and Ohio. The first railroad built

for steam power was 13 miles (21 kilometers) long.

5. The new machines also changed farming methods. Until the American Revolution, farmers used wooden plows and spades to turn over the soil. They used scythes to cut the grain. The scythe had a blade of hammered iron with a long wooden handle. With these tools, work was very hard. No wonder the workday on the farm was almost 16 hours long!

6. In the 1830s many farmers moved to the grassy plains of the Middle West. Special plows were needed to turn over the grassy soil. The wooden plow would not make furrows in the hard ground. The man who provided the new plow was John Deere of Illinois. He invented a plow with a steel blade that cut through the roots and turned over the soil quickly. Since farmers could plow more land, they were able to plant more seed. Thus, the improved plow meant more crops.

7. Now that more grain was being planted, a quicker way of harvesting the crop had to be found. The scythe was much too slow. The invention of the reaper by Cyrus McCormick filled this need. McCormick first tried out his reaper in West Virginia but moved to the Midwest where there was a demand for it. The first reapers were pulled by horses. The machine was made up of four long blades that turned as the machine moved. McCormick's invention met with success. The reaper replaced the scythe on the broad farms of the Middle West. It made it possible to grow more wheat and provide food for people in distant cities.

8. As the United States grew in size, there was a great need for sending news quickly. In 1844 an American artist and inventor, Samuel Morse, found a better way to send messages by electricity. He called his invention a telegraph. In a telegraph, electric current is sent through a wire. If the current is stopped, it causes a "buzz."

These "buzzes" or "dots and dashes" were formed into a code. Different series of dots and dashes meant different letters and numbers. This method of "writing" is known as the Morse code.

9. Congress gave Morse money to demonstrate his invention. He built a telegraph line between Washington and Baltimore. In 1844 he sent the first message over this telegraph line: "What hath God wrought!" The new invention proved to be most useful. It brought the people of this country into closer communication with one another. News could be flashed across the country in a matter of minutes. By 1861 telegraph lines had reached San Francisco on the West Coast. This great invention helped newspapers to bring up-to-date news to their readers. The new railroads used telegraph signals to make travel safer.

10. The first modern machines for making cloth were invented as early as 1750. Factories used the movement of falling water to power the machines. However, sewing clothing was still being done at

Cyrus McCormick giving a public demonstration of his invention, the reaper. Why was this invention important?

home. About one hundred years passed before a machine for sewing cloth was invented. The sewing machine was invented in 1846 by Elias Howe. It was of great use both to factory owners and to those who sewed clothing at home. New factories were opened to make clothing. Soon many families were able to buy their clothing instead of making it at home. Shoe factories began to use the sewing machine to sew leather for shoes.

11. With the invention of new machines and the growth of factories, more iron was needed. As late as 1840, iron was of very poor quality and was costly to make. Then a new way was found to use coal to turn iron into steel. In 1846 an American, William Kelly, found a way to make steel by blowing cold air into the heated iron. This method was improved in 1853 by Sir Henry Bessemer in England. The iron ore was placed in a furnace with a very hot fire. Cold air was blown through the iron to get rid of the impurities. Then it was melted and made into steel. The steel was harder than the iron and lasted longer. It was especially useful in farm machinery and rails for the spreading railroad systems.

12. There was also a growing demand for oil. The Indians had used oil for medicine long before the Europeans came to America. In the 19th century, people found that oil made the moving parts of the newly invented machines run better and longer. They found that oil could be changed into kerosene and gasoline. Kerosene was used to light lamps. At first, there was no use for gasoline and it was thrown away. Later, it was used as a fuel. In 1859 Edwin Drake dug the first oil well in Pennsylvania. Before long, oil fields were opened in nearby Ohio and West Virginia.

REVIEWING CHAPTER 1

Decide whether each statement describes life before or after the Industrial Revolution.

1. The United States is a land of farmers.
2. Machines do much of the heavy work for us.
3. The length of the working day is short.
4. Most work is done by hand.
5. People can buy more goods at a lower cost.
6. Everyone in the family works.
7. The members of the family spend much time making the things they need for the home.
8. Most of the heat for homes comes from fireplaces.

UNDERSTANDING CHAPTER 2

I. What is the main purpose of Chapter 2?

a. To describe how greater use was made of iron
b. To tell about some of the new tools on farms in the United States
c. To explain the changes brought about by the telegraph
d. To describe some of the important inventions before 1865

II. Choose the correct answer.

1. The new farm machinery helped people in the cities because it
a. provided more food
b. made more city people move to the farms
c. made it easier to travel to farms

2. There was a greater need for iron for
   a. use in stoves
   b. use in making machines
   c. fuel for the factories
3. The work of Kelly and Bessemer
   a. made steel possible
   b. opened the way for the clothing business
   c. improved communication in all parts of the country
4. Railroads were made safer through an invention of
   a. Samuel Morse
   b. Cyrus McCormick
   c. Elias Howe
5. All of these men made improvements in transportation EXCEPT
   a. Robert Fulton
   b. Peter Cooper
   c. Elias Howe
6. The government helped one invention by
   a. giving free land to Cyrus McCormick
   b. building a blast furnace for William Kelly
   c. giving Samuel Morse money to build a telegraph line

III. Decide whether each statement agrees or disagrees with what you have read. If the statement disagrees, explain why.

1. The invention of the reaper helped to develop the Middle West.
2. Eastern farmers had an immediate use for the reaper.
3. Steamboats became popular on the rivers of the United States.
4. English inventors played a great part in bringing about the Industrial Revolution.
5. The steamboat was invented before railroads came into use.
6. The first factories in the United States were built by the year 1800.
7. There were no railroads in the United States before 1800.
8. The steel industry in the United States began before the Civil War.

DEVELOPING IDEAS AND SKILLS **PICTURE SYMBOLS** These pictures should help you recall parts of the chapter you have just read. What is the main idea of each picture?

READING A BAR GRAPH

If you open a history book or a newspaper, you will probably find a graph. Graphs are an important way of showing information in a quick and simple form. Graphs show figures or numbers in a visual way. There are four main kinds of graphs: line graphs, bar graphs, pie graphs, and pictograms. Each one shows information in a different way.

Below is a bar graph. Bar graphs are useful for showing the quantities, or amounts of things. Bar graphs use bars or columns of different sizes. By looking at the lengths of these bars or columns, it is easy to compare things. Bar graphs can run up or down (vertical) or sideways (horizontal). Along one side of the graph, quantities or amounts are labeled. The things being compared are labeled along another side. The title of the bar graph tells what is being shown.

Look at the bar graph below. Then answer the following questions.

1. Is this a vertical or horizontal bar graph?
2. What does this bar graph show?
3. What are the numbers along the top of the graph?
4. How many miles could a passenger travel on a stagecoach in one day? On a railroad in one day?
5. How many times faster was railroad travel than stagecoach travel?
6. What period in our history does this graph describe?
7. Can you re-draw this information in a different kind of graph?

Number of Miles Traveled in One Day, 1860

NUMBER OF MILES PER DAY	0	50	100	150	200	250	300
Stagecoach							
Railroad							

Thinking It Through

How did the inventions described in this chapter help to strengthen ties between business people of the East and farmers of the West?

3 REFORMS ARE MADE

What kinds of reform movements got under way in the early 1800s?

1. While inventors were designing new machines, other men and women were seeking different kinds of changes in our country. These people wanted to improve the lives of Americans. Because they worked for reforms, these people were called reformers. They thought there should be good schools for all the people. They believed the new nation should take better care of the poor. During the time that Andrew Jackson was president, these reformers made the country aware that many Americans did not have the benefits they thought all people should share in a democracy.

2. The reformers did not work alone. They made certain that others learned about the country's prisons, hospitals, and schools. They spoke at public meetings. As more citizens became interested in the aims of the reformers, they started clubs and organizations. These organizations worked hard to correct some evils in our democracy. In the 1830s reformers were interested in better schools, better care of the insane, improvement in the treatment of lawbreakers and prisoners, and equal rights for women.

3. Many people thought that women were not entitled to the same rights as men. Women were expected to marry early, raise families, and give their property to their husbands. They were supposed to stay at home. For many years, women were not allowed to go to college, vote, or help in making laws.

4. Women began to demand more rights. Many women had joined the abolitionist movement to end slavery. With the knowledge gained from the antislavery movement, several women reformers joined forces to organize the first women's rights convention. It was held at Seneca Falls, New York, in 1848. Lucretia Mott and Elizabeth Cady Stanton were its leaders. This convention drew up a declaration of independence for women. In it, they listed what was wrong with the position of women in the United States:

a. Women had to obey the laws of the nation, although they had no voice in making them.
b. Once married, women had few legal rights.
c. Husbands took away their property rights, even the wages women earned.
d. Men took all the best jobs.
e. Women could not get a proper education, since all colleges were closed to them.
f. Worst of all, women had no power to change this. They could not vote.

In the following years, women such as Susan B. Anthony continued the long struggle for women's rights.

5. By the late 1830s a few colleges admitted women as students. In 1837 Mary Lyon opened Mount Holyoke, a school that became a college for women only. As women received an education, some became teachers and others took jobs in the business world. Women began to perform some of the tasks that only men had done before. For example, Elizabeth Blackwell became the first woman doctor in 1849. By the year 1851, several states had given women the right to own property. But women were still not allowed to vote.

6. Dorothea Dix was one of the more famous reformers. She spent most of her life trying to improve the care of prisoners

A laboratory at Mount Holyoke College in the late 1890s. Why did many people feel that women should not go to college?

for education for most people in the early 19th century. Children worked from 12 to 14 hours a day. Because they had to work on the farm, they had little time for school. In most schools, all classes and subjects were taught by one teacher who was poorly trained and poorly paid. The lessons consisted of reading, writing, and arithmetic. The whip and a few old textbooks were the only teaching tools found in most classrooms.

9. Except in New England, few schools were supported by the public. In most places, taxpayers were not willing to see education paid for by all the people. The parents who sent their children to public schools had to pay part of the expenses of the school. Parents who could afford it usu-

Dorothea Dix. What are some of the reforms she worked for? Why are reformers such as Dix so important in American history?

and the insane. She found terrible conditions in some of our prisons. Prisoners had no hope because they were sent to jail for long terms. They were housed in dark and dirty cells. Young prisoners were placed with hardened criminals. Food was poor. Prisoners were often overworked and treated harshly. They received little medical care, and the number of deaths in prison was high. Few efforts were made to help the prisoners when they were released.

7. Dorothea Dix also found that insane persons were crowded together in cold rooms as if they were animals. Sometimes they were jailed with criminals. They were treated badly and poorly fed. They were often chained, kept naked in cages, and whipped into obedience. Dix went from state to state reporting what she saw. In time, the states provided better care for the insane, keeping them apart from criminals.

8. Another important reform movement was the drive to obtain free education for all citizens. There were few opportunities

ally sent their children to private schools. In some of the large cities, societies conducted schools for the poorer children. Parents were not eager to send their children to these schools because they did not want to accept charity.

10. The movement for tax-supported schools grew stronger during the period when Andrew Jackson was president. It was led by men like Horace Mann of Massachusetts and Henry Barnard of Connecticut. They believed that a democratic government demanded opportunity for education for all. If the people govern, they should know how to govern. Labor organizations also helped the cause of free public schools. Many working people hoped that their children would make a comfortable living as a result of their schooling.

11. At first, many people did not like the ideas of Mann and Barnard. But in time, many communities began to accept them. Big cities led the way in opening tax-supported schools. The school term was lengthened. Schools were started for training teachers. Textbooks were improved. By 1850 most northern states had free public elementary schools. There was then a movement to spread free education to the high schools. Schools were established to take care of the handicapped, the blind, and the deaf.

12. Another reform movement grew in the 1830s. It was the temperance movement. Its members urged people to use fewer or no alcoholic drinks. They felt that too much liquor often led to crime, loss of jobs, and broken families. They tried to get the states to pass laws against such drinks. In 1846 Maine became the first state to prohibit alcoholic drinks. By 1855 Maine had been followed by 12 other states.

13. The first labor unions began during this period. While they were most interested in getting better pay and shorter hours, they also fought for many of the reforms of the Jacksonian period. At that time, people could be put in jail for not paying money they owed. Many of these debts were small. Partly through the efforts of early unions, laws were passed which forbade sending people to jail because they were unable to pay debts. However, these early labor unions did not last long.

REVIEWING CHAPTER 2

Who is identified in each statement?

Elias Howe   Robert Fulton   Cyrus McCormick
Peter Cooper   John Deere   William Kelly
                    Samuel Morse

1. I invented the first successful steamboat.
2. I helped the farmer in the Middle West by inventing a new kind of plow.
3. The clothing industry depended upon my invention.
4. I was one of the people responsible for the development of the steel industry.
5. I found a means of sending messages over wires.
6. With my invention, farmers could plant more crops, and harvest them, too.
7. I invented the first successful steam locomotive in America.

I. What is the main purpose of Chapter 3?

    a. To show how the life of the common people was improved
    b. To describe how schools were improved
    c. To discuss some of the advances in women's rights
    d. To describe how treatment of prisoners has changed

II. Choose the correct answer.

1. Dorothea Dix is remembered for her fight for
    a. rights for women
    b. improvements in public education
    c. better treatment of the insane
2. One of the early gains made by women in the 19th century was the
    a. right to vote
    b. election of women to Congress
    c. opening of colleges for women
3. Horace Mann was a leader in the
    a. fight for public education
    b. movement to provide homes for the aged
    c. improvement in treatment of criminals
4. The area of the country that first supported public education was
    a. the South
    b. New England
    c. the West
5. The first woman doctor in the United States was
    a. Dorothea Dix
    b. Elizabeth Blackwell
    c. Lucretia Mott
6. Why did reformers bring certain evils to the attention of the public?
    a. They were running for government offices.
    b. They were interested in improving conditions of the people.
    c. They wanted to get supporters for their political party.
7. Susan B. Anthony was a leader in
    a. the fight for the shorter workday
    b. President Jackson's cabinet
    c. the women's rights movement

III. Decide whether each statement agrees or disagrees with what you have read. If the statement disagrees, explain why.

1. The movement for public education was started by farmers on the frontier.
2. Dorothea Dix worked to improve conditions of prisoners and the insane.
3. A reformer is a person who is trying to gain a position in government.
4. Many reforms were demanded when Andrew Jackson was president.
5. Wealthy people often sent their children to private schools.
6. Elizabeth Cady Stanton opened Mount Holyoke, which became a college for women only.
7. The subjects taught in our early public schools included reading, science, history, and art.

Choose two of the women listed below. Make a brief report on the two women's contributions to American life in the 1800s. You may use an encyclopedia or other books to help you.

Emily Dickinson	Lucy Stone
Susan B. Anthony	Angelina Grimké
Harriet Tubman	Harriet Beecher Stowe
Elizabeth Cady Stanton	Margaret Fuller
Lucretia Mott	Louisa May Alcott
Emma Willard	Ida Wells-Barnett

REFORMS   Complete the following chart in your notebook.

REFORMS	THEN	NOW
Women's rights		
Treatment of prisoners and the insane		
Education		
Temperance movement		

Several reform movements mentioned in this chapter are still being conducted today; for example, movements for women's rights, better treatment of prisoners and the mentally disturbed. What kinds of changes are today's reformers demanding?

4 INVENTIONS CHANGED THE LIVES OF AMERICANS

What inventions made the transportation system in the United States grow after 1865? How was electricity used to improve life for Americans?

In 1869 the last rails of the Union Pacific and Central Pacific railroads were joined at Promontory, Utah. Why was this event cause for celebration? How did the results of this event affect people's lives?

1. After 1865 the United States became a leading industrial nation, a country of mills and factories. The number of inventions to improve transportation and communication increased. New uses for electricity were found. More farms and factories began to use the new machines. People left their farms and small shops to find work in factories. Goods were produced in greater amounts than ever before. The cities grew even larger.

2. By 1853 our nation had spread from one coast to another. People wanted to travel to the Far West. However, they wanted a faster and safer means of travel than the stagecoach. Railroads were needed west of the Mississippi. In 1862 Congress voted to give land or money to any railroad company that would build a line to the West Coast. In 1867 two railroad companies, the Union Pacific and the Central Pacific, accepted the offer. The Union Pacific started to build westward from the city of Omaha, Nebraska. (Most of its workers came from Ireland and Germany.) The Central Pacific built eastward from California. (Its workers were largely Chinese.) On May 10, 1869, after many hardships, the two railroads met at Promontory, near Ogden, Utah.

3. East and West were now united by a railroad that crossed the entire country. The transcontinental railroad, as it was called, brought larger numbers of people to the West. Villages and towns sprang up along the route of the railroad. The trains brought the tools and machines needed by settlers to the West. In turn, the railroads carried the products of western farms and ranches to the cities and factories of the Middle West and the East. Workers in cities came to depend on the distant farms for their food. The cities were able to grow larger because of the goods brought by the railroads.

4. The railroads themselves changed. Wood-burning engines gave way to coal burners. The type of car that looked like the stagecoach was replaced by the heavy passenger car. Sleeping and dining cars were added. Steel rails replaced iron rails. They gave a smoother ride. Gas lamps and steam heat became common in most passenger cars. In 1869 George Westinghouse invented the air brake. Its use increased passenger safety. The Westinghouse brake

used compressed air to stop the long, heavy trains quickly and smoothly.

5. During the 1890s several Americans tried to make horseless carriages. Henry Ford was among these auto makers. Most cars that had been built when Henry Ford started his work were expensive. They took a long time to build. A few men built them in little shops. Only a few people could afford to buy them. Ford wanted to make a car that everyone could afford. At the same time, he wanted to make a safe automobile. He developed a car that was strong and easy to drive. It had a gasoline engine.

6. In order to build his car in great numbers and at low cost, Ford improved the method of manufacturing called **mass production.** In an automobile factory, mass production works in the following way. A moving assembly line, or belt, runs from one end of the building to the other. At the beginning of the line are the frames of the cars. As each car frame moves along the line, workers add new parts to it. After each worker adds parts, the car moves on to other workers along the line until it is completely built. Each worker along the line has a separate job to do. This is called **division of labor.** The parts that make up the car—the wheels, engines, and bodies—are exactly alike for each car. These are called **standardized parts.** As early as 1800, Eli Whitney had used standardized parts to mass-produce army muskets on a nonmoving assembly line. In the 1860s sewing machines and McCormick reapers had been mass-produced. But it was Henry Ford who perfected the system of mass production on a moving assembly line.

7. The gasoline engine also made possible the modern airplane. People had first tried to float through the air in balloons. But balloons depended on the winds. They were difficult to steer. People then built gliders that they attached to their bodies. Gliders floated, too, for they had no engines. What was needed was an engine

An automobile of the 1920s. How has the automobile changed the way people live?

powerful enough to lift gliders off the ground, yet light enough to stay in the air.

8. Samuel Langley carried out some of the first American experiments with airplanes. He was not successful. Others were interested in making an airplane, too. Among these were the Wright brothers of Dayton, Ohio. Wilbur and Orville Wright owned a bicycle repair shop and factory. They had been experimenting with gliders as a hobby. They designed a gasoline engine and attached it to an improved glider. The Wrights took their airplane to the beach at Kitty Hawk, North Carolina. There, on December 17, 1903, Orville Wright made the first successful airplane flight. It lasted 12 seconds. Later that day, the Wright brothers' plane stayed in the air for almost a minute. A machine that was heavier than air could fly! The air age had begun!

9. Americans were not only traveling more quickly from one place to another. They were also benefiting from other kinds of inventions. These included inventions for sending messages from one place to another. These inventions depended on a new form of power called electricity. In the

363

late 18th and early 19th centuries, a number of European scientists studied this form of power. Electricity had first been produced by English scientists rotating coils of copper through magnets.

10. As you have learned, one important early electric invention was the telegraph. It was developed by Samuel Morse. At first, however, telegraph wires were strung only over land. There was no way of sending telegraph messages across the vast oceans. Beginning in 1854, an American named Cyrus W. Field tried to lay a cable of telegraph wires under the Atlantic Ocean. He hoped to connect Europe and America by telegraph. His first attempts did not succeed. The cable and wires were not strong enough to hold on the ocean bottom. Field did not give up. In 1866 he succeeded. The first successful cable between the United States and Europe was put in place.

11. Ten years later, a young man from Scotland, Alexander Graham Bell, surprised the world with another great invention—the telephone. He showed his telephone to the world for the first time at a great fair in Philadelphia, in 1876. It was an immediate success. People began to look for a way to send sound without using wires. The man who first succeeded in doing this was an Italian named Guglielino Marconi. In 1901 Marconi sent the first wireless signal across the Atlantic Ocean.

12. One of the most important results of Marconi's work was the radio. Marconi sent only "dot and dash" messages through the air. In 1906 an American, Lee De Forest, made a special tube by which words and music could be sent without wires. This is called broadcasting. The first radio station to start broadcasting as we know it was station KDKA in Pittsburgh. This station made history with its broadcast of the election of President Harding in 1920.

13. The man who learned to use electricity for light and power was Thomas Alva Edison. His first important invention was a machine that printed telegraph messages. He earned enough money to start his own laboratory at Menlo Park, New Jersey. He hired other people to help him work out his ideas. For example, Lewis H. Latimer, a black inventor who had helped Bell work on the telephone, was among the experts. Edison's laboratory at Menlo Park became a real "invention factory." Edison is best known for his invention of the modern electric light in 1879.

14. Edison had to find a way to provide power cheaply if people were to use his electric light. He put together the central power station. In this station, there were large machines called generators. These machines changed the energy of water, coal, or oil into electricity. The electric current was carried by wires to all parts of the city. Edison continued to find new uses for electricity. By the time of his death, Thomas Edison had invented over 1,300 different objects, including the first working phonograph and the first motion picture camera.

Thomas Edison and his motion picture camera.
Name some of his other inventions.

15. Electricity produced by the central power station was used not only to light homes but also to run machinery in factories. It was used to run street cars, once pulled by horses, and elevators, at first run by steam engines. The new power to lift elevators meant that buildings could be made higher. Electric power would soon make its way into homes. Before long, the American people at work and at home would enjoy many inventions run by electricity.

Decide whether each statement describes public schools before or after the reforms of Horace Mann.

1. Free schools were open to all children.
2. Girls attended high schools.
3. There were one-room schools, with all grades in one room.
4. School terms were a few months long.
5. Children attended school only when they were not working on the farm.
6. Reading, writing, and arithmetic were the only subjects taught.
7. Colorful, well-printed textbooks were given to children.
8. The young men with a few years of schooling became teachers.
9. Schools were established to train teachers.
10. History, geography, and shop subjects were taught.

I. What is the main purpose of Chapter 4?

a. To discuss improvements in transportation
b. To describe the work of Henry Ford
c. To describe changes in railroad travel
d. To describe important 19th- and 20th-century inventions

II. Choose the correct answer.

1. The completion of the transcontinental railroad in 1869
   a. helped the North win the Civil War
   b. helped the "forty-niners" to reach California
   c. joined the East to the West by rail.
2. The building of more railroads
   a. led to a decrease in farm production
   b. brought large numbers of people to the West
   c. caused a movement of people to the farms of the South
3. The laying of the cable under the Atlantic Ocean meant that
   a. ships could sail faster
   b. messages could be sent between Europe and North America
   c. fishing ships would be able to catch more fish
4. We remember Alexander Graham Bell because he
   a. developed the first use for the compressed air brake
   b. invented the telephone
   c. led the movement to improve schools in Massachusetts

5. Henry Ford is remembered as the man who
   a. made the first motorcar
   b. made cars cheaply
   c. discovered the process of hardening rubber
6. Which of these inventions made the modern airplane possible?
   a. Steam engine
   b. Gas-filled balloon
   c. Gasoline engine
7. Why did Edison set up a workshop?
   a. He needed the help of many workers to turn out his inventions.
   b. He wanted to rent his laboratory to other inventors.
   c. He hoped to start a school for young inventors.

III. Decide whether each statement is true or false. The underlined words are clues to help you decide. If a statement is false, change the underlined word or words to make it true.

1. Before the Civil War most of the nation's railroads were <u>east</u> of the Mississippi River.
2. The first transcontinental railroad was finished at <u>San Francisco</u>.
3. The compressed air brake for railroads was invented by <u>Peter Cooper</u>.
4. <u>Henry Ford</u> found a way to produce a safer and cheaper car.
5. In the moving assembly-line factory, each worker makes the <u>entire product</u>.
6. Radio broadcasting, as we know it, began <u>before</u> 1920.
7. The discovery of a use for <u>gasoline</u> led to the invention of the automobile and airplane.
8. Because of new <u>inventions</u>, life became easier for the American people.

PICTURE STUDY   There are several main figures in this picture. What do you suppose each person is probably thinking?

New Inventions

In your notebook, copy the following heads. Under the four headings, list several inventions or improvements in the order in which they occurred.

FARMING   COMMUNICATION   TRANSPORTATION   INDUSTRY

Thinking It Through

Make a list of at least ten jobs that resulted from the invention of the automobile. Also make a list of benefits and problems that have resulted from the invention of the automobile.

5 AMERICANS COME FROM ALL OVER THE WORLD

What problems have been faced by immigrants to the United States?

1. The United States would not have grown into such a great industrial nation without the help of immigrants, men and women who came to this country from other lands. They came to America for many reasons: to make a better living; to be free to think and worship as they pleased; to gain a better education for their families.

2. We have always been a nation of immigrants. Early settlers in the United States came chiefly from Britain. Beginning in the early 17th century, black people from Africa were taken to the British colonies and forced into slavery. There were also Dutch, German, and Swedish settlements along the Atlantic Coast. Most of the people began to speak English and live according to English customs. As a result, our language and many of our laws come from the English.

3. For a long time after the American Revolution, most of the immigrants came from countries in northern and western Europe. These people became known as the "old immigrants." They came to America when there was still a frontier and much available cheap land.

4. A great migration of Irish to the United States took place in the 1840s and 1850s. Millions of people left Ireland during these years because of a potato famine there. This was the period of improvements in transportation in America. Many of the Irish were able to find work building the new canals and railroads. At about the same time, large numbers of Germans came to

America. Many of these people settled in the Middle West, where land was cheap. People also came from Norway, Sweden, and Denmark to farm in the Middle West.

5. The years of the heaviest immigration were from 1870 to 1910. Twenty million people came to the United States during this period. Industries were growing rapidly. Jobs were plentiful. The United States needed people to do the heavy work in the factories. During this period greater numbers of people began immigrating from the countries of southern and eastern Europe.

6. The "new immigrants" included Italians, Slavs, Poles, Jews, and others from eastern and southern Europe. Their homelands were poor. They came to America at a time when the best farmlands had already been settled. Therefore, these immigrants settled chiefly in the cities and worked in

Thousands of Chinese laborers helped to build the early railroads. Others worked on farms and in factories and businesses.

factories. Many had to take jobs at very low wages. The newcomer to America has often had to take the hard and disagreeable tasks.

7. Immigrants from Asia also came to America in the late 1800s. The Chinese came first. In the 1850s and 1860s they worked in California mining camps and they helped to build the railroads. After 1890 Japanese immigrants also began coming to America. They settled on the West Coast and in Hawaii. At first, they also worked on the railroads. As these jobs disappeared, they began to work on farms. In time, they bought lands that nobody else wanted and turned them into fertile areas.

8. Most of the immigrants landed in New York City when they first came to America. In the harbor they saw the Statue of Liberty —a tall figure of a woman holding a torch high above her head. The people of France gave this statue to the people of the United States in 1876. On the base of the statue is written: "Give me your tired, your poor, your huddled masses yearning to breathe free. . . ."

9. When immigrants arrived in the United States, they often settled near people who had come from their own country. Neighborhoods made up of people from one country are called **ghettos.** In these ghettos, the people were likely to keep their own language and customs. In the shops and stores, the immigrants were among friends. When they left their neighborhoods, they were often laughed at, cheated, or mistreated by people who themselves had once been immigrants.

10. Many of the immigrants tried to continue the sort of life they had known in Europe. But slowly, they and their children came to be like those born in America. First, they had to send their children to public schools. In these schools, the children learned to speak English and to play with children of different backgrounds and religions. The children began to talk and dress like other American children. The

Immigrants arrive in New York. What problems did these people face upon settling in the United States?

schools also had night classes for the parents. In these classes, immigrants learned the English language and American history to help them become citizens.

11. Second, they were able to join settlement houses. A settlement house was a place where immigrants could learn the ways of the new land. Two of the most famous settlement houses were Hull House, started by Jane Addams in Chicago, and the Henry Street Settlement, started by Lillian Wald in New York City. They began day nurseries for children whose mothers worked. They opened clubs and playgrounds for the young people of the neighborhood.

12. Third, the immigrants often had to take jobs that took them far from their neighborhoods. On the job, they mixed with other Americans. They also joined labor unions. At union meetings, they

369

Immigrants taking the oath of citizenship in Boston. How does this reflect the spirit of the United States?

learned English and other customs of the country. Finally, the immigrants learned to help themselves. They built their own hospitals, schools, old-age homes, and self-help organizations. Many programs that now help people in need can be traced to these earlier efforts of immigrant groups.

13. Some native-born Americans, those born in America, were **prejudiced** against newcomers. They did not like people who spoke different languages, dressed differently, or had different customs. Some native-born Americans felt the immigrants could never become Americans as the people before them had done. They were also afraid the newcomers would take away their jobs. In the 1840s the Irish Americans, as Catholics, had a very hard time. In the 1880s Jews and Italian Americans could not rent or buy homes where they wanted. On the West Coast, the people talked of a "yellow danger." The Chinese and Japanese immigrants were often driven from their homes.

14. Starting in the 1880s, Congress passed laws to discourage immigration from certain places. From 1882 to 1943 Chinese workers were forbidden by Congress to immigrate to the United States. (In 1907 President Theodore Roosevelt made an agreement with Japan to stop Japanese workers from coming to the United States.) Beginning in 1917 only people who could read and write were allowed to immigrate. In 1924 Congress limited the number of immigrants from eastern and southern Europe. Congress also stated how many immigrants could come from *each* country. This is called a **quota system.** A 1929 law lowered the number of immigrants to 150,000 a year. A law passed by Congress in 1952 made a number of changes in earlier laws, however. It allowed a few Asian groups, including Japanese, to immigrate.

15. Congress passed new immigration laws in 1965 and 1976. Congress ended the old quota system. The laws now permit

about 290,000 people a year to come to the United States from all the world's countries. About 170,000 of them can come from countries outside the Western Hemisphere. About 120,000 can come from countries in the Western Hemisphere. Preference is given to people with special skills or with relatives living in the United States and to refugees. In recent years, immigration to this country has increased from Latin America, especially Mexico, and from Asia. The United States has taken in thousands of refugees from Cuba, Vietnam, and the Soviet Union in the past 20 years.

REVIEWING CHAPTER 4

Decide whether each statement is true or false. The underlined words are clues to help you decide. If a statement is false, change the underlined word or words to make it true.

1. Thomas Edison was born in <u>Ohio</u>.
2. Edison was interested in <u>making money</u> at an early age.
3. The most famous of Edison's inventions was the <u>phonograph</u>.
4. Latimer helped Bell work on the <u>television</u>.
5. De Forest's work led to the development of the <u>automobile</u>.
6. <u>Bell</u> invented the telephone.
7. Edison built a laboratory where he could <u>work alone</u>.

UNDERSTANDING CHAPTER 5

I. What is the main purpose of Chapter 5?

a. To describe the people who came to America from Asia
b. To explain how other Americans felt about the immigrants
c. To describe the jobs found by immigrants
d. To tell about the problems faced by immigrants

II. Choose the correct answer.

1. Why did the United States encourage immigration in the late 1800s?
a. It needed more soldiers in the growing army and navy.
b. It needed workers in the factories.
c. It needed people to settle the land in the West.
2. What was one of the reasons why Congress decided to limit immigration?
a. Indians protested about the loss of their land.
b. The countries of Europe did not want to see so many people leave for America.
c. Some people thought immigrants took jobs from those who had been in this country for a longer time.
3. Why did immigrants settle near earlier immigrants from their own country?
a. They shared the same language and customs.
b. They were not allowed to settle anywhere else.
c. The earlier immigrants had become citizens.

4. Many newcomers to America were faced with which of these problems?
   a. They had little knowledge of English.
   b. They were not allowed to attend American schools.
   c. They were not allowed to attend church with English-speaking people.
5. Some native-born Americans did not like the great wave of immigration because the new Americans
   a. could not read or write
   b. spoke different languages and dressed differently
   c. were skilled workers

GRAPH STUDY *Where Immigrants Came From*
Study the pictograph. Then decide whether these statements are true or false. If a statement is false, rewrite it so that it is true.

Where Immigrants Came From

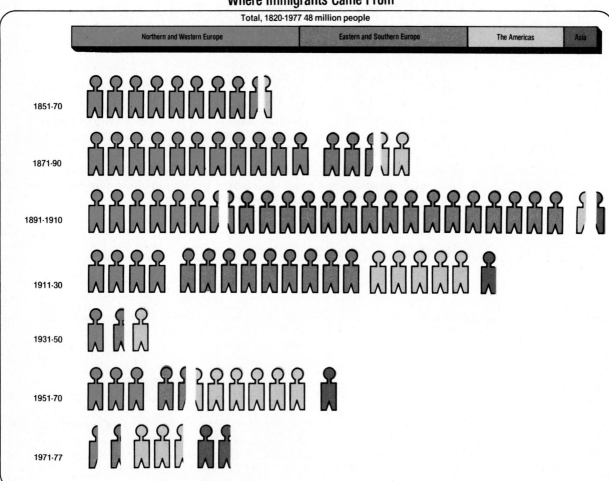

Each symbol equals 500,000 people.

1. There were no immigrants to the United States between 1930 and 1950.
2. Between 1911 and 1930, most immigrants to the United States were from Europe.
3. About five million people came to the United States between 1850 and 1870.
4. This graph tells us why immigrants came to the United States.
5. People from Asia cannot come to the United States.
6. The years 1891 to 1910 were the years of heaviest immigration.
7. Between 1971 and 1977 the number of Asian immigrants was about four times as large as the number from northern and western Europe.
8. Between 1871 and 1890, immigrants from northern and western Europe outnumbered immigrants from eastern and southern Europe.
9. We can tell from this graph how the immigration laws of our country are made.
10. Immigration dropped off sharply between 1930 and 1950.

SUMMING UP **CONTRIBUTIONS OF IMMIGRANTS** Choose ten of the immigrants. What contributions have these people made to the United States and the world? You may use an encyclopedia or other books to help you.

Alexander G. Bell	Joseph Pulitzer	Igor Stravinsky
Jacob Riis	Michael Pupin	John James Audubon
Andrew Carnegie	Carl Schurz	Enrico Fermi
John J. Astor	Nathan Straus	Henry Kissinger
Victor Herbert	James G. Bennett	Frances Xavier Cabrini
Albert Gallatin	Isaac M. Wise	Ieoh Ming Pei
John Ericsson	Nikola Tesla	Albert Einstein
Samuel Gompers	Louis Agassiz	Enrico Caruso
Louise Nevelson	David Sarnoff	

Thinking It Through

Why did immigrants come to this country during the 1800s? Why do you think people continue to immigrate to the United States today?

6 AMERICA BECOMES A LAND OF CITIES

What problems were created by the growth of cities in this country?

View of the New York Elevated Railroad, early 1880s. What are advantages and disadvantages of elevated railroads? Name two reasons why cities grew so fast.

1. A very important result of the Industrial Revolution in America was the growth of cities. Of course, there were cities in America before 1865. Some cities grew up near harbors, canals, rivers, and lakes. Others grew up where roads or railroads crossed. Some were factory towns where the workers lived. After 1865, however, cities grew even more rapidly as the United States became a leading industrial nation. By 1900 there were 77 cities with more than 50,000 people.

2. There were several reasons for the growth of cities. First, the nation's population was growing. Second, many people (including southern blacks) were moving from farms to the cities to work in factories. Third, as the immigrants came to America, many of them settled in cities. Fourth, now fewer farmers and ranchers were needed to feed the millions of people who chose to live and work in the cities. Finally, the railroads now could bring to the cities the large amounts of food, coal, oil, and other raw materials needed to keep a city going.

3. As the cities grew, there were many new problems. In the villages, the people got their water from wells. Their garbage was burned or taken away by themselves or a small company. In the city, huge tubes, or **aqueducts,** had to be built to bring in fresh water from lakes and rivers. Chemicals were added to the water to make it safe from disease. Pipes were laid to carry away water and waste. The city collected the garbage and built large furnaces to burn it.

4. When communities were small, fire fighting was done by volunteers. When cities grew large, they hired full-time fire fighters to stay on duty at all hours. In the station was the fire wagon pulled by horses. A steam engine was used to pump water onto the fires. The fire alarm box came into use. At the same time, cities began to hire full-time uniformed policemen to fight the growing problem of crime. These men were trained and were used to patrol the neighborhoods.

5. Many city people lived far from their place of work. They had to go to work in all kinds of weather. They needed better ways to travel to and from their work. Although some streets had been paved with cobblestones or wood blocks, others were not paved at all. But about 1900, asphalt streets began to replace cobblestones. Electric trolley cars appeared. Bridges were built across waterways that divided parts of large cities. The first elevated railway was opened in New York City in 1867. In 1897

Boston opened the first subway system of trains that ran underground. Despite these inventions, horse-drawn carriages and wagons remained, crowding the streets.

6. As the cities grew, land in the inner city became very expensive. There was a need to put up higher and higher buildings in the middle of crowded areas. The first skyscraper was built around 1900. Two inventions made the skyscraper possible. One was the elevator, which was run by electricity. The second was the steel frame for the tall buildings.

7. Living conditions for city people improved a great deal. About the year 1900, many city homes had built-in bathtubs, hot and cold running water, electric lights, and even telephones. Their rooms were warmed by steam or hot-water radiators. Their floors were covered with rugs or carpets. Their shopping was done in large general stores called department stores. Here city dwellers could find almost anything they needed. The chain stores began. These stores were able to sell goods at lower prices because they bought goods in large amounts. The Great A & P Company and the Woolworth Company were two of the earliest chain stores. Sewing clothing, canning food, baking cakes, and washing clothes, tasks once done at home, were now often done by large plants and factories.

8. As more people came to the cities, new schools had to be built. More people remained in school through high school. School buildings were larger and cleaner. Teachers were better trained and used many kinds of materials to interest pupils. Some schools began to teach trades to the children of the cities.

9. With both farm workers and people from foreign lands moving into the cities, many sections of the city became heavily crowded. Most of these new workers earned low wages because they were not skilled in higher-paying trades. Many of them could not buy new homes. Therefore, they crowded together in old buildings. Conditions in some sections of our large cities were miserable. These areas are called slums. Several families might live in a single flat or apartment. Many rooms had no windows. All of the families on a floor might have but one bathroom to be shared by everyone. As the inner parts of the city become overcrowded, some people moved to new neighborhoods outside the city. These sections are called suburbs.

The opening of one of the first five-and-ten-cent stores. What were the advantages of chain stores?

Decide whether each event below encouraged or discouraged immigration in the United States. Support your decisions.

1. The building of railroads and canals
2. The discovery of gold in California
3. Hard times in the United States
4. Cheap land available in the West
5. Beginning of interest in factories and mines
6. The quota system
7. The Civil War in the United States
8. The lack of political freedom in Europe

I. What is the main purpose of Chapter 6?

a. To tell about improvements in city life
b. To discuss improvements in education
c. To describe conditions in city slums
d. To describe the growth of American cities

II. Choose the correct answer or answers.

1. The growth of cities created which two problems?
   a. Poor housing
   b. Little time for entertainment
   c. More crime and fires
2. Cities before 1900 did not have
   a. paved streets
   b. a fresh water supply
   c. bus lines
3. After 1865 many people moved to the city to
   a. be near their place of work
   b. get more living space
   c. find better homes
4. The skyscraper became possible with the invention of the
   a. electric light and steam-powered elevator
   b. steel frame and electric-powered elevator
   c. neither answer a nor answer b

III. Do you agree or disagree? Give reasons for your answers.

1. The number of Americans living in cities fell sharply between 1865 and 1900.
2. People moved from the farms to the cities to work in factories and other businesses.
3. Many Americans found a new way of life in the cities.
4. As the cities grew, Americans found many new problems.
5. The needs of people living in the cities brought about changes in the ways of living.
6. As the cities became overcrowded, people left to live in the suburbs.
7. Making water safe to drink was a big problem for the growing cities.
8. Department stores were begun to provide goods to people living on farms and in the suburbs.

PICTOGRAPH STUDY *America Becomes a Nation of City Dwellers*
Study the pictograph. Then decide whether these statements are true or false. Rewrite the false statements to make them true.

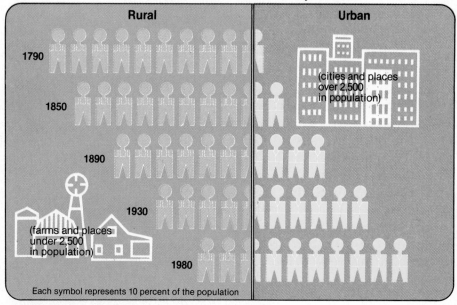

America Becomes a Nation of City Dwellers

Each symbol represents 10 percent of the population

1. In 1790 most Americans were farmers.
2. In 1890 most Americans lived in cities.
3. Rural is another word for living in the city.
4. Our cities did not grow between 1850 and 1890.
5. This graph tells you why people moved to the cities.
6. Our cities grew larger as more and more immigrants came to this country. (Review the pictograph on page 372 for help in answering this question.)

THEN AND NOW Complete the following chart in your notebook.

THEN (Villages)	PROBLEM	NOW (Cities)
	Sanitation	
	Education	
	Transportation	
	Fire and police protection	
	Water supply	
	Lighting and heating	

Thinking It Through

In the past 30 years, many people left the cities to live in the suburbs, sections outside the cities. What changes might bring these people back to the cities?

7 THE GROWTH OF INDUSTRY AFFECTS FACTORY WORKERS

How did business change after 1865? What methods did workers use to improve their working conditions?

1. From colonial times until the mid-1800s, a person who wanted to start a business could do so easily. Only a small amount of money was needed to get started. The business person had to buy materials, find a suitable building for a shop or workroom, and hire a few workers. The owner was generally close to the workers and called them by their first names. If the owner of a business wanted to enlarge it, going in with others as partners was the solution. If one partner became sick or died, the others could carry on the business.

2. After 1865 things began to change. Everything was done on a larger scale. Factories became larger. Business people bought more materials. They put in new power-driven machines. They hired more workers to tend the machines. All of this cost a lot of money. Few had enough money to set up these new factories and hire all the workers needed. To obtain such large sums of money, a new form of business began, called the **corporation.**

3. How is a corporation formed? The corporation starts with shares of stock. These shares are offered for sale to people. Those who buy the stocks become owners of the corporation. They are called stockholders or shareholders. Usually the stockholders pick a board of directors to manage the corporation. If the corporation succeeds, the stockholders make money. They receive a share of the profits of the business. Some of these corporations grew large and came to be called big business.

Andrew Carnegie, iron and steel manufacturer. He believed that the rich should use their wealth for the good of the public. Carnegie gave much of his money to education, research, and libraries.

4. The heads of the largest corporations were sometimes called **captains of industry.** Like the other pioneers in our history—the farmers, miners, and cattle ranchers—they helped America grow. They developed our coal, iron, and oil resources. They brought the country together by building railroads and telegraph and telephone lines. They brought many goods and comforts to the farmers and the city workers. By 1900 their ways of doing business had changed America into a land of factories and machines. Some of the pioneer leaders in American business were James J. Hill (railroads), Andrew Carnegie (steel), and John D. Rockefeller (oil). They helped make the United States the world's leading industrial nation.

5. The corporations also had some disadvantages. The few men at the head of big business grew richer and richer and had great power. A single corporation could control almost all of the oil produced in the country. A single man could own the mines, railways, and mills needed to make steel. When this was so, the corporation could charge the people whatever price it wanted for its goods. This is called a **monopoly.** A monopoly could even lower prices to make it hard for other people to succeed in businesses of the same kind. Once these others were driven out of business, the monopoly could raise its prices again.

6. The growth of factories after the Civil War was hard on the workers. Conditions in most of these factories were poor. The factories were badly lighted. Many of the machines were unsafe and many accidents took place. Women and children sometimes worked as much as 15 hours a day with low pay. Factory workers took home about $5.00 a week for their labor. Most young people did not graduate from high school, for they had to go to work to help the family. In order to keep costs as low as possible, many employers were not willing to improve conditions in their factories.

7. It became harder and harder for the workers to leave their jobs. Until 1890, if the workers did not like the factory they could make a change. They could go West and stake out a farm. After 1900 there was little free land in the West. With the cheaper land gone, job holders could not leave the factory jobs. Many immigrants were looking for work in the cities, so employers could find other workers to replace those who protested about conditions. Workers were still free to leave their jobs, but in many cases this meant they were free to starve.

8. Finally, the saddest fact about the Industrial Revolution was that machines often put people out of work. There were years when businesses found they could not sell the goods they made. If profits were small, the business needed fewer workers. These hard times are called **depressions.** Since the coming of the machine, more people suffer during a depression. The average person today depends upon other people for food and clothing. These items must be bought with money. If people are out of work, they cannot buy the things they need. Serious depressions in the United States took place during the years 1873–1878, 1893–1897, and 1929 through the 1930s.

9. What could the working people do to improve their conditions? Workers decided that the best thing they could do was to follow the example of the business people —join together. They formed what we call labor or trade unions. The first large union in the United States was begun in 1869. It was organized by Uriah Stephens and was called the Knights of Labor. It was open to all workers, whether or not they had a skill. Men, women, blacks, whites, farmers, and

Scene in a clothing factory, early 1900s. Why were factories such as these called "sweat shops"?

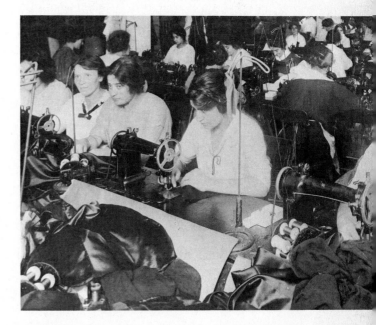

factory workers, were all allowed to join. Within 20 years the Knights of Labor had 750,000 members. Most of these were unskilled workers. However, the union began to lose members during the 1890s. It was difficult to keep people with so many different skills in the same union.

10. The first successful leader of the American working people was Samuel Gompers. Gompers had three ideas about a trade union. First, the union should be made up only of skilled workers. These workers are well-trained. Second, skilled workers should belong to a union of their own craft or trade. There should be a union of carpenters only; another of plumbers; another of locksmiths. Such unions came to be called **craft unions.** Third, workers and employers should try to settle their differences through **collective bargaining.** This takes place when the employers and the union leaders meet together and talk over their problems. Both sides can then come to an agreement about wages, hours, rules, and working conditions.

11. In 1886 Gompers started the American Federation of Labor, or A.F. of L. Many difficulties faced the unions. First, many employers did not believe they should be told how to run their businesses. They felt they should be able to hire and fire workers and set their wages. Employers often fired workers who joined a union. They called them "troublemakers." A large part of the public agreed with the employers. Second, the great number of immigrants provided a ready supply of workers. These newcomers were willing to take less money in order to get a job. Third, women worked for less pay than men who did the same job. Women took little interest in the labor union, for many expected to leave their jobs when they married. Fourth, many white workers would not join unions that also included blacks. Finally, the government was often against them. Government troops were sometimes used to break strikes.

12. Should collective bargaining fail to bring about an agreement, each side may take other action. The workers may refuse to work until their demands are met. This is called a **strike.** The strikers may picket their place of work. This means that workers place themselves at the entrance to the plant and try to persuade other workers not to go to work. They ask customers not to buy from the plant. They try to keep the employer from hiring other workers to take their places during the strike. Workers and people who favor the workers may **boycott,** or refuse to buy, the business's product.

13. In a strike, an employer might close the plant and refuse to talk with the workers. This is called a **lockout.** The employer might find out the names of the union members who were the leaders. The

The Homestead Strike, 1892, at the Carnegie Steel Company. Troops were sent to end this strike. Do you think it was right to use troops in this way? Do you think sending troops would be a good way to end strikes today? Why or why not?

employer might let other employers know who these people were. This is called a **blacklist.** Then other employers might not hire those people whose names were on the blacklist. Sometimes an employer refused to hire a worker unless he or she agreed in advance not to join a union. The worker pledged not to become a union member by signing a paper called a **yellow-dog contract.** To stop a strike the employer could ask for an **injunction.** An injunction is a court order to do or not to do something. The court could order that the workers stop their strike and return to their jobs.

14. The first big strike took place in 1877. At that time, four big railway lines in the East ordered a cut in pay for their workers. This was because of a serious business slowdown throughout the country. The men, making only $30 to $40 a month, were bitter. They went on strike. They were joined by other railroad workers in other states. Soon the trains did not run. There were fights between strikers and company officials. People were killed and wounded. Property was destroyed. The governors of four states asked for federal troops to stop the fighting. This was the first strike in which the army was used. The troops broke the strike and the strikers returned to work for less pay. Following this strike, there were many other long, costly, and bitter strikes.

15. The struggle for better working conditions and higher pay was a long and hard one. In 1900 most workers were earning about $400 to $500 a year and working about 10 hours a day. At first, the employers had the law on their side. Union members were thought to be little more than troublemakers. Not until the 1930s did the labor unions become strong enough to win better pay and improved working conditions for their members. In the meantime, the public was often caught in the middle of disputes between employers and workers.

REVIEWING
CHAPTER 6

Improvements in our way of life do not happen by chance. When something is needed, ways are found to fill this need. Listed in Column A are some conditions that called for action. In your notebook, list improvements asked for in Column B.

Column A
1. People wished to be able to get to work quickly.
2. People needed protection from crime and disease.
3. People wanted homes that were more comfortable.
4. People demanded better schools.

Column B
List three improvements in city transportation.
List three improvements in city law enforcement and sanitation.
List three improvements in city homes.
List three improvements in education in our cities.

UNDERSTANDING
CHAPTER 7

I. What is the main purpose of Chapter 7?

   a. To discuss the growth of big business and its effect on workers
   b. To tell how a corporation operates
   c. To describe laws passed by Congress
   d. To describe the contributions of business people

II. Choose the correct answer.

1. Big business has played a large part in the growth of America by
   a. helping to settle eastern lands
   b. developing the natural resources of the country
   c. opening schools in large cities
2. A depression usually means that
   a. large numbers of people are out of work
   b. people want to buy more goods than factories can make
   c. stockholders in a corporation are making money
3. The growth of big business led to
   a. the end of women and children working in factories
   b. better working conditions in factories
   c. a great variety of goods for the American people
4. The chief reason why workers formed unions was to
   a. improve their working conditions
   b. raise prices of factory-made goods
   c. create larger sales of manufactured goods
5. Corporations were formed because
   a. there was a large supply of workers
   b. stockholders wanted to share in forming the business
   c. operating a giant business took a large amount of money
6. With cheap land in the West already claimed and immigrants seeking jobs, workers found that they
   a. could move more easily from job to job
   b. could save money and become owners themselves
   c. were less secure in their jobs than they once were
7. Workers in early factories
   a. worked under safe conditions
   b. owned the tools they used
   c. worked long hours with little pay

DEVELOPING IDEAS AND SKILLS

PICTURE SYMBOLS   These pictures should help you recall parts of the chapter you have just read. What is the main idea of each picture?

MAP SKILLS   *Oil Resources of the United States*
Study the map on the next page. Then decide whether these statements are true or false. Explain your answer.

Oil Resources in the United States

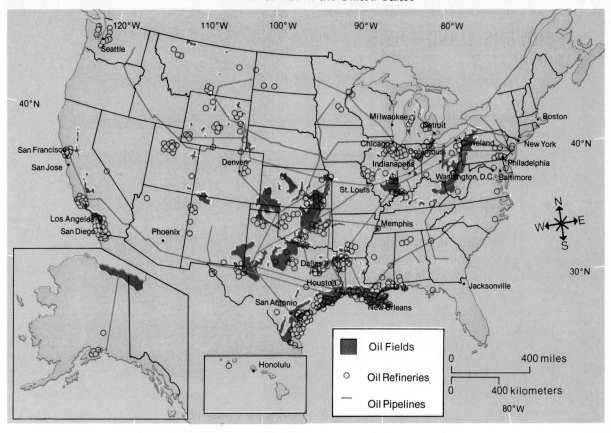

1. The largest oil fields are found north of Boston.
2. The most oil pipelines are found in the Northwest.
3. There are no oil fields on the West Coast.
4. Most states have oil deposits.
5. Most of the large cities are near oil fields.
6. An oil pipeline brings oil from Alaska to the East Coast.
7. There are oil fields near the Gulf of Mexico.
8. There are major oil refineries in Texas.

SUMMING UP **Complete this outline in your notebook.**

THE FACTORY SYSTEM

I. Advantages
   A.
   B.
   C.

II. Disadvantages
   A.
   B.
   C.

Thinking It Through

Many workers refused to join unions when they first started. Why do you think this was so? Joining a labor union today is protected by law. Nevertheless, the majority of American workers do not belong to labor unions. Why do you think this is so?

8 FARMERS HAVE THEIR PROBLEMS

What changes did machines bring to farm life?

1. After the Civil War, the machine came to many more farms. Within the next 50 years, many of the steps in growing and harvesting crops were done by machine. Gas engines took the place of horses in pulling the plows and reapers. Machines affected farming in two ways. First, fewer people were needed to work the farms. Second, these same few workers could produce more food. In 1850 one farmer, working alone, could farm 12 acres of ground. Because of the new machinery, by 1900 one farmer could farm 50 acres and produce more food per acre!

2. With so many new machines available, many farmers turned to lands they once thought too dry for farming, the Great Plains. They found that wheat was the best crop for the Great Plains. Farmers used irrigation, new farming methods, and a new kind of wheat brought back from Russia by Mark Carleton. This wheat could grow in very dry soil and did not get many plant diseases. These new farms on the Great Plains provided food for the growing population of our country and Europe. By 1900 the United States was known as the "breadbasket of the world."

3. In order to succeed, farmers became more and more like other business people. They no longer grew everything they needed. They began to specialize in one crop, which they grew to sell. This was called the money crop. They sold their money crop and bought manufactured goods that their farm could not supply.

This poster was published by the Grangers. What does it suggest are the gifts of the farmer?

Farmers became specialists just like the workers in the factories.

4. Farmers had their problems, too. They depended on a good price for their money crop. They often borrowed money to buy their machines and seed. If the price for their crops was low, farmers could not pay their debts. If they could not meet their payments, they might lose their farms.

5. They had other problems. Farmers depended on the railroads to get crops to market. They would get nothing for crops if the crops did not reach those who would buy them. Farmers felt that the railroads charged high prices for carrying their products. But they could not do without the railroad.

6. Farmers tried to make more money by raising larger amounts of wheat, cotton, and corn. The more they grew, the more they

had to sell. However, when there was too large a supply of farm goods, the prices for these goods dropped. Moreover, by continually using their land, farmers wore out the soil.

7. The prices for farm products were so low between 1865 and 1895 that farmers could not pay their debts. Thousands lost their farms. Then farmers began to work for laws that would help them. One organization of farmers was the Grange, founded in 1867 by Oliver H. Kelley. By 1875 there were 858,000 Grange members. They voted for lawmakers who agreed to get benefits for them. Soon the state governments of Illinois, Minnesota, Iowa, and Wisconsin were controlled by men who supported the farmers' program. These states passed laws that helped farmers in their fight against the railroads. The Granger laws did not last, for the Supreme Court said that states had no power to regulate railroads.

8. In 1887 Congress passed the Interstate Commerce Act to regulate railroads. It set up a commission that had little control over the railroads. However, it was the beginning of an effort by the government to limit the power of the railroads. At the same time, certain businesses were growing stronger by buying up smaller businesses. These new business giants were called **trusts.** Some trusts were soon able to set up monopolies in meat packing and flour milling. Farmers sold their goods to these large firms, but they were paid low prices. The farmers felt that these trusts should be broken up. In 1890 Congress passed the Sherman Antitrust Act. This act was intended to prevent businesses from joining together to control trade in a product.

9. When these laws did not help, many farmers joined the Populist party, which had a smaller following than the Democratic or Republican parties. Through the Populist program, farmers hoped to gain the support of the eastern workers. The Populists wanted a shorter working day, a tax on money earned (an income tax), and government control of the railroads. They also wanted a way of voting in which a person's own choice could be kept secret. There were other demands. The Populists never succeeded in electing a president. However, some of the changes they asked for have gradually been made into law.

Match the items in the left column with the explanations in the right column.

1. craft union
2. industrial union
3. collective bargaining
4. strike
5. lockout
6. captains of industry

a. Workers of a particular skill are organized.
b. The employer closes the factory.
c. Workers refuse to report to work.
d. Heads of large 19th-century corporations helped industry grow.
e. Representatives of the workers and the employer discuss their problems.
f. All the workers of an industry join one union.

I. **What is the main idea of Chapter 8?**

    a. To discuss problems and changes in farm life
    b. To tell about organizations of farmers
    c. To describe a modern farm
    d. To describe government action to help the farmer

II. **Choose the correct answer.**

  1. Congress passed the Interstate Commerce Act to
    a. improve conditions in factories
    b. stop unfair practices of the railroads
    c. prevent the selling of impure foods
  2. Farmers hoped to solve some of their problems in the late 1880s by asking the government to
    a. regulate railroads
    b. give them insurance against a poor crop
    c. pay them for land they did not cultivate
  3. Farmers supported the Populist party because farmers
    a. favored lower prices on farm products
    b. were opposed to unions
    c. could not get help from the older political parties
  4. The government passed the Sherman Antitrust Act to
    a. break up very large companies that were controlling trade
    b. raise taxes on goods coming from overseas
    c. take over certain large businesses in time of war
  5. One of the purposes of the Grange was to
    a. work for laws to benefit farmers
    b. speed railroad building on the Great Plains
    c. gain a shorter working day for farm workers
  6. When farmers have a "money crop,"
    a. they grow everything they need to feed their family
    b. they grow one special crop that they hope to sell to obtain the things they need
    c. they are members of the soil bank
  7. Farmers could turn out larger amounts of crops when they
    a. used machinery
    b. joined the Grange
    c. were supported by the Populist party

III. **Decide whether each statement agrees or disagrees with what you have read. If the statement disagrees, explain why.**

  1. After 1865 new machines were invented to help the farmer.
  2. The new machines made it possible for fewer people to farm larger plots of land.
  3. Farmers depended on many crops to make money.
  4. Most farmers made little money because of high railroad costs.
  5. Farmers began to feel that their problems were too big to solve by themselves.

MAP SKILLS *Agricultural Regions*
Study the map. Then decide whether these statements are true or false.
Support your decision.

Agricultural Regions

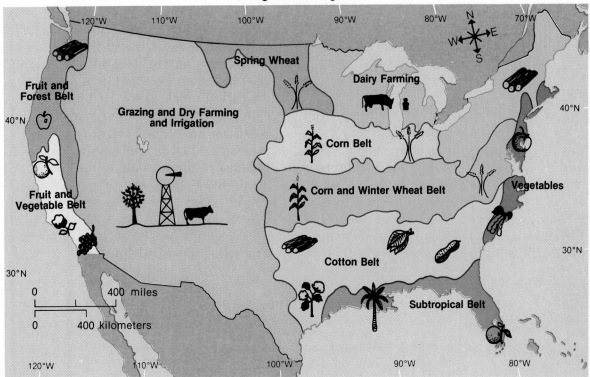

1. Irrigated land is found chiefly in the western part of the United States.
2. The Great Lakes area is an important dairy farming region.
3. Much of the western United States is suited to cattle grazing.
4. The cotton growing region is found only in the southern states.
5. Most of the land in the United States is suited for growing corn.
6. Spring wheat is grown in a cooler climate than winter wheat.
7. The northwest region has large forest areas.

THE FARM PROBLEM Below are some headings for an outline. In
your notebook, write two topics under each heading.

Headings:
A. How the Machine Changed Farm Life
B. Problems of the Farmer
C. Efforts to Solve the Problems of the Farmer

Thinking It Through

In what ways did farmers and factory workers take similar action to improve
their situations?

9 THE PROGRESSIVE MOVEMENT

How did a group of reformers try to solve some of America's problems?

1. The rapid growth of industry after 1865 brought many changes to American life. It gave Americans more goods, more machines, and more comforts. But the new ways of living brought serious problems as well. Many people thought that our form of government, democracy, was in danger. A few wealthy and powerful business leaders were able to influence government officials to pass laws in their favor. They were able to squeeze out owners of smaller businesses. They were able to sell goods of poor quality at high prices. They had no income taxes to pay. In addition, many people thought that the way officials were elected was not democratic enough. In short, there were few laws to correct these problems.

2. These and other problems facing the people were described by a group of writers called **muckrakers**. In 1906 Upton Sinclair published the most stirring of these writings, *The Jungle*, a story of the meat-packing industry. The public was shocked to learn of the unsanitary methods used to bring meat products to market. For example, meat was often stored in rooms where rats would race about. Poisoned bread would be set out to kill these rats. Then the poisoned bread, dead rats, and

This cartoon depicts the business trusts as the real bosses of the Senate. Why did many people think this was so?

THE BOSSES OF THE SENATE.

meats would all go into the meat grinder together.

3. Other well-known muckrakers were Frank Norris, Lincoln Steffens, Ida Tarbell, and Thomas Lawson. In his books, Frank Norris told how farmers suffered from the railroad and grain **trusts.** Lincoln Steffens showed how politicians in many cities got rich by giving favors to big business. Ida Tarbell wrote the *History of the Standard Oil Company*, which told how difficult it was for new companies to make a start against the giants of the business world. Thomas Lawson showed how a few men controlled most of the money in this country.

4. All over the United States, voices called for reform or change. Those voices seemed to say, "Come on Americans. We can do better than this." The call for reform was led by a new group of Americans, called **Progressives.** The Progressives were mainly middle-class Americans who wanted to correct some of those abuses. They did not like the growing power of big business. They felt that the cities were run poorly. They wanted to end child labor in the factories. The government's role, as they saw it, was to help them bring about reforms. Among the leading Progressives were Senator Robert La Follette of Wisconsin and Presidents Theodore Roosevelt and Woodrow Wilson.

5. The Progressives wanted the common people to have greater control over their local governments. In the larger cities, a new type of leader had appeared, the political boss. The bosses were full-time politicians. Sometimes they got themselves elected as mayors. But for the most part, they stayed in the background. They picked their own candidates for office. Then they made sure that the people in their district voted for these candidates. When their candidates were elected, the bosses were able to control them from behind the scenes. Once in power, these

Robert La Follette giving a radio campaign speech. What reforms did the Progressives want to make?

bosses often made fortunes for themselves and their families, always at the expense of the people they were supposed to serve.

6. In order to curb some of the worst abuses by political bosses, many Progressives worked to bring about the following changes.

a. *Civil Service Reform.* For a long time, government jobs were handed out to people who had helped elect a high official. They were given to people who had worked for the successful political party or had given money to it. They were not given out based on a person's ability. This practice is called the **spoils system.** In 1883 the Civil Service Act was passed. Under this law, a large number of government jobs were given only to people who passed an examination that proved their ability. This law made government workers feel safer in their jobs. Now they could not be removed if a political party other than their own won the next election.

b. *The Secret Ballot.* Although more people were voting than ever before, voting still took place in the open and each political party provided its own ballots. Each party had its own colored paper for its ballot. As a result, party workers could easily see who was voting for their party. Party workers could get a group of people together, show them how to vote, and make sure they voted as the party wished. Under the leadership of the Progressives, laws were passed requiring that voting be done in secret (in a polling booth). Furthermore, they required ballots to be all one color and supplied by the government.

c. *The Direct Primary.* For a long time most candidates for political office were chosen at private meetings of the party leaders. The Progressives wanted the people to have a greater voice in the selection of candidates. They urged that people use the direct primary. Under this method, an earlier election, called a **primary**, would be held. Voters of each party would choose the candidates they wished to represent them in the final election. Voters could also have the name of any candidates listed on the ballot if enough members of the party signed a petition for those candidates.

7. The Progressives also wanted to check the growing power of big business. Some earlier efforts to do so (the Granger laws in the 1870s, Interstate Commerce Act of 1887, Sherman Antitrust Act of 1890) had failed. A number of states began to pass laws to protect the worker. These laws reduced the number of hours that men, women, and children could work in factories. In some states, children under 16 years of age were forbidden by law from working in factories and mines. However, the courts did not allow some of these laws to stand. The Supreme Court said that a state could not pass laws that would inter-

fere with a business that was carrying on trade in more than one state.

8. The Progressives worked even harder to get Congress to pass national laws that cared for the needs of the people. In 1906 Congress passed the Pure Food and Drug Law. This law protected the people from unsafe foods and medicines. Shortly thereafter, Congress passed a law giving the government the power to inspect meats and other foods. In 1913 Congress passed the Federal Reserve Act, setting up the banking system that still exists today. In 1914 it passed the Clayton Antitrust Act. This act made it easier to break up the big trusts into smaller companies. It clearly stated what big businesses could and could not do. It also made it easier for workers to join labor unions and strike.

9. One of the greatest achievements of the Progressives was the passage of the 16th Amendment in 1913. This amendment gave Congress the power to place a tax on the money people earned. This is called an **income tax.** Only 18 years before, the Supreme Court had said that such a tax was unconstitutional because it was an attack upon the rich. The new income tax was graduated, which means that people paid according to their income. Those who made a lot of money were required to pay higher taxes than those who did not make much money.

10. In 1913 the Progressives were also successful in having the 17th Amendment added to the Constitution. Up until that time, United States senators were chosen by the legislatures of the states. As a result, senators were often elected by small groups of people in each state and did not represent the choice of the majority of voters. Under the 17th Amendment, United States senators were to be elected directly by the people of the states.

11. Demands grew for the right of women to vote. In 1869 the Wyoming Territory gave women in that region full vot-

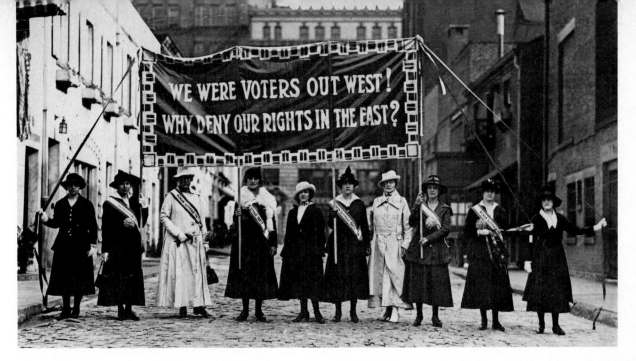

Women marching for the right to vote. Why did some people oppose women's right to vote?

ing rights. Many reformers joined the National Woman Suffrage Association. As its president, Susan B. Anthony continued her work for women's rights. But by 1898 women could vote in all elections only in Wyoming, Utah, Colorado, and Idaho.

12. In the early 20th century, supporters of the vote for women organized marches, petitions, and hunger strikes. More and more states, mostly in the West, passed laws giving women the right to vote. In 1912 the Progressive party came out officially in favor of women's **suffrage** (the right to vote). Carrie Chapman Catt became an important leader. She and other supporters worked hard to convince Congress to pass a constitutional amendment giving women the right to vote. Their work was finally successful. Congress passed the 19th Amendment. It became part of the Constitution in 1920.

13. At the same times these reforms were being made, there was a movement to save our natural resources. When the first settlers came to America, they found a land rich in soil, forests, and water. As the westward movement continued, the great resources of our land were used carelessly. There seemed to be so much natural wealth that people gave little thought to protecting nature's gift. Instead, they cut down whole forests. Miners dug only the richest veins of ore. Cattle and sheep were allowed to strip the grassy plains, turning them into "dust bowls." Beginning with President Theodore Roosevelt, the government took an active part in seeing that our natural resources were not wasted. Lands were set aside by the national government as parks. These lands were not to be settled. Rather they were to be used by all the people. This program of saving our natural resources is called **conservation.**

14. The Progressives had changed the attitude of the government toward business. For a long time, it had been felt that government should not interfere with business. However, the struggles of farmers and workers to improve their lot changed this idea. New laws brought the government

closer to the people. The people were given greater power in choosing public officials. There were laws that protected farmers and workers as well as those who used their goods. With the beginning of the 20th century, the government became more concerned with the welfare of all the people of the nation.

Decide whether each description below is associated with big-business people, workers, or farmers.

1. Supported the Grange
2. Wanted collective bargaining
3. Wanted the government to regulate railroads
4. Was helped by the Interstate Commerce Act
5. Did not want to see workers organized
6. Harmed when the price of their money crop dropped
7. Sometimes formed a monopoly
8. Used the strike to gain their demands
9. Formed corporations
10. Blacklisted union leaders

I. What is the main purpose of Chapter 9?

   a. To describe the laws that keep our food pure
   b. To discuss the changes brought about by the Progressive movement
   c. To discuss the work of certain governors in the Progressive movement
   d. To describe efforts to save our natural resources

II. Choose the correct answer.

1. The direct primary was supported by the Progressives in order to give
   a. women the right to vote
   b. the people a more direct voice in their government
   c. the states more power
2. The movement to save the natural resources of our country is called
   a. conservation
   b. the spoils system
   c. the direct primary
3. An income tax means that people pay a tax on
   a. goods brought into this country
   b. goods that are made in this country
   c. money they earned during the year
4. Government employees who get their jobs by taking examinations are under the
   a. Progressive system
   b. civil service system
   c. spoils system
5. A muckraker believed that
   a. slavery should be ended
   b. the government should not interfere in business
   c. power should not be in the hands of only a few

6. The states that first gave women full voting rights in the late 19th century are
   a. in the East
   b. in the West
   c. in the South

III. Decide whether each statement agrees or disagrees with what you have read. If the statement disagrees, explain why.

1. Farmers were among the first to fight big business.
2. United States senators are still chosen by state legislatures.
3. The Progressive movement brought about many reforms at the beginning of the 20th century.
4. The 16th Amendment was a great victory for the Progressives.
5. Many government workers must pass an examination to obtain their jobs.
6. The Progressive movement gave the people a greater voice in the nominations and elections of officials.
7. As a result of the Progressive movement, many people favored government regulation of big business.
8. During the early 20th century, the government began to protect people against harmful foods and drugs.
9. The muckrakers were a group of conservationists.
10. The Supreme Court has changed its thinking on some of the decisions it has made.
11. Women throughout the country gained the right to vote in 1920.
12. Carrie Chapman Catt led the fight for civil service reform.

DEVELOPING IDEAS AND SKILLS

PICTURE SYMBOLS These pictures should help you to recall parts of the chapter you have read. Describe the main idea of each picture.

SUMMING UP

Thinking It Through

Many of the ideas of the Progressive movement have reappeared during the past few years as consumerism. Individuals and groups are again calling for a look into the quality of goods being sold to the public. How is the public protected against bad food and water, cigarettes, dangerous medicines, and unsafe cars?

FROM BOOM TO BUST!

What was life like in the 1920s? How did the New Deal help people during the Great Depression of the 1930s?

Life in the United States. These scenes are from a large wall painting. They show life in the United States in the 1920s and 1930s. What do the scenes tell us about life during this time?

1. The Progressive movement came to an end in about 1917. Starting in the early 1920s, new changes took place in our way of life. More people had more money to spend than ever before. Many Americans came to feel that they had to go to the new movies at least once a week. Many thought that they had to have a package of cigarettes a day, a new car in their garage, and a new radio in their parlor. Americans were using many kinds of machines run by electricity—refrigerators, washing machines, and vacuum cleaners. More and more women were beginning to work in stores, offices, and factories. The 19th Amendment had given women the right to vote.

2. The automobile did much to change the way people lived. The demand for cars meant new highways, new industries, and new jobs to service them. People could drive to and from work. Cars even made it possible for people to work in the cities but live in the suburbs, new sections outside the main cities. Most people welcomed the new sense of freedom that the automobile gave them.

3. Americans of the 1920s enjoyed going to the movies. They went every week to watch their favorite movie stars in "silent" pictures. By the end of the 1920s, "talking" pictures, or movies with sound, appeared. Millions of people also enjoyed going to sports events such as baseball and football games and boxing. Sport figures like Babe Ruth, Jack Dempsey, Gertrude

Ederle, and Red Grange became great heroes to all Americans.

4. In 1919 a prize of $25,000 was offered to the pilot making the first nonstop flight from New York to Paris, a distance of 3,600 miles. Several fliers tried to win this prize. None succeeded. Then in May 1927, a 25-year-old air-mail pilot named Charles Lindbergh decided to try. His flight across the Atlantic Ocean was successful. Lindbergh, who came to be known as the Lone Eagle, became a hero overnight. Lindbergh's success brought Europe and America closer to each other. In 1928 Amelia Earhart was part of a crew that flew across the Atlantic. Four years later, Earhart became the first woman to fly across the Atlantic alone. She, too, became an American hero.

5. Looking back, the twenties may seem like a time when Americans were full of fun and ready to try new things. This is not the entire case. Some workers made very little money and could not give their families the goods they needed. Many farmers could not

sell all the crops they were growing. The 1920s were a time of lawlessness too. In 1919 the 18th Amendment was passed. This amendment made it illegal to sell or buy alcoholic drinks. Many Americans were against this amendment and they refused to obey it. Some of them bought bootleg, or illegal, liquor. Much of this liquor was supplied by gangsters who often fought "wars" among themselves to control this trade. People were sometimes killed openly on the streets.

6. The 1920s were also a time of fear. In 1915 a new Ku Klux Klan was started. Klan members covered their heads with white pillow slips and their bodies with sheets. They burned crosses near the homes of blacks, Jews, Catholics, and immigrants to frighten them. If that failed, Klan members turned to whipping them, burning their houses, and even killing them. Klan members came not only from the South but

When Charles Lindbergh returned to New York after his first transatlantic flight, the city welcomed him with a ticker-tape parade. Here he is in June 1927, sitting on the left on top of a car. Why do you think Lindbergh was a hero of his day?

from the other states as well. By 1924 the Klan had over 5 million members.

7. Many Americans were trying to get rich by buying the stocks, or shares, of large companies. As more people looked for stocks to buy, the shares began to sell for many times what they were really worth. As the prices rose, more and more people rushed to buy stocks. They hoped to make big profits as the stock prices continued to go up. In October 1929, the stock market crashed. The prices of stocks fell sharply, until the stocks were almost worthless. Many people and businesses that owned large amounts of stocks lost great sums of money.

8. The worst depression in our history began. It has become known as the Great Depression. Factories and mills closed. Millions were put out of work. Many families did not have the things they needed in order to live. Herbert Hoover, who was president, felt that there was nothing wrong with American business and that the depression would soon end. Hoover did ask Congress to set up a few programs to help out farmers, workers, and businesses. But he felt that the people could help themselves during the depression.

9. How did the depression affect the people? Conditions kept getting worse instead of better. By 1933 there were over 13 million people out of work. There were hunger marches on Washington, D.C. It grew harder and harder for men and women to find jobs. Millions of people turned to bread lines and soup kitchens in order to have any food at all. Finally, many of the states and cities began to give small amounts of money to people who were out of work so that they could buy food and clothing. This is called **relief.**

10. Farmers were also in trouble. Farm prices dropped even lower than in the 1920s. Farmers could not sell all their crops. Many farmers lost their homes and their land. Some became sharecroppers.

For many people, the Great Depression meant waiting in lines such as this for free food. Why did many people go on relief?

his leadership, Congress passed many laws to try to end the Great Depression. These laws were called the New Deal. The new laws tried to help farmers, workers, and business and factory owners. To put people back to work, Congress created many new jobs: building dams, highways, houses, and bridges. With money the workers earned, they could buy factory goods and provide work for others.

12. To help people take care of themselves during hard times, the Social Security Act was passed in 1935. Under this law, unemployed workers receive money during the time they are looking for a job. The money is raised by a tax paid by employers. The law also set up a fund for those who become too ill or too old to work. Both the employer and the worker give money to this fund. Now when workers 62 or over stop working full time, they can receive a pension. This means that they get an amount of money every month from the fund. The law also provides money for states to help the disabled and blind poor, and for needy children. Since the law was

Others became **migratory workers,** moving from place to place to find work. Black workers found it hardest of all. Even those jobs that white people had never before wanted were now taken by whites.

11. In 1933 Franklin D. Roosevelt became president of the United States. Under

Under President Franklin D. Roosevelt's leadership, Congress set up many programs to help the country out of the Great Depression. Name two programs.

passed, millions of people have become part of the Social Security plan.

13. To help farmers, the government asked them to plant fewer acres of their money-making crops. In turn, the government paid farmers to plant crops such as clover and alfalfa. These crops helped keep the soil fertile. The government asked farmers not to offer their entire crop for sale. Instead, the government bought part of their crop and kept it in storehouses or granaries. This is still done today, but it has become very costly. The government has given much of this food to needy people both in our country and overseas.

14. To help workers, Congress passed many laws during the 1930s. One of these ended child labor in factories, set 40 hours as the normal working week, and fixed 40 cents an hour as the minimum, or lowest, wage. Today the average work week is 35 hours and the federal minimum wage is over $3 an hour. Another law, the Wagner Act, stopped employers from firing workers who joined unions. Workers and employers were encouraged to settle their disputes by collective bargaining. Under this new law, unions grew rapidly in membership. At this time, John L. Lewis formed the Congress of Industrial Organizations (CIO). He believed that unskilled workers should also be able to join a union. He wanted all workers in the same industry (skilled and unskilled) to belong to the same union — an **industrial union.** The early CIO unions were formed in the steel, auto, and rubber industries.

15. The drive to save our natural resources continued under Franklin Roosevelt. There was a demand to rebuild areas that were ruined by floods. In the Tennessee River Valley, dams were built by the Tennessee Valley Authority (TVA). The dams not only control floods, but they provide electric power and a better life for millions of people nearby. More projects like the TVA have been planned.

16. The steps taken by the New Deal to save our human resources cost billions of dollars. Taxes increased. The national government had to borrow large sums of money. Some people did not agree with such spending. They pointed out that the debt of our national government had become greater than ever before in our history. There were others, however, who felt that our government should help citizens regardless of the debt. Some of them felt that the New Deal was a continuation of the Progressive movement. Indeed, many farmers, businesses, and workers were helped by the New Deal. Many agencies created under the New Deal still operate today.

REVIEWING CHAPTER 9 **Choose the correct answer.**

1. The reform movement that brought about many changes in American life at the beginning of the 20th century was called the
   a. Progressive movement
   b. New Deal
   c. Alliance for Progress

2. Which statement best describes how Presidents Theodore Roosevelt and Wilson felt about big business?
   a. The government should not interfere in business affairs.
   b. The government should take over certain businesses.
   c. The government should stop unfair business practices.

3. The Progressive movement did not ask for changes in
   a. the practices of big business
   b. voting procedure
   c. military spending
4. The 17th Amendment provided for
   a. the direct election of senators
   b. giving citizens over 21 the right to vote
   c. the ending of the poll tax
5. One of the reforms brought about by the Progressives was
   a. the ending of the electoral college
   b. the merit or civil service system
   c. the placing of a limit on the terms of office for the president.

UNDERSTANDING
CHAPTER 10

I. **What is the main purpose of paragraphs 9 and 10?**

a. To describe the new machines that Americans had in the 1920s
b. To describe the movement to save our natural resources
c. To explain how the 18th Amendment affected Americans
d. To discuss problems caused by the Great Depression

II. **Choose the correct answer.**

1. Franklin D. Roosevelt started a program of building highways, bridges, and other public works chiefly to
   a. improve transportation
   b. make sure the United States would be prepared if war came
   c. give people work when jobs were scarce
2. The TVA is a program to
   a. provide jobs for people in eastern cities
   b. improve the life of people near the Tennessee River
   c. irrigate the lands of the Southwest
3. The Social Security Act helps all of these people EXCEPT those who
   a. are out of work
   b. are 62 years of age
   c. are not U.S. citizens
4. Farmers did not share the good times of the 1920s because
   a. they did not use machines
   b. they were paying high shipping prices to the railroads
   c. they were growing more crops than could be sold
5. The CIO was organized because
   a. farmers wanted their own union
   b. a large number of unskilled workers were not union members
   c. government employees had no union

III. **Decide whether each statement agrees or disagrees with what you have read. If the statement disagrees, explain why.**

1. The American people have been careful to save their natural resources.
2. The New Deal increased government spending.
3. All groups were making more money during the 1920s.

4. Dams may be built for many reasons.
5. The people of the United States are considered resources of the nation.
6. Inventions often create many new jobs.
7. The government gave many people jobs building dams, highways, and bridges during the Great Depression.
8. Workers without skills cannot join a union.
9. In a depression, a large number of people are out of work.
10. During the 1920s the rights of many Americans were threatened by the Ku Klux Klan.

DEVELOPING IDEAS AND SKILLS

THE GREAT DEPRESSION AND THE NEW DEAL Complete the following chart in your notebook.

GROUP	HOW DID THE DEPRESSION AFFECT THESE GROUPS?	WHAT STEPS OR LAWS WERE TAKEN TO HELP THEM?
Factory workers		
Farmers		
Business people		

SUMMING UP

Thinking It Through

Are there any similarities between life in the 1980s and life in the 1920s? If so, what are they? Do you see similarities between the 1980s and the 1930s? If so, describe them. If not, explain why.

Using a Time Line

Study this time line. Then answer the questions that follow. Use the information you have studied in this unit to help you. You may also look at the time line on pages 346 and 347 if you need additional help.

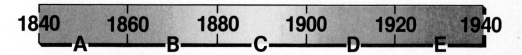

In which period of time (**A, B, C, D,** or **E**) did the following take place?

1. The Wright brothers flew their airplane for the first time at Kitty Hawk.
2. Mott and Stanton led the Women's Rights Convention at Seneca Falls.
3. The Great Depression occurred.
4. Morse invented the telegraph.
5. The Grange was founded.
6. The 20th Amendment giving women the right to vote became part of the Constitution.
7. Thomas Edison invented the light bulb.
8. Congress passed a law setting quotas on immigration.

Historical Novels

One of the most interesting ways to gain a better understanding of our history is to read a historical novel. This is a book of fiction in which the author has made up a story to describe life in a certain period of history. Most of the characters in the book did not exist, but very often the author has included real people to show an important historical event. The historical novel is written around historical fact.

The historical novel is entertaining. It teaches you about history as it tells a story of adventure or romance. This is one of the most interesting ways to read history. MacKinlay Kantor, one of our most famous authors, has written novels about the Civil War. His people did not really exist. But his description of their adventures helps you to know what it was like to live during that terrible war. *The Red Badge of Courage*, by Stephen Crane, is another famous historical novel. It is the story of a young man who develops courage he did not believe he had.

Your home library and your class library should have some of these historical novels. You will find them fun to read. Many such novels have been made into movies that you may have seen.

A list of some historical novels you might like follows.

HISTORICAL FICTION (Simplified)

AUTHOR	TITLE, PUBLISHER	DESCRIPTION
1. Cooper, James F.	*The Deerslayer*, Globe	An exciting story of a backwoodsman. Natty Bumppo, and his adventures among the Huron Indians.
2. Cooper, James F.	*Last of the Mohicans*, Scott, Foresman	A story of the French and Indian War.
3. Hawthorne, Nathaniel	*The Scarlet Letter*, Globe	A story of the early days of the Massachusetts Colony.
4. Jackson, Helen H.	*Ramona*, Globe	A story of an Indian marriage in the Southwest that was destroyed by American gold seekers.
5. Melville, Herman	*Moby Dick*, Sanborn	A story of whale hunting in the early 19th century.

HISTORICAL FICTION (Complete and Unabridged)

AUTHOR	TITLE, PUBLISHER	DESCRIPTION
1. Icenhower, Joseph B.	*The Scarlet Raider*, Clinton	A story of a boy's experiences with the Confederate Cavalry during the Civil War.
2. John, Annabel and Edgar	*Wilderness Bridge*, Harper & Row	A novel about a young bride's experiences in crossing the country to settle with the Mormons in Utah.
3. Mayrant, Drayton	*Always a River*, Appleton-Century	Problems of the life of a family in a Puritan town in a southern colony.
4. Speare, Elizabeth	*Calico Captive*, Houghton Mifflin	The adventures of Susanna Johnson after capture on an Indian raid on Charleston, New Hampshire, 1754.
5. Sterner, Emma	*The Long Black Schooner*, Scholastic Book Services	Story of a mutiny on board a slave ship, the voyage to Long Island, and the return to Africa.
6. Strachan, Winoma	*Johnny Codliner*, Watts	A novel of the American Revolution set among the fishermen of New England.
7. Webb, Robert N.	*We Were There Series*, Grosset and Dunlap	
	On the Nautilus	A novel of a trip on an atomic submarine.
	With the Mayflower Pilgrims	A family's adventures on the voyage to America on the *Mayflower*.
8. Wibberley, Leonard	*John Treegate's Musket*, Farrar, Straus	A boy's experiences in Boston during the colonists' fight against the British troops.
9. Writtens, Herbert	*The Warrior's Path*, Follett	Two boys are captured by Indians and escape in time to warn settlers of Boonesboro of an Indian attack.

BOOKS FOR UNIT VI

AUTHOR	TITLE. PUBLISHER	DESCRIPTION
1. Angel, Polly	*Pat and the Iron Horse*, American	The story of an immigrant boy in the days of the canal boats and railroads.
2. Coy, Harold	*Chicano Roots Go Deep*, Dodd, Mead	Chicanos of the Southwest and present attempts to retain their culture.
3. Dagliesh, Alice	*Ride in the Wind*, Scribner	The story of Lindbergh's early life and his famous flight across the Atlantic.
4. Davis, A. F.	*American Heroine*, Oxford	The work of Jane Addams at Hull House.
5. Dowdell, Dorothy and Joseph	*The Japanese Helped Build America*, Messner	Courage of Japanese immigrants, fighting discrimination, and gifts to American culture.
6. Finkelstein, M., Sandifer, J., and Wright, E.	*Minorities, U.S.A.*, Globe	Stories of a variety of religious and ethnic minorities who have helped build America.
7. Hano, Arnold	*Roberto Clemente: Battling King*, Putnam	The Puerto Rican athlete who died while helping victims of an earthquake.
8. Holland, Ruth	*Mill Child*, Crowell-Collier	The moving, bitter story of child labor in America.
9. Huthmacher, J. Joseph	*Nation of Newcomers*, Delacorte	Clear, well-written study of ethnic minority groups in American history.
10. Johnson, R. P.	*Chief Joseph, The Story of an American Indian*, Dillon Press	A fighter, guide, and peacemaker of a wandering and suffering people.
11. Judson, Clara I.	*City Neighbor*, Scribner	A picture of the work of Jane Addams at Hull House.

12.	Leipold, L. Edmond	*Founders of Fortunes,* Books I and II, T. S. Denison	Biographies of "captains of industry" in both the 19th and 20th centuries.
13.	Leipold, L. Edmond	*Famous American Indians,* T. S. Denison	Biographies of Americans of Indian descent in war, athletics, art, and politics.
14.	Lens, S.	*The Labor Wars,* Doubleday	The struggle of American workers for justice in working conditions.
15.	Marker, Dorothy	*The Little Giant of Schenectady,* American	The story of Charles Steinmetz and his remarkable work with electricity.
16.	Miers, Earl S.	*Black Americans,* Grosset and Dunlap	Accounts of famous black Americans and their contributions.
17.	Naden, Corrine J.	*The Triangle Shirtwaist Fire, March 25, 1911,* Watts	The blaze that changed an industry and brought laws to protect American workers.
18.	Nathan, Adele G.	*Building of the First Transcontinental Railroad,* Random House (Landmark Books)	The story of the men responsible for the first railroad across the continent.
19.	Shippen, Katherine	*Mister Bell Invents the Telephone,* Random House (Landmark Books)	One of the greatest inventions in the field of communication.
20.	Sobol, Donald J.	*The Wright Brothers at Kitty Hawk,* Thomas Nelson and Sons	The story of experiments of two pioneers in aviation.
21.	Time-Life editors	1870–1900, Time-Life Books	Magnificent pictorial account of America: frontier, entertainment, cities, law and order.
22.	Weems, John E.	*Death Song,* Doubleday	The last of the Indian wars, the closing decades of the 19th century.
23.	Wilson, D.	*Bright Eyes: The Story of Susette la Flesche,* McGraw	Omaha Indian fighting racism and atrocities committed against her people.

Unit VII

How Did the United States Become a Leader in World Affairs?

1870   1880   1890   1900   1910   1920

1867: Alaska purchased

1898: Spanish-American War ;
Hawaii annexed ;
Puerto Rico and
the Philippines obtained

1899: Open Door policy

1914: Panama Canal opened

1917: United States entered
World War I

1914–1918: World War I

1930   1940   1950   1960   1970   1980

1947: Marshall Plan

1973: Oil embargo

1945: United States dropped 2 atomic bombs on Japan ; United Nations founded

1962: Cuban missile crisis

1959: Alaska and Hawaii became states ; St. Lawrence Seaway opened

1941: Japanese attacked Pearl Harbor ; United States entered World War II

1950-1953: Korean War

1952: United States developed H-bomb ; Puerto Rico became a commonwealth

1962-1973: United States involvement in the Vietnam War

1979- 1980: Iran crisis

1939-1945: World War II

1949: NATO formed

1934: Good Neighbor policy

1948-1949: Berlin blockade and airlift

1979: United States recognized China ; Panama Canal treaties approved

1 THE UNITED STATES REACHES BEYOND NORTH AMERICA

How did the United States gain territories outside its boundaries? What happened to the Philippines, Puerto Rico, and Cuba after the Spanish-American War?

1. After the Civil War, most Americans were busy rebuilding farms, working in factories, or settling the plains. Some Americans, however, dreamed of opening new lands beyond our borders. One of these Americans was William Seward, secretary of state for the nation in the 1860s. In 1867 Russia offered to sell its territory of Alaska. Seward wanted the United States to buy it. He favored freeing the Americas of another foreign power. Seward was able to get the Senate to approve the purchase. Alaska became a possession of the United States for the price of $7,200,000. But many Americans did not agree with the purchase of Alaska. They thought the United States should not have colonies. They thought it was a waste of money. The sale was called Seward's Folly or Seward's Icebox. The people who called it this were wrong. Alaska's riches of fish, forests, oil, and minerals have added greatly to the wealth of the United States. In 1959 Alaska joined the United States as a state.

2. Toward the end of the 19th century, Americans became more interested in other parts of the world. They had settled their western lands. They were growing more cotton, wheat, and tobacco than they could use. Business people were looking for foreign markets in which to sell these goods. Some wanted to invest their money in foreign lands. Others saw that some nations of Europe were gaining colonies and trading rights in Asia and Africa. They were envious. They felt that the United States also should expand its territory and power. They thought that the United States had a duty or mission to carry its way of life to new lands and peoples. Other Americans disagreed. They believed that it was wrong to have colonies and rule other peoples. Despite their feelings, though, the drive to extend America's power abroad guided this country's relations with other peoples in the years ahead.

3. Although other Spanish colonies in Latin America gained their freedom, Cuba remained a Spanish colony. The Cuban people were not happy under Spanish rule, however. Attempted revolts against the Spanish failed. When a rebellion broke out in 1895, the Spanish government sent an army to crush it. Both the Spanish and the Cubans destroyed fields and towns and put prisoners to death. The Spanish turned whole towns into prisons in which they kept women, children, and old people. The people of the United States were shocked

The U.S. battleship *Maine* blew up in Havana harbor. What was the American reaction to this disaster?

The Charge of the Rough Riders at San Juan Hill, painted by Frederic Remington. Transportation problems caused the Rough Riders to leave most of their horses in Florida. They had to fight on foot.

when they read in their newspapers of the conditions in Cuba. They understood the desire of the Cubans to be free. Also, many Americans had money invested in Cuban sugar plantations and mines. War in Cuba was a threat to American property.

4. The stories coming out of Cuba disturbed the American people. When they read that the American battleship, the *Maine,* was blown up in the harbor of Havana in February 1898, they became angry. Americans demanded war. The cause of the explosion of the battleship is still not known. But the cry, "Remember the *Maine!*" was heard throughout the nation. On April 25, 1898, Congress declared war on Spain at the request of President McKinley.

5. The Spanish-American War was short. In the Pacific, an American fleet under Commodore George Dewey trapped the Spanish fleet in Manila Bay in the Philippines. Dewey's force destroyed all the Spanish ships without any loss of American ships. On the other side of the world, American warships sank another Spanish fleet in the harbor of Santiago, Cuba. On land, United States troops were just as successful. Theodore Roosevelt, who later became president, headed a group of soldiers who fought on horseback. He won fame by leading these Rough Riders in a charge at San Juan Hill. This charge opened the way for the army to enter Santiago and prevent the Spanish from escaping.

6. The war ended less than four months after it began. More Americans had died from impure food and tropical diseases than from enemy bullets. Spain lost all its colonies in America. As a result of Spain's defeat, the United States took temporary control of Cuba as a **protectorate,** that is, a territory to be governed and protected. In addition, the United States gained Puerto Rico in the Caribbean Sea and the island of Guam in the Pacific Ocean. Spain sold the Philippine Islands to the United States for $20,000,000. Spain no longer had colonies in the Americas.

7. The United States now had the problem of governing the new colonies. When the Filipinos learned that the United States

would not free them at once, they took up the fight for freedom. The revolt continued until their leader, Emilio Aguinaldo, was captured in 1901. When the rebellion ended, Congress helped the islands form their own government under the United States. In 1907 the Philippines elected their own assembly.

8. In 1916 Congress passed an act that led to the independence of the Philippines. It allowed the island people to elect their own legislature. This gave them experience in governing themselves and making their own laws. In time, the American people began to favor complete independence for the islands. But it was not until after World War II that the Philippines became independent. On July 4, 1946, the Philippines gained their freedom. The new nation agreed to allow the United States to keep army and navy bases on the islands for their protection.

9. In 1898 the United States gained Puerto Rico from Spain. It is a beautiful island southeast of Florida. The Puerto Ricans accepted the government of the United States immediately. Over the years, the United States has given the Puerto Rican people more and more power to govern themselves. It has allowed them to make their own laws. At first the United States appointed the governor of the territory. In 1948 the people began to elect their own governor. They chose Luiz Muñoz Marin as their first governor. Five years later, Puerto Rico became a **commonwealth.** As a commonwealth the Puerto Ricans elect their own government and pass most of their own laws. Puerto Ricans are American citizens and serve in the American armed forces. There are some Puerto Ricans who want complete independence from the United States. Others want their island to become a state of the Union.

10. During the Spanish-American War, Cuba suffered great damage. The American army remained in Cuba to help the people

Assembly line at a factory in Caguas, Puerto Rico. Manufactured goods make up about 80 percent of the value of products made or grown in Puerto Rico. When did Puerto Rico become a commonwealth?

recover from the war. The Americans built schools, hospitals, roads, railroads, and bridges. American and Cuban doctors attacked the problem of yellow fever, the cause of so many deaths during the war. Major Walter Reed proved that yellow fever was carried by a mosquito. Places where the mosquitoes laid their eggs were cleaned up. The disease was stopped on the island.

11. In 1902 American troops left Cuba, leaving a Cuban government to run the island. Cuba was free. However, the United States kept the right to send troops if there was trouble on the island. The American government wanted to protect American lives and property. Our country did enter into Cuban affairs in the years that followed. This was not welcomed by Cuban patriots. In 1934 under President Franklin Roosevelt, the right of the United States to enter Cuban affairs was ended. But the United States kept a great naval base at Guantánamo Bay.

12. As a result of the Spanish-American War, the United States had become a world power. At the beginning of the 20th century, it had colonies in both the Atlantic and Pacific oceans. Its interests extended from the Caribbean Sea to the Far East. From this time on, Americans had greater concern about happenings all over the world.

I. What is the main purpose of paragraphs 2 through 4?

a. To review the causes of the Spanish-American War
b. To identify the events in the purchase of Alaska
c. To describe the sinking of the *Maine*
d. To describe how the United States gained new territories

II. Choose the correct answer or answers.

1. Why did the United States become interested in foreign lands? (2 reasons)
   a. There was no more unsettled land in the United States.
   b. Business people were looking for places to sell their goods.
   c. Nations of Europe were starting colonies in South America.
2. Why were the people of the United States interested in Cuba's fight for freedom?
   a. They wanted to end slavery in Cuba.
   b. They agreed with Cuba's desire to be free.
   c. They wanted to add Cuba to the United States.
3. Why did some Americans make fun of Secretary of State Seward?
   a. They thought Alaska was a worthless land.
   b. They thought Alaska was too far from the other states.
   c. They felt the Senate would not approve the purchase.
4. Why did the United States go to war with Spain?
   a. Spanish ships blockaded our southern ports.
   b. The United States wanted more territory.
   c. Unrest in Cuba led to the sinking of an American battleship.
5. What was one of the results of the Spanish-American War?
   a. Cuba remained a colony of Spain.
   b. Cuba was promised and soon granted independence.
   c. Cuba immediately became independent.
6. How have conditions in Puerto Rico changed since 1898?
   a. The island is now independent.
   b. The island has returned to Spanish control.
   c. The people elect their own officials and make most of their own laws.

III. Decide whether each statement agrees or disagrees with what you have read. If the statement disagrees, explain why.

1. By 1900 Spain had lost all its colonies in America.
2. In 1823 the United States helped Spain when Spain's colonies revolted.
3. Most Americans agreed with Secretary of State Seward's purchase of Alaska.

4. The Spanish-American War gave more territory to the United States.
5. Cuba gained its independence as a result of the Spanish-American War.
6. The United States has a naval base in Cuba.
7. The Philippines gained its independence soon after the Spanish-American War.
8. About the year 1900, the United States began to take more interest in world affairs.

DEVELOPING IDEAS AND SKILLS

Answer the following questions about the cartoon.

1. Who might be Uncle Sam in this cartoon?
2. What is he doing in the first picture?
3. What is the meaning of the icebox?
4. Why is Uncle Sam surprised when he opens the icebox?
5. What is a good title for this cartoon?

SUMMING UP

THE SPANISH-AMERICAN WAR Using these headings, complete the outline in your notebook. List at least three topics under each heading.

Headings:
A. Causes of the war with Spain
B. Events of the war
C. Results of the war

Thinking It Through
When the Cubans tried to gain their freedom from Spain, Americans came to their aid. In which countries today are people trying to overthrow undemocratic governments? Should the United States give these people help? Explain your answer.

2 THE UNITED STATES IMPROVES RELATIONS WITH LATIN AMERICA

Why did the United States obtain the Canal Zone and build the Panama Canal? What kinds of relations has the United States had with Latin America?

Ships passing through the Panama Canal. Why was the canal so important?

1. During the Spanish-American War, the United States tried to send help to its fleet in Cuba. It ordered the battleship *Oregon* from the Pacific Ocean to Cuba in the Atlantic. The trip around South America took so long that the war was almost over by the time the *Oregon* arrived. The American government saw the need for a shorter route between the two oceans.

2. In 1882 a French company started to dig a canal across the **isthmus** of Panama. (An isthmus is a narrow strip of land, with water on both sides of it. It connects two larger bodies of land.) Panama was then a province of Colombia. The French made some progress but had to give up the job. Too many workers died of yellow fever and malaria. Also, the cost of building the canal was higher than the French had expected.

3. The United States wanted to continue the work started by the French. It had to receive permission from Colombia to build in Panama. At first, Colombia refused. But President Theodore Roosevelt wanted the canal built in Panama. The people of Panama wanted the canal, too. If the canal was built, the people of Panama would be helped by the trade that followed. In November 1903, Panama revolted from Colombia and declared itself an independent nation. President Roosevelt recognized the new nation and arranged for the purchase of a strip of land through Panama. This land, about 10 miles (16 kilometers) wide, stretched from the Atlantic to the Pacific. It was called the Canal Zone. The United States paid the new government of Panama $10 million for use of the land on which the canal was built. The United States also agreed to pay Panama yearly rent for the land. The Panama Canal was finished and opened to traffic in 1914.

4. The route between the Atlantic and Pacific oceans was now shortened by thousands of miles. Goods could now be sent more cheaply by water from coast to coast. The canal also became of great importance to the defense of the United States. Our navy could now protect both our shores. It could move warships from one ocean to another in a short time. In order to protect the canal, the United States bought the Virgin Islands from Denmark in 1917, at a cost of $25 million. The Virgin Islands are on the sea route from the Atlantic Ocean to the canal.

411

5. Not all the Latin-American countries were happy over the way the United States gained rights to build the canal. Some felt that the United States was too quick to recognize the independence of Panama. Some people believed that President Roosevelt had urged Panama to revolt. The whole affair caused distrust of the United States in Latin America. In 1921 the United States paid the government of Colombia $25 million to help make up for its loss of Panama. The United States increased its yearly rent payment to Panama for use of the canal. But this did not satisfy the people of Panama. They felt that the canal was like a "knife through their heart."

6. Over the years, the people of Panama made more demands for the return of the canal. They felt strongly that a foreign country should not rule part of their territory. Of course, many Americans disagreed. They felt that the United States had built the canal despite many hardships and, therefore, that the United States had a right to keep it. As time passed, the canal lost the importance it once had. In past wars, the United States needed the canal to send warships from one ocean to another. Today, there are separate American fleets in the Atlantic and Pacific oceans. Recognizing these changes, the United States and Panama signed two treaties in 1978. The first one gradually turns over the Panama Canal to Panama. By the year 2000 Panama will have complete control of it. The second one gives the United States the right to defend the canal even after that date.

7. For a long time, the United States has been interested in Latin America. First, we have a large trade with our Latin-American neighbors. They send us products that we need and enjoy, such as tin, copper, coffee, bananas, and chocolate. In turn, their people buy many products from the United States. Second, the United States has tried to keep the Americas free from foreign control. If a strong and unfriendly nation con-

trolled the nations near us, it would be a threat to the safety of the United States. As early as 1823, President Monroe had stated this policy of keeping European nations out. This policy became known as the Monroe Doctrine. (See page 215.) For these reasons, the United States has continued to take part in the affairs of Latin America.

8. After the Spanish-American War, the American people took an even greater interest in the Caribbean area. In 1902 several European countries sent warships to blockade the ports of Venezuela. Venezuela owed these countries money. President Theodore Roosevelt did not want any European nations to occupy Venezuela. Pointing to the Monroe Doctrine, he asked for a peaceful settlement of the dispute. When an agreement was reached, the European nations withdrew their warships.

9. Between 1905 and 1934, American troops were also sent to keep order in other Latin-American countries. These included the Dominican Republic, Cuba, Haiti, Mexico, and Nicaragua. The people of

Theodore Roosevelt said that the United States should follow the old saying, "Speak softly and carry a big stick; you will go far." How does the cartoon show this idea?

Latin America did not always want this kind of help. Many of them resented the power of the United States. They felt they were able to take care of themselves.

10. In 1889 a meeting had been held promoting friendship among all American nations. As a result of this meeting, an organization that came to be known as the Pan American Union was formed. Twenty-one American nations were members. The organization had headquarters at Washington, D.C. It held meetings in different countries every few years. For a long time, however, Latin Americans remained suspicious of the actions of the United States.

11. In 1934 President Franklin D. Roosevelt announced that our policy toward Latin America would be that of a "good neighbor." He believed that all American nations must cooperate with each other. He brought the Marines home from Haiti and Nicaragua. The United States treaty with Cuba was changed. The United States agreed not to intefere in the affairs of that country. However, the United States kept its great naval base at Guantánamo Bay in Cuba.

12. During World War II, the nations of the Americas felt threatened by the Axis countries. With the exception of Argentina, they cooperated to defeat the Axis countries. After the war was won, the American nations met at Rio de Janeiro, Brazil, and agreed that each nation of the Americas would help any other nation if it were at-

Students of a forestry training center in Ecuador receive instruction from an expert. Do you think the United States should send money and experts to help the people of other countries? Why or why not?

tacked by a foreign power. In 1948 the Pan American Union became part of the Organization of American States (OAS). The OAS works to improve living conditions and education. It also works for peace and human rights and defends the independence of its 28 member nations.

13. In 1961 the United States suggested that the American nations be partners in improving the living standards of Latin-American peoples. The United States offered a plan that was called the Alliance for Progress. In the 1960s and early 1970s, the United States provided billions of dollars in aid. The aid was used to bring more land, homes, and schools to the people of Latin America. In the 1980s, the United States continues to seek close cooperation with the countries of Latin America.

Choose the correct answer.

1. The United States declared war against Spain because of the
   a. sinking of the battleship *Maine*
   b. sympathy with the people of Puerto Rico
   c. blockade of Cuban ports

2. As a result of the Spanish-American War, the United States gained
   a. Hawaii and the Philippines
   b. the Philippines, Guam, and Puerto Rico
   c. Cuba, Haiti, and the Philippines

3. A chief reason for the new interest of the United States in world affairs was the
   a. desire for markets for goods
   b. rush of immigrants
   c. growing problems of the city workers
4. The United States purchased Alaska from
   a. Canada
   b. Spain
   c. Russia
5. The Spanish-American War took place in
   a. 1865
   b. 1898
   c. 1914

6. During the war with Spain, Manila was captured by
   a. Dewey
   b. Theodore Roosevelt
   c. Scott
7. The Philippines gained complete independence from the United States in
   a. 1898
   b. 1916
   c. 1946
8. The first elected governor of Puerto Rico was
   a. Theodore Roosevelt
   b. Luis Muñoz Marin
   c. Emilio Aguinaldo

UNDERSTANDING
CHAPTER 2

I. **What is the main purpose of Chapter 2?**

   a. To describe how the United States obtained the Canal Zone and built the Panama Canal
   b. To discuss the revolt in Panama
   c. To describe the beginning of the Pan American Union
   d. To discuss relations between the United States and Latin America

II. **Choose the correct answer or answers.**

1. The French failed to complete the canal across Panama because (2 reasons)
   a. the cost was higher than they expected
   b. they did not have skilled workers
   c. the land was not cleared of disease
2. The United States wanted a shorter route between the oceans because
   a. a battleship had been delayed during the war with Spain
   b. gold was discovered in California
   c. the Erie Canal had been so successful
3. The United States secured the Canal Zone
   a. as a result of the Spanish-American War
   b. by a treaty with Panama
   c. by purchasing the land from Colombia
4. The Latin-American countries supported the United States in World War II because
   a. they felt threatened by the Axis powers
   b. of the Pan American Union
   c. they were invaded by European nations
5. The use of the Monroe Doctrine has been changed because
   a. it is no longer of any value
   b. the United States has decided to treat the countries of Latin America as its equals
   c. the United States now has military bases in South America

6. The United States has a great interest in Latin America for which two reasons?
   a. The United States needs the products of Latin America.
   b. A friendly Latin America helps to protect the Panama Canal.
   c. Latin-American countries expect the United States to keep order in these countries.

MAP SKILLS   A. *The Caribbean Area*

Study the map. Then decide whether these statements are true or false.

The Caribbean Area

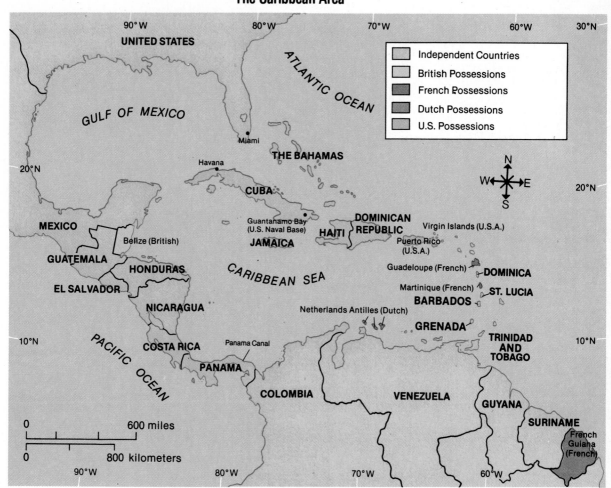

1. All the islands in the Caribbean are independent.
2. The Caribbean Sea is part of the Atlantic Ocean.
3. Haiti and the Dominican Republic are located on the same island.
4. Costa Rica is the largest country of Central America.
5. Puerto Rico is the largest island in the Caribbean Sea.
6. The Panama Canal is closer to Mexico than to the United States.
7. Cuba is an independent country.
8. The United States has a naval base in Haiti.
9. Cuba is closer to the United States than Puerto Rico is.

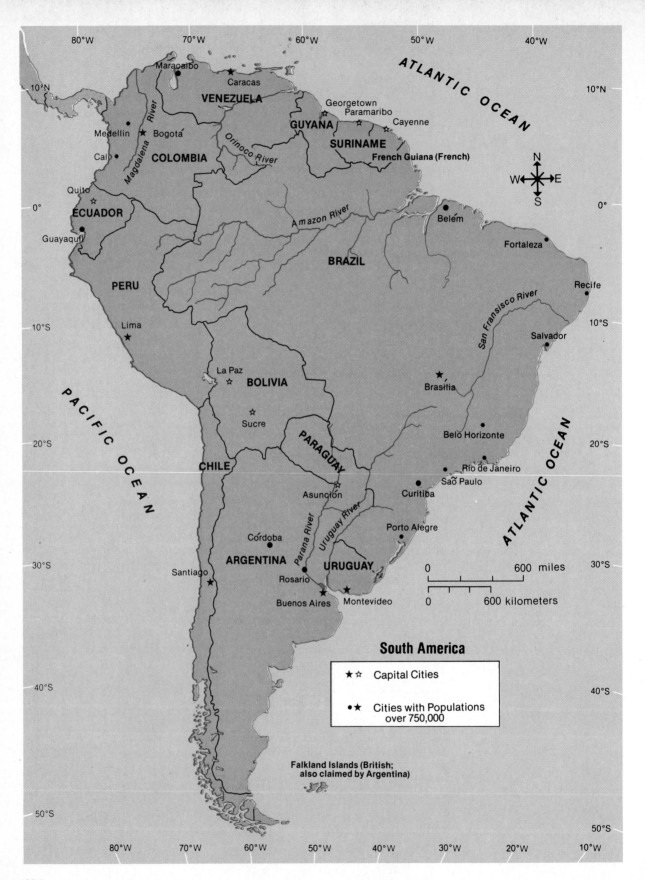

South America

★ ☆   Capital Cities

●★   Cities with Populations over 750,000

MAP SKILLS   B. *South America*

Study the map. Then decide whether these statements are true or false.

1. Buenos Aires is the capital of Brazil.
2. All of the countries of South America have a coastline.
3. The Amazon River drains the northeastern part of South America.
4. La Paz has a population of over 750,000.
5. Chile is in the western part of South America.
6. Argentina is the largest country in area in South America.
7. Most of South America's cities are found inland.

With the help of an encyclopedia and an atlas, answer these questions.

1. Where are the Andes Mountains located? How did they affect South America?
2. Why are the eastern coasts of South America generally wetter than the western coasts?
3. Where do most people in South America live? Why? Why do so few people live in the Amazon Basin?
4. Why do the people of Brazil speak Portuguese while most other South Americans speak Spanish?
5. When did South America become divided into many small countries?

SUMMING UP   **UNITED STATES POSSESSIONS**   In your notebook, make a chart using the titles suggested below.

TERRITORY	HOW AND WHEN IT WAS OBTAINED	VALUE TO THE UNITED STATES
Commonwealth of Puerto Rico		
Philippines (Before 1946)		
Alaska (Before 1959)		
Canal Zone (Before 1979)		
Virgin Islands		
Guam		

Thinking It Through

How can better understanding between the United States and Latin America be promoted?

3 THE UNITED STATES BECOMES INTERESTED IN THE FAR EAST

How did the United States gain control of Hawaii? Why did the United States suggest the Open Door policy?

A scenic view of Honolulu, Hawaii. Today tourism is one of Hawaii's most important businesses.

1. Two events in 1898 turned the interest of the United States toward the Far East. First, as a result of the Spanish-American War, the United States gained possession of the Philippines. These islands are about 500 miles (800 kilometers) from the China coast. Second, the United States annexed the Hawaiian Islands in 1898.

Queen Liliuokalani of Hawaii. She ruled Hawaii from 1891 to 1893. When did Hawaii become a state of the United States?

2. The Hawaiian Islands are located in the Pacific Ocean, about 2,000 miles (3,200 kilometers) southwest of California. (See the map on the next page.) In the early years of the 19th century, New England trading and whaling ships stopped at the islands. In 1820 a small group of American missionaries went to the Hawaiian Islands. They taught the people to read and write the English language. They gave them ideas about the American form of government. After the Civil War, more Americans went to Hawaii and invested in sugar and pineapple plantations. Sugar and pineapple became the chief crops of the islands. The rulers of Hawaii let the United States use Pearl Harbor as a place to repair and refuel its ships on the long trip across the Pacific Ocean to the Far East.

3. Early in 1893, Americans living in Hawaii, supported by United States Marines and some Hawaiians, led a revolt against Queen Liliuokalani. The revolt was

successful and a republic was established. The new government asked the United States to annex it. It was not until 1898, during the war with Spain, that Congress voted to annex the Republic of Hawaii. The islands soon became a territory of the United States.

4. In 1959 Hawaii became the 50th state of the Union. This was only a few months after Alaska was admitted as a state. The rich lands of Hawaii are now an important part of the United States. Almost a million people of many races live in Hawaii. Some are native Hawaiians. Thousands are the descendants of settlers from Japan, China, the Philippines, and the United States. Many people visit the islands. The flowers, trees, and fruits are part of Hawaii's great natural beauty. Pearl Harbor is still a great base for United States warships.

5. The United States opened trade with China in the 1800s. In the 1890s Russia, Japan, and some Western European nations began to take over parts of China. China was too weak to defend itself. Americans were worried that their trade with China would be stopped. Our government wanted to help China and to protect American trade. In 1899 Secretary of State John Hay suggested the idea of the "Open Door." By this idea he meant that China should be open to all nations that wished to trade or do business there. The European nations agreed to the idea, although they were not happy about it. In 1900 Hay added another idea to the Open Door policy. He said that the United States would help keep other countries from taking over any of China's territory. The Open Door policy won the friendship of the Chinese. For a time, the nations stopped dividing China among themselves.

The United States and Its Possessions

Asia
130°E   160°E   170°W   140°W   110°W   80°W   50°W
China
Alaska (1867; became a state in 1959)
ATLANTIC OCEAN
Japan
U.S. Virgin Islands (1917)
UNITED STATES
Puerto Rico (1898)
Philippines (1898-1946)
North America
South America
Guam (1898)   Mariana Islands   Midway Islands (1867)
PACIFIC OCEAN
Wake Island (1899)
0°
Caroline Islands
Hawaii (1898; became a state in 1959)
Panama Canal Zone (1903-1979)
0°
Marshall Islands
Trust Territory (1947)
N
W   E
S
0   3000 miles
0   3500 kilometers
Australia
American Samoa (1899)
160°E   170°W   140°W   110°W

Commodore Matthew C. Perry meeting Japanese royal officials in Japan in 1854. They agreed to a treaty to open up trade between Japan and the United States.

States and Japan. Perry brought with him many inventions. A small railroad and a small steam engine were two of them. He hoped these inventions would convince the emperor that it would help Japan to trade with the United States. The people of Japan were quick to learn to use the machines of the Western world. Within fifty years, they had greatly changed their ways of living. Japan became the strongest nation in the Far East.

7. Japan is a crowded nation. It has millions of people on its small islands, and yet there is little farmland to be used. In the late 19th century, Japan began to look for colonies. It looked toward Manchuria, a rich but weak province of North China. Japan also wanted Korea, a peninsula on the eastern coast of Asia. Russia wanted these same places, too. Early in 1904, Japan and Russia went to war over these territories. President Theodore Roosevelt offered to help settle the dispute. In 1905 both sides agreed to make peace. The Russians gave up their claims to Korea and Manchuria. Japan was now the most powerful nation in the Far East. A belief was growing that Japan might invade China.

6. The islands of Japan lie east of China. (See map on pages 4 and 5.) Tokyo, the capital of Japan, is about 500 miles from Shanghai. In 1853 and 1854 Commodore Matthew Perry took a fleet to Tokyo. He wanted to open trade between the United

REVIEWING CHAPTER 2

Choose the correct answer.

1. Most of the countries of South America at one time were colonies of
   a. France
   b. Spain
   c. Portugal
2. The Organization of American States works to
   a. build nuclear weapons
   b. improve living conditions and defend the independence of its members
   c. keep the 50 states of the United States together
3. The Panama Canal connects the Atlantic Ocean with the
   a. Caribbean Sea
   b. Amazon River
   c. Pacific Ocean
4. The Good Neighbor policy was promoted by President
   a. James Monroe
   b. Franklin D. Roosevelt
   c. James Polk

5. In 1823 President Monroe stated his famous doctrine that the United States should
   a. protect new independent countries in South America
   b. protect United States interests in the Panama Canal
   c. drive the French from Mexico
6. The Pan American Union was a
   a. policy of the United States
   b. union of all Spanish-speaking countries
   c. movement to bring about cooperation among all American nations
7. A narrow strip of land that connects two larger bodies of land is called a(n)
   a. strait
   b. peninsula
   c. isthmus
8. The president who made the building of the Panama Canal possible was
   a. Theodore Roosevelt
   b. James Monroe
   c. Franklin D. Roosevelt

UNDERSTANDING CHAPTER 3

I. **What is the main purpose of paragraphs 2 through 4?**

   a. To tell how the United States secured Hawaii
   b. To discuss American policy in China
   c. To describe United States relations with the Far East
   d. To describe changes in Japan

II. **Choose the correct answer.**

1. One of the reasons the United States wanted an Open Door policy in China was to
   a. gain a naval base for its ships
   b. keep China open for trade with the United States
   c. give the Chinese a chance to come to the United States
2. Hawaii was added to the United States
   a. as a result of the Spanish-American War
   b. by annexation
   c. by purchase from Spain
3. How did Japan change after the visit of Commodore Perry?
   a. Japan learned to use the inventions of the Western world.
   b. Japan was invaded immediately by China.
   c. European nations claimed parts of Japan.
4. China and the United States had friendly relations in the early 1900s because
   a. many Chinese came to the United States
   b. the United States had loaned China large sums of money
   c. the United States' Open Door policy made the Chinese feel they were being treated fairly

III. **Decide whether each statement below is a fact or an opinion. Explain why.**

1. President Theodore Roosevelt helped to end the war between Japan and Russia.
2. The United States became more interested in the Far East at the time of the Spanish-American War.

3. More schools to teach foreign languages should be established in the United States.
4. Secretary of State John Hay announced the Open Door policy.
5. Distant relatives of some Hawaiians once came from China and Japan.
6. The Atlantic and Pacific oceans protect the United States so that it need never fear invasion.
7. Hawaii is the most recent state to join the Union.
8. Latin America is more important to the United States than any other area in the world.

Answer the following questions about the cartoon.

1. What are the people doing around the table?
2. Who is the man at the door?
3. What country does he represent?
4. Why is he opening the door?
5. What is a good title for this cartoon?

POLICIES OF THE UNITED STATES Complete the chart below, giving information about important policies of the United States

POLICY	WHO STATED IT	WHEN	ITS PURPOSE
Monroe Doctrine			
Good Neighbor policy			
Open Door policy			

Thinking It Through

Many Americans felt sorry for Japan when the war with Russia began in 1904. After the war, many Americans thought the United States should "beware" of Japan. What was the reason for this change of attitude?

4 THE UNITED STATES TRIES TO STAY OUT OF WAR

How did the United States become involved in World War I?

1. By 1914 the United States was becoming one of the strongest nations in the world. It had almost 92 million people. It was producing a large share of the world's coal, iron, steel, and oil. The United States was selling its goods throughout the world. It had colonies in the Pacific Ocean and the Caribbean Sea. The United States had just completed the Panama Canal, connecting the two largest oceans in the world. In that same year, war broke out in Europe. Within a few years, the United States would be fighting in this world war.

2. How did such a terrible war begin? For many years, the nations of Europe did not trust each other. They had been building large armies and preparing for war. In order to protect themselves, they had formed groups, or **alliances.** Before World War I, two opposing alliances had been formed: the Allies and the Central Powers. England, France, and Russia were the Allies; the Central Powers consisted of Germany, Austria-Hungary, and Italy.

3. On June 28, 1914, an Austrian prince was killed by a man from Serbia, a small country in southeastern Europe. The death of this prince started the war. But it was not the real cause of the war. The real cause was that nations were afraid of and disliked each other. To punish Serbia, Austria-Hungary declared war. (See map on page 426.) Russia prepared to help Serbia defend itself. Germany, the partner of Austria-Hungary, declared war on Russia and its ally France. When German troops marched through neutral Belgium to attack France, Great Britain declared war on Germany. The French and British armies met the Germans in battle at the Marne River, not far from Paris. They defeated the German army at that point after a hard fight.

The archduke and archduchess of Austria were killed on June 28, 1914. How were these murders the spark that set off World War I?

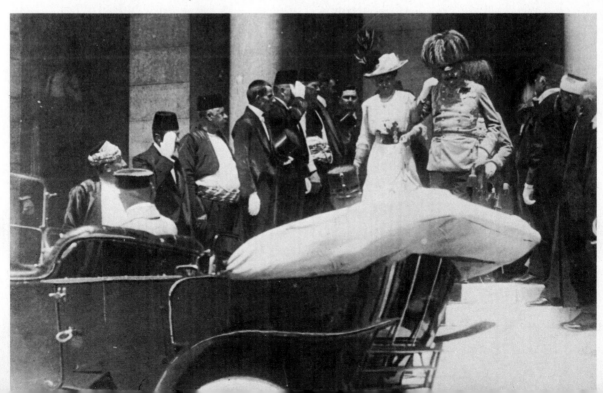

Rows of barbed-wire entanglements and trenches on the battlefields of France. Why was it difficult for armies to make major land advances while battling from behind trench lines?

4. Much of the fighting thereafter was called **trench warfare.** Both sides dug deep ditches, called trenches. The trenches were protected by barbed wire. Each side found it hard to push back the other.

5. President Wilson did not want the United States to be drawn into the war. He asked the American people to stay **neutral,** not to take sides. The war continued through 1915 and 1916. Both sides in the fighting spread stories of terrible actions committed by enemy soldiers. Speakers came to the United States to explain their side of the war. Each side pointed to the cruelties of the enemy. Few stories were proven true. We call this kind of story **propaganda.**

6. As the war went on, most Americans began to hope for a victory for the Allies — England, France, and now Italy. First, Americans did not like the fact that Germany had invaded Belgium, a neutral country. Second, Americans had been selling their products in England and France for many years. Germany, too, had wanted to buy tools of war from United States merchants. But the powerful British navy con-

trolled the ocean and would not let American ships trade with Germany. At first, the Allies paid for their supplies with gold. But, as the war continued, their gold supply ran low. The Allies borrowed money from the United States. Before long, Great Britain, France, and the other countries fighting against Germany were in debt to the United States. A victory for Germany might mean that these loans would never be repaid.

7. Third, Germany decided to break British control of the seas by the use of submarines. If enough British ships were sunk, the British might be starved into surrender. German submarines sank ships, at times without any warning. The Germans had said they would sink enemy ships on the seas, or those ships of neutral powers that might be carrying arms to the allies. Even American ships were not safe on the ocean. In May 1915, a German submarine sank the British ship *Lusitania.* More than a thousand lives were lost, including those of 128 American citizens. The United States began to fear the growing strength of Germany.

8. President Woodrow Wilson sent notes to the German ruler demanding that the submarine attacks be stopped. For a time the attacks came to a halt. In 1917, however, Germany decided on a last large-scale move to drive the British navy from the seas. They decided on submarine warfare against ships of all nations. Germany announced that there were certain waters around Europe that no ship could enter without fear of being sunk.

9. Germany believed that submarine warfare would defeat England. Germany knew that the United States was not prepared for war. If the United States did enter the war, Germany might win before American troops reached Europe. President Wilson repeated that his people desired war with no one. In early 1917 the British found out about a secret German telegram. It

showed that Germany was trying to get Mexico to fight against the United States. Germany promised that Mexico would get Texas, New Mexico, and Arizona. The British gave this information to President Wilson. This news turned the American people even more against Germany. In addition, in February and March 1917, German submarines sank more American ships.

10. President Wilson appeared before Congress to ask for a declaration of war against Germany. He stated that the United States wanted no land. The aim of the nation, Wilson said, was to make the world "safe for democracy." On April 6, 1917, Congress voted to declare war on Germany. The United States was now in the fight it had tried to avoid.

REVIEWING CHAPTER 3

Decide whether each item refers to United States relations with the Far East or Latin America.

1. The Good Neighbor policy
2. The Open Door policy
3. The warning of President Monroe
4. The announcement of Secretary John Hay
5. The expedition of Commodore Perry
6. The use of United States Marines to keep order
7. The formation of the OAS
8. The president's of the United States help in settling a war in the region
9. The exporting of oil, copper, coffee, and bananas to the United States

UNDERSTANDING CHAPTER 4

I. What is the main purpose of paragraphs 5 through 10?

a. To describe trench warfare
b. To discuss how the United States was drawn into World War I
c. To describe German submarine warfare
d. To discuss how Germany came to favor the Allies

II. Choose the correct answer.

1. The countries of Europe had built large armies before 1914 because they
   a. wanted to keep their colonies in Latin America
   b. distrusted one another
   c. wanted to keep peace in the troubled areas around the Mediterranean Sea
2. One reason the United States entered World War I was it
   a. feared the growing sea power of England
   b. wanted to acquire territory in Europe
   c. suffered losses from German submarine warfare
3. The United States began to favor the Allies in the war because
   a. the Allies were English-speaking nations
   b. it was promised land in Europe after the war
   c. it was selling goods and lending money to the Allies

4. Germany started unrestricted submarine warfare to
   a. bring the United States into the war
   b. cut off the Allies from overseas help
   c. stop U.S. attacks on German shipping
5. President Wilson said that the United States was entering the war to
   a. make the world safe for democracy
   b. completely destroy the German nation
   c. bring all nations under one world government

DEVELOPING IDEAS
AND SKILLS

MAP SKILLS *World War I*

Study the map. Then decide whether these statements are true or false. Explain your answers.

World War I

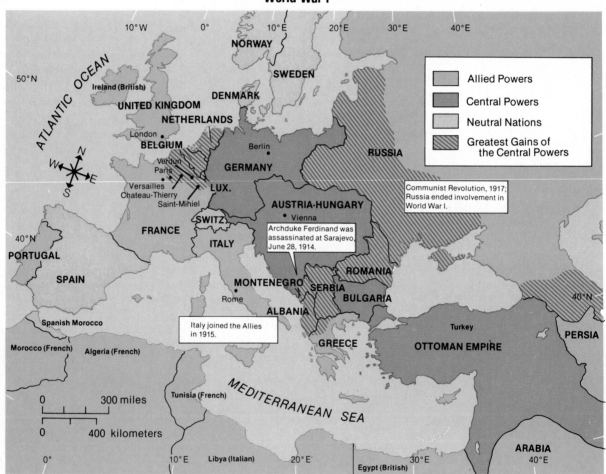

1. All of Europe took part in World War I.
2. Russia fought with the Allies until the very end of the war.
3. Spain fought on the side of the Allies.
4. The United Kingdom (England) is separated from the mainland of Europe.

5. Italy was an Allied power from the very start of World War I.
6. The Archduke Ferdinand was killed in Serbia.
7. The Central Powers occupied the heart of Europe.

SUMMING UP **A DEBATE** "The United States could have stayed out of World War I." Do you agree or disagree with this statement? List your reasons in your notebook under one of the headings below.

COULD HAVE STAYED OUT OF WAR	COULD NOT HAVE AVOIDED WAR

Thinking It Through

In 1917 President Wilson said, "Once you lead our people to war, they will forget about democracy." What did he mean? Do you agree or disagree with this statement? Explain your answer.

5 THE UNITED STATES IN WORLD WAR I

How did the United States help to end the war? What were the terms of peace?

1. The Allied nations were glad that the United States had entered the war on their side. How fast could the United States send help to the fighting fronts? A huge army was quickly raised and trained. Men from 18 to 45 years old were **drafted** into the service by the war's end. Over 4 million men were in the armed forces. The government sold Liberty and Victory Bonds to the people to help meet the cost of the war. In order to save food, the government declared days without meat and bread. The government took over management of the railroads and directed the building of ships. It used special powers during this period that it would not have used in peacetime.

2. The Russians had been involved in the war from its start, but they stopped fighting in late 1917. A revolution had overthrown the Russian czar, or king. A Communist government under Vladimir Lenin came to power. Thus Russia became the first Communist state. This means that the country's leaders and many of its people believed that the government should own all property. They also felt that people should share equally all the things they needed to live. The Communist government was a dictatorship.

3. The new Russian government signed a separate peace treaty with Germany. Now Germany could take its troops from the fighting against Russia and move them to the fighting in France. In the spring of 1918, the Germans began a drive to reach Paris. British and French armies had been fighting for almost four years. They were hard pressed and in need of help.

4. If the United States was to provide that help, it had to get troops to Europe before the big German drive. German submarines were a threat in moving troops to Europe. It would be a terrible loss to the Allies if the Americans could not get past the submarines. But in a short time, over a million American soldiers were in Europe. The navy brought them across the Atlantic without losing a single soldier to the German submarines.

5. Marshal Foch of France was now the commander of all the Allied forces in Europe. The Allies were fighting with their "backs to the wall." German armies were nearing Paris. American troops under General John Pershing were ordered into action. The German troops were stopped in the battles of Chateau-Thierry and Belleau Wood. (See map on page 426.)

6. By the fall of 1918, the number of American soldiers in Europe had reached almost the 2 million mark. The American

One of over 200,000 wounded American soldiers returning from World War I.

navy had brought them all across the ocean safely. On September 12, Americans won another famous battle at Saint-Mihiel. Pershing's army pushed on, driving the Germans back almost to the borders of Germany.

7. Germany's partners in the war, Bulgaria, Turkey, and Austria-Hungary, surrendered. German leaders now offered to end the fighting. Germany wanted to save its land from invasion. An **armistice,** or an agreement that stops the fighting, was arranged. It was signed on November 11, 1918, in a railroad car outside Paris. World War I was over.

8. The leaders of the Allied nations met at Versailles near Paris to decide on the peace treaty. President Wilson represented the United States at the peace conference. The terms of the Treaty of Versailles were announced early in 1919:

a. Germany was blamed for starting the war. It had to pay large amounts of money to the Allies. Germany was not to be allowed to have a strong army and navy.

b. Germany, Austria-Hungary, and Turkey had to give up much territory. Poland, Yugoslavia, Czechoslovakia, and several other nations once ruled by Russia or Austria-Hungary became free. Austria-Hungary became two separate countries, Austria and Hungary.

c. A League of Nations was set up. The League was to be an organization of all nations to keep peace in the world.

d. The Asian and African colonies that once belonged to Germany were now to be governed by the League of Nations.

9. The League of Nations was the part of the peace treaty that President Wilson wanted most. However, he alone could not make our nation join. Two-thirds of the Senate had to approve the treaty before the United States could belong to the league. To convince the Senate, President Wilson

Allied leaders met at Versailles in 1918 to draw up the peace treaty ending World War I. Seated from left to right are Vittorio Orlando of Italy, Lloyd George of Great Britain, Georges Clemenceau of France, and Woodrow Wilson of the United States.

traveled across the country. At each stop, he asked the American people to urge their senators to support the league. One night he collapsed. A blood clot had found its way to his brain. He was paralyzed. He had to give up and return to Washington, D.C.

10. Despite Wilson's efforts, the treaty was not accepted by the United States Senate. Many senators did not want the United States in the League of Nations. They said that membership in the league would involve the United States in the affairs of the rest of the world. In the election of 1920, Wilson's party was defeated. It would seem that most Americans agreed with the Senate. In July 1921, the United States made a separate peace treaty with Germany.

11. In 1920 the League of Nations opened its headquarters at Geneva, Switzerland. The membership in the league

grew to 60 nations in a short time. The league established the World Court to settle arguments among nations. This was separate from the league itself. A nation did not have to be a member to ask the World Court for a ruling. But a great weakness of the League of Nations was that it did not have the power to punish a nation that broke the rules of the organization.

12. Although the United States did not join the League of Nations, Americans still worked for peace. In 1921 and 1922 a conference of leading nations was held in Washington, D.C. Great Britain, France, Japan, Italy, and the United States agreed to limit the size of their navies for ten years. In 1928 these five nations signed the Paris Peace Pact. They agreed not to use war as a means of settling disputes.

13. The world, especially Europe, became a very different place after World War I. A large empire, Austria-Hungary, no longer existed. The rulers of Russia and Germany had been overthrown. Many governments in Europe had been turned upside down. The war had brought into use new and more deadly weapons, such as poison gas and airplanes. These weapons brought a new horror to war. Americans, whether they liked it or not, were watching their country become a world power. Life in the United States would not be the same again.

After the peace conference at Versailles, President Wilson toured the United States. He tried to convince the people to support the treaty and U.S. entry into the League of Nations. Why did many people want the United States to stay out of the league?

REVIEWING CHAPTER 4

Choose the correct answer.

1. The immediate cause of World War I was the
   a. assassination of an Austrian prince
   b. sinking of the *Lusitania*
   c. invasion of Belgian territory

2. The United States entered the war in
   a. 1914
   b. 1917
   c. 1918

3. Allies of the United States in the war were
   a. England and Austria
   b. England and France
   c. France and Austria

4. War was declared on Germany by the
   a. Congress
   b. president
   c. Senate

5. A reason for the United States' entry into the war was to
   a. increase the strength of the United States in Europe
   b. free colonies of European nations all over the world
   c. make the world safe for democracy

I. What is the main purpose of paragraphs 1 and 4?

    a. To describe how the United States helped end World I
    b. To explain the provisions of the Treaty of Versailles
    c. To explain how the United States got ready for war
    d. To describe the work of the League of Nations

II. Choose the correct answer.

1. The United States helped to end the war by
    a. sending troops and supplies to the Allies
    b. blockading German ports
    c. landing in Italy
2. The United States did not join the League of Nations because
    a. President Wilson opposed the idea
    b. the Senate did not approve the Treaty of Versailles
    c. Congress voted against paying taxes to the league
3. For a time, the Allies were in danger of losing the war because
    a. Germany discovered the secret of the atom bomb
    b. England had been occupied by German troops
    c. one of the Allies, Russia, left the war
4. Germany asked for peace because
    a. Russia had invaded its territory
    b. its ruler had died
    c. it did not want its land to be invaded
5. The purpose of the League of Nations was to
    a. explore outer space
    b. rule Germany after the war
    c. urge cooperation and peace among nations
6. Which of these was the policy of the United States toward other nations after the war?
    a. The United States took part in the League of Nations.
    b. The United States worked for peace through conferences and treaties.
    c. The United States soon joined the League of Nations.

III. Decide whether each statement agrees or disagrees with what you have read. If the statement disagrees, explain why.

1. The League of Nations hoped to prevent future wars.
2. In 1917 there was a revolution inside Russia.
3. Although the United States did not join the League of Nations, it did continue to work for world peace.
4. During World War I the United States government had powers that it did not have in peacetime.
5. The United States was well prepared for war when it entered World War I.
6. The Senate of the United States would not approve the Treaty of Versailles.
7. The United States was a weak nation in 1914.

Europe Before World War I

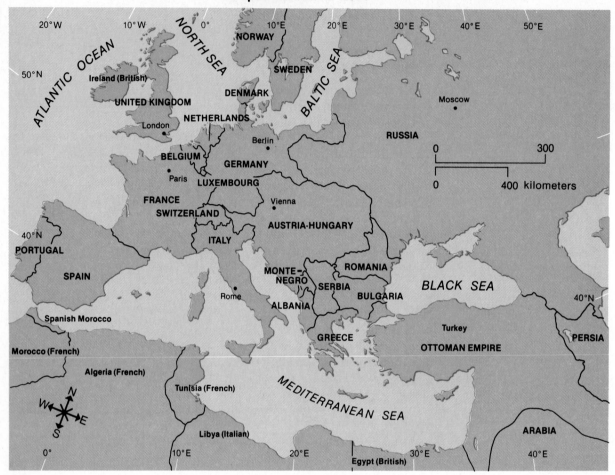

Answer the following questions.

1. What new countries were formed in Europe after World War I?
2. What countries in Europe lost territory as a result of World War I?
3. What was Russia's new name? How did this happen?
4. Where is Versailles located?
5. Which empire was separated into two countries after its defeat in World War I?

SUMMING UP   **WORLD WAR I**   Below are three headings for an outline. Place the topics listed on this page and the next under the correct heading.

Headings:
A. Causes of the War
B. Events of the War
C. Results of the War

Topics:
1. Marshal Foch commands the Allied armies.
2. European nations distrust each other.
3. United States enters the war.

Europe After World War I

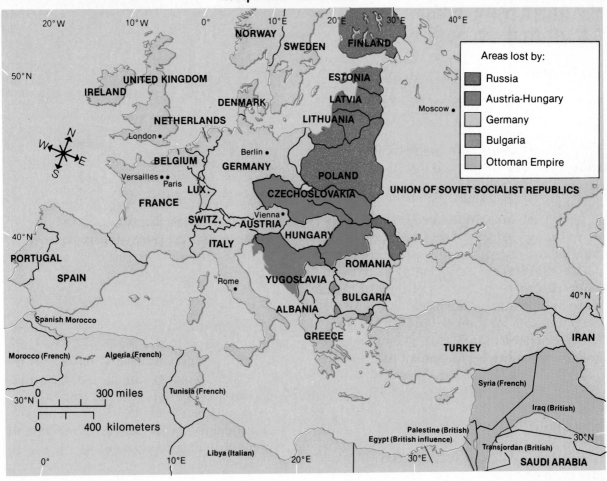

4. Unrestricted submarine warfare is declared.
5. Germany loses its colonies.
6. Austrian prince is killed.
7. Communist revolution overthrows the rulers of Russia.
8. League of Nations is formed.
9. Germany invades Belgium.
10. Trench warfare continues.
11. United States troops win the Battle of Belleau Wood.
12. Nations of Europe form alliances.

Thinking It Through

In World War I nations used new weapons such as poison gas, tanks, improved machine guns, and airplanes. Over 10 million people were killed. More than 20 million people were wounded. What can nations do to prevent such wars in the future?

6 DICTATORS LEAD THE WORLD TO WAR

What events led to World War II?

Mussolini and Hitler. While these dictators ruled, the lives of the people in Italy and Germany were under the total control of the government. Do you think dictatorships allow freedom of the press? Explain.

1. During the 1920s and 1930s, many countries in Europe fell on hard times. They had to rebuild after the war. The Great Depression began in 1929 and added to their problems. Many people in Europe were out of work and went hungry. Like Americans, the people in these countries wanted their governments to help them. Countries such as Great Britain and France were able to solve their problems and still keep freedom for their people. Other countries were not as successful. They turned to governments run by dictators.

2. The dictators ruled the country with the help of a loyal political party. They took away the freedom of the people and turned the country into a police state. Everyone had to obey the new leaders. If people protested against their government, the dictators used force to stop them. In Europe, the three most important nations ruled by dictators were the Soviet Union, Italy, and Germany. In Asia, Japan also had a powerful new government. It was controlled by a group of military leaders who were preparing their nation for war.

3. Russia was the first great power in Europe to become a dictatorship. For hundreds of years Russia had been ruled by czars. These czars had become hated. Russia suffered terrible defeats by the German army during World War I. This led the Russian people to revolt in 1917. They overthrew the czar and set up a new government. But the new government was weak. A new group, the Communists, led by Vladimir Lenin, seized control of the new government by force. Under Lenin's leadership, the Communists were able to bring all Russia under their rule. The Communists changed Russia's name to the Union of Soviet Socialist Republics (USSR). Many people use the name the Soviet Union, or even the old name Russia, when speaking of the USSR. The Communist government slowly took over the factories, mines, and farms of the nation. Lenin died in 1924. He was followed by another dictator, Joseph Stalin. During the 1920s and 1930s, millions of people who opposed the Communist dictator were killed or sent to harsh work camps.

4. In Italy, an ambitious young man, Benito Mussolini, organized a new political party, the Fascists. At first, the party was made up of young men who wore black shirts. Armed with guns and clubs, they often beat those who opposed them. Mussolini soon had a large following. People believed that he would give Italy a strong government and restore its greatness. In 1922 Mussolini marched to Rome and took control of the government. Once in power, he became a dictator. His secret police made certain that no one openly disagreed with him.

5. While Mussolini was gaining power in Italy, Adolf Hitler was organizing the Nazi party in Germany. Hitler told the German people he would get back the land lost by Germany in World War I. He blamed the Jewish people for Germany's defeat in the war. He also blamed the Jews for the hard times in Germany that followed the war. He told the German people that Germans were a "master race." He said that non-German people were inferior and should be killed or made into slaves.

6. Once in power in 1933, Hitler became a dictator. Like Mussolini, he depended on force to keep control. He made use of a secret police, the Gestapo. People who opposed him were thrown into prison or concentration camps. Thousands just "disappeared." In particular, Adolf Hitler had a great hatred for Jews. On his orders, the Nazis drove the Jews out of their schools, their businesses, their jobs, and even their homes. The Nazis sent the Jews to **concentration camps** where they died from starvation and horrible tortures.

7. The Nazi party set out to control every aspect of the people's lives. It told factory owners what to make. It told workers they could not join labor unions or strike. Germans were allowed to read and hear only what their leaders wanted them to know. Schools taught German youth to serve Hitler and the state. Many church schools were closed when they protested Hitler's methods. A new German army was created under the slogan, "Germany today, tomorrow the world!" A country such as Nazi Germany where everything is controlled by the government is a **totalitarian state.**

8. In 1931 Japan invaded Manchuria, a province of China. When the League of Nations said that Japan was wrong, Japan simply left the league. The member nations were not willing to send troops to stop Japan. They had hoped they might convince Japan by peaceful means, but they could not. When Germany and Italy saw that other nations would not fight against them, they began their attempts to conquer territory.

Japanese troops march on China. Why was the League of Nations unable to stop the Japanese invasion?

9. In 1935 Mussolini's armies invaded Ethiopia, a small nation in Africa. When the League of Nations protested, Italy left the league. In 1936 Germany sent troops into German land west of the Rhine River. This had been forbidden by the peace treaty ending World War I. Later the same year, Germany signed a treaty with Italy and Japan. These nations agreed to help each other. The alliance became known as the Rome-Berlin-Tokyo Axis. In 1937 Japan sent troops into the mainland of China.

10. The Nazi attempt to conquer Europe began in March 1938. Nazi armies marched into Austria. Hitler said that Austria should be a part of Germany because many Germans lived there. He claimed that all Germans belonged under one government. The nations of Europe did not stop Hitler. They did not want war. They thought that Hitler might be satisfied with Austria. Most Americans wanted to be neutral in these European troubles. They thought the Atlantic Ocean would protect them from the problems of Europe.

11. Czechoslovakia was next on Hitler's list. Hitler demanded a piece of territory, the Sudetenland, from Czechoslovakia. This territory was close to the German border and had a large number of German-speaking people. England and France protested. A conference was held at Munich, Germany. Prime Minister Chamberlain of Great Britain and Premier Daladier of France went to the conference. These leaders agreed to allow Germany to have the Sudetenland. They believed this would save the world from war. On his return to England, Chamberlain said that the agreement meant "peace in our time." Winston Churchill, who was to follow Chamberlain as prime minister, claimed that the conference at Munich would only lead to war.

12. Six months later, in March 1939, Germany occupied the rest of Czechoslovakia. Then Hitler made demands on Poland, which had been restored as a free nation in 1919. Poland refused Hitler's demands. On September 1, 1939, the German armies entered Poland. Great Britain and France now rushed to the defense of Poland. World War II had begun.

REVIEWING CHAPTER 5

Decide which events are results of World War I.

1. The League of Nations was formed.
2. Submarine warfare was forbidden in the future.
3. Germany was made to pay for the damages of war.
4. The president of the United States became the leader of the League of Nations.
5. New nations were established.

Which statements apply to the part played by the United States in World War I?

1. The battles of Belleau Wood and Chateau-Thierry are fought.
2. The armies of Germany are defeated.
3. Men and women are drafted into the army.
4. The government operates the railroads.
5. Troops fight in France for three years.
6. The government used the atomic bomb to end the war.

I. What is the main purpose of Chapter 6?

    a. To identify some of the events that led to World War II
    b. To tell how Germany took over Austria
    c. To describe the meeting at Munich
    d. To describe Hitler's rule of Germany

II. Choose the correct answer.

1. Why did the United States remain neutral during the 1930s?
    a. The United States was only interested in the Far East.
    b. The nation had no large army.
    c. Americans did not want to become involved in the affairs of Europe.
2. Why did France and England give in to Hitler at Munich?
    a. They felt Germany was too strong.
    b. They wanted to avoid war at all costs.
    c. Germany had promised to pay its debts of World War I.
3. In which of these did both Mussolini and Hitler believe?
    a. The use of force and secret police
    b. The need for a world organization to keep peace
    c. The right of a people to select their own leaders
4. Why did France and England declare war on Germany?
    a. Germany broke the Treaty of Versailles.
    b. Germany left the League of Nations.
    c. Germany invaded Poland.
5. Which of these actions did Hitler take first?
    a. He annexed Austria.
    b. He invaded Poland.
    c. He divided Czechoslovakia.
6. What was one reason why Mussolini came to power in Italy?
    a. He was elected by a great majority.
    b. He convinced the people he would make Italy great.
    c. He had been a general in World War I.

III. Decide whether each statement agrees or disagrees with what you have read. If the statement disagrees, explain why.

1. Dictators depend on force to keep themselves in power.
2. The United States thought that the wide oceans would protect it from troubles in Europe and Asia.
3. Hitler's actions showed him to be an enemy of religion.
4. England and France approved of Hitler's actions when he seized other lands.
5. Fascism is a form of government in which the lives of the people are tightly controlled by the government.
6. Japan showed that it wanted to rule Asia by invading Manchuria in 1931.
7. Before World War II, the Axis countries seized other lands.

STEPS TO WORLD WAR II In your notebook, arrange these events in
the order in which they happened.

Rise of Hitler and Mussolini
Hitler invades Austria
Japan invades Manchuria
Germany, Italy, and Japan become
 partners
Mussolini invades Ethiopia
Germany takes over all of Czech-
 oslovakia.

1. Treaty of Versailles

2.

3.

4.

5.

6.

7.

8. Hitler attacks Poland

Thinking It Through

What was new and different about the governments that came to power in
Russia, Germany, and Italy after World War I? How did they differ from
democratic governments? Do such dictatorial governments exist today? If
so, where? Should force be used to stop such governments if they invade
other countries? Why or why not?

7 THE NAZIS OVERRUN EUROPE

Which countries fell to the Nazi armies?

London and other British cities were bombed heavily by the Germans. What kinds of attitudes would be necessary for people to survive this kind of destruction?

1. A week before Germany invaded Poland, Hitler and the Soviet Union made an agreement. Each nation promised not to attack the other. The world was shocked. Nazi Germany and Communist Russia were supposed to be enemies. A secret part of the agreement was the plan to divide Poland between Germany and the Soviet Union. When Germany invaded Poland from the west, Russian troops crossed Poland's borders on the east. (See map on page 443.) The Germans showed the world a new kind of war, the **blitzkrieg**, or "lightning war." German planes bombed soldiers, factories, and whole cities. After the air attack, the army quickly followed in tanks and armored cars. Within four weeks, Germany and the Soviet Union defeated Poland and divided it between themselves.

2. The powerful German armies then overran Denmark and Norway. On May 10, 1940, Hitler struck at France through Holland and neutral Belgium. His armies moved around the Maginot Line. This line of forts was supposed to protect the eastern border of France. After a month of the Nazi blitzkrieg, Holland was conquered, the Belgian army surrendered, and France was defeated.

3. The German march into France separated the French and British armies. It seemed as if the British forces were trapped. They retreated to the French coast. They gathered at the seaport town of Dunkirk. There the British armies waited while the British people gathered every boat they could find to get their soldiers

back to England. Finally, 300,000 men were brought home safely! But they left behind on the beaches the heavy equipment of war. It was a terrible defeat for the Allies.

4. After seeing this great German victory, Mussolini declared war on France. On June 22, 1940, France had to sign an armistice with Germany. Germany divided France. The Germans occupied Paris and about two-thirds of the country. They allowed the French to set up a "puppet government" in the rest of the country. The headquarters of this government was at Vichy. In other parts of the world, French people continued their fight against the Nazis. These Free French were led by a general named de Gaulle.

5. The Nazis now tried to knock England out of the war. They began an all-out air attack. German planes bombed entire cities. Buildings and homes were destroyed.

439

Thousands of people were killed, but the British refused to give up. The British Air Force, the RAF, destroyed so many enemy planes that the air raids became fewer. In speaking of the British air force, Prime Minister Winston Churchill, wartime leader of Great Britain, said "Never in the field of human conflict was so much owed by so many to so few."

6. Great Britain stayed in the war. But the powerful Axis armies swept over most of Europe by the spring of 1941. Mussolini seized Albania. Germany invaded Yugoslavia and Greece. German and Italian troops occupied most of North Africa.

7. In the United States, the spread of German victories caused a change of feeling toward the war. Americans began to wonder if their own country was safe. Only England stood between America and a nation that was threatening the democratic way of life. Wherever the Nazis appeared, people lost their freedom. Non-Germans were considered inferior to the German "master race." They were forced to work in the fields and factories to supply the German war machine.

8. No person was important to the Nazis unless he or she could serve the state. There was no concern for the aged or young children. Those who could not work were not cared for. The Nazis saved their greatest hatred and cruelty for the Jews. The Nazi government's aim was to wipe out all

Terrible conditions in Nazi concentration camps shocked people around the world. Why is it important that the world never forget these horrors?

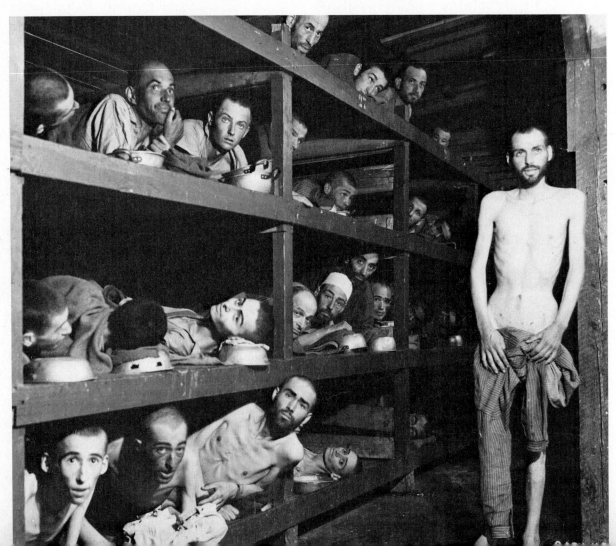

the Jewish people in the lands it conquered. The Germans built huge camps. They brought the Jewish people to these camps. The Jews were branded, tortured, and put to death in gas chambers and furnaces. At first, the treatment of the Jews seemed too horrible to be believed. Only later, when American and Russian soldiers entered these camps, did the world get to see the scenes of the Nazi crimes. When the war ended, the truth about the Nazi cruelties was made known. Six million defenseless and innocent Jews had been killed by the Nazis. This killing of so many Jews has been called the **Holocaust.**

9. The United States began to prepare for war in 1940 and 1941. Young men were given training in the army, navy, and the air corps. President Roosevelt and Prime Minister Churchill met aboard a battleship in the Atlantic in August 1941. They drew up their plan for a better world. It was called the Atlantic Charter. The charter stated that England and the United States would seek no territory as a result of the war. It assured all people the right to choose their own form of government.

10. Hitler wanted to seize the natural resources of the Soviet Union. Russia has rich resources of grain, coal, iron, and oil. Hitler also wanted to be sure that the Russian armies would not be used against him. Despite the treaty with the Soviet Union, the Nazis invaded Russian territory in June 1941. Russian armies retreated before the invaders while destroying everything that could be used by the Nazis.

11. On the other side of the world, the Japanese had taken a large part of China. The Japanese wanted to set up a new order in Asia. United States relations with Japan had grown worse since 1939. When the American government opposed Japan's invasion of Indochina, all hope of peace seemed gone. On December 7, 1941, Japanese planes bombed the American naval base at Pearl Harbor, Hawaii. The attack was a surprise. A large part of the United States fleet was sunk in the bombing. The next day, Congress declared war on Japan. Three days later, Japan's partners, Germany and Italy, declared war on the United States. Our country had entered World War II.

REVIEWING CHAPTER 6

Decide whether or not each statement applies to a dictatorship. Explain your answer.

1. We believe in a strong government, controlled by one person.
2. We believe that the law should treat all people equally.
3. We believe that people should know only what their rulers want them to know.
4. We believe that a person's religion is his or her own business.
5. We believe that the chief purpose of everyone's life is serving the government.

6. We believe that all people have certain rights that no one may take from them.
7. We believe that no one should be allowed to criticize the government.
8. We believe in the use of terror and secret police.
9. We believe that newspapers should print the truth.
10. We believe that the TV and radio stations should tell citizens only what the government wants them to.

I. **What is the main purpose of Chapter 7?**
   a. To discuss how the United States prepared for war
   b. To describe how France was defeated
   c. To describe the battle to invade Great Britain
   d. To tell how the Nazis overran most of Europe

II. **Choose the correct answer or answers.**

1. One reason why Germany attacked the Soviet Union was that
   a. Germany needed oil and food
   b. Germany disputed the boundary of Russia
   c. Russia wanted all of Poland
2. Germany overran Europe so quickly because
   a. other nations were waiting for American help
   b. Germany had developed a new method of fighting
   c. Germany had the greatest population in Europe
3. President Roosevelt and Winston Churchill met in 1941 to
   a. discuss the war aims of England and the Allies
   b. arrange for a treaty of peace
   c. decide how to divide territory after the war
4. One of the reasons why Japan attacked the United States was that the United States
   a. had blockaded the Japanese islands
   b. would not give up Hawaii
   c. disapproved of Japan's ambitions in Asia
5. The United States had begun to prepare for World War II for which two reasons?
   a. Germany continued unrestricted submarine warfare.
   b. England was the only nation that stood in the path of Nazi control of all of Europe.
   c. Japan had continued its conquests in Asia.

III. **Decide whether each statement is true or false. The underlined words are clues to help you decide. If a statement is false, change the underlined word or words to make it true.**

1. Germany attacked Pearl Harbor on December 7, 1941.
2. Germany invaded Russia to seize rich supplies of oil and wheat.
3. Trench warfare was developed by the Germans during World War II.
4. For the second time in a world war, Germany invaded the neutral country of France.
5. When Germany invaded Poland, England and France declared war.
6. The wartime leader of Great Britain was Winston Churchill.
7. In 1941 Roosevelt and Churchill published a statement called the 14 points.
8. In 1941 Japan sank a large part of the British fleet.
9. Hitler carried out a terrible persecution of the Jewish people.
10. After the fall of France, General de Gaulle led the Free French.

MAP SKILLS *The March of the Dictators, Early 1941*
**Study the map. Then decide whether the statements are true or false.
Explain your answer.**

The March of the Dictators, Early 1941

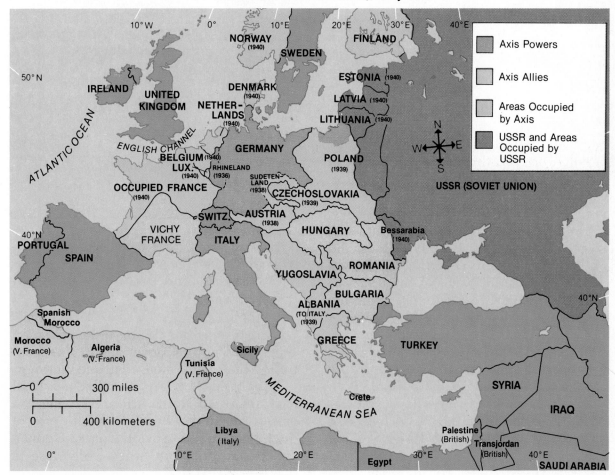

1. Most of central and eastern Europe was under Axis control in 1941.
2. Germany and the Soviet Union divided Poland between themselves.
3. Germany and Italy were called the Axis nations.
4. By 1941 France was still independent.
5. The Axis nations controlled many ports in the Mediterranean and the Adriatic seas.
6. Only the English Channel separated England from Axis-controlled land.
7. All Europe had been conquered by the Axis nations in 1941.

Thinking It Through

What Nazi actions during World War II shocked the rest of the world? Was it right for the Allies to remain silent during the war, even though they had learned that terrible things were taking place?

8 THE DICTATORS FALL

How were the Axis armies in
Europe defeated?

During World War II, many women went to work in
factories. Why did it become easier for women to
obtain factory jobs during that time?

1. The leader of the United States during World War II was Franklin D. Roosevelt. He was born in Hyde Park, New York. His parents were wealthy, and young Franklin received a fine education. He was interested in government. During World War I, he served as assistant secretary of the navy. Not long afterward, he suffered an attack of infantile paralysis, or polio. His illness did not end his career in government. He was elected governor of New York in 1928. In 1933, during the Great Depression, he became president of the United States. Under his leadership, Congress passed many laws to bring the hard times to an end. These laws became known as the New Deal. He also started the Good Neighbor policy toward Latin America. In 1940 Roosevelt was elected president for a third time. One year later, the United States was at war with the Axis powers.

2. The United States began to plan for a long war. The army and navy grew larger as men between the ages of 18 and 45 were drafted into service. Many women joined the armed forces. Factories started to make guns, airplanes, and tanks. The people at home were shown how to take care of themselves in case of air attacks. There were fewer goods in the stores. The needs of our army and navy came first. **Rationing** was started. Under this plan, the scarcer articles, such as sugar, meat, and gasoline, were divided evenly among the people. Without rationing, only people who were able to pay the highest prices could have

bought scarce goods. In order to keep prices down, the government also controlled the cost of food, rent, and clothing.

3. By 1942 Germany controlled nearly all of Europe and North Africa. The German armies faced the Russians at the city of Stalingrad in the Soviet Union. German and Italian troops in Africa were close to the Suez Canal in Egypt. President Roosevelt decided that the United States would act with the Allies against Germany. In October 1942, the British, under General Montgomery, attacked the Germans under General Rommel in North Africa. The British drove the German army back over 1,000 miles (1,600 kilometers) to Tunisia. In November 1942, American troops under General Dwight D. Eisenhower landed in North Africa. They were joined by the Free French soldiers of General de Gaulle and the British under Montgomery. These armies completed the defeat of the Axis forces in Africa.

4. In the meantime, the Russians turned back the Germans at Stalingrad. They trapped a Nazi army of 300,000 and forced them to surrender. Many say that this victory at Stalingrad was the turning point of the Nazi advance. Russia now attacked the German armies and started to push them back to the German border.

5. From North Africa, the Allies invaded Sicily, an island south of Italy. (See map on page 448.) In July 1943, the Allies landed in southern Italy. Mussolini fled to northern Italy; the Italian Fascist government fell. Mussolini was later captured and killed by the Italian **underground,** patriots who fought secretly against the dictator. The new Italian government surrendered to the Allies. But fighting in Italy continued. Hitler sent his own troops into Italy. He wanted to keep the Allies away from Germany. The new Italian government joined the Allied side in the fight against Germany.

6. By the end of 1943, the United States had a large air force in Great Britain. It carried on air raids over German-held terri-

May 8, 1945, known as V-E day, marked victory in Europe for the Allies. General Dwight D. Eisenhower, Supreme Allied Commander, made his V-E Day speech.

tory hour by hour. The main targets were factories that made war supplies. With the control of the air in their hands, the Allies now planned to invade France, which was under German control.

7. On June 6, 1944, D-day, American and British armies under General Eisenhower invaded Europe from bases in England. The huge force landed in Normandy, on the northwest coast of France. (See map on page 448.) Four thousand ships and 11,000 planes took part as 176,000 troops went ashore. The invasion was called the second front. (The Soviet Union had already been fighting Germany for three years on the eastern, or first, front.) The fighting in France took some German troops away from the fight against the Russians on the eastern front.

8. In August 1944, another Allied force invaded the southern part of France. These troops marched northward to join those who had landed at Normandy. They soon freed France. In September, the Allied armies pushed into Germany. In December, the Germans made one last attack at the Battle of the Bulge in Belgium. The at-

United States troops in France fire a blast at the enemy. How did the fighting in France help the Russians?

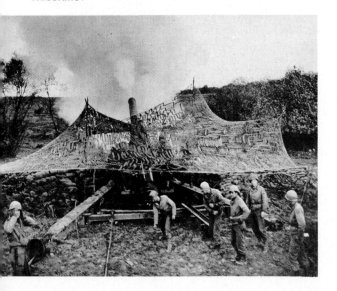

tack failed, and American armies continued their advance eastward. In April 1945, the Russian troops and the Western Allied forces met and cut Germany in two. On May 7, 1945, Germany surrendered. Adolf Hitler was not found. He had taken his own life to avoid capture by the Russians who had just entered the city of Berlin. The war in Europe was over, but the war in the Pacific continued.

Winston Churchill of England (left), Franklin D. Roosevelt of the U.S. (center), and Josef Stalin of the USSR (right) met at Yalta in early 1945 to discuss plans for the postwar world. Why do you think these leaders were called the "Big Three"?

REVIEWING CHAPTER 7

Choose the correct answer.

1. The United States entered World War II when
   a. Germany invaded Poland
   b. France surrendered
   c. Japan attacked Pearl Harbor

2. One of the aims of the Allies, as stated in the Atlantic Charter, was to
   a. gain territory
   b. establish a world government
   c. assure to all peoples the right to choose their own form of government

3. *Blitzkrieg* means
   a. lightning war
   b. trench warfare
   c. hour-by-hour bombing

4. The British were able to fight against the German air attacks because of the
   a. death of Adolf Hitler
   b. heroic work of the British Air Force
   c. arrival of troops from the United States

5. Which of these was NOT true of Nazi Germany?
   a. Secret police terrorized the people.
   b. The newspapers and radio were controlled by the government.
   c. Free elections were held every few years.

UNDERSTANDING CHAPTER 8

I. **What is the main purpose of Chapter 8?**

   a. To discuss the bombing of German territory
   b. To tell how Italy and Germany were defeated
   c. To describe the invasion of North Africa
   d. To describe the victory at Stalingrad

446

II. Choose the correct answer or answers.

1. The Battle of Stalingrad was important because
   a. Stalingrad was the first step of the Nazi advance into the Soviet Union
   b. Italy was then finished in the war
   c. a great German army was forced to surrender
2. The United States invaded North Africa to
   a. help the British drive out the Nazi army
   b. recover lost United States territory
   c. for both of these reasons
3. The first dictator to fall was
   a. Hitler
   b. Mussolini
   c. Stalin
4. D-Day was an important event in the war because
   a. it opened a second front in Europe
   b. the United States entered German territory
   c. Germany was far from victory at that time
5. Which two statements about Franklin D. Roosevelt are true?
   a. He was president of the United States during World War II.
   b. He served more than two terms as president.
   c. He refused to cooperate with the British leaders during the war.

III. Decide whether each statement agrees or disagrees with what you have read. If the statement disagrees, explain why.

1. World War II ended when Germany surrendered.
2. The Allied armies invaded Europe through ports in Spain.
3. Warfare destroys people and homes as well as military targets.
4. Women became part of the United States armed forces during World War II.
5. The government of the United States used more of its power during the war than it had during peacetime.
6. The Fascist government of Italy was overthrown before Germany surrendered.

DEVELOPING IDEAS AND SKILLS

THE WAR IN EUROPE   In your notebook, outline the war to defeat Germany and Italy, using these major headings. List at least two topics or events under each heading.

A. How the War Began
B. The War in Europe
C. The War in Africa
D. The Defeat of Germany

World War II in Europe: The Allies Defeat the Axis Powers

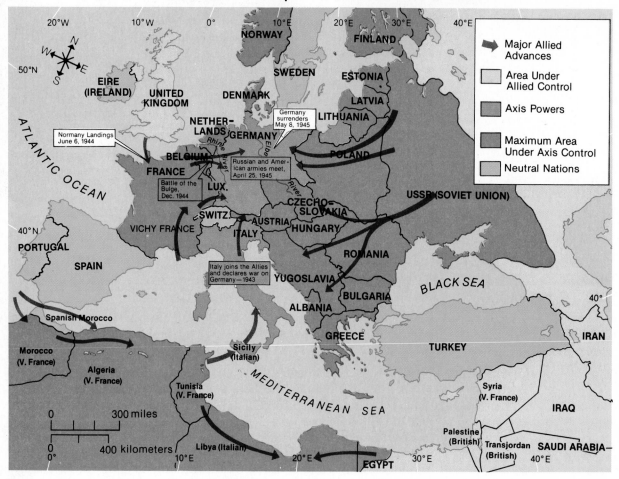

1. Allied armies did not invade German soil during the war.
2. The Soviet Union pushed westward toward Germany.
3. The Allies invaded Europe at several points.
4. Spain was one of the Axis powers.
5. Allied forces entered Germany from Italy.
6. The Allies invaded France from bases in England.
7. Germany invaded Great Britain.
8. The campaigns in North Africa and Sicily were part of a plan to invade southern Europe.
9. Every country in Europe took part in World War II.

SUMMING UP   **Thinking It Through**

During wartime, the United States government has often used powers it doesn't use in peacetime. Why has this been so? Do you think such action is necessary? Is it dangerous in any way? Explain.

9 THE DEFEAT OF THE JAPANESE EMPIRE

How was the war conducted in the Pacific?

General Douglas MacArthur (center) waded ashore at Leyte Island in the Philippines in 1944. He fulfilled a promise to return he had made more than two years earlier.

1. At the beginning of the war, the Japanese were very successful. After they attacked Pearl Harbor, the Japanese invaded the Philippine Islands. A small force of American and Filipino soldiers fought bravely against the invaders. They could not hold out. The Philippines passed into the hands of the Japanese. General Douglas MacArthur, the American commander in the islands, escaped to Australia. There he trained a new force to recapture the lost territories in the Pacific. Meanwhile, Japan advanced through British, Dutch, and French colonies in the Pacific. (See map on page 453.) The British bases of Hong Kong and Singapore fell. The Japanese advanced into New Guinea and the Solomon Islands and threatened Australia.

2. In May 1942, a Japanese fleet appeared in the Coral Sea, northeast of Australia. It was sailing toward Port Moresby, a base in southern New Guinea. The fleet was attacked by planes from United States aircraft carriers. The planes sank or damaged several Japanese ships. For the first time, ships fighting in battle did not see each other. Each side sent out planes to attack the other side's ships. The Battle of the Coral Sea saved Australia from Japanese invasion. (See map on page 453.)

3. Shortly after this success in the Coral Sea, the American navy won another victory at Midway Island. The Battle of Midway marked the turning point of the war in the Pacific. The Japanese navy was still strong, but it had lost control of the Pacific Ocean. General MacArthur planned to drive the Japanese armies back to their home islands. The army, navy, and marines worked together. The American forces took island after island from the Japanese—first Guadalcanal, then the Carolines, the Marianas, and Iwo Jima.

4. Early in 1945, after desperate fighting, American forces recaptured the Philippines. Bombers from the Marianas and the Philippines dropped thousands of tons of bombs on Japan. In June, they captured the island of Okinawa. This island lies about midway between the Philippines and Japan. Naval forces then sailed close to Japan and shelled the islands. The war had been carried to the Japanese homeland at last.

5. In 1939 some American scientists became aware that the Germans were trying to develop a new bomb, an atomic bomb. This bomb's tremendous explosive force would come from splitting the atom. One of the scientists in the United States, Albert Einstein, a German-born Jew, wrote Pres-

Hiroshima after the explosion of the atomic bomb on August 6, 1945. The United States hoped that dropping the atomic bomb would bring the war to a quick end and thereby save the lives of thousands of American servicemen. Considering the destruction and suffering the bomb caused in Japan, do you think the United States did the right thing? Why?

ident Roosevelt. He told him what the Nazis were doing. President Roosevelt immediately started a secret project in laboratories around the country. He wanted to beat the Germans in developing an atomic bomb. In 1942 the scientists working on the project sent Roosevelt a secret message. They told him that Enrico Fermi, an Italian-born scientist working in a laboratory in Chicago, had brought about the first nuclear reaction. By 1945 three atomic bombs had been built. One was secretly tested in July 1945 in the New Mexico desert. The Atomic Age had begun.

6. The United States then warned that Japan faced destruction unless it surrendered. Japan refused to give up. President Harry Truman made the decision to drop the atomic bombs. Truman had taken office when Franklin D. Roosevelt died suddenly in April 1945. On August 6, 1945, an American airplane flew over the Japanese city of Hiroshima and dropped an atomic bomb. In a flash, most of the city was wiped out. Three days later, a second atomic bomb de-

stroyed the city of Nagasaki. The entire world was stunned by the news. The bombs had destroyed entire cities and had brought death and injury to hundreds of thousands of people.

7. On August 8, 1945, Russia declared war on Japan. The Russian armies overran Manchuria. The Japanese leaders saw that Japan could not continue in the war. On August 10, the Japanese government asked for peace, and on August 14, it announced its surrender. Japan's official surrender was received in writing by General MacArthur aboard the battleship *Missouri* on September 2, 1945. So ended the worst war in history.

8. World War II was different from any other war that had been fought. First, it was a total war. It was fought not only by armies and navies, but by the people at home. Second, the war was global. It was fought all over the world. Third, much more than in any other war, nations made use of scientific discoveries. They used new instruments of war: radar, rockets, guided

missiles, magnetic mines, and the atomic bomb. Many lives were saved through such medical discoveries as blood plasma, penicillin, and sulfa drugs.

9. What were some of the important results of the war? After the war the Soviet Union became one of the powerful nations of the world. Although they overcame their enemies, Great Britain and France were weakened by the war. They were not able to hold their colonies in Africa and Asia.

The leaders of the United States came to realize that our country could not withdraw from world affairs. Unlike its reaction after World War I, the United States was now ready to take part in a world organization to keep peace. The United Nations Organization was formed. Even before the war ended, President Roosevelt had helped to start this organization. He hoped that the UNO, or the UN as it is now known, would find ways to keep peace in the world.

REVIEWING CHAPTERS 7 AND 8

What person or group of people is identified in each statement?

Winston Churchill	Dwight Eisenhower	Douglas MacArthur
Adolf Hitler	RAF	Josef Stalin
Franklin Roosevelt	Benito Mussolini	Free French
	Charles de Gaulle	

1. I formed part of the Axis alliance with Germany.
2. I was the commander of Allied forces in Europe.
3. I was the wartime leader of Great Britain.
4. We turned back the German bombers over Britain.
5. I commanded the Allied forces in the Pacific war.
6. I was the dictator of the Soviet Union.
7. We refused to surrender and fought against Germany even after our country was defeated.
8. I was the leader of the powerful war machine that almost conquered all Europe.
9. I led the French people who continued to fight against Germany.
10. I was the wartime leader of the United States government.

UNDERSTANDING CHAPTER 9

I. What is the main purpose of Chapter 9?

a. To list the results of World War II
b. To describe the defeat of the Japanese navy
c. To tell how Japan was defeated
d. To describe the use of the atom bomb

II. Choose the correct answer or answers.

1. How did the United States plan to defeat Japan?
   a. By capturing island after island until it reached the Japanese mainland
   b. By blockading Japanese ports
   c. By trapping Japanese armies in China

2. One of the reasons why Japan was forced back to its home islands was that
    a. its navy was defeated in several important battles
    b. American troops landed in Japan
    c. American bombers attacked Japan's cities during the early days of the war
3. Japan surrendered after
    a. its fleet was completely sunk
    b. its ships could not leave port
    c. atomic bombs wiped out two of its cities
4. World War II was called a global war because
    a. its cost ran into billions of dollars
    b. the war was fought on almost every continent
    c. even those who were not in the armed forces were involved in the war
5. World War II was different from other wars in that
    a. fewer nations took part
    b. greater use was made of scientific inventions
    c. much of the fighting took place in Europe
6. Which two were results of the war?
    a. France and Great Britain were weakened.
    b. Australia became the most powerful nation in the Pacific.
    c. The Soviet Union became a world power.

III. Decide whether each statement agrees or disagrees with what you have read. If the statement disagrees, explain why.

1. The final fighting in World War II took place in the Pacific.
2. The first years of World War II in the Pacific were successful ones for the United States
3. The first atomic bomb used against an enemy was dropped on a Japanese city.
4. The dropping of the atomic bomb brought a sudden end to the war.
5. Russia declared war against Japan at the start of World War II.
6. Americans soldiers fought in Europe, Africa, and Asia during the war.
7. The airplane was not an important weapon in the war against Japan.

DEVELOPING IDEAS AND SKILLS

MAP SKILLS *World War II in the Pacific*
Study the map. Then decide whether these statements are true or false. Explain your answer.

1. Japan overran parts of China and Australia.
2. The Japanese islands lie east of the Asian mainland.
3. The Allies bypassed the Pacific islands on their way to Japan.
4. The United States continued to fight Japan in 1946.
5. Hawaii was captured by Japan.
6. The Coral Sea is located near Hawaii.
7. Parts of Japan lie within 500 miles (800 kilometers) of the Soviet Union.

World War II in the Pacific

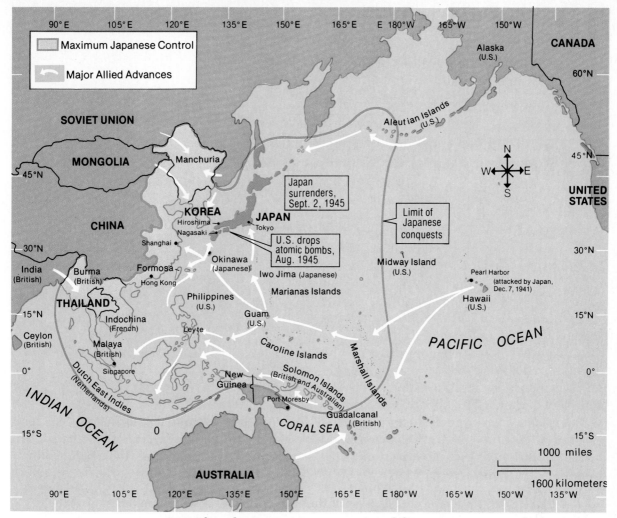

8. At first the Japanese were successful in conquering southeast Asia.
9. The Japanese captured some of the Alaskan islands known as the Aleutian Islands.
10. The atomic bomb was used early in the war.
11. Japan captured some lands belonging to Great Britain, France, and the Netherlands.

SUMMING UP   **Thinking It Through**

How did the dropping of atomic bombs in World War II change the history of the world?

10 THE UNITED NATIONS

What are the purposes of the
United Nations?

Headquarters of the United Nations in New York. On the left is the General Assembly, in the center is the 39-story Secretariat, and on the right is the Dag Hammarskjold Library. Why was the United Nations created?

1. Over 45 million people were killed during World War II. More than this number were wounded. Whole cities were destroyed. People were left homeless. Because of this terrible loss of life and property, world leaders knew that future wars had to be prevented. The Allies brought some of the German and Japanese leaders to trial for crimes against peace, humanity, and the laws of war. Some of these war criminals were put to death. But world leaders felt that a new organization to handle disputes among nations had to be formed. As early as 1942, President Roosevelt began to make plans for such an organization of nations. He hoped it would be stronger and more effective than the old League of Nations. This time the United States would join the organization. This time the organization would have an army and navy to enforce its decisions. The leaders of England, the Soviet Union, and China met with Roosevelt during the war to plan for the new organization.

2. In April 1945, the representatives of 51 nations met in San Francisco to establish the new organization. The war had not ended; there was still fighting in the Pacific. Before the meeting began, President Roosevelt died. The nations continued their work and soon drew up the **charter,** or constitution, for a permanent peace organization to be known as the United Nations. The headquarters of this organization was established in New York City. The old League of Nations ended its existence when the United Nations began its activities.

3. The United Nations has six major parts: the General Assembly, the Security Council, the Economic and Social Council, the Trusteeship Council, the International Court of Justice, and the Secretariat. The General Assembly is made up of representatives sent by all the nations that belong to the UN. It discusses the problems of the world and suggests ways of settling these problems. Most nations have one vote in the General Assembly. The expenses of the United Nations are paid for by the members. Each nation's share of the costs depends on its ability to pay. Many of the UN's new members are newly independent countries in Africa, the West Indies, and the Pacific Ocean region. In 1984 there were 158 member nations in the organization.

4. The Security Council is composed of 15 members. Five nations are permanent members: the United States, the Soviet

Union, China, France, and the United Kingdom (Great Britain). These are known as the Big Five. It would be difficult to run the UN without the support of these powerful nations. There are 10 other members of the council. These are elected by the General Assembly for a term of two years. All of the Big Five must approve all major decisions of the council. Any one of the Big Five may veto or block any action that it disapproves. The chief duty of the Security Council is to keep peace in the world.

5. The Economic and Social Council is a group of agencies that work to improve living conditions in the world. The most important agencies are the World Health Organization (WHO), the International Labor Organization (ILO), and the United Nations Educational, Scientific, and Cultural Organization (UNESCO). The Trusteeship Council took care of the many lands taken from defeated nations in both world wars. Some Pacific islands once owned by Japan are the only remaining trust territories. They are "held in trust" by the United States until plans for their self-government are completed.

6. The International Court of Justice tries to settle disputes among nations. The court hears cases brought before it by member nations. However, it hears only cases in which all parties agree to live by the decision of the court. The court is located in the Netherlands.

7. The Secretariat is the administrative, or working, staff of the UN. The Secretariat has over 3,000 workers from all parts of the world. It is headed by the secretary general. The secretary general is named by the Security Council and elected by the General Assembly for a five-year term. He or she must keep informed of world conditions that might cause war. The secretary general reports to the Security Council on those matters that may cause trouble in the world. The secretary general tells the General Assembly what the UN is doing.

8. Since World War II there have been many differences between two groups of countries. One group is made up of the free and democratic nations led by the United States. The other is made up of the Soviet Union and other Communist nations. Since 1950 a third group of nations has been taking shape. Many of these nations were once colonies of the European powers. Often they do not want to side with either major group. They are known as the Third World nations. (India is an example of a Third World nation.) Because of their growing number in the UN, the votes of Third World nations have become important. Both the United States and the Soviet Union have tried to gain their support.

9. Despite differences among the "Big Powers," the United Nations has had some successes:

1947–48   Helped set up the new state of Israel
1949   Helped gain freedom for Indonesia from the Netherlands
1950–53   Sent troops to Korea to prevent a Communist takeover of South Korea

United Nations peacekeeping forces in the Sinai Peninsula, January 1957. In what parts of the world today are there UN peacekeeping troops?

1956–57	Sent troops to Egypt to keep peace between Israel and Egypt
1960–64	Sent troops to the Congo to stop civil war
1964	Sent troops to Cyprus to keep peace between Greek and Turkish Cypriots
1974	Sent troops to guard cease-fire lines between Israel, Egypt, and Syria
1977	Sent troops to Lebanon to patrol the border near Israel

10. At first, most Americans were eager to support the work of the United Nations. They had learned from two world wars that people must work together to keep peace in the world. In recent years, however, the American government has become less happy with the UN. There are several reasons for this. First, the large nations cannot always agree on what action should be taken. For example, Soviet troops invaded Afghanistan in late 1979. But the Soviet Union blocked Security Council demands for the troops to leave.

11. Second, the United Nations has no real power to enforce its decisions. In the 1970s, the UN tried to stop trade with Rhodesia because of that country's treatment of its black people. Nevertheless, many nations ignored the UN's demands. Third, some nations do not give their full share of money to support the United Nations. The United States pays about 25 percent of the UN's costs. Other nations sometimes withhold their share. Fourth, almost every nation, regardless of its size or population, has one vote in the General Assembly. As a result, the small nations can often join together and vote for policies unfavorable to the United States and its allies. These problems must be solved if the United Nations is to regain the respect it once had and be an effective leader of nations.

REVIEWING CHAPTER 9

Decide whether each event mentioned below took place in Europe, Africa, or the Pacific.

1. The United States recaptured the Philippines.
2. British soldiers were helped to escape from Dunkirk.
3. The Battle of the Coral Sea was fought.
4. Six million Jews were killed.
5. The RAF destroyed hundreds of enemy planes.
6. German forces were driven out of Tunisia.
7. The islands of Guam, Iwo Jima, and Okinawa were captured.
8. The first invasion by United States troops under General Eisenhower was made.
9. The Battle of Stalingrad was fought.
10. Germany and Italy threatened the Suez Canal.
11. Normandy was invaded.
12. An atomic bomb was dropped on Hiroshima.

UNDERSTANDING CHAPTER 10

I. What is the main purpose of paragraphs 3 through 8?

a. To describe the failure of the League of Nations
b. To explain the duties of the secretary general
c. To tell how the UN began
d. To describe how the UN operates

II. Choose the correct answer.

1. The League of Nations failed to keep peace because
   a. it had no power to punish nations that disobeyed the league
   b. it had no leadership
   c. only a few nations belonged
2. The United Nations was formed to
   a. punish Germany and Japan for their part in World War II
   b. keep peace in the world
   c. make plans to help nations who asked for aid
3. The General Assembly is an important part of the United Nations because
   a. all problems can be discussed there
   b. it makes laws for all member nations
   c. it takes military action to settle disputes among nations
4. The United Nations sent troops to Korea because
   a. Japan had regained control over Korea
   b. Communist forces tried to take over South Korea
   c. the disorders in Korea were harming efforts to build dams, highways, and bridges
5. The United Nations has not always been successful in ending disputes because
   a. it is located in the United States
   b. there are too many members in the General Assembly
   c. the large nations do not always agree on what action should be taken

DEVELOPING IDEAS AND SKILLS

COMPARING EFFORTS FOR PEACE   The following chart shows some features of the League of Nations. In the column next to these features, show how the UN improves on the League of Nations. Complete this chart in your notebook.

LEAGUE OF NATIONS	UNITED NATIONS ORGANIZATION
1. The United States was not a member.	
2. All member nations had to agree before action could be taken.	
3. The charter was part of the treaty of peace.	
4. It had no military force to enforce its decisions.	
5. It paid little attention to social problems and the rights of people in the world.	

PICTOGRAPH STUDY *Organization of the United Nations*

Study the pictograph. Then decide whether these statements are true or false. Rewrite the false statements to make them true.

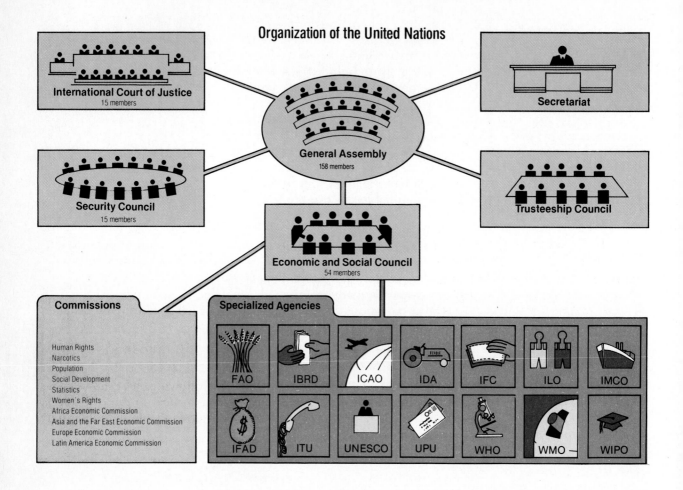

Organization of the United Nations

International Court of Justice
15 members

General Assembly
158 members

Secretariat

Security Council
15 members

Trusteeship Council

Economic and Social Council
54 members

Commissions

Human Rights
Narcotics
Population
Social Development
Statistics
Women's Rights
Africa Economic Commission
Asia and the Far East Economic Commission
Europe Economic Commission
Latin America Economic Commission

Specialized Agencies

FAO   IBRD   ICAO   IDA   IFC   ILO   IMCO

IFAD   ITU   UNESCO   UPU   WHO   WMO   WIPO

1. The UN has six main parts.
2. The Economic and Social Council does its work through committees and agencies.
3. The Security Council has six members.
4. Every member of the Security Council is also a member of the General Assembly.
5. The WHO is concerned with medical research and world health problems.
6. The Secretariat is the working staff of the UN. It is headed by the secretary general.

SUMMING UP   **Thinking It Through**

Has the UN helped the world? If so, in what ways? If not, why not?

11 THE COLD WAR IN EUROPE

Why did a cold war develop after World War II?

1. During World War II, the Allied leaders held several meetings. One of these meetings was held at Yalta in southern Russia, and another was held at Potsdam in Germany. At each conference, they made plans for the occupation of Germany after the war. They agreed that Germany should be disarmed and the Nazi leaders punished. They agreed to divide Germany into four parts, or **zones,** of occupation. Russia would use troops to occupy eastern Germany. England, France, and the United States would place troops in western Germany. Berlin, which was surrounded by the Russian zone, would be occupied by all four nations.

2. Real peace was not to come to the world. The Western nations and the Communist countries moved farther apart in their relations with each other. The Soviet Union had occupied many countries in Eastern Europe in its march toward the heart of Germany in 1945. Russia refused to give up control of these occupied countries: Poland, Hungary, Romania, Bulgaria, Yugoslavia, and Albania. These countries became Russian **satellites.** That means that they were under Russia's control. In these satellite countries, farms and factories were turned over to the state. Thousands of people who opposed the Communist party were killed or sent to labor camps. Personal freedom was not allowed. Winston Churchill called attention to what Russia was doing. He said that the Russians were stretching an **"iron curtain"** of secrecy around Eastern Europe. This was the beginning of the **cold war.** Although there was peace, there was also a feeling that fighting could start at any time.

3. The Soviet Union's government is a dictatorship run by the leaders of the Communist party. The Communist party is the only political party allowed in Russia. The Soviet government has a strong voice in deciding what work people may do, where they will work, and what they will be paid. In the United States, each person is free to choose his or her life's work. Nearly all Russian factories are controlled by the government. Factories in the United States are owned by private individuals or corporations.

4. The first effort by the United States to stop the spread of communism into other countries came in 1947. President Harry S. Truman announced that the American government would give aid to Turkey and Greece. He wanted to assist these nations in holding up against communism. This policy became known as the Truman Doctrine. The United States wanted to keep the Soviet Union from gaining bases in the Mediterranean Sea.

5. In June 1947, Secretary of State George Marshall announced a new plan. The United States would lend money to the nations of Europe to help them recover from the damages of the war. He offered aid to the Soviet Union and its satellites, but it was refused. Sixteen other nations accepted help. Congress voted to spend billions of dollars to help the nations that asked for this assistance. These nations used the money to restore farmlands and rebuild railroads and factories in Europe. The Marshall Plan played a great part in keeping some of the nations of Europe from turning to communism for help.

6. By 1948 the Western powers felt they could not reach an agreement with Russia over Germany. The three Western nations combined their zones of occupation into

one. They prepared plans for a German government in the western part of Germany. Russia then cut off all roads and railroads leading to the city of Berlin. This blockade, Russia hoped, would force England, France, and the United States to give up their occupation of Berlin.

7. Berlin is a problem for the West, for it lies 100 miles (160 kilometers) inside the Communist zone. Two million people live in the sections occupied by England, France, and the United States. They depend on West Germany for the goods they need in order to live. These goods must be brought through part of East Germany. If the means of transportation were closed down, the people of Berlin would not be able to get food and supplies. The United

Europe Today

*In 1966 France withdrew its forces from NATO but remained a member of the alliance.

Legend:
- Countries Having a Military Alliance (NATO) With the United States
- Communist Countries Having a Military Alliance With the USSR
- Communist Countries Without a Military Alliance With the USSR
- USSR

The Berlin Wall, looking into East Berlin. This concrete and barbed-wire wall was built in 1961 to stop East Germans from traveling freely to the West. Why do you think East Germans wanted to leave East Germany?

States decided to fight the blockade. American planes began to bring supplies into Berlin entirely by air. The Berlin Airlift was a success. Russia gave up the blockade after a year. However, in August 1961, Russia built a wall in Berlin to stop East Germans from moving through East Berlin into West Berlin.

8. Early in 1948, Communists overthrew the democratic government of Czechoslovakia. Czechoslovakia became another Russian satellite. This increased fear among the people of the democratic countries about the Communist movement. Finally, in 1949 the Western nations encouraged the formation of the Federal Republic of Germany (West Germany) with Bonn as its capital. Russia followed by establishing the German Democratic Republic (East Germany). West Germany has a democratic government. East Germany is a Communist dictatorship. East Germany is smaller and has fewer people than West Germany.

9. The Berlin blockade and the spread of communism to Czechoslovakia aroused the Western nations. Believing that Western Europe was in danger, 12 nations, including the United States, met in 1949 to sign a treaty. They formed the North Atlantic Treaty Organization (NATO). These nations agreed to help each other in case of attack. The members of NATO also created an army to defend their freedom. General Eisenhower was appointed the first commander of the NATO forces. By 1955 NATO had 15 member nations. In 1966, however, France decided to drop out of most NATO activities.

10. The nations of Western Europe began to realize they could increase their wealth and strength by joining together as trading partners. In 1957 they drew up a plan for sharing resources. This plan is called the Common Market. Six countries joined—France, Italy, West Germany,

NATO troops. The NATO treaty states, "An armed attack against one . . . shall be considered an attack against . . . all." Why did the United States join NATO?

461

Belgium, the Netherlands, and Luxembourg. They agreed to lower tariffs on goods traded among their group. The plan has been a success. In 1973 Britain, Ireland, and Denmark joined the Common Market. In 1979 Greece signed a treaty to become a full member starting in 1981. Portugal and Spain may also be admitted. Europe could now become stronger and more prosperous than ever.

11. The power of the Soviet Union continued to grow. Their armed forces became larger and better equipped. They easily put down revolts in Hungary (1956) and Czechoslovakia (1968). They sent arms abroad to nations in Latin America, Africa, and Asia. Recognizing Russia's growing might, in 1963 the United States signed a Nuclear Test Ban Treaty with the Soviet Union. In this treaty, the two nations agreed not to carry out nuclear tests in the air, in outer space, or under water.

12. In 1972 President Nixon signed the first Strategic Arms Limitation Talks (SALT) agreement with the Soviet Union. In this treaty both nations laid the groundwork for limiting several kinds of weapons. At that time Nixon favored a policy of improving relations between the two countries. In 1979 President Carter signed a second SALT agreement with the Soviet Union. He sent the agreement to the Senate for approval. However, Carter withdrew the agreement from consideration after the Soviet Union invaded Afghanistan in late 1979. Instead, he urged Congress to strengthen American forces to meet Soviet threats throughout the world.

REVIEWING CHAPTER 10

Choose the correct answer.

1. The person who directs the work of the United Nations is the
   a. president of the General Assembly
   b. chairman of the Security Council
   c. secretary general

2. The Economic and Social Council
   a. settles disputes among member nations
   b. decides what nations may become members
   c. works for better living conditions in the world

3. The International Court of Justice
   a. hears cases of disputes among nations
   b. advises the Security Council on action to be taken
   c. passes laws that all nations must obey

4. The Security Council
   a. settles disputes only among the Big Five
   b. tries to keep peace in the world
   c. sends engineers to underdeveloped countries

5. The section of the United Nations that helps lands that do not have their own governments is the
   a. secretary general
   b. Trusteeship Council
   c. Economic and Social Council

I. What is the main purpose of Chapter 11?

  a. To describe the cold war in Europe
  b. To describe the results of the Marshall Plan
  c. To discuss what happened to Germany after World War II
  d. To review the differences between communism and democracy

II. Choose the correct answer.

1. The Truman Doctrine was a plan to
   a. give help to the poorer peoples of the world
   b. train more doctors and nurses in this country
   c. protect Greece and Turkey from communism
2. The chief purpose of the Marshall Plan was to
   a. sell U.S. coal and steel at lower prices
   b. help Europe recover from the damages of World War II
   c. build air bases in Europe and Asia
3. The "iron curtain" refers to
   a. the spread of communism since World War II
   b. the building of a huge army in the Soviet Union
   c. Russia's efforts to keep the world from knowing what goes on behind its borders and the borders of its satellites
4. NATO was formed to
   a. unite Western nations against the danger of a Communist attack
   b. develop the newest weapons of war
   c. unite the nations of North and South America against an attack by any enemy
5. The United States changed its attitude toward the Soviet Union after World War II because
   a. Americans were not allowed to travel in the Soviet Union
   b. many countries in Eastern Europe had fallen under the control of the Soviet Union
   c. the Soviet Union had refused help through the Marshall Plan
6. The Berlin Airlift was necessary because
   a. tourists were forbidden to enter Russia by railroad
   b. railroads into Berlin had been badly damaged
   c. the entrances to Berlin were blockaded by the Soviet Union

LEADERS OF THE WORLD   The people listed below were world leaders in the years shortly after World War II. Using the encyclopedia as your reference, choose one person and write a paragraph describing this person's contributions as a world leader.

David Ben-Gurion	Jawaharlal Nehru
Josip Tito	Charles de Gaulle
Francisco Franco	Sukarno
Konrad Adenauer	Jomo Kenyatta
Mao Zedong (Mao Tse-tung)	Harry S. Truman

PICTOGRAPH STUDY *The United States and the Soviet Union*

Study the pictograph. Then decide whether these statements are true or false. Explain your answers.

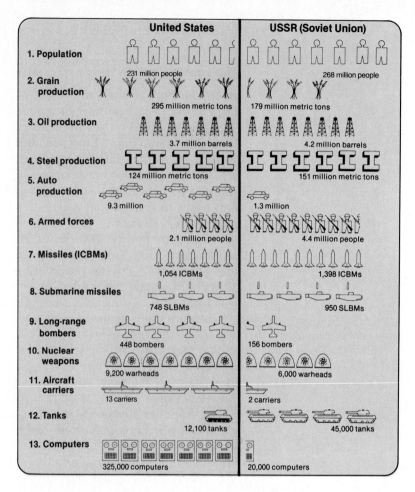

1. The United States has more people in its armed forces than does the Soviet Union.
2. The United States has more than twice as many long-range bombers as does the Soviet Union.
3. The United States produces more cars than the Soviet Union.
4. The Soviet Union leads in the production of steel and oil.
5. Both the Soviet Union and the United States have the resources to be leading industrial powers.
6. The United States has more than three times the number of tanks as does the Soviet Union.
7. The Soviet Union is behind the United States in food production.

SUMMING UP   **Thinking It Through**

In 1945 American and Russian troops met at the Elbe River in Germany. They shook hands in friendship. Today, Germany is divided with American troops in the west and Communist troops in the east. How did this happen?

12 THE COLD WAR SPREADS

What changes took place in Asia and Latin America since 1945? How did the United States get involved in the Korean and Vietnam wars?

United States troops helping South Koreans. What was the result of the conflict in Korea?

1. World War II caused great changes in Asia. During the war, the Japanese had overrun eastern Asia. They had driven out most of the Western powers. However, the people of mainland Asia hated Japanese rule. But the Asians also disliked the rule of the English, the Dutch, and the French. When the war ended, Asians did not want the Western powers to rule them again. This desire of a people to rule themselves, this pride in one's nation, is called **nationalism.** For example, growing nationalism forced England to give up its colonies in southern Asia after World War II. Burma, India, Pakistan, Malaysia, Singapore, and Sri Lanka (the island of Ceylon) all gained their freedom from England.

2. When World War II ended, a Chinese civil war that had been going on since the 1920s continued. Communist Chinese led by Mao Zedong fought the Nationalist Chinese led by Chiang Kai-shek. The United States supported the Nationalists and sent aid to Chiang Kai-shek. But by 1949 the Communists gained control of China. The Nationalists fled to the nearby island of Formosa (Taiwan). Although driven from the mainland, the Nationalist government of Chiang Kai-shek continued to represent China in the United Nations for many years. In 1971 the Nationalists were voted out of the UN. The Communist government on mainland China was voted in.

3. Korea is another Asian country that has been a scene of conflict. After the defeat of Japan in World War II, Korea was divided into two zones of occupation. North Korea was occupied by the Soviet Union. South Korea was occupied by the United States. South Korea held an election and set up its own government, the Republic of Korea. In the North, Communists controlled the government. The Soviet Union would not cooperate in an election to make a single government for all Korea. In time, American and Soviet troops left this divided Korea.

4. In June 1950, North Korea invaded South Korea. President Truman ordered American troops to help the South Koreans. The United Nations also sent armed forces to help them. Under the leadership of General MacArthur, the United Nations' armies drove the invading North Koreans almost to the border of Manchuria, a part of China. At this point, Communist Chinese "volunteers" entered the fight on the side of the North Koreans. The war went on for three years. The end of the fighting did not bring

465

victory to either side. But the military action of the United States and other United Nations' members prevented a Communist takeover of South Korea. Korea was left divided.

5. After the Communists gained control of China, many Americans began to worry about Communists within the United States. In 1950 Senator Joseph McCarthy of Wisconsin accused the government of employing many Communists. He also accused many well-known Americans of helping the Communists. Many Americans felt Senator McCarthy was pointing out a real danger. Others did not like what he was doing. However, they were too frightened to speak out. They feared that they, too, might be accused of being Communists. McCarthy became bolder. He claimed that there were Communists in the army. Finally, President Dwight Eisenhower and the Senate turned against him. In a long Senate hearing, shown on TV for 36 days, it became clear that his charges could not be supported. By 1954 Senator McCarthy had lost his power to frighten the American people. Still, the word *McCarthyism* has become part of the American language. It means accusing people of wrongdoing with little or no real proof.

6. In 1951 the United States made a treaty with Japan. After World War II, the United States had occupied and ruled Japan. When the Japanese got their own government back in 1952, they allowed the Americans to keep troops and bases in Japan. Over the years, the Japanese and Americans have grown to be friends again. Japan is now the United States' second most important trading partner. In 1972 the United States returned the island of Okinawa to the Japanese.

7. In the 1960s, the cold war moved closer to home. It reached the island of Cuba, which is only 90 miles southeast of the state of Florida. Since 1933 Cuba had been ruled by a dictator. In 1959 the dicta-

tor was overthrown in a revolt led by Fidel Castro. Castro then set up his own dictatorship. His followers ran the army, the police forces, and the schools. He turned to the Soviet Union for aid. His policies had driven many Cubans out, chiefly to the United States. Many of these Cubans planned to return to Cuba to end Castro's rule. The United States helped to train them for this purpose. In 1961 they invaded Cuba but were defeated by Castro's army. Later that year Castro announced that he was a Communist. Cuba moved even closer to the Soviet Union.

8. In 1962 the United States discovered there were soldiers and missiles of the Soviet Union in Cuba. President John Kennedy asked the Soviet Union to remove them. To back up his demand, he ordered a naval blockade around the island. Rather than risk nuclear war, the Soviet Union agreed to take out its missiles. While the United States won a cold war victory over the Soviet Union, the Communist government of Cuba survived. Over the years, Castro's rule has become stronger. He has sent Cuban troops to fight in Angola and Ethiopia, countries in Africa. He is supporting the new Sandinista government in Nicaragua. The United States believes he is trying to overturn other governments in Central America.

9. French Indochina also suffered from the spread of Communism. Before World War II, Indochina was a French colony. During World War II, the Japanese invaded Indochina. They drove out the French. Many native Indochinese fought a **guerrilla** war against the Japanese. (In a guerrilla war, soldiers hide in mountains and jungles. They strike suddenly in small groups. After a brief battle, they return to their hiding places.) When Japan lost World War II, the French returned. The people of Vietnam, which is part of Indochina, wanted to be free of any foreign control. They started

U.S. paratroopers fire against Communist troop positions in Vietnam.

United States felt it had to stop communism as it had in Korea. In 1962 President John Kennedy sent about 8,000 troops to train the South Vietnamese army, but not to take part in the actual fighting. In August 1964, North Vietnamese patrol boats attacked American navy ships in the Gulf of Tonkin, about 30 miles off the coast of North Vietnam. An angry Congress gave President Lyndon Johnson the power to send more troops. By 1968 there were almost 500,000 American troops in South Vietnam. They took over much of the fighting. At the same time, the Vietcong got more and more help from North Vietnam, the Soviet Union, and China. The war had **escalated,** or widened.

a revolt against French rule. The leader of the revolt was Ho Chi Minh, a Communist.

10. To give the people more self-rule, the French divided Indochina into three separate states. The states were Cambodia, Laos, and Vietnam. This did not end the revolt. Despite American aid, the French could not stop Vietnamese Communists from gaining control of the northern part of Vietnam. In 1954 the French had to leave after their defeat at Dien Bien Phu. The two sides then signed a peace agreement at Geneva, Switzerland. The agreement divided Vietnam into two sections, North and South Vietnam. It set up a Communist government, led by Ho Chi Minh, in the North. It set up a non-Communist government in the South. The agreement also called for elections to bring the country together.

11. The government of South Vietnam refused to hold the elections. Ho Chi Minh increased his aid to the South Vietnam Communists. They were known as the Vietcong. By 1960, the Vietcong had won control of a large part of South Vietnam. The

Southeast Asia in 1960

467

Southeast Asia Today

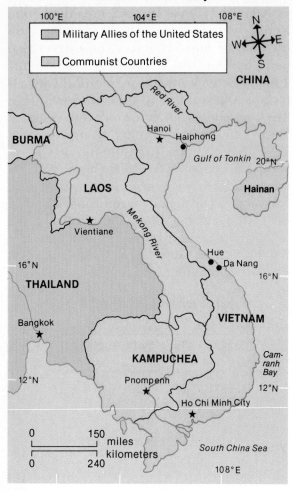

Southeast Asia Today

100°E   104°E   108°E

- Military Allies of the United States
- Communist Countries

N W E S

CHINA

Red River

BURMA

Hanoi ★ Haiphong ●

Gulf of Tonkin   20°N

LAOS

Hainan

Vientiane ★

Mekong River

16°N

Hue ●
Da Nang ●

16°N

THAILAND

VIETNAM

Bangkok ★

KAMPUCHEA

Cam-
ranh
Bay

12°N

Pnompenh ★

12°N

Ho Chi Minh City ★

0   150
miles
kilometers
0   240

South China Sea

108°E

12. The war deeply divided the American people. Many Americans supported the government's actions. They felt the United States had to stop the spread of Communist power. Other Americans, however, did not share these feelings. They argued that South Vietnam's rulers were dictators. They said that American bombs were killing too many innocent people. To back up their protests, they marched in antiwar demonstrations. Young men sometimes burned their draft cards.

13. In 1969 Richard Nixon became president. He began to withdraw some of the American troops. The South Vietnamese took over more of the fighting. In the meantime, the war spread to nearby Cambodia and Laos. At home, demonstrations against the war increased. Some young people were killed during demonstrations on college campuses in Ohio and Mississippi. In 1973 a **cease-fire,** or stopping of the fighting, was arranged. Like the French before them, all American troops had to leave. In 1975, the North Vietnamese defeated the South Vietnamese troops. Vietnam was united under Communist rule in 1976. Communists also took power in Laos and Cambodia (renamed Kampuchea).

14. Under Communist rule, the South Vietnamese suffered even more. The new Communist government began to force thousands of them from their lands and businesses. They fled the country in small boats. Neighboring countries did not want to let the Vietnamese in. Many small boats with hundreds of people in them drifted on the open seas and often sank. The United States, however, took in a large number of these "boat people." Many of them had fought bravely with U.S. troops in the Vietnam War. The Vietnamese have started new lives and businesses in the United States. Many have learned English and have found jobs they could only dream of in Vietnam.

15. After the war in Vietnam, the United States began to reexamine its foreign policy. For many years the United States had refused to recognize the People's Republic of China and its Communist leader Mao Zedong. But in the 1960s and 1970s American leaders watched as a growing split developed between the two giant Communist powers, the Soviet Union and China. Even while the American troops fought in Vietnam, President Nixon visited China in 1972. In 1979 President Carter recognized the Chinese Communists as the official rulers of China. Ties between China and the United States continue to grow closer.

Decide whether each statement is true or false. The underlined words are clues to help you decide. If a statement is false, change the underlined word or words to make it true.

1. The city of Berlin is surrounded by the <u>Communist-held</u> part of Germany.
2. The cold war involves the <u>United States</u> and the Soviet Union.
3. One of the main differences between the United States and the Soviet Union is the <u>form of government</u> of each nation.
4. The capital city of West Germany is <u>Berlin</u>.

5. <u>NATO</u> is a group of nations that have formed an organization to defend themselves against communism.
6. <u>Germany</u> is now divided into two separate nations.
7. The <u>Common Market</u> is an economic plan among nations in Western Europe.
8. After World War II, <u>France</u> became a scene of cold war tensions.

I. **What is the main purpose of Chapter 12?**

a. To describe the Korean War
b. To describe the great changes in Asia and Latin America since World War II
c. To tell why Vietnam is divided

II. **Choose the correct answer.**

1. United States troops were sent to Korea to
   a. collect debts owed by the Korean government
   b. stop North Korea's invasion of South Korea
   c. defeat the Chinese
2. Until 1971 the Chinese were represented in the United Nations by
   a. the Nationalists
   b. Mao Zedong
   c. the Communists
3. Before World War II, Indochina was a colony of
   a. Britain
   b. France
   c. the United States
4. After the Cuban missile crisis,
   a. American troops invaded Cuba
   b. Castro lost power
   c. Cuba remained a Communist state
5. Why did the United States send troops to Vietnam?
   a. To prevent a Communist takeover of South Vietnam by the Vietcong
   b. To train American soldiers for guerrilla wars
   c. To try out new weapons of war
6. How did the war in Vietnam affect Americans at home?
   a. Everybody worked to help the South Vietnamese win the war
   b. The American people were deeply divided over taking part in the war
   c. All Americans went willingly to fight in the war

469

7. In a guerrilla war
   a. large numbers of soldiers must fight on each side
   b. soldiers use the jungles or mountains to hide from the enemy
   c. a strong navy is needed to blockade the coast

III. Decide whether each statement is true or false. The underlined word or words are clues to help you decide. If a statement is false, change the underlined word or words to make it true.

1. The <u>Nationalists</u> took over China after World War II.
2. Mao Zedong was the leader of the <u>Nationalist</u> Chinese.
3. <u>Korea</u> is a divided country.
4. Fidel Castro has turned Cuba into a <u>democratic</u> state.
5. The American people were <u>united behind</u> the war in Vietnam.
6. The United Nations helped <u>North Korea</u> defend itself.
7. The United States came to <u>South</u> Vietnam's aid to prevent a Communist takeover.
8. <u>India</u> became an independent nation after World War II.

DEVELOPING IDEAS AND SKILLS

PICTURE SYMBOLS These pictures should help you recall parts of the chapter you have just read. What is the main idea of each picture?

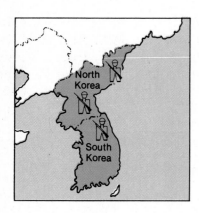
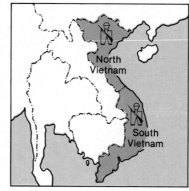
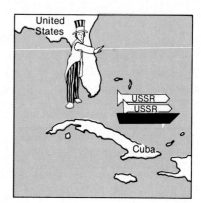

SUMMING UP

Complete the following chart in your notebook.

AMERICA'S WARS SINCE 1945

NAME OF WAR	DATES	CAUSES	RESULTS
Korean War			
Vietnam War			

Thinking It Through

What are some of the challenges of change in Asia and Latin America? How can the United States meet these challenges?

13 A TROUBLED MIDDLE EAST

How do events in the Middle East affect the world?

1. For the most part, the Middle East is a desert region that lies east of the Mediterranean Sea. It is actually southwestern Asia. It consists largely of many Arab nations and the Jewish state of Israel. The nation of Israel was formed in 1948 through the efforts of the United Nations. This started a war. The Arab nations invaded Israel, but they were thrown back. The two sides agreed to a **truce** – a stopping of the fighting. Ralph Bunche, an American working for the United Nations, arranged the truce. For this work, Bunche became the first black to win the Nobel Peace Prize.

2. During the fighting of 1948, thousands of Arabs fled Israel. Today, more than 2 million of them live in neighboring Jordan, Lebanon, Egypt, and other Arab countries. They are **refugees,** people who have fled their homeland. Many of these Palestinians, as they call themselves, live in camps supported by the United Nations. (Palestine is the ancient name for the area that is now Israel and Jordan.) Others work in nearby Arab countries.

3. Some of the young people have formed **commando** groups. They are trained to use violence to reach their goals. They attack Israelis. Sometimes they attack other Arabs who disagree with them. The most powerful of the Palestinian groups is the Palestine Liberation Organization (PLO). They want a Palestinian state for themselves, formed from land now held by Israel. They do not recognize Israel's right to exist.

4. The Middle East is important to the world. First, the Suez Canal is located there. The canal is very important. It provides a short route between the Mediterranean Sea and the Red Sea and Indian Ocean. Without it, ships going between Europe and Asia would have to travel all the way around Africa. Second, the region has the richest oil deposits in the world. The United States, the nations of Western Europe, and Japan need the oil for their homes and factories. At present, American companies work the oil fields with the permission of the Arab rulers. The Soviet Union also has a deep interest in all of the Middle East. It has tried to extend its power in this area for many years. Syria, Iraq, and Southern Yemen are now receiving much help from the Soviet Union.

5. In 1956 trouble developed over the Suez Canal. Egypt seized the canal from the private company that ran it. Most of this company was owned by the British government and French citizens. Egypt had refused to let Israeli ships go through the canal since 1948. In addition, Egypt increased its border raids on Israel. Within days Israel invaded Egypt. Then England and France also attacked Egypt. They hoped to regain control of the canal. The United States and the Soviet Union asked the UN General Assembly to help solve the problem. The UN ordered the three nations to take their troops out of Egypt. After they did, UN forces moved in to keep peace between Egypt and Israel. Egypt remained in control of the Suez Canal. It agreed to pay the former owners of the canal company.

6. In 1967 Egypt ordered the UN to withdraw its peace forces. Egypt then blockaded the Gulf of Aqaba, Israel's only entrance to the Red Sea. Egypt also began moving tanks and troops toward Israel. In June 1967, Israel attacked Egypt and Egypt's allies, Jordan and Syria. Within six days, Israel overran parts of Egypt, Jordan, and Syria. The UN ordered a cease-fire. The Six Day War was over. For the next few years there were border raids by both sides.

President Carter and Egyptian and Israeli leaders sign the Camp David Peace Treaty. Why was this such an important event?

But the cease-fire held until October 1973. Then Egypt and Syria suddenly attacked Israel. The Egyptian and Syrian troops made some gains before they were stopped. The Soviet Union supplied the Arab side with arms. The United States supported Israel. The fighting lasted three weeks before the UN called for another cease-fire. A UN peace-keeping force moved into the area between Egypt and the Israeli troops. New cease-fire lines were drawn through the efforts of Henry Kissinger, the American secretary of state.

7. In the war of 1973, the other Arab nations found a new and effective way to help Egypt and Syria. They cut down on their oil shipments to the Western industrial nations. They placed an **embargo** on oil to the United States. This means that they did not allow their oil to be shipped to the United States. They also raised the price of oil. The Arab methods were successful. Rather than be without oil, most industrial nations moved closer to the Arab position. Within a few months the Arabs once again began shipping oil to the United States. However, the price for this oil is continually rising. Much of the Western world's wealth is being turned over to the Arabs to pay for the oil.

8. Anwar El-Sadat, the leader of Egypt, made a historic visit to Israel in 1977. He and Menachem Begin, the Israeli prime minister, agreed to try to work out a plan for peace in the area. Encouraged by President Carter, the two leaders held talks at Camp David in Maryland in 1978. In 1979 the two nations signed a peace treaty. The Israelis agreed to return the Sinai Peninsula to Egypt in exchange for the promise of peace. (See map on page 475.) Egypt agreed to allow Israel to use the Suez Canal. They also agreed to work together to help solve the Palestinian problem.

9. The other Arab nations were angry about the treaty. Except for Egypt, no Arab state recognizes Israel. That means they have no official dealings with Israel. They want Israel to give up all the land it captured during the 1967 Arab-Israeli War. They also demand the setting up of a Palestinian state in what is now Israel. Nevertheless, Egypt and Israel are carrying out the treaty. Israel has returned the Sinai Peninsula. Egypt has kept the peace and Israeli ships now use the Suez Canal.

10. The Middle East continued to boil over. In January 1979, the people of Iran overthrew their ruler, the shah. He fled the country. In November 1979, a group of young Iranians overran the American em-

Americans sending a huge valentine to the hostages in Iran. Why was the world outraged at Iran's taking of hostages?

472

bassy in Teheran, Iran's capital city. The 63 Americans inside were taken as hostages, or captives. This act of terrorism was supported by the Ayatollah Khomeini, the new religious leader of Iran. The terrorists shortly let a few Americans go, reducing the number of captives to 53. However, they said they would not release the remainder until the United States returned the shah to Iran for trial. (He had gone to the United States for medical treatment.) The shah died in 1980. The Americans were finally let go on January 20, 1981, the day Ronald Reagan was sworn in as the new president.

11. In December 1979, the Soviet Union invaded Afghanistan, a Muslim country lying east of Iran. The fighting between rebels in Afghanistan and Soviet troops is still going on. In 1980, Iran and Iraq became involved in a long, terrible war. In 1982, Israel invaded Lebanon, its northern

Troops of the USSR invade Afghanistan.

neighbor. The Israelis wanted to end the PLO attacks coming from that country. Israeli forces quickly reached Beirut, Lebanon's capital. The PLO was forced to depart. The Israeli troops withdrew southward. Their place in Beirut was taken by troops from the United States, France, Italy, and Great Britain. These troops had to leave after many terrorist attacks. Lebanon continues to be torn by violence.

REVIEWING
CHAPTER 12

Choose the correct answer.

1. To *escalate* means to
   a. use ships to block a port
   b. increase the level of fighting
   c. bring a war to an end
2. Satellite nations are countries controlled by
   a. the United States
   b. the Soviet Union
   c. Cuba
3. The leader of the North Vietnamese was
   a. Mao Zedong
   b. Chiang Kai-shek
   c. Ho Chi Minh
4. The president who ended American participation in the Vietnam War was
   a. John Kennedy
   b. Lyndon Johnson
   c. Richard Nixon

5. As a result of the Korean War
   a. Korea remained divided
   b. the Communists took over all of Korea
   c. Korea was united under a non-Communist government
6. For several years after World War II Japan was
   a. divided between a Communist north and a non-Communist south
   b. occupied by U.S. troops
   c. dictatorship
7. After overthrowing a dictatorship in Cuba, Fidel Castro
   a. formed a military alliance with the United States
   b. set up a Communist dictatorship
   c. blockaded American ports

I. What is the main purpose of Chapter 13?
  a. To describe the wars and the search for peace in the Middle East
  b. To tell about the Soviet attack on Afghanistan
  c. To explain the role of the UN in the Middle East
  d. To describe the importance of oil to the Western world

II. Choose the correct answer.

1. Why is the United States concerned over unrest in the Middle East?
  a. The United States has naval bases in the area.
  b. The Arab-Israeli wars may lead to a larger world war.
  c. Most countries in the area have set up Communist governments.
2. The Middle East is an important area for all of these reasons EXCEPT:
  a. The Suez Canal is located there.
  b. The area has large resources of gold.
  c. The world's largest oil reserves are located there.
3. The goal of the Palestine Liberation Organization is to have
  a. the UN take over Israel
  b. the United States help Israel in case of war
  c. a nation of their own
4. As a result of the Six Day War in 1967
  a. new oil wells were discovered
  b. Israel occupied land once belonging to Egypt, Jordan, and Syria
  c. the Palestinian refugees returned to Israel
5. Since Israel was created in 1948, most Arab nations have
  a. accepted Israel
  b. not recognized Israel
  c. joined with Israel in developing the resources of the desert
6. The Middle East is now troubled by all these events EXCEPT:
  a. the revolution in Iran
  b. the holding of the Olympic Games in Moscow
  c. the Soviet invasion of Afghanistan
7. American hostages were held at the American embassy in
  a. Egypt
  b. Afghanistan
  c. Iran

III. Decide whether each statement agrees or disagrees with what you have read. If the statement disagrees, explain why.

1. The nation of Israel was formed after World War II.
2. Many Palestinian refugees live in camps supported by the United Nations.
3. Since 1948 several wars have been fought between the United States and the Arab nations.
4. The Arab nations opposed the new nation of Israel.
5. The nations of the world depend heavily on Arab oil for their homes and factories.
6. The Suez Canal is a waterway in Panama important to the world.
7. In 1956, 1967, and 1973 the United States sent troops to Israel to defend it against the Arabs.
8. The Soviet Union now controls most of the Arab oil fields.

MAP SKILLS *The Middle East Today*

Study the map. Then answer the following questions.

The Middle East Today

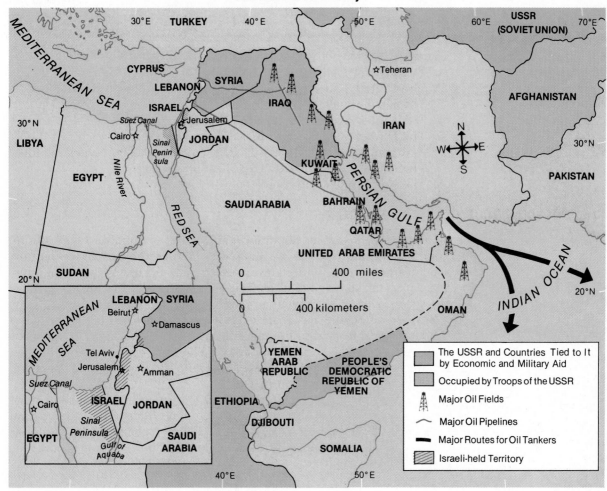

1. Which countries are major oil producers?
2. What are the countries that border Israel?
3. Which countries received economic and military aid from the Soviet Union?
4. What city is the capital of Iran?
5. About how many miles (and kilometers) are Soviet troops from the Persian Gulf?

Suppose the president offered you a job as a member of the State Department. What suggestions would you make to bring about peace in the Middle East? What actions might you advise the president to take on oil? What would you suggest the United States do about the invasion of Afghanistan by the Soviet Union?

Using a Time Line

Study this time line. Then answer the questions that follow. Use the information you have studied in this unit to help you. You may also look at the time line on pages 404 and 405 if you need additional help.

In which period of time (**A, B, C, D, E,** or **F**) did the following take place?
1. The Panama Canal was opened to traffic.
2. The United States declared the Open Door policy toward China.
3. The Japanese attacked Pearl Harbor.
4. The United States fought in the Vietnam War.
5. The United States bought Alaska from Russia.
6. Arab countries cut off their oil to the United States for several months.
7. The North Atlantic Treaty Organization was set up.
8. The Nazis under Hitler took over in Germany.

EXTENDING YOUR READING — VII

Using the Newspaper

Current events are an important part of your learning in social studies. Your teacher may often ask you to look in the newspaper for a report or a special article. Along with radio and television, the newspaper is an important source of knowledge of current events. To read the newspaper well takes skill. Do you know how to read a newspaper carefully?

Besides news, the newspaper has other sections or features, such as sports, movies, television programs, and advertising. There is an index to help you locate the section you want. When you turn to the right page, headlines help you find the article you want. The most important news articles are on the first or front page.

Each newspaper has an editorial or opinion page. On this page, the newspaper gives its thoughts about many of the news items. There are columns by writers who report on current affairs. There may also be an "editorial" cartoon. Finally, there may be a "letters to the editor" column for the readers of the newspaper.

BOOKS FOR UNIT VII

AUTHOR	TITLE, PUBLISHER	DESCRIPTION
1. Brau, M. N.	*Island in the Crossroads*, Doubleday	History of Puerto Rico.
2. Dareff, Hal	*From Vietnam to Cambodia: The Struggle in Southeast Asia*, Parents'	A background book about war in Southeast Asia.
3. Feurlicht, Roberta S.	*America's Reign of Terror*, Random House	World War I, bringing terror to many thought to be different: aliens, minorities, dissenters.

4. Feurlicht, Roberta S.	*In Search of Peace,* Messner	The story of four Americans who won the Nobel Peace Prize.
5. Foster, Genevieve	*Theodore Roosevelt,* Scribner's	The "Rough Rider," president, and conservationist.
6. Galt, Tom	*How the United Nations Works,* Crowell	Good account of how the United Nations began.
7. Gersh, Harry	*Women Who Made America Great,* Lippincott	Ten women, each famous for a different reason, who dared to change their times.
8. Giers, J.	*Franklin D. Roosevelt: Portrait of a President,* Doubleday	The president who was elected four times.
9. Leckie, Robert	*The Story of World War I,* Random House	Adapted from the American Heritage *History of World War I,* with excellent illustrations.
10. Levinger, Elma E.	*Albert Einstein,* Messner	The biography of one of the greatest scientists in history.
11. Mann, P.	*Ralph Bunche, UN Peacemaker,* Coward, McCann	An American diplomat who led the solution to problems of the founding of Israel.
12. Meltzer, M.	*Never to Forget,* Harper	The horrors of the Holocaust, Nazi Germany.
13. Rink, Paul	*The Land Divided, The World United,* Messner	Victory over nature; heroism of building the Panama Canal.
14. Shirer, William L.	*Rise and Fall of Adolf Hitler,* Random House (Landmark Books)	The story of the German dictator.
15. Snyder, Louis L.	*First Book of World War II,* Watts	Simple, clear account of the most important events of World War II.
16. Weinstein, Irving	*Shattered Decade, 1919–1929,* Scribner's	The glamour and reality of life in the United States in the years following World War I.
17. Zassenhaus, H.	*Walls: Resisting the Third Reich,* Beacon	Woman who led Norwegian and Danish refugees to safety in the Hitler years.

Unit VIII
How Can the United States Meet the Future?

$$\frac{=P(\varepsilon}{P_2}$$

$$\langle\frac{P_{18}-P_2}{}$$

$$\frac{402}{-42}$$

INDI
POW

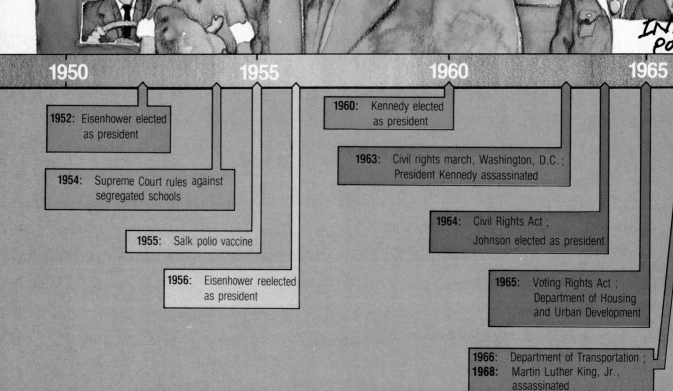

1950   1955   1960   1965

1952: Eisenhower elected as president

1954: Supreme Court rules against segregated schools

1955: Salk polio vaccine

1956: Eisenhower reelected as president

1960: Kennedy elected as president

1963: Civil rights march, Washington, D.C.; President Kennedy assassinated

1964: Civil Rights Act; Johnson elected as president

1965: Voting Rights Act; Department of Housing and Urban Development

1966: Department of Transportation;
1968: Martin Luther King, Jr., assassinated

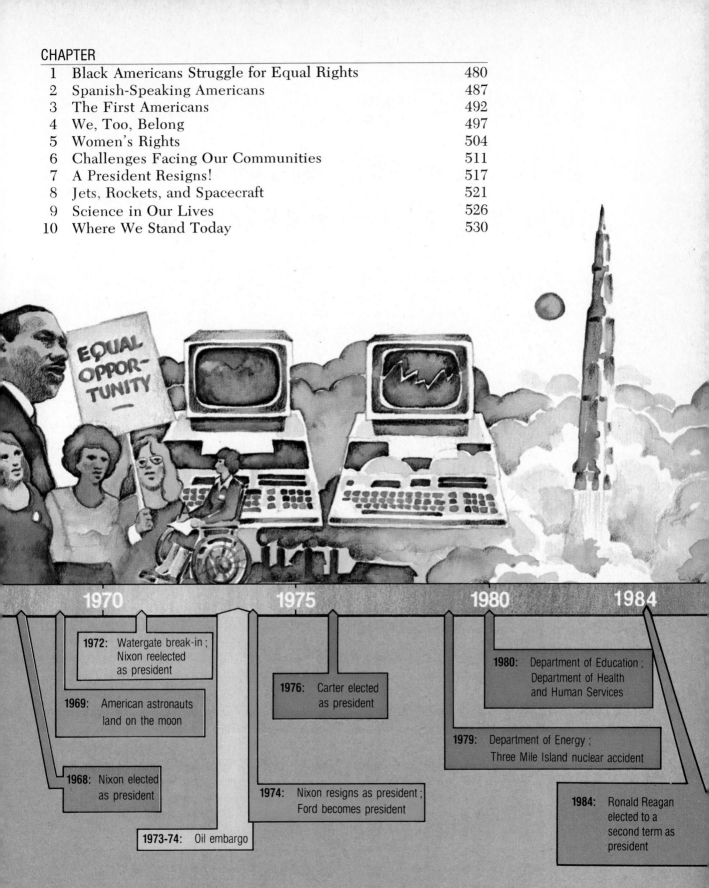

1970   1975   1980   1984

1972: Watergate break-in;
Nixon reelected
as president

1969: American astronauts
land on the moon

1968: Nixon elected
as president

1973-74: Oil embargo

1976: Carter elected
as president

1974: Nixon resigns as president;
Ford becomes president

1980: Department of Education;
Department of Health
and Human Services

1979: Department of Energy;
Three Mile Island nuclear accident

1984: Ronald Reagan
elected to a
second term as
president

1 BLACK AMERICANS STRUGGLE FOR EQUAL RIGHTS

How did the civil rights movement develop in the United States?

A sit-in at a lunch counter in the early 1960s. What was the purpose of such protests?

1. After World War II, the income of the average American family increased. Most people were able to buy more goods and live more comfortably. Not everyone shared in this prosperity, though. This was the case for many black Americans. The 1950s became a turning point for blacks. They were angry at being treated as "second-class" citizens. Many blacks could not travel where they wished and could not eat where they chose. They often could not live where they wanted and could not vote. In short, they were denied certain **civil rights** enjoyed by other Americans.

2. In 1954 the Supreme Court ruled that **segregated,** or separate, public schools for blacks and whites were unlawful and had to end. Some states moved promptly to carry out this decision. Others moved very slowly.

3. In 1955 Mrs. Rosa Parks, a black woman from Montgomery, Alabama, boarded a bus on her way home from work. The bus was segregated, with black people in the back and white people in the front. The bus driver asked her to take a seat in the back. He wanted her to move to make room for a white person. A city law allowed him to do this. Parks refused to move to the back. She was arrested. On learning of the arrest, blacks in Montgomery decided to **boycott,** or refuse to ride, the buses in that city. They said they would not ride the city's buses until black people were treated

the same way as white people. They also demanded that the bus company hire black bus drivers. One of their leaders was a young minister named Martin Luther King, Jr. He believed in nonviolent methods and peaceful action to win equal rights. The homes of some of the black leaders were bombed. King and other leaders were arrested for leading the boycott.

4. The Parks case went to the courts. After a year of the boycott, the courts ruled that Montgomery must end segregation of the buses. So the city changed its law to allow **integrated** seating, that is, seating that is not segregated. Also, black bus drivers were hired. The boycott ended. After this, Martin Luther King, Jr., became one of the most important leaders in the civil rights movement.

5. Encouraged by this development, the civil rights movement began to pick up speed. In 1960 black and white students began to stage sit-ins. They would sit down together at white-only lunch counters and

demand service. They would not leave unless they were served. As with the bus boycott, their protests were nonviolent. Soon civil rights workers, as they were called, began to go on "freedom" rides. They rode on buses in the South. They tried to stop segregation on the buses by sitting, blacks and whites, together. By the end of 1961, the federal government ordered a stop to segregation on all trains and buses between states.

6. Civil rights workers tried to end segregation in waiting rooms and rest rooms. They also tried to end segregation in public libraries, theaters, parks, and churches. They continued to use peaceful methods. The civil rights workers went wherever the signs said "For Whites Only." They were always in danger of being beaten or killed. However, they did not fight back. Their protests were nonviolent. By 1962 most colleges were integrated.

7. In August 1963, black leaders organized a peaceful march of 200,000 black and white people in Washington, D.C. They wanted to show their support for President Kennedy's civil rights bill. As millions of people watched on television, Dr. Martin Luther King, Jr., said, "I have a dream that one day the sons of former slaves and the sons of former slave owners will be able to sit down at the table of brotherhood and sing in the words of the old Negro spiritual, "Free at last! Free at last! Thank God Almighty, we are free at last!"

8. On November 22, 1963, President Kennedy was shot to death while visiting Dallas, Texas. The next president, Lyndon Johnson, moved quickly to carry out a civil rights program. Congress passed the Civil Rights Act of 1964. This law forbade segregation in hotels, restaurants, parks, and other public places. It outlawed discrimination by businesses and labor unions. While the bill was still in Congress, three civil rights workers were killed trying to help blacks register to vote. Even after the law was passed, many black Americans still had trouble voting. In 1965 Martin Luther King, Jr., led a march of 20,000 whites and blacks from Selma to Montgomery, Alabama. He wanted to dramatize the need for full voting rights for blacks.

9. In 1965 Congress passed the Voting Rights Act. This law forbade the use of reading tests to prevent Americans from voting. The law also gave the government the power to register black voters when local officials refused to do so. It greatly increased the number of black voters in the South. Congress passed the Civil Rights Act of 1968. This outlaws discrimination in the selling or renting of houses or apartments.

10. The work of certain organized groups made many of these gains possible. Two of the older groups were the National Associa-

President Johnson and Dr. Martin Luther King, Jr., shake hands at the signing of the Civil Rights Act of 1964.

tion for the Advancement of Colored People (NAACP), led by Roy Wilkins, and the National Urban League, led by Whitney Young. Two of the newer groups were the Congress of Racial Equality (CORE), led by James Farmer, and the Southern Christian Leadership Conference (SCLC), led by Martin Luther King, Jr. In 1964 Dr. King received the Nobel Peace Prize for his work. On April 4, 1968, he was shot and killed in Memphis, Tennessee. This was a serious blow to the nonviolent civil rights movement.

11. The civil rights movement of the 1950s and 1960s had given blacks hope. It had guaranteed their voting rights. But it had not done much to help them earn a better living. Many blacks were still poor and still living in crowded ghettos. During the 1960s there were terrible riots in Los Angeles, Newark, Detroit, and other American cities. The rioters, mostly jobless young blacks, burned homes, looted shops, and shot at police. In many cases, federal and state troops had to be called in. Before the riots ended, many people, most of them black, died.

12. Many blacks felt they could no longer work closely with whites. They wanted to work only with other blacks. They were called black separatists. One of the largest separatist groups was the Black Muslims. It was led by Elijah Muhammad from the 1930s into the 1970s. He called for a separate state or "black nation" within the United States.

13. In the 1960s, other black leaders began to speak about getting black rights by more forceful action. They called for black power. They wanted blacks to organize and vote for programs that would benefit blacks. They said that black power meant that black people should run their own communities and businesses. They urged blacks to learn more about Afro-American history and culture. They worked to increase black pride and self-respect.

Black political leader, Jesse Jackson. He was born in South Carolina in 1941.

14. Many blacks were bitter because living conditions did not improve fast enough. Yet the civil rights movement brought many gains. There are more black office holders today than ever before in this century. Many large cities have black mayors. Many black people hold office in the federal government. Some are ambassadors and members of the president's cabinet. Thurgood Marshall became the first black to sit on the Supreme Court. Companies that once refused to hire blacks have begun drives to get more black employees. Many blacks are now working as salespeople, receptionists, TV performers, airline flight attendants, fashion models, and business managers. These are positions that very few blacks held before 1960.

15. Blacks are now putting their mark on all aspects of American life. In 1984, Jesse Jackson, a black civil rights leader, ran for the Democratic nomination for president. Twenty-five years ago he could not eat at a whites-only lunch counter in his home-

town. Black astronauts have recently been part of the space shuttle crew. Congress has made the birthday of slain civil rights leader Martin Luther King, Jr., a national holiday. Despite these success stories, black Americans have a long way to go. Too many blacks still live in poor housing. Too many young blacks drop out of school or cannot find useful work. Too many black families live chiefly on welfare. But as more blacks vote, they will obtain the political power to overcome these problems.

UNDERSTANDING
CHAPTER 1

I. **What is the main purpose of Chapter 1?**

   a. To describe our immigration laws
   b. To describe what World War II did for blacks
   c. To describe the struggle for equal rights by black Americans after World War II
   d. To describe the Supreme Court decision of 1954

II. **Choose the correct answer.**

1. Why were new civil rights laws needed?
   a. Women could not vote.
   b. The government had become too powerful.
   c. Many black Americans were being treated as "second-class" citizens.
2. The Supreme Court decision of 1954 was important because it
   a. ended the poll tax
   b. gave blacks the right to vote
   c. ordered an end to segregated public schools
3. Why was the 1963 march on Washington held?
   a. To fight for better housing in the cities
   b. To show the need for civil rights laws
   c. To demand that gasoline taxes be reduced
4. Martin Luther King, Jr., became world-famous as the man who
   a. led American troops in the Korean War
   b. led the fight for civil rights in the United States
   c. became the first black member of the Supreme Court
5. What does the word *segregation* mean?
   a. The working together of blacks and whites in business and government
   b. The belief that blacks and whites should get equal treatment
   c. The separation of people by race, especially in schools, housing, public places, and private businesses
6. Black Muslims believe that
   a. blacks and whites should live separately
   b. blacks and whites should work together
   c. blacks should return to Africa

III. Decide whether each statement agrees or disagrees with what you have read. If the statement disagrees, explain why.

1. Martin Luther King, Jr., led marches and boycotts to dramatize demands for equal rights for blacks.
2. Violence was sometimes used against workers in the civil rights movement.
3. In 1954 the Supreme Court said that segregated public schools were lawful if they were "separate but equal."
4. During the 1960s black Americans made important gains toward getting equal rights.
5. Many gains made by black Americans were made possible by the efforts of black civil rights groups.
6. During the 1960s serious riots took place in several large cities.
7. New laws passed by Congress made it even harder for blacks to vote.
8. By 1980 there were more black officeholders and government officials than in 1960.
9. Blacks and whites worked together in the civil rights movement.
10. Some black leaders felt that nonviolent methods of gaining rights were too slow.
11. The federal government did little to end discrimination in the 1960s.

DEVELOPING IDEAS AND SKILLS

A. GRAPH SKILLS *Average Incomes of Full-time Working Blacks and Whites, 1982*
Study the graph. Then decide whether each statement is true or false. If the statement is false, explain why.

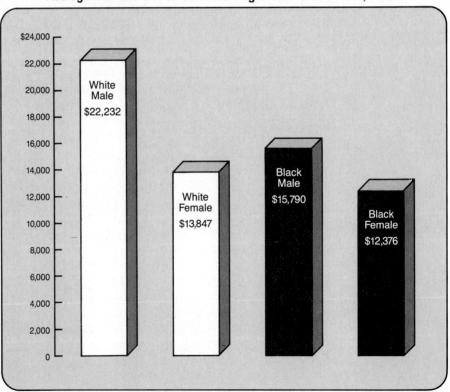

Average Incomes of Full-time Working Blacks and Whites, 1982

White Male $22,232
White Female $13,847
Black Male $15,790
Black Female $12,376

1. The average income of black and white women was almost the same in 1982.
2. The average income of black men was over $3,000 more than that of black women.
3. Black men earn about $3,000 less than white men.
4. Black women had a lower average income than any other group on the graph.

B. **GRAPH SKILLS** *Years of Education Completed by Blacks, 1970 and 1982*

Study the graph. Then decide whether each statement is true or false. If the statement is false, explain why.

Years of Higher Education Completed by Blacks, 1970 and 1982

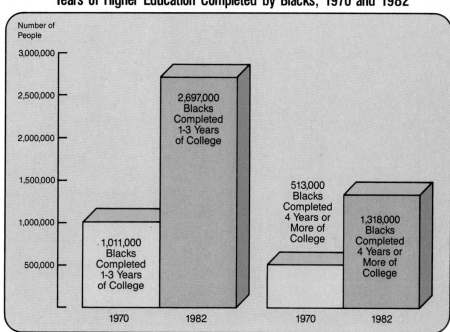

1. In 1982 there were over 2 million black Americans who had completed one to three years of college.
2. The number of black Americans who completed one to three years of college more than doubled between 1970 and 1982.
3. The number of black Americans who completed four years or more of college tripled between 1970 and 1982.

Select six of the following black Americans. Briefly describe their contributions to American life. You may use reference books to help you.

Thurgood Marshall	Eleanor Holmes Norton
Charles Richard Drew	Matthew A. Henson
Jackie Robinson	Shirley Verrett
Patricia Roberts Harris	Eubie Blake
A. Leon Higginbotham, Jr.	A. Philip Randolph
Samuel L. Gravely, Jr.	Kenneth Clark
Muhammad Ali	James Baldwin
Mary McCleod Bethune	Ella Fitzgerald
James Meredith	Shirley Chisholm
Maynard Jackson	George E. Carruthers

Thinking It Through

What are the chief problems black Americans face today? If you were a member of the president's cabinet, what suggestions would you make to solve them?

2 SPANISH-SPEAKING AMERICANS

Who are the Spanish-speaking Americans? What problems do they face?

Mayor Henry Cisneros of San Antonio, Texas. He is the first Mexican American mayor of a large United States city.

1. Blacks are not the only minority group that has made it clear that there are large gaps between the American dream and their real way of life. Spanish-speaking Americans also call for equal rights and a greater share of the nation's wealth. After the blacks, Spanish-speaking citizens make up the largest and fastest growing minority in the United States. These 14 million Spanish-speaking Americans are often called Hispanic Americans.

2. There are several different groups of Hispanic Americans. The largest—about 8 million—are Mexican Americans. Many Mexican Americans prefer to call themselves Chicanos, which comes from the Spanish word for Mexican. Others refer to themselves as *La Raza*, which means "the race" or "the people."

3. Most Mexican Americans live in the southwestern states. These include California, Arizona, New Mexico, Colorado, and Texas. Many of their ancestors were here hundreds of years before settlers came from the eastern states. They are a mixture of the early Spanish settlers, the American Indians of that region, and the blacks brought as slaves by Spain to its New World colony. Chicanos were the first settlers in many of the cities of the Southwest.

4. In 1848 the United States took over the Southwest after the war with Mexico. Over 75,000 Mexicans found that the United States was now their government. Thousands of English-speaking settlers from the East came to the Southwest, especially after the Civil War. The English-speaking settlers learned much about cattle raising, sheep raising, and irrigation from the Mexican Americans. But most Mexican Americans lost their land to the new settlers.

5. Thousands of other Mexicans came to the United States after 1900. They came because they were unable to make a living in Mexico. Many farmers, railroads, and mining companies offered them work. Living conditions were bad. The pay was low. But they could make more money working in the United States than in Mexico. Today large numbers of Mexicans are still coming north. They are coming secretly, looking for better paying jobs. If they are caught, they are sent back.

6. Most Mexican Americans live in the large cities of the Southwest. They are concentrated in sections called **barrios.** Most of them are poor. Some own small businesses in the neighborhood. Most, however, work at low wages doing unskilled labor. Their language at home is Spanish. In recent years

487

some public schools have begun to teach them in Spanish as well as in English. Many Mexican Americans are trying to improve the schools, housing, and health care in their communities.

7. Mexican American migrant farm workers have special problems. Migrant workers move from place to place to harvest various crops. The whole family usually travels and works. Families may live in a camp set up for them near the farms where they work. Such families are often overworked, underpaid, and poorly fed. To improve their working conditions, some migrant workers joined a labor union organized by Cesar Chavez in the 1960s. Chavez and his United Farm Workers work hard to make other Americans aware of the problems of the migrant farm workers.

8. The next largest Spanish-speaking group in the United States is made up of Puerto Rican Americans. As you have learned, the United States took Puerto Rico from Spain in 1898. Since then, the United States has allowed the Puerto Rican people more and more self-government. In 1948 the people began to elect their own governor. In 1952 the Commonwealth of Puerto Rico adopted its own constitution. As a commonwealth the Puerto Ricans elect their own government and pass their own laws. Puerto Ricans are American citizens. About 2 million Puerto Ricans live in the United States. They can vote in United States elections. Another 3½ million live on the home island. Many want their island to become a state of the Union. Some Puerto Ricans want Puerto Rico to be completely independent from the United States.

9. In the early 1950s, Puerto Ricans began to come to the United States in large numbers. At that time, Puerto Rico depended mainly on its sugarcane crop. There were few jobs on the island. Puerto Ricans came to the United States looking for jobs. They wanted to improve their lives. Unlike other immigrants, they were

Herman Badillo was born in Puerto Rico and earned a law degree in New York City. He is a lawyer, accountant, and former member of Congress.

citizens and they came largely by plane. Most settled in the East, in large cities such as New York and Philadelphia.

10. But for many Puerto Ricans who made the trip, the rewards were not very great. Many had trouble finding good housing. English-speaking Americans often did not want to rent or sell them homes. Most could only afford to live in the poorer neighborhoods of the city. Since the neighborhoods were old, they had all the problems that came with living in a slum. These problems included buildings that needed repairs, crime, drugs, and a lack of health services. Like other Spanish-speaking Americans, Puerto Ricans faced language problems in school and at work.

11. Despite these problems, many Puerto Ricans opened small businesses to serve their communities. Others found

jobs, often low paying, in the cities. Some became leaders in city government, sports, and the arts. Herman Badillo, Roberto Clemente, and Rita Moreno are just a few of the outstanding Puerto Ricans. In the past decade, more Puerto Ricans than ever before have become high school and college graduates. Beginning in 1974, more Puerto Ricans moved back to the home island than moved from Puerto Rico to North America. The jobless rate in Puerto Rico is high. Yet, manufacturing rather than farming is now more important.

12. The third largest group of Spanish-speaking Americans are the refugees from Cuba. They have been streaming into Florida since 1959 when Fidel Castro came to power in Cuba. The largest group of Cubans, about 800,000, live in widely scattered neighborhoods in and around Miami,

Florida. Many Puerto Ricans and Mexicans came to the United States in search of jobs. The Cuban refugees, however, were fairly well to do. They did not leave because of poverty. They left to escape a Cuban government they did not like. For a time they waited for the Castro government to fall or be overthrown. In 1961 the United States supported a Cuban refugee invasion of Cuba. The invasion was unsuccessful. This made the refugees realize that Miami might be their home for a long time. They got jobs, started new businesses, built homes, and became American citizens. They made some neighborhoods in Miami thoroughly Cuban. In 1980, over 100,000 more Cubans left Cuba for the United States. Most of them arrived in Florida in small boats. The United States has given the Cubans a chance to rebuild their lives.

REVIEWING CHAPTER 1

Decide whether each statement is true or false. The underlined words are clues to help you decide. If a statement is false, change the underlined word or words to make it true.

1. Martin Luther King, Jr., received the Nobel Peace Prize.
2. The march on Washington in 1963 was a protest against a decision of the Supreme Court.
3. Equal treatment for all people in public places was guaranteed by the 15th Amendment.
4. In 1964 the Supreme Court ruled that separate schools for blacks and whites were unlawful and had to be ended.
5. President Lyndon Johnson was shot to death in 1963.
6. Elijah Muhammad was the leader of a black separatist group called CORE.

UNDERSTANDING CHAPTER 2

I. What is the main purpose of Chapter 2?

a. To describe the problems of Spanish-speaking Americans
b. To describe life in a barrio
c. To explain why Puerto Ricans came to the United States
d. To describe why Cuban refugees came to the United States

II. Choose the correct answer.

1. In which part of the United States do most Mexican Americans live?
a. Northeast
b. Middle West
c. Southwest

2. Puerto Ricans faced all of these problems EXCEPT:
   a. They spoke a different language from that spoken by most people in the United States.
   b. They are not citizens of the United States.
   c. They often had to live in the poorer sections of the cities.
3. Cesar Chavez heads a union trying to protect the interests of
   a. skilled workers
   b. office workers
   c. migrant farm workers
4. Most Hispanic Americans are
   a. Americans born in Spain
   b. Spanish-speaking Americans
   c. Cubans
5. A *barrio* is a
   a. town where migratory workers live
   b. camp for children with problems
   c. section of a large city where Mexican Americans live
6. Most Cubans came to the United States
   a. in order not to be ruled by the Communist government in Cuba
   b. to practice their religion freely
   c. to attend schools in the United States
7. The fastest growing minority group in the United States are:
   a. Asian Americans
   b. Hispanic Americans
   c. black Americans
8. In Puerto Rico, most jobs are now in
   a. sugarcane farms
   b. tobacco farms
   c. manufacturing

III. **Decide whether each statement agrees or disagrees with what you have read. If the statement disagrees, explain why. What paragraph in the chapter helped you in making your decision?**

1. Most Mexican Americans make their living as farm workers.
2. Puerto Ricans can come freely to the United States.
3. Spanish-speaking Americans are guaranteed the same rights as all other American citizens.
4. Many Spanish-speaking citizens live in their own neighborhoods.
5. Unlike the blacks, Spanish-speaking citizens have few housing or education problems.
6. Many Mexican families were living in the Northwest long before English-speaking settlers came.
7. Cuba is a colony of the United States today.

DEVELOPING IDEAS AND SKILLS

MAP SKILLS *20th Century Migrations*
Study the map. Then decide whether these statements are true or false.

1. Many white Americans are moving westward and southward.
2. Many Puerto Ricans who come to the United States settle in the North.
3. Many black Americans now live in the large northern cities.

20th Century Migrations

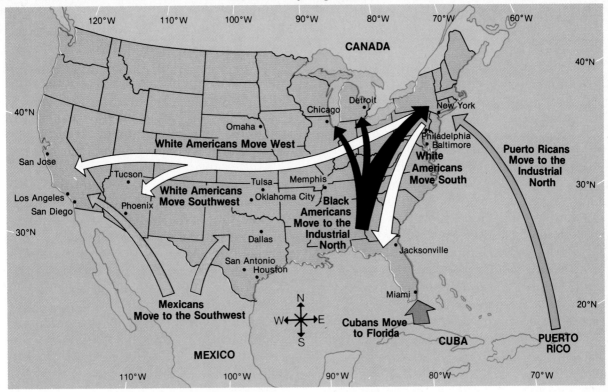

4. Many Mexican Americans live and work in the Southwest.
5. During the 20th century, many blacks left the South.
6. Many newcomers settle in the East, Southwest, and West, where they do farm work.
7. Cuban Americans live largely in the state of Texas.
8. Puerto Rico got its freedom soon after the Spanish-American War.

SUMMING UP   Complete the following chart in your notebook.

SPANISH-SPEAKING AMERICANS

GROUP	WHERE THEY SETTLED	WHERE THEY CAME FROM
Mexican Americans		
Puerto Ricans		
Cubans		

Thinking It Through

In what ways are the problems faced by Spanish-speaking Americans similar to those faced by black Americans? In what ways are the problems different?

491

3 THE FIRST AMERICANS

What problems do Indians face today?

1. As you remember from the first chapters of the book, the Indians were already here when the Europeans came. Their way of life was different from the Europeans. Many Indians did not wish to see the forests cleared of trees and wildlife or the plains emptied of buffalo. They wanted to hunt and fish as they had always done. Some Indians got much of their food from farming. Indians raised maize (corn), peas, beans, squash, pumpkins, and tobacco. Other Indians were nomads. Every year they wandered from place to place in search of food and a good life. Most early white groups, on the other hand, wanted to settle down on the land, plant crops, and build settlements. They wanted to take over the land the Indians used.

2. A large part of American history is a story of how the white settlers drove the Indians from their lands. On many occasions, white people broke the treaties and agreements they had made with Indians. The Indians fought for a long time to hold on to their homes and their customs. But they were defeated and often destroyed. They were forced to live on **reservations**. Reservations are areas of land set aside for a special purpose. These reservations were controlled by the government. Here the government gave the Indians food and whatever other goods and services it thought they needed. The Indians had little to say about how or where they lived.

3. Partly as a reward for their services in World War I, the Indians were made American citizens in 1924. Some had already become citizens by earlier laws. But citizenship did not make their lives much better. Of course, from time to time mineral discoveries on some of their lands brought riches to a few Indians. But for Indians as a whole, life was hard. Their death rate was higher and their education poorer than other Americans.

4. In the 1930s the federal government adopted a new Indian policy. It put a stop to its practice of breaking up the reservations. It encouraged the Indians to practice self-government and to develop their own way of life on the reservations. Government workers taught the Indians to use their land more wisely. Encouraged by the new policy, many Indian peoples began to rebuild their tribal way of life. During World War II, about 25,000 Indians served in the armed forces.

5. Since World War II, the Indian population has grown rapidly. There are about one million Indians living in the United States today. Indians are no longer required to live on reservations, although many still do. They may travel, work, and live where they please. About one-half now live in cities. Although Indians live in almost every state of the Union, most live west of the Mississippi River.

6. On the reservations, the Indians are gaining a greater voice in running their own affairs. In the reservation schools, the young people can learn their native languages and about their heritage. Although many Indians are poor, some Indian lands contain minerals, woodlands, and other valuable resources. These include much uranium, oil, gas, and coal. Some companies have made arrangements with the federal government to use these resources. This has made the Indian leaders angry. They feel that whites are taking advantage of them once again.

7. Encouraged by the gains made by other groups in the civil rights movement, the Indians also protested. In 1969 a group of Indians took over part of Alcatraz Island

Wounded Knee, early 1973. What conditions have led Indians to organize protests in recent years?

in San Francisco Bay. The federal government had given up its prison there, and the Indians occupied it for a few months. In 1973 another group of Indians occupied the village of Wounded Knee, South Dakota. They held the village for over two months. Wounded Knee was the place where in 1890 about 200 Indians had been killed by soldiers. In 1978 about 1,000 Indians made their way across the United States. They marched into Washington, D.C. Why did the Indians hold these protests? Why did they take this "long walk"? What did they want?

8. They wanted to show the public and members of Congress how bitter Indian life was in America. They wanted to hold hearings on government treaties with Indians. Indians have lived in America longer than any other group in the United States. Yet

The Wampanoag Indian Tribal Council meeting in Massachusetts. Today there are more than one million American Indians in the United States.

even today, they do not enjoy the same rights as other Americans. They continue to be the poorest group in the United States. Their children are still the least educated. They find it harder than other Americans to find jobs. Their rights as citizens are more limited than those of any other minority.

Some Indians are trying to make the government honor their treaty rights. They want their land returned. To do this, they are taking their cases to court. As one Indian leader said recently, "All we want is the right to govern ourselves on our own lands, a right that other Americans have."

Choose the correct answer or answers.

1. Migrant workers are people .who
   a. own their own land
   b. work in factories
   c. go from farm to farm to work
2. The largest group of Spanish-speaking Americans is made up of
   a. Puerto Ricans
   b. Mexican Americans
   c. Cuban Americans
3. Cesar Chavez organized a union to help
   a. migrant workers
   b. auto workers
   c. farm owners
4. Puerto Rico was acquired by the United States after
   a. the Civil War
   b. World War II
   c. the Spanish-American War
5. A barrio is a
   a. Spanish-speaking neighborhood in a large city
   b. school in Havana, Cuba
   c. Spanish labor union

I. What is the main purpose of Chapter 3?

   a. To describe some important Indian leaders
   b. To describe how Indians live on reservations today
   c. To describe problems that Indians have faced and still face today
   d. To describe government policy toward Indians today

II. Choose the correct answer.

1. Early American Indians wanted to
   a. use their land for hunting, fishing, and farming
   b. build large cities on their land
   c. mine their own minerals
2. Indians are often called the first Americans because they
   a. fought in the Revolutionary War
   b. helped settle the plains
   c. came to America long before any other people
3. Which statement best describes the condition of Indians today?
   a. They are the largest minority group in the United States.
   b. They must remain on reservations.
   c. Many live in great poverty, are poorly educated, and are out of work.

4. When did most Indians become American citizens?
    a. 1924
    b. 1965
    c. 1876
5. What has been the purpose of Indian protests and court cases in the 1970s and 1980s?
    a. To get jobs for Indians in the cities
    b. To regain control of their hunting rights
    c. To draw the rest of America's attention to their problems and to get land returned to them

III. Do you agree or disagree? Give reasons for your answers.

1. The Indians would like a larger share of America's wealth.
2. The Indians are better off than most other minorities in America.
3. Indians held protests at Alcatraz and Wounded Knee.
4. Indian tribes are found only in the Southwest.
5. Indians served in the armed forces in both world wars.
6. Many Indians still do not want to adopt the white people's way of life.
7. Some Indians were denied their civil rights even after 1924.
8. Some Indian reservations consist of land with valuable resources.
9. The government broke many treaties and agreements with Indians.

DEVELOPING IDEAS
AND SKILLS

Study the photograph. Then answer the following questions.

1. Why do you think these Indians have gathered in Washington, D.C., to protest?
2. How do you think these Indians feel? Explain.
3. What is a good title for this photograph?

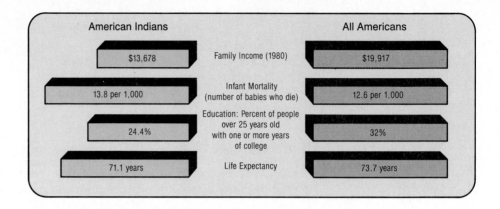

1. What does this chart show about American Indians today?
2. Do you agree or disagree with this statement, "As a group, Indians have one of the lowest incomes and least amount of higher education of all Americans." Explain your answer.
3. What could be done to help American Indians?

Thinking It Through

Do you think that Indians will help solve their problems by joining protest groups? Why or why not?

4 WE, TOO, BELONG

How did other minority groups help the United States grow?

1. America has always been a land of minority groups. Even in early colonial times, there were settlers from many different countries. Most people came to America to better their lives. Usually, the newcomers worked at the hardest jobs for little pay. Each group found that at first they were not accepted by Americans who had been born here or whose families had lived here for a long time. Each group suffered prejudice and discrimination. But the good outweighed the bad. Immigrants kept on coming, and many prospered. Here is the story, in brief, of six such minority groups.

2. In the early 1800s many Irish people came because there was not enough land for them to support their families in Ireland. In Ireland, the people depended on the potato for food. In the late 1840s the potato crop failed because of a plant disease. Nearly one million people starved to death in Ireland. Another 800,000 Irish came to the United States. They settled in the East. Most lived in the large port cities such as New York, Philadelphia, and Boston. They often saw signs announcing jobs. But the signs read, "No Irish need apply." They had to take jobs requiring heavy labor. They became dock workers, ditch diggers, and builders of the nation's canals, railroads, and highways. Many others, especially women and girls, became house servants. Often the newcomers could afford to live only in the worst slums.

3. Despite their hardships, Irish Americans made great strides. Irish-American workers played an important part in the early labor unions such as the Knights of Labor and the United Mine Workers of America. They also went into city politics, largely as members of the Democratic party. Sometimes Irish-American political leaders found jobs for newcomers and gave them help when they were sick or out of work.

4. Irish Americans also relied on the Catholic Church to help them get ahead. Their hard-won earnings went into the building of **parochial** schools. In these private religious schools their children learned about the Catholic religion as well as the subjects taught in the public schools. Irish Americans built such colleges and universities as Fordham, Holy Cross, Villanova, Notre Dame, and Georgetown. These schools, and public schools as well, trained Irish Americans to move ahead in business, the professions, sciences, and the arts. Irish Americans continued to face discrimination in housing and jobs. They were opposed by the Ku Klux Klan (**KKK**). The **KKK** was violently anti-Catholic as well as being antiblack.

5. Gradually, there was less prejudice against Irish Americans. Many Irish Americans became important leaders. In 1928 Al Smith ran for president. Although he lost the election, Smith was the first Irish Catholic to run for president. Eugene O'Neill and George M. Cohan wrote plays for the Broadway theater. George Meany became head of the giant group of labor unions known as the AFL-CIO. Bing Crosby sang some of America's favorite songs. In 1960 John F. Kennedy was elected as the first Catholic president of the United States.

6. As Irish Americans began to move out of the slums, their place was taken by the "new immigrants" from southern and eastern Europe. Italians made up the largest of all the "new immigrant" groups. Although America got its name from an Italian explorer (Amerigo Vespucci), by 1850 there

Mario Cuomo, an Italian-American, was elected governor of New York State in 1982. Cuomo was born and raised in New York City. He played minor league baseball for a short time after graduating from high school. Cuomo went on to receive a law degree and entered politics in the 1970s.

were only about 4,000 Italian Americans in the United States. It was not until after 1880 that large numbers of Italians arrived here. By 1920 over 4 million Italians had come to the United States. Like the Irish, they settled in the cities of the East. Most lived in the poorest sections. They faced discrimination in housing, jobs, and education. Like the Irish, they suffered from anti-Catholic prejudice. Before 1885 they often relied on the padrone, or work boss, to get them jobs. A padrone was also from Italy, but he had been in America longer. Italian Americans also had to take the jobs that required heavy work with low pay. They helped build bridges and subways in the big cities.

7. Italians settled in neighborhoods where other Italians already were. This was the same pattern followed by most immigrant groups. The father took whatever job he could find. Boys sold papers, ran errands, and shined shoes. Women broke with the old ways of life and took jobs in sweatshop factories. Despite these early hardships, the Italians worked hard to keep their strong family ties. In time they learned the ways of their new homeland and got better jobs. They joined labor unions. They became mechanics, plasterers, bakers, and butchers. When Mussolini became the dictator of Italy, the vast majority of Italian Americans rejected him. Over 400,000 Italian Americans fought bravely in World War II.

8. As their voting strength grew, Italian Americans went into politics. Fiorello La Guardia won fame as the mayor of New York City (1934–45). By the late 1970s and early 1980s, Italian Americans were leaders at the state and national level. In the field of music, Arturo Toscanini was a leading orchestra conductor. Frank Sinatra thrilled millions with his songs. In science, Enrico Fermi helped introduce the world to the atomic age. He won the Nobel Prize for Physics and worked on the atomic and hydrogen bombs. One of many outstanding business people was Amadeo Giannini. He built his small California bank into the Bank of America, the largest bank in the United States. Italian Americans are now doctors, lawyers, teachers, and other professionals. For example, in 1979 Yale University chose A. Bartlett Giamatti to be its president.

9. There are now about 5½ million Jewish Americans in the United States. This is the largest Jewish community in the world today. The first Jews came to this country in the 1600s. After the Revolutionary War, the United States was the first nation in modern times to give Jews equal civil rights. Jews began to come to the United States in large numbers after 1880. They were escaping religious persecution in eastern Europe

and Russia. Like the Irish and the Italians, the Jews, too, faced many problems. They were kept out of many neighborhoods, schools, clubs, and jobs. They had to take low-paying jobs in the sweatshops.

10. Through the efforts of the labor leaders Sidney Hillman and David Dubinsky, they organized labor unions such as the Amalgamated Clothing Workers of America and the International Ladies Garment Workers Union. They relied heavily on the public schools and their own self-help organizations. Today about eight out of every ten Jewish workers are business people or professionals (doctors, lawyers, teachers, engineers, and social workers). Only a few neighborhoods now remain closed to them.

11. Jews have fought in every one of America's wars since the Revolutionary War. They built up the clothing and newspaper industries. Jews pioneered in the radio, movie, and television industries. Five Jews, including Louis Brandeis and Felix Frankfurter, have served on the Supreme Court. In the field of science, Jews have been well known. These scientists include Albert Einstein (atomic energy), Jonas Salk (polio vaccine), Selman Waksman (streptomycin), and Edward Teller (hydrogen bomb). Despite these contributions, some Jewish Americans still feel insecure. They were badly frightened by the slaughter of 6 million Jews in Europe during World War II. They fear for the safety of the Jewish state of Israel in the Middle East. Although most Americans do not approve of **anti-Semitism** (hatred of the Jews), it still exists in some areas of the United States.

12. In terms of numbers, Asian Americans of Chinese, Japanese, and Vietnamese origin form three of the smaller minority groups in the United States today. There are about 600,000 Japanese, 435,000 Chinese, and 300,000 Vietnamese living in the United States today. The Chinese were the first immigrants from the Far East. In the 1850s and 1860s, they came to work on the railroads and in the mines in the West. Many other Americans did not like them. Their language, religion, dress, and customs were different. They were also members of a different race. In bad times when many people were out of work, some white Americans rioted against the Chinese. People seemed to want to blame their troubles on Asian immigrants. In 1882 Congress passed a law ending Chinese immigration. The law also said that Chinese people could not become citizens. This kind of law was in effect until 1943. Cities and states passed laws to keep Chinese from getting certain kinds of jobs. Many Chinese lived in ghettos in the cities of New York and San Francisco. They traded with each other because no one else would do business with them. They could not join labor unions. Since the Chinese could not vote, political bosses paid no attention to them.

13. The Japanese came later, in the 1880s and 1890s. They, too, were limited to such jobs as small farmers, cannery workers, gardeners, and servants. They, too, found many white Americans to be anti-Asian. The U.S. government pressured Japan to slow down Japanese immigration. In 1924 a new U.S. immigration law cut it off altogether. Despite these hardships, native-born Japanese Americans (Nisei) tried to get ahead by going to school. As relations between the United States and Japan grew worse in the 1930s, the distrust of Japanese Americans grew. After Japan's attack on Pearl Harbor, over 100,000 Japanese (most of them American citizens) were removed from the West Coast to ten **detention camps** inland. They were treated almost like prisoners and kept behind barbed-wire fences. Both President Franklin Roosevelt and the Supreme Court approved. Despite this unfair treatment, many young Japanese Americans volunteered to serve in the armed

forces. They had an outstanding record, especially in the fighting against Italy.

14. World War II proved to be a turning point for most Asian Americans. During the war, many Chinese Americans found work in the nation's airplane plants and factories. Japanese Americans fought bravely in Europe. After the war, many other Americans were ashamed of what had happened to the Japanese Americans. The old immigration laws were ended. Hawaii was admitted as the 50th state in 1959. Over one-third of its people were of Chinese and Japanese origin.

15. Today, it is much easier for Asian Americans to get better jobs and find better housing. There is much less discrimination. Asian American families value education. As a result, Asian Americans have gone to college and become doctors, pharmacists, lawyers, and engineers. Outstanding Chinese Americans include the scientists Tsung Dao Lee and Chen Ning Yang, who won the Nobel Prize for Physics. I. M. (Ieah Ming) Pei is one of the country's most important architects. Japanese Americans have made equally outstanding achievements. Samuel T. Hayakawa of California and Daniel K. Inouye of Hawaii were elected senators. Isamu Noguchi is a world-famous sculptor. Seiji Ozawa is one of the country's leading orchestra conductors.

16. Since World War II, over 12 million people have legally come into the United States. When the Communists put down protests in Hungary, Czechoslovakia, and Poland, thousands fled to America. In 1979 and 1980, more than 50,000 Jewish refu-

Japanese Americans being sent to detention camps during World War II. They had to sell at low prices the homes and property they left behind.

gees came to the United States from the Soviet Union. After the Korean War, 300,000 Koreans came to America. Since Castro took power in Cuba in 1959, about 1,000,000 Cubans have landed on United States shores. In the late 1970's, after the Vietnam War, about 600,000 Vietnamese traveled halfway around the world to start a new life in the United States. In the past 30 years, over 2,000,000 Mexicans have moved north in search of better jobs. There can be little doubt that many of the world's people want to live in the United States.

Vietnamese refugees beginning a new life in the United States. How does this reflect the spirit of America's history?

REVIEWING CHAPTER 3

Fill in the missing word or words in the sentences below.

1. The first people living in North America were _____.
2. One of the important foods that some Indian tribes raised was _____.
3. When white people first met them, American Indians made a living largely through small farming, _____, and fishing.
4. The Indian tribes on the Great Plains depended largely on horses and _____.
5. White people broke many treaties with Indians in order to get the Indians' _____.
6. Indians fought various _____ to hold off the white settlers, but they did not succeed.
7. The special lands set aside for Indian use are called _____.
8. In 1924 Congress passed a law by which Indians finally became American _____.
9. In recent years, many Indian groups have taken their cases to court in order to get _____ returned to them.
10. There are about _____ Indians living in the United States today.

UNDERSTANDING CHAPTER 4

I. **What is the main purpose of Chapter 4?**

   a. To give a brief history of several minority groups in America
   b. To describe America's immigration laws
   c. To describe the contributions of various Americans
   d. To describe various religions in America

501

II. Choose the correct answer.

1. All the following are true of Jewish Americans EXCEPT:
   a. They are concerned about the state of Israel.
   b. The first Jews came to this country in the 1600s.
   c. Most are poorly educated.
2. A person who is anti-Semitic is one who hates
   a. Jews
   b. people because of their skin color
   c. the Catholic Church
3. All the following are true of Chinese Americans EXCEPT:
   a. They first came to work in the mining camps and on the railroads.
   b. They bought large farms in the South.
   c. They have made much progress since the 1950s.
4. All of the following are true of Irish Americans EXCEPT:
   a. They received support from the Catholic Church.
   b. They came in large numbers in the middle of the 1800s.
   c. They met little discrimination once they were here.
5. All the following are true of Italian Americans EXCEPT:
   a. At first, many relied heavily on a padrone to get them jobs.
   b. They remain one of America's smallest minority groups.
   c. They helped build bridges and subways in the big cities.
6. During World War II members of which minority group were put in concentration camps in the United States?
   a. Filipinos
   b. Japanese Americans
   c. Chinese Americans
7. Which group of Asians arrived in the United States in great numbers in the late 1970s?
   a. Japanese
   b. Vietnamese
   c. Chinese

III. Decide whether each statement agrees or disagrees with what you have read. If the statement disagrees, explain why.

1. Asian Americans have always been treated fairly.
2. Many immigrants worked for low wages in sweatshops, mines, and factories, or on roads and railways.
3. All minority groups were always welcomed in the United States.
4. Jews began coming to America in colonial times.
5. Minority groups have made important contributions to our country.
6. The Irish and Italians settled largely in the farmlands of the West.
7. As a war measure, Japanese Americans were sent to detention camps in the 1940s.
8. Many new immigrants settled in neighborhoods near people from their native country.
9. The United States took in thousands of boat people after the Vietnamese War.

Answer the following questions.

1. What minority groups are shown in this cartoon?
2. Why did these groups come in large numbers to the United States?
3. What problems did they face at first?
4. According to the cartoon, what has helped them to overcome their problems?
5. What problems do minority groups still face?

SUMMING UP

At one time, many Americans thought that immigrants had to give up their traditional customs and beliefs in order to become "good" Americans. By the 1970s, this feeling had changed. What do you think? Must members of a minority group give up their "old way of life" completely to be good Americans? Or, can they hold on to the ways of their group and still be good Americans? Give reasons for your answer.

Thinking It Through

The people of the United States come from many different kinds of backgrounds. In this chapter, for example, we discussed only six of the many immigrant groups. Millions of Germans, Austrians, Hungarians, Canadians, Russians, British, Swedes, Filipinos, West Indians, and others also came. People are different in their religion, race, beliefs, and way of life. What are three things Americans can do to get along with each other and respect one another's rights, freedom, and ways of life?

5 WOMEN'S RIGHTS

What rights have women fought for over the years?

Carrie Chapman Catt voting for the first time. What amendment gave women the right to vote?

1. From colonial days women had worked side by side with men in building a new country. Yet women did not have the same rights as men. As you have already learned, in the 19th century, some women began to organize themselves to fight for women's rights. Before the Civil War, some of these leaders were also active in the antislavery and temperance movements. Angelina and Sarah Grimké, Lucretia Mott, Sojourner Truth, and Elizabeth Cady Stanton were among them. Mott and Stanton organized the Women's Rights Convention in Seneca Falls in 1848. (See page 357.) These women wanted equal rights under the law. They wanted women to have the opportunity for good jobs and a good education. Most of them wanted women to have the right to vote.

2. During the early part of the 19th century, most women who worked outside their homes were household servants or hired farm hands. But the Civil War was a turning point for many women. With the coming of the war, women went into government service and into offices. Thousands of others began working in factories. There they made clothing, blankets, bandages, and other supplies. Some women worked in the army camps as nurses, cooks, and launderers. Some served in the field as spies and scouts. After the war, more colleges opened their doors to women. (The first had done so in the 1830s.) As the number of women high-school and college graduates increased, the number of women teachers, doctors, and lawyers grew. In the

offices, women quickly mastered the new equipment—telephones and typewriters. Still, by 1900, a woman working outside her home was most likely to be a household servant or a factory worker. These were low-paying jobs. Men who did the same kinds of work got paid more.

3. In the late 19th and early 20th centuries, women often led reform movements. Frances Willard and Carrie Nation fought to make the use of alcoholic drinks illegal. Jane Addams and Lillian Wald founded settlement houses. They worked with the poor immigrants who crowded into the city slums. Mary Church Terrell organized a nationwide group of black women to work for better schools and hospitals. Others, like Rose Schneiderman, joined the labor movement. They tried to organize the large number of unskilled, underpaid working women into trade unions.

4. Despite gains in other fields, women failed to get the right to vote. Yet women continued to work actively for the right to

vote. (See page 391.) Under the leadership of Susan B. Anthony, Elizabeth Cady Stanton, and Carrie Chapman Catt, voting became the symbol of all that women hoped to achieve for themselves. These women led marches to demand the right to vote. But many men and women opposed them. Nevertheless, women won the right to vote by means of the 19th Amendment in 1920.

5. During World War I, many more women began working in the nation's shops, offices, and factories. When the war ended, some women lost their jobs to men returning from the war. Yet during the 1920s, many more women joined the work force. These new jobs were usually in business offices rather than in factories. Thousands of women became sales clerks, librarians, and social workers. In the 1920s a new style for women emerged—the "flapper." She was a woman with a short skirt and bobbed hair (a kind of short haircut), who danced to the new fast music. Most women, however, did not follow all the fashion styles of the flappers.

6. The depression of the 1930s ended much of this new freedom. As unemployment swept the nation, women were among the first to be fired. Nevertheless, the New Deal brought a few women into high government jobs. Eleanor Roosevelt, wife of President Franklin D. Roosevelt, took the lead. Frances Perkins, as secretary of labor, became the first woman cabinet member. Mary McLeod Bethune directed black affairs in the government.

7. In the early 1940s, women returned to factories and offices as men went off to fight in World War II. At the end of the war, women once again lost their jobs to men returning from the war. During the 1950s and 1960s more labor-saving machines for the home became available. As a result, some women had more time for jobs outside the home. Others took new jobs to earn money needed for themselves or their families.

Mary McCleod Bethune and Eleanor Roosevelt. Bethune served as the president's adviser on minority affairs. In the late 1940s, Roosevelt became a delegate to the UN.

By 1960 over 23 million women were working outside the home.

8. Beginning in the 1960s, new women leaders such as Betty Friedan spoke out. They argued that home and family need not be a woman's only concerns. There was an active effort known as the women's liberation movement to end discrimination against women in all fields. For example, one of the goals for women was, and still is, to get equal pay for equal work. In 1982, for example, the average income for women who had completed four years of college was $17,400. The average income for men with the same amount of education was $28,000.

9. Laws were passed to protect women's rights. The Civil Rights Act of 1964 forbade sex discrimination in hiring. In the late 1970s and early 1980s women seemed to be winning some of the battles for equal

Associate Justice of the Supreme Court Sandra Day O'Connor. She is the first woman to serve on the Supreme Court.

rights. Growing numbers of women became lawyers, doctors, and military officers. Women were increasing their activity in politics. For the first time voters had elected women to one out of every ten seats in state legislatures. Chicago and San Francisco elected women as their mayors. Sandra Day O'Connor became the first woman to serve on the Supreme Court.

10. In their personal lives, women have undergone major changes. Fewer women are getting married. Women who do are doing so at a later age. They are also having fewer children. Women are no longer remaining at home. More than two out of three women between the ages of 25 and 50 now hold jobs outside the home. If they are working mothers, child care is important to them. Thus, the number of children in nursery schools has doubled since 1970. More and more companies now have child-care programs for children of employees.

11. In 1972 Congress passed the Equal Rights Amendment. Despite hard work by its supporters, the ERA was not passed by the required 38 states. However, this has not stopped the leaders of the women's rights movement. They feel that ERA will be adopted one day. As Shirley Chisholm, the first black woman elected to Congress, said, "It took us 70 years to get the right to vote. If it takes us another ten years to pass ERA, we won't go away mad."

REVIEWING
CHAPTER 4

Choose the correct answers.

1. Many Irish immigrants came to the United States in the mid-19th century because
   a. they wanted religious freedom
   b. the potato crop failed in Ireland
   c. free ship tickets were given to all immigrants

2. The first Catholic president of the United States was
   a. Al Smith
   b. Herbert Hoover
   c. John F. Kennedy

3. Italian immigrant women often took jobs
   a. in sweatshop factories
   b. as lawyers or doctors
   c. in cotton and rice fields

4. The word *ghetto* means
   a. a neighborhood in which members of a minority group live, often as a result of discrimination
   b. a settlement house in a slum neighborhood
   c. a Catholic private school
5. For what explorer is America named?
   a. Columbus
   b. Cabot
   c. Vespucci
6. Where did most Irish and Italian immigrants settle when they first came to the United States?

a. In the farmlands of the West
b. In the cotton fields of the South
c. In the big cities of the East

7. Between 1882 and 1943 Congress did not allow the immigration of
   a. Japanese
   b. Filipinos
   c. Chinese
8. Many Vietnamese refugees came to the United States in the
   a. 1950s
   b. 1960s
   c. 1970s

UNDERSTANDING CHAPTER 5

I. **What is the main idea of Chapter 5?**

   a. To explain which rights women have fought for over the years
   b. To show how women won the right to vote
   c. To show the part they played in America's wars

II. **Choose the correct answer.**

1. Which statement best expresses the position of women in the 1840s?
   a. They did not have the same rights as men.
   b. They were not taught how to read or write.
   c. They were forced to work in factories.
2. Women took part in all the following reform movements EXCEPT the
   a. movement to abolish slavery
   b. fight against the use of alcoholic drinks
   c. abolition of the income tax
3. Which statement best describes the women's rights movement today?
   a. The women's rights movement is trying to gain equal rights for women in all fields of life.
   b. The only goal of the women's rights movement is to elect women to office.
   c. The main purpose of the women's rights movement is to prevent women from remaining at home.
4. As a result of the 19th Amendment, women
   a. gained equal rights with men
   b. became citizens of the United States
   c. won the right to vote
5. For what will Susan B. Anthony be remembered?
   a. She fought for women's right to vote.
   b. She organized women workers into labor unions.
   c. She was the first woman doctor in the United States.

6. What is the Equal Rights Amendment about?
   a. Equal voting rights for blacks
   b. Equal rights for women
   c. Limiting each state to an equal number of members of Congress
7. What part did women play in the Civil War?
   a. They fought in the armed forces.
   b. They invented new weapons of war.
   c. They worked as nurses and as factory workers.
8. In many cases, women with the same skills and education as men now earn
   a. more money than men
   b. the same amount of money as men
   c. less money than men
9. The first black woman elected to Congress was
   a. Betty Friedan
   b. Jane M. Byrne
   c. Shirley Chisholm
10. Which statement is true of women in America today?
   a. Most still remain at home.
   b. Most are raising large families.
   c. More are becoming doctors and lawyers.

III. Do you agree or disagree? Give reasons for your answers.

1. In colonial times, women had few rights.
2. In the early 1800s, women were among the leaders of the antislavery movement.
3. Women quickly won the right to vote.
4. The women's rights movement is not as active as it once was.
5. Women played an active role in both world wars.
6. Lawmakers ignored the demands of women for many years.
7. In the 1800s few women found work outside their homes.
8. Today, more women are working outside the home than ever before.
9. Women face many of the same problems as minority groups do.
10. Women cannot serve in the armed forces as men do.

DEVELOPING IDEAS AND SKILLS

PICTURE SYMBOLS   These pictures should help you recall parts of the chapter you have just read. What is the main idea of each picture?

GRAPH STUDY *Number of American Women Working Outside the Home, 1880-1984* and *Percentage of American Mothers (with children under 18) Who Work Outside the Home*

Study the two graphs below. Tell whether the following statements are true or false. If a statement is false, rewrite it so that it is true.

1. By 1984 about 46 million American women worked outside the home.
2. Between 1940 and 1960 the number of American women working outside the home almost doubled.
3. In the hundred years between 1880 and 1980, the number of American women working outside the home increased by about 30 million.
4. In 1950 about a third of all American mothers with children under 18 years old worked outside the home.
5. In 1984 over one-half of American mothers with children under 18 years old worked outside the home.

Percent of American Mothers (with children under 18) Who Work Outside the Home

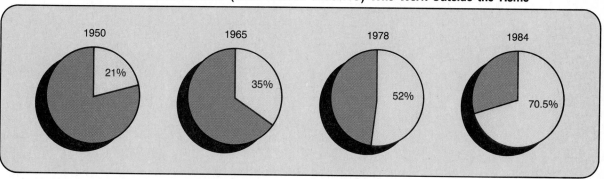

Number of American Women Working Outside the Home, 1880-1984

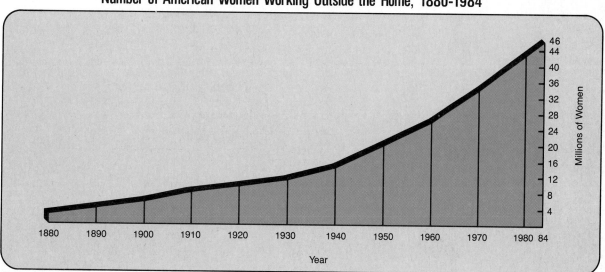

Choose six of the women from the following list. Tell what contributions they made to American history. If you need additional help, look them up in the encyclopedia.

WOMEN	CONTRIBUTIONS
1. Dorothea Dix	
2. Susan B. Anthony	
3. Eleanor Roosevelt	
4. Helen Keller	
5. Elizabeth Blackwell	
6. Betty Friedan	
7. Mary Church Terrell	
8. Maria Tallchief	
9. Rosalyn S. Yalow	
10. Belva Lockwood	

Thinking It Through

In what ways are the growing number of women in the work force a kind of revolution?

6 CHALLENGES FACING OUR COMMUNITIES

What are the major problems of our cities, suburbs, and rural areas?

Los Angeles, California is one of the leading cities in the Sunbelt.

1. The rapid growth of American cities began during the Industrial Revolution in the 19th century. This growth continued at an even faster rate after World War I. To provide housing for the increasing number of people in the cities, apartment buildings were built. New skyscrapers rose even higher as more office space was needed for growing businesses. Cities became overcrowded.

2. Starting in the 1930s, a change began to take place in the city. The automobile freed the wealthier middle class from living near their places of work. They began moving out of the crowded cities into the suburbs. The suburbs around some cities grew very large. There was little or no farmland between one city and its suburbs and nearby cities and their suburbs. Instead, there were great stretches of houses, factories, and stores. Such an almost unbroken strip of cities and suburbs is called a **megalopolis.** During the day people living in the suburbs came to the central, or inner, city to work. At night, they returned to their homes on tree-lined streets. The movement to the suburbs became even more rapid after World War II.

3. In the late 1970s and early 1980s, many new factories were built in the countryside *beyond* the suburbs of the large cities. (This area beyond the rim of the suburbs is called **exurbia.**) Many people moved to smaller towns to be near the new factories. These towns had to provide housing and other services for their newcomers.

4. At the same time, many people were moving out of the older cities and towns to the **Sunbelt.** This is the area made up of California, Texas, Florida, and Arizona. They were both young and old Americans. The young people were looking for jobs in the space, oil, and computer fields. America's elderly are now healthier and living longer than ever before. To have a better life when they retire, or stop working, many moved to the South and Southwest to enjoy the warmer climate of those regions.

5. In the meantime, other people moved into the cities. Hundreds of thousands of these newcomers were Puerto Ricans, Mexican Americans, and blacks. They hoped to find a better life in the cities. Instead, they often found a city that was old and worn down by problems. The problems of the cities were as difficult to solve as those that the pioneers of old faced.

511

6. One of these problems is the growing lack of clean air and water. Most factories are in or near cities. These factories send smoke and fumes into the air. As a result, the air people breathe is loaded with harmful dirt and gases. This is called air **pollution.** Also, factories often pour their wastes into nearby rivers and streams. As a result, the water becomes unfit for drinking, bathing, and fishing. The situation has become so serious that many Americans now realize that they must do something to clean up the air and water.

7. A second problem is the need for better housing. Much of the housing in the inner cities is bad. As people left the inner city for new homes in the suburbs and countryside, poorer people often moved into older, run-down city buildings. Some cities have replaced the old buildings with new apartment buildings for poor and middle-income people. This is called **urban renewal.** Rebuilding housing in our cities costs a great deal of money. In 1965 Congress created a new department to help our nation's housing needs. It is called the Department of Housing and Urban Development (HUD). This department supplies much of the money needed by the cities to build new low-cost public housing.

8. Pollution and the lack of enough good housing are not the only problems. A third problem is the need for better schools. Education is as important in American life as ever. Public schools depend on local taxes for money. In some big cities and country areas, not enough taxes are collected for schools. Therefore, the schools may not be able to pay for all the teachers and programs that students need. But the people in these areas are determined to provide a good education for their children. If the schools cannot do this job, then students may choose to "drop out" instead. Both the state and the federal governments provide some aid to local schools. In 1980 a separate federal Department of Education was set up to give special help in the cities and states. By 1984 over 60 million Americans attended schools, colleges, or universities.

9. A fourth problem is the control of traffic. People living in the central city and the suburbs must get to work each day. Millions of people have to reach their places of work by car, railroad, bus, or subway. A few even use helicopters. Moreover, thousands of trucks use city streets. They bring in foods and materials daily. As quickly as new roads and highways are built, they become choked with traffic. Ways must be found to move and direct traffic and to provide places where workers can park. Local, state, and federal governments have provided funds for more highways. Some people want the government to spend more money on public **mass transit.** Mass transit includes buses, railroads, and subways, forms of transportation that can carry large numbers of people.

The subway system in Washington, D.C. is one of the newest in the nation. Why is there a need for better public transportation?

10. A fifth problem is poverty. Americans today make more money and eat better foods than do most people in the world. However, not all Americans enjoy the comforts of modern living, proper housing, or medical care. There are about 35 million poor people in the United States. Many of the poor are workers who cannot find jobs. Others are broken families. Still others are the old, the blind, and the disabled.

11. Since the 1930s, American presidents and the Congress have tried to solve the problems of poverty. As a result, poor people today receive money from their local government. This **welfare** enables them to buy food and clothing and to pay rent. The state and federal governments have job training programs. Medicaid and Medicare programs help provide health care for poor and older citizens. Medicaid provides health care for the poor and disabled. Under Medicare, people over 65 receive health services for a small fee.

12. A sixth problem is crime. Crime is growing rapidly in our cities and suburbs. We hear or see reports of terrible crimes: murder, robbery, assault. As a result, some city dwellers, especially the elderly, are increasingly afraid to go out. Young people commit many of the crimes. Some criminals are drug users. They steal and even murder to get the money they need to pay for their drugs. Others are poor. They want the good things of life that they feel most Americans have. To them, crime seems the only way to get these things. People in cities, towns, and suburbs are demanding more police protection. Some say the courts should work faster on criminal cases. Others want criminals to get longer sentences. Still others say that the problems of poverty must be solved before violent crime can be reduced.

13. Cities are finding it difficult to pay for all the services they provide. City governments, like state and federal governments, get their money from taxes. As city

Urban housing being improved. Why is this kind of effort so important to cities?

problems increase, both people and businesses move out. Thus the city's tax base is reduced. In order to keep going, the city government must either raise taxes or cut its work force. Cutting the work force often means the city has fewer firefighters, police, and teachers. In 1975 New York City almost went bankrupt when it could not pay the money it owed. With federal help, New York was able to borrow money and continue its services. Other cities, such as Cleveland, Ohio, and Chicago, Illinois, are having similar problems.

14. The problems of our cities, towns, suburbs, and rural areas are serious. Many of these problems fall hardest on minority groups. During the summer of 1967, there were terrible riots in American cities. What did these riots mean? They told us that urban problems had become so big that many people could no longer live with them. In 1964 President Lyndon Johnson called for a War on Poverty. Under his

leadership, the government started a number of new programs: Head Start for preschool children, the Job Corps for school dropouts, the Model Cities program, legal services for the poor, neighborhood health centers, and many other community action programs. In 1972 President Nixon and Congress started a **revenue-sharing** program. This meant that the federal government gave money to the states every year. The states could then spend the money on whatever programs they wished. Today, the monies set aside for Social Security, Medicare, and other social service programs take up a large part of our national budget. This shows our nation's deep concern for these problems.

A community cleanup. Are there community action programs in your area? What form do they take?

REVIEWING
CHAPTER 5

Match the items in Column A with those in Column B. There is one extra item in Column B.

COLUMN A
1. Grimké sisters
2. Jane Addams
3. Susan B. Anthony
4. Carrie Nation
5. Rose Schneiderman

COLUMN B
a. Temperance movement
b. Settlement house
c. Women's right to vote
d. Trade unionism
e. Care of the mentally ill
f. Abolition movement

UNDERSTANDING
CHAPTER 6

I. What is the main idea of Chapter 6?

a. To describe the problems of keeping our air pure
b. To tell how to save our water and air resources
c. To identify some of the problems faced by Americans in our cities, towns, suburbs, and rural areas
d. To describe the need for government help to education

II. Choose the correct answer.

1. President Johnson's plans for a War on Poverty included
   a. helping farm owners
   b. community action programs for the poor
   c. letting more immigrants come to the United States

2. What major change has taken place in the United States since 1945?
    a. The country has acquired new territory.
    b. More people are living in cities and nearby suburbs.
    c. The standard of living is lower.
3. Why is education important to people?
    a. It means they will have more leisure time.
    b. It means they will be able to get better jobs.
    c. It means they will not have to pay taxes.
4. Why haven't new highways solved all the traffic problems?
    a. They do not connect large cities.
    b. Auto owners must pay for their use.
    c. Highways are jammed as soon as they are built.
5. Which statement is *true* of cities today?
    a. Many people are finding it hard to get housing they can afford to rent or buy.
    b. Little poverty is found in the cities.
    c. Many cities lack the money to provide all the services needed.
6. Americans are now moving to the Sunbelt in order to:
    a. obtain jobs in new industries
    b. take advantage of a warmer climate
    c. for both of these reasons

III. Do you agree or disagree? Give reasons for your answers.

1. Most cities today are noisy, crowded, and smoky.
2. It will cost a lot of money to solve our cities' problems.
3. Many of the poor are the old, blind, or disabled.
4. Living conditions in the inner cities are often bad.
5. The problems of air and water pollution are only city problems.
6. Crime is a rising problem in cities and suburbs across America.
7. Housing must be rebuilt in many cities.
8. Many people have moved to small towns to be near the new factories in the countryside.

DEVELOPING IDEAS AND SKILLS

COMMUNITY SERVICES The following list contains a number of services provided by most communities. Select one and write a report answering the following questions.

Health	Social welfare	Schools
Government	Housing	Communication
Fire and police Protection	Recreation	Power

1. Where is this service located in your community?
2. How can you, or your friends, or your parents make use of this service?
3. How is this service supported?
4. Who is in charge of this service?
5. Does this service meet the needs of the community?
6. What can you, or your friends, or your parents do to improve this service?

Study the graphs. Then decide whether these statements are true or false. Rewrite the false statements to make them true.

The Federal Budget Dollar, 1985

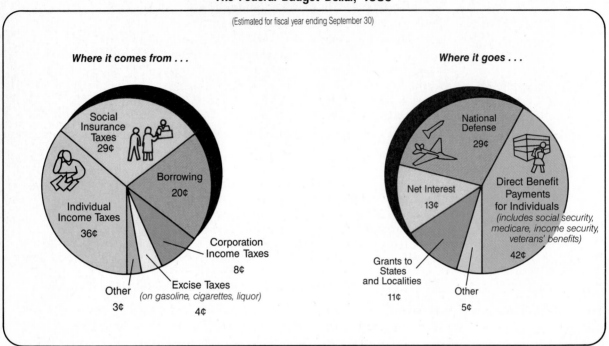

(Estimated for fiscal year ending September 30)

Where it comes from . . .

Social Insurance Taxes 29¢

Borrowing 20¢

Individual Income Taxes 36¢

Corporation Income Taxes 8¢

Other 3¢

Excise Taxes (on gasoline, cigarettes, liquor) 4¢

Where it goes . . .

National Defense 29¢

Net Interest 13¢

Direct Benefit Payments for Individuals (includes social security, medicare, income security, veterans' benefits) 42¢

Grants to States and Localities 11¢

Other 5¢

1. The largest percentage of the budget dollar comes from taxing people's incomes.
2. Business and industry are not required to pay taxes to the government.
3. About 11 cents out of every tax dollar is spent on grants to states and localities.
4. About 10 cents out of every tax dollar comes from excise taxes.
5. The government spends the greatest proportion of money on the national defense.
6. The government spends more on paying the interest on what it has borrowed than on grants to states and localities.

SUMMING UP   **Thinking It Through**

Choose one of the problems discussed in this chapter. What steps do you think should be taken to solve this problem?

7 A PRESIDENT RESIGNS!

How did the Watergate affair lead Richard Nixon to resign as president?

Senators Howard Baker and Sam Ervin led the Senate investigation into the Watergate affair. How did the outcome of this affair prove that the Constitution "works"?

1. In August 1974, Richard Nixon became the first American president to resign his office. He had been chosen president by a large majority of voters in November 1972. Yet two years later, he had to leave his office. How had this come about? The answer is Watergate.

2. In 1972 President Nixon had begun planning his reelection campaign. He had run in two close races for the presidency in the past. He had lost the first one in 1960. But he had won the second in 1968. He was determined not to lose the third, the election of 1972. For that purpose, he decided not to use the usual Republican party committee. Instead, he formed a special Committee to Reelect the President (CRP). It was headed by his friend, former Attorney General John Mitchell. The committee collected a great deal of money.

3. On June 17, 1972, five men were caught breaking into the headquarters of the Democratic National Committee in Washington, D.C. The offices were in one of the group of buildings called Watergate. The five burglars were arrested. Money found on them was traced to the CRP. Representatives of President Nixon declared he had no connection with the break-in. The public was successfully kept in the dark about the facts behind the crime. This hiding of the facts was called a cover-up. In November 1972, Nixon was reelected as president by a very large majority.

4. The burglars were tried and found guilty. On March 23, 1973, they were sentenced to prison by Judge John Sirica.

Shortly thereafter, one of President Nixon's aides, John Dean, began talking to the FBI about a cover-up. Two reporters for the *Washington Post*, Robert Woodward and Carl Bernstein, also began to write stories about the Watergate affair, as they called it. In order to calm the people's growing concern, Nixon fired two of his chief aides, H. R. Haldeman and John Ehrlichman. A special prosecutor, Archibald Cox, was appointed to investigate the whole affair.

5. In the meantime, the Senate began its own investigation. Senate committee members asked John Dean what he knew. Dean claimed that he had informed the president of the illegal cover-up in March. When the president failed to follow up, Dean had gone to the FBI. At first there seemed to be no way to prove Dean's story. Then another witness told the committee that many of President Nixon's conversations had been taped. This was a normal

practice of the president. The tapes would help to answer many questions about the cover-up.

6. The Senate committee, Judge Sirica, and Prosecutor Cox asked for the tapes. President Nixon refused to surrender the tapes. The president then fired Cox. Leon Jaworski was named the new special prosecutor. Jaworski surprised Nixon. He also wanted the tapes. Nixon finally handed some of the tapes over to the court. But some tapes were missing and parts of others had been erased.

7. On October 10, 1973, Vice-President Spiro Agnew resigned his office. It was discovered that he had taken bribes while he was governor of Maryland in the 1960s. He had also failed to report this extra money to the government. Nixon then used the 25th Amendment to replace Agnew. President Nixon chose Gerald R. Ford, a respected member of Congress from the state of Michigan, to be the new vice-president.

8. President Nixon continued to say he knew nothing about the break-in. Nevertheless, he refused to give up the complete tapes. He claimed they contained secret information. The House of Representatives began to talk of impeaching him, that is, accusing him of wrongdoing in office. On July 24, 1974, the Supreme Court ordered Nixon to give up all the tapes. The Court said that the tapes did not contain any secrets that would threaten the nation.

9. President Nixon obeyed the Court decision and released the tapes. They showed that he had known about the break-in from an early date. He had also ordered his aides to keep secret their part in the Watergate break-in. By this time, President Nixon had lost his support in Congress. The House was moving toward impeachment. On August 8, 1974, Nixon appeared on television. He told the country he was resigning.

10. Vice-President Gerald Ford became

President Nixon went before the nation on television to announce his resignation. How did the Watergate affair show the value of a free press?

the next president. He selected Nelson Rockefeller as his vice-president. For the first time in American history, the United States was headed by a president and a vice-president who had not been elected. Ford said he wanted to restore the people's trust in government. In September 1974, Ford pardoned Richard Nixon for all federal crimes Nixon had "committed or may have committed" while president. However, many other officials involved in the cover-up were tried and sent to prison. For most Americans, the Watergate affair was a sad moment in our history. However, it did show two things. First, no person, not even the president of the United States, is above the law. Our system of government, set up almost 200 years ago by the Constitution, still works. Second, a free press is as important today as it was in Peter Zenger's time. A free press tells citizens what the government is doing.

Match each item in Column A with its description in Column B. There is
one extra item in Column B.

COLUMN A	COLUMN B
1. megalopolis	a. dirt that spoils our environment
2. welfare	b. sections bordering a city
3. urban renewal	c. President Johnson's program against poverty
4. slums	d. government money that provides the poor with food, clothing, and shelter
5. suburbs	e. rebuilding parts of cities
6. pollution	f. an almost unbroken strip of cities and suburbs
	g. the crowded, dirty sections of the city where poor people live

I. What is the main idea of Chapter 7?

a. To describe the presidential election of 1972
b. To explain why President Nixon had to leave office
c. To describe a burglary in Washington, D.C.

II. Choose the correct answer.

1. President Nixon set up the CRP in 1972 in order to
    a. advise him on foreign policy
    b. prepare new programs for the cities
    c. make sure he would be reelected as president
2. What happened in one of the Watergate buildings in 1972?
    a. Burglars broke into the headquarters of the Democratic party.
    b. Jimmy Carter was nominated as the next president.
    c. A bomb exploded, killing two people.
3. What part did John Sirica play in the Watergate affair?
    a. He headed the CRP.
    b. He published special papers on the Vietnam War.
    c. He was the judge that sentenced the Watergate burglars to jail.
4. The Supreme Court decided that President Nixon
    a. could keep the tapes
    b. had to release the tapes to the public
    c. had to resign from office
5. After President Nixon's resignation, he was replaced as president by
    a. Gerald Ford
    b. Spiro Agnew
    c. Jimmy Carter

III. Decide whether each statement is true or false. The underlined words are clues to help you decide. If the statement is false, change the underlined word or words to make it true.

1. Nixon was elected president for a <u>second</u> term in 1972.
2. <u>Gerald Ford</u> was appointed vice-president under Richard Nixon.

3. Watergate is a group of buildings in <u>New York City</u>.
4. At first, President Nixon <u>denied</u> any connection with the burglary at Watergate.
5. Vice-President Spiro Agnew resigned as vice-president because of <u>Watergate</u>.
6. <u>John Mitchell</u> decided to talk about the Watergate cover-up to a Senate committee.
7. The <u>army</u> ordered President Nixon to give up the tapes.
8. President Nixon resigned his office rather than face <u>going to prison</u>.

DEVELOPING IDEAS AND SKILLS Study the following cartoon. Then answer the questions.

1. Who is the main figure in this cartoon?
2. What happened to him in 1972?
3. Why does the cartoonist show him as a lion?
4. Why did the main figure leave the White House in 1974?
5. Why does the cartoonist also show him as a lamb?
6. What did the American people learn from the event that the cartoonist shows?
7. What is a good title for this cartoon?

SUMMING UP   What part did the president, Congress, and the Supreme Court each have in the Watergate affair?

Thinking It Through

During the Watergate affair, one of Nixon's aides said that "the government has a right to lie." Do you agree or disagree with this statement? Why or why not?

8 JETS, ROCKETS, AND SPACECRAFT

What are some of the important developments in air and space flight?

1. During World War II a new type of plane was developed. It is called the jet plane. Earlier planes had propellers that "pulled" the plane in flight. But airplanes with propellers cannot go much faster than about 500 miles an hour (800 kilometers per hour). Jet engines can "push" airplanes through the air at much greater speeds.

2. The jet engine is a wheel with blades. The wheel is turned by a stream of burning fuel. The wheel turns a fan. The fan draws in air from the front and blows it out behind the airplane. As the air escapes, it pushes the plane forward. This stream of air is called a jet. Today, almost all large airplanes have jet engines. The fastest jet airliner, the SST Concorde, now crosses the Atlantic Ocean in three hours. Most powerful nations now have jet fighter planes and bombers as part of their modern air force.

3. As fast and powerful as jet engines are, a different kind of engine was needed to fly in space. There is no air in space. Without air, the jet plane cannot fly. The layer of air around the earth reaches out for only a few hundred miles. Beyond this layer of air is space. In space are the moon and the planets.

4. To fly through space, another kind of engine was invented. This engine can run without outside air. It is the rocket engine. The rocket carries its own air, or oxygen, in a tank. It carries fuel in another tank. The fuel and oxygen meet and are "burned in a furnace." As early as 1919, Robert Goddard suggested that people could build a rocket that could go to the moon. In 1926 Goddard flew one of the first rockets with liquid fuel on his aunt's farm in Massachusetts. He frightened the neighbors so much they called him "moon-mad" Goddard. Goddard died in 1945. During World War II the Germans also developed rockets. They used the rockets to bomb cities in England. After World War II the U.S. armed forces developed many rockets using both Goddard's and the German scientists' ideas. In the past few decades the United States, the USSR, and a few other countries have produced thousands of rockets. These rockets can carry A-bombs and H-bombs.

5. On October 5, 1957, the Soviet Union successfully sent the first human-made "moon," or **satellite** into space. It was powered by a rocket engine. It traveled, or orbited, around the earth. Many consider the launching of Sputnik to be the beginning of the Space Age. Not to be outdone, the United States soon placed its first satellite, Explorer I, into orbit. Since that time, several nations have successfully launched satellites and other objects into space. The satellites carry instruments that tell scientists much about outer space. Satellites also record facts about the weather and about crops and natural resources on earth. Some satellites connect continents by way of TV relays. Others are spy satellites. The USSR and the United States use satellites to watch each other's military activities.

6. In the early 1960s, the United States and the Soviet Union began training people to explore space. In the United States these people are called **astronauts.** In 1961 the Soviet Union sent the first man into space. Yuri Gagarin was the first space pioneer. His spacecraft orbited the earth and returned safely. The United States followed with a similar flight by John Glenn in 1962.

7. Since that time, both nations have continued to send up spacecraft. Both nations had "walks in space." During these "walks" men have left their spaceship and

A space shuttle crew, 1983. Dr. Sally K. Ride was the first American woman to take part in a space flight. Astronauts go through difficult training before they can travel in space.

worked outside the craft. In 1963 the Soviet Union sent the first woman into space. In 1965 the American astronauts Frank Borman and James Lovell orbited the earth for almost 14 days. In 1965 the United States thrilled the world when it successfully sent a spaceship to link up with a satellite already in orbit.

8. In 1969, the last moon practice flight was made as two astronauts flew to within 9 miles (almost 15 kilometers) of the moon. The next flight, Apollo 11, would go to the moon. On July 16, 1969, thousands made their way to Cape Kennedy, Florida, to see the launching of Apollo 11. The launch went off on time. On July 19, the Apollo 11 spacecraft reached the moon and went into orbit. Astronauts Neil Armstrong and Edwin Aldrin entered the lunar module (LM), a small ship with four legs. This module would land them on the moon's surface. The other astronaut was Michael Collins. His job was a lonely one—to re-

main in the Apollo II command ship orbiting the moon.

9. The LM landed safely on the moon. Armstrong was the first person to walk on the moon. As he stepped down, he radioed back, "That's one small step for a man, one giant leap for mankind." A few minutes later, Aldrin also stepped out. Armstrong described the moon's surface as follows: "The surface is fine and powdery. I can kick it up loosely with my toe." Millions of people watched all this on TV. The astronauts set up an American flag, picked up rock samples, and then returned to the command ship. They returned safely to earth on July 24.

10. Other successful space flights have followed. In 1973 three Americans lived in space for 59 days aboard Skylab, an orbiting space station. In 1975 American and Soviet astronauts circled earth together. Space probes have been sent to explore other planets. In this way scientists have learned

much about Mars, Venus, Jupiter, Saturn, and Uranus. In 1981, the United States launched a space shuttle. The shuttle was made to enter space and return, over and over again. It rides on two booster rockets and a big fuel tank. As the shuttle orbits in space, its used-up rockets drop off. After its mission, the space shuttle returns to earth as a regular jet would. The shuttle is able to launch new satellites into space, get them back, and repair them. On April 11, 1984, the first such service call in space was made. As the shuttle flights are safely carried through, they will help scientists all over the world take advantage of the knowledge to be gained in space.

REVIEWING CHAPTER 7

Match the term in Column A with its description in Column B. There is one extra item in Column B.

COLUMN A
1. impeach
2. campaign
3. investigate
4. resign
5. bribe

COLUMN B
a. to seek information
b. to quit or give up one's office or job
c. to give or offer to give money to someone to get him or her to do something against the law
d. to actively seek to win an election
e. to do something wrong
f. to draw up a list of charges against a government officer

UNDERSTANDING CHAPTER 8

I. **What is the main idea of paragraphs 4 through 11?**

   a. To describe space exploration
   b. To describe the important inventions of World War II
   c. To describe the first moon landing
   d. To describe some changes in education

II. **Choose the correct answer.**

1. A jet airplane has no
   a. wings
   b. fuel
   c. propellers
2. The Space Age began during which period of time?
   a. 1900 to 1910
   b. 1930 to 1945
   c. 1955 to 1970
3. The men who flew the first spaceships may be compared to the pioneers of the American West because they
   a. helped to settle far-off lands
   b. braved unknown dangers
   c. performed their jobs without the help of science
4. The first space satellite was launched by the
   a. Soviet Union
   b. United States
   c. United Nations

5. A satellite can be described as a
   a. platform in space
   b. human-made moon that orbits the earth
   c. jet engine
6. Nations could not explore space until they had learned how to
   a. make telescopes
   b. build rockets
   c. predict the weather
7. As a result of the space program
   a. there are now colonies in space
   b. human beings have landed on the moon
   c. new planets have been discovered

III. Decide whether each statement agrees or disagrees with what you have read. If the statement disagrees, explain why.

1. An astronaut is a person who travels in outer space.
2. Where the layer of air ends, space begins.
3. The invention of the gasoline engine made space travel possible.
4. The United States made the first successful moon landing in 1969.
5. The moon landing made the United States a leader in exploring space.
6. The United States is the only nation exploring space.
7. Robert Goddard was a pioneer in developing space travel.

DEVELOPING IDEAS
AND SKILLS

Answer the following questions about the cartoon.

1. Who is the main figure in the cartoon?
2. Some people feel that the space program costs too much money. They say that the money is needed at home. What do you think?
3. What is a good title for this cartoon?

Voyager II is a space probe. It has already flown by the planets of Jupiter and Saturn. It is due to fly past Uranus in 1986 and Neptune in 1989. During this time, Voyager II will radio information back to earth. After that it will wander through space on its own. On board the Voyager is a message describing life on earth. The message is on a copper record. Suppose the scientists who prepared this record had asked you to briefly describe your life in the United States. What things would you put on the record?

Thinking It Through

Recent movies such as *Star Wars, Close Encounters of the Third Kind,* and *The Empire Strikes Back* have been very popular. They deal with life in space. Why do you think people are so interested in this topic? Do you think there is life in space? If so, what kind of life do you think it might be?

9 SCIENCE IN OUR LIVES

What are some of the most recent scientific discoveries?

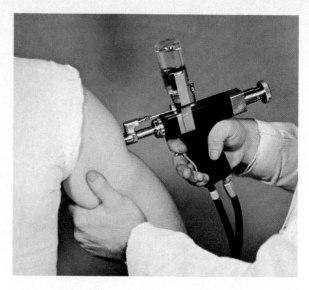

Vaccination being given by an injection gun. Medical research has done much to prevent and cure diseases. What are some diseases that can now be prevented by vaccination?

1. Even before people found a way to travel in space, they had invented machines that helped them see into outer space. One of these space "eyes" is the radio telescope. It is unlike the optical telescope, which depends on light waves. Instead, the radio telescope uses the fact that objects in space send out radio waves. Radio signals have been received from the stars, the moon, and planets such as Venus, Mars, and Jupiter. Astronomers are learning a lot about the universe by means of the radio telescope. Some scientists are even using the radio telescope to search for clues of life on other planets.

2. In addition, scientists are trying to set up a way of communicating with other planets. They are using **lasers,** light beams of great strength. Lasers are different from the light of the sun or the light sent out by ordinary electric bulbs. The sun and light bulbs send out light in all directions. A laser, however, sends out a narrow beam of light in only one direction. Because the laser beam concentrates its light waves, it produces intense heat. Lasers are used in medicine to burn away diseased tissues. Lasers are used in industry to cut and make holes in metals. Signals for navigation can also be sent by laser beams.

3. In 1960 the United States launched a huge balloon, Echo I, into space. This was a relay station outside the earth's layer of air. This balloon made it possible to bounce television and radio signals back to earth. Later in the year, the United States also put television cameras into space to take pictures of weather conditions from hundreds of miles above the earth's surface. In 1962 the United States put a communications satellite, Telstar, into orbit around the earth. Since then the United States has put other such satellites into orbit. These satellites make it possible to send both pictures and voices of events across the world the moment those events are taking place.

4. Closer to home, American scientists made discoveries about the nature of life. Through many experiments and tests, they found new drugs that can destroy many of the germs that cause diseases in humans. These drugs proved highly effective in checking infections and saving millions of lives. Among the most famous of these drugs are the **antibiotics** such as the penicillins and the tetracyclines.

5. Scientists also developed new **vaccines** as a method of preventing disease. Vaccines are made from dead or weakened germs. Once inside the body, a vaccine helps prevent a regular case of the disease. In 1954 young Americans began to receive shots against polio. The vaccine was discovered by Dr. Jonas Salk and his fellow workers. Soon after that, Dr. Alfred Sabin

developed an antipolio vaccine that could be taken by mouth. Scientists also have developed vaccines to prevent such diseases as measles, mumps, and certain kinds of flu.

6. Scientists are also learning more about our own bodies. They are pointing out which foods keep people healthy. They are urging Americans to exercise more. They are also showing the relationship between cigarette smoking and such diseases as lung cancer and heart disease. Scientists are explaining the role of the nucleic acids, DNA and RNA, in determining the kind of body we have. Surgeons have learned to keep people alive by replacing diseased organs such as kidneys and hearts with healthy ones. Pacemakers now help provide normal heartbeats for people with heart problems. Machines help diseased kidneys work better.

7. Perhaps the most amazing scientific discovery in the 20th century has been the use of the power locked in the atom. An American born in Germany, Albert Einstein, suggested using this new source of power. Atoms are like unseen building blocks. All things are made of atoms. When the tiny atom is split, it releases tremendous energy. An atomic reactor is the heart of the new power source. In the reactor, the atoms are split and heat is released. The heat changes water into steam. The steam turns a generator to produce electricity. Starting in the mid-1950s, the United States began to build power plants and submarines run by atomic power.

8. About 40 years ago, people began building machines that could solve problems. Some thought that these machines "with brains" might take over part of the work of men and women. Today, this idea has come true. These machines are called **computers.** Computers have many advantages. They can be very, very small. Some are so small they can fit on your thumbnail. Computers are very speedy. They can work out problems in a billionth of a second. Computers can store huge amounts of infor-

mation. Computers now do many kinds of jobs. They sort mail, design autos, send rockets into outer space, control traffic lights, check and keep records, and solve very difficult problems dealing with numbers.

9. Computers are the "brains" behind other developments in the factory, namely **automation.** Automated machines no longer need workers to operate them. The machines run by themselves. They also check themselves, spot mistakes, and make corrections. **Robots** are being used in auto factories to do some of the jobs once handled by workers. These jobs include painting cars and welding metal. As more factories become automated or use robots, the way of turning out goods will be completely changed.

10. Many of these new computers are based on the science of electronics. One of the important electronic inventions is the **transistor.** Transistors are very tiny, about half the size of a pea, or smaller. Made of wire and plastic, they can take the place of vacuum tubes. They are much smaller, last much longer, and need less power. Transistors have made possible many new ma-

Robot arms on the left are assembling auto engines. Why do you think robots are becoming more important in industry?

chines, or appliances, now found in the American home. These include the television set, the tape recorder, the electric calculator, the microwave oven, and the record player.

11. As a result of these discoveries, many changes have taken place in the way Americans live. First, Americans are living longer and healthier lives. For example, a female born in 1900 lived on the average about 48 years. A female born today can be expected to live about 78 years. Second, they are using machines and materials unheard of by their parents. Third, computers are taking away much of the mental work that used to take people so long to do. Finally, Americans are now living through a cultural explosion. Television sets, records, tapes, and books are now found in most American homes. Americans of today have more of these products than any people ever did before.

REVIEWING
CHAPTER 8 Match each item or name in Column A with its description in Column B. There is one extra description in Column B.

COLUMN A
1. orbit
2. astronaut
3. satellite
4. Robert Goddard
5. Neil Armstrong

COLUMN B
a. a machine launched into orbit around the earth by rockets
b. the "father" of space flight
c. the first person to land on the moon
d. a missile that carries an A-bomb
e. to travel in a path around another body
f. a pilot or member of a crew of a spaceship

UNDERSTANDING
CHAPTER 9

I. What is the main purpose of Chapter 9?

a. To describe how science has made it possible for people to live longer
b. To review changes in industry
c. To describe the advances in science
d. To discuss changes in education

II. Choose the correct answer.

1. Atomic power now provides energy to run all of these EXCEPT:
   a. submarines
   b. airplanes
   c. factories or plants
2. Albert Einstein suggested using the power that could be found in
   a. atoms
   b. electricity
   c. ocean tides
3. Dr. Jonas Salk discovered a means of preventing
   a. cancer
   b. polio
   c. heart disease

4. *Automation* is a word that refers to
    a. the Industrial Revolution
    b. machines taking the place of people in industry
    c. a new method of launching space satellites
5. What advances have been made in medicine in the recent past?
    a. The microscope has been invented.
    b. Pacemakers have been invented to help keep the heart beating properly.
    c. The vaccine for smallpox has been developed.

III. **Decide whether each statement is true or false. The underlined words are clues to help you decide. If a statement is false, change the underlined word or words to make it true.**

1. The <u>optical</u> telescope makes it possible to look farther into space.
2. <u>Lasers</u> are now used in surgery to burn away diseased tissue.
3. It is now possible to send television pictures across the world because of the <u>space shuttle</u>.
4. Dr. Albert Sabin discovered an oral vaccine for preventing <u>measles</u>.
5. Although the atomic bomb was first used in World War II, <u>atomic power</u> has peacetime uses also.
6. <u>Computers</u> can now solve problems in a fraction of the time it once took people to solve them.

DEVELOPING IDEAS AND SKILLS

PICTURE SYMBOLS   These pictures should help you recall parts of the chapter you have read. What is the main idea of each picture?

SUMMING UP

Many of the things that make modern life healthful or comfortable were unknown to your grandparents when they were your age. One of these is polio vaccine. Another is television. What other examples can you think of? How have these inventions or discoveries affected your life?

Thinking It Through

Imagine you had the chance to put objects in a time capsule to be opened by people in the year 2500. What would you place in it to show people of the future what life is like today?

10 WHERE WE STAND TODAY

What events troubled the American people in recent years?

1. The Vietnam War was a terrible blow to the confidence of Americans. Many were disappointed that the United States with all its military might could not defend a weak government against the forces of a Communist government. Others, watching the war on television every night, were shocked by the violence. Finally, many were saddened by what took place at home —the protests, the burning of draft cards, the shooting of college students, and the flight of young Americans out of the country. Americans were deeply troubled by the war.

2. As the Vietnam War ended, the scandal of Watergate was uncovered. In June 1972, five men were caught breaking into Democratic party headquarters in Washington, D.C. At first, most Americans gave little thought to the incident. Spurred on by reporters, federal officials began to investigate. They found out that the burglars were working for aides to President Nixon. They also learned of other break-ins, enemy lists, illegal wire taps, and tapings. The investigation into Watergate led to the fall of President Nixon. Faced with a bill of impeachment accusing him of "blocking justice and misusing his power," President Nixon resigned in August 1974.

3. Another worry to Americans was the slow down of the nation's economy. Although American farmers were still able to grow more than enough food for the American people, the country's raw materials were becoming scarcer. The people of the United States make up only six percent of the world's population. Yet they were using up a major share of the world's most needed natural resources.

4. The heavy drain on resources had led to a big increase in pollution. Smoke from factories and automobile exhausts poisoned the air. These poisons, or pollutants, turned into acid in the atmosphere. The acid falls to the earth with rain or snow. It kills fish,

The Vietnam War memorial in Washington, D.C. The names of the war dead are engraved on this wall.

destroys forests, and changes the soil. Pollutants from the United States crossed the border and fell as acid rain on the lakes and farmlands of Canada. In addition to acid rain, factory wastes, chemicals, and insecticides were dumped into landfills, ponds, and pits. They threaten our food and water supplies. Huge piles of garbage, old cars, and used machinery rose everywhere. Americans began to understand that they were paying a high price for the increase in goods. Their health and their country's natural beauty were in danger. **Ecology** took on new importance. Ecology is the study of the relationship between living things and the environment.

5. In 1973, a war in the Middle East made Americans more aware of their great need for energy sources. The United States and its allies, Western Europe and Japan, depend heavily on Middle Eastern oil. During the war, the Arab rulers of the Middle East cut off their oil from the United States and its friends. As oil became scarcer, prices became higher and long lines of cars appeared at gas pumps. After the war ended, the Arab nations once again began to supply oil. However, the oil prices remained high.

6. In 1976, Americans chose Jimmy Carter to be their president. Carter got Congress to approve the Panama Canal treaties (see p. 412) and helped the leaders of Egypt and Israel work out a peace treaty (see p. 472). Carter also set up full relations with mainland China (see p. 468). In addition, he signed an arms control agreement with the Soviet Union (SALT II). Last but not least, Carter promoted human rights abroad.

7. As part of its search for new energy sources, the United States built nuclear power plants. About 80 nuclear power plants have been built in the United States since the mid-1950s. In 1979, the use of nuclear power suffered a setback. An accident occurred at the Three Mile Island

A telephone powered by energy from the sun. Why is it important for the United States to find other sources of energy?

nuclear power plant in Pennsylvania. For a while, it was feared that dangerous **radioactive** material (the waste material from a nuclear power plant) might spread over Pennsylvania and neighboring states. Radioactive material gives off powerful rays that are harmful to living things. Luckily, nuclear scientists brought the reactor core under control. Only a small amount of radioactive gas and water escaped. Public support for more nuclear power plants dropped sharply after the accident.

8. The late 1970s had its share of troubles for Americans. In November 1979, an Iranian mob seized the United States embassy in Teheran (see p. 472). The Americans held prisoner were not let go until 14 months later. In December 1979, the Soviet Union invaded and occupied Afghanistan, a country east of Iran. The oil-rich region of the Middle East—so important to the United States and others—was in danger. At home, the automobile industry was facing strong competition from Japan and Germany. Both of these

countries were producing cars at lower cost than the United States. Large numbers of American auto workers were losing their jobs. In addition, the prices of goods seemed to be going higher.

9. In 1980, Ronald Reagan, a former screen actor and governor of California, became president. Reagan promised to make America "walk tall again." He built up the armed forces. He also cut taxes. Prices began to drop steadily and more people were able to find work. Reagan sent American troops to Lebanon, a small country north of Israel (see p. 473). They were withdrawn, however, after a bomb explosion killed over 200 Marines. Troops were also sent to Grenada, an island in the Caribbean Sea (see map, p. 415). They removed the Communist leaders and helped return the country to a more democratic form of government. In Central America, President Reagan gave aid to rebels fighting the Soviet backed government of Nicaragua. In El Salvador, however, Reagan gave aid to the government so it could fight rebel forces.

10. As 1984 came near, President Reagan chose to run for a second term. The Democratic party knew that President Reagan was very well liked by the American people. They looked for a "ticket" (the party's choices for office) to beat him. For a while, the Reverend Jesse Jackson, a black civil rights leader, made a strong bid for the nomination. However, the Democrats chose Walter Mondale, former vice-president under President Carter, to run against Reagan. Mondale chose Geraldine Ferraro as his vice-presidential running mate. She was the first woman chosen by a major party for the vice-presidential job. The Democrats ran a strong campaign. Despite their efforts, President Reagan won re-election easily. With this vote of confidence, President Reagan promised to build a rich nation for all to enjoy, to strengthen freedom and democracy in the world, and to avoid nuclear war.

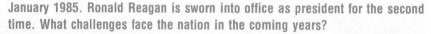

January 1985. Ronald Reagan is sworn into office as president for the second time. What challenges face the nation in the coming years?

I. Choose the correct answer.

1. As a result of the radio telescope, scientists
   a. found life on the planet
      Mars
   b. discovered mineral re-
      sources in Antarctica
   c. are able to "see" objects far
      away in space
2. The laser is
   a. more popular than the atom
      bomb
   b. the heart of the computer
   c. a very narrow beam of light
3. Antibiotic drugs are used to
   a. prevent such diseases as
      polio and smallpox
   b. kill germs that cause dis-
      eases in people
   c. put people to sleep
4. Computers can
   a. work faster than human
      brains in solving problems
   b. store a great deal of infor-
      mation
   c. do both of the things men-
      tioned in *a* and *b*
5. As a result of new medical discoveries
   a. the average person lives
      longer
   b. people can now travel from
      place to place
   c. the average person lives to
      the age of 58

II. Choose the correct answer.

1. The war in Vietnam
   a. deeply troubled the American people
   b. ended in victory for South Vietnam
   c. led to the end of the United Nations

2. The Watergate scandal led to
   a. the resignation of President Nixon
   b. the end of the Republican party
   c. a tax revolt by the American people

3. All of the following were achievements of President Carter EXCEPT:
   a. the United States treaty with Panama over the future of the Panama
      Canal
   b. the peace treaty between Egypt and Israel
   c. the release of the American hostages in Iran

4. After the nuclear accident at Three Mile Island,
   a. public support for nuclear power plants fell
   b. the plant was taken apart
   c. the government stepped up the building of nuclear power plants

5. President Reagan's program included all of the following EXCEPT:
   a. a buildup of the armed forces
   b. a strong stand against the spread of communism
   c. an increase in taxes

Answer the following questions about the cartoon.

1. Who is the figure in the cartoon?
2. What do the pins represent?
3. Which of these problems has been solved? Which ones remain to be solved?
4. What is a good title for the cartoon?

SUMMING UP

1. Think about the American history you have studied in this book. Then answer the following questions.
   a. Which period in American history would you most like to have lived through? Why?
   b. What do you think are some of the most important events of the past five years? Why?
   c. Do you think our age will be remembered as one of the great times in American history? Why or why not?

2. Choose three names from the following list. Then answer the questions.

Harriet Tubman   Neil Armstrong   Thomas Edison
Martin Luther King, Jr.   Enrico Fermi   Clara Barton
Fidel Castro   Thurgood Marshall   Jackie Robinson
George Washington   Jane Addams   Susan B. Anthony
Mao Zedong   Joseph Pulitzer   Jonas Salk
  (Mao Tse tung)   Abraham Lincoln   Eleanor Roosevelt
                            Adolf Hitler   Sandra Day O'Connor

a. Discuss the ways in which these people have made history. You may use an encyclopedia to help you.
b. List five people you would add to this list of history makers. Why?

USING A TIME LINE   Study this time line. Then answer the questions that follow. Use the information you have studied in this unit to help you. You may also look at the time line on pages 478 and 479 if you need additional help.

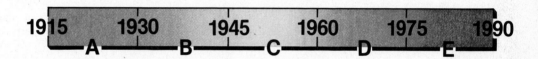

1915   1930   1945   1960   1975   1990
        A   B   C   D   E

In which period of time (A, B, C, D, E, or F) did the following take place?

1. Richard M. Nixon resigned from the office of the presidency.
2. Women gained the right to vote by the passage of the 19th Amendment.
3. The Supreme Court ruled that segregation in public schools must end.
4. Jimmy Carter was elected president.
5. Congress passed a law giving American citizenship to American Indians.
6. The United States landed astronauts on the moon.
7. Arab countries cut off their sale of oil to the United States for several months.
8. President John F. Kennedy was assassinated.
9. Puerto Rico became a commonwealth.
10. Ronald Reagan was elected to a second term as president.

BOOKS FOR UNIT VIII

AUTHOR	TITLE, PUBLISHER	DESCRIPTION
1. Allen, S.	*The Ground Is Our Table*, Doubleday	The poverty of migrant workers.
2. De Leeuw, Adele	*The Barred Road*, Macmillan	A novel about a young girl who moves to a new town and faces a tradition of racial discrimination.
3. Deloria, V., Jr.	*Behind the Trail of Broken Treaties*, Delacorte	An Indian Declaration of Independence
4. Drotning, Philip T.	*Up From the Ghetto*, Cowles	Fourteen blacks tell how they fought the ghetto and succeeded in various fields.
5. Goode, S.	*Guerrilla Warfare and Terrorism*, Watts	Informing us of the dead problems of nations throughout the world.
6. Graham, F., Jr.	*Since Silent Spring*, Houghton Mifflin	What have we done about pollution warnings?
7. Hoag, Edwin	*American Cities*, Lippincott	Fine story of our great cities, their beginnings, growth, and problems.
8. Martinez, E. S., and Vasquez, E.	*Viva La Raza*, Doubleday	The struggle of Mexican Americans for acceptance.
9. Sachen, J.	*Movers and Shakers*, Quadrangle	American women thinkers and activists.
10. Sterling, Philip and Brau, Maria	*The Quiet Rebels*, Doubleday	Four Puerto Rican leaders and how they have contributed to heir homeland.
11. Time-Life Editors	*1960–1970*, Time-Life	Magnificent pictorial account of these ten years; science, war, protests, youth, assassinations.

Appendix

GLOSSARY OF HISTORICAL TERMS

The meanings given are the ones used in the book.

abolish   To do away with.

abolitionists   People who worked to end slavery in the United States.

adobe   Sun-dried brick.

alliance   An agreement among nations to help each other.

almanac   A yearly book and calendar of facts and figures about the weather, the tides, the position of the sun, moon, and stars, and other information.

amendments   Additions or changes in a document.

annex   To add or join territory to a country.

antibiotics   Chemicals that can stop the growth of or kill germs that cause diseases.

apprentice   A person who works for another in order to learn a trade or business.

aqueduct   A human-made channel or large pipe for bringing water from a distance.

armistice   An agreement to stop fighting.

Articles of Confederation   The first written constitution for the national government of the United States, 1781–1789.

assembly   A lawmaking body. Also a gathering or meeting of persons.

assembly line   A moving belt or track in a factory. As it moves, each worker adds a part until the product is finished.

astrolabe   An instrument used at sea for determining the position of a ship.

astronaut   A person who is trained for space flight.

atom bomb   A powerful bomb that uses the energy suddenly released when atoms are split.

automation   The use of machines to control the production of goods.

barrios   Mexican-American neighborhoods in towns and cities.

bee   A play-work party.

Bill of Rights   The first 10 amendments to the U.S. Constitution. These amendments guarantee to U.S. citizens important freedoms such as the freedoms of speech, press, and religion.

blacklist   A list of persons who are disproved of or are to be punished or boycotted.

blitzkrieg   Sudden, violent attacks of war. German for "lightning war."

blockade   To prevent ships or people from entering or leaving a place.

blockhouse   A log fort or building with a second story. It had holes to shoot from.

bounty   A reward from a government.

boycott   To refuse to buy certain goods.

cabinet   A group of advisers chosen by the president to help the president.

canal   A human-made waterway across land.

capital   A city serving as a seat of government.

carpetbaggers   Northerners who came to the South after the Civil War. They gained power in government as a result of unsettled conditions.

cease-fire   An order to stop fighting.

charter   (1) An official government document granting special rights to a person or company, such as permission to settle in a certain land. (2) A written plan, such as the United Nations charter, that states the laws and purposes of an organization or government.

check   To hold in control or stop the action of.

checks and balances   The limits placed on each branch of government by the other branches.

Chicanos   Mexican Americans.

citizen   A person who is a member of a state or nation.

civil rights   The rights and privileges of a citizen.

civil service   Government jobs that require workers to pass a special examination.

cold war   The rivalry between the United States and the Soviet Union for world leadership after World War II.

collective bargaining   Meetings of employers' and workers' representatives to discuss wages, hours, work conditions, and so forth.

colonists   A group of people who leave their homeland to settle in another land. They are ruled, however, by the country that controls the land they settle on.

commando   A fighter trained to carry out surprise, hit-and-run raids.

commonwealth   A self-governing territory associated with the United States. Puerto Rico became a commonwealth in 1952.

communism   A way of life controlled by the Communist party. Under this system, the government (not individuals or private businesses) owns and manages industry and farming.

compact   An agreement.

compass n instrument with a magnetic needle that always points north. The compass tells the traveler the direction in which he or she is traveling.

compromise Settlement (of a quarrel or difference of opinion) by both sides giving up something.

computer A machine run by electricity. It can store great amounts of information and solve difficult problems very quickly.

concentration camps Places where political prisoners are kept, usually without trial. During World War II the Nazis killed millions of Jews and others in concentration camps.

Conestoga wagon A large covered wagon used by settlers to travel to the frontier. This type of wagon was first built in the Conestoga Valley of Pennsylvania.

Confederacy The government of the southern states that seceded from the Union during the Civil War.

congregation A gathering of people for worship.

Congress The lawmaking body of the United States.

conquistador A Spanish conqueror in North or South America during the 16th century.

conservation The protection and wise use of natural resources.

constitution The basic rules according to which a country or state is governed.

Constitution The written plan of government of the United States.

Continental Congress The First Continental Congress was a meeting of delegates of the American colonies in 1774. The Second Continental Congress (1775–1781) was the government of the United States during most of the American Revolution.

conventions Large meetings of delegates.

corporation A large business organization. In order to raise money, the corporation sells shares in the business to people.

cotton gin A machine invented by Eli Whitney that separates the seeds from the fibers of cotton.

council A body of persons chosen to give advice or make laws.

craft unions Unions formed by skilled workers of a certain craft or trade.

Crusades A series of wars fought by the Christians to take back Palestine, the Holy Land, from the Turks.

culture Way of life. It includes learned ways of behavior and beliefs, which can be handed down from one generation to the next.

debtors People who owe money.

declaration A statement.

Declaration of Independence A document written chiefly by Thomas Jefferson during the American Revolution. It proclaimed the independence of the American colonies.

delegate One who represents a group of people.

democracy A form of government in which laws are made by the people or their representatives.

depression A time when businesses do poorly and many people are out of work.

detention camps Special, guarded places where West Coast Japanese Americans were forced to live during World War II.

dictatorship A government ruled by one person or one party. The people have few rights.

discriminate To recognize a difference between; to show prejudice in one's attitude or actions.

division of labor A separation of jobs. Each worker does one of the many jobs needed to finish a product.

doctrine A set of ideas that are taught.

draft The choosing of people for military service.

ecology The study of the relationship between living things and their environment, or surroundings.

elect To choose one of two or more candidates for office by vote.

elector A person who is chosen to elect the president. Electors generally select the candidate who has received the most votes of the people.

Emancipation Proclamation An order issued by President Lincoln during the Civil War freeing the slaves in the states that were fighting the Union.

embargo An order of government forbidding ships to enter or leave its ports.

empire A group of lands under the rule of one nation.

escalated Increased, expanded, or speeded up.

excise tax A tax on goods made and sold in the country.

executive Dealing with enforcing and carrying out the laws.

executive branch The branch of the national government that enforces the laws passed by Congress.

exports Goods sent to other countries for trade.

exurbia The area beyond the suburbs.

federal government A government in which powers are divided between the national and state governments.

flatboat A large boat with a flat bottom used by pioneers to carry their farm and household goods.

fleet A group of ships.

forty-niners People who rushed to California in search of gold in 1849.

freedmen The newly freed black men, women, and children after the Civil War.

frontier   The border, or edge, of settled country.

ghettos   Neighborhoods made up of people of one racial group or of people from one country.

Good Neighbor policy   A term used to describe the friendly policy of cooperation and relations between South America and the United States under Franklin D. Roosevelt.

guerrilla war   A war fought by rebels who attack the enemy with surprise raids and sabotage.

Holocaust   The organized killing of 6 million Jews by the Nazis during World War II.

homesteaders   Farmers on the Great Plains who got their land through the Homestead Act.

House of Burgesses   The colonial representative assembly of Virginia; the first representative assembly in the 13 colonies.

House of Representatives   The house of Congress whose members are elected according to the population of each state.

hydroelectricity   Electricity produced by water power.

immigrants   People who settle in a country where they were not born.

impeach   To charge an officer of the government with misconduct.

imports   Goods made and brought in for sale from another country.

impressment   The seizure of sailors on the high seas before and during the War of 1812.

inaugural address   The speech made by a person at the beginning of his or her term of office.

inaugurate   To begin, as a term of office.

income tax   A tax on the money people earn.

indentured servant   A person who was willing to work usually seven years in order to come to America. At the end of that time, he or she was supposed to be freed and allowed to be a member of the colony.

indigo   A blue dye obtained from certain plants.

Industrial Revolution   The change from the making of goods at home to the manufacture of goods in factories.

industrial union   A union open to all the workers of a certain industry.

injunction   A court order to do or not do something. The court can order that workers stop their strike and return to their jobs.

integrated   Having all races share together in the opportunities and facilities of a community, such as jobs, housing, schools, travel.

interdependent   Needing and depending upon each other.

interstate commerce   The shipping goods from one state to another.

iron curtain   A term used to describe t imaginary "wall" raised by the Soviet Union to se off Communist-controlled lands from infoation and ideas of democratic countries.

irrigation   The watering of dry land by ans of ditches and canals.

judicial   Dealing with justice and courts law.

judiciary   The system of courts of law; t branch of government that explains the meaning laws.

justices   The Supreme Court judges.

labor union   An association of workers oanized to improve working conditions.

lasers   Light beams of great strength.

League of Nations   Organization of natio formed after World War I to keep peace.

legislative   Dealing with lawmaking.

legislature   A lawmaking body.

lock   A section of a canal where boats a raised or lowered to another level of water.

lockout   The employer's closing of his oer factory and refusal to open it until the workersneet the employer's demands.

log   A daily record of a ship's voyage.

long drive   The movement of cattle herd from the ranches to the railroads.

long hunters   Daring men who spent lor periods of time in the forest, hunting game. They arried long rifles.

loom   A machine for weaving threads in cloth.

Loyalists   Colonists who remained loyal the English king and supported England duing the American Revolution.

lynched   Killed by a mob, usually by har ging, without a trial to consider whether or n t the person was really guilty of a serious crine.

manufacture   To turn raw materials into useful goods by hand or machine.

Marshall Plan   A United States plan to elp European nations repair the damage to their homes and farms as a result of World War II.

mass production   The method of manufacturing large amounts of goods at a low cost.

mass transit   Public transportation, such as buses, railroads, subways, that can carry large numbers of people.

Mayflower Compact   An agreement by the Pilgrims to form a government for their colony.

media   Communications: radio, television, movies, newspapers.

megalopolis   An almost unbroken strip of cities and suburbs.

mercantilism A plan of action by which a nation tried to gain power by getting as much gold and silver as possible. It did this by controlling businesses and developing agriculture. It tried to export as many products as possible and import as little as possible.

merchant A trader; a person who buys and sells goods.

mestizo A person who is partly Spanish and partly American Indian.

Mexican Cession The land in the Southwest that the United States obtained from Mexico after the Mexican War.

Middle Colonies The American colonies between New England and the colonies of the South. They included New York, New Jersey, Pennsylvania, and Delaware.

migratory workers People who move from place to place to find work.

Minutemen Colonial patriots who pledged to be ready to fight the British on a minute's notice.

missile A weapon or other object thrown or shot into the air.

missionaries People who bring their religion to those who are not members of their faith.

missions The buildings or headquarters of religious groups sent to places to carry out religious work.

money crop A crop that a farmer raises for sale. He or she depends on this crop to buy the goods that the farm does not supply.

monoply Exclusive control of a product or service.

Monroe Doctrine A policy announced in 1823 aimed at keeping European nations out of the Americas.

mountain men Trappers who explored the western streams and mountains for furs.

muckrakers A group of writers who wrote about conditions in government and business needing reform.

nationalism A strong feeling of pride in one's nation or government and the desire that one's own country be independent.

NATO North Atlantic Treaty Organization. An alliance of western nations formed in 1949. NATO members have agreed to help each other in case of attack.

natural resources Materials found in or on the land, such as soil, water, minerals, forests.

naval base A harbor where ships can be repaired or refueled.

naval stores Products used in making wooden ships: tar, pitch, turpentine.

neutral Not taking sides in an argument.

New Deal President Franklin D. Roosevelt's program of helping workers, farmers, and businesses during the Great Depression of the 1930s.

New England Colonies That group of the original 13 colonies located in the northeastern section of the United States. The New England colonies included Massachusetts, Connecticut, Rhode Island, and New Hampshire.

nominating convention A meeting of delegates to choose the candidates of their party for office.

Northwest Ordinance A 1787 act of Congress. It set up a plan for governing the Northwest Territory until parts of it were admitted as states.

nullify To set aside or declare no longer in effect.

Open Door policy A policy announced in 1899 to keep China open to trade with all nations.

Oregon Trail A route used by pioneers who crossed the continent to settle the far Northwest.

overseer A person hired to direct the work of the plantation.

palisade A fence of pointed logs to protect a settlement.

Pan Americanism The movement for cooperation among all the American nations.

Parliament A lawmaking body, such as in Britain or Canada.

patriots The one-third of the colonists in the 13 colonies who supported the fight for independence from England; people who love and support their country.

picketing The act of standing or walking outside a building in order to voice protest.

pillory A wooden frame with holes in which the hands and head of the lawbreaker were locked. In colonial times, a pillory was used as a punishment.

pioneers The first people to go into or settle a region.

plantation A large farm on which one main product is usually grown.

planters People who own plantations.

political party A group of people brought together by the same ideas of government. A political party chooses candidates to run for public office and works for the election of these candidates.

poll tax A tax that people were sometimes required to pay before they could vote.

pollution The dirtying of water, air, and other resources.

Pony Express A system for sending mail between Missouri and California by relays of horsemen.

pope The head of the Roman Catholic Church.

port A harbor; a city or place where ships arrive and depart.

prejudiced Having an opinion formed without taking time and care to judge fairly.

president The head of the executive branch of the United States government.

presidio A fort built by the Spanish in America.

primary The election process by which people choose a political party's candidates to run for office.

privateer An armed ship owned by private persons with government permission to attack and capture enemy ships.

Progressives Supporters of reform in the late 19th and early 20th centuries. Progressives were in favor of such goals as popular control of government, the secret ballot, civil service reform, and limiting the power of big business.

propaganda Ideas spread deliberately to help one's cause or damage an opposing cause.

proprietary colonies Colonies that were given to an individual or group by the British monarch.

proprietors Owners of the land in a proprietary colony given to them by the monarch of England.

proslavery In favor of slavery.

prospectors Miners.

protectorate A nation or territory that is ruled and protected by a stronger nation.

pueblo An Indian village in the Southwest; or an adobe or sun-dried brick building.

quota system An immigration plan that was part of the laws passed by Congress in the 1920s. It stated how many immigrants could come from each country to the United States.

racial prejudice The false belief that one race is better than another.

radar A device for locating and tracking objects by means of radio waves.

radioactive Giving off powerful rays.

ranch A large area of land used for raising cattle, sheep, or horses.

ratify To give official approval to.

rationing Dividing scarce goods among the people so that not only those who are able to pay the highest prices can get scarce goods.

reaper A machine for cutting grain.

Reconstruction The period of rebuilding the South after the Civil War.

reformers Men and women who work to bring about reforms or changes for the better.

refugees People who have fled their homeland.

regions Sections or parts of the country or world.

relief Money, food, or other help given to the poor by the local, state or federal government.

repeal To cancel.

representative A person chosen to act for another person or group of people. Members of Congress, and sometimes specifically, members of the House of Representatives, are called representatives.

representative government The kind of government in which people elect others to speak or act for them.

republic A nation in which people choose representatives to make their laws.

reservations Lands set aside by the United States government as homes for Indian tribes.

revolution A great change. A complete change in government.

robot A machine that does routine tasks on command.

rocket A high-speed missile that has its own power (engine).

route A path or road.

royal colony A colony ruled by the monarch or his or her representative.

satellite An object in space that moves around, or orbits, another object.

satellite nations Nations that are controlled by and depend upon a more powerful one.

scalawags White southerners who held office in southern Reconstruction governments after the Civil War.

secede To leave or withdraw.

segregated Separated by race in housing, schools, eating places, and elsewhere.

seigneur A landowner in the colony of New France.

self-governing colony A colony in which some of the people were allowed to elect their own governor and make some of the laws.

Senate The house of Congress in which there are two senators from each state.

settlement An area where people make their homes.

settlement house A place that offers advice, training, and recreation for the people of a poor neighborhood.

sharecroppers Farmers who live on and farm land not their own and who give the landowner a share of the crop for rent.

slave A person owned by another.

slum A shabby, run-down section of a city where the poor live crowded together.

smuggling Bringing goods into or out of a country secretly and illegally.

Social Security A government program for giving money or medical care to old, poor, and handicapped people and workers who are not able to work.

social worker A person who works to improve the social conditions of other people, especially poor people.

Sons of Liberty A group of colonists who opposed the strict English tax laws and supported moves toward American independence.

spoils system The practice of a winning political party of rewarding friends and supporters by appointing them to government jobs.

stagecoach A large horse-drawn carriage that had a regular route from town to town for carrying passengers and mail.

stampede A sudden, wild running off of a frightened cattle herd.

standardized (or interchangeable) parts. Parts of a machine made exactly alike so that they will fit any machine of the same kind.

stockade A four-sided fence of pointed logs built by the pioneers and also by some Indian tribes to protect their settlements against enemy attacks.

stocks (1) A wooden frame with holes in which the legs of the lawbreaker were locked. In colonial times, stocks were used as a punishment. (2) Shares of ownership in a business.

strike A refusal of workers to work until their demands are met.

suffrage The right to vote.

Sunbelt The area made up of the Southeast and Southwest.

Supreme Court The highest and final court of appeal in the United States.

surplus crops Extra food plants over and above what farmers need to feed themselves.

tallow The hard fat of certain animals such as cows or sheep, used to make candles and soap.

tariff A tax on goods brought in for sale from another country.

tax Money paid to support government expenses.

telegraph A machine for sending messages by wire.

tepee A tent made of buffalo skins and used by the Plains Indians.

territory Any large area of land; a region of land controlled by the United States that had not yet become a state.

toll Money paid for using a road or canal.

Tories *See definition for* Loyalists.

totalitarian state A country whose government is controlled by one political party. People's lives are closely regulated by the government. Such a dictatorship tries to crush all those who oppose it.

town meeting A meeting at which people come together to discuss the problems of their town or village.

trade To exchange goods.

trading company A company formed to make money through trade with distant lands.

trading post A place where goods are exchanged.

transcontinental Across the continent.

transistor A tiny object used in computers, radios, TVs, and other electronic equipment. A transistor controls the flow of electric current.

trapper A person who catches animals for their fur.

travois A wooden A-shaped frame used by Plains Indians to carry loads. It was pulled by a dog or a horse.

treason Betrayal of one's country.

treaty An agreement between nations.

trench warfare A method of fighting in World War I. Long narrow ditches called trenches were dug to protect the soldiers from enemy gunfire.

triangular trade One of several trade routes between the American colonies, Europe, and Africa. The most important triangular trade was the rum-molasses-slave trade among the New England colonies, Africa, and the West Indies.

truce An agreement to stop fighting for a certain amount of time.

trusts Large businesses controlled by a group of people who had monopolies on producing some goods or services.

turnpike A road on which a toll is paid at various points.

tutor A private teacher.

unconstitutional Against the Constitution.

Underground Railroad A chain of secret hiding places set up by antislavery people to help slaves escape to Canada or other places of safety before the Civil War.

Union A name given to the United States of America; a "union" of states.

unite To join together.

United Nations The organization founded after World War II to keep world peace.

urbanization The growth and development of cities.

urban renewal The process of rebuilding rundown areas of cities.

vaqueros Cowboys or herdsmen.

veto To reject or forbid.

viceroy The governor of the Spanish colonies.

vigilantes People who illegally try to enforce law and order.

Vikings Sea warriors from northern Europe.

voyage A trip by sea.

wagon trains Lines of horse-pulled wagons used to carry pioneers westward.

water power Power obtained from flowing or falling water and used to run machinery.

welfare Money for food, clothing, and shelter given by the government to people who are poor and in need.

writs of assistance Warrants allowing soldiers to search homes of colonists for smuggled goods.

yellow-dog contract An agreement between a worker and an employer in which the worker promised not to join a union. In return, the employer would hire the worker.

zone part of a city or country.

THE PRESIDENTS OF THE UNITED STATES

NAME	STATE	YEARS IN OFFICE
1. George Washington	Virginia	1789–1797
2. John Adams	Massachusetts	1797–1801
3. Thomas Jefferson	Virginia	1801–1809
4. James Madison	Virginia	1809–1817
5. James Monroe	Virginia	1817–1825
6. John Quincy Adams	Massachusetts	1825–1829
7. Andrew Jackson	Tennessee	1829–1837
8. Martin Van Buren	New York	1837–1841
9. William Henry Harrison	Ohio	1841
10. John Tyler	Virginia	1841–1845
11. James K. Polk	Tennessee	1845–1849
12. Zachary Taylor	Louisiana	1849–1850
13. Millard Fillmore	New York	1850–1853
14. Franklin Pierce	New Hampshire	1853–1857
15. James Buchanan	Pennsylvania	1857–1861
16. Abraham Lincoln	Illinois	1861–1865
17. Andrew Johnson	Tennessee	1865–1869
18. Ulysses S. Grant	Illinois	1869–1877
19. Rutherford B. Hayes	Ohio	1877–1881
20. James A. Garfield	Ohio	1881
21. Chester A. Arthur	New York	1881–1885
22. Grover Cleveland	New York	1885–1889
23. Benjamin Harrison	Indiana	1889–1893
24. Grover Cleveland	New York	1893–1897
25. William McKinley	Ohio	1897–1901
26. Theodore Roosevelt	New York	1901–1909
27. William Howard Taft	Ohio	1909–1913
28. Woodrow Wilson	New Jersey	1913–1921
29. Warren G. Harding	Ohio	1921–1923
30. Calvin Coolidge	Massachusetts	1923–1929
31. Herbert Hoover	Iowa	1929–1933
32. Franklin D. Roosevelt	New York	1933–1945
33. Harry S. Truman	Missouri	1945–1953
34. Dwight D. Eisenhower	Texas	1953–1961
35. John F. Kennedy	Massachusetts	1961–1963
36. Lyndon B. Johnson	Texas	1963–1969
37. Richard M. Nixon	California	1969–1974
38. Gerald R. Ford	Michigan	1974–1977
39. Jimmy Carter	Georgia	1977–1981
40. Ronald Reagan	California	1981–

GEOGRAPHIC TERMS TO REMEMBER

basin	Land drained by a river and its branches.
bay	A part of the ocean protected by the land around it.
bed	Bottom of a river, lake, or stream.
belt	A region favorable for growing a particular product, for example, corn belt, wheat belt, cotton belt.
canyon	A deep narrow valley surrounded by high cliffs.
cape	A piece of land reaching out into the sea.
climate	The average weather over a long period of time.
coastline	The land along the sea or ocean.
continent	The largest bodies of land on earth: North America, Asia, Africa, etc.
current	A steady flow of water.
delta	Soil carried by a stream and piled up at its mouth.
desert	A large area of very dry land.
downstream	In the direction that the stream is flowing.
equator	Imaginary line around the earth halfway between the North and South poles.
fertile	Able to grow crops.
forest	Thick growth of trees. Also called woodland.
gap	A pass or low place in the mountains.
growing season	The length of time from the planting of crops until they are harvested. From spring to fall.
gulf	A body of water partly surrounded by land—usually larger than a bay.
harbor	A body of water protected by land, safe from storms.
island	Land entirely surrounded by water.
isthmus	Narrow strip of land joining two larger bodies of land.
lake	A body of water surrounded entirely by land.
latitude	The distance north or south of the equator.
legend	A guide, or help, in reading a map.
longitude	The distance east or west of the prime meridian.
lowland	Low or level country.
mainland	The continent.
mountain range	A line of mountain peaks.
mouth of a river	Where the river flows into the sea.
peak	The top of a high mountain.
peninsula	A piece of land almost entirely surrounded by water.
plains	Broad stretches of level or almost level land.
plateau	A large area of high land not as rugged as mountains.
pole	The extreme northern or southern end of the earth.
prairie	A grassland.
scale of miles or kilometers	Tells how far one place is from another on a map.
source of a river	Where the river begins.
strait	A narrow passage of water that connects two larger bodies of water.
temperate	Mild; neither hot nor cold.
tropical	Hot and rainy; often describes areas near the equator.
upstream	Toward the source of the river; against the current.
valley	The land between ranges of mountains.

THE CONSTITUTION OF THE UNITED STATES

Those parts of the Constitution that are no longer followed are enclosed in brackets and printed in italic type, like this: [*which shall be determined*].

PREAMBLE

WE THE PEOPLE of the United States, in order to form a more perfect union, establish justice, insure domestic tranquillity, provide for the common defense, promote the general welfare, and secure the blessings of liberty to ourselves and our posterity, do ordain and establish this Constitution for the United States of America.

ARTICLE I: Legislative Department

SECTION 1. Congress

All legislative powers herein granted shall be vested in a Congress of the United States, which shall consist of a Senate and House of Representatives.

SECTION 2. The House of Representatives

All legislative powers herein granted shall be vested in a Congress of the United States, which shall consist of a Senate and House of Representatives.

a. How a representative is elected. The House of Representatives shall be composed of members chosen every second year by the people of the several States, and the electors in each State shall have the qualifications requisite for electors of the most numerous branch of the State Legislature.

b. Who may be a representative? No person shall be a Representative who shall not have attained to the age of twenty-five years, and been seven years a citizen of the United States, and who shall not, when elected, be an inhabitant of that State in which he shall be chosen.

c. The number to be chosen. Representatives and direct taxes shall be apportioned among the several States which may be included within this Union, according to their respective numbers, [*which shall be determined by adding to the whole number of free persons, including those bound to service for a term of years, and excluding Indians not taxed, three fifths of all other persons*].[1] The actual enumeration shall be made within three years after the first meet-

ing of the Congress of the United States, and within every subsequent term of ten years, in such manner as they shall by law direct. The number of Representatives shall not exceed one for every thirty thousand, but each state shall have at least one representative; [*and until such enumeration shall be made, the state of New Hampshire shall be entitled to choose three; Massachusetts, eight; Rhode Island and Providence Plantations, one; Connecticut, five; New York, six; New Jersey, four; Pennsylvania, eight; Delaware, one; Maryland, six; Virginia, ten; North Carolina, five; South Carolina, five; and Georgia, three.*]

d. Filling vacancies. When vacancies happen in the representation from any State, the Executive authority thereof shall issue writs of election to fill such vacancies.

e. The House officers; their power to impeach. The House of Representatives shall choose their Speaker and other officers; and shall have the sole power of impeachment.

SECTION 3. The Senate

a. Each state has two senators; term of office. The Senate of the United States shall be composed of two Senators from each state, [*chosen by the legislature thereof,*][2] for six years, and each Senator shall have one vote.

b. One-third of the Senate is elected every two years. Immediately after they shall be assembled in consequence of the first election, they shall be divided as equally as may be into three classes. [*The seats of the Senators of the first class shall be vacated at the expiration of the second year, of the second class at the expiration of the fourth year, and of the third class at the expiration of the sixth year,*] so that one third may be chosen every second year; and if vacancies happen by resignation, or otherwise, during the recess of the legislature of any State, the Executive thereof may make temporary appointments [*until the next meeting of the legislature, which shall then fill such vacancies.*][3]

c. Who may be a senator? No person shall be a Senator who shall not have attained to the age of thirty years, and been nine years a citizen of the United States, and who shall not, when elected, be an inhabitant of the State for which he shall be chosen.

---

[1] Changed by the 14th Amendment.

[2] Method of election changed by the 17th Amendment.
[3] Changed by the 17th Amendment.

d. The president of the Senate. The Vice President of the United States shall be President of the Senate, but shall have no vote, unless they be equally divided.

e. The Senate chooses its officers. The Senate shall choose their own officers, and also a President *pro tempore*, in the absence of the Vice President, or when he shall exercise the office of President of the United States.

f. The Senate tries impeachments. The Senate shall have the sole power to try all impeachments. When sitting for that purpose, they shall be on oath or affirmation. When the President of the United States is tried, the Chief Justice shall preside; and no person shall be convicted without the concurrence of two thirds of the members present.

g. What punishment may be given for conviction. Judgment in cases of impeachment shall not extend further than to removal from office, and disqualification to hold and enjoy any office of honor, trust or profit under the United States; but the party convicted shall nevertheless be liable and subject to indictment, trial, judgment and punishment, according to law.

Section 4. Elections and Meetings of Senators and Representatives

a. Rules for holding elections. The times, places and manner of holding elections for Senators and Representatives shall be prescribed in each State by the Legislature thereof; but the Congress may at any time by law make or alter such regulations, except as to the places of choosing Senators.

b. Congress meets once a year. The Congress shall assemble at least once in every year, [*and such meeting shall be on the first Monday in December,*] unless they shall by law appoint a different day.[4]

Section 5. Rules of Procedure for Both Houses

a. How the houses are organized. Each house shall be the judge of the elections, returns and qualifications of its own members, and a majority of each shall constitute a quorum to do business; but a smaller number may adjourn from day to·day, and may be authorized to compel the attendance of absent members, in such manner, and under such penalties, as each house may provide.

b. Each house makes its own rules. Each house may determine the rules of its proceedings, punish its members for disorderly behavior, and, with the concurrence of two thirds, expel a member.

[4] The time of meeting changed by the 20th Amendment.

c. Each house keeps a journal. Each house shall keep a journal of its proceedings, and from time to time publish the same, excepting such parts as may in their judgment require secrecy; and the yeas and nays of the members of either house on any question shall, at the desire of one fifth of those present, be entered on the journal.

d. Closing. Neither house, during the session of Congress, shall, without the consent of the other, adjourn for more than three days, nor to any other place than that in which the two houses shall be sitting.

Section 6. Privileges and Restrictions of Members

a. The members of Congress are paid. The Senators and Representatives shall receive a compensation for their services, to be ascertained by law, and paid out of the Treasury of the United States. They shall in all cases except treason, felony and breach of the peace, be privileged from arrest during their attendance at the session of their respective houses, and in going to and returning from the same; and for any speech or debate in either house, they shall not be questioned in any other place.

b. Members of Congress cannot hold other offices. No Senator or Representative shall, during the time for which he was elected, be appointed to any civil office under the authority of the United States which shall have been created, or the emoluments whereof shall have been increased during such time; and no person holding any office under the United States shall be a member of either house during his continuance in office.

Section 7. Method of Lawmaking

a. Money bills start in the House. All bills for raising revenue shall originate in the House of Representatives; but the Senate may propose or concur with amendments as on other bills.

b. How a bill becomes a law. Every bill which shall have passed the House of Representatives and the Senate shall, before it become a law, be presented to the President of the United States; if he approve he shall sign it, but if not he shall return it, with his objections, to that house in which it shall have originated, who shall enter the objections at large on their journal, and proceed to reconsider it. If after such reconsideration two-thirds of that house shall agree to pass the bill, it shall be sent, together with the objections, to the other house, by which it shall likewise be reconsidered, and if approved by two-thirds of that house, it shall become a law. But in all cases the votes of both houses shall be determined by yeas and nays, and the names of the persons voting for and against the bill shall be entered on the journal of each house respectively. If any bill shall not be returned by the President within ten days (Sundays excepted) after it shall have been presented to him, the same shall be a law, in like manner as if he had signed it, unless the Congress by their adjournment prevent its return, in which case it shall not be a law.

c. The president's part in lawmaking. Every order, resolution, or vote to which the concurrence of the Senate and House of Representatives may be necessary (except on a question of adjournment) shall be presented to the President of the United States; and before the same shall take effect, shall be approved by him, or being disapproved by him, shall be re-passed by two thirds of the Senate and House of Representatives, according to the rules and limitations prescribed in the case of a bill.

SECTION 8. **The Powers of Congress**

The Congress shall have power

a. To lay and collect taxes, duties, imposts, and excises, to pay the debts and provide for the common defence and general welfare of the United States; but all duties, imposts and excises shall be uniform throughout the United States;

b. To borrow money on the credit of the United States;

c. To regulate commerce with foreign nations, and among the several States, and with the Indian tribes;

d. To establish a uniform rule of naturalization, and uniform laws on the subject of bankruptcies throughout the United States;

e. To coin money, regulate the value thereof, and of foreign coin, and fix the standard of weights and measures;

f. To provide for the punishment of counterfeiting the securities and current coin of the United States;

g. To establish post offices and post roads;

h. To promote the progress of science and useful arts by securing for limited times to authors and inventors the exclusive right to their respective writings and discoveries;

i. To constitute tribunals inferior to the Supreme Court;

j. To define and punish piracies and felonies committed on the high seas and offences against the law of nations;

k. To declare war, grant letters of marque and reprisal, and make rules concerning captures on land and water;

l. To raise and support armies, but no appropriation of money to that use shall be for a longer term than two years;

m. To provide and maintain a navy;

n. To make rules for the government and regulation of the land and naval forces;

o. To provide for calling forth the militia to execute the laws of the Union, suppress insurrections, and repel invasions;

p. To provide for organizing, arming, and disciplining the militia, and for governing such part of them as may be employed in the service of the United States, reserving to the States respectively the appointment of the officers, and the authority of training the militia according to the discipline prescribed by Congress;

q. To exercise exclusive legislation in all cases whatsover, over such district (not exceeding ten miles square) as may, by cession of particular States, and the acceptance of Congress, become the seat of the government of the United States, and to exercise like authority over all places purchased by the consent of the legislature of the State, in which the same shall be, for the erection of forts, magazines, arsenals, dockyards, and other needful buildings;—and

r. To make all laws which shall be necessary and proper for carrying into execution the foregoing powers, and all other powers vested by this Constitution in the government of the United States, or in any department or officer thereof.

SECTION 9. **Powers Denied to the Federal Government**

a. [*The migration or importation of such persons as any of the States now existing shall think proper to admit, shall not be prohibited by the Congress prior to the year one thousand eight hundred and eight, but a tax or duty may be imposed on such importation, not exceeding ten dollars for each person.*]

b. The privilege of the writ of habeas corpus shall not be suspended, unless when in cases of rebellion or invasion the public safety may require it.

c. No bill of attainder or ex post facto law shall be passed.

d. No capitation, or other direct, tax shall be laid, unless in proportion in the census or enumeration herein before directed to be taken.

e. No tax or duty shall be laid on articles exported from any State.

f. No preference shall be given by any regulation of commerce or revenue to the ports of one State over those of another: nor shall vessels bound to, or from, one State be obliged to enter, clear, or pay duties in another.

g. No money shall be drawn from the Treasury, but in consequence of appropriations made by law; and a regular statement and account of the receipts and expenditures of all public money shall be published from time to time.

h. No title of nobility shall be granted by the United States: and no person holding any office of profit or trust under them shall, without the consent of the Congress, accept of any present, emolument, office, or title, of any kind whatever, from any king, prince, or foreign state.

SECTION 10. Powers Denied to the States

a. No State shall enter into any treaty, alliance, or confederation; grant letters of marque and reprisal; coin money; emit bills of credit; make any thing but gold and silver coin a tender in payment of debts; pass any bill of attainder, ex post facto law, or law impairing the obligation of contracts, or grant any title of nobility.

b. No State shall, without the consent of the Congress, lay any imposts or duties on imports or exports, except what may be absolutely necessary for executing its inspection laws; and the net produce of all duties and imposts, laid by any State on imports or exports, shall be for the use of the Treasury of the United States; and all such laws shall be subject to the revision and control of the Congress.

c. No State shall, without the consent of Congress, lay any duty of tonnage, keep troops, or ships of war in time of peace, enter into any agreement or compact with another State, or with a foreign power, or engage in war, unless actually invaded, or in such imminent danger as will not admit of delay.

ARTICLE II: Executive Department

SECTION 1. President and Vice President

a. The president is elected for four years. The executive power shall be vested in a President of the United States of America. He shall hold his office during the term of four years, and together with the Vice President, chosen for the same term, be elected as follows:

b. The president is chosen by electors. Each State shall appoint, in such manner as the legislature thereof may direct, a number of electors, equal to the whole number of Senators and Representatives to which the State may be entitled in the Congress; but no Senator or Representative, or person holding an office of trust or profit under the United States, shall be appointed an elector.

How the president was first elected. [*The electors shall meet in their respective States, and vote by ballot for two persons, of whom one at least shall not* *be an inhabitant of the same State with themselves. And they shall make a list of all the persons voted for, and of the number of votes for each; which list they shall sign and certify, and transmit sealed to the seat of government of the United States, directed to the President of the Senate. The President of the Senate shall, in the presence of the Senate and House of Representatives, open all the certificates, and the votes shall then be counted. The person having the greatest number of votes shall be the President, if such number be a majority of the whole number of electors appointed; and if there be more than one who have such majority, and have an equal number of votes, then the House of Representatives shall immediately choose by ballot one of them for President; and if no person have a majority, then from the five highest on the list the said house shall in like manner choose the President. But in choosing the President the votes shall be taken by States, the representation from each State having one vote; a quorum for this purpose shall consist of a member or members from two thirds of the States, and a majority of all the States shall be necessary to a choice. In every case, after the choice of the President, the person having the greatest number of votes of the electors shall be the Vice President. But if there should remain two or more who have equal votes, the Senate shall choose from them by ballot the Vice President.*][5]

c. Date of elections. The Congress may determine the time of choosing the electors, and the day on which they shall give their votes; which day shall be the same throughout the United States.

d. Who may be president? No person except a natural born citizen, [*or a citizen of the United States, at the time of the adoption of this Constitution,*] shall be eligible to the office of President; neither shall any person be eligible to that office who shall not have attained to the age of thirty-five years, and been fourteen years a resident within the United States.

e. The vice-president succeeds the president in certain cases. In case of the removal of the President from office or of his death, resignation, or inability to discharge the powers and duties of the said office, the same shall devolve on the Vice President, and the Congress may by law provide for the case of removal, death, resignation, or inability, both of the President and Vice President, declaring what officer shall then act as President, and such officer shall act accordingly, until the disability be removed, or a President shall be elected.

f. The president shall be paid. The President shall, at stated times, receive for his services, a compensation, which shall neither be increased nor dimin-

[5] Changed by the 12th Amendment.

ished during the period for which he shall have been elected, and he shall not receive within that period any other emolument from the United States, or any of them.

g. The president takes an oath of office. Before he enter on the execution of his office, he shall take the following oath or affirmation:—"I do solemnly swear (or affirm) that I will faithfully execute the office of President of the United States, and will to the best of my ability, preserve, protect and defend the Constitution of the United States."

SECTION 2. **Powers of the President**

a. The president is in charge of the armed forces. The President shall be commander in chief of the army and navy of the United States, and of the militia of the several States, when called into the actual service of the United States; he may require the opinion, in writing, of the principal officer in each of the executive departments, upon any subject relating to the duties of their respective offices, and he shall have power to grant reprieves and pardons for offences against the United States, except in cases of impeachment.

b. The president makes treaties and appointments. He shall have power, by and with the advice and consent of the Senate, to make treaties, provided two thirds of the Senators present concur; and he shall nominate, and by and with the advice and consent of the Senate, shall appoint ambassadors, other public ministers and consuls, judges of the Supreme Court, and all other officers of the United States, whose appointments are not herein otherwise provided for, and which shall be established by law; but the Congress may by law vest the appointment of such inferior officers as they think proper, in the President alone, in the courts of law, or in the heads of departments.

c. The president fills vacancies. The President shall have power to fill up all vacancies that may happen during the recess of the Senate, by granting commissions which shall expire at the end of their next session.

SECTION 3. **Duties of the President**

The president reports to Congress once a year. He shall from time to time give to the Congress information of the state of the Union, and recommend to their consideration such measures as he shall judge necessary and expedient; he may, on extraordinary occasions, convene both houses, or either of them, and in case of disagreement between them with respect to the time of adjournment, he may adjourn them to such time as he shall think proper; he shall receive ambassadors and other public ministers; he shall take care that the laws be faithfully executed, and shall commission all the officers of the United States.

SECTION 4. **Impeachment**

Officers of the United States may be impeached. The President, Vice President and all civil officers of the United States shall be removed from office on impeachment for, and conviction of, treason, bribery, or other high crimes and misdemeanors.

ARTICLE III: Judicial Department

SECTION 1. **The Federal Courts**

The courts of the land. The judicial power of the United States shall be vested in one Supreme Court, and in such inferior courts as the Congress may from time to time ordain and establish. The judges, both of the Supreme and inferior courts, shall hold their offices during good behavior, and shall, at stated times, receive for their services, a compensation, which shall not be diminished during their continuance in office.

SECTION 2. **Powers of the Federal Courts**

a. The powers of the federal courts. The judicial power shall extend to all cases, in law and equity, arising under this Constitution, the laws of the United States, and treaties made or which shall be made, under their authority;—to all cases affecting ambassadors, other public ministers and consuls;—to all cases of admiralty jurisdiction;—to controversies to which the United States shall be a party;—to controversies between two or more States;—[*between a State and citizens of another State;*]—between citizens of different States;—between citizens of the same State claiming lands under grants of different States, and between a State, or the citizens thereof, and foreign states, citizens or subjects.[6]

b. The Supreme Court's powers. In all cases affecting ambassadors, other public ministers and consuls, and those in which a State shall be a party, the Supreme Court shall have original jurisdiction. In all the other cases before mentioned, the Supreme Court shall have appellate jurisdiction, both as to law and fact, with such exceptions, and under such regulations as the Congress shall make.

c. How trials are held. The trial of all crimes, except in cases of impeachment, shall be by jury; and

---

[6] This clause has been modified by the 11th Amendment.

such trial shall be held in the State where the said crimes shall have been committed; but when not committed within any State, the trial shall be at such place or places as the Congress may by law have directed.

SECTION 3. Treason

a. **What is treason?** Treason against the United States shall consist only in levying war against them, or in adhering to their enemies, giving them aid and comfort. No person shall be convicted of treason unless on the testimony of two witnesses to the same overt act, or on confession in open court.

b. **How it is punished.** The Congress shall have power to declare the punishment of treason, but no attainder of treason shall work corruption of blood, or forfeiture except during the life of the person attainted.

ARTICLE IV: The States and the Federal Government

SECTION 1. State Records

Full faith and credit shall be given in each State to the public acts, records, and judicial proceedings of every other State. And the Congress may by general laws prescribe the manner in which such acts, records, and proceedings shall be proved, and the effect thereof.

SECTION 2. Rights of Citizens

a. **Privileges.** The citizens of each State shall be entitled to all privileges and immunities of citizens in the several States.

c. **Extradition.** A person charged in any State with treason, felony, or other crime, who shall flee from justice, and be found in another State, shall, on demand of the executive authority of the State from which he fled, be delivered up, to be removed to the State having jurisdiction of the crime.

c. **Runaway slaves.** [*No person held to service or labor in one State, under the laws thereof, escaping into another shall in consequence of any law or regulation therein, be discharged from such service or labor, but shall be delivered upon claim of the party to which such service or labor may be due.*]

SECTION 3. New States and Territories

a. **How a state is admitted.** New States may be admitted by the Congress into this Union; but no new State shall be formed or erected within the jurisdiction of any other State; nor any State be formed by the junction of two or more States, or parts of States, without the consent of the legislatures of the States concerned, as well as of the Congress.

b. **The power of Congress over territories and lands.** The Congress shall have power to dispose of and make all needful rules and regulations respecting the territory or other property belonging to the United States; and nothing in this Constitution shall be so construed as to prejudice any claims of the United States, or of any particular State.

SECTION 4. Guarantees to the States

The United States shall guarantee to every State in this Union a republican form of government, and shall protect each of them against invasion; and on application of the legislature, or of the executive (when the legislature cannot be convened) against domestic violence.

ARTICLE V: Methods of Amendment

How the Constitution is amended, or changed. The Congress, whenever two thirds of both houses shall deem it necessary, shall propose amendments to this Constitution, or, on the application of the legislatures of two thirds of the several States, shall call a convention for proposing amendments, which, in either case shall be valid to all intents and purposes, as part of this Constitution, when ratified by the legislatures of three fourths of the several States, or by conventions in three fourths thereof, as the one or the other mode of ratification may be proposed by the Congress; provided that [*no amendments which may be made prior to the year one thousand eight hundred and eight shall in any manner affect the first and fourth clauses in the ninth section of the first article; and that*] no State, without its consent, shall be deprived of its equal suffrage in the Senate.

ARTICLE VI: General Provisions

a. **The public debts will be paid.** All debts contracted and engagements entered into, before the adoption of this Constitution, shall be as valid against the United States under this Constitution, as under the Confederation.

b. **The Constitution is the highest law of the land.** This Constitution, and the laws of the United States which shall be made in pursuance thereof; and all treaties made, or which shall be made, under the authority of the United States, shall be the supreme law of the land; and the judges in every State shall be bound thereby, anything in the Constitution or laws of any State to the contrary notwithstanding.

c. The oath of office; no religious test. The Senators and Representatives before mentioned, and the members of the several State legislatures, and all executive and judicial officers, both of the United States and of the several States, shall be bound by oath or affirmation, to support this Constitution; but no religious test shall ever be required as a qualification to any office or public trust under the United States.

ARTICLE VII: Ratification of the Constitution

Approving the Constitution. The ratification of the conventions of nine States shall be sufficient for the establishment of this Constitution between the States so ratifying the same.

AMENDMENTS TO THE CONSTITUTION

1st AMENDMENT (*adopted 1791*)
Freedom of Religion, Speech, Press, Assembly, and Petition

Congress shall make no law respecting an establishment of religion, or prohibiting the free exercise thereof; or abridging the freedom of speech, or of the press; or the right of the people peaceably to assemble, and to petition the government for a redress of grievances.

2nd AMENDMENT (*adopted 1791*)
Right to Keep Arms

A well-regulated militia, being necessary to the security of a free State, the right of the people to keep and bear arms, shall not be infringed.

3rd AMENDMENT (*adopted 1791*)
Sheltering of Troops

No soldier shall, in time of peace, be quartered in any house, without the consent of the owner, nor in time of war, but in a manner to be prescribed by law.

4th AMENDMENT (*adopted 1791*)
Limiting the Right to Search and Seize; Warrants

The right of the people to be secure in their persons, houses, papers, and effects, against unreasonable searches and seizures, shall not be violated, and no warrants shall issue but upon probable cause, supported by oath or affirmation, and particularly describing the place to be searched, and the persons or things to be seized.

5th AMENDMENT (*adopted 1791*)
Rights of Persons Accused of Crimes

No person shall be held to answer for a capital, or otherwise infamous crime, unless on a presentment or indictment of a grand jury, except in cases arising in the land or naval forces, or in the militia, when in actual service in time of war and public danger; nor shall any person be subject for the same offense to be twice put in jeopardy of life or limb; nor shall be compelled in any criminal case to be a witness against himself, nor be deprived of life, liberty, or property, without due process of law; nor shall private property be taken for public use without just compensation.

6th AMENDMENT (*adopted 1791*)
Right to a Speedy, Public, and Fair Trial by Jury

In all criminal prosecutions, the accused shall enjoy the right to a speedy and public trial, by an impartial jury of the State and district wherein the crime shall have been committed, which districts shall have been previously ascertained by law, and to be informed of the nature and cause of the accusation; to be confronted with the witnesses against him; to have compulsory process for obtaining witnesses in his favor, and to have the assistance of counsel for his defense.

7th AMENDMENT (*adopted 1791*)
Jury Trials for Property Disputes

In suits at common law, where the value in controversy shall exceed twenty dollars, the right of trial by jury shall be preserved, and no fact tried by a jury, shall be otherwise re-examined in any court of the United States than according to the rules of common law.

8th AMENDMENT (*adopted 1791*)
Bail and Fines that Are Too Heavy and Cruel Punishments Forbidden

Excessive bail shall not be required, nor excessive fines imposed, nor cruel and unusual punishments inflicted.

9th AMENDMENT (*adopted 1791*)
Rights Kept by the People

The enumeration in the Constitution of certain rights, shall not be construed to deny or disparage others retained by the people.

10th AMENDMENT (*adopted 1791*)
Powers Left to the States and the People

The powers not delegated to the United States by the Constitution, nor prohibited by it to the States, are reserved to the States respectively, or to the people.

11th AMENDMENT (*adopted 1798*)
Law Suits Against the States

The judicial power of the United States shall not be construed to extend to any suit in law or equity, commenced or prosecuted against one of the United States by citizens of another State, or by citizens or subjects of any foreign state.

12th AMENDMENT (*adopted 1804*)
Election of President and Vice-President

The electors shall meet in their respective States, and vote by ballot for President and Vice President, one of whom, at least, shall not be an inhabitant of the same State with themselves; they shall name in their ballots the person voted for as President, and in distinct ballots the person voted for as Vice President, and they shall make distinct lists of all persons voted for as President, and of all persons voted for as Vice President, and of the number of votes for each, which lists they shall sign and certify, and transmit sealed to the seat of government of the United States, directed to the President of the Senate;—the President of the Senate shall, in the presence of the Senate and House of Representatives, open all the certificates and the votes shall then be counted;—the person having the greatest number of votes for President shall be the President, if such number be a majority of the whole number of electors appointed; and if no person have such majority, then from the persons having the highest numbers not exceeding three on the list of those voted for as President, the House of Representatives shall choose immediately, by ballot, the President. But in choosing the President, the votes shall be taken by States, the representation from each State having one vote; a quorum for this purpose shall consist of a member or members from two thirds of the States, and a majority of all the States shall be necessary to a choice. And if the House of Representatives shall not choose a President whenever the right of choice shall devolve upon them, [*before the fourth day of March next following*] then the Vice President shall act as President, as in the case of the death or other constitutional disability of the President.—The person having the greatest number of votes as Vice President, shall be the Vice President, if such number be a majority of the whole number of electors appointed, and if no person have a majority, then from the two highest numbers on the list, the Senate shall choose the Vice President; a quorum for the purpose shall consist of two thirds of the whole number of Senators, and a majority of the whole number shall be necessary to a choice. But no person constitutionally ineligible to the office of President shall be eligible to that of Vice President of the United States.

13th AMENDMENT (*adopted 1865*)
Slavery Abolished

SECTION 1. **Slavery is ended**

Neither slavery nor involuntary servitude, except as a punishment for crime whereof the party shall have been duly convicted, shall exist within the United States, or any place subject to their jurisdiction.

SECTION 2. **Enforcement**

Congress shall have power to enforce this article by appropriate legislation.

14th AMENDMENT (*adopted 1868*)
Rights of Citizens

SECTION 1. **Who is a citizen?**

All persons born or naturalized in the United States, and subject to the jurisdiction thereof, are citizens of the United States and of the State wherein they reside. No State shall make or enforce any law which shall abridge the privileges or immunities of citizens of the United States; nor shall any State deprive any person of life, liberty, or property, without due process of law; nor deny to any person within its jurisdiction the equal protection of the laws.

SECTION 2. The number of representatives to be chosen

Representatives shall be apportioned among the several States according to their respective numbers, counting the whole number of persons in each State, excluding Indians not taxed. But when the right to vote at any election for the choice of electors for President and Vice President of the United States, Representatives in Congress, the executive and judicial officers of a State, or the members of the legislature thereof, is denied to any of the male inhabitants of such State, being twenty-one years of age, and citizens of the United States, or in any way abridged, except for participation in rebellion, or other crime, the basis of representation therein shall be reduced in the proportion which the number of such male citizens shall bear to the whole number of male citizens twenty-one years of age in such State.

SECTION 3. How citizens may lose some rights

No person shall be a Senator or Representative in Congress, or Elector of President and Vice President, or hold any office, civil or military, under the United States, or under any State, who, having previously taken an oath, as a member of Congress, or as an officer of the United States, or as a member of any State legislature, or as an executive or judicial officer of any State to support the Constitution of the United States, shall have engaged in insurrection or rebellion against the same, or given aid or comfort to the enemies thereof. But Congress may by vote of two thirds of each house, remove such disability.

SECTION 4. The public debt of the United States will be paid; the Confederate debt will not be paid

The validity of the public debt of the United States, authorized by law, including debts incurred for payment of pensions and bounties for services in suppressing insurrection or rebellion, shall not be questioned. But neither the United States nor any State shall assume or pay any debt or obligation incurred in aid of insurrection or rebellion against the United States, or any claim for the loss or emancipation of any slave; but all such debts, obligations, and claims shall be held illegal and void.

SECTION 5. Enforcement

The Congress shall have power to enforce by appropriate legislation the provisions of this article.

15th AMENDMENT (adopted 1870)
Right of Voting

SECTION 1. Citizens cannot be kept from voting because of race, color, or because they had been slaves

The right of citizens of the United States to vote shall not be denied or abridged by the United States or any State on account of race, color, or previous condition of servitude.

SECTION 2. Enforcement

The Congress shall have power to enforce this article by appropriate legislation.

16th AMENDMENT (adopted 1913)
Income Tax

The Congress shall have power to lay and collect taxes on incomes, from whatever source derived, without apportionment among the several States, and without regard to any census or enumeration.

17th AMENDMENT (adopted 1913)
Direct Election of Senators

a. How a senator is elected. The Senate of the United States shall be composed of two Senators from each State, elected by the people thereof, for six years; and each Senator shall have one vote. The electors in each State shall have the qualifications requisite for electors of the most numerous branch of the State legislatures.

b. Filling vacancies. When vacancies happen in the representation of any State in the Senate, the executive authority of such State shall issue writs of election to fill such vacancies: *Provided* that the legislature of any State may empower the executive thereof to make temporary appointments until the people fill the vacancies by election as the legislature may direct.

c. When it becomes effective. This amendment shall not be so construed as to effect the election or term of any Senator chosen before it becomes valid as part of the Constitution.

18th AMENDMENT (*adopted 1919*)
National Prohibition

SECTION 1. Alcoholic drinks cannot be made, sold, or transported

[*After one year from the ratification of this article the manufacture, sale, or transportation of intoxicating liquors within, the importation thereof into, or the exportation thereof from the United States and all territory subject to the jurisdiction thereof for beverage purposes is hereby prohibited.*]

SECTION 2. Enforcement

[*The Congress and the several States shall have concurrent power to enforce this article by appropriate legislation.*]

SECTION 3. Limited time for approval

[*This article shall be inoperative unless it shall have been ratified as an amendment to the Constitution by the legislatures of the several States, as provided in the Constitution, within seven years from the date of the submission hereof to the States by the Congress.*]

19th AMENDMENT (*adopted 1920*)
Women's Right to Vote

SECTION 1. Women's right to vote

The right of citizens of the United States to vote shall not be denied or abridged by the United States or by any State on account of sex.

SECTION 2. Enforcement

The Congress shall have power to enforce this article by appropriate legislation.

20th AMENDMENT (*adopted 1933*)
The "Lame Duck" Amendment

SECTION 1. When the terms of the president, vice-president, and Congress begin

The terms of the President and Vice President shall end at noon on the 20th day of January, and the terms of Senators and Representatives at noon on the 3d day of January, of the years in which such terms would have ended if this article had not been ratified; and the terms of their successors shall then begin.

SECTION 2. Meetings of Congress

The Congress shall assemble at least once in every year, and such meeting shall begin at noon on the 3rd day of January, unless they shall by law appoint a different day.

SECTION 3. Who succeeds the president?

If, at the time fixed for the beginning of the term of the President, the President elect shall have died, the Vice President elect shall become President. If a President shall not have been chosen before the time fixed for the beginning of his term, or if the President elect shall have failed to qualify, then the Vice President elect shall act as President until a President shall have qualified; and the Congress may by law provide for the case wherein neither a President elect nor a Vice President elect shall have qualified, declaring who shall then act as President, or the manner in which one who is to act shall be selected, and such person shall act accordingly until a President or a Vice President shall have qualified.

SECTION 4. Choice of president by the House

The Congress may by law provide for the case of the death of any of the persons from whom the House of Representatives may choose a President, whenever the right of choice shall have devolved upon them, and for the case of the death of any of the persons from whom the Senate may choose a Vice President whenever the right or choice shall have developed upon them.

SECTION 5. Effective date

Sections 1 and 2 shall take effect on the fifteenth day of October following the ratification of this article.

SECTION 6. Time limit for approval

This article shall be inoperative unless it shall have been ratified as an amendment to the Constitution by the legislatures of three fourths of the several States within seven years from the date of its submission.

21st AMENDMENT (*adopted 1933*)
Repeal of Prohibition

SECTION 1. Repeal of the 18th Amendment

The eighteenth article of amendment to the Constitution of the United States is hereby repealed.

SECTION 2. **States protected**

The transportation or importation into any State, territory or possession of the United States for delivery or use therein of intoxicating liquors in violation of the laws thereof, is hereby prohibited.

SECTION 3. **Ratification**

This article shall be inoperative unless it shall have been ratified as an amendment of the Constitution by conventions in the several States, as provided in the Constitution, within seven years from the date of the submission hereof to the States by the Congress.

22nd AMENDMENT (*adopted 1951*)
Two-Term Amendment for President

SECTION 1. **The presidential term limited to two terms**

No person shall be elected to the office of the President more than twice, and no person who has held the office of President, or acted as President, for more than two years of a term to which some other person was elected President shall be elected to the office of the President more than once. But this article shall not apply to any person holding the office of President when this article was proposed by the Congress, and shall not prevent any person who may be holding the office of President, or acting as President, during the term within which this article becomes operative from holding the office of President, or acting as President during the remainder of such term.

SECTION 2. **Ratification**

This article shall be inoperative unless it shall have been ratified as an amendment to the Constitution by the legislatures of three-fourths of the several States within seven years from the date of its submission to the States by the Congress.

23rd AMENDMENT (*adopted 1961*)
Extending the Vote to the District of Columbia

SECTION 1. **Granting vote to qualified people in District of Columbia**

The district constituting the seat of government of the United States shall appoint in such manner as the Congress may direct: A number of electors of President and Vice President equal to the whole number of Senators and Representatives in Congress to which the district would be entitled if it were a State, but in no event more than the least populous State; they shall be in addition to those appointed by the States, but they shall be considered, for the purpose of the election of President and Vice President, to be electors appointed by a State; and they shall meet in the district and perform such duties as provided by the twelfth article of amendment.

SECTION 2. **Enforcement**

The Congress shall have power to enforce this article by appropriate legislation.

24th AMENDMENT (*adopted 1964*)
Poll Tax Banned in National Elections

The right of citizens of the United States to vote in any primary or other election for President or Vice President, for electors for President or Vice President, or for Senator or Representative in Congress shall not be denied or abridged by the United States or any state by reason of failure to pay any poll tax or other tax.

25th AMENDMENT (*adopted 1967*)
Succession of the Vice-President to the Presidency

SECTION 1. **When the vice-president can take over the presidency**

In case of the removal of the President from office or his death or resignation, the Vice President shall become President.

SECTION 2. **Appointment of a new vice-president**

Whenever there is a vacancy in the office of the Vice President, the President shall nominate a Vice President who shall take the office upon confirmation by a majority vote of both houses of Congress.

SECTION 3. **How the president can transmit powers to the vice-president**

Whenever the President transmits to the President pro tempore of the Senate and the Speaker of the House of Representatives his written declaration that he is unable to discharge the powers and duties of his office, and until he transmits to them a written declaration to the contrary, such powers and duties shall be discharged by the Vice President as Acting President.

How the vice-president can take over the powers of the president

Whenever the Vice President and a majority of either the principal officers of the executive departments, or of such other body as Congress may by law provide, transmit to the President pro tempore of the Senate and the Speaker of the House of Representatives their written declaration that the President is unable to discharge the powers and duties of his office, the Vice President shall immediately assume the powers and duties of the office as Acting President.

Thereafter, when the President transmits to the President pro tempore of the Senate and the Speaker of the House of Representatives his written declaration that no inability exists, he shall resume the powers and duties of his office unless the Vice President and a majority of either the principal officers of the executive departments, or of such other body as Congress may by law provide, transmit within four days to the President pro tempore of the Senate and the Speaker of the House of Representatives their written declaration that the President is unable to discharge the powers and duties of his office. Thereupon Congress shall decide the issue, assembling within 48 hours for that purpose if not in session. If the Congress, within 21 days after the receipt of the latter written declaration, or, if Congress is not in session, within 21 days after Congress is required to assemble, determines by two-thirds vote of both houses that the President is unable to discharge the powers and duties of his office, the Vice President shall continue to discharge the same as Acting President; otherwise, the President shall resume the powers and duties of his office.

26th AMENDMENT (*adopted 1971*)
Voting Age Lowered to 18

SECTION 1. **Granting vote to those eighteen years of age or older**

The right of citizens of the United States, who are eighteen years of age or older, to vote shall not be denied or abridged by the United States or by any State on account of age.

SECTION 2. **Enforcement**

The Congress shall have power to enforce this article by appropriate legislation.

A GUIDE TO THE U.S. CONSTITUTION, THE LAW OF THE LAND

The Constitution is divided into three parts: the preamble, the seven articles, and the amendments. (These are sometimes called the introduction, the body of the Constitution, and the additions.)

PREAMBLE	The Constitution is made by the people of the United States.
ARTICLE I – *Legislative Department* SECTION 1	The legislative shall be made up of two groups or two houses, the House of Representatives and the Senate.
SECTIONS 2–6	The members of the House of Representatives are elected every two years; one third of the Senate is elected every two years. Senators are in office for six years. The chief officer of the House is the Speaker; the leader of the Senate is the Vice-President. Congress must meet at least once a year.
SECTION 7	This section describes how a bill becomes a law. The President can approve or disapprove (veto) bills.
SECTION 8	Under the Constitution, Congress has many powers. Among them are the power to: tax the people give patents to writers borrow money and inventors deal with the Indians set up lower courts

| | coin money   declare war |
| | |

coin money   declare war
establish post offices build an army and navy

SECTION 9	Congress cannot pass a law to hold a person in jail without evidence. Congress cannot punish a person without a trial. Congress cannot tax goods sent out of the country. Congress cannot give titles of nobility to citizens.
SECTION 10	The States cannot make treaties, coin money, tax exports or keep troops without the consent of Congress. States may enter into agreements with each other if Congress approves.

ARTICLE II—*Executive* SECTION 1	The President is the head of the government. If the President dies, he or she is followed by the Vice-President. The president is chosen by electors. The president is elected every fourth year.
SECTIONS 2–4	The President is commander in chief of the Armed Forces. He or she can make treaties with other countries, but these treaties must be approved by the Senate. The President appoints officers of the government other than members of Congress. The President must report to Congress once a year. He or she must carry out all the laws passed by Congress.

ARTICLE III—*Judicial Department* SECTIONS 1–2	The Supreme Court is the highest court in the land. The Court explains the meaning of the Constitution and hears cases from lower courts.
SECTION 3	Treason—to fight against the United States or help its enemies—can be punished by death or prison.

ARTICLE IV—*Relations Among the States* SECTIONS 1–4	Each state will respect the laws of another state. Congress may admit new states. Congress has power to sell the public lands and to set up governments for territories and colonies of the United States. Every state shall have a republican form of government.

ARTICLE V—*Methods of Amendment*	The Constitution can be changed or amended to meet the needs of the people.

ARTICLE VI—*General*	The Constitution is the highest law of the land. There shall be no religious test for office. (A person of any religion can hold office.)

ARTICLE VII—*Ratification*	The Constitution had to be approved by nine states before it became the law of the land.

AMENDMENTS 1–2	*The Bill of Rights*—Congress cannot deprive a person of his or her freedom of religion, speech, press, assembly, and petition, or the right to keep guns.

3	Congress cannot shelter troops in a person's home without the owner's consent.
4	Homes and property cannot be searched or seized without a warrant.
5–6–7–8	An accused person has the right to: a. not be tried twice for the same crime b. not be forced to be a witness against himself or herself c. not have his or her life, liberty, or property taken away unless according to due process of law d. have a speedy and public trial by a fair jury e. be told what he or she is being accused of f. know the witnesses against him or her g. obtain witnesses in his or her favor h. have a lawyer to defend him or her i. have a trial by jury in lawsuits of over $20 j. not be forced to pay overly heavy bail or fines k. not be punished in cruel or unusual ways
9–10	The people and the states have other rights not mentioned in the Constitution.
11	A citizen can sue a state in the courts of that state.
12	The electors must vote twice; the first vote is for President, the second for Vice-President.
13	Slavery is ended in the United States.
14	Blacks are made citizens of the United States. The states cannot take away citizens' rights. The states cannot take away a citizen's life, liberty, or property without due process of law. People have the right to equal protection of the laws.
15	A person cannot be deprived of the right to vote because of his or her race or color.
16	Congress has the power to tax the money earned by people and businesses.
17	Senators shall be elected by the voters of their state.
18	The making or selling of alcoholic drinks is forbidden.
19	Women may vote.
20	Congress must start its session on January 3. The President's term of office shall begin on January 20.
21	The 18th amendment is repealed.
22	The President is limited to two terms in office.
23	Citizens in Washington, D.C., can vote.
24	A citizen may vote for candidates for office in the national government without paying a poll tax or other tax.
25	If the President is removed from office, dies, or resigns, the Vice-President becomes President. The Vice-President becomes the acting President when the President is disabled.
26	Qualified citizens eighteen years of age or older may vote.

INDEX

De Forest, Lee, 364
de Gaulle, Charles, 439, 444
Delaware, 62, 65, 72, 97, 110
Delaware River, 60-61, 83, 151
Democratic party, 236-237, 385, 497
Democratic-Republicans, 184-185
Dempsey, Jack, 394
de Niza, Marcos, 34
Department of Education, 512
Department of Housing and Urban Development (HUD), 512
Department stores, 375
Depressions, 379, 395-397
De Smet, Pierre, 235
De Soto, Hernando, 35-36
Dewey, George, 407
Dias, Bartholomeu, 16
Dictators, 434-436, 439-441, 445-446, 459-462, 466
Direct primary, 390
Dix, Dorothea, 325, 357-358
Douglas, Stephen A., 306, 311-312
Douglass, Frederick, 301
Draft: Civil War, 325; World War I, 428; World War II, 444
Drake, Edwin, 354
Drake, Francis, 45, 235
Dubinsky, David, 499
Du Bois, W.E.B., 338
Dutch, 60-61, 72, 97, 368. *See also* Holland.

Earhart, Amelia, 394
East Germany, 460-461. *See also* Germany.
Ecological movement, 530-532
Edison, Thomas Alva, 364
Education: of black slaves, 286-287; end of segregation, 480-483; of freed black slaves, 337; of immigrants, 369, 370; of Indians, 207, 492, 493; of Irish Americans, 497; of Jews, 499; in New England colonies, 88-89; public, 194, 357-359, 375, 512; in southern colonies, 94; in Spanish colonies, 225-227; of Spanish-speaking Americans, 487-489; of women 357; 504-505. *See also* Colleges.
Egypt, 444, 456, 471-472
Eighteenth Amendment, 395
Einhorn, David, 300-301
Einstein, Albert, 449-450, 499, 527
Eisenhower, Dwight D., 444, 445, 466
Electricity, 348, 362-365, 394, 397
Electric light bulb, 364, 375
Elevated railways, 374
Elevators, 365, 375
Elizabeth I, Queen, 45
El Salvador, 532
Emancipation Proclamation, 320, 326. *See also* Lincoln, Abraham.

Embargo Act, 210
England, 20, 215, 216, 240, 282, 287, 295, 352, 434, 436; in Cold War, 459-462; colonies in America, 45-47, 50-52, 55-57, 60-62, 65-67, 72, 92-94, 97-99, 108-110; in Common Market, 462; in French and Indian War, 118-120; immigration from, 368; in Middle East, 471; in Oregon Territory, 235, 236; in United Nations, 454, 455; in World War I, 423-425, 428-430; in World War II, 434, 436, 444-446
Equal Rights Amendment (ERA), 506
Ericson, Leif, 20
Ericsson, John, 319
Erie Canal, 196, 352
Estevanico, 34
Europe, 471; cold war, 459-469; immigration from, 368-370, 497-499; World War I, 423-425, 428-430; World War II, 434-436, 444-446
Executive branch of government, 181-182. *See also* Congress, Government, House of Representatives, Senate.

Factories, 220, 300, 301, 313, 333, 348, 369, 512; children in, 296, 389; in Civil War, 326; cloth-making, 282, 287, 295-296, 353-354; in communist countries, 459; in Great Depression, 395-397; growth of cities, 374, 375; meat-packing, 260; minorities working in, 498-499; in Nazi Germany, 435; reforms in, 389-390; in South, 336-338; in Soviet Union, 434, 459; women working in, 296, 504, 505; workers in, 378-381; in World War II, 444
Fallen Timbers, battle at, 196
Far East, 15, 409; U.S. relations with, 418-420. *See also* China, Japan.
Farming, 177, 348, 362, 391, 487; in California, 255; in communist countries, 459; in Depression years, 394-397; in French colonies, 113; on the frontier, 195, 200, 261; machinery for, 352-353, 384-385; in Middle Colonies, 97-98; in New England, 50, 51, 84; in Oregon Territory, 236; organization of farmers, 385; in Southern colonies, 92-94; in Soviet Union, 434, 459; in Spanish colonies, 225-227; workers move to cities, 374, 375
Farragut, David, 318, 319
Federal Bureau of Investigation (FBI), 517
Federalists, 184
Federal Reserve Act, 390
Fermi, Enrico, 450, 498
Ferraro, Geraldine, 532
Field, Cyrus W., 364
Fifteenth Amendment, 332

Fishing industry, 87, 113, 114, 406
Florida, 20, 25, 26, 36, 66, 173, 215, 312, 408, 489
Foch, Ferdinand, 428
Food stamp program, 513
Ford, Gerald, 518
Ford, Henry, 363
Forests, 87, 236, 391, 406
Forts: Bridger, 231; Donelson, 320; Duquesne, 118-120, 147; Hall, 231; Henry, 318; Laramie, 231; McHenry, 211; Orange, 60; Sumter, 313; Sutter, 227; Ticonderoga, 134, 151
Forty-niners, 254
Fourteenth Amendment, 331-332
France, 241, 411; in cold war, 459-462; colonies, 110, 113-114; in Common Market, 461; French and Indian War, 118-120; Louisiana Purchase, 200; in Middle East, 471; Napoleon, 200; Panama Canal, 411; Revolutionary War, 147-148, 152, 157, 162-163; in United Nations, 455; War of 1812, 210-212; War in Indochina, 466-467; World War I, 423-425, 428-430; World War II, 436, 439-441, 445, 449, 451
Frankfurter, Felix, 499
Franklin, Benjamin, 98-99, 118-120, 137, 147-148, 163, 173
Freedmen, 331-333
Freedom: of assembly, 182; in the Northwest Ordinance, 194; of the press, 110, 182; of religion, 109-110, 182; of speech, 182; of trial by jury, 182
Frémont, John, 245
French and Indian War, 118-120, 124, 147
Friedan, Betty, 505
Frontier, 102-104, 124-125, 156-157, 220-222, 230-232, 235-237
Fugitive Slave Laws, 279, 301, 305
Fulton, Robert, 352
Fundamental Orders of Connecticut, 56, 108
Fur trade, 61, 71-72, 87, 102, 113-114, 124-125, 156, 173, 230-232, 235, 236, 259

Gadsden Purchase, 245
Gama, Vasco da, 16, 21
Garrison, William Lloyd, 300-301
Gasoline engine, 363, 384
Gates, Horatio, 151
George III, King of England, 125, 137-138
Georgia, 66-67, 83, 92, 162, 221, 222, 282, 312, 324
Germany, 267, 362, 521; in American Revolution, 137, 152; in cold war, 459-462; immigration from, 66, 72, 97, 368; World War I, 423-425, 428-430; World

Silver, 30-31, 34, 225, 245, 259
Sinclair, Upton, 388
Singapore, 449
Sirica, John, 517, 518
Sitting Bull, Chief, 261
Six Day War, 471, 472
Sixteenth Amendment, 390
Skylab, 522
Skyscrapers, 375
Slater, Samuel, 295
Slavery, Civil War, 325-326; colonial 276-279; Constitution, 331-332; Dred Scott decision, 306; education in, 277, 286-287, 292; Emancipation Proclamation, 320, 326; Fugitive Slave Law, 279, 301, 305; history, 276-279, 282; life in, 286-287; in Northwest Ordinance, 194; slave trade, 25, 73; struggle against, 277-278, 291-292, 299-301, 305, 307, 311-313; in Texas, 240-241, 244, 245. *See also* Abolitionists, Compromise of 1850, Lincoln, Abraham, Missouri Compromise.
Slaves, 368
Smith, Al, 497
Smith, Jed, 230
Smith, John, 46
Smith, Joseph, 250
Social Security Act, 396-397
Society of Friends. *See* Quakers.
Solar energy, 531-532
Solomon Islands, 449
Sons of Liberty, 128-129
South: the American Revolution, 162-163; Civil War, 318-320, 324-326; colonies, 92-94; Constitutional Convention, 176-178; cotton growing, 281-282; Reconstruction period, 331-332, 336-338; tariff, 299-300
South America. *See* Latin America.
South Carolina, 66, 72, 92, 110, 162, 282, 312
South Dakota, 201, 261
Southern colonies, 82, 92-94
South Korea, 456, 465-466
South Pass, 230, 236
South Vietnam, 467-468, 501
Soviet Union. *See* Russia.
Space Age, 521-523
Space satellite, 521, 522, 523, 527
Space shuttle, 523
Spain, 20, 21, 164, 173, 200, 205, 488; Armada, 45; colonies, 25-27, 34-37, 45, 110, 120, 225-227, 235, 240, 487; in Common Market, 462; conquistadors, 30-31, 34-37, 225; contributions to Indian agriculture, 227; Empire, 225-227; explorers, 20-21, 25-27, 34-37; missionaries, 225-227; slavery, 276; Spanish-American War, 406-409; treaty with U.S., 215
Spalding, Henry and Elizabeth, 235

Spanish-American War, 406-409, 411, 412, 418
Spanish-speaking Americans, 487-489
Spoils system, 221, 389
Sputnik, 521
Stagecoach, 255-256, 362
Stalingrad, Soviet Union, Russian victory at, 444, 445
Stalin, Joseph, 434
Stamp Act, 128
Stamp Act Congress, 128
Standish, Miles, 51
Stanton, Elizabeth Cady, 357, 504
"Star-Spangled Banner, The," 211
States, power under Constitution, 181
Statue of Liberty, 369
Steam engine, 295, 352, 365, 374, 420
Steel, 336, 348, 354, 397, 423
Steffens, Lincoln, 389
Stephenson, George, 352
Stephens, Uriah, 379
Steuben, Friedrich von, 152, 163
Stockholders, 378
Stock market, 395
Stony Point, New York, 163
Stowe, Harriet Beecher, 301
Strait of Magellan, 26
Strategic Arms Limitation Agreements (SALT), 462
Strikes, 380-381. *See also* Labor unions.
Strip mining, 531
Stuyvesant, Peter, 60-61
Submarines, 424-425, 428
Suburbs, 375, 394, 512-514
Subways, 375, 498, 512, 513
Suez Canal, 444, 471-472
Suffragists, 390-391
Sugar, 195, 276, 407, 418, 488
Sumner, Charles, 306
Sunbelt, 511
Supreme Court, 181-182, 216, 222; Civil rights movement, 480-483; Dred Scott decision, 306; Grange laws, 390; Watergate affair, 518. *See also* Judicial branch of government.
Sutter, John A., 227, 254
Sweden, 267; immigrations from, 60-61, 72, 97, 368
Syria, 471-472

Tarbell, Ida, 389
Tariffs, 299-300, 462
Taxes, 110, 125, 128-129, 138, 147, 332, 397; under Articles of Confederation, 172; under Constitution, 176, 177, 182; income, 385; poll tax, 337; for public education, 358-359
Taylor, Zachary, 244
Tecumseh, Chief, 211. *See also* Indians.
Teheran, Iran, 473
Telegraph, 256, 349, 353, 364

Telephone, 364, 375, 378
Television, 528
Teller, Edward, 499
Telstar, 526
Temperance movement in the United States, 359, 395, 504
Tennessee, 104, 200, 221, 241, 313, 318-319
Tennessee River Valley Authority, 397
Tepees, 206
Terrell, Mary Church, 504
Texas, 34, 35, 227, 244-245, 267, 282, 305, 312, 319, 487
Thames River, battle at, 211
Thanksgiving Day, 51
Third World nations, 455
Three-Fifths Compromise, 177
Three Mile Island, Pennsylvania, 531
Tobacco, 47, 61, 66, 73, 83, 92-93, 125, 226, 276, 281-282, 336, 492
Tokyo, Japan, 420
Toleration Act, Maryland, 66, 110
Tom Thumb, 352
Tories, 138, 146, 164
Toscanini, Arturo, 498
Town meetings, 108, 132
Townshend Acts, 128-129
Trade, 200; under Articles of Confederation, 173; with China, 419; with England, 125; with Japan, 420, 466; in Spanish colonies, 230-232; under U.S. Constitution, 177, 182. *See also* Fur trade.
Trade Unions. *See* Labor unions.
Trail of Tears, 222
Transistors, 527
Transportation, 98, 254-256, 352, 362-365, 368; airplane, 349, 363, 444; automobile, 363, 394, 397, 512; canals, 411-412, 471-472; in cities, 512-513; highways, 394, 512, 513; railroads, 245, 362; stagecoach, 255-256; subways, 498, 512, 513; wagon train, 251, 254-255
Travis, William B., 241
Treaties: Camp David, 472; under Constitution, 182; with Indians, 196, 222, 493, 494, with Japan, 466; with Mexico, 245; Revolutionary War, 163-164; with Spain, 215; War of 1812, 212; World War I, 429
Treaty of Versailles, 429
Trench warfare, 424
Trenton, New Jersey, 151
Trial by jury, 182
Truman Doctrine, 459
Truman, Harry S., 450, 459, 465
Trusts, 385, 390
Truth, Sojourner, 300, 504
Tubman, Harriet, 301
Turner, Nat, 291-292
Tuskegee Institute, 337

ACKNOWLEDGMENTS

6, Union Pacific Railroad; 7, United Air Lines; 8 (top), International Harvester; 8 (bottom), Union Pacific Railroad; 10 (top left), Mark Kane; 10 (top right), Coronet Instructional Media; 10 (bottom left), IBM Corporation; 10 (bottom right), Coronet Instructional Media; 14, Louis Goldman/Photo Researchers; 15, The Bettmann Archive; 16, Trustees of the British Museum; 20, The Bettmann Archive; 21, The New York Public Library; 25, The Bettmann Archive; 26, Pan American Union; 30, Gianni Tortoli/Photo Researchers; 31 (top), Coronet Instructional Media; 31 (bottom), The American Museum of Natural History; 34, State of Arizona Dept. of Library Archives & Public Records; 35, Coronet Instructional Media; 36. The Granger Collection; 40, The Bettmann Archive; 41, The Bettmann Archive; 42, The Bettmann Archive; 45, Katherine Young; 46 (top), Library of Congress; 46 (bottom), The National Portrait Gallery; 50, Coronet Instructional Media; 51 (top), The New York Historical Society; 51 (bottom), Culver Pictures; 55, The Bettmann Archive; 56, The Bettmann Archive; 59, The Bettmann Archive; 60, American Museum of Natural History; 61, Historical Pictures Service, Chicago; 62, The Bettmann Archive; 65, The Bettmann Archive; 66, Culver Pictures; 67, The Granger Collection; 71, The American Museum of Natural History; 72, John T. Hopf/Touro Synagogue; 73, The American Antiquarian Society; 83, The Bettmann Archive; 84, Coronet Instructional Media; 88 (top), The Bettmann Archive; 88 (bottom), Governor Dummer Academy, Byfield, Mass.; 89, The Bettmann Archive; 93, The Metropolitan Museum of Art, Gift of Edgar William & Bernice Garbisch, 1963; 94 (right), The National Gallery of Art; 94 (left), The Bettmann Archive; 98, The Bettmann Archive; 99, The Bettmann Archive; 102, National Gallery of Art; 103, The New York Historical Society; 104, Washington University Gallery of Art; 108, Colonial National Historical Park; 109, The Bettmann Archive; 114, The National Gallery of Canada, Gift of the Estate of the Hon. W. C. Edwards, Ottawa, 1928; 115, The National Gallery of Art; 118 (top and bottom), George Roos; 119, The State Historical Society of Wisconsin; 124, American Antiquarian Society; 125, The Granger Collection; 128, The Bettmann Archive; 129 (top and bottom), The Bettmann Archive; 132, The Bettmann Archive; 133, Brown Brothers; 137, Coronet Instructional Media; 138, The Bettmann Archive; 140, Coronet Instructional Media; 146 (top and bottom), The New York Historical Society; 151, Katherine Young; 152 (top), Valley Forge Historical Society; 152 (bottom), Library of Congress; 156, Indiana Historical Society; 157, The Bettmann Archive; 160, The Bettmann Archive; 163, Coronet Instructional Media; 164, The Henry Francis Dupont Winterthur Museum; 165 (left and right), Coronet Instructional Media; 172, The American Antiquarian Society; 173 (top), The Bettmann Archive; 173 (bottom), The Bettmann Archive; 177, The Bettmann Archive; 181, Linda Bartlett/Photo Researchers; 183 (top left and right), Editorial Photocolor Archives, Inc.; 183 (bottom left), Wide World; 183 (bottom right), William S. Clark, Jr.; 195, The Library of Congress; 196, The Metropolitan Museum of Art, Gift of Mrs. John Sylvester, 1936; 200, The Bettmann Archive; 201 (top), The Bettmann Archive; 201 (bottom), Chicago Historical Society; 205, Washington University Gallery of Art; 206 (top), The Smithsonian Institution; 206 (bottom), Philbrook Art Center; 209 The American Museum of Natural History; 211, The Bettmann Archive; 212, The Bettmann Archive; 216 (top), The Bettmann Archive; 216 (bottom). The National Portrait Gallery; 220, The Bettmann Archive; 221, The Bettmann Archive; 225, Pan American Union; 226, Society of California Pioneers; 230, The Bettmann Archive; 231, Coronet Instructional Media; 235, Coronet Instructional Media; 236 (top), Coronet Instructional Media; 236 (bottom), The Bettmann Archive; 240, Coronet Instructional Media; 241, The Bettmann Archive; 244, The Thomas Gilcrease Institute of American History & Art, Tulsa, Oklahoma; 245,

The Thomas Gilcrease Institute of American History & Art, Tulsa, Oklahoma; 251, The Bettmann Archive; 254, Bancroft Library; 260 (top and bottom), Coronet Instructional Media; 266, The Bettmann Archive; 267, Coronet Instructional Media; 276, Chicago Historical Society; 277, The Bettmann Archive; 278 (top), Maryland Historical Society; 278 (bottom); Collection of Erving & Joyce Wolf; 281, The Bettmann Archive; 282, St. Louis Art Museum; 286, Louisiana State Museum; 287, The New York Historical Society; 291, The Granger Collection; 292, The Bettmann Archive; 294, The Bettmann Archive; 295, The Bettmann Archive; 296, Yale University Art Gallery; 299, The Bettmann Archive; 300 (top and bottom), Smith College, Sophia Smith Collection; 301 (top), Cincinnati Art Museum; 301 (bottom), Historical Pictures Service, Chicago; 306, Kansas State Historical Society, Topeka; 307 (top), Library of Congress; 307 (bottom), The Bettmann Archive; 311, Library of Congress; 312, The Bettmann Archive; 313, Katherine Young; 319, The Bettmann Archive; 320 (top and bottom), Library of Congress; 324, The Bettmann Archive; 325 (top), M. & M. Karolik Collection, © 1978, Museum of Fine Arts, Boston; 325 (bottom), Historical Pictures Service, Chicago; 326, Chicago Historical Society; 330, The Bettmann Archive; 331, The Bettmann Archive; 332, Coronet Instructional Media; 333, Wide World; 336, Brown Brothers; 337, The Bettmann Archive; 338 (top and bottom), The Bettmann Archive; 348, Union Pacific Railroad; 349, Coronet Instructional Media; 353, International Harvester; 358 (top), Mount Holyoke College; 358 (bottom), Brown Brothers; 362, Union Pacific Railroad; 363, Coronet Instructional Media; 364, Con Edison; 368, Denver Public Library; 369, National Archives; 370, Wide World Photos; 374, Museum of the City of New York; 375, John Hancock Mutual Life Insurance Company; 378, The Bettmann Archive; 379, National Archives; 380, The Bettmann Archive; 380, The Bettmann Archive; 384, The Library of Congress; 388, The Bettmann Archive; 389, The Bettmann Archive; 391, The Bettmann Archive; 394, The New School for Social Research; 395, United Press International; 396 (top), United States Information Agency; 396 (bottom), The Bettmann Archive; 406, The Bettmann Archive; 407, Remington Art Museum, Ogdensburg, New York; 408, Commonwealth of Puerto Rico; 411, Coronet Instructional Media; 412, The Theodore Roosevelt Collection, Harvard College; 413, United National; 418 (top), American Airlines; 418 (bottom), The Bettmann Archive; 420, The Bettmann Archive; 423, Wide World Photos; 424, National Archives; 428, United Press International; 429, National Archives; 430, National Archives; 434, United States Information Agency; 435, The Bettmann Archive; 439, The Bettmann Archive; 440, The Bettmann Archive; 444, The Bettmann Archive; 445 (top), United States Army; 445 (bottom), Wide World Photos; 446, United Press International; 449, United States Army; 450, National Archives; 454, United Nations; 455, United Nations; 461 (top), Coronet Instructional Media; 461 (bottom), Wide World Photos; 465, Wide World Photos; 467 (top), United States Army; 468, Dennis Brack/Black Star; 472 (top), Owen/Black Star; 472 (bottom), Wide World Photos; 473, Barrel/Sipa/Black Star; 480, Wide World Photos; 481, United Press International Photo; 482, FPG/Spencer Burnett; 487, Mayor's Office, City of San Antonio; 488, Oscar Buitrago/Black Star; 493 (top), Irene Stern; 493 (bottom), Wide World Photos; 495, United Press International Photo; 498, FPG/Hans Jordan; 500, The Bettmann Archive; 501, © Lawrence Frank/Black Star; 503, The Bettmann Archive; 504, Brown Brothers; 505, United Press International Photo; 506, FPG/S. Casteel; 511, American Airlines; 512, Leo de Wys, Inc./Everett C. Johnson; 513, Alpha/ C. Bacot; 514, FPG; 517, Fred Ward/Black Star; 518, Leo Choplin/Black Star; 522, National Aeronautics and Space Administration; 526, Armed Forces Institute of Pathology; 527, Leo de Wys; 530, FPG/H. Yaeger; 531, Leo de Wys; 532, Wide World; 545, Wide World.

SUX.